THE MEIJI RESTORATION

W. G. BEASLEY

THE MEIJI RESTORATION

STANFORD UNIVERSITY PRESS

STANFORD, CALIFORNIA 1972

Stanford University Press
Stanford, California

Printed in the United States of America
ISBN 0-8047-0815-0
LC 72-78868

Acknowledgments

In the course of the past fifteen years, during which I have been working—at least intermittently—on the topics that form the subject matter of this book, I have incurred debts of gratitude to many persons, far more than I could appropriately list here. To many of them I have expressed my thanks on other occasions. I therefore do not propose now (for the most part) to name individuals, but rather to describe my indebtedness in more general terms.

First, writing this book would have been impossible without the help of many Japanese scholars, not merely because of their books and articles, essential though these are, but also because of their willingness to talk about problems, answer questions, and give guidance about materials. In particular, I want to thank my friends at the Historiographical Institute (Shiryō Hensanjo) of Tokyo University, where I have often worked, some of whom, especially Professors Numata Jirō and Konishi Shirō, have been my advisers ever since my work on Japanese history began. Another special debt is to those who helped me when I visited Kōchi and Kagoshima, as well as to librarians in all three places, who were so generous with their facilities and time.

In England, too, I have had help of many kinds: from archivists and librarians (at the Public Record Office, the British Museum, and the School of Oriental and African Studies); from colleagues and students at the university, who have contributed questions and discussion (and have sometimes forced me to clarify ideas by simply looking puzzled); and from the School of Oriental and African

Studies as an institution, in that it has contributed financial and administrative support, as well as granting me substantial periods of leave of absence. To them all I am grateful. So I am to my wife, who not only has helped with my work in many time-consuming ways, but has also had to live with it, which was a greater imposition than any.

W.G.B.

London
December 1971

Contents

Explanatory Note

Japanese names are given in the customary Japanese form, that is, family name followed by given name, e.g., Matsudaira Keiei. Many given names have variant readings, e.g., Keiei, which is also read Yoshinaga. Moreover, most lords and samurai had several given names, sometimes of the same kind, but at different dates, sometimes of different kinds for use in different circumstance. Thus Matsudaira Keiei is more often known as Matsudaira Shungaku. For any one individual, I have used one version throughout the book, even at the cost of anachronism. Variants will be found in the index and, where appropriate, in the Biographical Notes (Appendix B).

Before January 1, 1873, a lunar calendar was in use in Japan for specifying month and day, years being identified by means of an era-name (*nengō*), followed by a serial number. Wherever possible I give the correct Gregorian equivalent, e.g., Ansei 5, 6th month, 19th day is given as July 29, 1858. Where only year and month occur in a Japanese text I give the Gregorian year, followed by the lunar month, with Gregorian equivalents in brackets, e.g. Ansei 5, 6th month, becomes 1858, 6th month [July 11–August 8].

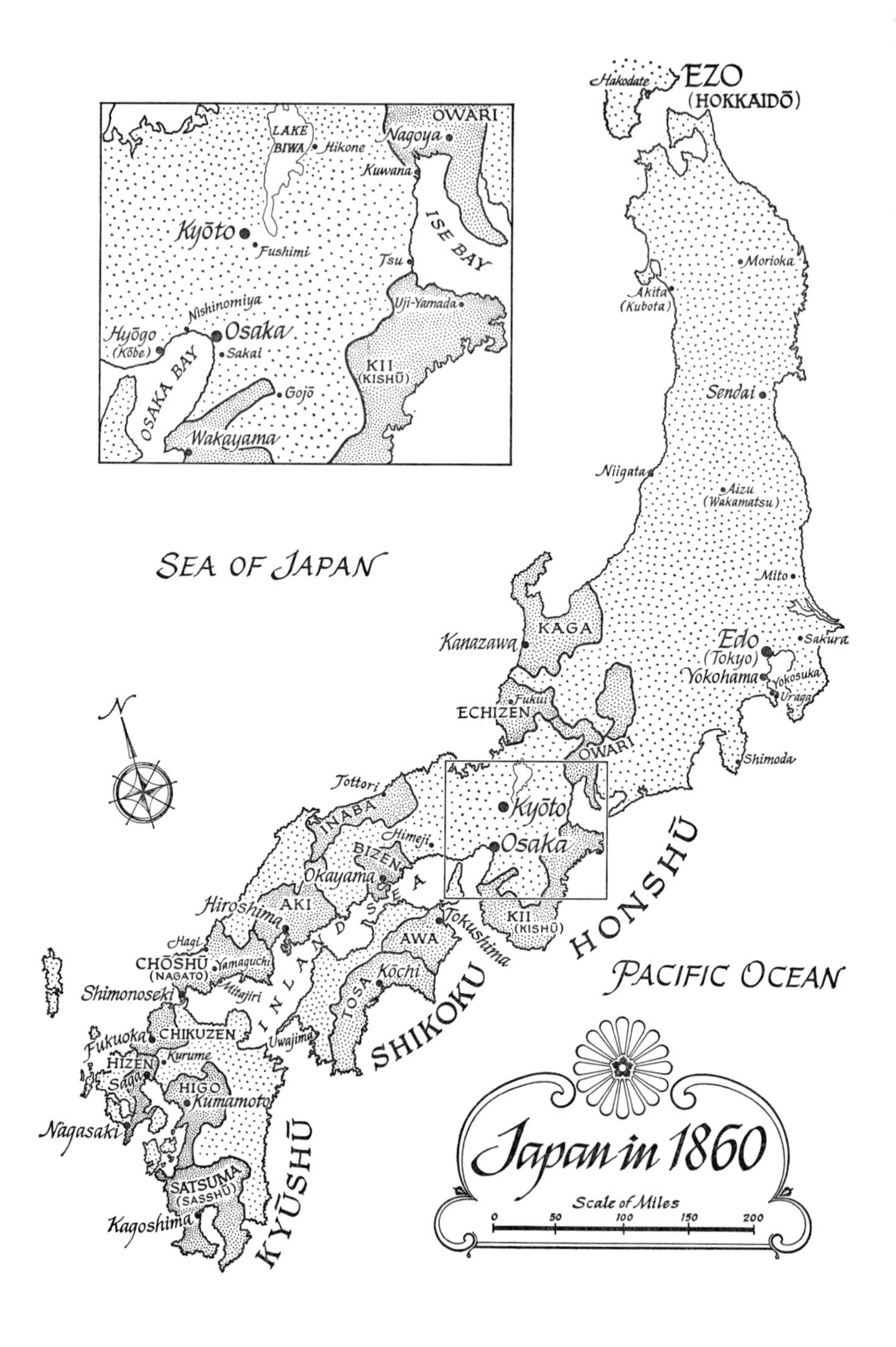
Japan in 1860
Scale of Miles
0
50
100
150
200
SEA OF JAPAN
PACIFIC OCEAN
EZO
(HOKKAIDŌ)
Hakodate
HONSHŪ
SHIKOKU
KYŪSHŪ
INLAND SEA
Morioka
Akita
(Kubota)
Sendai
Niigata
Aizu
(Wakamatsu)
Mito
Edo
(Tokyo)
Sakura
Yokohama
Yokosuka
Uraga
Shimoda
KAGA
Kanazawa
ECHIZEN
Fukui
OWARI
Kyōto
Osaka
KII
(KISHŪ)
Tottori
INABA
Himeji
BIZEN
Okayama
AKI
Hiroshima
Hagi
CHŌSHŪ
(NAGATO)
Yamaguchi
Mitajiri
Shimonoseki
AWA
Tokushima
TOSA
Kōchi
Uwajima
CHIKUZEN
Fukuoka
HIZEN
Kurume
Saga
HIGO
Kumamoto
Nagasaki
SATSUMA
(SASSHŪ)
Kagoshima
LAKE
BIWA
Hikone
Nagoya
Kuwana
ISE BAY
Fushimi
Tsu
Uji-Yamada
Nishinomiya
Hyōgo
(Kōbe)
Sakai
OSAKA BAY
Gojō
Wakayama
N

PRINCIPAL DOMAINS IN 1860

This list includes all the domains officially assessed at 200,000 koku or more, plus a few others that were politically important in the Restoration period. They are arranged geographically, roughly from north to south. The names given in the second column are names of provinces, commonly used instead of the name of the castle town in designating the very largest domains. However, this was a conventional usage, in that the domain and province boundaries did not necessarily coincide: the Kanazawa domain included most of Kaga, Notō, and Etchū provinces; Nagoya comprised Owari plus parts of Mino and Shinano; Wakayama comprised Kii plus southern Ise; Tottori comprised Inaba and Hōki; Hiroshima comprised Aki plus about half of Bingo; Yamaguchi comprised Nagato and Suō, together known as Chōshū; Kagoshima included Satsuma, Ōsumi, and part of Hyūga. Fukui, Okayama, Tokushima, Kōchi, Fukuoka and Kumamoto each comprised most or all of the relevant province, but Saga was only the eastern half of Hizen. The boundaries shown on the map are approximately those of the domains, not the provinces. The letters in parentheses after the family name indicate the type of daimyo house: S stands for sanke; K, kamon; F, fudai; and T, tozama.

Castle town	Alternative name	Land assessment (in koku)	Daimyo family
Northeast Honshū			
Akita (Kubota)		205,000	Satake (T)
Morioka		200,000	Nambu (T)
Sendai		625,000	Date (T)
Aizu (Wakamatsu)		230,000	Matsudaira (K)
Kanazawa	Kaga	1,022,000	Maeda (T)
Kantō and Central Honshū			
Mito		350,000	Tokugawa (S)
Sakura		110,000	Hotta (F)
Fukui	Echizen	320,000	Matsudaira (K)
Nagoya	Owari	619,000	Tokugawa (S)
Hikone		350,000	Ii (F)
Tsu		323,000	Tōdō (T)
Kuwana		110,000	Matsudaira (K)
Wakayama	Kii (Kishū)	555,000	Tokugawa (S)
Himeji		150,000	Sakai (F)
Western Honshū			
Tottori	Inaba	325,000	Ikeda (T)
Okayama	Bizen	315,000	Ikeda (T)
Hiroshima	Aki	426,000	Asano (T)
Hagi or Yamaguchi	Chōshū (Nagato)	369,000	Mōri (T)
Shikoku			
Tokushima	Awa	257,000	Hachisuka (T)
Kōchi	Tosa	242,000	Yamauchi (T)
Uwajima		100,000	Date (T)
Kyūshū			
Fukuoka	Chikuzen	520,000	Kuroda (T)
Kurume		210,000	Arima (T)
Saga	Hizen	357,000	Nabeshima (T)
Kumamoto	Higo	540,000	Hosokawa (T)
Kagoshima	Satsuma (Sasshū)	770,000	Shimazu (T)

THE MEIJI RESTORATION

Introduction

During the middle decades of the nineteenth century China and Japan both faced pressure from an intrusive, expanding West. This entailed, first, a political and military danger, manifested in two Anglo-Chinese wars and in the use of force on many other occasions, threatening their independence; and second, a challenge to their traditional culture from one that was alien in many of its fundamental concepts, as well as superior in technology and science. Emotionally and intellectually, Chinese and Japanese reacted to the threat in similar ways: with simple hostility, with manifestations of cultural chauvinism, with a grudging recognition of their own inferiority in "wealth and power." Yet they differed greatly in the kind of actions that this response induced. In China, the Confucian order proved strong enough to inhibit change, whether in polity or ideas, thereby bringing about a union of conservatism at home with concession abroad that led eventually to dynastic decline and an age of revolutions. In Japan, men succeeded in "using the barbarian to control the barbarian" so as to initiate policies that produced a "modern" state, powerful enough in the end to meet the West on equal terms. Hence Japan, unlike China, moved to empire and industry, not poverty and civil war.

The Meiji Restoration is at the heart of this contrast, since it was the process by which Japan acquired a leadership committed to reform and able to enforce it. For Japan, therefore, the Restoration has something of the significance that the English Revolution has for England or the French Revolution for France; it is the point from which modern history can be said to begin. For this reason it has been much studied. Equally, it has been the subject of enduring controversy, for its significance—and thus the way in which it is to be explained—has changed with every change of attitude toward the society that it brought into being.

Questions of interpretation are linked with those of definition. There was a time when to speak of the Meiji Restoration was to identify nothing more than a coup d'état carried out in Kyōto on January 3, 1868, that put control of the Imperial Court into the hands of men from some of the great feudal princedoms of west and southwest Japan. At their bidding a decree was issued terminating the hereditary office of the Tokugawa Shogun and reasserting the Emperor's direct responsibility for governing the country, a "restoration of imperial rule," or *ōsei-fukko,* which was then confirmed by victory in a civil war.

Yet even in this, the narrowest definition of the Restoration, there is an implication of wider meaning. The leaders who emerged as a result of these events were, after all, themselves the makers of the new Japan. During their lifetimes and under their direction, feudal separatism gave way to centralized bureaucracy, the social order was reconstructed, a conscript army replaced the samurai house-band as the ultimate instrument of authority, factories were established, trade was encouraged, and a Western style of education was fostered in a system of state schools. In consequence, Japan was able within a generation to claim a place among the powerful and "enlightened" countries of the world. The slogans characterize the age: *fukoku-kyōhei,* "enrich the country, strengthen the army"; *bummei-kaika,* "civilization and enlightenment." Both expressions, at least for the period down to about 1880, can be subsumed under that of "renovation," or *ishin.*

The relationship between *ōsei-fukko* ("restoration") and *ishin* ("renovation") caused no great difficulty to Japanese writers of the later nineteenth century, to whom it was axiomatic that reform followed from the transfer of power. Nor did they mean by this merely a statement about the mechanisms of decision. What, after all, were the salient characteristics of the society the Restoration had produced, as they saw them? One was its "imperial" quality, an emphasis on the role of the Emperor as ruler and as the focus of national aspirations. Another was its novelty, the long list of ideas, habits, and institutions in which the old was ousted by the new, the traditionally Japanese by the alien Western. These, then, were the things the historian had to explain. Because they were clearly aspects of a single whole, essential contributions to a process of "national regeneration" in the face of a hostile world, his explanation had to relate them to each other. The simplest, and intellectually most satisfying, way of doing this was to treat them as part of the same chain of cause and effect, to identify the forces that had brought about "restoration" with those that shaped "renovation" after it.

Among the earliest and most influential attempts to expound this viewpoint was Taguchi Ukichi's *Short History of Japanese Civilization* (Nihon kaika shōshi), published between 1877 and 1882.[1] Its argument, which is not so very different from that still put forward by historians of a conservative or traditional frame of mind, is worth summarizing at some length.

During the long Tokugawa peace, Taguchi said, loyalty (*chūgi*) became Japan's basic virtue. Confucian schools officially encouraged it, some notable literary works took it as their theme, the popular literature of plays and novels extended it to all levels of society. This, of course, was a feudal loyalty, that which was owed by a vassal to his lord; but it was capable of being transferred under the right conditions from lord to lord's lord, from Shogun to Emperor, a process that began to take place in the latter part of the Tokugawa period under the influence of the "national scholars" (*kokugakusha*).

Even so, the change from a feudal to an imperial loyalty (*kinnō*) was not itself enough to overthrow the Tokugawa. This had to wait upon the emergence of external threat, identified chiefly with the activities of Britain in China, as a result of which the transfer of loyalty from lord to Emperor was supplemented by a shift in the focus of patriotism from domain to country. This was so, at least, among the more able and active samurai, the *shishi*, or "men of spirit." The Tokugawa Bakufu (i.e., the Shogun's administration), Taguchi explained, proved itself incapable of implementing the policies that these men thought necessary for the country's survival. Equally, it failed to suppress or restrain those who challenged its authority on that account. It thus forfeited the right to rule. More, the feudal lords for the most part showed no greater spirit or capacity, with the consequence that only the Emperor was left to give Japan the unity through which the West might be successfully resisted. The destruction of the Bakufu, followed by that of the domains, was thus the inevitable concomitant of imperial "restoration."

In all this Taguchi reflected the official outlook of his day, condemning the past and glorifying the present, as befits the chronicler of a successful revolution. Yet it would be wrong to conclude that his attitude stemmed from nothing more than a sycophantic deference to a victorious Meiji government. For one thing, his condemnation of the Tokugawa was by no means total.[2] More important, his concept of what had taken place clearly fitted into the theme that runs all through his work (and is implicit in its title), that of man's progress from barbarism to civilization. The Meiji Restoration was to him a major step toward enlightenment, something that had raised Japan to the next higher rung on the social evolutionary ladder.

Essentially, Taguchi accepted the Restoration as he accepted the society deriving from it, as a good. So did most of his successors in the early twentieth century. Inobe Shigeo, the greatest of them, probed more deeply into the nature of loyalist and anti-foreign attitudes, clarifying the relationship between them and illuminating the origins of reform, but he did not in any fundamental sense challenge Taguchi's thesis. To Inobe, too, "restoration" and "renovation" were in the last resort a response to foreign threat and the means by which his own (satisfactory) society had been created.[3]

This was even true of those who approached the results of the Restoration from what was politically a much more critical standpoint. For example, the authors of the *Jiyūtō-shi* (1910), a history of one of Japan's earliest political parties, were at some pains to argue that the Restoration movement had been led by samurai of little rank or wealth, with at least tacit support from the more well-to-do farmers, and that it was therefore an attack on the selfish monopoly of power by the Tokugawa and on the whole system of family status (*mombatsu*) buttressing it. It was, they said, aimed at both "a restoration of imperial rights of government" and "a restoration of the people's liberties."[4] The second of these tasks had not yet been achieved. Accordingly, bodies like the Jiyūtō had been left to finish it, to fulfill the vision that the foreign threat had inspired originally in the lesser samurai. And what was that vision? It was the creation of a polity in which imperial authority and popular liberties could be so brought together as to give Japan a genuine unity, through which she could confront the world on equal terms. This was to deny that the Restoration had fully achieved its ends but was not in other respects so very different from Taguchi. It was certainly not a denial of Meiji society's central values.

Indeed, it was not political opposition that was first to prompt a substantial reassessment of Japan's immediate past, but industrial development. Between 1914 and 1930 the Japanese economy entered a stage at which it became possible for the first time to speak of the country as predominantly industrial and capitalist. Not surprisingly, there soon emerged a concept of the Meiji Restoration appropriate to the change, focusing, not on political structure and reform, but on the transformation of a feudal into a capitalist society. Beginning with detailed studies of the Tokugawa period by scholars like Tsuchiya Takao,[5] which demonstrated how the feudal economy broke down under the stresses caused by commercial growth, there developed a full-fledged theory of economic causation similar to those being used by contemporary Western historians in the study of late medieval and early modern Europe.

The new theory was conveniently summarized by Takahashi Kamekichi in an article published in 1929.[6] Elements of capitalism, Takahashi said, were already emerging in the Tokugawa economy by the middle of the nineteenth century, but their development was restricted by Japan's economic isolation. As a result, feudalism was weakened. But it was not completely overthrown; there was unrest, not revolution. Into this situation there was then injected a political and economic challenge from the West that revealed the weaknesses of Bakufu and upper samurai leadership, so bringing men to question the social order. It also imposed a financial burden (for items like defense works and indemnities) that neither Bakufu nor domains had the resources to sustain. By contributing to a sharp rise in commodity prices, this gave a new impetus and direction to existing discontents, prompting a political movement that led to "restoration," then "renovation." Renovation in turn hastened the process by which a fully capitalist society was brought into being from the seeds already planted in the old.

The effect of introducing economic interpretations of this kind was to leave Japanese with a choice of three different, even discrete, explanations of their country's modern history. Some still argued that the nation's essence was the imperial polity, from which all else stemmed, and that this had been restored as a result of the overwhelming moral indignation of loyalists over the wrongs of Tokugawa rule. Such a view provided the basis for a critique of contemporary society that was to assume a crucial importance in the 1930's (though its relevance is rather to the study of nationalist politics than to the historiography of the Restoration). A second school, following Taguchi, saw "restoration" and "renovation" as part of a chain of primarily political events, one that brought into existence a Meiji state shaped by a concern for national dignity and strength. This was to place emphasis on the foreign threat and on the international consequences of Japan's success in meeting it. But to economic historians, offering yet another version, this foreign threat was more catalyst than cause. Surveying the historical process over a period that began in the eighteenth century and extended to the twentieth, they concerned themselves with institutional change, not everyday politics, and envisaged an end-product that was to be identified in the Japan of Taishō (1912–25), not that of Meiji (1868–1912). In other words, Japan's achievement as they saw it was capitalist and bourgeois rather than military and diplomatic.

Marxist historical writing, which made its appearance in Japan soon after these three lines of argument had taken shape, denied this distinction, asserting that Meiji and Taishō were part of a single—and unacceptable—sociopolitical whole. Unlike the rest, this view sprang from genuine dissent, that is, from a rejection of modern Japanese society and a desire to change it; and though its origins can be traced to writers of the 1930's,[7] it owes its full development to Japan's defeat in World War II and the searching criticism to which Japanese intellectuals thereafter subjected their country's immediate past. The men and the institutions they rejected as having brought the country to ruin were identified as imperialist and capitalist, absolutist and bureaucratic. These, then, were the qualities that a study of the nineteenth century had to explain. The story even had its ready-made villains: the Emperor, the bureaucrats, the parasitic landlords, the monopolist bourgeoisie, all those, in fact, who were targets of wrath in the suddenly democratic postwar scene.

The upshot of this radical reassessment was the concept of Meiji "absolutism" (*zettaishugi*), something that was said to have emerged because of the balance achieved at the end of the Tokugawa period between the forces of a declining feudalism and those of a growing, but not yet developed, bourgeoisie. Exploiting this balance, it was said, a minority, acting in the Emperor's name, established an authoritarian state defended by a powerful standing army. The new leaders claimed to represent (or to transcend) the interests of both parties, but once in office they used their position to maintain the existing divisions in society and so perpetuate their power. Thus feudal lords became pensioners of a bureaucratic government, landlords and industrialists its clients. Both joined in an alliance to suppress or subvert the "natural" growth of democracy, whether in its bourgeois or its proletarian form.

Briefly, the Meiji Restoration was taken to be the process by which this kind of society came into being. This view involved subjecting the Restoration to a new type of analysis, designed to identify the origins of absolutism in the class relationships of late-Tokugawa Japan, a task that was first effectively undertaken by Tōyama Shigeki in a book published in 1951.[8] Tōyama's starting point is the so-called Tempō reforms, which had been undertaken by the Bakufu and some of the domains in the 1830's and 1840's. These, he says, were not solely concerned with finance. Nor were they mere manifestations of feudal reaction, for all that they were prompted by a fear of peasant revolt. Rather, they were an attempt by lower-ranking feudal officials to come to grips with the problems posed by economic change, an attempt that led them in a number of instances to seek the cooperation of the "rich farmers" (*gōnō*), who in reality controlled the countryside. In this were the seeds of an "absolutist" alliance directed against both feudal lords and restless peasantry.

The alliance's further development took place in the context of the dangers posed by an aggressive and capitalist West. As Tōyama sees it, these threatened not only Japan, but also the feudal structure, thereby stimulating a demand for reform from both the upper and the lower levels of the samurai class. The former—Bakufu and lords—showed during the 1860's that they could not act together long enough to preserve their power. The latter—lesser samurai and some non-samurai supporters—at first found political identity in the demand for *sonnō-jōi*, "honor the Emperor, expel the barbarian"; but when events proved this to be an ineffective policy, they turned instead to destruction of the Bakufu through control of a few powerful domains, notably Satsuma and Chōshū. During this phase they also worked out the policy of fukoku-kyōhei, "enrich the country, strengthen the army," as a realistic alternative to "expulsion" of the foreigner.

The coup d'état of January 1868 was followed, in Tōyama's view, by measures to involve as many elements as possible of the ruling class in the new administration. However, as the government's military position became stronger its personnel became more cohesive and its actions less conciliatory. Facing ominous manifestations of feudal separatism and a renewal of peasant revolt, it abolished the domains in 1871, thereby effecting a second coup d'état. This opened the way for reforms that were designed to free the leadership from dependence on the pre-Meiji social structure as well as to strengthen Japan against the West: land-tax reform, which gave the state a reliable revenue and confirmed the position of its landlord allies in the village; conscription, which provided a means of suppressing unrest while appealing to "popular" participation; education, which made it possible to inculcate appropriate civic virtues in addition to technical skills. The result was a state in which the bureaucratic oligarchy could promote modernization, even economic growth, without effectively having to share its power.

Tōyama's thesis has had a profound effect on later writers, including those who have disagreed with him. Some of what he said about the Tempō reforms has been shown to be at the least an oversimplification.[9] Further work on the landlords has revealed considerable regional variations in the nature and extent of both their economic and their political influence.[10] The relationship between sonnō-jōi and *tōbaku* ("destroy the Bakufu") has proved less easy to spell out in detail than Tōyama made it seem.[11] Nevertheless, among historians of the left the general outline of his approach has stood the test of time remarkably well.

There are those, however, who firmly reject Tōyama's view, and their voices have grown stronger as Japan has moved away from the long postwar malaise into a more affluent and self-confident era. Outstanding among them is Sakata Yoshio, whose work is characterized by a precision of detail and a respect for textual statement rather than a taste for theorizing.[12] Sakata sees the origins of the Restoration more in terms of anti-Bakufu and anti-foreign sentiment than in terms of social change. He emphasizes that the reformers of the Tempō period (and later) were greatly influenced by the desire to prepare defenses against an expected foreign attack, and that the assault on the Bakufu came from those who condemned its inability to strengthen the country to this end. It was for this reason that they sought an alternative political structure. That many of them, if not most, were lesser samurai, he says, was not remarkable, since lesser samurai comprised over 80 per cent of the samurai class; and the village elite, though important in the movement, did not take part as such, being recruited as quasi-samurai, student-swordsmen, and dissident intellectuals. Nor were socioeconomic factors the main determinants of Meiji policy. Indeed, the creation of a bureaucratic state after 1868 is to Sakata the product, not of social pressures, but of political compromise. It sprang from the need to avoid both a new Bakufu, headed by Satsuma or Chōshū, and a necessarily inefficient feudal assembly; and the far-reaching social reforms it instituted in its early years represent the successful manipulation by a handful of Western-trained modernizers of a widespread acceptance of the proposition that above all else the country needed to be strong.

Sakata, then, maintains that one must separate two different strands. One of them was a political movement, prompted essentially by fear of the West. It sought both national unity, involving the overthrow of the Bakufu, and military strength, involving the adoption of Western types of organization and technology. The other was a movement of reform, more far-reaching in its implications, that took inspiration and impetus from the West but materialized only after "imperial rule" had been achieved. Social and economic change, though important as the background to both movements, did not determine the success of either.

The theme of foreign pressure has also been pursued in recent years by scholars who, unlike Sakata, treat it as having been capitalist in both character and consequence, that is, as an aggression effected as much through economic as military means, which resulted in Japan setting herself on a capitalist path.[13] This new treatment is partly a reflection of a modern world in which imperialism is seen to be economic and its chief exponent the United States. Partly it stems from a recognition that Japan's own achievement is outstandingly the creation of an industrial state, so that one must reassess its Meiji origins in terms of ishin, "renovation," rather than ōsei-fukko, "the restoration of imperial rule."[14] Both elements prompt a critical examination of twentieth-century Japanese imperialism, arguably the child of Restoration, about which inhibitions are becoming fewer and documents more plentiful as the thing itself recedes in time.

A non-Japanese historian, being less emotionally involved, can to some extent free himself from a compulsion to condemn or exculpate the Japanese past because of his view of the Japanese present. It has to be said, however, that his dependence on the work of Japanese scholars may provide him with prejudice as well as evidence. More, he brings to his task some preconceptions of his own. One is a natural interest in the process by which Western influence and ideas were extended to the rest of the world.[15] Pursuit of this interest can lead, if unwittingly, to undervaluing the factors that were sociological and Japanese. Almost the converse is an academic taste for comparative and institutional studies in which a knowledge of the Japanese experience is sought in order to better understand general phenomena: the nature of "modern" society, the typology of revolutions, the determinants of modernization itself.[16] The two interests are not easy to reconcile, any more than the large questions of interpretation that we have here been discussing are easy to resolve.

Nevertheless, it is in such a context that this book must be set. And since it has been the purpose of this introduction to identify the problems with which we are to deal, rather than to afford a survey of the relevant literature, it might be proper now to abandon bibliography and recapitulate what the problems are.

First, there are questions concerning the role and relative importance of internal and external factors in the pattern of events. Did the activities of the Western powers prompt changes in Japan that would not otherwise have taken place? Or did they merely hasten a process that had already begun? Similarly, did Western civilization give a new direction to Japanese development, or do no more than provide the outward forms through which indigenous change could manifest itself? Was it a matrix, or only a shopping list?

Second, how far was the evolution of modern Japan in some sense "inevitable"? Were the main features of Meiji society already implicit in the Tempō reforms, only awaiting an appropriate trigger to bring them into being? More narrowly, was the character of Meiji institutions determined by the social composition of the anti-Tokugawa movement, or did it derive from a situation that took shape only after the Bakufu was overthrown? This is to pose the problem of the relationship between day-to-day politics and long-term socioeconomic change. One can argue, paraphrasing Tōyama, that the political controversy about foreign affairs provided the means by which basic socioeconomic factors became effective; or one can say, with Sakata, that the relevance of socioeconomic change is that it helped to decide the manner in which the fundamentally political ramifications of the foreign question were worked out. The difference of emphasis is significant.

Finally, have recent historians, in their preoccupation with other issues, lost sight of something important in their relative neglect of ideas *qua* ideas? Ought we perhaps to stop treating loyalty to the Emperor as simply a manifestation of something else? After all, the men whose actions are the object of our study took that loyalty seriously enough, certainly as an instrument of politics, if not as an article of faith.[17]

CHAPTER I

Tokugawa Political Society

To UNDERSTAND the fall of the Tokugawa rulers of Japan, one must first understand their strength. Their most remarkable characteristic, after all, was their ability to survive, since their rule endured, not entirely unchanging by any means but essentially so, for over two centuries and a half. During that period fifteen successive members of the Tokugawa family held office as Shogun, exercising a degree of authority that persuaded European visitors to think of the Shogun as Emperor and of the Emperor as a kind of pope; and this authority had itself to be broken before the power of the Tokugawa could be brought to an end.

Once it was broken, the way was open for a largely feudal state, possessing a highly developed status structure and committed to Confucian norms, to be transformed into a centralized "imperial" and bureaucratic one, offering its citizens a career open to talent in the pursuit of modernizing goals. To state the contrast so baldly is to oversimplify, of course. Nevertheless, it helps to identify the features of the *ancien régime* with which we need to start, those that had to be changed to bring the Meiji state into being. They are the Tokugawa political system and the distribution of power that it embodied; a social structure resting on inherited position; and the ideology that supported the whole. This preliminary chapter will briefly examine the nature of these three elements.

BAKUFU AND DOMAINS

The key to political stability in Tokugawa Japan was the relationship between the central government, known as the Bakufu, and the domains, or *han*.[1] That relationship had originated in the long period of intermittent civil war beginning in 1467 and ending in the early seventeenth century, during which a new generation of feudal lords, or daimyo, had emerged, carving out for themselves territories of substantial size and establishing an autocratic control over the land and all who lived on it. From bases that were capable of supporting sizable armies of samurai retainers, the more considerable daimyo were able to engage in a struggle for all Japan. One, Tokugawa Ieyasu (1542–1616), had at last succeeded in halting, first by preponderance of arms, then by enduring institutional arrangements, the constant process by which each potential ruler in turn was challenged and overthrown by a coalition of rivals.

Throughout his career Ieyasu's main concern was with the seizure and retention of power. To this end he sought to establish the legitimacy of his position *vis-à-vis* the Imperial Court, so giving legal validity to what he had gained by force; to devise mechanisms for maintaining an advantage over his recently defeated peers; and to ensure that his retainers would remain agents of his own and his family's will rather than pursue ambitions of their own. The solutions he devised set the pattern of Japanese government for some 250 years.

By taking the title Shogun in 1603, as other feudal rulers had done before him, Ieyasu became in name an imperial official: the Emperor's military deputy, head of the military class, de facto ruler of Japan. As such he was able to control the Imperial Court and even the Emperor's person. Both were treated with respect and given an air of consequence. Both were also granted larger revenues than hitherto, the land designated for this purpose being increased from 10,000 *koku* in 1601 to 99,000 koku by the end of the century and 130,000 koku at the time of the Restoration.* In return, how-

* Webb, *Japanese Imperial Institution*, pp. 126–28. These figures represent the estimated annual crop of the land earmarked for Court maintenance, not the revenue derived from it. This was characteristic of all Tokugawa valuations of landholding or rights in land, applying equally to Court, Shogun, feudal lords, samurai, and farmers; in making valuations for official purposes, administrators used an estimate of the total crop, expressed in rice (other crops being converted to rice equivalents) and measured in koku (about five bushels). This figure was known as the *kokudaka* of the land in question. The actual revenue or income derived from a given kokudaka might vary with a number of factors (e.g., the degree of control exercised over the

ever, they had to surrender what little political influence had been left to them by the centuries of feudal rule. Senior posts at Court, especially the highest, that of Kampaku, could only be filled in consultation with Tokugawa officials.* The courtiers generally were kept in strict seclusion, the Emperor himself being expected to remain within the palace grounds, so that opportunities for intrigue with feudal lords were minimal. A Tokugawa vassal was established as governor, or Shoshidai, of Kyōto, the imperial capital.

These arrangements held certain latent dangers for the Tokugawa, as the nineteenth century was to show. There was nothing in them that openly denied the Emperor's sovereignty or the Shogun's formal subordination to him. Hence a challenge to Tokugawa authority, once it became strong enough, might gain legitimacy by an appeal to the Emperor's patronage, as the Tokugawa themselves had originally done. Yet when this eventually happened, it was a *result* of Bakufu weakness, not its cause. In practice, so long as the Shogun retained the substance of power he was able to exploit the imperial prestige on his own behalf in his relations with the feudal lords. He was, for example, able to underline the special character of his own position by a careful allocation of Court ranks and titles.

Tokugawa power did not depend on this kind of device, to be sure, any more than it depended, except initially, on victory in civil war. Rather, it rested on the far-reaching redistribution of domains that victory had made possible. By 1650, after three generations of manipulation, carried out on a variety of pretexts, the Shogun himself controlled land assessed as producing a crop equivalent to 4.2 million koku of rice out of a national total of about 26 million. His holdings, combined with the 2.6 million koku in the

land by the recipient, or regional and local differences in agriculture), but for most members of the ruling class, including the Emperor and members of the Court, it was commonly received in the form of payments made from the Shogun's or feudal lord's treasury at a standard rate. This rate was usually something like 40 per cent of the kokudaka, i.e., the putative yield from a 40 per cent tax on the land.

* The office of Kampaku had developed as the chief executive office of the Court under the Fujiwara family in the 9th century and might be described as that of regent to an adult Emperor. When the Emperor was a minor, the same functions were carried out by the Sesshō. Both posts could be held only by members of five senior families of Court nobles, all being branches of the Fujiwara house. Technical terms of this kind are briefly explained in Appendix A.

hands of his direct retainers, came to something over 25 per cent of the whole. Apart from a few hundred thousand koku allocated to the Imperial Court and a number of shrines and temples, the rest was held by feudal lords. Some 36 per cent (9.3 million koku) was held by other members of the Tokugawa family and its branches (*shimpan*), together with the so-called *fudai daimyo* (82 of them in 1614; 145 in 1853), who were vassals of the Tokugawa. The remaining 9.8 million koku were in the hands of about 100 *tozama daimyo*, those who had submitted to the Tokugawa only after Ieyasu's victories. In other words, rather less than 40 per cent of the land remained to those lords, the tozama, who were thought most likely to become rivals of the dominant house.

Nor was this all. The Tokugawa and fudai lands were concentrated in strategic areas: in the provinces surrounding the Shogun's own capital at Edo; around Kyōto; and along the famous highway, the Tōkaidō, that connected the two. Great castles protected the approaches to this central belt and the key points within it. Moreover, throughout the country the largest landholdings of the later sixteenth century had been broken up. By the time of the eighth Shogun, Yoshimune (r. 1716–45), only sixteen lords still held domains of 300,000 koku or more. Of these, five were members of the Tokugawa family or its branches. One, Ii of Hikone, was the senior fudai. The rest were tozama, no fewer than seven of them being located in western Japan, the area where Tokugawa and fudai power was weakest. They included Shimazu of Satsuma (770,000 koku), Mōri of Chōshū (369,000 koku), and Nabeshima of Hizen (357,000 koku); retainers from these three families were to play a leading part in nineteenth-century politics.

The balance maintained between tozama and fudai did not only depend on regulating the total amount of land they held. The tozama, though retaining fiefs* that were on average a good deal

* Though there is some doubt whether Tokugawa society as a whole can be called feudal in the full sense in which the word is applied to medieval Europe, it is quite clear that some of its institutions can properly be described in feudal terminology. Thus a daimyo can be said to have held his lands in fief from the Shogun, even though his han was in some cases more akin to a princedom and certainly included nothing comparable with the European manor. On this question in general, see Hall, "Feudalism."

larger than those of the fudai, were relegated to areas remote from the centers of power and were excluded from office in the Shogun's government. The Shogun's closest relatives were similarly without office as a rule, though their lands were in the central region and were therefore strategically better placed. The three most important were the Tokugawa houses of Owari (619,000 koku), Kii (555,-000 koku), and Mito (350,000 koku). By contrast, the fudai, whose individual holdings rarely exceeded 100,000 koku, had a monopoly of senior posts in the administration. This was clearly intended to give them a vested interest in the maintenance of the regime.

All daimyo, whether tozama or fudai, were subject to a code of detailed regulations. Marriage alliances between them required the Shogun's permission. So did the building or repair of castles. From 1649 a decree laid down the maximum military establishment that a domain of any given size could keep. Moreover, the accession of each new generation made necessary the renewal of a written oath of allegiance by the daimyo and the issuance by the Shogun of an itemized confirmation of the lands the daimyo held in fief. Ceremonial gifts, minutely prescribed, confirmed the relationship at each new New Year and on occasions like coming of age and marriage. Yet the daimyo were not formally taxed, except for one brief and unsuccessful period of experiment under Yoshimune. The only substantial contribution they made to the cost of government—which could be a punitive one at times—was the carrying out of such public works as might be allocated to them (e.g., irrigation, defense, the rebuilding of a palace).

The most conspicuous instrument of Bakufu control, however, was the system known as *sankin-kōtai*, or "alternate attendance," which developed from pre-Tokugawa practices requiring feudal service in the capital and the giving of hostages.[2] These practices were systematized and made compulsory for tozama in 1635 and were extended to fudai in 1642. Thereafter, a lord was usually required to spend alternate years in Edo and in his own domain, leaving his wife and family in the capital when he himself was absent from it. There were a few exceptions; certain fudai lords, for example, were allowed to alternate every six months. There were also occasional temporary dispensations in cases of hardship or urgent need. But for the most part the system continued unchanged—again, except for about eight years under Yoshimune—until 1862. It helped to make Edo one of the world's great cities. It gave the feudal lords and a considerable number of their retainers a taste for urban life, a development that was to have important economic repercussions. It provided, in a society that was characterized by regional separatism and by an emphasis on the vertical relationships between man and man, one of the few means by which ideas could circulate and personal contacts could be made outside the confines of the domain or province. For all these reasons, as we shall see, it was important to the politics of the Meiji Restoration.

The supervision of sankin-kōtai and of the Shogun's relations with the daimyo generally was one of the tasks of the Edo government, the Bakufu. This was normally under the direction of four or five councillors, the Rōjū, who were appointed from among fudai daimyo with domains of about 25,000 to 50,000 koku, though in times of crisis a regent, or Tairō, might briefly supersede them. He would commonly be a Tokugawa relative or very senior fudai. Under the Rōjū were a number of offices responsible for such matters as finance, the administration of the city of Edo, and the governing of Bakufu ports like Nagasaki. These offices were filled by *hatamoto,* that is, Tokugawa retainers just below the rank of daimyo. It was often in such posts that men of the greatest ability were to be found, for they were the highest to which the career bureaucrat of fairly modest birth could aspire; but the scope for the exercise of talent was limited by the fact that every office of any consequence, including that of Rōjū, was held simultaneously by two or more incumbents, who took it in turn to carry out the assigned functions. The same restrictive attitude to the exercise of responsibility was to be seen in the creation of a separate office, that of Metsuke, to seek out evidence of subversion or misgovernment. All this helped to protect the Tokugawa from their own officials, as no doubt it was designed to do, but it made administration a very slow and cumbersome business.[3]

The Shogun not only staffed the Bakufu from among his own retainers, but also financed it from the revenues of his own lands, these being collected by a small army of stewards and other local officials, many of whom controlled areas equivalent in size to a daimyo's han. Such men, like those in Edo, performed their duties in the name of feudal service, their emoluments being hereditary and dependent on rank, not on the office they filled. In practice, however, it was evident that there could often be no exact correlation between a man's inherited status and the responsibilities he was asked to bear, despite complicated rules about eligibility for appointment. As a result, the payment of salaries gradually became common. In the form that became standard in the eighteenth century, such salaries were decided by fixing a norm of income for a given post, then supplementing the value of the incumbent's hereditary fief or stipend where necessary to bring it up to the norm. For example, a samurai of 200 koku holding an office rated at 500 would be granted an additional kokudaka of 300 koku during the period of his tenure. A similar system operated in most of the domains. Because of the importance of such salaries to the individual's comfort, many samurai, especially later in the period, became engaged in a struggle for promotion that was essentially bureaucratic rather than feudal, leaving them with attitudes and experience that were highly relevant to the nature of the Meiji state.

Though the Shogun's authority derived nominally from the Emperor, his administration did not in actuality concern itself with the whole Japanese people or with all they did. This was true even within his own domains, where apart from the vital matter of tax-collecting the details of town and village government received little attention from Bakufu officials. Tax was assessed on each village or district as a unit. The amount of tax assigned to each household, the settlement of civil disputes between local residents, arrangements concerning roads and irrigation, all these were questions for the village headman (or his urban equivalent), who was chosen from a leading family of the locality. Only nonpayment of taxes or evidence of unrest was likely to bring intervention from the headman's samurai superiors.[4]

At a more exalted level, the same principle held good in the relations of the Shogun with the daimyo. Control was exerted over the person of the feudal lord through such devices as sankin-kōtai. If he failed in his administrative duties (and especially in the earlier years of Tokugawa rule) he might find himself transferred to a smaller fief, reduced in territory in his existing one, or forced to retire in favor of his heir; but there was no precedent for the Bakufu to assume, either in whole or in part, the responsibility for administering his domain itself, except by way of punishment and outright confiscation.[5] This, too, was significant for the politics of the later Tokugawa period, since it meant that Edo had no direct and simple means of asserting its authority within a han. If a daimyo was unable or unwilling to suppress anti-Bakufu activities within his own boundaries, if his samurai showed themselves ready to jeopardize their lord's position because of their own political views, if neither lord nor samurai proved amenable to the kind of pressures Edo could normally put on them, then there was no way short of using force by which the Bakufu could remedy the situation. In the last resort it had to choose between ineffectiveness and civil war.

One might make the point differently by saying that Japan under the Tokugawa had not one government but many, each exercising authority within its own territorial limits. Each han was in some respects a little Bakufu.[6] It is easy to exaggerate the divisive effect of this system, of course. In normal times Edo's authority went unchallenged and its example, in both policy and institutions, was everywhere followed. It took a major upheaval in the nineteenth century to make things otherwise. All the same, it remains true that a daimyo had a real measure of independence, enjoying within his own domain something like the power wielded by a Shogun, even to the extent in the larger ones of enforcing a system of sankin-kōtai for his more powerful dependents. His retainers owed the same duty of service and filled the same kind of offices as those in Edo. His relatives and most trusted vassals served, when required, as senior councillors; samurai of the next lower level filled an important middle range of bureaucratic posts; and a host of lesser men, all claiming at least a semblance of samurai rank, acted as clerks, messengers, and guards. Administratively, the parallels between

Bakufu and han were close. Moreover, the relationship between feudal government and the affairs of villagers and townsmen was the same on a daimyo's lands as on the Shogun's: government was primarily a matter of collecting taxes and maintaining order.

There were other similarities, too. Throughout Japan, though in differing degree in different areas, the civil wars of the fifteenth and sixteenth centuries had begun the process of detaching samurai from the land. The need to have an army more or less on call had led the daimyo to insist that their followers live round a central stronghold. This samurai community became in many cases the nucleus of a castle town. When peace was restored under the Tokugawa, the practice continued, partly because of its administrative convenience, partly because it strengthened a lord's authority over his men. As a result the majority of samurai became townsmen, resident in or around the castle, except when they were sent to serve in Edo (another castle town, though on the grand scale) or were employed as officials in a rural area. Most of them even ceased to be landholders in any real sense. In 1690–91 only about one-sixth of the domains still maintained the custom by which samurai held fiefs in land.[7] For the rest they either held quasi-fiefs, drawing from the domain treasury an income that in theory derived from a piece of land, though it no longer reflected a personal connection with it, or else received outright stipends that were not even nominally related to the land. Even in Chōshū, where fief-holding remained more common than in most areas, records show that it declined greatly in relative importance: in 1625 it accounted for 57 per cent of samurai revenues, in the nineteenth century only about 28 per cent.[8] By 1800, indeed, only a handful of senior families in any domain were likely to hold fiefs in land, except by special dispensation.

The political consequences—leaving aside the economic ones for later discussion—were ominous. Samurai who no longer lived in the countryside had increasing difficulty in controlling it, as peasant unrest and the emergence of a new rural elite began to demonstrate. Earlier regimes in Japan had made the same mistake of allowing a new leadership to interpose itself between themselves and the land. Always the results had been fatal to their power. In the nineteenth century it began to look as if the Tokugawa, in their anxiety to control the samurai, might come to the same end.

CLASS STRUCTURE

One factor that contributed to the durability of the Tokugawa system was a highly formalized social order based on inherited position. At its top were the Emperor and Court nobility, together with the Shogun and daimyo. The rest of society was divided—the categories are contemporary and in descending order of importance—into samurai, farmers, artisans, and merchants, each group being subdivided in its turn. Indeed, the longer the peace lasted the more detailed and more rigid the subdivisions became. Details of how a man lived and spoke, as well as how he worked, varied with his place in this stratification. So, ideally, did his wealth and power. In practice, however, there were certain anomalies in the equation from the beginning, and two centuries of economic change introduced more. Since these anomalies are of importance in any analysis of the Restoration movement, we need to pay them some attention.

The Court nobles (*kuge*), partaking of the Emperor's prestige, outranked all other groups.[9] Their upper segment, coming just below the imperial princes, comprised nearly 150 families in the nineteenth century, all of them entitled to a place in the Emperor's presence on ceremonial occasions. Of these, the highest were the five Fujiwara houses, whose members were qualified to fill the office of Kampaku. Their land assessments ranged from 1,500 to 3,000 koku. Next came nine houses eligible for appointment as Chancellor (Dajō-daijin), including the house of Sanjō (469 koku), which figured prominently in the Restoration movement. Below this were five ranks, most of them held by families with stipends ranging from 100 to 300 koku, though a few had more. These, too, included some famous Restoration names, like Saga (Ōgimachi Sanjō) and Iwakura. The rest of the kuge, forming a lower segment without the right of imperial audience, were poorer and more numerous, and rarely got their names into the histories. They fell into three main divisions: the staff of the palace itself; the secretaries and clerks of the various ministries and bureaus (which had long since lost all practical importance); and the personal retainers of the upper kuge, corresponding to samurai.

Many of these men, for all that their means were modest, held Court ranks as high as those of feudal lords.* Indeed, of the feudal nobility only the Shogun and a few of his relatives had the rank to move in the highest circles at Kyōto, though a number of daimyo —by no means all—could meet at least the middle ranks of the kuge on equal terms. This situation encouraged a degree of arrogance on the part of the Court that accorded ill with its lack of power.

Among the daimyo themselves the real test of a man's standing was his relationship, not with the Court, but with the Tokugawa.[10] In formal terms this relationship was reflected in the allocation of various state apartments in Edo castle on those occasions when the presence of the lords was required. The three senior branches of the Tokugawa, the *sanke*, were assigned to the first chamber. Then, in what was called the *tamari-no-ma*, were accommodated other Tokugawa cadet houses, together with the leading fudai. At the third level, in the *ōhiro-ma*, were housed the first tozama (those having the highest Court rank) and more fudai. The sequence continued through another four rooms and ended with a group that had no "place."

This, like the superiority of kuge over daimyo, was a ranking that did not depend on wealth. As we have seen, few of the Shogun's relatives and only one of the fudai had domains rated at over 300,000 koku, a good deal less than the leading tozama houses with which in this ranking they stood on an equal footing. (For a list of the principal domains, see p. xi.) More realistic in economic and military terms was another system of categories that depended broadly on the size of a man's fief and the nature of his stronghold. It recognized five grades, the highest of which, *kunimochi*, comprised eighteen lords (other than sanke) whose lands covered a whole province or more and whose headquarters was a castle. Of

* Webb, *Japanese Imperial Institution*, pp. 97–99, makes the point that kuge incomes were higher than the kokudaka figures would make them seem, since most Court families were able to use their social prestige to improve their economic status, e.g., by teaching traditional arts like calligraphy and flower arrangement, by entering into marriage alliances with the wealthy but lower born, by patronage of certain merchant houses.

the domains that played a key part in late-Tokugawa politics, five were those of kunimochi: Satsuma, Chōshū, Tosa, Hizen, and Echizen. There was also an informal grading of domains by kokudaka, the "great" han being those with 400,000 koku or more, the small ones those with under 100,000 koku.

Turning to the samurai, one should begin, perhaps, by emphasizing their total numbers. So far, taking senior kuge and daimyo together, we have been considering only a few hundred families. The samurai class, including wives and children, accounted for as much as 5 or 6 per cent of a total population in the nineteenth century of something like thirty million people.[11] The Bakufu's orders of 1649, putting restrictions on the military establishment of domains, laid down a formula that worked out at approximately twenty-two men under arms for every thousand koku.[12] If applied evenly, this would have meant about 570,000 men for the country as a whole, a figure that accords reasonably well with the estimate of samurai households totaling about two million persons at the time of the Restoration.

However, the distribution of samurai among different domains was not as even as this calculation would suggest. The Shogun and his retainers, holding 6.8 million koku, could put a force of 80,000 men in the field, an average of twelve per thousand koku. The figures for the Tokugawa branch house of Owari and the related (shimpan) house of Aizu were broadly similar. By contrast, Satsuma averaged close to thirty men per thousand koku and Chōshū only a fraction less.[13] Indeed, if one takes the 1826 returns at their face value, almost one-third of the inhabitants of Satsuma belonged to families that had some sort of claim, however tenuous, to samurai rank.[14]

The disparity in these averages reflects a difference of historical experience. One group, the Tokugawa and fudai, had been victors in a civil war and had sought to extend their control over as wide an area as possible. They were inevitably spread thin. The other, Satsuma and Chōshū, were the defeated, deprived of part of their lands but not, commensurately, of retainers, so that they had to crowd within their narrower boundaries a larger than average samurai population. This accounts for some of their economic difficulties, as well as their continuing resentment of the Tokugawa. A superfluity of men qualified for office may also help to explain the high level of political activity among their samurai at the time of the Restoration.

Because of the very large number of persons claiming membership in the samurai class, it is important to consider how the class was subdivided.[15] Contemporaries talked vaguely of "upper" and "lower" samurai but did not always mean the same thing by these terms or define very clearly the line to be drawn between them. Domain administration tended, usually by implication, to identify three sections, which one might label "upper," "middle," and "lower." This in some ways makes a convenient starting point for discussion, so we will use it here; but the reader should be warned that neither Tokugawa writers nor modern scholars have established an accepted usage in this matter. The subject remains full of pitfalls.

One can distinguish with some confidence a group at the very top of the samurai class, those whom all would agree were upper samurai. Their numbers, as one would expect, were relatively small. In both Satsuma and Chōshū, for example, this segment comprised about 70 families, some of them branches of the daimyo house, others its senior vassals.[16] Most of them still held fiefs in land. All had various ceremonial privileges in relations with their lord. Moreover, for the first part of the Tokugawa period these families had a monopoly of senior administrative posts, and they maintained a near monopoly in most domains even in the nineteenth century. In this, as in other respects, they corresponded to the senior hatamoto in the Bakufu.[17] There were some 5,200 Tokugawa hatamoto (retainers having the right of audience), of whom a small minority, the *kōtai-yoriai* and *yoriai*, had fiefs of 3,000 koku or more. About a third of the hatamoto had 500 koku and above, nearly all in the form of fiefs rather than stipends. These can be taken to be upper samurai in the narrower sense.

The next, or middle, stratum was that of *hirazamurai* ("ordinary" samurai), or *heishi*, men of full samurai rank having the right of audience with their lord but distinguished in several ways from those described above. In Satsuma they numbered nearly 3,900 families, which were organized in three subdivisions, and in Chōshū about 2,500 families, which held no fewer than eleven different ranks. A strict comparison in terms of status within each system, taken separately, would be with the Bakufu's middle-ranking hatamoto, that is, those below the rank of yoriai; but it is probably more realistic to compare them with the rather smaller number of hatamoto holding less than 500 koku, of whom there were something like 3,500. A more straightforward comparison is with Owari, a Tokugawa domain that was about the same size as Satsuma measured by assessment of crop, and about twice the size of Chōshū. Like Chōshū, Owari had about 2,500 hirazamurai, against some 3,900 in the comparably sized Satsuma. This supports the view that on the Tokugawa lands there were usually fewer hirazamurai in relation to the value of the domain.*

The hirazamurai families were all of some consequence in castle-town society and were sometimes described rather loosely as being part of the "upper" samurai. They filled the middle range of domain offices and had stipends (occasionally fiefs) up to about 300 koku. Sometimes, as in the Bakufu and Tosa, they went as high as 500 or 600 koku.[18] The lower limit seems to have been about twenty koku in Chōshū and Tosa, thirty koku (later raised to fifty) in Owari, and fifty koku in Satsuma. I have not been able to identify a lower limit for the hatamoto.

Below the hirazamurai—and leaving aside some small groups of semi-samurai that are very difficult to classify—the picture becomes more complex. The lower samurai, in fact, need to be treated under three separate headings. Most straightforward are the *ashigaru*, who can be taken as the extension downwards of the system described so far: on the field of battle, foot soldiers; in civil gov-

* On Owari, see *Hansei ichiran*, 1: 287; and Shimmi, *Kakyū shizoku*, especially pp. 43–46. Taking the *omotedaka* for the three domains, that is, the public or formal figures for assessed value (770,000 koku for Satsuma, 619,000 for Owari, 369,000 for Chōshū), one gets 4 hirazamurai families per thousand koku in Owari, 5 in Satsuma, and almost 7 in Chōshū. However, the *uchidaka* assessment (i.e., the "private" kokudaka as estimated by domain tax collectors) gives a very different result. On the figures reported in *Hansei ichiran* (869,000 koku for Satsuma, 853,000 for Owari, no less than 988,000 for Chōshū), the proportions become 3 hirazamurai per thousand koku in Owari, 4.5 in Satsuma, and only 2.5 in Chōshū. This suggests that the unevenness of distribution may have been more apparent than real in some cases, or rather, that it was modified by increases in taxable yield, which did not vary in the same pattern as political relationships.

ernment, messengers and clerks. Numbers varied considerably, but they were commonly, as in Chōshū, about the same in total as the hirazamurai. Stipends ranged from three koku up to about seven koku in Tosa, ten koku in Chōshū, and twelve koku in Owari. Among the Bakufu's retainers at these lower levels, there were, in addition to the hatamoto, a little over 17,000 *gokenin*. One is tempted to rank these with ashigaru because they lacked the right of audience and were described in status terminology that was applied elsewhere to lesser samurai, but their stipends ranged from as little as 15 to as much as 230 koku, which put them economically—and therefore to some extent socially—in a substantially better position.

The other two categories overlap to a degree with the middle samurai group. The *baishin*, or rear-vassals, who were retainers of the senior families that still held land in fief, might include some who ranked with, but immediately after, the hirazamurai, as well as some who were clearly ashigaru. In Chōshū, for example, about half the 6,000 or so baishin were treated as having full samurai status, though their stipends did not rise above 150 koku.[19] By contrast the Satsuma baishin were more numerous (some 11,000 houses) and poorer (about 4 koku to a family), which made them all roughly equal to ashigaru. Not very much is known about equivalents elsewhere.

Finally there were the *gōshi*, or "rural" samurai, who varied widely in type as well as in status and income.[20] All were nominally resident in the countryside, not the castle town—it was this that gave them their name—but beyond this it is hard to generalize. Some were survivals from an earlier period when the samurai had also been farmers, and most were little better off than the farmers themselves. Satsuma provides much the best-known example, with 25,000 such men (in 1826), totaling with their families over 100,000 persons. Their lands averaged no more than five koku a family, but they played an important military role as a local defense force and as reserve units, with the result that they held a position clearly higher than that of mere tillers of the soil. Pockets of similar groups existed elsewhere in the country, such as Yamato, where they took part in a loyalist revolt in 1863.

The Tosa gōshi are equally famous, though of very different kind from the Satsuma and Yamato groups. Some were retainers of a former daimyo family who had been allowed to settle in the villages with quasi-samurai status. Much the greatest number, however, were men, sometimes of samurai origin, sometimes not, who were granted gōshi rank as a reward for land reclamation or contributions to the domain revenue. Some even began life as merchants, the lowest of social groups, and lived in the castle town. What is more, many had substantial incomes. Figures for six of Tosa's seven districts in the nineteenth century show 749 gōshi families with average landholdings of 54 koku. Of these, 89 had 100 koku and over.[21] The figures would be appropriate for hirazamurai.

From all this it is clear that the term "lower samurai" as used in this chapter so far covers a very wide spread of differing circumstance. Indeed, domain officials themselves found the group difficult to define. After 1868, when they were required by the Meiji government to classify the population into three general categories, *shizoku, sotsu,* and *heimin* (the first two corresponding roughly to samurai and ashigaru, the third being "commoners"), and then to reduce the categories to two (shizoku and heimin), there were many disagreements because of differences in local practice.[22] Making proper allowance for the activities of pressure groups, which no doubt met with varying success, this still implies that even to contemporaries the lines of demarcation were blurred.

To sum up, the samurai class of Tokugawa Japan was very much larger than one would have expected in a European aristocracy, whether medieval or modern, and was divided into three major divisions: upper samurai, accounting for perhaps one samurai family in fifty and including daimyo; middle samurai, representing about half the total; and lower samurai.* The lower samurai have to be further subdivided into ashigaru (foot soldiers), baishin (retainers of subvassals), and gōshi (rural samurai).

* Fukaya, *Kashizoku,* pp. 154–57, gives the following figures for shizoku and sotsu at the beginning of 1872: shizoku, 258,952 households, comprising 1,282,167 persons; sotsu, 166,875 households, comprising 659,074 persons. Since shizoku are known to have included, at least in some cases, not only former upper and middle samurai, but also some who had been lower samurai, it seems probable that lower samurai, that is, those below hirazamurai rank, had earlier accounted for a rather larger percentage of the whole than the sotsu do in these figures.

Modern scholars have sometimes tried to simplify the pattern by adopting instead a classification based only on economic criteria, arguing that a fief or stipend of 100 koku might reasonably be taken to mark the lower limit of the upper samurai (in a two-part division of the class), since Tokugawa writers maintained that this was the point at which a family's pressing financial worries came to an end. But such a classification also poses problems. For one thing, a man's income varied not only with his rank, but also with the size of his lord's domain. Thus an upper samurai holding office as Karō, equivalent to the Bakufu's Rōjū, would probably have 10,000 koku or more if he were in Satsuma or Owari, between 2,000 and 10,000 koku in Tosa, perhaps 1,000 koku in a domain of moderate size like Yanagawa. In a really small domain he would have only a few hundred koku. Similar disparities existed, as we have seen, at the lower levels. Against this, it has to be acknowledged that income is relevant in trying to assess a family's real standing in the community. For example, a middle samurai of minimal stipend, i.e., with about twenty koku, would find it difficult enough to feed, clothe, and house a family, still less provide for the cost of his ceremonial and military obligations. In fact, it is probable that a majority of hirazamurai households felt their standing to be at risk on financial grounds, since comparatively few attained the security of the 100 koku level. Thus in Chōshū 661 hirazamurai families in 1858 had 100 koku or more, out of a total of about 2,600. A further 541 had over 50 koku; 472 had between 40 and 50 koku; and no fewer than 925 had below 40 koku. Nor was Chōshū the worst case; a Satsuma list of 1639 describes only 320 out of nearly 4,000 hirazamurai families there as having 100 koku or more.[23]

Yet despite all this, there was a real sense in which the hirazamurai's right of audience with his lord, which was not directly related to income, marked him off from those below him in the formal orders of rank. It denoted eligibility for domain offices important enough to be itemized in tables of administration; it was often a line of demarcation between different types of stipend or ways of paying them; and it affected questions like inheritance and adoption. Without this right a man could not be classed as a middle or upper samurai however affluent he may have been. Moreover, contemporaries recognized the distinction as having genuine meaning.

Sasaki Takayuki, a Tosa hirazamurai, commented at some length on the subject in his memoirs.[24] So did Fukuzawa Yukichi, who came from a lower samurai family in Nakatsu. In his autobiography, Fukuzawa commented that most people accepted these social divisions without question, "almost as though they were laws of nature rather than inventions of man."[25]

Social mobility was plainly at a minimum in such a structure, though not altogether lacking.[26] A man could be moved down the scale for a variety of reasons: poverty or ill health, making it impossible for him to accompany his lord on sankin-kōtai; the lack of a male heir, necessitating a deathbed adoption to perpetuate his line; even by way of punishment for political activities. Inevitably, upward movement was more difficult, since the Tokugawa peace eliminated what had earlier been its chief lubricant, civil war. Marriage or adoption offered a way to promotion for an able younger son. An ambitious man might move up the ladder by his efficiency in office, rather slowly if he remained within the normal bureaucratic hierarchy, much more quickly if he could gain the personal favor of his lord and a household post.* As a rule, his own rank would be increased to the level appropriate to the highest office he held. Yet *hereditary* rank usually lagged behind in such circumstances and could even remain unchanged. In Satsuma it took three generations of personal promotion to secure a permanent increase in family rank.[27] A similar rule operated in the Bakufu for promotion to hatamoto from gokenin.[28] In fact, it was generally much more difficult to move from lower samurai status to middle samurai or from middle to upper than it was to gain a rather higher standing within one of these major divisions.

The same kind of considerations held good concerning entry to the samurai class from outside. It was relatively easy for a samurai to become a merchant or farmer, though few ever wanted to. The reverse process was in theory quite exceptional; and the fact that the transition was made, if to a limited degree, by quite large numbers of people in the nineteenth century was widely regarded as

* One should note the importance of the right of audience, i.e., hirazamurai rank, in securing posts within the daimyo's household. Without this right, it was much more difficult to get on the bottom rung of the ladder.

evidence that the country was on the brink of chaos. This represented, after all, a blurring of the most important line in Japanese society. In theory, to be sure, the samurai were the highest of four classes of "the people." In practice they were the dominant part of a duality: farmers, artisans, and merchants comprised, as they were to do in Meiji law, an entity that could be labeled "commoners." They were therefore expected to behave with docility in the face of samurai rule.

One must emphasize at this point that the relationship between the samurai and other classes was not an exclusively feudal one. Most samurai, we have said, had been separated from the land. This weakened them individually *vis-à-vis* their lords because it deprived them of the measure of independence that the true fief provided. Collectively, however, it strengthened them enormously against the rest of the population, which they confronted not as an agglomeration of petty lords of the manor, but as quasi-bureaucratic representatives of a powerful administrative machine.

In this capacity, their first concern was the village, the source of tax. By tradition its heart was the *hombyakushō,* a farmer-cultivator with fields rated at perhaps five or ten koku, sometimes a little more, who lived in the village and paid his full share of the dues the community owed to the domain. Below him were those who owned neither house nor fields, being laborers and tenants. Above him were a few families of elders, from whose number the headman would be chosen. It was an object of government to maintain this pattern, especially to uphold the position of the hombyakushō, which was thought to be basic to the preservation of order in the countryside.

Economic change, however, made maintaining this traditional structure difficult.[29] In two centuries very considerable areas of new land were brought under cultivation, not necessarily by those who already had the chief stake in a given community. Moreover, new outlets for economic activity appeared in local trade and some forms of manufacture. The men who profited from them eventually formed a class of "rich farmers" (*gōnō*) whose inherited status did not necessarily match their wealth: they lived well; they educated their sons to dress and behave like samurai; and they sought, not unnaturally, to acquire some of the formal privileges that would give official blessing to the position they had won. Those among them who could claim samurai descent, even if remotely, were from an early date able to acquire rank as gōshi. This happened, for example, in both Tosa and Chōshū, where such men were recruited as village headmen.[30] Others, chiefly in the eighteenth and early nineteenth centuries, by subscribing generously to the loans for which every domain appealed from time to time, were able to acquire those fundamental badges of membership in the samurai class, the right to wear a sword and use a family name. Still more used their money to bribe their way into existing samurai families, usually those of lower samurai, by marriage or adoption. There was actually in some domains a market in the sale of status, with a recognized scale of fees.[31]

The result was that Japanese rural society in 1850 differed markedly from the ideal cherished by Tokugawa statesmen and philosophers. Most important, from the point of view of later politics, there now existed in many parts of the country a network of links between the "rich farmers" and the lower samurai. Thus a number of gōshi families in Tosa included among their friends and kinsmen some who were still farmers, others who were village headmen, and perhaps a local doctor or a priest. In addition, they frequently had relatives who had secured the kind of minor samurai rank that went with posts on the staff of the district magistrate, himself a hirazamurai from the castle town. In this position it was not impossible for them to secure the distinction of serving in their lord's entourage when it went to Edo, albeit in a humble capacity.

The network often extended to merchants of the castle town as well. Like every other class in Tokugawa Japan, these, too, had their substrata. There were those who owned both a residence and the land it stood on; those who owned the building but rented its site; and those who rented both. Broadly, the divisions corresponded to different rights of participation in urban government. As was also true of Japan's feudal rulers, however, formal differences were often less important than disparities of wealth.

For merchants, too, as one would expect, economic change had

had the effect of disrupting the equation between wealth and status. It produced rich merchants (just as it produced rich farmers), some of whom developed a special relationship with the Bakufu or their own domain, acting as agents in matters of finance or monopoly trading.[32] For these services they were frequently rewarded with grants of samurai rank. Others invested their profits in the purchase or reclamation of land, thereby becoming entitled to apply for rank as gōshi. As such they were officially landowners. It was not uncommon, however, for them to remain resident in the castle town and to continue to exercise supervision of the family business through a relative or proxy.[33]

There was, therefore, a link between the ostensibly rural gōshi and the urban merchants. Yet this is not to say that the two had identical interests, either economic or political, or that they acted together. Merchants of the great cities like Edo and Osaka were in some respects rivals of those of the castle towns, though both had the same concern to maintain their monopolies against any challenge from the countryside. Gōshi might be drawn from any of the groups, or none. Some gōshi, indeed, represented an older landed interest, hostile to the incursion of commercial practices into the village altogether. In other words, the fact that some merchants, rich farmers, and lower samurai, including gōshi, can be treated as having a similar place in the spectrum of Japanese society does not inevitably mean that they behaved as a single class or were willing to cooperate in a political alliance.

It matters, of course, to any discussion of late-Tokugawa politics that the realities of social structure no longer accorded with traditional doctrine. The hierarchy of status, on which the regime's strength had depended for generations, was becoming less clear-cut; and to the extent that this was so, the regime itself was being weakened. Moreover, the attempt to maintain status distinctions or reassert them—the inevitable response of those who felt their positions threatened—had the result of uniting in opposition others who regarded their status as being less than their wealth or ability warranted. Nevertheless, the effect of this, as we shall see, was not simply to range all samurai on one side and all non-samurai on another, however great the tensions between the two groups. Social structure was not in the end the only factor that decided political allegiance.

POLITICAL ATTITUDES

Since one of the principal objectives of the Tokugawa system was to maintain the authority of samurai over commoner, of daimyo over samurai, and of Shogun over daimyo, it is not surprising that it had an ideology appropriate to these ends. One of the ingredients of that ideology was loyalty, the primary feudal duty. Loyalty, however, was a highly personal bond and as such did not necessarily lend itself to the maintenance of order in the state, as the record of earlier feudal history amply showed. Moreover, the nature of the Tokugawa polity posed some special problems of its own. What, for example, if loyalty to one's lord and loyalty to the Shogun were at variance? Worse, what if Emperor and Shogun were in conflict with each other? These were to become central issues of late-Tokugawa politics.

In part, the Tokugawa rulers afforded one answer to such questions by developing a hierarchical concept of the political structure, which was expressed by a nineteenth-century scholar, Fujita Yūkoku, as follows: "If the shogunate [Bakufu] reveres the imperial house, all the feudal lords will respect the shogunate. If the feudal lords respect the shogunate, the ministers and officials will honour the feudal lords. In this way high and low will give support to each other, and the entire country will be in accord."[34] Loyalty in this form was incorporated in Bushidō, the samurai code.[35] It was reinforced, as the very wording of the passage indicates, by a social ethic derived from the Neo-Confucianism of the Sung scholar Chu Hsi, whose ideas were introduced into Japan in the early years of Tokugawa power and soon acquired official patronage. One element in Chu Hsi's philosophy that was highly relevant to the Tokugawa ideology was the emphasis on subordination: that of subject to ruler, of son to father, of wife to husband, of younger to elder. Another was filial piety, which was also related to the inculcation of habits of obedience. More widely, Confucianism provided a philosophical framework within which to set the new role of the samurai in Japanese society, that of government rather than war; or to put it another way, substituting ethical leadership for naked military force. Good government, the Chinese tradition held, "was largely a matter of correct moral dispositions on the part of governors."[36]

It was of course necessary to persuade the samurai themselves of this, a task that was increasingly undertaken by official domain schools, where members of the ruling class received an education in the Confucian classics.* By the nineteenth century most samurai attended these schools, though a few upper samurai were taught at home and in some areas the lower-ranking samurai, the ashigaru and their like, were specifically excluded. In fact, the status divisions of society were clearly reflected inside the school: in seating arrangements, in a refusal to encourage competition between men of different rank, in the content of the instruction given.

Nevertheless, education was one of the few instruments of social mobility. Samurai reformers like Ogyū Sorai argued that there should be minimum standards for appointment to office; a few domains, late in the period, applied educational tests to such matters as adoption and the right of succession to family headship; and even in the Bakufu some of the more able scholars, despite comparatively humble birth, were able to rise to offices of considerable importance. It was a process known as "climbing by one's brush."[37] Because of it, teachers, unlike most people, seem to have been able to move about the country fairly freely, serving under different lords. Indeed, students were also able to travel and were encouraged to do so, if they showed promise, in order to continue their studies in the schools of Edo, Osaka, and Nagasaki. This peripatetic intelligentsia played a part in evolving a greater uniformity of culture, a fact that had considerable significance for the development of nineteenth-century nationalism. So did the fact that most men of

* In 1750 there were official schools in only 32 han. By 1800 the number was 107, and by 1850 it was 178, out of something over 250 han. In general, the largest domains acted earliest in this matter. Indeed, over 50 per cent of domains under 20,000 koku still did not have such schools in 1865. See Dore, *Education*, tables, p. 71.

education possessed a common political vocabulary, derived from the Chinese classics.[38]

Some of these advantages were shared by a number of commoners, who though rarely admitted to the official schools—and then only if they were men on the fringes of the samurai class, like village headmen and privileged merchants[39]—had access to the private schools of good scholastic standing that were found in the cities and larger towns. These schools were often more enterprising in their choice of curriculum and more stimulating in the way they taught than the official ones, but they were no more likely to challenge the values of samurai society. Most of their members, both teachers and pupils, were conscious of belonging, at least in prospect, to a ruling class. This made them wary of too much education for the lower orders. As the author of a treatise of 1817 put it, when the lower classes acquired "a little skill at letters," they tended to become arrogant, to "look down on their fellow-men, despise their elders and superiors and question the instructions of the authorities."[40]

Still less were the established values likely to be challenged in the many local schools (*terakoya*) that were established during the later years of the Tokugawa period by samurai, priests, and village headmen. These schools provided no more than an elementary training in reading, writing, and arithmetic, together with some slight indoctrination in the socially desirable virtues of filial piety and obedience. Nevertheless, their work was of great, if somewhat contradictory, significance in the longer term. On the one hand, they gave a substantial segment of the population, possibly as much as 40 per cent of boys and 10 per cent of girls by 1868,[41] the beginnings of literacy, something that had important implications for the development of technology and public opinion in the Meiji period. On the other, by facilitating the dissemination of orders and information and by helping to inculcate an acceptance of authority, they made Japan easier to govern. They were in this sense an important adjunct to "absolutism," both before and after 1868.

In fact, for the greater part of the Tokugawa period schools of all kinds were an instrument for spreading the ethic of the ruling class throughout society, contributing to a general acceptance of samurai norms, even by wealthy and ambitious commoners.* We have already seen that it was possible, if difficult, for men of substance in both urban and rural Japan to obtain a measure of samurai rank. This encouraged them to adopt samurai standards of behavior. By so doing, they helped in turn to determine the ambitions of those who were lower in the scale of status than themselves. Craig cites the example of Yamagata Bantō (1748–1821), a writer on Western science, who, though himself a rich merchant, accepted in his writings the concept of a class structure that subordinated the merchant to both the samurai and the farmer.[42] Even Ishida Baigan (1685–1744), who is always thought of as a defender of the merchant against those who decried him as parasitic, did so in terms that made it clear he felt the respect the merchant ought to enjoy depended on loyal service to the state and conformity to its code, not on a new set of values.[43]

In fact, it is surprising how little open criticism of the political and social structure is to be found in writings of the Tokugawa period.[44] Clearly, radical economic reformers like Honda Toshiaki and Satō Shinen[45] and the Rangakusha, or "Dutch" scholars, whose subject matter occasionally embraced Europe's politics as well as its science, advanced ideas that were potentially subversive of the existing order. So did the advocates of a Shintō revival, whose attacks on the corrupting influence of Confucian thought were accompanied by an apparently dangerous emphasis on the Emperor's divinity. All the same, they cannot be said to have tried deliberately to overturn the society into which they were born. Nor was their failure to do so entirely due to fear of the Bakufu's police. It was rather that the men themselves were passive—with respect to political questions at least—and have a reputation as rebels only because of the uses to which their arguments were later put.

* Notwithstanding what is said on this subject here, it will become apparent later that schools also provided many of the turbulent young activists of the 1850's and 1860's. I do not regard this as a contradiction, because I believe that the "crisis" of those years effected a fundamental change in the outlook of many Japanese. It is perhaps as well, however, to emphasize that what I have been saying above about the social function of Tokugawa education refers to the period before 1853.

To such men and their political influence we shall have to return later in this book. Here it is more useful by way of conclusion to consider briefly some of the implications of pre-Restoration ideology, especially those aspects of it that are most relevant to the regime's fall. For it was, strangely enough, from the Confucian scholars, a group one would have thought to be committed to society's existing ways, that there came the kind of criticism that had the greatest impact on the Restoration movement in its early stages.

One reason for this apparent paradox is to be found in the attempt to make Confucianism the orthodoxy of a feudal class. In China, after all, Confucianism was the ideal statement of a political and social structure that was dominated by scholar-gentry, whose function was defined in bureaucratic terms. Confucianism provided both the sanction for their authority and the test of their fitness to rule. To attack it was to attack tradition and established order. None of this was true of Japan; for the samurai, Confucianism did no more than reinforce a claim to power that rested fundamentally on other grounds. Hence in the last resort it could be relegated to the position of a mere code of ethical behavior because it did not comprise the whole of society's beliefs. It could be made to coexist with Western scientific thought, for example, without putting in question, as it did in China, a system of ideas on which the fabric of society was believed to depend.

More immediately to our purpose, the adoption of Confucianism in Japan produced anomalies that could not be indefinitely ignored. For the Japanese Confucian scholar, as for his Chinese counterpart, the material of philosophy was history. But it was *Chinese* history. Thus the Japanese Confucianist had constantly to deal with concepts like the Mandate of Heaven and the dynastic cycle, that is, with Chinese theories about the legitimacy of Emperors and the reasons for their rise and fall. For example, the doctrine of the Mandate (*t'ien-ming*) held that the Emperor possessed his authority by the will of Heaven, subject to his governing the country well, and that withdrawal of the Mandate, because of "bad government" (defined in Confucian terms), would be manifested in heavenly portents and popular unrest. A Japanese scholar, familiar with the literature in which such ideas were expressed, could hardly avoid as a consequence some consideration of the respective roles of Emperor and Shogun in Japan. And he might do so in a variety of ways. He might argue, as Tokugawa supporters sometimes did, that the Shogun's part had been that of the loyal and able minister, "restoring" the imperial order after a period of corruption and decline.[46] Or he might say that such notions as the Mandate applied to the source of the Shogun's authority itself, that the Emperor represented Heaven in relation to a Shogun ruler, validating his power (and perhaps even taking it away). Significantly, as we shall see, Mito loyalism, which became an attack on the Tokugawa, had Confucian origins of this kind.

Tokugawa scholars were also forced by the nature of their studies to recognize that Chinese and Japanese institutions were far apart in a number of other ways. One of the most obvious was that Japan was governed through a feudal system (*hōken-seido*), whereas China had long since abandoned feudalism in favor of an arrangement of provinces and districts (*gunken-seido*) administered by appointed officials of the Throne. Critical discussion of the relative merits and defects of the two systems involved questioning either the overall superiority of Chinese civilization or the virtues of what was done in Japan, a difficult choice for any man who was both samurai and Confucian scholar.[47] More, the difficulty extended also to the evaluation of his own place in the scheme of things. In Chinese theory, authority and status depended primarily on talent, insofar as this was measured in a series of Confucian-oriented examinations that gave access to office. In Japanese practice, despite its Confucian veneer, power accorded normally with birth. The Confucian scholar of Bakufu or domain, no matter how much he saw himself as a "man of talent," belonged characteristically to the middle or even lower samurai, able to exercise influence, to be sure, but rarely in the highest posts. His duty as a samurai enjoined acceptance of this situation. But Chinese doctrine implied that it was wrong—and was to that extent subversive. Certainly in the nineteenth century many samurai became unhappily aware of the conflict between these two components in their value system when the emergence of foreign and domestic threats to the world they lived in made it vital that Japan be at once united and efficient. The one entailed a strengthening of the bonds that held society together, the other a weakening of them so far as would give power to "men of talent"; and in this situation, Confucianism, though it justified for some a resistance to all things new, became for others an ingredient in a complex of ideas that was reformist, if not revolutionary.

CHAPTER II

Troubles at Home

To many Japanese in the middle of the nineteenth century it seemed that their country was facing the classic combination of domestic unrest and foreign attack that had so often brought about the downfall of Chinese rulers. A Chinese phrase, rendered in Japanese as *naiyū-gaikan*, "troubles at home and dangers from abroad," occurs frequently in their books and other writings. By *naiyū* they meant the rising level of turbulence in Japanese society, occasioned by economic changes that threatened both the political and the social order. *Gaikan* implied a belief that the expansion of the West's temporal power in Asia would sooner or later culminate in an attempt to subdue Japan. The experience of India and China, which was familiar to them, argued that the attempt would succeed.

It is the coming together of these two strands that gives a special character to the period of Japanese history starting in 1853. They are the major theme of this book. However, before considering the relationship between the two and the political context in which it was worked out, we should examine the background and nature of each separately. We begin, therefore, with naiyū, turning first to a phenomenon that has a special importance because it occurs at the point where political and economic history interact, namely, the impoverishment of both the samurai as a class and the governments to which they gave allegiance.

FINANCIAL PROBLEMS

Tokugawa Japan was an agrarian society. The samurai was himself in origin a farmer-soldier; it was to the farmer that he looked for his own income and for the revenue to maintain his government; and much the largest proportion of the country's wealth and population was agricultural. Against this, it was during the years of Tokugawa rule that the economy first developed a commercial sector of significant size. True, there had been trade and traders for several centuries. As early as the Muromachi period (1392–1573) they had begun to be of some importance. Nevertheless, it was under the Tokugawa that trade received so substantial a stimulus that it became a source of conspicuous wealth, a development to which contemporaries were able to attribute most of the country's ills. Nor was this coincidental. Commercial growth was not only a response to the restoration of peace and stability after civil war; it was also a natural outcome of the Tokugawa system.

Since samurai were required to live in the vicinity of their lord's principal stronghold, the samurai community frequently became the nucleus of a castle town (*jōkamachi*), attracting to itself the artisans and shopkeepers who catered to the needs of a relatively affluent ruling class.[1] As an administrative center, the castle town established a network of communications with the surrounding countryside, becoming both a political and an economic focus for its area. It was also linked to the two great cities of Edo and Osaka, thereby forming part of a larger complex.

The rules of sankin-kōtai, as we have seen, required each daimyo to spend alternate years in the Shogun's capital. While there he was attended by a notable retinue, and at all times he had to maintain there an establishment of some size to house his family and officials. As a result, Edo took on all the characteristics of an enormous castle town. By the eighteenth century it had a population of well over a million persons, half of them in samurai households whose daily spending made the city one of the greatest consumer markets in the world. Since the money they spent derived from the tax revenues of over 200 domains, ways had to be found of transferring resources from the provinces to the capital, preferably in cash. In addition, Edo itself had to be provided with the supplies of food, clothing, and other commodities its population needed, which were far beyond the capacity of its immediate hinterland to provide. Thus the city became the center of two separate but interlocking economic systems. One comprised the machinery for selling domain surpluses on the wholesale market in Osaka and making the credits so acquired available for use in Edo. The other was an elaborate series of arrangements for producing, shipping, and distributing the goods for the city's shops. In time the second of these extended to the larger provincial jōkamachi, too, for tastes acquired in Edo were soon carried back to the castle town, affording profitable outlets to a growing class of local merchants.

By 1700 Japan's merchants were already highly specialized. Some dealt chiefly in domain finances, handling the sales of tax rice in Osaka and the banking operations arising from them. Often they were in a position to make substantial advances against future crops. Others were wholesalers in any of a wide range of commodities or engaged in large-scale transport and warehousing. Below them ranged the retailers and local brokers, many of whom acted as financial agents for individual samurai, together with the shopkeepers, pawnbrokers, journeymen, and clerks. All these occupational groups had their counterparts in the castle towns. At least a few had connections with the villages, where a number of residents began to devote part of their time to trade. Indeed, the needs of the townsfolk gradually brought fundamental changes in the pattern of rural life. Beginning with the production of food for urban markets, cultivators in many areas turned away from subsistence farming to the raising of commercial crops: wax for candles, cotton and silk for textiles, indigo for dying. Before long, rural entrepreneurs, like those in cities, had also taken up certain forms of manufacture. Saké-brewing was one of the most lucrative and widespread, as was the production of rape-seed oils, but spinning and weaving in the textile trades were being organized through a cottage-industry system well before the end of the period. Some processes were even carried on in workshops in the more advanced localities by the nineteenth century.

An economic life as complex as this inevitably became more tightly organized. Merchants, relegated to the bottom of the social structure, sought a measure of security through collective action, forming guilds (*za*) to protect themselves against exploitation by their samurai masters.[2] They also tried to set up monopolies in specific goods or services, often receiving official sanction in this enterprise in return for an annual fee. In most domains one or two of the great merchant houses were appointed as financial agents. Others obtained special privileges as official contractors and suppliers. Everywhere, in fact, the conduct of business came to involve the handling of an intricate web of personal or corporate "rights," as well as technical detail.

This is one reason the samurai was reluctant to enter into it, quite apart from his natural distaste for a way of life beneath his station. He quite simply lacked the necessary knowledge. For example, in different parts of the country or under different circumstances, a price might be quoted in koku of rice, in gold *ryō*, in silver *momme*, in copper *mon*. For bookkeeping purposes it was possible to assume a standard set of values for these units; during much of the period one koku of rice was worth about one ryō, or 60 momme, or 1,000 mon. Yet actual market values were capable of wide and rapid movement, not least because of periodic debasement of the coinage. Thus rice prices regularly varied from the 60 momme norm by as much as 10 or 20 per cent on either side, and were subject at times to periods of still more violent fluctuation.[3] The nineteenth century was especially "abnormal" in this respect, showing a range of about 80 to 180 momme per koku in the 1830's; 65 to 100 in the 1840's; 75 to 120 in the 1850's; and then a final burst of inflation that brought prices from 150 momme in 1860 to over 200 in 1864 and nearly 1,000 by 1867. One has to remember, too, that there were two other kinds of variation of great importance to both family and domain budgets: regional differences, which depended a good deal on transport facilities, and seasonal price changes related to the harvest.

The market price of rice was vital to samurai standards of living. The vast majority, living on fixed stipends or the nominal yield from quasi-fiefs, had no direct connection with the land. Hence they could do little to increase their incomes by better management of agricultural production. Nor could they simply use the rice they received from the domain for food, providing for other needs by barter. All castle-town samurai had to serve at one time or another in Edo, where their bills could only be paid in cash, and it was not long before the money economy of the city had spread to provincial towns and villages as well. In this situation the samurai suffered from a number of disadvantages. Because of his relative ignorance of commercial practices, any profits to be made from dealings in the rice that comprised his stipend usually went to the merchant who acted as his agent. Moreover, other prices rose faster than those of rice, partly because the samurai himself contributed to an increase in the level of demand. Urban life gave him new tastes and opportunities and indulging them became part of his way of life, even though he could not easily afford them. Extravagance in matters of "style" thus became a major factor in the impoverishment of the feudal class. For samurai, keeping up appearances involved, as Ogyū Sorai said of daimyo, "the manner in which they are dressed on various occasions, their garments, food and drink, their household furnishings and apartments, the servants they employ, the elegance of their wives, their forms of address, the status of their messengers and the size of their retinue in processions through the city."[4] Competition in such items brought many men into the hands of the moneylenders. Thereafter, high interest rates made it unlikely that they would ever escape from debt.

There is ample evidence that samurai were not only in debt, but indeed in poverty, from quite early in the period. In Chōshū, for example, those with less than 200 koku were given permission in 1669 to live in the villages to cut down costs. The family of one of the Restoration leaders, Inoue Kaoru, seem to have taken advantage of this, for they apparently farmed some of their own land at times when he was young.[5] In Satsuma, too, samurai were sometimes allowed to recoup their fortunes by returning to the land. Ōkubo Toshimichi's ancestors did so for 70 or 80 years in the seventeenth century.[6] Moreover, in these and other areas there are numerous cases of samurai supplementing an inadequate income by engaging in a cottage industry, like the manufacture of lanterns or umbrellas. Others even relinquished their samurai status altogether to become farmers or merchants. This was true of the family of Matsukata Masayoshi, famous as Finance Minister during the middle of the Meiji period; his father, of Satsuma gōshi origin, abandoned his small fief and made a successful career in trading with the islands to the south.[7]

The same factors that brought penury, or at least hardship, to a considerable proportion of samurai households also operated, if more slowly, on the finances of daimyo and domains. For a daimyo even more than for a samurai, sankin-kōtai made inevitable an involvement in the money economy through the expenditure of large sums in cash.[8] A single journey to Edo in 1801 cost Satsuma no less than 14,100 gold ryō, equivalent to the whole annual revenue of a fief of 35,000 koku. To be sure, this was an exceptionally large amount—Satsuma was farthest from the capital of all the domains—but even quite small domains spent sums that were comparable in relation to their income. To this had to be added the cost of maintaining an establishment in Edo, perhaps more than one. Kaga, richest of the tozama lords, kept four, with grounds totaling over 250 acres and a staff of several thousand persons.

One of the Bakufu's reasons for enforcing this system of residence in the capital was precisely to prevent the emergence of "overmighty subjects" by ensuring a constant drain on domain finances. The policy was notably successful. It was reinforced by intermittent demands for the carrying out of public works, many of which were not only exceedingly expensive but also unpredictable and therefore difficult to budget for. Equally unpredictable—though in this case the Bakufu could not be held responsible—were the consequences of fire, flood, and earthquake. Since there was a high incidence of such calamities, this was an item not by any means to be ignored.

To meet extraordinary expenditures of this kind, the domains had rather less revenue at their disposal than their reputation for imposing very high tax rates might lead one to think. By the time the nominal value of the land (kokudaka) had been adjusted to exclude the value of sub-fiefs, which no more paid taxes to the daimyo than did the daimyo to the Shogun, and to take account of regular expenses like samurai stipends and administrative salaries, what was left yielded a *disposable* revenue of surprisingly small proportions. Thus the Chōshū treasury received in 1840, taking regular and supplementary sources together, a net revenue after deductions of only a little more than 75,000 koku. This was on an assessed land value of 895,000 koku.[9] Satsuma in the nineteenth century averaged between 120,000 and 130,000 koku a year from an assessed total of about 890,000, making no allowance for the costs of salaries.[10] By the same type of calculation, Kaga in 1868 raised about 250,000 koku on its 1,380,000 koku of land.[11] This represents approximately an 8.4 per cent yield for Chōshū, a 14.6 per cent yield for Satsuma, and an 18 per cent yield for Kaga.

Much of this disposable income was available for use in Edo. So were other kinds of revenue, most of which were actually raised in cash, either directly or indirectly from taxation of commerce. In fact, separate accounts were usually kept of the domain's income and expenditure in gold or silver, ignoring for this purpose the portion of the land tax that could not be converted to such use. Figures for Tosa in 1834–38 will serve as an example. During these years tax rice averaged 141,700 koku, of which 45,600 koku remained after subtracting earmarked items. This produced 4,848 *kamme* of silver, to which was then added the yield from miscellaneous dues, bringing the total up to 6,179 kamme. Against this were set expenditures of 7,169 kamme, giving an annual deficit of nearly 1,000 kamme.[12]

Significantly, no less than 4,465 kamme of Tosa's money was debited to expenditure in Edo. T. G. Tsukahira's calculations suggest that the proportion was not unusual. Taking five typical fudai domains, he shows that they were spending something on the order of 80 per cent of their available cash revenue on sankin-kōtai and associated items in the late-Tokugawa period. In the same period five large tozama domains spent about 71 per cent, if one includes their expenses in Kyōto and Osaka, which were incurred largely for the same purpose.[13] Given this drain on cash resources, it is easy to see why most samurai officials showed a marked preference for financial policies that promised not merely an increase in revenue in general, but an increase in the domain's stock of gold and silver in particular.

Nevertheless, the effects of these heavy charges were in some degree balanced by a steady growth in the yield from land tax. The main reason for this was a rise in what one might call taxable values, occurring as new land was brought into cultivation and entered on the registers. All domains had two different sets of valuations (kokudaka). One of these, called *hondaka* ("basic" value) or *omotedaka* ("public" value), was the valuation that was entered on the Shogun's grant of fief and usually represented the result of land surveys at the beginning of the Tokugawa period. Though originally fairly accurate, it eventually became notional, since no change seems ever to have been made for increases in cultivated area or yield per acre. The other, most commonly known as *jitsudaka* ("true" value), *uchidaka* ("private" value), or *kusadaka* ("total" value), was the valuation recorded by the tax collector. His figure was kept up-to-date to the extent of allowing for the new fields (*shinden*) added to the total. Sometimes it also reflected changes in the system of measurement or differences in the degree of efficiency with which surveys were carried out. Certainly it was in many cases substantially at variance with the figure that the Bakufu recorded.

Chōshū is probably the most extreme example of the variance in recorded valuations, for its omotedaka was falsified in the first place, being reported in 1610 as only 369,000 koku when the domain's own valuation was already over 500,000 koku. A fresh survey raised the domain's self-valuation to 658,000 koku in 1625; and by 1868 it was no less than 988,000 koku, that is, over two-and-a-half times the omotedaka, which had remained the same since 1610.[14] Tosa also showed a great disparity, with a jitsudaka of over 490,000 koku in 1868 against an omotedaka of 242,000. By contrast, Satsuma was rather below the national average, with about 870,000 koku against a theoretical 770,000, that is, a rise of less than 13 per cent.

To give some idea of the range of variation in the country as a whole, let us take sixteen of the largest domains, nominally of 200,000 koku or more, for which the 1868–69 figures are available in print. At this date, their "true" assessments (jitsudaka) compared with their "public" assessments (omotedaka) as follows: in three cases, the jitsudaka was over 100 per cent higher; in two cases, it was between 50 and 100 per cent higher; in four cases, it was between 20 and 50 per cent higher; in the remaining seven cases, it was less than 20 per cent higher.[15]

Tax rates on these assessments were high but varied a great deal, both nationally and locally. Contemporary writers talk of the farmer handing over as much as 50, 60, or even 70 per cent of his crop to his lord in the nineteenth century. It is doubtful, however, whether such figures were at all common. Averages based on the returns made to the Meiji government in 1868–69 suggest that over much of the country land tax was between 35 and 45 per cent of the jitsudaka, with some areas rather lower and others a little higher.[16] Support is given to this view by the fact that in most domains samurai were paid 40 per cent, or very near it, on the kokudaka of their stipends and fiefs.[17] Evidence on particular domains and villages conforms to the same broad pattern.[18]

It seems on balance unlikely that domains were able to make any substantial increase in the actual percentage of the crop they received as tax during the Tokugawa period, despite considerable efforts in this direction by local officials.[19] Their rule had never been lenient, even in the seventeenth century, so that there was little scope for a raising of tax rates. Nor does the actual administration of the tax system appear to have become greatly more efficient with time. What is more, as we shall see, commercial wealth was taxed insofar as it was taxed at all by other devices; there is no sign, for example, of attempts to tax the profits of local trade by artificially high assessments on the land of those who engaged in it.

Yet the domain as such did manage to improve its financial position relative to that of its retainers. For one thing, it contrived to retain for its own use an increasing share of normal revenue, as compared with that portion it distributed in stipends. Stipends, after all, remained fixed in value except where they were changed by way of reward or punishment. Accordingly, if the total kokudaka of the domain rose—and the great majority did—the lord's share of this increase accrued to the treasury, not to his samurai. The effect of this can be seen in Satsuma, where the treasury's share of the kokudaka increased by about 60 per cent between 1648 and 1849 as against a rise of only about 15 per cent in the total allocated to stipends.*

In addition to this long-term trend, domains were also able to use their authority to require special contributions from their sa-

* *Kagoshima-ken shi*, 2: 68–81. It is interesting to note that the increase for castle-town samurai was only about 8 per cent over the whole period, all of which took place by 1771, whereas the gōshi increase was 36 per cent, spread fairly evenly through time. This suggests that the former group suffered severely by its detachment from the land.

murai. These usually took the form of cuts in stipends, which began in some areas as early as 1700 and were widespread by the end of the eighteenth century, the extent varying both with time and place. Satsuma, for example, was one of the earliest to adopt this practice—levies had already been made intermittently there long before they were regularized in 1704—and its requirements were among the lowest, with an official norm of about 8 per cent, though this was sometimes raised to 13 or 15 per cent in years of financial crisis.[20] In Kaga there was a sliding scale based on size of stipend, with lower rates for the poorer families. Between 1794 and 1866 its rates varied from a minimum of 5 to 10 per cent to a maximum of 8 to 18 per cent.[21] Tosa also had a sliding scale but set at a much higher level. It was instituted in 1728 with a complex system of grades right up to 50 per cent; and though samurai opposition sometimes brought the maximum down to 25 per cent, the original system seems to have been what the domain government generally aimed at.[22]

It is clear from all this that the daimyo, or more accurately the domains as entities, were in a better position to meet the growing cost of urban life than were their retainers. They profited from the increase in jitsudaka, both relatively and absolutely. They were also able to put pressure on farmers and samurai to pay larger sums by way of tax or take smaller ones by way of stipend. This explains why domain debts were a rather later phenomenon than samurai debts. Even so, they were already of significant size as early as 1700 and became the main preoccupation of administrators at all levels in the following 100 years. Words like "policy" and "crisis" and "reform" came to be used almost exclusively in the context of finance, which in the first half of the nineteenth century became the focus of some bitter struggles.

It is not difficult to find examples to illustrate the problems the domains faced. Thus Shōnai, a fudai fief of 140,000 koku, already had debts of over 80,000 gold ryō in the early eighteenth century, with an annual deficit, excluding interest payments, of 12,000 ryō (equivalent to roughly 12,000 koku).[23] Kaga, with its much greater resources, had a regular deficit on current account by 1800; and it often ran as high as 3,000 kamme of silver in the next 50 years, that is, about 65,000 koku.[24] Satsuma in 1818, after a period of retrenchment, still had debts that totaled nearly one million ryō and was finding it difficult to get credit in Osaka. By 1827 the figure was said to have risen to five million ryō,[25] though one is tempted to wonder whether such a startling increase could really have taken place in so short a time. Finally, Chōshū's debts totaled 85,000 kamme of silver in 1840, when interest and repayments amounted to more than the domain's entire cash revenue from taxation.[26] At about this time a contemporary writer, noting that the estimated national total of domain debts of some 60 million ryō in gold required the sale of three million koku of rice a year in service charges alone (i.e., three-quarters of the quantity that was shipped annually to the Osaka market from all areas), commented that the daimyo had become little more than stewards to the great financiers, who were the real "owners" of Japan.[27]

The Bakufu was beset with the same kinds of financial troubles as the domains, though they developed more slowly, thanks to the Shogun's greater authority and greater wealth in land.[28] Years of extravagance and misfortune in the second half of the seventeenth century wasted inherited reserves; and this, since it came at a time when it was no longer easy to expand the Bakufu's landholdings at the expense of the feudal lords, put the government in some financial difficulties. All the same, the situation was by no means irretrievable, as the eighth Shogun, Yoshimune, demonstrated. By careful administration, rather than by any financial genius, he achieved an annual surplus in both rice and cash. From the time of his death in 1751, however, the situation deteriorated rapidly. In the second half of the eighteenth century, rice revenue fell while cash expenditure rose a good deal more quickly than cash income. As a result, by 1800 the Bakufu was actually showing a small annual deficit in terms of gold. The exceptional commercial growth of the early nineteenth century did much to accelerate this trend, so that by 1837–41 the Bakufu's accounts were showing an annual deficit of well over half a million ryō.

In one respect the Bakufu seems to have been worse off than many of the great domains because of long-term trends in agricultural production. Between the seventeenth and nineteenth centuries, assessed tax values (jitsudaka) increased much more in the predominantly tozama areas of southwest, west, and northeast Japan than they did in the central region, where most of the Tokugawa and fudai holdings were to be found.[29] This reflects differences in the nature of the economic development taking place at the country's center and periphery. At the periphery the increase in wealth that occurred during the Tokugawa period stemmed mostly from a rise in agricultural production of the traditional kind (the increase in jitsudaka being evidence chiefly of an increase in the area under cultivation). In tax terms, this meant that many of the more powerful tozama were able to improve their revenue substantially by the use of tried and familiar methods. At the center, by contrast, there was characteristically a growth of commerce (including commercial agriculture), which left the Bakufu with the much more difficult problem of devising ways to tax new forms of wealth. Its inability to do so effectively created an anomaly: despite the fact that the most economically advanced provinces were under its control, the Bakufu ended in no better a plight financially than its potential rivals, and perhaps a worse one.* Indeed, it could well be argued that it was actually weakened by the growing wealth of those who lived on its lands, because the accompanying social changes posed political and administrative problems that took up much of its energies. As was to be true also in the field of foreign affairs, responsibility for public policy *in a situation of failure* was to be anything but a source of strength.

The Bakufu and the domains used a number of devices that were not, strictly speaking, forms of taxation to supplement their regular dues, all having it in common that they exploited, as best they could, the commercial sector of the economy. Most important to the Bakufu was the device of recoinage, that is, debasement of the currency, which was first carried out in 1695 and repeated frequently if irregularly thereafter. The profits from this practice were very large: for example, more than 1.6 million ryō in the two years 1841–42 alone.[30] The domains, having no such recourse open to them

* Totman, *Politics*, pp. 62–63, points out also that by the 19th century the Bakufu's lands had become quite widely scattered and fragmented, so that the old "central fortress" had been nearly destroyed. This weakened the Bakufu economically as well as militarily because of the administrative difficulties it caused.

since coinage was a Bakufu monopoly, managed to secure some of the same advantages by issuing paper money.

Both Bakufu and domains also made extensive use of their power to call for *goyōkin,* or "forced loans." The Bakufu first used this technique in 1761–62, when it raised 700,000 gold ryō from Osaka merchants, but it was in the nineteenth century that the practice really became general. Ōyama Shikitarō records that the Shogun's government collected 1.4 million ryō in goyōkin between 1853 and 1860, nearly 900,000 ryō of it coming from the two cities of Edo and Osaka.[31] There was a further levy in 1865 in which a good many of the contributors were village headmen or farmers, suggesting that the device was a means of tapping the profits of rural as well as urban commerce. Data on Chiaraijima, a village on a fudai domain in Musashi, bear this out. Over the thirty-year period ending in 1868 two branches of the Shibusawa family there, one dealing in indigo, the other in silk, appear to have contributed goyōkin to their lord in amounts considerably in excess of the whole village's land tax assessment.[32] From the frequent references in biographies to the way in which rural families of standing acquired samurai status by such means, there can be no doubt that something of the kind was happening elsewhere as well.

Revenue was also derived from merchant organizations and monopolies, which became of increasing importance during the second half of the Tokugawa period.[33] Yoshimune had granted special rights to some merchant groups, largely in an attempt to control their activities. His successors did so for the purpose of raising money. In addition, the Bakufu itself exercised monopolies—in silver and copper, for example, and certain herbs—which were operated for it by privileged merchants. The larger domains followed suit, using their political authority to enhance the profits of undertakings that contributed substantially to their finances.

Sometimes a domain simply granted certain merchants a monopoly and helped to enforce it. In Himeji, for example, all cotton cloth was acquired from the producers in return for the domain's own paper money, then sold in Edo, the treasury taking its share of the profits from the sale in cash. In other cases, official intervention was more direct, as in the paper monopolies of Tosa and Uwajima.[34] Here officials were used to control the process of production and shipping, though marketing in Osaka was left to wholesale merchants. Once again, the domain made payment in its own paper and received its returns in cash. These were the most frequent types of monopoly arrangement, though in a few cases the whole process, including marketing, remained directly in the hands of the domain. At the same time, it was not uncommon to use merchants as officials in this context, so that monopolies, whatever their outward form, almost always involved cooperation of some kind between samurai and merchants. Often they brought in the village headmen as well to ensure control of a local crop, like mulberry, sugar, and even rice.

A mercantilist element was common to all these undertakings, since one object was to achieve a yield in gold and silver that would be available for use in Edo.* Accordingly, the monopolies were usually in "export" commodities, those that had a ready market outside the domain. In the eyes of officials, indeed, this may well have been a monopoly's most valuable function. It is true that a good deal of the profits found their way into the hands of the merchants who helped to make them. In some instances, moreover, the profits were apparently quite small, either because the monopoly was easy to evade or because it was so tightly administered as to kill the trade that gave rise to it. Nevertheless, where the system was successful, it became vital to domain finances. Satsuma's sugar monopoly, for example, is estimated to have yielded profits of about 120,000 gold ryō a year at the beginning of the nineteenth century, very nearly equal in value to the domain's whole disposable revenue from land tax after payment of stipends.[35] With sums like this at stake it is no wonder that monopolies became a major preoccupation of samurai officialdom.

CRITICISM AND UNREST

One of the disadvantages of the monopoly system, as of other policies designed exclusively to tap commercial development for the benefit of revenue, was that it attacked only one of the prob-

* Murata Seifū of Chōshū once remarked: "The first principle of finance is to sell all the goods produced in Chōshū to other *han* in exchange for gold and silver and not to let any gold or silver produced in Chōshū out of the *han*" (Craig, *Chōshū*, p. 74).

lems created by economic change, namely, that of government finance. Another equally critical problem, that of samurai impoverishment, was little touched by it. Indeed, though from one point of view it was to the advantage of government to stimulate commercial growth in order to tax it, when this was done the samurai as an individual remained subject to all the disabilities arising from the possession of a fixed rice income in a money economy; and as the merchant became richer his wealth, it seemed to many, bade fair to undermine not only samurai solvency, but also samurai dominance of society at large. There was in this a cause for concern that raised public, as well as private, issues.

Nor was this the only challenge to the established order. The same pressures that were changing the relationship between merchant and samurai were also modifying the nature of life in the village,[36] for as more and more farmers began to raise crops for the market differences in their ability to cope with fluctuations in price or to improve the productivity of their land led to a greater separating out of rich and poor. The clumsiness of the tax machinery enabled a man who increased his crop by the use of fertilizer or who turned to another crop that gave a relatively better yield to reduce substantially his effective rate of tax, leaving himself a margin of income for saving and investment.* Much the same was true of a man who engaged in local trade or manufacture, since these, too, were activities that were never fully taxed.[37] At the other end of the scale, those who failed to seize such opportunities were left to bear the full weight of feudal dues and often fell into debt to their more prosperous neighbors. This led almost inevitably to tenancy and sometimes to a total loss of land. Accordingly, as the few became rich the many became poorer, eking out a living as part-time or full-time agricultural laborers, working as employees in a local industry like saké-brewing, or taking refuge in flight to the town or city. Satō

* Seki, *Hansei kaikaku*, pp. 56–66, points out that the effective levels of tax in Chōshū in the economically advanced areas around Yamaguchi and Mitajiri were for this reason no more than 40 per cent, compared with 50 or 60 per cent in other parts of the domain. More striking still, Furushima, "Seiritsu-ki kisei jinushi-sei," pp. 18–19, cites the example of a family engaged in cotton growing in Kawachi whose tax on that part of their land they cultivated themselves for raising cotton (as distinct from the part that was let to tenants) was only 11 per cent of the income they drew from it.

Nobuhiro, writing in 1827, claimed that 30 or 40 per cent of farmers had already lost their land in this way.[38]

The separating-out process was faster in those parts of the country that had the closest ties with the urban economy, such as the provinces around Edo and Osaka, and those where the soil and climate favored particular commercial crops.[39] But even in the remotest areas it was not entirely unknown, so that almost everywhere the middle farmers, the traditional cultivators of tax rice, began to decline in numbers.* At the same time, a new elite began to take over village government, sometimes after a struggle with those they displaced.[40] Their origins were diverse, and varied from place to place: in Kumamoto and Tosa, for example, either commercial or landed wealth could open a route to gōshi status and village office; in Aizu, it was landlords, cultivating land with paid labor, who retained control; in Chōshū, some villages were dominated by former merchants, others by landlords who drew their income from tenancy, and still others by a new class of prosperous middle farmers.[41]

These men and those who were closely associated with them provided many of the rank-and-file of the anti-Bakufu movement after 1858. Their participation in the running of business and of village affairs gave them a greater practical knowledge of the country's needs and problems than was possessed by most samurai of the castle town, while their comparatively low social standing made them ready to reform society in the name of ability rather than rank. At the same time, they were by no means representative of the lower orders, whose unrest they feared. Consequently, they were perfectly willing to take the side of authority once they had won acceptance in the ruling class.[42] Against this, it has to be said that in some respects their interests, like their origins, were diverse. Some derived income primarily from the land, in rice or rents, and were therefore concerned vitally with the level of land tax. Others depended on their links with the monopolies, which they accordingly wished to retain or develop. Others, again, were hostile to monopo-

* In some areas, however, commercial cropping led to the virtual disappearance of both rich and landless residents in the village, leaving it almost entirely to a new type of middle farmer–producer. See, for example, the figures for a paper-producing village in Mito cited in Shibahara, *Meiji ishin*, pp. 120–23.

lies, either as traders outside the ring or as producers seeking a free (and more profitable) market.

Their importance in our present context is that their emergence contributed to a rising level of turbulence in the countryside. The events that historians list as peasant revolts in Tokugawa Japan often include what would now be regarded merely as mass protest meetings, some of them even led apparently by village headmen;* but there is no doubt that after the middle of the period villagers were increasingly being driven to violence to express dissatisfaction, whether their grievances sprang from the severity of tax collectors or arose from the shifting pattern of class relationships in rural society.[43]

Nearly 400 incidents have been recorded for the years between 1813 and 1868, some of which involved thousands of farmers. For example, it is estimated (a little improbably) that some 100,000 men took part in a march on Wakayama in 1823, which led to attacks on rice dealers, pawnbrokers, and village headmen. High rice prices were largely the issue in this instance, as they were in a similar affair in Kai in 1836, when local Bakufu representatives had to seek military reinforcements from neighboring provinces before order could be restored. Also on Bakufu territory was a large-scale rising in Ōmi in 1842, this one provoked by attempts to increase land-tax revenue. Even more alarming was a series of incidents in 1837 following the disclosure that a minor Bakufu official in Osaka, Ōshio Heihachiro, had been plotting a rising to bring home to his superiors his sense of the justice of popular discontent. Ōshio was betrayed and committed suicide, and the affair seemed likely to end there, causing only minor disturbances in the city. But news of it prompted risings in the area around and as far afield as the province of Echigo on the Japan Sea coast. What is more, Ōshio had raised issues that were to be of increasing importance in later years. Himself married into a rich farmer family, he had gathered the sons of such families into a school he had founded, where he lectured with zeal about the

* One should not make too much of this fact, since the headman was uneasily placed between an officialdom that held him responsible for breaches of the peace and a population that blamed him for the actions of officialdom. See Befu, "Duty," pp. 28–46. Still, there is evidence that by the 19th century many village headmen were in fact discontented with their lot. See Jansen, "Tosa," pp. 331–47.

moral evils of Bakufu rule, appealing against them to Confucian ethics and the Emperor's justice, much as the "men of spirit" of the 1860's were to do.[44] In other words, his activities set a new pattern, affording evidence that rural wealth might well become linked with political subversion in a context in which both Bakufu officials and urban merchants would be objects of distrust.

On fudai domains, there were outbreaks at Takeda in Bungo in 1811–12 and at Miyazu in Tango in 1822. In both cases merchants and local officials concerned with the monopoly system were attacked. Among the tozama, Chōshū had no fewer than nine risings of one kind or another in the early nineteenth century, culminating in a major one in 1831 that is said to have forced the domain to undertake reforms.

This Chōshū rising, in fact, which has been much studied,[45] serves to illustrate the difficulty of generalizing about the causes and nature of these events. It started, like many others, as a protest against domain monopolies, specifically against a plan to extend their operation that had been put into force the previous year. But by no means all those who took part in it were protesting against the same thing. In the economically advanced areas along the Inland Sea, where the disturbances began, one of the grievances was an increase in rice prices, which brought hardship to those farmers who no longer grew rice because they had turned their land over to crops like rape-seed and indigo. Other causes of complaint were the monopoly itself (which prevented the free marketing of such commercial crops and limited the producer's profit) and abuses in the monopoly's administration. In such areas the revolt can be characterized, perhaps, as "bourgeois." Elsewhere, especially in the backward mountain districts, to which unrest rapidly spread, it reflected rather the simple farmer's incoherent sense of the injustice of local merchant exploitation, manifested in an appeal for the domain to ease his lot by reducing its tax demands on him.

Taking Japan at large the causes of unrest were more varied still. Sometimes, as in Chōshū, it was the domain monopolies that were the objects of resentment. Sometimes it was the level of taxation or local maladministration or the failure of officialdom to take full account of an exceptionally bad harvest. Not infrequently it was some quite trivial local grievance that brought men, made desperate by poverty, to the point of violence. Certainly the "revolts" were not revolutionary in the sense of being movements directed to overthrowing or changing the regime, even though it was often officials who were under attack. Indeed, if there can be said to be any single thread running through them at all, it was that the anger of the farmers, whatever its initial cause, commonly was vented against their nearest enemies—the "rich farmers," who were so often pawnbrokers, and the village headmen, who might also be landlords or agents for the domain monopolies—and that it was to their lord they turned for justice or relief.

The dangers implicit in all this—in merchant wealth and samurai impoverishment, in peasant revolt and rural social change—were clear enough to the feudal administrators of Tokugawa Japan. From the seventeenth century on, they sought solutions that would both preserve the privileges of their class and meet the financial requirements of their lords, finding them, often enough, in measures designed to check or stifle commercial growth. With this were sometimes associated plans for the resettlement of samurai on the land.[46] Kumazawa Banzan (1619–91) was the first to urge such a policy, which he envisaged as a means of reviving military morale, as well as cutting down on the samurai's household costs. It should be accompanied, he said, by a relaxation of the requirements for sankin-kōtai so as to reduce the expenses incurred in Edo. Another samurai reformer, Ogyū Sorai (1666–1728), supported this policy but saw more clearly than Kumazawa the threat it might pose to Bakufu control of the provinces. Accordingly, his plans for restoring self-sufficiency to the economy of the domains were accompanied by others for reasserting the status divisions within society, especially the superiority of samurai *vis-à-vis* merchants and farmers. Later writers followed much the same line, so that "agrarianism" of this kind became a familiar ingredient in the literature of reform.

There is no evidence of any attempt to put such "back-to-the-land" proposals fully into practice.[47] What did happen, however, was that hostility toward urban life came to be an element in the conception of reform in the later part of the period. If samurai could not be returned to the land, the feeling was, they ought at least to be discouraged from spending too freely in the towns. Hence, sumptuary laws became a regular phenomenon. Similarly, merchants ought to be brought under closer supervision so as to limit their ability to profit at the samurai's expense, and made to disgorge part of their wealth for the benefit of samurai and farmers. In the villages themselves there should be a return to subsistence farming. "It is a good farmer who does not know the price of cereals," wrote Shōji Kōki in the nineteenth century.[48] In fact, any device that was calculated to check the growth of cities and force population back into the countryside, there to increase the productivity of the land, was assumed to be a contribution to solving the problems of society. As Yamagata Bantō put it in a book published in 1820, "It is good government to encourage agriculture and discourage commerce and industry, with a view to causing the decline of urban districts."[49]

Not all samurai could be brought to agree with this, however. Many liked life in the towns and cherished no desire to practice frugal virtues in a village. Moreover, they were prisoners in a web of debts and interest payments, of salaries and side-employment, which it seemed rather easier to live with than to destroy. Accordingly, they were willing to give their support to those officials who saw the solution to society's ills in a more efficient exploitation of the commercial economy by the feudal class, not its restriction or abolition in the name of an agrarian ideal.[50] This, too, became an element in late-Tokugawa reform.

So did the resentment of the samurai over the consistent failure of any of these policies to better their position appreciably. Tokugawa literature is full of their complaints of poverty, their bitterness against merchants, their haughty strictures on the behavior of those commoners (in the countryside as well as in the town) whose wealth enabled them to ape their betters. It is also replete with warnings about the political dangers of the situation, including hints at the possibility of samurai disaffection.

As early as the seventeenth century Kumazawa Banzan wrote: "If the daimyo are bankrupt and the samurai are impoverished, their exactions from the people are heavier and the farmer suffers. If the peasantry is impoverished, the merchants and artisans likewise will suffer. In addition, great numbers of unemployed samurai (*rōnin*) will be produced and will be exposed to hunger and cold. Thus society as a whole will be afflicted with poverty and the heavens will cease to favour the shogun."[51] The last sentence of this passage, by implication, applies the Chinese doctrine of the Mandate of Heaven to Tokugawa rule: for the ruler to fail in the duty of succoring his people is to imperil his right to power. Ogyū Sorai was too firm an adherent of the Shogun to go quite so far. Yet even he could write: "When one is so poor that one is in want of food and clothing, one loses all regard for propriety. Unless there is respect for propriety among the lower orders, it is obvious that there must be unrest, and eventually civil war."[52]

In another writer, Honda Toshiaki (1744–1821), one finds ideas that are so critical of authority in this context as to seem positively subversive. The farmers, he said, were deprived by their lords of the greater part of their harvest, "the product of their tears of blood and their hardships of a year," only to see it handed over directly to the merchants to whom the daimyo was in debt.[53] However, the results of this, namely, "that the farmers are dying of starvation and that good fields are turning into wasteland," was the responsibility, not of the daimyo, but of the Shogun.[54] It was the Shogun, therefore, who in the last resort must face the consequences: "The daimyo are now all impoverished and unable to pay their retainers their stipends. The farmers are exhausted by severe taxation, and practice infanticide in order not to add mouths to feed. It is certain then that both the lords and the farmers hate the ruler. . . . Unless the merchants are brought under the ruler's control, the wrath and pent-up indignation of the samurai and the farmers will burst forth, and anything may happen."[55]

One product of this sense of grievance was a growing demand in the late-Tokugawa period for "the promotion of men of talent." This, too, was Confucian orthodoxy, though it fitted less well than most Confucian tenets into a society like Japan's, where status was determined by birth.[56] Ogyū Sorai, who wrote about this subject more vehemently than he had approached the question of the Shogun's sovereignty (perhaps because as a man of low rank and great ability himself he felt a stronger personal commitment), was scathing in his description of the upper samurai: "Set apart from those below by their high rank, they are uninformed of conditions among the people. Brought up amidst the constant flattery of those around them, they pride themselves on their wisdom without in truth having any."[57] Ogyū thought it inevitable that ability should disappear from the upper levels of society, since ability was developed only by the need to exercise it, that is, by contact with adversity. What is more, its disappearance, if not compensated for by the promotion of able men from lower ranks, would endanger the regime:

> But if the men in high positions try to postpone the time when they should give place to others, and are so foolish as to attempt to keep things as they are by laying it down that the families which are in a superior position and those which are in an inferior position shall remain in that state for ever, they will be acting against the principles of natural order. As a result of this, persons of ability will disappear from among the upper class and in the course of time an age of disorder will come, in which men of ability will appear among the lower classes and overthrow the dynasty.[58]

Though presented as a lesson drawn from Chinese history, this analysis seems prophetic, if not threatening. It provides an excellent example of how orthodox Confucian thought, expounded by one who was clearly loyal to the regime, could in a Japanese setting provide the beginnings of a revolutionary rationale.

As a result of this kind of Confucian writing, it had become a commonplace in Japan by the nineteenth century that "promotion of men of talent" was a desirable policy, for all that it might run counter to the status system.* And as turbulence and the problems of government grew there was more inclination to give it reality. In a few domain schools practical training in administration was introduced and greater recognition was given to intellectual prowess. Thus a Chōshū memorial of 1840 states: "The success or failure of the school depends entirely on its production of talented men."[59]

Moreover—after 1853 especially—many samurai were promoted, by both the Bakufu and the domains, to posts of far greater conse-

* One must remember that the expression could be interpreted—and was so interpreted by conservatives like Matsudaira Sadanobu—as no more than an injunction to select the most able of those qualified by birth.

quence than those to which their inherited rank entitled them.[60] Others were encouraged to take up the study of Western military science and technology with a view to entering fields that would normally have been reserved to hereditary "experts." As Hosoi Heishū (1728–1801) observed: "There are times of turbulence and times of peace. . . . In time of turbulence, irrespective of nobility or baseness of rank, one promotes those who are useful and will help to win tomorrow's battle and strengthen the domain."[61] To many samurai, indeed, this was of the essence of politics: "the shapeless future would take care of itself if men of ability were to occupy positions of practical responsibility."[62] The lack of interest in "programs" that this implies was to characterize much of the Restoration movement.

THE TEMPŌ REFORMS

As has been suggested above, by the nineteenth century economic change had produced a number of actual or potential conflicts in Japanese society, all of great political significance. The new "men of substance," the rich merchants and farmers, whose interests accorded with neither the samurai's nor each other's, pursued activities that tended to increase the burdens imposed on the rural mass by adding rent, usury, and commercial profits to feudal dues. What is more, whereas some samurai preferred their comforts, which implied a willingness to maintain an essentially symbiotic relationship with urban wealth, others sought to restore a dominance that they believed to rest of necessity on an agrarian base. Among the latter, moreover, one must distinguish between those who urged a seventeenth-century ideal, that is, subsistence agriculture, and those who shared the economic ambitions of an emergent village upper class.

One consequence of this state of affairs was turbulence. Another was "reform," namely, policies designed to change Japan's existing economy and society, not simply maintain the even tenor of government. On several occasions in the eighteenth and nineteenth centuries, the administrators of the Bakufu and a number of domains set out to discover solutions to one or other of the problems, usually the financial ones, that seemed to threaten their way of life.

They did so by a variety of devices; gave support to several different social groups; offered various justifications for their actions; and have thereby provided the historian with a number of "explanations" to choose from. The last such attempt at reform came in the Tempō period.* Since much of what then took place is held to have established patterns that were significant for the nature of the Restoration movement, we must obviously discuss it. Before entering on generalization, however, it might be as well to summarize what actually occurred. We begin with the Bakufu.

Tokugawa Yoshimune, who was Shogun from 1716 to 1745, had created precedents for most of the "reforms" of his successors: retrenchment, sumptuary laws, recoinage, manipulation of prices, efficient tax collection, encouragement of the military virtues, everything that served to increase Bakufu revenue on the one hand and restrain samurai consumption on the other. His grandson, Matsudaira Sadanobu, chief minister from 1786 to 1793 and the country's next major reformer, put his emphasis on the control of public and private spending, though without achieving any lasting effect on government solvency or the habits of the samurai class. Accordingly, when Mizuno Tadakuni, fudai lord of Hamamatsu (60,000 koku), became senior Rōjū in July 1841 and announced his intention of seeking to reduce the annual deficit by policies based on those of Yoshimune and Sadanobu, he was not only giving notice of a program of reform, but also indicating its probable nature, that is, an attack on extravagance in all its guises.[63]

During the next two years there was a constant stream of edicts regulating standards of food and dress, hair styles, the giving of presents, all the expensive habits of the world of theaters and brothels into which the samurai seemed to be so easily lured. In addition, an attempt was made to check the drift of population into Edo from

* The Japanese habitually designated years serially by reference to era-names (*nengō*), chosen for their auspicious meanings. Tempō ("Heavenly protection") was one of these, in use from 1830 to 1843 (these two years being the first and fourteenth years of Tempō, respectively). The era-names are often used as chronological labels for notable events that occurred in or are associated with the period in question. Thus the reforms here discussed are known as "the Tempō reforms," just as the foreign treaties of 1854–58 concluded in the Ansei period (1854–59) are known as "the Ansei treaties" and the restoration of imperial authority that occurred in the first year of the Meiji period (1868–1912) is known as "the Meiji Restoration."

the countryside by banning new immigrants and ordering men without fixed employment to return to the farm; a ceiling of 10 per cent a year was put on the interest rates that could be charged on the debts of Tokugawa samurai; and an ambitious campaign was launched to reduce prices in the city's shops. The last of these measures was supported by some unprecedented acts of interference in the working of the commercial economy, including orders for the dissolution of the merchant guilds (*kabu-nakama*) on the grounds that their monopoly operations were forcing up prices.

These measures had the same weakness as those directed against samurai consumption, namely, that they attacked the symptoms, not the cause. It was rising demand in a situation of relatively static production that sent up prices, not the manipulations of the Edo kabu-nakama, however much the merchants were concerned to maximize their profits. Hence it was doubtful from the outset whether Mizuno's policy would achieve the ends he had in mind. Nor, indeed, did he have the administrative machinery to see that it was properly carried out. Samurai connived at interest rates higher than those the law allowed because they could not live without loans. Merchants evaded the price regulations or simply failed to bring their goods to market. What is more, the Bakufu's intervention in the very complex organization by which the life of Edo received finances and supplies disrupted the normal processes of credit and distribution, thereby almost bringing commerce to a halt.

All this spelled failure. Mizuno's financial policy, based on recoinage and forced loans, was effective in the short term but could hardly be described as popular. His Draconian sumptuary laws were no more so, offending as they did most of Edo's inhabitants, not least those who lived in the Shogun's castle. In addition, lack of judgment on particular issues led to quarrels with members of the Tokugawa house. None of this would have mattered so much, perhaps, had Mizuno been a man of very high personal rank, or one who found it easy to make friends. Being neither, he could depend only on results; and these, for all his ability, he did not produce. The Bakufu's Tempō reforms ended with his dismissal from office in November 1843.

What Mizuno tried to do for the Bakufu, others attempted in

the domains, sometimes even by the same techniques. In Tosa, for example, reformers were directly inspired by Mizuno's methods and suffered a similar fate.[64] By contrast, in Hizen, where reforms had been initiated some years earlier by retainers of the new daimyo, Nabeshima Naomasa, the familiar policy of retrenchment, aimed at restricting both samurai and domain expenditure, was supplemented by an attack on landlordism in the villages, designed to strengthen the position of the farmer-cultivator. This was conceived to be in the interests of both feudal stability and the production of rice, which was Hizen's principal cash crop. And in the short run, at least, it seems to have been effective in preserving the traditional patterns of living in the countryside.[65]

Mito, another domain that was destined to play a leading part in mid-nineteenth century politics, affords certain parallels with Hizen. Reform there was stimulated by the succession of a new daimyo, Tokugawa Nariaki, and included steps, implemented through a land survey, to limit the wealth of the richer landlords. Unlike Hizen, however, Mito maintained and strengthened its monopolies (in paper and tobacco); gave gōshi status to village leaders who took part in the monopolies and the survey; and made a start on settling samurai on the land as the nucleus of a militia force charged with maintaining order in the countryside. These measures were accompanied by an attack on inefficiency in the domain's financial administration—in the manner of Mizuno Tadakuni, with whom Nariaki cooperated in the Bakufu's own reforms—and by steps to improve samurai education and morale.[66]

The Tempō reforms in Chōshū provide yet another variation on the traditionalist theme. Throughout the eighteenth and early nineteenth centuries there had been a steady growth of commercial activity in Nagato and Suō (the two provinces that comprised Chōshū), especially along the Inland Sea coast.[67] This led to the emergence of powerful merchant groups in the castle town of Hagi and the creation of monopolies at various times in such things as paper, wax, cotton cloth, and rape-seed oil; but the domain nevertheless got further and further into debt, until by the 1830's it owed something like 80,000 or 90,000 kamme of silver, equivalent to about a million and a half gold ryō. In 1830 an attempt was made to reduce these debts by instituting an ambitious monopoly plan that put all the trade of a wide range of commodities in the hands of five groups of privileged merchants in return for an annual payment of 360 kamme. This scheme, however, provoked widespread peasant unrest and soon had to be abandoned. Even so, sporadic outbreaks of peasant revolt continued for the next few years.

It was in these circumstances that in 1838 the new daimyo, Mōri Yoshichika, called on Murata Seifū, a hirazamurai, to carry out financial reforms.[68] Murata's first actions were fairly conventional, consisting of economies in expenditure, better budgeting procedures, and improvements in financial administration; but in 1840 he launched a more far-reaching program, which included abolishing some of the monopolies and changing the character of others, as well as sumptuary laws and measures designed to restore the samurai to a proper sense of their military duties. In sum, Murata favored traditional virtues and the farmer-cultivator against "decadence" and the merchant-monopolist, so far as the financial interests of the domain allowed.

Murata did not, it is true, markedly reduce the domain's debts. However, he succeeded in repudiating some of them, apparently, and in building up cash reserves in an emergency fund, which largely financed Chōshū's military expenditure in later years.* Moreover, withdrawal of the domain's support from most of the monopolies eased to some extent the burdens placed on farmers. In addition, part of the gains from the administrative economies were also passed on: supplementary levies on farmers were reduced from 5 per cent to 3 per cent, and there were progressive reductions in the cuts the domain had been making in samurai stipends. Both measures served to improve morale and help to explain why Chōshū had only four peasant revolts in the following forty years. Certainly, then, one can say that Murata left Chōshū stronger than he found it in a number of ways, whatever its position in strictly fiscal terms.

The same can be said of the Satsuma reformer Zusho Hiromichi,

* The chief source of these reserves was the yield from an office (Koshinagata) set up to exploit Chōshū's access to, and control of, one of Japan's key shipping routes (that through the Shimonoseki Straits). In this instance—perhaps because the profits were greater—Murata's supposed hostility to monopolies was not in evidence. See Craig, *Chōshū*, p. 69.

though in matters of policy the two men differed greatly.[69] In 1831, when Zusho instituted his reforms, Satsuma was not only paying some 350,000 gold ryō a year as interest on existing debts, but also running an annual deficit of 50,000 ryō on current account. The Osaka financial houses were reluctant to extend further credit. Two of them, however, finally rallied to Zusho's support, providing money for immediate use. Further, with their help plans were drawn up for the gradual funding of what was owed to the city merchants, largely through the profits from monopoly trade. Zusho's role in this program, one that he admirably fulfilled, was to make sure the trade was efficiently run. Indeed, better administration of existing sources of revenue was the key to his success in general. By improving the quality and the handling of the rice that was shipped for sale to Osaka, he doubled its market price. A similar result was achieved by more careful refining of wax, which was now made a monopoly. Above all, the trade in sugar from Ryukyu and Ōshima was reorganized and made more profitable.

Sugar had been received as tax from these islands long before the end of the eighteenth century, by which time any part of the Ōshima crop that was not actually being paid as dues was a domain monopoly.[70] Zusho's contribution was to strengthen the ban on private dealing, which was made a capital crime, punishable by death; and to revise the arrangements both for payment to the producers and for sale of the crop in Osaka, so as to provide the greatest possible yield to the Satsuma treasury. Samurai officials maintained a close inspection of the crop, the whole of which had to be surrendered to them at fixed prices. In return, they provided the islanders with all other commodities they needed at prices fixed in relation to that of sugar in order to ensure a very low purchase price for the sugar in real terms. Since the domain's own ships were used to carry the sugar to Osaka, where it was then sold by competitive tender, it is clear that a substantial part of the return was to the domain's immediate benefit; and though we lack complete figures on actual profit, from those we do have it would seem not unreasonable to assume that Zusho achieved annual profits of about 100,000 ryō, a sum that his successors, exploiting what he had done, greatly exceeded. Certainly his work as a whole, including the yields from other monopolies, not only reduced in some degree the Satsuma debts, but also led to the accumulation of a large cash reserve, similar to Murata's in Chōshū. Satsuma's later leaders were able to use these funds for military reform, the purchase of Western arms, and a number of costly experiments in the use of modern technology.

It has long been accepted that this is one of the keys to the political significance of the Tempō reforms, namely, that by their relative success some domains, notably Satsuma and Chōshū, increased their own strength *vis-à-vis* the Bakufu and so put themselves into a position to challenge Bakufu authority when the opportunity offered. Mizuno failed, it is said, because the Bakufu held the rich heartlands of the country, where commerce was more fully developed and therefore more difficult to subordinate to the needs of the feudal class; whereas Murata and Zusho succeeded because their territories, in addition to being more compact and hence more easily administered, were economically rather less advanced so that it was possible to reassert samurai dominance there and exploit commercial growth for the benefit of the domain.[71]

The argument has substance, of course. Without a war chest of considerable size, Satsuma and Chōshū would have been unable to build up their armaments to the point of risking a trial of strength. It is, nevertheless, an oversimplification. In terms of relative military capacity, the willingness to adopt Western organization and technology was as important as the money to finance them; and this was a feature, not primarily of the Tempō reforms, but of those that came in the Ansei period (1854–59) and after.[72]

One marked difference between the Bakufu and the domains that does emerge in the Tempō reforms is a political one, the fact that in the domains, but not in Edo, men of middle samurai rank gained authority and administrative experience. Even in Satsuma, which was conservative in these matters, Zusho rose from hirazamurai rank, via posts in his lord's household, to that of Karō (senior councillor) and a stipend of 1,000 koku. His successor as the central figure of Satsuma politics (though admittedly a distant relative of the daimyo house) did the same.[73] Albert Craig has shown that most of the leaders of Chōshū politics after about 1840, starting with Murata, were also hirazamurai, with stipends ranging from 40 to 200 koku.[74] The standing of Nariaki's chief supporters in Mito was much the same, though their stipends were higher (200 to 300 koku).[75] The Hizen reforms, too, were undertaken by hirazamurai of the daimyo's entourage.[76]

Given the nature of domain political structures, the rise of such men naturally centered on their relationship with their lord. He was always an autocrat in theory, whatever he might be in reality, and most offices were therefore his to grant. Accordingly, his personal favor, manifested perhaps through nomination to a household appointment, was the commonest way for a man of relatively humble birth to overcome the disabilities of hereditary status, or for one group to oust another whose policies it rejected. Largely for this reason, succession disputes, made more frequent by lack of a clear rule of primogeniture, became a familiar occasion for factional strife. Thus when Tokugawa Narinaga of Mito died without an heir in 1829, his younger brother Nariaki was made his successor with the help of a reform party of middle samurai against the opposition of a group of upper samurai conservatives, who wanted as their lord one of the sons of the Shogun Ienari.[77] Shimazu Nariakira of Satsuma, another of the great reforming lords of the 1850's, also came to power after a political controversy, in this case one that was connected with his criticism of Zusho's policies.[78] It involved a rivalry with his half brother, Hisamitsu; the support of a middle samurai faction, to which Ōkubo Toshimichi's father belonged; and the intervention of the Bakufu leader Abe Masahiro.

In some domains, including those we have just been discussing, political events served to underline the existence of a rivalry between upper samurai on the one hand and middle or lower samurai on the other. Nor is this division surprising. Most upper samurai, having power, were conservative in both political and economic matters. It follows that proposals for reform or an attempt by any other group to secure a share of power involved an attack on them. Nevertheless, one must be careful not to extend this argument into an assertion that all men of lower rank were united in demanding reform or meant the same thing by it. For example, in Chōshū Murata Seifū and Sufu Masanosuke, who was Murata's successor as leader of the "enlightened" party, preached a return to the agrarian ideal, whereas their "conservative" opponents, Tsuboi Kuemon and Mukunashi Tōta, upheld the symbiosis between castle-town samurai and privileged merchants. Yet all four were hirazamurai of about the same economic standing. Murata's stipend was 91 koku, Sufu's 68; Tsuboi's was 100, Mukunashi's 46. On this evidence, at least, it would be difficult to maintain that the policy disputes were manifestations of a class struggle, or even a struggle between upper and lower levels of a single class.[79]

This, however, is not the whole story. One is still left with other important questions about the social background to the Tempō reforms. All modern writers are agreed that one element in the reforms was an official hostility toward monopolies and those who profited from them, which led either to their abolition, ostensibly as a means of lowering prices and interest rates, or to attempts to harness them more strictly to the service of feudal finance. It is also agreed that this was by way of reaction against the situation that had developed in the first part of the nineteenth century, when there had been a rapid increase in monopoly trading. From this it is a short step to asserting that the reforms took shape as the result of an "alliance" between the domain and those groups in the village which were opposed to the monopolies (like the middle farmer–producer of commercial crops in an area like Chōshū), and that this alliance replaced a previous one between the domain and the privileged merchants.

In one variant, Seki Junya argues that the feudal class, finding its merchant allies becoming too strong, sought alternative supporters who would be too weak to challenge its authority themselves. In another, Horie Hideichi sees the process as an abandonment by the domain of an alliance with the old village leadership in favor of one with those who were beginning to attack it in the name of economic freedom. Both see the lower samurai as being the natural spokesmen for the new alignment, since it was they, like the middle farmers, who had suffered most from the rise of the merchant class.

With a different emphasis, Shibahara Takuji and Tōyama Shigeki maintain that the reforms represent a coming together of those in both the village and the castle town who felt themselves threatened by the tide of peasant revolt.[80]

This kind of approach raises the issue, not of divisions within the samurai class, but of the extent to which the relationships between samurai and non-samurai groups give a class significance to castle-town politics. It is an issue that is not easily resolved. One might begin by questioning the applicability of the word "alliance" in this context, since it implies a degree of cooperation between self-conscious and independent entities that is not reflected in the records (which describe only samurai initiatives). More fundamentally, one must have doubts about any generalized explanation that purports to apply to the whole of Japan in view of the considerable differences of policy and circumstance our summary of the reforms has shown. This disparity, indeed, is reflected in the disagreements among Japanese historians, which are often founded on differences in the geographical basis of their studies. So Tanaka Akira is probably right in saying that though all the Tempō reforms were attempts to maintain or restore feudal authority, the local variations in the nature of the challenge to that authority led to wide variations in the response.[81] It may well be impossible in the present state of our knowledge to find a thesis any more elaborate than this that would fit all the domain patterns.

All the same, the socioeconomic argument cannot be summarily dismissed. Village society *was* changing, and in ways that were likely to affect the balance of political power. Feudalism *was* facing a crisis in that its political forms had outlived its economic base. A price revolution, accompanying the commercialization of the economy, *had* produced a number of phenomena for which a properly ordered Tokugawa society had no place: samurai who were driven by debt to become ambitious place-seekers or impoverished umbrella-makers; rich urban merchants enjoying feudal patronage and, in some measure, feudal status; farmers exploiting new and lucrative opportunities as producers and entrepreneurs, or failing to do so and hence declining into tenancy and wage labor. All these things were at variance with the accepted canons. They represented a divorce between the actual and the ideal that was *potentially* revolutionary and that led immediately to dissatisfaction and unrest. If they do not necessarily justify the postulation of an "alliance" to explain the overthrow of the Tokugawa, they are clearly relevant to some of the major acts of policy for which the Restoration opened the way: abolition of the domains, land-tax reforms, a new social structure. Hence any general view of the Restoration must take them into account.

CHAPTER III

Dangers from Abroad

WHEN JAPAN'S rulers in the early seventeenth century decided to cut off their country's relations with the outside world, except those that could be maintained through a carefully regulated trade with the Dutch and Chinese at Nagasaki, they did so in the belief that foreign religion and foreign trade held dangers. Both might serve as adjuncts to foreign attack. Both might be valuable weapons in the hands of a daimyo who sought to supplant his overlord. The one, they argued, should therefore be suppressed, the other rigidly controlled.

These attitudes still persisted in the nineteenth century, though rather with reference to the foreign than the domestic threat. Aizawa Seishisai's *Shinron* (1825), the most influential piece of political writing of the late-Tokugawa period, stated them as follows: "When those barbarians plan to subdue a country not their own, they start by opening commerce and watch for a sign of weakness. If an opportunity is presented, they will preach their alien religion to captivate the people's hearts."[1] The point was made again and again in the debates on foreign policy that were prompted by the Perry expedition in 1853–54. So was the economic objection to foreign trade, which stemmed partly from Confucian agrarianism, characterized by contempt for any activity directed solely at the pursuit of profit, and partly from a mercantilist distrust of exporting bullion in return for goods. As Aizawa's lord, Tokugawa Nariaki, put it in 1853: "To exchange our valuable articles like gold, silver, copper and iron for useless foreign goods like woollens and satins is to incur great loss while acquiring not the smallest benefit."*

These specific arguments against resuming relations with the West were reinforced by a form of cultural chauvinism that developed from, and rivaled, China's. To Confucian scholars, whether Chinese, Japanese, or Korean, the world comprised a natural hierarchy of the "civilized" and the "barbarian" in which China, together with the countries to which she had transmitted her culture, represented the first and the West, replacing the nomads of the steppe, the second.† By this estimate, Japan was civilized. In her case, however, there was another source of pride that was uniquely Japanese: a sense of the divine origin of the land, its people, and its rulers, deriving from ancient myth and embodied in Shintō doctrine. It led the scholar Hirata Atsutane (1776–1843) to assert that "Japanese differ from and are superior to the peoples of China, India, Russia, Holland, Siam, Cambodia and all other countries of the world" because Japan is "the homeland of the gods."[2] Yet though the tradition originated with Shintō, its expression was by no means confined to those, like Hirata, who regarded that faith as irreconcilable with Chinese scholarship. Indeed, the Confucian scholar Yamaga Sokō (1622–85)—who was largely responsible for elaborating the samurai code, Bushidō, in its later form—said of Japan, using terms not so very different from Hirata's, that "the qualities of its people are supreme throughout the eight corners of the earth."[3] And nearly two centuries later another Confucianist, Aizawa Seishisai, writing in the preface to *Shinron*, declared that

* Beasley, *Select Documents*, p. 104. The reasoning stems originally from China, and a classic statement of it is to be found in Lin Tse-hsü's famous letter to Queen Victoria in 1839: "Of all that China exports to foreign countries there is not a single thing which is not beneficial to people. . . . On the other hand, articles coming from outside to China can only be used as toys" (Teng and Fairbank, *China's Response*, pp. 25–26).

† Again, the Chinese and Japanese attitudes are very close. An anti-foreign placard in Canton in 1841 said of the British: "You are ignorant of our laws and institutions, ignorant of right principles. . . . Except for your ships being solid, your gunfire fierce, and your rockets powerful, what other abilities have you?" (Teng and Fairbank, *China's Response*, p. 36). For a brief discussion of the Chinese attitude, see Hsü, *China's Entrance*, pp. 3–12; and on the Japanese attitude, see Blacker, "Ōhashi Totsuan," pp. 166–67.

"Japan's position at the vertex of the earth makes it the standard for the nations of the world."[4]

It is not surprising to find a period of seclusion, in which the country's development had been introverted for generations and its institutions submitted to no external test save that of comparison with China, breeding attitudes of this kind. Nevertheless, the fact needs to be given emphasis, for it is vital to an understanding of the nineteenth-century crisis. Once seclusion was challenged by countries that not only possessed an overwhelming military superiority, but also espoused ideas in total contradiction to the fundamentals of Japanese thinking,* then Japan, like China, became involved in a struggle for her cultural, as well as her political, survival. A consciousness of this double threat, emotionally charged by a sense of dishonor on the part of what was, after all, a *military* ruling class, made foreign policy for a time the essential focus of Japanese politics. Gaikan, the danger from abroad, came to overshadow naiyū, the turbulence at home.

SECLUSION CHALLENGED

Japan's seclusion went long unquestioned, chiefly because her neighbors were preoccupied elsewhere and Europe's expansion took other channels. In the second half of the eighteenth century, however, these conditions ceased to obtain. In the north Russia began to explore the possibilities of what are now her easternmost territories and to extend her power gradually into the islands of the North Pacific. In the south Britain, having established herself in India, moved into Malaysia and built up a China trade. The newly created United States of America, too, acquired trading interests on the China coast. All these events had ominous implications for Japan. They were also well known to the Japanese, both from Chinese books and from the annual reports the Dutch were required to

* It would be difficult, for example, to imagine a statement that was in greater contrast with Japanese views on the nature and importance of trade than the following passage from the *Edinburgh Review* (October 1852, p. 383): "The compulsory seclusion of the Japanese is a wrong not only to themselves, but to the civilized world. . . . The Japanese undoubtedly have an exclusive right to the possession of their territory; but they must not abuse that right to the extent of debarring all other nations from a participation in its riches and virtues."

submit through Nagasaki. And hearsay was confirmed by incident as foreign ships, seeking trade, diplomatic relations, or merely stores, appeared with increasing frequency in Japanese harbors.[5]

The Russian problem, which was the first to emerge, was also in many ways the most familiar. It sprang from the appearance of Russian settlements on the islands to the north of Ezo (Hokkaidō), which then marked the extreme limit of Japanese political authority; and it raised issues of defense and frontier demarcation, of which, for all that Tokugawa officials had no direct experience of them, the histories afforded plenty of examples. A Russian envoy coming to Matsumae in 1793 and another to Nagasaki in 1804 were sent away without concessions. Russian attacks on some scattered Japanese posts in the islands during 1806–7 were countered by the seizure of a Russian surveying party in 1811. Ezo itself was put under direct Bakufu administration for twenty years in order to ensure proper military surveillance.

As it transpired, these measures, though slight enough, were sufficient to ward off Russia's very tentative advances, with the result that after 1813 Russo-Japanese relations remained almost devoid of incident until the 1850's. British activities were of a different order. For one thing, they were maritime and commercial. For another, they threatened much more than they performed, at least in the early years. In 1808 a British frigate—a commerce raider seeking out Dutch ships—entered Nagasaki harbor and behaved in a notably high-handed manner to obtain supplies of food and water; in 1813–14 Thomas Stamford Raffles, as lieutenant governor of Java during its British occupation, tried without success to bring the Nagasaki trade of the Dutch under British control; and in 1837 a joint Anglo-American expedition, organized by merchants and missionaries with some semiofficial backing, sought to secure an entry to Uraga on the pretext of taking home a group of Japanese castaways. From time to time, moreover, British (and American) whaling crews came into conflict with Japanese villagers, as they did on the coast of Mito in 1824. Yet though these events helped to give color to Japanese fears, there was little in them directly to suggest that the conquerors of India had territorial designs on Japan.

There was little to suggest it, that is to say, until 1839. From that date, the Opium War, resulting in the seizure of Hong Kong and the enforced opening of treaty ports as far north as the Yangtze, changed the whole position. British naval survey vessels began to appear in the seas around Japan. Disturbing reports circulated in Japan of British—and also French—interest in the Ryukyu islands, starting as early as 1843. In 1844 Japanese officials received a letter from the Dutch King, obviously inspired by these events, urging Japan to give heed to what was happening around her and take steps to end her seclusion before the decision was forced on her from outside. Two years later an official American mission, led by Commodore James Biddle, arrived in Edo Bay to ask for the opening of ports to trade. To be sure, Biddle, like the Dutch, accepted without demur the Bakufu's ungracious refusal of his overtures; but two formal approaches in as many years were a clear sign that foreign governments were unlikely to remain satisfied with such replies for long. Indeed, had the Japanese known it, the British government had already in 1845 approved proposals for a mission to open treaty relations with Japan, to be put into effect as soon as a sufficiently imposing naval force could be assembled to support it.

Thus America's plans for an expedition under Commodore Perry, publicly announced and reported to Edo by the Dutch in 1852, did not by any means lack antecedents. Nor had there been a lack of discussion in Japan of the wider problems that Perry's arrival was bound to pose. From about 1790, books and pamphlets bearing on foreign affairs, some published, some circulated in manuscript, had appeared with fair regularity. Knowledge of them and concern about them were limited, admittedly, to quite small numbers of officials, scholars, and feudal lords. All the same, these were men of influence, in some cases men of power, so that the views they expressed, varied and often conflicting though they were, were likely to carry weight when Japan was finally confronted with the need to make decisions.

One broad segment of opinion, as it developed in these years, was based on an interest in Western technology and military science. It emerged chiefly in the last quarter of the eighteenth century, forming part of a reaction against current orthodoxy and the unquestioning acceptance of Chinese models, which brought, for example, the "Shintō revival"—an attempt to restore the purity and prestige of Japan's native religion—as well as a fresh interest in "Dutch studies" (Rangaku).[6] Both movements turned from China to seek inspiration in a different cultural tradition, in the one case that of ancient Japan, in the other that of Europe. Both were careful to avoid any direct assertion that their search for other roots was intended as an attack on the established order. Both were nevertheless revolutionary in the effect they had on the thinking of certain individuals. Rangaku, in particular, moved rapidly beyond the study of Western medicine, language, astronomy, and clocks to matters that had more immediately political implications, like the application of science to warfare and the nature of society. By so doing it gave some men an opportunity to escape from the personal frustrations of life in a tradition-bound environment* and opened to others the possibility of changing that environment itself.

Outstanding examples of Dutch specialists in the earlier years were Hayashi Shihei (1738–93) and Honda Toshiaki (1744–1821).[7] In 1791 Hayashi wrote a book urging the need for the use of Western military science to defend the north against Russian encroachment, in which he argued that reform at home, involving encouragement of agriculture and trade, relaxation of sankin-kōtai, and reeducation of samurai, was an essential concomitant of defense. For this apparently innocuous statement the Bakufu ordered his arrest and the destruction of the blocks from which his book was printed. Honda, perhaps because of Hayashi's experience, reserved his own, more radical proposals for private circulation. A samurai, but of very modest status, Honda was an outspoken critic of the incapacity of upper samurai officials. "Since the regulations insist that administrators be chosen from among persons of high rank," he wrote, "it is natural that there are few men of ability among them."[8] He therefore saw one solution to the country's ills in the promotion of able men from the lower levels of the samurai class.

* Fukuzawa Yukichi, speaking of his decision to leave his castle town to study Rangaku in Nagasaki, said: "I would have welcomed anything, literature or art or anything at all, so long as it gave me an excuse to get away" (Blacker, *Japanese Enlightenment*, p. 4).

Another was the exploitation of Western techniques in a vast economic effort. He specifically suggested the use of gunpowder to blast navigable channels in rivers and the development of shipping and foreign trade under close government supervision so as to restrict or even reverse the flow of bullion from the country. This program was to be reinforced by the establishment of colonies, first in nearby islands, then as far afield as the Aleutians and North America, to serve as defensive outposts and sources of raw materials. He even envisaged the eventual transfer of the capital to Kamchatka as the natural center of a Japanese-controlled North Pacific.

A generation later another Japanese student of Western science, Satō Nobuhiro (1769–1850), devised a similar but still more grandiose plan for the conquest of an empire in eastern Asia.[9] It was to begin with an invasion of China: "With proper spirit and discipline on our part," Satō argued, "China would crumble and fall like a house of sand within five to seven years."[10] Thereafter, Burma, India, and Central Asia would rapidly submit. Even more startling was the political program that went with all this. Where Honda had recognized a need for feudal society to be reformed or reinforced, Satō saw it as something to be replaced entirely—replaced, moreover, by a terrifyingly modern and totalitarian structure. Government was to be conducted by a number of specialist departments and bureaus, which would control all economic and military activities, along with the appropriate segments of the population. A university, including Western studies in its curriculum, would provide officials to staff the bureaus. A network of local schools—one for every 20,000 koku of land—was to train the rest of the people in skills and attitudes suitable to their hereditary functions.

It is not possible to trace any direct transmission of Satō's ideas to the Meiji leaders, tempting though it is to try, but with another of the "Dutch" scholars, Sakuma Shōzan (1811–64), the connection is unmistakable.[11] Through two equally famous pupils, Katsu Awa (who became his brother-in-law) and Yoshida Shōin, Sakuma made an important contribution to the shaping of Meiji policies. A samurai administrator, he was adviser to his lord, Sanada of Matsushiro, in the latter's capacities as daimyo and Bakufu councillor. Perhaps because of this Sakuma, like many who held high office after 1868, was a conservative in his social and political attitudes, practical and military in his approach to the civilization of the West. He made his own camera, took personal charge of cannon founding, compiled a dictionary. All these undertakings he regarded as being relevant to Japan's defense (even the dictionary, since it contributed to a military need, the learning of "barbarian" tongues).

By contrast, Confucian scholarship, no matter how vital to questions of moral behavior, Sakuma thought militarily irrelevant. China had failed in the Opium War, he said, "because foreign learning is rational and Chinese learning is not."[12] Nor were Japan's own initial preparations any more effective. As he described them in 1854, just after the signing of the Perry treaty: "The existing coastal defense installations all lack method; the pieces of artillery that have been set in array are improperly made; and the officials who negotiate with the foreigners are mediocrities who have no understanding of warfare."[13] Consequently, in his view the study of Western techniques could be effective only if political steps were taken to ensure that the lessons learned were properly carried out. "Men of talent in military strategy, planning, and administration" should be appointed to positions of responsibility. Indeed, so great was the incapacity of the majority of samurai that special army units should also be recruited, drawn from members of "old, established families not in the military class."[14]

This idea contained the seeds of later proposals, developed by Katsu Awa and Yoshida Shōin, then by Takasugi Shinsaku and Ōmura Masujirō, that represented a much more serious blow to the samurai's position in society than Sakuma seems to have intended. In the long run, a new military science was to involve new forms of military organization and recruitment, ending in conscription, which would help to destroy the hereditary privileges of the samurai class.

Sakuma, however, had not thought the problem this far through. To him, as he revealed in a memorial on coast defense in 1842,[15] the essence of the matter was technology, a technological defense made necessary by a technological threat. He wanted the building of coast batteries and the suspension of copper exports to make the metal available for them; the construction of Western-style ships and a special financial levy on domains to pay for it; the creation of a navy (much like that Peter the Great had fashioned in Russia, an example to which he often refers); and close regulation by the Bakufu of marine transport and foreign trade. New schools to train the Japanese people, just administration to "unify their minds," the employment of "men of talent" from the domains in the Shogun's service, all these were needed; but Sakuma's demand for them reflected more the frustrations he encountered as a man of modest middle samurai birth in getting his ideas accepted, than a conscious program of radical social change. His men of talent, after all, were still to be samurai. Their ethical training was to remain Confucian. It was simply that in his view Japan, having for many centuries "adopted the strong points of China," thereby making herself strong enough to resist any possible Chinese attack,[16] must now transfer her apprenticeship in the same sense to the West. "The barbarians of today," he commented, "have excelled China by far in both science and technology."[17]

For all the far-reaching implications of these ideas, it was not those who studied the West, like Hayashi, Satō, and Sakuma, whose response to the foreign threat introduced the main disruptive element into late-Tokugawa politics, but a group of Confucian scholars connected with Mito. The first of them, Fujita Yūkoku (1773–1826), whose commentaries on problems of defense gave a new direction to Mito thinking in the latter part of the eighteenth century, can claim the distinction of having furnished many of the ideas and slogans on which the Japanese debate was to focus in the following 80 years.[18] It was he, for example, who specifically applied the phrase naiyū-gaikan, "troubles at home and dangers from abroad," to the Japanese situation. By the first part of it he meant the financial difficulties of the domains and the hardships these inflicted on the farmer; by the second, the activities of Russia in the north. The solution to both, he said, was fukoku-kyōhei, "enrich the country, strengthen the army," though he did not mean by this the same thing later writers meant. Enriching the country to him involved a kind of agrarianism: restricting trade and subordinating merchants, discouraging urban life, returning the population to the land. Strengthening the army required a restoration of morale and military virtue among the samurai. This, since it implied a return to frugality, was the key to fukoku, as well as to the suppression of unrest, so that the two parts of the solution were really one, just as the two parts of the problem were.

Aizawa Seishisai (1781–1863), Fujita Yūkoku's pupil, inherited and extended these ideas, notably in his book *Shinron* (New Proposals), written in 1825.* More impressed by the external threat than his mentor had been, Aizawa saw Britain and Russia, perhaps acting in collusion, making use of trade, Christianity, and eventually arms to subdue both China and Japan. Nor did he believe that salvation lay in the proposals of the "Dutch" scholars, who to his mind had been bemused by their studies into seeking ways of "transforming our civilized way of life into that of the barbarians."[19] Rather, it had to be pursued through armed preparedness (including the use of Western-style weapons) and a policy of *jōi*, "expelling the barbarian." This meant above all the inculcation of a will to resist. Not only was Japan weak as a result of centuries of peace, Aizawa said, but she would never be strong until her people could be made united and resolute. Unity and resolution, in turn, would come only by making it clear from the outset that the country would fight if attacked: " 'Put a man in a position of inevitable death, and he will emerge unscathed,' goes the saying. . . . So I say, let a policy for peace or for war be decided upon first of all, thus putting the entire nation into the position of inevitable death."[20]

Responsibility for taking this critical decision—as for the other measures that were needed in order to strengthen the country, such as promoting men of ability and relaxing the conditions of sankin-kōtai—rested, in Aizawa's view, squarely with the Bakufu. After all, was not the first part of the Shogun's title *sei-i*, "barbarian subduing"? It was therefore for the Shogun to give a lead, to show the way to national unity by demonstrating that this particular duty transcended all lesser loyalties, to lord or lineage or domain. Above

* The work was first circulated in manuscript. It was finally printed in 1857, some 30 years after Aizawa wrote it, and became a text regularly used in domain schools. In the late 1850's and 1860's it was said that no man deserved the designation *shishi*, "man of spirit," unless he possessed a copy. See Earl, *Emperor and Nation*, pp. 91–92.

all, the Shogun must show that the Tokugawa were ready to subordinate their own "selfish" interests, including the preservation of their shogunal authority, to the wider interests of the people as a whole, manifesting a devotion to the concept of sonnō, "honor the Emperor," which would ensure that the Emperor, the symbol of the "national polity" (*kokutai*), would again "govern the land and control the people . . . , bringing the entire realm under his sway."[21]

Aizawa, then, went far beyond his predecessors in spelling out the political implications of certain kinds of response to the problems of foreign affairs. Notwithstanding the surface meaning of what he wrote, he did not really envisage the overthrow of the Tokugawa and a restoration of imperial rule, but he had certainly sown the seeds of such an argument for others to nurture. In doing so, he had completed the political vocabulary of the Restoration movement. Sonnō and jōi were to come together as a single slogan, "honor the Emperor, expel the barbarian," to summarize the objectives of loyalist samurai in the 1860's. Kokutai, the national polity, with its connotations of a mystical unity between Emperor and people, was to become a constitutional ideal (that to which political action was designed to give reality) and also the essence of what jōi sought to defend.

Shaping these generalizations into an argument that was immediately relevant to foreign demands for the opening of Japanese ports was the work of Yūkoku's only son, Fujita Tōko (1806–55). In a book called *Hitachi-obi*, written in 1845 in the knowledge of the Opium War in China, he examined various proposals that his contemporaries were putting forward about foreign policy in this new situation.* First, there was the idea of appeasing the foreigners by granting them the right to trade so as to give Japan time to arm herself in order to expel them. This, said Tōko, was the policy of a weakling, postponing to a future generation what ought to be done today. Moreover, it was self-defeating, for it would provide an opportunity for trade and Christianity to sap Japan's morale,

* The argument of *Hitachi-obi* is summarized in Inobe, "Mito," pp. 142–44. Its title, like those of many other books of the period, is not very meaningful in translation—"The Sash of Hitachi," the name being that of the province the Mito domain controlled. I do not propose as a rule to offer translations of such titles.

thus making it certain that expulsion would never come.[22] Second, there was the plan for opening Japan to the world with a view to studying and adopting those elements of Western civilization that would make her strong enough to demand equality on the international scene. This, too, Tōko said, risked corruption of the national spirit. Its most likely result was that Japan in her weakness and inexperience would fall into the foreigners' toils. Finally, there was the straightforward policy of expulsion, a war in defense of the "land of the gods." Even this Tōko rejected, because it was negative. Instead, he urged that jōi (which in this context might be better translated "*repelling* the barbarian"), once it had fulfilled the crucial function of rallying the people behind preparations for defense, should be succeeded by *kaikoku*, "opening the country." In other words, "expulsion" was not to be an end in itself. It was the first step in a process that would enable Japan to face the world on equal terms: rearmament, political reform, the cultivation of a loyalty to the Emperor on which true national unity could be founded.

Such attitudes, expressed though they were in a framework of highly respectable Confucian concepts and terminology, were by no means as typical of samurai thinking at the time as they seem in retrospect, any more than were the views of Rangakusha like Sakuma Shōzan. The majority, indeed, almost certainly sympathized more readily with the conservatives among the Confucian scholars, those whom R. H. van Gulik has so aptly described as "arid and uncompromising."[23] It is true that these scholars contributed little to the history and ideas of the Meiji Restoration movement, for all that their principles were eventually embedded deeply in the social doctrines and education system of the Meiji state. Yet we cannot entirely afford on that account to ignore them here, if only because the stridency of their attacks on Western culture, deriving partly from China's cultural chauvinism (through the circulation in Japan of Chinese books) and partly from the recognition of Western science as a challenge to their own professional self-interest, helped considerably to heighten the emotional atmosphere of the foreign policy debate.

On of the best known of them was Shionoya Tōin (1810–67), who had been an adviser to Mizuno Tadakuni in carrying out the Tempō reforms. Britain, Tōin predicted in a work dated 1846, would soon turn her attention from China to Japan, sending surveying vessels, asking for the provision of stores, making raids on the coast, engaging in fact in all the devices that made up "the art of subjugating by intimidation,"[24] until she was in a position to send an expedition and demand the opening of ports to trade. By then it would be too late to resist effectively. China's mistake, Tōin asserted in a later book, *Kakkaron*, published in 1859, had been to grant the West an initial foothold at Macao. Once this was gained, trade and Christianity had worked together to exploit it, a task in which the barbarians were aided by "foxes within"—the officials and others whose blindness and inefficiencies had contributed so greatly to China's weakness.

For not only had China failed to recognize the foreign danger and prepare against it in the military sense, she had also failed to put her house in order at home. Had her rulers retained the support of the people, Tōin said, "then, even if the foreigners tried to allure them with a hundred means, they would not have a chance of conquering them. If there are poor people in a state, it is as if there were sick children in a household; and if there are malcontent people in a state, it is as if there were a profligate son in a family. Now the sick child has not been given medicine, the profligate son is not called to order. . . . To whom shall the blame accrue?"[25] The moral was plain: Japan needed not merely military science, but also Confucian ethics, the basis of a stable society; for it was not Confucianism that was to blame for defeat, but a failure to live by it.

Ōhashi Totsuan (1816–62), writing at about the time of Perry's arrival, was even more insistent on this point.[26] Western civilization, as he saw it, was preoccupied with profit to the exclusion of duty, with science—that is, external forms—rather than moral essence. It neglected the proper distinctions between man and man, just as it challenged the proper hierarchy of "civilized" and "barbarian." On all counts, therefore, it was destructive of the social order. Indeed, even the study of it was corrupting. Hence, though the West unquestionably had great power, an attempt to combine "Western science" with "Eastern ethics" (Sakuma Shōzan's slogan) could lead only to destruction. "To say that we can accept Western science although we must reject Western moral teaching as evil and wrong," Ōhashi wrote, "is like telling people that although the mainstream of a river is poisoned yet they can safely drink from the sidestreams."[27]

Ōhashi demonstrated the strength of his convictions by becoming a political activist after 1858, dying in 1862 as a result of the treatment he received in prison. Sakuma Shōzan, by contrast, was assassinated by an anti-foreign fanatic in 1864. It would be hard to find better examples from which to argue the political relevance of the opinions here discussed. All the same, it is dangerous to emphasize the ideas that divided men, if this means overlooking the things they had in common. That some in Japan respected, and others despised, Western civilization is true, just as it is that some were willing to temporize and others not. Their disputes were bitter, as we shall see. Yet the disputes took place within a conceptual framework on which there was a considerable measure of agreement. That Japan was in danger of armed attack by one or another of the Western powers, that to save herself she needed to revamp her armies and institute reforms at home, that in doing so she must beware of destroying her traditional ethos—all these were propositions to which many, if not most, of the better informed samurai would have subscribed by the time of Perry's arrival in 1853, however much they differed on almost everything else. Events in the following five years were to extend these convictions to a widening circle, as dangers, hitherto prospective, materialized in actual foreign demands.

THE PERRY EXPEDITION

The fact that it was an American squadron which eventually opened Japanese ports to foreign ships is not so surprising as the earlier Japanese preoccupation with Britain and Russia might make it seem. There was a long-standing, if modest, American interest in Japan, enough to have got Biddle sent there in 1846. Moreover, his unsuccessful attempt to establish relations with Japan was followed by a series of events that led to a rapid increase in America's concern with and access to the Pacific: the transfer of the Oregon Territory, the independence of California and its subsequent entry into the union, the gold rush of 1849. These stimulated talk of a transcontinental railway and a steamship route from San Francisco to Shanghai, giving a new importance to Japan, which was known not only as a potential hazard to shipping, but also as a source of coal. Thus, in April 1849 an American naval vessel, the *Preble*, calling at Nagasaki to repatriate the crew of a shipwrecked whaler, sought permission to establish a coaling station for trans-Pacific steamers. The request, like Biddle's, was brusquely refused.

It is against this background that one must set the instructions given to Commodore Matthew Perry when he was appointed to command an expedition to Japan in 1852. He was to ensure protection for American seamen, to gain access to Japanese ports for provisions and coal, and to seek rights of trade, if only on a temporary basis. In doing so, however, he was to be careful of Japanese sensibilities. As the presidential letter that he was to deliver to the "Emperor" of Japan stated: "I have particularly charged Commodore Perry to abstain from every act which could possibly disturb the tranquillity of your imperial majesty's dominions."[28] Yet Perry himself seems to have been far from impressed by the need for such restraint. Partly, no doubt, this was because his experiences on the voyage from Norfolk, Virginia, to Hong Kong in the winter of 1852–53 had confirmed him in his view of the overriding importance of having coaling stations under American control, since he had been greatly inconvenienced by the fact that most of those along his route had been preempted by Britain. Partly it was because he shared, or rapidly acquired, China coast prejudices about the role of force or threats of it in oriental diplomacy.

Certainly by the time Perry reached Uraga, accompanied by two steam frigates and two sailing vessels, on July 8, 1853, he was prepared to take a very firm line with any Japanese attempts at procrastination or evasion. Japanese officials, seeking to persuade him to go to Nagasaki, were told that if they would not make proper arrangements to receive his letters, he would go ashore "with a sufficient force" and deliver them in person, "be the consequences what they might."[29] What is more, in the letter he had written to accompany that of the President he expressed the hope "that the Japanese government will see the necessity of averting unfriendly collision between the two nations,"[30] which it could best do by accepting his proposals. He was willing to come back for an answer in the spring of 1854, he said, "with a much larger force," if no reply could be given immediately.

Perry's actions caused consternation in Japan, notwithstanding the discussions of the previous decade or more, which had anticipated just such an eventuality. A Japanese chronicler, writing in 1864, described the reaction in this way:

> The military class had during a long peace neglected military arts; they had given themselves up to pleasure and luxury, and there were very few who had put on armour for many years. So that they were greatly alarmed at the prospect that war might break out at a moment's notice, and began to run hither and thither in search of arms. The city of Edo and the surrounding villages were in a great tumult; in anticipation of the war which seemed imminent, the people carried their valuables and furniture in all directions to conceal them in the house of some friend living farther off.[31]

Nor was the alarm confined to those outside official circles. On July 10 the Bakufu began a round of agitated meetings to decide whether or not to insist that Perry go to Nagasaki. The discussions continued late into the next night, July 11, breaking off only when news arrived that Perry's squadron had entered Edo Bay. Fear of hostilities then brought the last of the waverers to accept the inevitable: authorization for the governor of Uraga to receive the letters and to promise a reply for the following spring. The documents were duly handed over at Kurihama on July 14 with appropriate ceremony.

This, of course, was not the same thing as agreeing to Perry's terms, a subject on which officialdom was still very much divided. Abe Masahiro, senior member of the Bakufu council since 1845, was himself convinced that Japan could not for long resist Western demands for trade—he is reputed to have given Satsuma secret permission to open negotiations with the French through Ryukyu in 1846[32]—but he recognized that for Edo to accept the American proposals without demur would arouse a great deal of anti-Bakufu feeling in the country. In an attempt to overcome this difficulty he took the unprecedented step of calling on all officials and feudal lords to submit memoranda on the situation, confident that in so doing the majority, if only out of deference to his own opinions, would advise against hostilities and thereby provide a "popular" base for a compromise settlement. In this, as it transpired, he was wrong. For all the Bakufu's authority in such matters, some of those consulted proved ready to urge, even to insist on, a policy of their own.

Translations of the American letters were circulated at the beginning of August 1853, and comments on them were received by the Bakufu during the next three months. Sixty-one of the replies from daimyo are extant, summarized by Inobe as follows: nineteen expressed a willingness to accept trade and the opening of ports in some form; nineteen urged outright rejection of Perry's requests; fourteen reflected a primary concern with the need to avoid war; seven stated rejection to be the ultimate aim but envisaged the adoption of temporary expedients meanwhile; and two simply bowed to Bakufu orders, whatever these might be.[33] One cannot, to be sure, assume that the other 200-odd feudal lords were divided on exactly these lines. Nevertheless, it is clear from the replies we have that Abe found no consensus, not even a "public" consensus such as might have stemmed from simple acceptance of the Bakufu's right to decide. What is more, each of the main groups included men whose advice he could not ignore.

Among those who agreed to the opening of Japanese ports, for example, was Hotta Masayoshi, a fudai lord who was to be Abe's successor as senior minister two years later. He believed, as Abe himself was inclined to do, not only that Japan was incapable of offering military resistance to the West, but also that she might find trade to her advantage.[34]

Ii Naosuke, most powerful of the fudai lords, was no less forthright. Japan, he said, would condemn herself to inevitable defeat if she passively awaited a foreign attack: "When one is besieged in a castle, to raise the drawbridge is to imprison oneself and make it impossible to hold out indefinitely."[35] The proper course was not so much to open Japan's own ports as to build steamships and use them for trading overseas, thereby acquiring the experience and skills needed to create a navy. This done, the country could defend its independence and act "so as to make our courage and prestige resound beyond the seas."[36]

Kuroda Narihiro of Chikuzen, a tozama daimyo holding over 500,000 koku in Kyūshū, made similar proposals. He believed that it would be possible by careful diplomacy—"using the barbarian to control the barbarian," in the traditional Chinese manner*—to avoid major concessions long enough for Japan to follow the example of Peter the Great of Russia. "Summoning numbers of artisans concerned with cannon and warships from Holland and America," he wrote, "we must order them to undertake construction and to train Japanese artisans, until the work can be carried out by Japanese."[37]

Kuroda's relative Shimazu Nariakira of Satsuma, whose domain of nearly 800,000 koku was second in size only to that of Maeda of Kaga, also emphasized the importance of Western military science, especially in connection with maritime defenses, since it was clear that Japan faced essentially a naval attack. About the political aspects of foreign affairs, however, he was more cautious, urging the Bakufu to delay any decision about treaties—three years, he thought, would be enough—until defense preparations were complete.[38]

By contrast, Yamauchi Yōdō of Tosa (242,000 koku), a tozama lord who was related to the Tokugawa by marriage, coupled a recommendation for the employment of Dutch experts in shipbuilding and cannon-founding with a total opposition to the Perry proposals. Once the foreigners had forced the opening of trade, he said, they would exploit their advantage, "seducing the ignorant by demonstrations of goodwill until in the end they have made Japan completely subservient to their wishes."[39] The solution was to keep them out altogether, at least until Japan was strong enough to handle them with impunity.

Yamauchi's argument was not so very different from that of Tokugawa Nariaki, head of the Mito house (350,000 koku), whose me-

* The phrase originated as a description of Chinese frontier policy in Central Asia, but in the 19th century writers like Wei Yüan applied it to the diplomacy of playing off one Western power against another. See Teng and Fairbank, *China's Response*, pp. 34–35. Japanese writers also used it to describe plans for employing Western technology against the West.

morial of August 14, 1853, was a classic application of the Mito school's "expulsion" views to the particular question of the American negotiations.[40] Nariaki stated briefly the traditional objections to Christianity and trade, and underlined the dishonor that would result if the Bakufu succumbed to threats—the foreigners were "arrogant and discourteous, their actions an outrage." But, he insisted, there *was* a way out, if Edo would only take it. Since weapons were useless without the will to use them, the first requirement for the country's defense was for the government to make it clear that it would fight. To follow the advice of the temporizers and the lovers of foreign ways could only bring disaster: "If we put our trust in war the whole country's morale will be increased and even if we sustain an initial defeat we will in the end expel the foreigner; while if we put our trust in peace, even though things may seem tranquil for a time, the morale of the country will be greatly lowered and we will come in the end to complete collapse."[41] Failure might also threaten the reputation and authority of the Tokugawa house. Conceivably "Bakufu control of the great lords would itself be endangered." Success, on the other hand, would enable Japan "to go out against foreign countries and spread abroad our fame and prestige."

To Abe, the man responsible for formulating a policy, the key element in this memorial was its complete rejection of compromise with Perry as a means of buying time for Japan to complete her defenses. The Mito objections to foreign trade, after all, though they certainly had powerful support,[42] need not in themselves have precluded a settlement. Had not the American President suggested only a *temporary* raising of the Japanese ban, which might be reimposed if the experiment proved unsuccessful? Nor did Nariaki's views on coast defense pose problems, in the sense of being likely to meet with fundamental disagreement from the Bakufu or other feudal lords. He did not deny the value of Western military technology—his own domain, like Satsuma and Hizen, had already made considerable progress in Western-style ship-building and cannon-founding under the tutelage of the "Dutch" scholars — he merely denied that the opening of ports was necessary to it.

In fact, for all that trade and defense were matters of serious debate on which men differed profoundly, it was the opening of the ports that was the immediate issue. Here Nariaki had the support in one degree or another of some very powerful tozama lords who were as opposed to the American demands for a treaty as he was. He was also backed by one of his young collateral relatives, Matsudaira Shungaku of Echizen (320,000 koku). To Shungaku, as to Nariaki, compromise would threaten both Japan and the Tokugawa. To decide in the name of expediency to conclude a treaty with Perry, he said, "would give the appearance of having fallen into the foreigners' toils simply from fear of their military might," leading men to "question the competence of our rulers."[43]

The career officials of the Bakufu thus found themselves in a very difficult position. On the one side were the great fudai lords like Abe Masahiro, Hotta Masayoshi, and Ii Naosuke, all members of a group that customarily dominated the council of state. They advocated a "realistic" foreign policy, which implied a compromise arrangement with Perry, followed by active steps to strengthen Japan by exploiting the newly established relationship with the West. Opposing them were a few powerful members of the Tokugawa family itself, led by Nariaki and backed by some of the more active tozama, who insisted that the dangers of such a settlement outweighed its advantages, in other words, that long-term military needs precluded a short-term diplomatic compromise. The situation was complicated by the existence of a long-standing tension between the fudai and the Tokugawa relatives. As Bakufu councillors, the fudai had at heart the interests of the "administration" more than those of the "house." As great lords, the Tokugawa branch houses, almost as much as the tozama, felt the attractions of independence from central control.

It is perhaps for this reason that Nariaki found few supporters among Bakufu officials below the very highest ranks. Some of them, especially the more able ones who owed their promotion directly to Abe's patronage,* clearly declared for the kaikoku policy of their

* They included Mizuno Tadanori, Toki Yorimune, Kawaji Toshiaki, Inoue Kiyonao, Iwase Tadanari, Nagai Naomune, and Tsutsui Masanori. All played an important part in the foreign policy decisions of 1857–58, which are discussed in the next chapter. On the activities and attitudes of these men in 1853–54, see Tabohashi, *Kindai Nihon*, pp. 494–511, 535–47.

seniors, which indeed they had done much to shape. There were even a few who urged still more radical solutions, notably Mukōyama Gendayū, whose son was to be a leading foreign affairs expert in the 1860's. In a long memorandum written in the summer of 1853, Mukōyama put together two elements that seem to be some years before their time: a recognition that the foreign crisis made necessary political unity and economic reform at home, the one being dependent to some extent on the other; and a plea for regarding foreign trade, since it was a source of revenue and a means of importing scientific knowledge, as the proper basis for national wealth and strength (fukoku-kyōhei). The fact was, he wrote, "the profits from trade are greater than the profits to be made from seizing [another country's] land and increasing [agricultural] production. . . . If we now want to pursue a policy of 'enriching the country and strengthening the army,' there can be no better way of doing so than by establishing trade."[44]

This was not at all the sort of proposal to appeal to the conservative majority among Edo officials, who were preoccupied with seeking a solution that would not involve them in anything so dangerous as a choice between the two extremes. This is clearly reflected in a memorial submitted by an influential group headed by the Edo city magistrates (Machi-bugyō) on August 26, 1853.[45] It began by rejecting Perry's demands, save that concerning the treatment of castaways. It then went on to argue that the manner of the refusal must be as friendly as possible, since Japan was in no position to precipitate hostilities. Assuming that Perry remained adamant, as well he might, the document continued, there remained the question of how to avoid war long enough to give time for the Bakufu's defense preparations to be completed. The answer lay in diplomatic subtlety, that is, in offering trade privileges to America on condition she secure promises from all the other powers to recognize an American monopoly. This plainly would be "quite impossible to accomplish." It would, however, gain time.

One gets the impression from all this—not for the last time, by any means—that many Bakufu officials were at this stage more aware of their political difficulties at home than of the realities they faced abroad. Certainly they spent much of the winter of 1853–54 seeking a basis of agreement between Abe Masahiro and Tokugawa Nariaki in terms that suggest concern, not with policy, but with verbal formulae. Nariaki, however, remained unhelpful, even in private discussions. His position, as he described it in a letter to Matsudaira Shungaku on September 13, 1853, was that he wanted "war at home, peace abroad."[46] This meant undertaking ostentatious preparations for war within Japan while pursuing a course calculated to postpone the risk of hostilities when dealing with the foreigners. On the face of it, it was not so very far from the position taken by the officials supporting Abe's views, who argued that Japan for all her efforts could not be ready to fight for several years; and had it not been for the rigidity of status requirements, which prevented a personal confrontation between the men concerned, it is quite possible that a compromise could have been worked out.[47] As it was, an exchange of memoranda, supplemented by talks conducted through intermediaries, left the two parties still suspicious of each other. The officials thought Nariaki rash, perhaps a warmonger. Mito was sure that the Bakufu was weak and hesitant. Not even a decree permitting the domains to build warships, which was in part a concession to Nariaki's wishes, convinced him otherwise.[48]

The outcome of these exchanges was a Bakufu announcement on December 1, 1853, that tried, but tried in vain, to bridge the gap between them.[49] In the present state of Japan's defenses, it said, every effort would have to be made to avoid a conflict with Perry when he returned. However, if negotiations then broke down, all Japanese must be ready to defend their country. The effect was to make public the caution, favored by the majority in Edo, that was the very reverse of Nariaki's wishes; and early in the new year he commented in a letter to Matsudaira Shungaku that what he had all along feared was now about to come to pass, namely, that Japan was again to enter into negotiations unprepared.[50]

The cause of his despair was the return of Perry to Uraga, accompanied this time by all eight of his available ships. As Perry observed in his official report, he had "made every preparation to distinguish the occasion of his second landing in Japan by all necessary parade, knowing, as he did, the importance and moral influence of such show upon so ceremonious and artificial a people as the

Japanese";[51] and he spared no pains to impress on the Japanese negotiators in the series of meetings that began on March 8, 1854, his determination to secure a treaty. Nor did the Japanese make much objection to this, for the Bakufu had already ordered its representatives to accept many of the American demands, notably those relating to castaways and ports of call.

Surprisingly, the question of trade was quickly settled, too. Perry proposed a commercial agreement based on the American treaties with China; the Japanese rejected it; and Perry turned to other matters.* The only real difficulty, in fact, arose over the choice of the ports to be opened, chiefly because Perry would have nothing to do with Nagasaki. Eventually, Shimoda and Hakodate were selected, the former to be opened at once, the latter after the lapse of a year, and with this settled the negotiations were virtually at an end. The treaty, duly drawn up in English, Dutch, Chinese, and Japanese, was signed on March 31, 1854, at a brief ceremony in the specially built hall at Kanagawa where the talks had taken place.[52]

Both sides seemed well enough pleased with what they had done. Perry's report claimed roundly that "Japan has been opened to the nations of the West."[53] It also viewed the future with some optimism. "The Japanese are, undoubtedly, like the Chinese, a very imitative, adaptative, and compliant people," it said, "and in these characteristics may be discovered a promise of the comparatively easy introduction of foreign customs and habits, if not of the nobler principles and better life of a higher civilization."[54] For their part, the Japanese negotiators could boast a number of petty triumphs—"the agreement was concluded in the names of the four envoys without any official document from the Rōjū"[55]—and one solid achievement, the exclusion of any clear-cut right to trade. This had been done, moreover, without provoking hostilities. It is true that Nariaki and his followers were horrified at the extent of the con-

* Perry's report describes this as an attempt to secure "so much of trade as Japanese jealousy could be brought to concede" (Hawks, *Narrative*, 1: 389). However, according to a Japanese account, Perry specifically stated that trade was subordinate to other issues, using the following words: "Commerce brings profit to a country, but it does not concern human life. I shall not insist upon it" (see "Diary of an Official," p. 106). Since Hawks was seeking to defend Perry against criticism on this point, it is not surprising that he failed to mention such a statement.

cessions that had been made without their knowledge, especially on such matters as consular representation,[56] and that even so forthright a kaikoku advocate as Sakuma Shōzan severely criticized Edo for its disgraceful weakness in succumbing to Perry's threats.[57] It is also true that Japan soon had to sign similar agreements with Russia and Britain,[58] which further increased the number of ships using Japanese ports and hence the chances of a clash. Nevertheless, the Bakufu had succeeded in what it had set out to do, that is, gain time. It remained to be seen what Japan would do with that time.

CHAPTER IV

Unequal Treaties

COMMODORE PERRY's arrival at Uraga in 1853 marked the beginning of both a new phase in Japan's relations with the West and the politics surrounding them. It is true the agreement he negotiated was not as exploitative and one-sided as the agreements the powers had extracted from China in the moment of victory or indeed those Japan herself was to sign in 1858. All the same, many Japanese found it unacceptable—and a confirmation of their fears. Because of it, discussion of anticipated dangers, which we considered in the previous chapter, became debates about actual events. Disagreements among scholars became struggles between men of power, both officials and lords. Above all, the geographical and social boundaries of the argument were greatly extended, so that the issue became a truly "national" one, charged with emotion.

The process had three stages. In the first, as we have seen, Perry's demands led the Bakufu to call for the views of feudal lords, who thus became publicly involved in the making of policy. In the second, to which we now turn, there was a gradual evolution of the Bakufu's own attitudes—without much consultation of the lords—which culminated in the signing of full commercial agreements with the powers, the so-called unequal treaties, in the summer of 1858. This was in one sense a measure of Edo's "realism," acquired through experience of diplomacy. However, *politically* it revealed a gap between the ideas of the Bakufu and those of a large part of the feudal class, a gap that brought bitter recrimination. In the final phase, therefore, objections to the treaties became grounds for opposing the men who made them, even the regime to which they belonged; and as a result, foreign affairs became the crux of domestic politics for most of a decade.

NEGOTIATING

That the Perry treaty and other agreements modeled on it would not long satisfy the Western powers was soon clear to all concerned with them, both Japanese and foreign. Indeed, the next step might well have come more quickly had not the two countries with most at stake in the Far East, Britain and Russia, become involved in hostilities over the Crimea in 1854, which were followed immediately by a British conflict with China, the so-called Arrow War. Together these two events kept the attention of the powers—even those not directly a party to them, like America in the first and Russia in the second—focused on Europe and China rather than Japan, turning the breathing-space the Bakufu had won by its negotiations into a period of relative immunity from foreign interference, lasting into 1858.

This is not to suggest that the interval was without incident or importance for Japan. For one thing, both Bakufu and domains initiated military reforms designed to ensure that when the next confrontation came they would be better prepared to meet it. The Bakufu, for example, founded a naval training school with Dutch instructors at Nagasaki and a shipyard at Uraga; and several of the great domains, including Mito, Satsuma, and Hizen, set up plants for building ships and making cannon in the Western manner. Paralleling this, officials began to work out an acceptable foreign policy, one that would depend less on reconciling the differences of opinion existing within Japan and more on a realistic appreciation of the international situation.

They did so under a new senior member of the Tokugawa council, Hotta Masayoshi (1810–64), whose promotion reflected a small but significant shift in the balance of power in Edo. Abe Masahiro found it increasingly difficult after March 1854 to maintain his position in the face of a growing conflict between the two groups whose disagreements had already begun to emerge in their memorials on foreign policy during the previous year: on the one hand, the senior fudai lords associated with Ii Naosuke who were concerned to develop Japan's external relations as much for the Bakufu's as for the country's sake; on the other, one or two Tokugawa relatives, led by Nariaki, who urged a policy that was at once more militant and more in accord with their interests as quasi-independent princes.

Abe inclined in outlook and background to the Ii supporters, though he recognized, as they apparently did not, the importance of Nariaki to the implementation of any decisions that were taken. He was not the man, however, to resist the pressures of the fudai for long or to overcome them by decisive action. In November 1855 he appointed Hotta to the council and resigned the chief seat to him, gradually handing over the effective conduct of affairs, until by the end of 1856 a full transfer of responsibility had taken place.

One result of this shift in power was to complete the estrangement of Tokugawa Nariaki from the Bakufu council, so removing some of the restraints on the formulation of a more "liberal" policy. It did not, however, involve any great change in the outlook of the men in office. Hotta, like Abe, was a reformer. As the young daimyo of Sakura (110,000 koku) he had instituted a reform program there at the end of 1833 that brought, in addition to the financial economies common in such cases, measures to encourage "Dutch" studies in the fields of medicine and military training. In June 1855, under the impact of Japan's first experience of the West's diplomacy, he also authorized a reorganization of the domain's military force, which retained its feudal command structure but was reequipped with Western-style weapons and divided into specialized cavalry, artillery, and infantry units.[1] All this provided a clear indication of the direction in which Hotta's ideas on Bakufu policy were likely to lead.

Moreover, Hotta inherited from Abe Masahiro a team of able Bakufu officials of middle rank whose attitudes accorded closely with his own.[2] Among them were Toki Yorimune, who had served under Abe in various capacities since the end of 1843 and was appointed Ōmetsuke (Great Censor) in September 1855; Mizuno Tadanori, who had seen duty at both Uraga and Nagasaki before being made Kanjō-bugyō (Finance Magistrate) in February 1855; Kawaji

Toshiaki, a man of fairly humble background—he was the adopted son of a Tokugawa houseman (gokenin) of only 90 koku—who had risen remarkably high to become Kanjō-bugyō in October 1852; his brother, Inoue Kiyonao, also an adopted son, who was governor of Shimoda from May 1855; and Iwase Tadanari, a younger man, quite well connected in Bakufu official circles, who held office as Metsuke (Censor) from February 1854.

Toki, Mizuno, Kawaji, and Iwase all held key posts in the Edo hierarchy, since Ōmetsuke and Metsuke, though nominally concerned with the seeking out of disaffection and maladministration, were commonly used as commissioners at large to deal with special governmental problems, whereas the Kanjō-bugyō controlled government revenue and expenditure, a function that gave them a vital role in the execution of policy. What is more, during the next few years these men became, because of their experience, the first of Japan's modern diplomatic specialists. All except Toki were to be appointed to the newly created office of Gaikoku-bugyō (Foreign Commissioners) after the signing of commercial treaties in the summer of 1858, thereby becoming what British observers described as "Under-Secretaries of Foreign Affairs."

Their first opportunity to take an active part in the shaping of Japanese foreign policy came in 1856, when the Dutch representative at Nagasaki, Donker Curtius, wrote to the Bakufu to urge a fundamental reconsideration of the question of Japan's external trade.[3] To continue to do nothing, he said, would mean sooner or later incurring the risk of war. Sir John Bowring, Britain's superintendent of trade at Hong Kong, who was known to have orders to negotiate a commercial agreement with Japan, was not a man to flinch from the use of force, and as Curtius saw it, Japan's best chance of avoiding a conflict was to come to an agreement with Holland on lines that Bowring might then be persuaded to accept.

It was an argument that gained a ready hearing in the capital, where officialdom was already to some degree conditioned to accept it by the debates of the past two years. Early in September the leading officials of the central government, together with the governors of Nagasaki, Uraga, Shimoda, and Hakodate, were sent a circular calling for their views, the wording of which made it clear that the issue was genuinely open to discussion, as it had not been previously. Moreover, on November 17, despite the continued opposition of Tokugawa Nariaki, a special commission was appointed to study the problem. It had Hotta at its head and six of Abe's "men of ability" among its other ten members.

It is not easy to judge how quickly the work of the commission would have progressed had it been left entirely to itself. There was certainly an air of hesitancy about the Bakufu's approach to the matter (induced perhaps by an awareness of Nariaki's hostility) that was far from promising. In the event, however, the commissioners were prompted into haste by news from China. In February 1857 Curtius heard of the British operations around Canton, which had followed the "Arrow" dispute; and in passing on the information to the Nagasaki Bugyō he did not fail to point the moral. The fate that was overtaking China, he urged, must assuredly overtake Japan unless she mended her ways.

Nor did Edo deny it. In March there came another circular to officials, this time making it absolutely clear that "the policy we have pursued so far cannot long be maintained," for fear that "Japan might suffer the fate of Canton."[4] Hotta himself expanded on the point in an accompanying memorandum. First, trade was inevitable, he said, so Japan had best decide the most advantageous terms on which to grant it. Second, the country's salvation depended on making policy decisions before a crisis occurred, not afterwards: "If we on our side have neither plan nor purpose, we will find ourselves in the end unable to do anything but accept foreign proposals as they stand. This would put our national strength in lasting jeopardy."[5]

The debates that followed took place chiefly within the inner circle of Bakufu officials, especially among those who had a special responsibility for defense and foreign affairs, and started from the assumption that the object now in view was to determine the manner, not the fact, of extending trade relations with the West. Nevertheless, there remained substantial disagreements. One group, which included Toki Yorimune and Iwase Tadanari, wanted Japan to exploit her newfound opportunities to the full, permitting trade free of government interference and opening it to the domains as well as the Bakufu. By this means, its members argued, Edo "could bring the whole country under control and also lay the foundations of national wealth and military strength."[6] Another group, led by Kawaji Toshiaki and Mizuno Tadanori, was more cautious, seeing trade as necessary, not desirable. Admittedly, this group said, the change in world conditions had made the opening of Japan's ports inevitable. Nevertheless, there were still powerful arguments in favor of seclusion. First, to abandon it would be to change something basic to the national structure, bringing "unforeseen weakness" of the kind that arises from trying to replace the pillars or foundations of a building. Second, such action would require for its success a great and original ruler to carry it out, whereas the Bakufu's role was rather that of successor and caretaker: its proper policy was "to preserve tranquillity and issue orders only after full consultation, thus uniting high and low in preserving with care the system handed down by generations of Shogun."[7] Accordingly, however necessary it might be for the Bakufu to *act* in new ways, it must not on that account abandon traditional *attitudes*: "Its ideas and its inner thoughts [must] be rooted in the former system."

It is interesting to see in these two documents how a similar premise—the inadequacy of existing institutions—could lead to such different conclusions: in the one case an argument that only radical reform could save the Bakufu's authority, in the other a belief that the Bakufu's own failings made it incompetent to effect real change. Both had in common, one should note, a commitment to the preservation of Bakufu power, together with a recognition that foreign policy decisions were relevant to it; and in the long run this was to be more important than the points on which the two groups disagreed. Immediately, however, their differences gave them a contrasting approach to the question of negotiations with Holland, the one cautious, the other optimistic. Shrewdly, Hotta chose a member of each, Mizuno Tadanori and Iwase Tadanari, to represent him in Nagasaki.

Officially, their task was to investigate the problem of trade in consultation with Donker Curtius, but as their discussions took shape during the summer of 1857 it soon became clear that they were in the process of drafting a commercial treaty. What is more, the joint persuasions of Curtius and Iwase gradually overcame Mizuno's suspicions, so that the draft agreement they eventually worked out marked a considerable departure from past practice. It opened Nagasaki and Hakodate to trade free of official interference, the trade to be without limit on its value and open to all Japanese merchants, not merely a monopoly ring; and although there was still to be a good deal of control over Dutch ships and persons, as well as a 35 per cent customs duty on all "private" imports, it seemed to both parties that so great an improvement on the old Deshima arrangements could hardly fail to be acceptable to the other foreign powers.*

This, of course, was the nub of the matter. Notwithstanding the views of Iwase and a few others of like mind, the only chance of getting such a treaty approved in Edo was to present it as a means of forestalling something worse. Mizuno and Iwase made this clear in letters seeking permission to sign the agreement at the end of August.[8] Haste was essential, they said, because a British squadron might appear at any time to demand a treaty and would certainly not accept as a model one that existed only in draft, unsigned. So confident were they of this fact, indeed, that they proposed to sign the treaty in the last resort on their own responsibility, should a British envoy arrive before the Bakufu's instructions.

In Edo, only Iwase's colleagues supported the proposals as they stood, the rest of the officials expressing reservations about one point or another, with the majority unable either to accept in their entirety the conclusions reached by those who were in direct communication with the foreigners or to formulate a clear alternative themselves.[9] This left the decision to Hotta personally. At the beginning of October he approved the Iwase-Mizuno draft.

Meanwhile, a Russian envoy, Rear Admiral E. V. Putiatin, had arrived at Nagasaki and requested a commercial treaty. Mizuno

* The Dutch trade at Deshima had long been subject to severe restrictions. The Japanese limited the number of Dutch ships that could come each year (usually to one, sometimes two); imposed a ceiling on the annual value of the trade; banned some exports and limited others (especially metals); required all transactions to be conducted through a merchant guild supervised by the Bakufu's local governor; and closely regulated any travel by the Dutch outside their "factory." Almost all these controls were ended by the new treaty, which was signed on Oct. 16, 1857. An English text of it is given in Beasley, *Select Documents*, pp. 149–55.

and Iwase promptly informed the Bakufu that since Russia was as greatly to be feared as Britain, they would if necessary also sign an agreement with Russia, thus furnishing two models against a British envoy's arrival instead of one. Nor was it long before they had to do so as the pressures from Curtius and Putiatin increased. Still not in receipt of the instructions Hotta had approved, which were slow in reaching them, but knowing from their private correspondence that they had powerful support in the capital, Mizuno and Iwase fulfilled their promises. The Dutch treaty was signed on October 16, followed by a similar agreement with Russia eight days later. It was, as Mizuno wrote, "an act of the greatest temerity" to have done this without specific orders, justifiable only by the nature of the crisis that they faced. After all, "nothing could be worse than to cause the Bakufu further difficulties."[10]

There can be no doubt that the Dutch and Russian agreements of 1857 represented the extreme limit of the concessions the Bakufu was likely to make under any ordinary pressure. Indeed, even this much was achieved only by virtue of Hotta's own authority, resolving differences within officialdom. Whether the decision could have been imposed on the lords and samurai at large must be open to question in view of what happened in the following year. However, we need hardly speculate about this, since the two treaties were quickly overshadowed by another, made with America, that pushed Japan further along the road toward a "Chinese" treaty pattern and made the subject of foreign relations once again a matter of public controversy.

This further development was the almost single-handed work of Townsend Harris, America's first consul in Japan, who had established himself at Shimoda in September 1856.[11] Within a few weeks of his arrival he gave notice of his intention to pursue commercial negotiations, sending the Shimoda Bugyō a Dutch translation of the American agreement with Siam, which was modeled on those with China, and requesting permission to go to Edo to deliver a letter from the President and open talks on "a most important matter." Edo's response was not encouraging, since it was obvious enough what Harris wanted, and only Iwase Tadanari and his colleagues favored it. He was told to deal exclusively with the Shimoda Bugyō, even on major issues. Nor did his repeated requests thereafter get any better treatment, at least until the decision was taken to enter into a discussion of trade with Curtius in 1857.

Even then the Bakufu's first consideration of the question was inconclusive, and it took a strong memorial from the Shimoda Bugyō—Kawaji Toshiaki's brother, Inoue Kiyonao—backed by Toki Yorimune, to secure a ruling in favor of the Edo visit.[12] This concession, which was by no means a small one in Japanese eyes, was communicated to Harris on August 27, 1857, though it was another month before a provisional date was set. When the news was at last publicly announced in Edo on October 1, it brought immediate protests from a number of powerful daimyo. These Hotta chose to ignore. Still, it was not until late November that Harris left Shimoda for Edo, where on December 7 he had a brief formal audience with the Shogun, Iesada, clearing the way for serious diplomatic business.

The Bakufu had intended to offer Harris (and Bowring, if he should come) a treaty modeled on that with Holland. However, at an interview with Hotta on December 12 Harris at once rejected this possibility. Instead, he asked for more liberal arrangements about trade, an increase in the number of open ports, and the right to appoint a resident minister in Edo. Britain, he said, would certainly accept no less; and since Bowring would bring with him the fleet assembled for the war against China, which he would undoubtedly be willing to use, Japan would then have to yield or fight. There would be a great difference, Harris pointed out, between "a treaty made with a single individual, unattended, and one made with a person who should bring fifty men-of-war to these shores":[13] to submit openly to force "would humiliate the Government in the eyes of all the Japanese people, and thus actually weaken its power."[14]

For two hours Harris lectured Hotta on the state of the world and the way the development of modern industry had changed it, on the threat from Britain—he could produce private letters from Bowring to demonstrate it—and the benefits to be derived from negotiation with America. He had a receptive audience, as Bakufu handling of the Dutch treaty had shown. He had also won access to the man who made decisions, which made his position markedly different from that of Curtius earlier in the year; and within a few days Hotta had drafted a memorandum for the information of Bakufu officials that made it clear he found Harris's arguments convincing.

Simply to accept foreign demands because of Japan's weakness, Hotta said, would be to invite eventual disaster. To oppose force with force, out of pride, would be equal folly, leading to economic and military collapse. Hence Japan must not only sign treaties, she must put them to use: "Our policy should be to stake everything on the present opportunity, to conclude friendly alliances, to send ships to foreign countries everywhere and conduct trade, to copy the foreigners where they are at their best and so repair our own shortcomings, to foster our national strength and complete our armaments, and so gradually subject the foreigners to our influence until in the end all the countries of the world know the blessings of perfect tranquillity and our hegemony is acknowledged throughout the globe."[15]

This policy was not quite, perhaps, what Harris had in mind when he described himself as being "engaged in teaching the elements of political economy to the Japanese."[16] Nor was it necessarily agreeable to majority opinion in Edo, as future events were to show. It meant, however, that negotiations could take place with some hope of reaching an acceptable conclusion.

There were to be a number of points of detail on which the Bakufu bargained stubbornly. On January 16, 1858, Harris had another interview with Hotta, at which Hotta agreed in principle to Harris's three main demands, albeit with reservations about the place at which a diplomatic representative should reside and the number of ports to be opened. Next day Inoue Kiyonao and Iwase Tadanari were appointed plenipotentiaries. But a week later, when the actual talks began, Harris found to his surprise and mounting irritation that he was having to fight the battle to get rid of the Dutch treaty "model" all over again. There were objections to the opening of Edo and Osaka, still more to the opening of Kyōto. There was a proposal that the American minister should live in

Shinagawa or Kanagawa, not Edo. There was absolute opposition to the idea of granting foreigners the right to travel freely in the interior of the country. Throughout there were delays and adjournments as the "plenipotentiaries" withdrew to consult their seniors and a constant reiteration of argument and counterargument, which led Harris to record in his journal: "I shall confine myself to the main leading facts of actual transactions, omitting the interminable discourses of the Japanese where the same proposition may be repeated a dozen times; nor shall I note their positive refusal of points they subsequently grant, and meant to grant all the while; nor many absurd proposals made by them, without the hope, and scarcely the wish, of having them accepted."[17]

Despite these problems, Harris succeeded in gaining most of what he asked. His demand for the opening of Kyōto was dropped, as was the question of the right of travel in the interior, except for officials. However, the minister, it was agreed, was to reside in Edo; Edo itself, with Osaka, Kanagawa (Yokohama), Nagasaki, Niigata, and Hyōgo (Kōbe), were all to be opened to trade between July 4, 1859, and January 1, 1863; customs duties were fixed at 5 or 20 per cent for the majority of imports; and American citizens in Japan were to be subject to American consular courts, not Japanese law.[18] It was in fact essentially the China treaty pattern, modified by a prohibition of opium and a specific provision for the toleration of Christianity (though limited to foreign residents). Acceptance of these terms was bound to draw Japan into the network of economic and political relationships the West had established in its dealings with China.

SIGNING

Seen from the perspective of the twentieth century and in the knowledge of what happened elsewhere in Asia, it is not difficult to identify the risks Japan ran in signing an agreement of the kind Harris had drawn up. If the demands of trade were to disrupt her economy, then a hostile political reaction among the Japanese, or simply chaos within the country, could provoke intervention in defense of the West's economic "rights." From this it was but a short step to becoming a European colony or protectorate. Alternatively, if Japan's economy were to adjust smoothly to the new situation, she might, as the weaker partner in an outwardly symbiotic relationship, become so subordinated to external control as to acquire a "semicolonial" status. Foreign economic superiority, in other words, buttressed by such devices as extraterritoriality and a regulated tariff, could gradually undermine the country's political independence as well as its economic independence. Between these two hazards, the colonial and the semicolonial, the path of safety was extremely narrow.

Contemporary Japanese did not see the problem in quite these terms, of course, but enough of them were alarmed at the dangers they *did* see in the treaty to make acceptance of it neither quickly nor easily to be won. This was already apparent by February 25, 1858, when the draft text was finally made ready for submission to the Bakufu; and it caused Inoue and Iwase, acting on instructions, to propose to Harris a delay in signing the agreement in order to give Hotta time to pacify opinion by securing the approval of the Imperial Court.

Late in December 1857 Hotta had decided to circulate to officials and feudal lords a summary of the statement Harris had made to him—much as Abe had done with the American letters in 1853—thereby taking a step that greatly extended the scope of a debate hitherto confined largely to the Bakufu's inner group. Within this group, as we have seen, there were already some who expressed dismay at the options open to Japan, which seemed to offer a choice between exposing the country to inevitable corruption by the West and fighting in the confident expectation of defeat. If the few were dismayed, however, the majority of officials reacted with something like despair.[19] Even Mizuno Tadanori, who had helped to negotiate the Dutch treaty a few months earlier, was unhappy about the risks that were now to be taken. To admit resident diplomats to Edo, he argued, would give them access to the great lords, which was politically dangerous. Moreover, to let them practice Christianity in the city might well bring accusations of weakness on the part of government, "whereupon those who have always been turbulent and discontented may seize the opportunity to stir up disaffection," endangering Tokugawa rule.[20] Nevertheless, the only practical suggestion he could make was to keep the foreigners out of places like Edo and Osaka and to try to limit them to obscure harbors in the Kii peninsula.*

Among the daimyo, too, such attitudes were not uncommon, though in many cases their alarm stemmed from a lack of knowledge of the West rather than from an awareness of a genuine dilemma. One or two of them had not changed at all in the past four years. Date of Sendai, for example, still rejected trade on economic grounds, as he had in 1853, and therefore would accept no part of what Harris pleaded.[21] More characteristically, a joint memorial from a group of influential fudai lords and Tokugawa branch houses proposed accepting the American terms in principle but seeking ways of delaying their implementation in practice.[22] Matsudaira Yoshitomo of Tsuyama (*kamon;*† 100,000 koku) actually put forward a line of argument for achieving this goal that was not so very different from the one the Bakufu was to use in 1862. Since the opening of the ports would encourage trade to the detriment of agriculture, he said, farmers would leave the land to engage in it, so contributing to the country's weakness. This in turn would bring unrest and ultimately attacks on foreigners; but if foreigners could be made to understand that these were the consequences of what they did, they might be brought to recognize that their demands, being unreasonable, ought to be withdrawn or modified.[23]

Perhaps the most notable change was that Tokugawa Nariaki now dropped his demand for resistance *à l'outrance,* notwithstanding his continued hostility to the opening of more ports and the establishment of foreign consulates in Edo. Yet his only contribution to the shaping of immediate policy was a proposal so unrealistic as to be almost derisory. The Bakufu might overcome the worst of its difficulties, he suggested, by sending him, as a senior member of the Tokugawa family, and a staff of rōnin, criminals, and younger sons of merchants and farmers to America to set up a trading post. This would give the foreigners what they wanted most, namely,

* Mizuno's arguments against admitting foreigners to Edo have a strong family resemblance to those used by Chinese conservatives in opposing foreign diplomatic representation at Peking during Lord Elgin's negotiations at Tientsin later in the year. See Hsü, *China's Entrance*, pp. 57–66.

† One of the categories of shimpan houses, junior branches of the Tokugawa.

trade, while keeping them out of Japan. If similar arrangements could be made with other countries as well, he thought, it might give Japan time, even at this late hour, to strengthen her defenses.[24]

There was, then, strong support among the feudal lords for those Bakufu officials who sought ways of moderating what they believed to be the most dangerous of America's terms while avoiding a hopeless military adventure. But there was also support for those who took a quite different view. Of these, the lead was once again taken by Iwase Tadanari, who in January 1858 submitted a memorial outstanding in the frankness of its attack on Bakufu indecision. Iwase, too, recognized in the situation a threat to both Japanese independence and Tokugawa power. He did not, however, believe that it could be met by splitting hairs or engaging in "trifling arguments about detail." To try to find distant and obscure harbors to open to foreign trade or to postpone a decision altogether seemed to him useless and provocative. Better by far to grasp the nettle, he said, to declare at once a willingness to open Yokohama to trade on generous terms, thereby gaining a tactical initiative in the negotiations with Harris and demonstrating Edo's responsibility for the country's government. By taking such a step "the Bakufu would in fact be reasserting its authority in overall supervision of national affairs, would be carrying out a policy that would be to our lasting advantage and would be laying the foundations of national wealth and strength."[25]

This positive approach to the problem had the enthusiastic backing of the kamon lord Matsudaira Shungaku, whose ideas had developed a good deal since 1853. Where he once had been firmly set against a treaty with Perry, he now wrote: "In dominating men or being dominated by them, the issue turns simply on the question of who has the initiative." [26] In the context of Japan's foreign relations this meant active measures to develop trade—"a wealthy country is the basis of military strength"—with the ultimate object of being able to "shatter the selfish designs of the brutish foreigners." Hence the Bakufu must accept Harris's demands where they were reasonable. It must also, however, institute a program of reform at home, for this alone would put Japan in a position to exploit the opportunities a treaty would open up.

Shungaku was by no means alone in urging this course. Another Tokugawa relative, Matsudaira Katamori of Aizu (kamon; 230,000 koku), argued that the time was one of challenge as well as crisis, a time when resolute action as the ports were opened would make it possible to "enrich the country and strengthen the army."[27] Shimazu Nariakira of Satsuma (tozama; 770,000 koku) and Tachibana Akitomo of Yanagawa (tozama; 119,000 koku) also advocated trade for the sake of national strength, coupling it with reform at home.[28] Kuroda Narihiro of Chikuzen (tozama; 520,000 koku) sent a secret and personal memorial on similar lines, written without consulting his family or retainers (a procedure he thought to be so unorthodox that he asked for the memorial to be destroyed after reading).[29]

From these documents it is clear that the situation Hotta faced in 1858 was in some respects quite different from that with which Abe had had to deal in 1853. Instead of a simple clash between two minorities, the one urging the opening of the ports, the other the expulsion of the foreigner, against a background of traditional and undifferentiated anti-foreign feeling, there was now a substantial recognition, at least among those close to the centers of power, of the inevitability of foreign trade and diplomatic relations.* What divided the more influential members of the ruling class was how far to make a virtue of necessity, or how best to save the things they valued, whether tradition or power.

However, the new appreciation of the situation in official circles did not necessarily make it easier to get approval for the Harris treaty. Some men condemned it as weakness in the face of threats, others because it was not part of a plan for Japan's regeneration. In fact, "progressives" were as critical of the treaty as "reactionaries." This Hotta discovered when he met with the leading feudal lords in Edo on February 12 and 13, 1858, to outline his policy. On February 18, therefore, he wrote to Harris to propose a delay in the signing of the agreement, asserting—as far as one can judge, sincerely—that imperial approval, which he now intended to secure, would silence all the treaty's opponents. They were, he believed,

* This was not true, as we shall see, of "public opinion" more broadly conceived. Indeed, the distinction that Kuroda made between his own views and those of his domain already hints at the existence of a different kind of division.

more misguided than malicious. As Inoue Kiyonao put it in talks with Harris, much of the opposition was bigoted, coming from men who, "like the obstinate of more enlightened countries," refused to listen to reason.[30] The only way of reaching them was through the Emperor's traditionalist prestige. Nor was there any danger that the Emperor would refuse his consent, when asked. The Bakufu, Inoue observed, "had determined not to receive any objections from the Mikado."[31]

In this estimate of the situation, Edo proved wrong.[32] By the time Hotta arrived in Kyōto on March 19, 1858, accompanied by Kawaji Toshiaki and Iwase Tadanari, there had already been some discussion of his proposals in Court circles. Of the twenty or so senior Court nobles (kuge) who had been consulted about the treaty, five had wholly rejected it and about half wanted no action taken until the great lords had clearly expressed their consent. The Emperor in person had committed himself to the latter view and had said that he was prepared, if necessary, to authorize "expulsion" of the foreigner.[33] As a result, on April 6 Hotta received a decree stating that sanction for the treaty would be withheld until further consultations with the lords had taken place.

For the next few weeks Hotta worked hard to get the Court decree modified. Through his influence with the Kampaku, Kujō Naotada, and the former Kampaku Takatsukasa Masamichi, he finally got a new draft prepared that recognized Edo's ultimate responsibility in such matters. This Kujō and Takatsukasa forced on their colleagues and the Emperor, who formally approved it on April 24. At this point, however, the Emperor let it be known privately that he viewed the revised draft with disfavor. In consequence, a meeting of 80 or more lower-ranking kuge, organized by Ōhara Shigenori and Iwakura Tomomi, passed a resolution condemning it. That action led Kujō to eliminate from his text the controversial passage about Bakufu responsibility; thus it was in a much less helpful form that the document reached Hotta on May 3. The treaty, if signed as now proposed, it said, "would make impossible the preservation of national honour."[34] The Bakufu must consult the lords and make a fresh submission.

One reason for this debacle was that many kuge had been deeply influenced by Mito writings in the past few years and thought that their action would strengthen the influence of Tokugawa Nariaki in the Bakufu's counsels. Another was that several daimyo, including Nariaki himself and Matsudaira Shungaku, had been intriguing in Kyōto (see chapter 5); and though it is true that their object was not so much to secure rejection of the American treaty as to increase the prospects of reform at home, a reform that in their view was necessary if the treaty was to become an instrument of Japan's revival, yet in the result, perhaps because some of the subtleties of the argument were lost on the politically inexperienced nobles of the Imperial Court, it was the rejection of the treaty that they actually brought about.

What they achieved, in fact, was not a reorientation of Bakufu policy but Hotta's downfall. Before leaving Kyōto, he reached a secret understanding with the Kampaku and other leading Court officials that in the event of a crisis he would sign the treaty, disregarding the imperial orders, so that in the context of foreign policy all was not entirely lost. Nevertheless, he had suffered an open rebuff that had seriously undermined his power. By the time he arrived back in Edo on June 1, 1858, steps were already in train to replace him as chief minister; and three days later Ii Naosuke was appointed Tairō, or Regent, relegating Hotta to second place.

The change of leadership made little immediate difference to the Bakufu's approach to foreign affairs: the signing of the treaty remained its prime concern. During June Iwase and Kawaji were set to work drumming up support for it among the daimyo in order to justify a fresh application for imperial approval. Testifying to their success, a joint memorial was submitted on June 25 by an impressive list of tozama—they included Ikeda of Bizen, Uesugi of Yonezawa, Asano of Aki, Arima of Kurume, Date of Uwajima, and Yamauchi of Tosa, men whose domains totaled nearly one and a half million koku—acknowledging that the Harris agreement ought not to be left unsigned. Many others wrote in terms that at least left the Bakufu free to claim it had their backing. Indeed, only Nariaki was irreconcilable, arguing that the Emperor's known opinions were the final confirmation of his own.

This was the position when the crisis against which Hotta and his colleagues had been preparing ever since the previous year at last materialized. On July 23 an American warship arrived at Shimoda and informed Townsend Harris that peace had been restored in China, and that the British and French plenipotentiaries were leaving at once to open negotiations with Japan. Harris lost no time in going to Kanagawa, where he conveyed this news to Inoue and Iwase. They in turn went back to Edo for instructions, urging that the treaty be signed immediately. Most of the other diplomatic specialists within officialdom agreed with them.

Nevertheless, some members of the council, which was summoned on July 29, still had difficulty making up their minds, and even Ii Naosuke, conscious of the political dangers he was running, expressed doubts about acting without the Court's consent. Consequently, there followed a long and difficult debate, which only the Regent's sense of Bakufu responsibility (reinforced, perhaps, by a knowledge of Hotta's secret bargain in Kyōto) brought to a positive conclusion. Better, Ii said at last, to act against the Emperor's wishes than to fight a losing war. Nor must the council deny its duty: "State policy is the responsibility of the Bakufu, which in an emergency must take such administrative action as seems expedient."[35] On these grounds Ii instructed Inoue and Iwase to return to Kanagawa and sign the treaty if they saw no possibility of further delaying it. They did so later the same day.

Demonstrating that the threat of British action was this time no mere rumor, Lord Elgin (who had superseded Bowring as British plenipotentiary in China) reached Edo about two weeks later, albeit without the large fleet that had been reported as likely to come with an English envoy. By August 26, with the help of Harris's secretary, Hendrik Heusken, he was able to sign a treaty based on Harris's own. A few days earlier, similar agreements had been made with Curtius for Holland and Putiatin for Russia. A French treaty followed in October. As a result, thanks largely to the decisions that Harris's demands had compelled the Bakufu—or rather its more open-minded officials—to take, Japan found herself committed to opening her ports within the next twelve months and entering into full commercial relations with five of the Western powers. Unlike China, she had been brought to this position without any overt use of force. Also unlike China, she was to react at once to the inequalities that had been imposed on her. Accordingly, 1858 marked the beginning, not the end, of her real struggle with the West, as well as the beginning of a political conflict at home that had many of the hallmarks of revolution.

CHAPTER V

Reforming Lords

THE "UNEQUAL" TREATIES signed in the summer of 1858 caused an immediate public outcry in Japan. Knowledge of them, after all, was by no means confined to men possessing office or high status. Many middle and some lower-ranking samurai were involved in one way or another in the discussions and intrigues surrounding them, sometimes as confidential messengers of the relatively small number of politically active lords, like Tokugawa Nariaki and Matsudaira Shungaku, but more often because the drafting of replies to Bakufu circulars made necessary a process of consultation with retainers. When these discussions took place in Edo—the sankin-kōtai system ensured that both daimyo and samurai were present in the city in considerable numbers—it was not difficult for individuals to follow them up by acquiring information about the negotiations and the treaties as they were taking shape. In fact, as long as the Bakufu itself felt a need for consultation, almost nothing could be kept secret. Nor was the circulation of news confined to Edo. All domains maintained a permanent establishment there, so that even in the absence of the daimyo and his entourage there was still a channel through which reports could reach the provinces.

The manner in which news was transmitted—through private meetings between samurai in Edo, in letters to friends or colleagues remaining in the castle towns, by oral accounts from those who transferred from one center to another — ensured that reliable knowledge of what was going on was restricted at first to members of the samurai class, since such exchanges took place between men of more or less equal standing. More slowly, the publication of books and pamphlets like Shionoya Tōin's *Kakkaron* in 1859 provided a basis for discussion by those who were literate, whether samurai or not.*

However, an extension, if a limited one, of the social boundaries of the debate did not have to wait on this development. Many samurai of fairly humble rank, including gōshi and ashigaru, as well as sons of village headmen and even well-to-do farmers and merchants, regularly went from all over the country to Edo or one of the other great cities to complete their education.[1] There they formed a society quite distinct from that of the official domain establishments: less regulated, more open to communication with men from other regions, and more flexible in outlook because less bound by status. It was a society in which the discussion of foreign affairs became a subject of absorbing, even passionate interest during the years after 1853. And because its members had contacts with relatively well-informed middle samurai on the one hand and with members of the semi-samurai or non-samurai upper class of the villages and provincial towns on the other, criticism of the treaty settlement assumed through them almost national proportions.

The wider implications of this we must leave to be worked out in later chapters. Here it is necessary only to emphasize that "public opinion," so defined, was hostile to the Harris treaty, to the way in which it had been signed, and to the men who signed it. Sakuma Shōzan, for example, who advocated the opening of Japan to Western influences on a scale far greater than was envisaged by the majority of men in office, wholeheartedly condemned Edo for giving way to foreign threats.[2] His pupil Yoshida Shōin, whose ideas were to have a revolutionary impact on the young radicals of the 1860's, blamed a "barbarian-subduing" Shogun for failing in his proper task: "Ignoring the distress of the nation, heedless of the shame of the nation, he disobeys the Imperial command."[3] Others used still more violent language, the temper of which by no means moderated as time went by. In 1860 a group of Mito samurai wrote of "the dishonor to our divine land."[4] *Genji Yume Monogatari* referred in

* As noted earlier, Aizawa Seishisai's *Shinron*, though written in 1825, was not published until 1857, when it caused something of a sensation.

1864 to "the anger of the gods at the continual pollution of our country by the visits of the outer barbarians."[5] Hirano Kuniomi, one of the samurai activists, condemned Bakufu subservience to the barbarians for threatening to make Japan "a subject state, stinking of the smell of foreign meat,"[6] and his associate Takechi Zuizan accused Edo officials of a total neglect of Japanese interests: "Acceding more and more to the insatiable demands of the foreigners, they take no account of the country's impoverishment or the people's distress. They show no trace of patriotic feeling."[7]

The importance of these examples—which could be multiplied many times, in documents ranging from state papers to personal diaries—is that they reflected not policy, but emotion. At the conclusion of the British negotiations in 1858 Lord Elgin's secretary, Laurence Oliphant, remarked shrewdly that treaties granted out of fear would not be easy to enforce. The Japanese officials, he said, "fancied they saw impending over them the fate of India, and they believed that the only alternative was to grant us concessions such as we had already wrung from China"; but once the immediate source of their fear was removed, they would almost certainly come under pressure at home, "even at the expense of good faith, to retreat from engagements they would never willingly have entered into."[8] What Oliphant did not foresee, any more than the Bakufu, was that the pressure would take the form not only of political argument in the councils of the great, but also of a "popular" campaign of threats and violence. Such a campaign, motivated by a strength of feeling that overrode prudence, was to be a crucial element in Japanese politics during the next few years.

It was not, however, the only element. Interlocking with the attacks on foreigners and those who had dealings with them was a political struggle of a very different kind. Many Japanese, as we have seen, reacted to the dangers that they envisaged as arising from renewed relations with the West by calling for reform at home; but they disagreed greatly about what constituted reform (apart, perhaps, from a new kind of military preparedness, entailing the adoption of Western weapons and techniques). Some felt the country's regeneration could be accomplished within the existing framework of society provided it was modestly modified to allow more effective leadership than had been evidenced by the Bakufu hitherto. Others, because of humbler status or a keener appreciation of the magnitude of the task, or both, insisted on a much more radical program requiring major institutional change, without which they saw no possibility of achieving national unity and strength. The first of these attitudes, that of conservative reform, was associated with a group of relatively able daimyo and their retainers whose demand for *kōbu-gattai*, "unity of Court and Bakufu," implied some limitation of the Shogun's power but was not an attack on the system as such. The second characterized the activities of the loyalists, turbulent lower samurai for the most part, whose interpretation of the Mito slogan *sonnō-jōi*, "honor the Emperor and expel the barbarian," gave it a new and iconoclastic meaning.

The political history of Japan from 1858 to 1865, with which the next chapters of this book will deal, centers on the conflict between the two groups and on their dealings with Edo. None of the regime's opponents in this period, whether barons or lower samurai, were fully to achieve their aims. The loyalists, emerging in the aftermath of the crisis of 1858, bade fair to dominate the scene in 1862 and 1863 but were defeated and scattered by the end of the following year. By contrast, the daimyo of the kōbu-gattai party, who seemed briefly to be the victors both before and after these events, proved unable in the long run to maintain a middle ground between the Bakufu's tenacity of power and the continued extremist assaults on their own moderation. We shall need to give detailed attention to the various confrontations that this situation involved and their significance for the Bakufu's fate. Before doing so, however, let us first examine separately the nature and objectives of each movement, beginning with that of the reforming lords.

TECHNOLOGY AND REFORM

Though the more emotional Japanese responses to the diplomacy of the years 1854 to 1858 owed much to the Mito school's advocacy of jōi, "expel the barbarian," many of the practical ones, from which there was to stem one strand of the proposals for political reform, developed from the work of the "Dutch" scholars and their allies, those who wished to open the ports. Defense, it was widely recognized, involved an organized study of the West. As Shimazu

Nariakira, daimyo of Satsuma, put it in 1856: "At this time when defence against the foreign barbarians is of crucial importance it is the urgent duty of all samurai both high and low to co-operate in learning of conditions in foreign lands so that we may adopt their good points to supplement our deficiencies, reinforce the military might of our nation and keep the barbarian nations under control."[9] Not surprisingly, his own domain, which already had a long tradition of promoting "Dutch studies," was one that took the lead in this process, sending students to work under specialist teachers in Nagasaki, Edo, and Osaka; translating and publishing Western books, including works on science and navigation; and providing for the teaching of such subjects in its official school.

Similar programs, usually on a more modest scale, were undertaken by other lords, among them Tokugawa Nariaki of Mito, Matsudaira Shungaku of Echizen, Nabeshima Naomasa of Hizen, and Mōri Yoshichika of Chōshū.[10] Often the introduction of Dutch medicine, providing practical benefits like smallpox vaccination (which was in use in several areas before 1853), opened the way for the later development of studies with a more military bias, since it stimulated the learning of relevant languages in addition to at least an elementary knowledge of scientific method. So, too, did mathematics and astronomy, which lent themselves readily to a shift of interest from calendars to navigation. It was therefore of considerable significance that such studies were so widespread in Japan toward the end of the Tokugawa period. One estimate puts the number of domain schools teaching "Western" subjects as high as 60 by the time of the Restoration.[11] The Bakufu itself founded a translation bureau in 1856 that quickly became a major center for the study of Dutch, English, French, and German, together with military science, metallurgy, and even Western-style art.* Oliphant thus had some grounds for observing in 1858 that "whereas the

* The plan originated in 1855 in discussions between Abe Masahiro, head of the Tokugawa council, and advisers like Mizuno Tadanori and Kawaji Toshiaki. The bureau, under the name Bansho-shirabesho (Office for the Study of Barbarian Books), was established in March 1856 and formally opened as a school in February 1857, its stated purposes being the study of foreign military systems, weapons, and weapons production, as well as the training of officials for a diplomatic service. Its staff was drawn initially from the domains where such studies had long been pursued. Samurai from other domains, however, were admitted as students. See Numata, *Bakumatsu yōgaku shi*, pp. 55–61; and Jansen, "New Materials."

Chinese are steadily retrograding and will in all probability continue to do so until the Empire falls to pieces, the Japanese, if not actually in a state of progressive advancement, are in a condition to profit by the flood of light that is about to be poured in upon them."[12]

Application of the new knowledge to Japan's military and economic needs, though not uncommon, was not always as rapid or widespread as its role in education might lead one to expect. Takashima Shūhan, for example, a Bakufu official at Nagasaki, took a personal initiative in learning gunnery and military organization from the Dutch during the 1820's but got little encouragement from his superiors before the Opium War and had to wait until after Perry's arrival before they gave his proposals much effect.[13] In the interval, however, his methods had become influential in a number of domains, especially through the teaching of another Bakufu expert, Egawa Tarozaemon, who had studied under Takashima. Once again Satsuma provides the clearest illustration. In 1847 a training school was established there to introduce Takashima's ideas in gunnery and drill. Simultaneously, steps were taken to build new coast batteries, and in 1848 there was a reform of military administration aimed at strengthening the supervision exercised by senior officials and ensuring a more efficient allocation of duties among castle-town samurai. After Shimazu Nariakira became daimyo in 1850, this work was continued and extended. The artillery force was reorganized, and Western training methods were adopted for it; rifle companies were formed; and a new-style cavalry unit was created on the lines laid down in a Dutch edition of the French cavalry manual, which had been translated by a Bakufu interpreter at Nagasaki.[14]

Satsuma also took an active part in naval training, though in this the lead was taken by able young officials in the Bakufu, notably Mizuno Tadanori.[15] In 1854 they arranged for the Dutch warship *Soembing* to be available to give naval instruction on a temporary basis at Nagasaki; in the following year they bought the ship in order to put the arrangement on a permanent footing and hired a team of twenty Dutch instructors. The naval school so formed was opened to men from the domains as well as the Bakufu, and many took advantage—or were ordered to take advantage—of the opportunity. The largest contingents came from Chikuzen (twenty-eight men) and Hizen (forty-eight men), these being the domains traditionally responsible for defending Nagasaki, but there were also sixteen from Satsuma (Nariakira offered small supplementary stipends to lower-level hirazamurai who undertook this duty) and fifteen from Chōshū. The school remained at Nagasaki for five years, and in that time it gave some of Japan's later "modernizers" a valuable introduction to Western maritime and scientific techniques: the young Bakufu retainer Katsu Awa, for example, and Godai Tomoatsu of Satsuma. It also produced a ship's company capable of taking a vessel to San Francisco in 1860 "without help," as Fukuzawa Yukichi proudly observed, "from foreign experts."[16]

In what we have said so far there is little that need be thought remarkable, perhaps, since Japan had a feudal ruling class that took its military labels seriously (in contrast with China, where the strong civilian bias within officialdom may well have inhibited any such development). Feudalism in this sense may even explain an initial interest in industry and manufacture. The story goes that Shimazu Nariakira, learning in 1854 that Perry's presents to the Shogun included a cavalry rifle, asked to see it—out of curiosity, as he explained. He then took the rifle back to his Edo residence, where he kept men working all night to make detailed drawings, before returning it with an air of innocence next day. His purpose, we are told, was to make it possible for Satsuma to manufacture similar weapons—and there is ample evidence that this attitude was not his alone. Satsuma, Chōshū, Hizen, Mito, the Bakufu itself—all founded Western-style industries, mostly industries that had a military application, before 1868 and in several cases even before 1853.[17] In 1850, for instance, after some years of experiment, Hizen completed Japan's first successful reverberatory furnace, an achievement that made it possible for the domain's artisans to cast iron cannon in substantial numbers in the next few years. Satsuma and Mito, with Hizen's help, were able to follow this example. Chōshū and Tosa tried and failed. The Bakufu, having a political right of sorts to share Hizen's technological secrets, also acquired a reverberatory, though only because Egawa Tarozaemon built one on his own initiative in the district he governed.

In ship-building the first attempts at using Western techniques were made by Satsuma and Mito, both having undertaken preliminary studies to this end before the Perry treaty. The raising of the Bakufu's ban on such activities in October 1853—largely at the urging of Tokugawa Nariaki and Shimazu Nariakira, it should be noted—enabled the two domains to complete their shipyards at Kagoshima and Ishikawajima, from which within a year or so they had launched their first Western-style ships. Satsuma's was a steamer, though the problem of manufacturing suitable marine engines for it was never satisfactorily solved. Hizen was slower getting started in this field than in cannon-founding, if more ambitious: it ordered a complete shipyard plant from Holland in 1856, which arrived and was installed in 1858. However, financial difficulties (and probably problems with an imported technology too advanced for Japanese skills) led to the project being almost at once abandoned.

The machinery Hizen had imported was handed over to the Bakufu for use in its own Nagasaki yard, which had been started in 1855 on the recommendation of local officials and was more an ironworks, engaged in ship repairs and gun casting, than a shipyard proper, though it did produce a small wooden-hulled steamer in 1857. There were also at that time Bakufu yards of modest size and limited facilities at Shimoda and Uraga. However, it was not until nearly a decade later, when the Bakufu built yards at Yokohama and Yokosuka with technical assistance provided by the French, that Japan possessed an establishment at all comparable in scale and equipment with some of those in Europe. Meanwhile, Japanese yards, like the ships they produced, remained in Heusken's words "rather old-fashioned."*

There are some respects in which the term "old-fashioned" can also be applied to the daimyo who were patrons of the new technology. At first sight a man like Shimazu Nariakira—surprisingly, in view of his rank—was an outstanding innovator. He took up photography, using an imported camera and an instruction book translated from the Dutch. He installed a telegraph between two

* Heusken, *Japan Journal*, p. 136. The comment was recorded at the end of 1857. Recognition by Japanese of the inadequacies of Japanese-built ships, once the opening of the ports provided more direct opportunities for comparison, led to a preference on the part of the Bakufu and the domains in the 1860's for buying ships from abroad instead of building them at home.

buildings of his castle-residence in Kagoshima and had gas lighting fitted in the grounds. He founded a combined factory and technical institute, the Shūseikan, at which, apart from the manufacture of cannon and rifles, work was carried out on metal-plating processes, the making of guncotton and sulfuric acid, the distillation of alcohol, the production of various kinds of glass, pottery, and agricultural implements. By the time of his death in 1858 it employed about 1,200 persons.

What is more, no doubt prompted by advisers like the "Dutch" scholar Matsuki Kōan (who later became Foreign Minister in the Meiji period under the name of Terajima Munenori), Nariakira showed himself a man of some imagination in matters of foreign affairs.[18] His most practical ideas concerned Ryukyu, an area Satsuma had long known well because the Shimazu claimed it as part of their fief. In the summer of 1857, during the negotiations with Holland and America, Nariakira put it to the members of his entourage that if Hyōgo and Osaka could not be opened—and the objections of the Court made it unlikely that they could—then it would be to Japan's and Satsuma's advantage to open Ryukyu to foreign trade. Indeed, he said, something of the kind ought to have been done when the Dutch first urged the opening of Japanese ports in 1844. Soon after this conversation Nariakira appointed a member of his entourage to take preliminary steps toward establishing contact with the French in Ryukyu and increasing the trade of the islands with China through Foochow.* On another occasion, turning to matters territorially more remote, he argued a case for the settlement of Hokkaidō as a defense against Russia. It would involve, he thought, not only a closer political control of the region, but also the development of its natural resources, like fisheries, timber, and mines.

To set against all this there is evidence that Nariakira, if enlightened, was still very much the feudal lord. In matters of domestic politics, his outlook was certainly as much that of the traditionalist as that of the reformer. Recognizing that debt and debauchery had

* French interest in the Ryukyu islands had begun as early as 1844; and the disputes within Satsuma, as a result of which Nariakira eventually became daimyo, were closely related to the question of how to respond to French requests for trade. See Sakai, "Shimazu Nariakira," pp. 211–24.

wrought havoc with samurai morale, he sought a solution partly in a Confucian education that would inculcate proper habits and behavior and partly in a "cleansing" of the system: the appointment of men of ability to office; the abolition of unnecessary and meaningless distinctions between different kinds of samurai; the development of a plan to enable those who were poor to regain their self-respect by returning to the land.[19] He opposed the granting of samurai rank to merchants, honored the farmer as the basis of the state, saw agriculture as the key to the economy, though in the agrarian context his relative openness to new ideas manifested itself again in a willingness to import better strains of seed and encourage improved techniques. He is credited, for example, with introducing the American sweet potato into Satsuma, as well as fresh varieties of sugar cane from China and Taiwan.[20]

Nariakira did not in fact see any contradiction in a "liberal" foreign policy, conservative politics, and technological innovation. Like Sakuma Shōzan, he regarded Western technology as something capable of making a contribution to Japan's wealth and strength, not as something inimical to the existing order. In other words, the measures necessary to ensure Japan's defense against the foreigner, including some that were wholly alien to the Japanese tradition, were practical and material things—like weapons and the way they were made, crops and the way they were grown. As such they were politically "neutral," touching little, if at all, on such critical, wider issues as the authority of Shogun and feudal lords over their retainers and samurai dominance of Japanese society at large. Nor, save for the removal of a few anomalies, need they involve an attack on hereditary status.

Accordingly, Nariakira's idea of a national program, including though it did an awareness that defense policies had certain implications for "reform," was conceived almost entirely within the framework of things as they were. In the first place, there must be a regeneration of Bakufu leadership, he said. In 1853 he envisaged this as being accomplished by making Tokugawa Nariaki the country's commander-in-chief, in 1858 by nominating Nariaki's younger son, Keiki, who had become by adoption the head of the Hitotsubashi house, to be the ailing Shogun's heir. After all, united action by the great lords, without which the country could never be saved, would come only if government was in the hands of men they could respect. By the same token, the lords had a duty to sink their sectional differences and rally to the Bakufu's support. This, Nariakira thought, would be easier to achieve under the aegis of the Emperor's approval.[21] Hence he urged increases in the grants made to the Court, supplemented, perhaps, by contributions from some of the great domains; arrangements for the Shogun to visit Kyōto every few years as a token of respect; improvements in the defenses of Osaka and the imperial capital, again with help from the domains; and a limitation of Edo's power to the extent implied by submission of all major policy decisions for the Emperor's consent.[22]

Many of the policies Nariakira argued for in domestic politics stemmed apparently from the writings of the Mito School, so that they had much in common with those of Tokugawa Nariaki.[23] Nariaki, too, was an agrarian reformer, one who sought to improve the lot of the farmer in order to prevent unrest and halt the flight of labor from the land. As a corollary, in the hope of decreasing the attractions of urban life, he manifested an official hostility toward merchants and commerce, at once minimizing the kind of economic activities he thought served to corrupt samurai morale and stimulating those that contributed more directly to the revenue of the domain. The pattern is a familiar one in late-Tokugawa reform, as we have seen in discussing the Tempō period.

Equally familiar is the concern for the moral training of the samurai, a concern that Nariaki shared with Nariakira, just as he shared Nariakira's willingness to patronize Western military science. To both men, then, Confucian ethics and military technology were instruments for strengthening Japanese society against the dangers that beset it; but whereas Shimazu devoted himself to devising the technological means to this end through his interest in what Aizawa Seishisai had disparagingly dubbed "novel gadgets,"[24] Tokugawa Nariaki, as Aizawa himself had recommended, sought rather to evoke the will to use them. This led him to emphasize what was politically, rather than technologically, necessary to Japan's survival.

One requirement, Nariaki maintained, was the preservation of law and order within Japan, a task that depended on the efficiency of the country's ruling class. "When superiors ignore the hunger and death of farmers in bad years," he told the Bakufu in 1839, "when they are remiss in making military preparations, when the samurai are weak and idle, then inferiors hate their superiors *and do not fear them.*"[25] The result was peasant revolt and a country weakened by unrest.

Another essential, as Nariaki saw it, was national unity, which he thought of as resting on an acceptance of social hierarchy and political authority in their existing forms. Without these, society might well disintegrate. However, unity also required—to an extent greater than it had been customary to grant—a recognition of the imperial dignity that gave the existing order sanction. In a letter to Mizuno Tadakuni in 1842 Nariaki wrote: "If the Shogun takes the lead in showing respect for the throne, the whole country will inevitably unite in so doing; but it is vital that in this each should observe his proper place. The samurai shows respect for his lord, the lord shows respect for the Shogun, the Shogun shows respect for the Emperor. To forget one's place and take matters into one's own hands is an evil act, worthy of the name of rebel."[26]

By this estimate the Emperor existed to reinforce a social cohesion that relied fundamentally on feudal loyalties. Nevertheless, Nariaki did not see this as an *automatic* process, operating if the Shogun merely showed a proper attitude toward the throne (as some Confucian scholars might have done). In another letter, this one to Abe Masahiro in 1846, he commented that ever since the seventeenth century Japan had been "a Tokugawa country," then observed that there was no immutable law saying it must always remain so. Should the Bakufu fail to act "when the safety of Japan is at stake," there were others, like the great tozama lords, who might act themselves and accuse the Bakufu of dereliction of duty, perhaps even bringing it down. To avoid such a catastrophe, he insisted, Edo could not afford simply to be passive, awaiting the outcome of events.[27]

Despite this apparent concern for Bakufu authority—significantly, it was expressed to the senior member of the Tokugawa council—Nariaki, like Shimazu Nariakira, was more concerned to preserve a political order in which daimyo like himself had power than to protect the narrower interests of the house to which he belonged. As a feudal lord, he had three things to fear: peasant revolt from below; Bakufu encroachment from above; and foreign attack. A rehabilitation (*chūkō*) of traditional society, if successful, would defend him from all three.[28]

Shimazu also accepted this proposition, differing only in the greater weight he gave to the external danger and the specifically technological means of meeting it; he was no less baronial than Nariaki. Indeed, both men were later to claim that they sought to assert their own autonomy in order to make good Edo's negligence and save Japan. In other words, despite their difference of emphasis, both saw an essential connection between the threat to seclusion and the need for reform. In 1858 this was to make them allies, opposing a Bakufu that appeared to prefer diplomacy.

THE HITOTSUBASHI PARTY

During the 1840's the ideas of political and technological reform upheld by Tokugawa Nariaki of Mito and Shimazu Nariakira of Satsuma became the subject of pressure on the Bakufu by a group of great lords. It was a small and self-consciously able group,[29] made up of men who were not only powerful in their own right but exceptionally influential in feudal society through their family ties. Nariaki himself, who was usually spokesman for the rest in Edo, was head of one of the three senior Tokugawa branch families, that of Mito (350,000 koku), and had several sons who had become daimyo by adoption, including the lords of Inaba (tozama; 325,000 koku) and Bizen (tozama; 315,000 koku). Another son, Keiki, was head of the Hitotsubashi house (100,000 koku) and as such a possible heir to the Shogun. In addition, Nariaki had sisters and daughters who had married into leading daimyo families, notably the Date houses of Sendai (tozama; 625,000 koku) and Uwajima (tozama; 100,000 koku). The head of the Uwajima house, Date Muneki, was himself a member of the reforming group. So was Matsudaira Shungaku, son of one of the secondary Tokugawa branches, that of Tayasu, and lord of the powerful Echizen fief (kamon; 320,000 koku). He was a nephew of a Shogun, Ienari, and related by marriage to the head of the Tokugawa council, Abe Masahiro. Another of Nariaki's associates, Shimazu Nariakira, had succeeded in 1851 to Satsuma, the second-largest of the tozama domains (770,000 koku). His brother Narihiro had become by adoption a member of the Kuroda family and daimyo of Chikuzen (tozama; 520,000 koku). One of Nariakira's daughters married the Shogun Iesada.

Unlike most daimyo, the members of this group also had close ties with nobles at the Imperial Court. Tokugawa Nariaki's younger sister was married to Takatsukasa Masamichi, who held office as Kampaku from 1823 to 1856. The Shimazu house had a centuries-old relationship with the house of Konoe, which had recently been reinforced by a marriage alliance with Konoe Tadahiro, holder of several high Court offices and a future Kampaku (1862–63). Yamauchi Yōdō of Tosa (tozama; 242,000 koku), another daimyo ally, was son-in-law to Sanjō Sanetsumu, whose posts were only a little less senior than Konoe's in the years before 1858. Sanjō's son, Sanetomi, played a crucial part in loyalist politics after 1860 and became one of the most distinguished of the Meiji leaders.

Despite differences of emphasis, in which Shimazu's more outspoken belief in Western technology is to be set against Tokugawa Nariaki's greater concern with samurai morale, these great lords were generally in accord on the need for a regeneration of Japanese society—always, to be sure, with the thought of defending, if not improving, their own position within it. More, they were prepared to take active steps to bring about regeneration, especially after the Perry expedition had made clear the nature of the Western threat to all they had inherited. Consulting each other by letter or messenger, they concerted the advice they gave individually to the Bakufu, notably in recommending that Nariaki be entrusted with the country's defense preparations in 1853–54. By similar means they conducted secret talks on policy matters with the Bakufu's leaders, or rallied their relatives and other daimyo to support the measures they proposed, acting as a pressure group, which, lacking office or any direct responsibility, nevertheless tried to influence officialdom at a number of points. Both Abe Masahiro and Hotta Masayoshi owed them a good deal in overcoming conservative opposition within the feudal class. Equally, the more enlightened Bakufu officials like Mizuno Tadanori and Iwase Tadanari could count on their backing and respect.*

However, this relationship between "liberal" officials and "reforming" lords began to break down in 1857. This was partly because of a growing conviction among the reformers that the Bakufu was submitting to threats in its negotiations with the foreigners, not laying the foundations of national revival. Edo, on its side, came gradually to suspect that the lords were serving baronial self-interest, not a common cause. For example, the lords sought a reduction in the requirements of sankin-kōtai, that is, in the amount of time they were forced to spend in Edo, arguing that this modest diminution of Bakufu control over daimyo was necessary as a means of diverting more of each domain's resources to defense. In addition, they called for a far-reaching program of military and administrative changes, designed avowedly to "enrich the country and strengthen the army." As Matsudaira Shungaku summarized it in a memorial of January 10, 1858: "The services of capable men must be enlisted from the entire country; peacetime extravagance must be cut down and the military system revised; the evil practices by which the daimyo and lesser lords have been impoverished must be discontinued; [defense] preparations must be made on both land and sea, not only in the main islands, but also in Ezo [Hokkaidō]; the daily livelihood of the whole people must be fostered; and schools for the various arts and crafts must be established."[30]

This was a program that threatened officialdom's power, since it called in question the Bakufu's authority over domains, hereditary rights to Bakufu office, and almost everything that comprised responsibility for framing policy. Hashimoto Sanai, one of Shungaku's retainers and his trusted agent in political matters, made the nature of the challenge even plainer in a letter he wrote in January 1858. Leadership, he said, should now be entrusted, not to the Bakufu

* For example, on January 9, 1857, Date Muneki wrote to Matsudaira Shungaku commending the views put forward by Iwase in a recent conversation. Iwase had said that foreign trade must be so organized as to benefit the domains as well as the Bakufu, and that there must be a revision of the "feudal system" if Japan was to be made truly strong. Both statements were in marked contrast to the "selfish" approach of the majority of Edo officials, Date commented. See *Sakumu kiji*, 2: 58–65, at pp. 61–62.

council, but to three of the great lords, Tokugawa Nariaki, Matsudaira Shungaku, and Shimazu Nariakira, who should be made chief ministers. A fourth lord, Nabeshima of Hizen (tozama; 357,000 koku), should be given charge of the country's foreign affairs. Only in this way would it be possible to ensure the promotion of men of talent, the pursuit of wealth and strength (to be undertaken with the help of foreign advisers), and the creation of an effective pattern of defense.[31]

Within the context of this program, Nariaki and his colleagues turned from persuasion to intrigue, trying first to manipulate dynastic and familial influence so as to overbear a council that they no longer trusted, then, when this seemed likely to fail, seeking to bring the Imperial Court into the struggle and thus work on the Bakufu from outside. By so doing they brought about a crisis.

The issue was the need to nominate an heir for the Shogun, Iesada, now childless and ailing. Probably under normal circumstances Yoshitomi, the eleven-year-old head of the Kii branch of the Tokugawa, would have been chosen without much demur, since he was the candidate with the strongest claim by blood. In Tokugawa practice, however, blood relationship was not the only test, as Kii's rivals quickly pointed out. In times of danger and upheaval it might well be more important to choose a Shogun whose greater age and known abilities gave hopes of a firm direction of affairs—a man like Hitotsubashi Keiki, Nariaki's son, who at the age of twenty already had a reputation of some promise. This at all events was how Keiki's father and his reformer friends began to argue the case late in 1857, making themselves "the Hitotsubashi party."

Matsudaira Shungaku took the initiative in this cause, his collateral relationship with the Tokugawa giving him standing in such a family matter. In writing to Hotta, however, Shungaku took care to emphasize that he did not stand alone. Weak leadership, he said, might at the present juncture result in civil war, so greatly was the country divided on this question.[32] Reinforcing the argument, Shimazu sent one of his retainers, Saigō Takamori, to Edo to act as intermediary between Shungaku and the Shogun's Satsuma wife, while Shungaku's representative, Hashimoto Sanai, organized support among the other feudal lords.[33]

To many of the fudai daimyo this was demonstrably an attempt to get power out of the hands of "the responsible officials" into those of men who by tradition had only an advisory function, or none at all. They closed their ranks, therefore, in defense of established procedures and the Kii claim. Hotta, though head of the council, was preoccupied with the American treaty and remained aloof from the argument, perhaps hoping not to commit himself to either side, but Ii Naosuke began to speak for the fudai, increasing the dangers of a confrontation.* As a result, Nariaki and Shungaku decided early in 1858 to appeal to Kyōto, just as Hotta was doing over foreign affairs, in the hope of exploiting the imperial prestige to resolve the issue in their favor. Their decision brought the two questions, that of the treaty and that of the succession, into sudden relationship with one another. It also made Kyōto, rather than Edo, temporarily the center of political maneuvers.

In March 1858, acting on Shungaku's orders, Hashimoto Sanai went to Kyōto armed with an introduction to Sanjō Sanetsumu from Yamauchi. At about the same time—this was a few days before Hotta's arrival in the capital to seek imperial sanction for the American treaty—Shimazu Nariakira wrote to seek Konoe Tadahiro's help. Tokugawa Nariaki, meanwhile, was already in correspondence with his brother-in-law, Takatsukasa. Thanks to these initiatives, three powerful Court nobles, briefed in detail by Hashimoto, were soon acting in the Hitotsubashi interest. Against them stood the Kampaku, Kujō Naotada, whose support for the Kii party was largely attributable to the persuasions of his relative by marriage, Ii Naosuke, represented in Kyōto by a retainer called Nagano Shuzen.

To make an already complicated situation even more so, the daimyo and the Bakufu were urging simultaneously on the Court views on foreign policy that cut across the lines of their other differences. Thus Shimazu Nariakira and Matsudaira Shungaku, in effect supporting Hotta, consistently argued that the Emperor must

* George M. Wilson, "Bakumatsu Intellectual," p. 260, quotes a letter from Ii to Nagano Shuzen, dated April 9, 1858 (text in *Ishin-shi*, 2: 442–43), arguing as follows against the Hitotsubashi case: "To nominate a lord because of his intelligence is to have inferiors choose their superior and is entirely the Chinese style."

approve the American treaty because of the danger of foreign attack if it was rejected and because of the risk of a civil war if the Court refused the Bakufu's request.[34] Ii Naosuke, too, for all that he opposed the others on the succession issue, had actually sent Nagano to Kyōto in the first instance to persuade Kujō to accede to Hotta's proposals.[35] Tokugawa Nariaki for his part expressed an unvarying hostility toward the treaty while looking, much as Shimazu and Matsudaira did, to a Hitotsubashi succession, followed by an accord between Court and Bakufu, as the basis for an eventual strengthening of Japan.[36]

These crosscurrents left the Court in a state of some confusion, if not alarm. Accustomed to the idea of ratifying everything the Bakufu proposed, the kuge did not find it easy to take decisions about matters that were at once important and disputed. It was still less easy when the decisions involved a choice between inclination—Kyōto prejudices accorded closely with those of Nariaki on foreign affairs—and the Bakufu's advice. In the circumstances, it is no wonder that such men as Konoe and Kujō sought desperately for some kind of accommodation between the policies being thrust on them.

By the middle of April 1858 they thought they had found one: a reply to Hotta that would express disapproval of the treaty and ask the Bakufu to reconsider it in consultation with the lords, while recognizing Edo's final responsibility in the matter; and, coupled with it, an imperial decree recommending, albeit without mention of Hitotsubashi's name, that a successor be found for Iesada who would be able, adult, and of good repute. In this way, Hotta and Ii would get their treaty, since it could be assumed that they would sign it in the end; Nariaki would get the Hitotsubashi succession; the Bakufu would have its authority confirmed; and Shimazu and Shungaku, because of the injunction that Edo must consult the lords, would be given an opportunity to secure the kind of reforms they thought essential to the country's future.

In practice, the compromise, though superficially attractive, turned out to have no stable political foundation. On the treaty question, as we have seen in the previous chapter, the Emperor's personal intervention, backed by an overwhelming majority of the Court nobles of middle and lesser rank, forced the removal of the clause recognizing the Bakufu's responsibility for decisions. Thus what Hotta actually received on May 3, 1858, was a command that the treaty proposal be reconsidered in the light of advice from the feudal lords. On the succession issue, Nagano Shuzen, acting on his own initiative—he had no time to get fresh instructions from Ii Naosuke once he realized what was going on—persuaded the Kampaku, Kujō Naotada, to delete the phrase about age and ability from the final draft of the decree. Accordingly, in the form in which it was issued on May 5 the document referred neither to the name nor to the qualities of a suitable heir, leaving it open to the Tokugawa to choose either candidate and claim imperial sanction for their choice.

The affair thus ended with a settlement of a very different kind from the compromise that the senior kuge had originally conceived: Hotta, Ii, and the Bakufu were frustrated about the treaty, and Tokugawa Nariaki, Shimazu Nariakira, and Matsudaira Shungaku made no headway in the matter of the Shogun's successor. Equally significant, the Court had failed to impose any pattern on the events surrounding the agreement, so that the Emperor, brought into politics for the first time in many generations, appeared less a symbol of unity than a political shuttlecock.

If the Court, prompted by the great lords, had begun to reflect during these weeks a doubt about the Bakufu's competence to lead the country, the Bakufu had certainly acquired reasons for questioning Hotta's ability to lead the Tokugawa council. Not only had he failed—publicly—in the avowed object of his mission, he now began to show signs privately of throwing in his lot with the Hitotsubashi party in order to secure their support for the treaty. At one stage he even proposed the appointment of Matsudaira Shungaku as Tairō. This was a betrayal of the collective interests of the fudai —to them, after all, a weak child Shogun was not unwelcome, since his weakness would be the bureaucracy's strength—and almost at once cost Hotta his authority in Edo. By the time he arrived in the city on June 1 steps had already been taken to nominate Ii Naosuke to fill the regency, and on June 4 the appointment was officially announced.[37]

Until this moment the Hitotsubashi lords had been confident of ultimate success, despite the debacle in Kyōto. However, the unheralded and altogether unexpected elevation of Ii Naosuke, which effectively blocked their access to the centers of decision, crucially upset their plans. From this time on, their allies and potential allies like Hotta, though still in office, were no longer in positions of trust; and Ii made it absolutely clear that he would brook no interference with his policies from any outside quarter.

Against so resolute and "correct" an attitude, influence at Court was little to the purpose. Indeed, on June 11, only a week after Ii's appointment, the Shogun informed the council of state that he had chosen Yoshitomi of Kii as his heir. On July 11—the delay having been occasioned by fears that a premature public statement might hamper the efforts to secure daimyo backing for the American treaty—an announcement was made to the Tokugawa branch houses and the leading fudai. On August 4 the decision was made generally known.

Ii Naosuke could not fail to be aware that his action concerning the succession would be criticized, perhaps contested, as would the signing of the American treaty, which had taken place a few days earlier. He accordingly took steps to see that his more powerful rivals and opponents were removed as quickly as possible from the scene. Already in June two of Hotta's ablest lieutenants, Toki Yorimune and Kawaji Toshiaki, had been demoted. Hotta himself, who had been kept in office until the beginning of August, was now blamed for the treaty and dismissed, as was another Rōjū with some pretensions to leadership, Matsudaira Tadakata. Both were replaced by new councillors of little character or ability. Even more startling, in view of his rank, Tokugawa Nariaki was ordered into house arrest on August 13 and forbidden to correspond with his former colleagues. On the same day Hitotsubashi Keiki was banned from Edo castle and hence from public life, while Matsudaira Shungaku and Tokugawa Yoshikumi of Owari (who had been a Hitotsubashi supporter in the later stages) were required to stand down as heads of their domains.

Early the next year Yamauchi Yōdō was also forced into retirement, a fate that Shimazu Nariakira would probably have suffered, too, had he not died at the end of August 1858. As it was, his agent, Saigō Takamori, was driven into exile on an island south of Kyūshū. Shungaku's man, Hashimoto Sanai, did not get off so lightly; he was arrested and executed. All told, considerable numbers of daimyo, officials, and samurai who had been connected in one way or another with the Hitotsubashi party were punished in degrees of varying severity. The "Ansei purge," as it is called, lasted well into 1859 and extended even to Kyōto, where Sanjō, Konoe, and Takatsukasa were all relieved of office.[38] The Kampaku, Kujō Naotada, by contrast, was given an increase of stipend as a reward for loyalty.

Parallel with these events, Ii Naosuke took steps to secure Court recognition of his actions in order to reconcile opinion generally to his position. In a letter to Kujō on August 6, 1858, he stated his reasons for the purge, referring to "plots" and "misconduct" among Bakufu officials and arguing that "unless those responsible are set aside we shall be unable to pursue a strong policy with respect to the barbarians."[39] By similar arguments he attempted later in the year to secure retrospective imperial approval of the treaties, knowing that the manner of their signing was the issue on which criticism, even within the Bakufu, chiefly focused.* His agent in this campaign was one of his own nominees to the council, Manabe Akikatsu, who was sent to "explain" the whole matter to the Emperor in October.

Manabe found, as he might have expected, that Ii's attacks on men whom Kyōto regarded as its loyal friends made headway difficult. He claimed in several long memorials that throughout the negotiations with the West the Bakufu had been a prisoner of circumstance, not acting willingly. But this argument failed to elicit any sympathy. In a personal letter to the Kampaku, which was obviously meant to be directed to Manabe's attention, the Emperor Kōmei

* Throughout the debate over the American treaty at the end of July Ii had shown himself fully aware of the political dangers of signing without imperial permission (see, for example, Beasley, *Select Documents*, pp. 181–83); and as early as August 2 he had written to Tokugawa Nariaki urging him to accept the treaty and cooperate in uniting national opinion (*BGKM*, 20: 534–37). Accordingly, one can accept his willingness to negotiate with Kyōto on this question as being genuine, though it was aimed at unity *on his own terms*, that is, subject to the preservation of Bakufu authority.

described the opening of the ports, "be it but for a day or even half a day," as inexcusable, an action that by arousing popular anger might even threaten the political stability of Japan.[40] To this Manabe responded in a much more forthright manner than he had before, commenting bluntly that the Shogun, "faced with a choice between war and peace," had taken action "in accordance with his hereditary responsibility"; and the decision, once incorporated in treaties, could not be reversed, "whatever the orders of the Court may be." The only solution was for the Court to recognize and accept reality, for the Bakufu to promise to secure "withdrawal" of the foreigners at some future time, and for both to agree to work together for the good of Japan. Manabe's recommendation was accompanied by dark hints about the inadvisability of listening to "base and idle rumors."[41]

For another month the deadlock continued, with no sign of Manabe being willing to move from the position he had taken. This left the Emperor, who seems to have played a much larger part in the shaping of Court policy than was usual, in a dilemma. On the one hand, he genuinely feared the consequences of admitting foreigners to Japan, especially to the ports in the neighborhood of Kyōto. On the other, he believed that these were primarily matters for the Shogun to decide. In the end, partly because of Ii's success in removing, or bribing, those who advocated a different viewpoint, the constitutional considerations prevailed, pushing Kōmei to accept in substance what Manabe proposed. An imperial decree dated February 2, 1859, though describing the American treaty as "a blemish on our Empire and a stain on our divine land," nevertheless agreed that in view of the Shogun's avowed intention to revert to seclusion once the opportunity arose and the importance of "greater unity between Court and Bakufu," the treaty would be recognized publicly—as a matter of necessity, not of choice. The Emperor, the decree declared, would "exercise forbearance on this occasion."[42]

If the imperial pronouncement was a source of some embarrassment for the Bakufu, it marked an out-and-out defeat for the Hitotsubashi party in its only remaining center of strength. Kyōto, like

Edo, had come under Ii Naosuke's control. Bribery and threats, coupled with a certain loss of nerve on the part of the great lords—or perhaps a recognition that if they pushed things to extremes they might destroy a political edifice in which they had a considerable share of power—had served to defend the authority of the Tokugawa from those who wished to dilute it to serve their own ends. Or had done so, at least, for a time. As events soon proved, the victory depended too much on one man, Ii Naosuke, to be enduring.

CHAPTER VI

Dissenting Samurai

ONE CONSEQUENCE of the recognition by Japanese of an external threat to their country was, as we have seen, a call for "conservative" reform by a number of Bakufu officials and great lords, men who proclaimed political unity, as well as Western technology, to be vital to national strength but were unwilling to sacrifice to it any essential part of their privileges under the existing order. Another consequence, to which we now turn, was a movement that by implication was much more radical, for it questioned Japan's feudal leadership itself. The seeds of this movement can be detected in the earlier struggles in a number of domains for that Confucian panacea, the promotion of "men of talent"; but it was above all the treaties, by arousing emotions strong enough to transcend sectional boundaries and feudal loyalties, that changed the character of Japanese politics. Principally, this was because they brought into political life a segment of the population that had not previously had, or expected to have, a voice in the conduct of affairs.

By 1858 foreign policy had become a "public" issue in Japan, discussion of which could no longer be confined to a small elite. Concern about foreign policy and involvement in it were extended outside the ranks of the policy-makers—the lords and senior officials—to men of lesser rank, who in the next ten years took a very different line, resorting to attacks on foreigners and terrorism at home in the hope of bringing about a reassessment of Japan's relations with the outside world. Almost all of these men were members or near-members of the dominant samurai class. They could not otherwise have found opportunities to act. Moreover, they came mostly from domains whose daimyo had been connected with the Hitotsubashi party, that is, those where the lord, by setting an example, had helped to give his retainers the political habit.*

It was a heritage that Ii Naosuke's purge confirmed, since his treatment of the reforming lords made the Bakufu an object of hatred to their loyal followers.[1] In addition, the readiness with which senior officials of many domains emulated him in meting out punishment—the banishment of Saigō Takamori, for example, was ostensibly at least a Satsuma decision, not a Bakufu one—brought down on them, too, the charge of having betrayed a patriotic duty. Hence the kind of criticism that men like Tokugawa Nariaki and Shimazu Nariakira had leveled against Bakufu councillors, namely, that they were neglecting the country's interests for the sake of defending their own, was soon being repeated at a humbler level by samurai as a charge against the governments of their domains. It was in this sense that *sabaku*, "pro-Bakufu," became a term of abuse.

The existence of such hostility toward feudal superiors, interlocking with the anti-foreign movement, raises important questions about the nature of the Restoration and the forces that lay behind it. It has always been accepted that samurai took the lead in overthrowing the Tokugawa and subsequently in remaking Japanese society, a task that included destroying the domains, i.e., "abolishing feudalism." What is much less a matter of agreement is the role and significance of the "loyalists" in this transformation. To some historians, they were just what the label implies, men whose actions reflected a ground swell of feeling that focused on the Emperor's person and his symbolic position in the national life. To others, they were linked with the shift from a feudal to a bourgeois stage of development, hence with an emergent merchant class or with "modern" landlords. Still others see connections with "proletarian"

* The correlation is not exact. Chōshū, which later produced large numbers of loyalists, was not very active in the politics of the 1850's. Hizen, whose lord played an important part down to 1858 and whose samurai became key members of the Meiji government ten years later, produced few of the better known activists in between. Kurume, which contributed a number of famous loyalists in the 1860's, had had no obvious links with the Hitotsubashi party. Nevertheless, it is significant that out of more than 250 domains only a few provided activists in any number, and that those few included most of the domains concerned in the 1858 crisis.

revolutionary protest, manifested in peasant revolt and urban riot.[2] It is against this background of variant interpretations that the advocates of sonnō-jōi, "honor the Emperor and expel the barbarian," have to be studied.

As a first step toward resolving some of the difficulties that surround this subject, it seems desirable to attempt to give with as much accuracy as possible an account of the attitudes and social origins of the men who played an active part in loyalist politics immediately after 1858. In other words, to look at who they were, what they sought to achieve, and with what elements in society they were most closely associated. We can then turn to a discussion of political activities and techniques, examining the way in which the loyalists set about attaining the ends they had chosen for themselves.

LOYALISM

Ii Naosuke's purge and the signing of the American treaty had the effect of bringing more order into a political scene that had hitherto been confused by several crosscurrents of opinion—of polarizing it, in fact. Differences over foreign policy—between those who wanted to open the country (kaikoku) and those who wanted to resist the West (jōi), both courses seen as a means to national survival—came now to focus on a single question. Was the Bakufu's action in signing the treaties acceptable? Those who answered that it was, that Edo had had no choice about what to do in the face of overwhelming foreign pressure, became *sabaku*, the Bakufu's supporters. Those who rejected the Bakufu's actions, whether out of blind hatred of the foreigner or in the more rational belief that a treaty signed from fear was no way to set about restoring Japanese strength, became its critics. Ii thus moved the exponents of both "expulsion" and "opening the country" into opposition. At the same time, he gave them the opportunity to claim political reform as their exclusive property. The actions he took against the Hitotsubashi party caused anti-Bakufu sentiment to become linked with the interests of the great lords, including some who were closely related to the Tokugawa house, against the official machine, traditionally controlled by the fudai. Ii therefore made the Bakufu not only a symbol of appeasement of the foreigner, but also the defender of the Bakufu-domain structure in its existing form. In consequence, those who opposed Edo on *either* count tended to come together.

Yet coming together was none too easy, in view of the great divergences of motive among the regime's enemies. Because of this, the everyday politics of the following decade came to center on two main issues: first, whether Edo's opponents could sufficiently reconcile their own differences to agree on an institutional alternative to Tokugawa power; and second, whether they could then muster the strength to impose their solution on the Bakufu and the country as a whole. In both processes, loyalism and its slogan, sonnō, "honor the Emperor," had a key part.

The anomaly of having both an Emperor who in theory recognized only divine restraints on his authority and a Shogun who behaved in practice like an autocrat had given a good deal of difficulty to Tokugawa writers.[3] Some simply recognized the Shogun as ruling as of right, leaving the Emperor with an ill-defined "superiority" of no great political significance that could be ignored in describing the structure of government. Thus Ikeda Mitsumasa, daimyo of Bizen, wrote in the seventeenth century: "The Shogun receives authority over the people of Japan as a trust from heaven. The daimyo receives authority over the people of the province as a trust from the Shogun. The daimyo's councillors and retainers should aid the daimyo in bringing peace and harmony to the people."[4] Others, beginning with the seventeenth-century writers Kumazawa Banzan and Yamaga Sokō, asserted instead the existence of an imperial mandate, by virtue of which the Shogun ruled Japan. A nineteenth-century expression of the argument in a Bakufu document ran as follows: "The emperor entrusts to the *taikun* [Shogun] all political powers and awaits his decisions in silence; the *taikun*, holding all the political powers of the country, maintains the virtue of humility and upholds the emperor with the utmost respect."[5] By the late-Tokugawa period it was the second of these views that was the more widely held.

It was not, however, unchallenged. For example, a different emphasis had been given by another seventeenth-century writer, Yamazaki Ansai (1618–82), who held that the Emperor, being of divine descent, commanded reverence as well as service and hence possessed an inalienable authority. This was to bring into Confucian philosophy a Shintō concept in such a way as to stress the conditional character of the imperial mandate and the fact that it might presumably be withdrawn. Many loyalists of the 1860's were greatly influenced by Yamazaki's school, as they were also by the teaching of two eighteenth-century scholars, Takeuchi Shikibu (1712–67) and Yamagata Daini (1725–67), who had been severely punished—Takeuchi exiled, Yamagata executed—for pointing out the potential conflict between loyalty to Emperor and loyalty to Shogun, and claiming that loyalty to the Emperor took first place.

It was also in the eighteenth century that the influence of the Shintō element in political thought had been strengthened by the work of the kokugakusha, or "national" scholars, whose attempts to reassert a native tradition against that of China, primarily in religious terms, had as one of its products a wider awareness of the ancient prerogatives of the throne.[6] Kamo Mabuchi (1697–1769) began the process, commenting with disapproval—and breathtaking inaccuracy—that as a result of the introduction of Chinese ethical and political ideas the Japanese Emperor had been reduced to "the intellectual level of a woman," becoming "an utter nullity."[7] This observation Motoori Norinaga (1730–1801) developed into the argument that the Emperor, as a descendant of the sun goddess Amaterasu and able at all times to consult the gods by divination, was himself a god. He ought therefore to be accorded the absolute obedience of which alien influences had deprived him. "Simply to obey, venerate, and serve him," Motoori wrote, "is the true Way."[8]

The nineteenth-century scholar Hirata Atsutane, taking a further step, claimed divine origin for the Japanese people as a whole. Because of this, he said, they were superior to all other people in the world, their culture an improvement not only on Chinese culture, but also on that of all countries, just as their Emperor was above all other rulers. Thus he envisaged a relationship between patriotism and loyalty that made the Emperor central to both, while evoking a national consciousness based on resentment of Chinese dominance that could be applied in due course to the cultural and political menace of the West.

This is not to say that kokugaku directly inspired an anti-foreign or anti-Bakufu movement. Indeed, one might more accurately claim it was the growth of such a movement in the nineteenth century that made kokugaku retrospectively of political importance, though this, too, would be an overstatement.* Certainly Motoori and Hirata were no rebels, even frustrated ones. To them the power of Shogun and daimyo, though it detracted from the Emperor's own, was shown by its very existence to be the will of the gods.

Nevertheless, the kokugakusha undeniably created a rationalization of imperial authority that rebels could cite and a climate of opinion within which they could find support. Hirata, in particular, was a successful publicist who had several thousand "pupils" in the Restoration years; and the fact that his beliefs involved in part an attack on the official Confucian ideology of the samurai class gave them a special appeal to those who were outside that class or on its fringes. As a result, his ideas gained a substantial following among the rich farmers and merchants, who as we shall see provided recruits and sympathizers for the extremist groups, indicating that those who aspired to samurai standing without fully achieving it might well be attracted to a scheme of things in which service to the Emperor (kinnō) became an alternative to samurai birth as a measure of one's place in society.†

This being so, it is not surprising to find that the samurai themselves, who provided, after all, most of the leaders of the rebels, were influenced less by the kokugaku of Motoori and Hirata than by the loyalism of the Mito school, which brought Shintō tradition

* Craig, *Chōshū*, pp. 137–43, points out that the numbers of Hirata's "followers" rose sharply after 1853; and Dore, *Education*, pp. 157–59, observes that the introduction of kokugaku into the curriculum of domain schools (which was in any case on a modest scale) was apparently speeded up by the effects of the Perry expedition. Both facts suggest that kokugaku was given a significance and popularity by the coming of the West it had not enjoyed before.

† A table showing the geographical distribution of the Hirata "school" in Craig, *Chōshū*, p. 142, indicates that the largest concentration was in some of the economically advanced provinces of the central region, reflecting the relatively large numbers of rich village headmen (*shōya*) and farmers Hirata had recruited there after being rebuffed by the Mito scholars. Outside this area there were substantial groups in Satsuma, Chikuzen, and Tosa but few in Chōshū and Hizen. One cannot, therefore, establish a direct correlation between the spread of Hirata influence and the kinnō movement of the 1860's.

to terms with Confucian thought.[9] The key element in the Mito philosophy was the concept of *taigi-meibun*, which is commonly translated "loyalty and duty." Taigi was fulfilling one's obligations toward the Emperor, both as ruler and as ethical exemplar. Its immediate political implications, however, were controlled by meibun, one's standing, a matching of behavior to status, which meant that loyalty had to be observed in accordance with one's place in society. As Fujita Yūkoku put it: "If the shogunate reveres the imperial house, all the feudal lords will respect the shogunate. If the feudal lords respect the shogunate, the ministers and officials will honour the feudal lords. In this way high and low will support each other, and the entire country will be in accord."[10]

The polity (kokutai), so ordered, was reinforced by filial piety, a respect for ancestors who were themselves supposedly loyal requiring loyalty on the part of a descendant. It was also strengthened by an element of reciprocity in the relation of ruler to ruled, in that the "loyalty" of the one had as its concomitant the "benevolence" of the other. It was here, however, that Mito was forced to depart most sharply from the orthodox Chinese model. In China a failure of imperial benevolence might entail loss of the Mandate of Heaven and the downfall of a dynasty. In Japan an Emperor of divine descent could never legitimately be removed. To quote once more from Aizawa Seishisai's *Shinron*: "Revering the ancestor [i.e. the sun goddess Amaterasu] and reigning over the people, the sovereign becomes one with Heaven. Therefore, that his line should endure as long as Heaven endures is a natural consequence of the order of things."[11]

This left a Confucian loyalist with the problem of reconciling two potentially conflicting ideas, that of the Mandate and that of the Emperor's divine descent. How was it done? In effect by substituting an imperial mandate for a heavenly one and identifying the Shogun as its recipient. In Mito doctrine it became the Shogun's duty to show reverence toward the Emperor and benevolence toward the people as a condition of his monarchical power; and since benevolence entailed not only protecting the population from hardship, but also defending it from foreign attack, sonnō, honoring the Emperor, logically included jōi, expelling the barbarian.

From this one can see that by the time of the Perry expedition the Mito scholars had already brought together all the ingredients necessary to justify an attack on the Bakufu for its handling of foreign affairs. By signing dishonorable and disadvantageous treaties with the West in contravention of an imperial command, the Shogun, it could be argued, failed simultaneously in the duties of loyalty and benevolence.

Nevertheless, to Aizawa Seishisai and his lord, Tokugawa Nariaki, as to the daimyo who cooperated with Mito in the disputes surrounding the shogunal succession in 1858, the Bakufu's failure in this regard did not necessarily imply that it had to be destroyed, or that feudalism had to be abolished in an effort to restore direct imperial rule, notwithstanding Aizawa's assertion that the Emperor "should govern the land and control the people."[12] It meant, rather, a diminution of the Bakufu's prestige and an increase in that of the Court, under the shadow of which the great lords might secure a voice in deciding policy; a public manifestation of respect for Kyōto in the interests of national unity against the foreigner (sonnō for the sake of jōi); and a strengthening of the pyramid of Japanese society, achieved by directing loyalty consciously toward the Emperor, the last stronghold of authority in a changing world (sonnō for feudalism's sake, in fact, enabling the Tokugawa and the lords to retain the substance of power).

Yet in men of another temper the ideas of Mito, tinged with kokugaku, were capable of producing attitudes of a much less conformist kind. One might cite, for example, Rai Sanyō (1780–1832), who in 1829 wrote an exceedingly popular, if inaccurate, history of Japan designed to exemplify the principle of imperial loyalism and castigate those who had at any time contravened it.[13] Even more influential was the Chōshū samurai Yoshida Shōin (1830–59).[14] A teacher, eclectic in the derivation of his thought, he was also a radical, an activist, a "man of spirit" (shishi) who showed as great a willingness to put his proposals into effect as did more respectable "legal" reformers like Aizawa Seishisai and Sakuma Shōzan.

As a very young man Shōin traveled to Edo to study, working for a time under Sakuma and establishing a connection with Aizawa (a tie that cost him his samurai rank and 57-koku stipend because of an unauthorized visit to Mito). In 1853 Shōin, like many other students, went to see Perry's ceremonial landing at Kurihama. This inspired him (with Sakuma's encouragement) to try to leave Japan with the American squadron in order to continue his studies abroad; but the Americans, who found him "courteous and highly refined,"[15] refused to take him, and he ended in prison. First in Edo, then in Hagi, the Chōshū castle town, Shōin remained in custody until the beginning of 1856, when his sentence was reduced to house arrest, and he began teaching in his uncle's school on the outskirts of the town. There many of those who were to be leaders of Chōshū in the following decade—and of Japan after 1868—came to study under him. Teaching, however, was not enough. At the end of 1858 Shōin planned the assassination of Manabe Akikatsu, Ii Naosuke's emissary to Kyōto; but the plot was discovered and the plotters arrested. Shōin, the ringleader, was sent to Edo in June 1859 and executed in November. He was not yet thirty years old.

Shōin's writings were in some respects as turbulent and unorthodox as his career. Like Sakuma Shōzan, he was deeply moved by the foreign danger to Japan and responded to it by demanding that the country's military technology be improved. "In studying the learning of Europe and America," he wrote in 1855, "to adore and idolise the barbarians . . . must be rejected absolutely. But the barbarians' artillery and shipbuilding, their knowledge of medicine, and of physical sciences, can all be of use to us—these should properly be adopted."[16] Shōin thought it insufficient, however, merely to increase the country's military capacity. Japan must also be provided with such control over neighboring territories as would make her defenses impregnable and enable her to meet the Western powers on equal terms: "If the sun is not ascending, it is descending. If the moon is not waxing, it is waning. If the country is not flourishing, it is declining. Therefore to protect the country well is not merely to prevent it from losing the position it holds, but to add to it the positions which it does not hold."[17] Kamchatka, Manchuria, Korea, Ryukyu, Taiwan, the Philippines, even China and India, all figured in his plans, "an enterprise which must continue eternally so long as the earth shall last."

To this was added an insistence on reform at home as a basis for national unity and the regeneration of morale. Defense, after all, was a *national* task, not one that depended only on the narrower loyalties of samurai to lord. It was therefore something essentially for Bakufu and Court to undertake. "If anyone whosoever in the entire realm is insulted by the foreign barbarians," Shōin said, "it is a matter of course that the Shogun, naturally leading all the lords of the realm, must wipe out this disgrace to the nation *and bring tranquillity to the mind of the emperor.*"* Accordingly, reform should comprise elements designed to bring about such unity, together with effectiveness in foreign affairs. This meant those that were put forward by the Mito scholars: good government, the promotion of "men of talent," and an adjustment of the relationships between Emperor, Shogun, and lords.

It did *not* mean the removal of the Bakufu as such or an attack on the network of feudal vassalage that centered on it. Even if the Shogun should so fail in his duties of loyalty and national defense as to require admonishing, Shōin argued, the initiative in any punitive action was for the lords to take: "If, when every effort has been exhausted, he [the Shogun] still does not appreciate his guilt, then unavoidably there will be no other course than for my lord, together with those other daimyo who realise the crime, to present this matter to the Imperial Court and to carry out the emperor's command."[18] In other words, during the period of treaty negotiations with the West, when all these statements were made, Shōin manifested the same political conservatism as his teachers, Sakuma and Aizawa, and held similar concepts of reform. He was not yet a radical in the sense in which the word can be used of many men in the 1860's.

It was the crisis of 1858 that changed him. The treaties, the purge, the failure of either lords or samurai to act against the Bakufu when it took measures opposed to everything they stood for convinced Shōin of the need for a program far more drastic than he had contemplated hitherto. Not only were the Tokugawa "more and more

* Earl, *Emperor and Nation*, pp. 179–80. Italics mine. The expression "bring tranquillity to the mind of the emperor" is characteristic of a great deal of loyalist writing in the next few years and was communicated to other kinds of writing, too, such as Bakufu memorials, especially those that were written with a thought to their public impact.

extending the sway of their evil power," he said, and the daimyo acting in a manner clearly subservient to them; the whole samurai class was betraying its duties by acceding without protest to what was being done. "In the lower ranks," he wrote, "even among loyal samurai . . . it does not happen that any, taking the initiative over his lord, plans righteous undertakings."[19]

Earlier Shōin had believed that the proper political action for loyalist samurai in Chōshū in face of the foreign crisis was to try to pressure the domain government into mediating between Court and Bakufu in the national interest. But now, with Court and Bakufu seemingly in open conflict while the lords stood idly by, he felt the shishi, the "men of spirit," had to choose sides and act for themselves. No reliance could be put on Shogun, or daimyo, or domain officials: "To wear silk brocades, eat dainty food, hug beautiful women, and fondle darling children are the only things hereditary officials care about. To revere the emperor and expel the barbarian is no concern of theirs."[20] In fact, the only hope for the country lay in those who were outside officialdom, the men whom Shōin called—without defining them—*sōmō eiyū*, "humble heroes." They must abandon the domain and demonstrate their sincerity in the only way left open to them: by a "rising" in the Emperor's name.

Shōin died before he could spell out in any detail who or what he meant by all this, though his plan for the assassination of Manabe is an indication of how his thinking ran. Certainly the intemperateness of his proposals during the last months of his life in 1859—especially, no doubt, his apparent willingness to abandon the samurai of influence and position in exchange for the help of "humble heroes"—cost him the support of many of his pupils.[21] Respectable Chōshū hirazamurai like Kido Kōin and Takasugi Shinsaku proved just as reluctant to jeopardize the position of their lord and their domain by acting rashly as their loyalist counterparts in Satsuma and other domains.

Nevertheless, Shōin was by no means without influence or followers in the next few years, both in Chōshū and outside it. The young, notably the students of rather less than hirazamurai status in the many military schools of Edo and the castle towns, found his teaching an inspiration and his example a call to arms. To them, expelling the foreigners became a sacred mission, one that only the Emperor could lead, and that only the shishi were willing to carry out. The Shogun and the lords, controlling as they did the military forces that would eventually be needed against the West, must be driven from their supine passivity and put into a position of *having* to act, whether they wanted to or not, the loyalists claimed; and there must therefore be risings and plots and attacks on foreigners, calculated to provoke a confrontation. Here was the argument that was to provide the rationale for terrorism in the 1860's.[22]

What is conspicuously absent from it, as from the writings of Yoshida Shōin, is a plan for the revision of basic political institutions, such as one would expect in a truly revolutionary movement. One can see the same negative quality in other "men of spirit." It marks, for example, the memorial Ii Naosuke's assassins drew up in March 1860 to explain the reasons for their deed (about which we shall have more to say in the next chapter). It was an emotional document, written shortly before they committed suicide to avoid capture and disgrace, which narrated in detail the circumstances of the negotiation of the unequal treaties, blamed Ii for the shame he had brought on Japan and for his persecution of their former lord, and condemned the Bakufu for its neglect of the Emperor's wishes. Then at the end it turned from recriminations to remedies. The Shogun, it said, should once again seek the advice of the men best qualified to help him, his relatives in Mito, Owari, Hitotsubashi, and Echizen, for instance, and the tozama lords of Satsuma, Tosa, Uwajima, and Chōshū. Each had an appropriate role to play. "If, on the one hand, the related houses assist the Shogun in conducting the administration, and, on the other, the great lords put forth their efforts loyally in military preparation, it is beyond all doubt that the dishonor of our divine land will be purged and the Emperor's mind will be set at rest."[23] This was really no more than a plan for the Hitotsubashi party's resurrection, emanating from retainers of Tokugawa Nariaki, who had been the party's leader. As such it looked less to the future than to the past, was concerned less with institutions than with feudal politics.

One might be inclined to disregard such a document altogether in this particular discussion, on the grounds that it was a mere variant of filial piety attached to an act of feudal revenge, were it not that a study of the principal activists and loyalists of the period 1862–63, those who avowedly sought "a restoration of imperial rule" (*ōsei-fukko*), reveals a similar dearth of truly revolutionary thinking. Their "restoration," though radical in its implications and totally unacceptable to Edo, fell a long way short of what actually happened after 1868. They did not envisage, for example, any more than Yoshida Shōin before them, the abolition of the domains or the dismantling of feudal society.[24] On the contrary, most of them went out of their way to express a preference for feudalism (hōken-seido), as against the Chinese-style provincial system (gunken-seido), which had been introduced into Japan in the seventh century and was much more truly "imperial."

Thus in 1861 Maki Izumi of Kurume, one of the most influential of the loyalists, described "restoration" as a matter of "rectifying names" within the feudal structure, that is, abolishing the titles held by feudal lords because they were bound up with the relationship between Shogun and daimyo and substituting for them earlier—but equally feudal—titles used in the period before the importation of Chinese institutions.[25] In other words, he proposed a continuation of feudalism, but with the difference that it should center on the Emperor, not the Shogun. In another document, written in the summer of 1863, he amplified this: there should be an imperial army, consisting of contingents provided by the domains and officered by Court nobles and loyal samurai; and all the provinces west of Owari should be removed from Bakufu control, those around Kyōto being put directly under imperial administration.[26]

Other shishi provided variations on Maki's central theme without contradicting it in fundamentals. Hirano Kuniomi of Chikuzen, urging the seizure of Kyōto in May 1862, claimed his object was to ensure action against the foreigner, which could be done only by "extending the imperial authority to all parts of the country." This itself, he said, depended on destroying the Shogun's power: "He should be stripped of office, reduced in rank and revenue, and given the same standing as the other great feudal lords."[27]

Kusaka Genzui of Chōshū, Yoshida Shōin's pupil, was more specific about what was to be aimed at and how it could be achieved—he recognized, for instance, that the violence of the shishi must supplement, not replace, the efforts of the domains[28]—but he was no less bound by traditional concepts of the nature of society. Like members of the Hitotsubashi party, he sought a relaxation of sankin-kōtai in order to reduce the Shogun's powers over the lords. Also like them, he envisaged a continuation of the Bakufu as the executive arm of government, even though a substantial measure of responsibility for making policy was to be transferred to Kyōto. As he wrote in a long memorial in August 1862:

> The [Shogun's] right of distributing territories under the vermilion seal ... and of bestowing official titles on the feudal lords must be exercised only on application to the Imperial Court, so affording evidence that the Bakufu repents of its two centuries or more of arrogance and discourtesy.... The powers of government must be restored to the Court by establishing an administrative headquarters in the Kinai [the provinces around Kyōto] and referring to the Court all matters of importance ... for discussion by the Court nobles and officials assembled there.[29]

The Tosa loyalist Takechi Zuizan, in a document written two months later, brought all these threads together, setting out the scope and limitations of what he and his friends—they were, after all, in frequent correspondence with one another—proposed for the government of Japan.[30] Once again the argument began with the Bakufu's failures in foreign affairs. "Bakufu officials, out of fear of the foreigners, follow a policy of makeshift," Takechi said. "They take no account of the country's impoverishment or the people's distress and show no trace of patriotic feeling." Their policies had so aroused resentment among men of spirit throughout the land "that there is even a risk of civil war." Only radical reforms, designed to accomplish expulsion, could calm their anger.

First, said Takechi, there must be proper provision for the defense of the Imperial Court by putting the provinces around Kyōto under imperial administration. The area should be divided among senior Court nobles, who would be supported by shishi and supplied with arms by "the rich men of Osaka." Then there must be a reduction in the time the lords were required to spend in Edo on sankin-kōtai so as to ease the financial burden on domains. Finally, "the proper functions of ruler and minister should be restored," that is, government must be conducted from the Court, as it was before the creation of the first Bakufu in the twelfth century, and the daimyo must fulfill their ceremonial obligations at Kyōto instead of Edo. It was clear to Takechi that the Tokugawa would not accept such a change willingly or even in response to an imperial command. Therefore, he argued, they must be faced with overwhelming force, which was to be provided by an alliance of domains from Kyūshū and west Japan. Only then would it be possible, "using benevolence and righteousness on the one hand to turn the Bakufu from its arrogance, invoking authority on the other to beat down its bluster," to bring Edo to obey.

From these examples, which are taken from the writings of the most famous loyalists of the early 1860's, one is bound to conclude that their vision of sonnō represented an attack on the Bakufu, not on feudalism. It implied a shift in the balance of power that would make the Emperor a focus of feudal loyalty and give the great lords a share in the making of decisions. It signified administrative changes in the affairs of the Court, such as would make it less dependent for finance on the good will of the Tokugawa or the domains (and would afford opportunities for the shishi themselves to acquire positions of some influence). Above all, it required the curtailment or outright abolition of the Shogun's authority, on the grounds that he had failed in the very tasks on which it was based.

That the loyalist position was more extreme, more violent in its challenge to the Tokugawa than anything the Hitotsubashi party offered is obvious. Yet nowhere in it, any more than in the program of the reforming lords, does one find the concept of a centralized state, focused on the Court and involving the abolition of the domains, such as was to emerge after the Tokugawa were overthrown. Still less is there any idea of a society in which the hereditary status of lord and samurai would disappear.

The "men of spirit," in fact, differed from the reforming lords not so much in putting forward conflicting institutional objectives, as in asserting more emphatically the political functions of the Imperial Court and expressing a willingness to go to much greater lengths than the reformers to bring about change. Kusaka Genzui once wrote to Takechi Zuizan, "Even if your domain or mine is destroyed because of this, it is nothing if we conduct a righteous and loyal cause."[31] He thus manifested a rejection of his society that was extreme enough to justify its destruction, if need be, in the attempt to save Japan. But this was iconoclasm, not revolution.

In the result, it is true, much of what the "men of spirit" did was revolutionary, since old institutions, once weakened and destroyed, had to be replaced by new ones, not by slogans; but it would be wrong to attribute such consequences to a grand design. Indeed, by temperament most of the loyalists were more rebels and roisterers than revolutionaries. Marius B. Jansen describes them as "brave, casual, carefree . . . given to wine and to women,"[32] men without care for the morrow; and it is abundantly clear from the record of their activities that their feelings about the Emperor and the foreigner were direct, simple emotions, far removed from the more "responsible" concerns of those who held authority in the Bakufu and the domains. It was this—a carelessness, even a contempt, in their approach to established order—rather than political ideology in the more formal sense that brought them into conflict with their lords.

THE LOYALISTS

Before we can fully accept the thesis sketched above, namely, that the loyalists' devotion to the imperial cause was in essence neither "anti-feudal" nor "modern," we need to ask who the loyalists were, whether their position in society accords logically with the views they held, and whether a distinction should be made between one kind of loyalist and another. To this end, it is useful to start by looking at what happened after 1858 in a few of the most important domains.

In Satsuma, to begin with an area in which loyalism in one of its forms was eventually successful, a number of young samurai had enthusiastically supported Shimazu Nariakira's plans before Ii Naosuke was appointed Regent, working closely with the Mito leaders in Edo, as well as with Hashimoto Sanai and other retainers of Matsudaira Shungaku's domain, Echizen.* Outstanding among the Satsuma men was Saigō Takamori, thirty years old at the time of Ii Naosuke's purge and already famous as a swordsman. A powerful, warmhearted man, he had many of the qualities of the traditional hero of romance: "quick temper, a coarse and earthy humour, provocative silences that could pass for contempt or wisdom."[33] Next in importance was Ōkubo Toshimichi, four years younger than Saigō and correspondingly less experienced, but in many respects a shrewder politician. There was about him "a core of coldness" and "an obsessive desire to forge ahead in life,"[34] a combination that made him a calculating and single-minded manipulator of his fellow men.

Both Saigō and Ōkubo came from houses of the *koshō-gumi,* the lowest rank of Satsuma middle samurai, and depended heavily on Shimazu Nariakira's personal favor for their influence.† As a result, Nariakira's death at the end of August 1858 was a serious blow to their ambitions. The intrigues Saigō was conducting in Edo and Kyōto in the interest of the Hitotsubashi party were cut off abruptly as the conservatives took control in Kagoshima, Satsuma's castle town. Saigō was sentenced to exile, though ill health kept him in Satsuma until early 1859, and his associates and followers, led by Ōkubo, were dismissed from their posts in the administration. Accordingly, they were left to seek methods of promoting their policies without access to office or the daimyo's patronage.

It was in these circumstances that they began to contemplate the possibility of insurrection, or at least of such use of force as might precipitate an anti-Bakufu coup d'état. Rumor had it, though doubtfully, that Nariakira had been thinking in these terms before he died.[35] Saigō had certainly done so, for he had written to two of his colleagues in October 1858 outlining a plan for a loyalist rising to

* Evidence of the importance of the Mito contact is to be seen in the frequency with which meetings with Mito scholars are proudly recorded in letters, diaries, and memoirs. For example, Kaeda Nobuyoshi of Satsuma devotes over forty pages of his autobiography to an account of his first meeting with Fujita Tōko and an exposition of Tōko's views (see Kaeda, *Ishin,* 1: 20B–45B). For materials on Satsuma politics, see the references given for Chapter 7, pp. 178–79, 184–86, below, where the subject is further discussed.

† Both families had supported Nariakira's claim in the succession dispute before he became daimyo.

seize Kyōto and hold it pending the arrival of troops from the great domains.[36] Thus the idea of a recourse to violence was respectably sponsored. To a group of young men incensed by the signing of treaties they regarded as a national dishonor, learning daily of fresh arrests among those they considered heroes and sages, and frustrated by the impossibility of getting the officials who now ruled them to act, the attractions of violence were almost overwhelming.

It is true that by this time Saigō had begun to recommend a degree of caution, concerned, no doubt, at the effectiveness of the purge.[37] Against that, there were a good many Satsuma men—not only young ones—who were inflamed, rather than sobered, by Saigō's punishment and to whom restraint or too calculating an assessment of risks seemed simple cowardice. By the end of 1859 some of them had again made plans for a rising in Kyōto. Before the venture could be carried out, however, news of it leaked to the Satsuma authorities, and the new daimyo, Nariakira's nephew Tadayoshi, issued orders forbidding it. Ōkubo, convinced that action without the backing of the domain was futile, decided to obey. With some difficulty he persuaded most of the other conspirators to do the same.[38]

This incident marks a turning point in the history of the Satsuma loyalists. Thereafter a party under Ōkubo, whom Saigō joined on his recall from exile in 1862, concerned themselves with winning the support of their lord for the anti-Bakufu cause—a task that entailed a willingness to compromise with those of less adventurous outlook—while another group broke away to engage in extremist activities outside the domain, which their daimyo had prohibited. The first provided a number of members of the Meiji government after 1868, the second some of the martyrs of the intervening decade. Accordingly, a comparison of them in terms of age and social composition might well provide a pointer to the nature of the movement of which both formed part.

It is possible to identify twenty-two men as belonging to the Saigō-Ōkubo party (see Table 1).[39] Of these, nine definitely and eight probably belonged to middle samurai families, if one includes the two leaders themselves; another three were upper samurai, including Iwashita Masahira, who eventually became Karō; and one, Ma-

TABLE 1
Background and Age of Satsuma and Tosa Loyalists

Background/age	Satsuma: Saigō-Ōkubo party (22)	Satsuma: Activists (22)	Tosa: Takechi party (22)	Tosa: Activists (55)
FAMILY BACKGROUND				
Upper samurai	3	—	—	—
Middle samurai	17	16	7	5
Lower samurai				
Ashigaru, etc.[a]	—	3	5	15
Gōshi[b]	1	3	10	9
Shōya and village officials	—	—	—	11
Other[c]	1	—	—	15
AGE IN 1862–63				
35 and over	5	4	4	1
26–34	15	9	14	17
25 and under	1	8	2	37
Not known	1	1	2	—

SOURCE: Beasley, "Politics and the Samurai Class in Satsuma, 1858–1868," *Modern Asian Studies*, 1 (1967): 47–57; Beasley, "Political Groups in Tosa, 1858–68," *Bulletin of the School of Oriental and African Studies*, 30 (1967): 382–90.

NOTE: I have ignored differences between lunar year and Gregorian year in calculating the age groups. About half of the figures on family background for Satsuma and about four-fifths of those for Tosa are confirmed by specific reference; the others are based on reasonable probability.

[a] One of the Satsuma men was a merchant/baishin; the other 2 were baishin.

[b] The 4 Satsuma men were merchant/gōshi.

[c] The non-classified Satsuma man was a Shintō priest. Of the 15 non-classified Tosa men, 1 was a Buddhist priest, 1 was a doctor, 1 was a farmer, and 1 was a merchant. The background of the other 11 is unknown.

tsukata Masayoshi, was a lower samurai, the son of a rural samurai (gōshi) who had abandoned his land to engage in trade. Even Matsukata achieved hirazamurai rank before the Restoration, so it is reasonable to describe the group in general as being of full samurai standing, though several of its members, including Saigō and Ōkubo, were very much at the lower limits of the middle samurai.* In age, taking as a datum the years 1862–63 when loyalist agitation

* Ōkubo's family, though of samurai descent, had been forced by poverty to live outside Kagoshima "on the land" for several generations. His own branch of it had only recently returned and regained castle-town samurai status as koshō-gumi. Saigō's family had had this status longer but was nevertheless in considerable financial difficulties in his youth. There is a useful account of the youth of both men in Craig, "Kido Kōin," pp. 268–90.

first appeared openly on a national scale, about two-thirds were between twenty-five and thirty-five, and most of the rest a little older.

By contrast, the extremists, or activists, those who wanted to break away from domain politics altogether,* tended to be both lower in rank and younger. Their leader was Arima Shinshichi, born into a gōshi family in 1825 but adopted into a related house of middle samurai as a very small child. Of the rest—again the identifiable individuals total twenty-two—fifteen seem to have had a broadly similar hirazamurai background to Arima's own, though information about them is rather less precise than one would like. The others, equally tentatively, can be classed as lower samurai, though four of them had a merchant background or connections. One of these was Moriyama Shinzō, a wealthy townsman of gōshi origin who helped to finance the group. Moriyama was just over forty in 1862 and Arima was thirty-seven, but no fewer than eight of their associates were then under twenty-five, two being actually under twenty. The fact that only five of them survived into the Meiji period, compared with eighteen of the men who followed Ōkubo, is an interesting comment on the relative hazards of politics and revolt.

A different picture emerges when one turns to Yamauchi Yōdō's fief of Tosa.[40] Because Yōdō had been less active than Shimazu Nariakira in the Hitotsubashi succession dispute, there was no nucleus of men in his domain around which the activists could rally, like that provided in Satsuma by Saigō and his friends. As a consequence, attacks on the domain government in Tosa came much more from "outside," that is, from those whose loyalist convictions were less directly prompted by the political opinions of their lord. They came, indeed, substantially from the rural samurai (gōshi) and village headmen (shōya) whose control of the countryside, coupled

* There is a large subjective element in compiling lists of loyalists because the hagiography of the Restoration often includes men whom one suspects of having subsequently exaggerated, perhaps even invented, their own contribution to events or of having had this service performed for them by their biographers. There is also the difficulty that some men were activists at one time and bureaucrats, for example, at another (like Saigō's younger brother, Tsugumichi, whom I have counted as a loyalist-activist because he was involved in the Teradaya affair, but who was later a domain bureaucrat and Meiji statesman). Nevertheless, I do not believe that the picture I give here is greatly distorted by such factors.

with low formal status, had bred in them a resentment of the social and economic privileges enjoyed by the samurai of the castle town.

The Tosa gōshi families were of three main kinds.[41] Oldest were the descendants of some sixteenth-century samurai houses that had been resident in Tosa before the Yamauchi became daimyo and had been made gōshi in the seventeenth century in order that they might contribute to the preservation of stability in the countryside. Next came a number of relatively wealthy farming families, often of samurai descent, that had been raised to gōshi status for such services as land reclamation. Finally, there were the families of former merchants who had acquired gōshi rank, mostly in the late eighteenth century or early nineteenth century, for land reclamation, like the farmers, or by purchase. All three types were represented among the loyalists.

The presence of these men in the loyalist movement serves to emphasize the fact that Tosa political divisions in the late-Tokugawa period fell approximately along the lines of an existing tension in the samurai class. Evidence of that tension had appeared in several incidents earlier in the century, when protests from gōshi had forced the domain government to recognize their rights against the hirazamurai. Verbally, it was reflected in the articles of association of a league of village headmen in 1841. "Should we not say," the document claimed, "that the *shōya,* who is the head of the commoners, is superior to the retainers who are the hands or feet of the nobles?"[42]

There was, in fact, a considerable hostility in Tosa toward "men of birth" (mombatsu) from those who saw their own privileges as resting primarily on function. Nevertheless, those who manifested it felt themselves to be part of a ruling class, had a samurai education, accepted samurai values, and in many cases adopted a samurai way of life. Moreover, for all that they represented the interests of the rural well-to-do against the interests of their urban and bureaucratic superiors, they expressed their views, once the treaties had polarized politics, in terms that were virtually indistinguishable from those used by the Satsuma middle samurai: a nationalist sentiment that condemned both Bakufu and domain for their weakness toward the foreigner, and a local and feudal loyalty that condemned

Kōchi, the castle town, for its subservience to Edo. In this the Tosa loyalists *behaved* as samurai, even though in strict contemporary terms their right to the label was questionable.

Their leader, Takechi Zuizan, was himself a gōshi, one of those whose family was descended from retainers of the former feudal lords of Tosa, the Chōsogabe. He was a teacher of fencing, tall and intense, a little uncouth. His studies in Edo during 1856–57 had furnished links with activists from other domains, and his swordsmen-pupils provided him with a core of regular followers. Despite his activist links, it was only slowly that Takechi reacted to the situation created by the treaties and the Ansei purge. In 1861 he formed a loyalist league pledged "to reactivate the Japanese spirit" and "bring about the rebirth of our nation,"[43] which at one point had nearly 200 members. However, it was not until May 1862, when he engineered the murder of the domain's chief minister, Yoshida Tōyō, that Takechi began to exercise much influence on Tosa policy. This he did through the help of a few sympathizers who were high enough in rank to hold office in the domain government, as Takechi himself could never do; but the device was a clumsy one, often outflanked by the subtleties of the ex-daimyo, Yamauchi Yōdō, and never gave him a hold at all comparable with that which Ōkubo, for example, secured in Satsuma.

Indeed, many of the Tosa loyalists soon became impatient with the lack of progress. Like their leader, they were better agitators than politicians, with the result that they were always being tempted into adventures in Kyōto and elsewhere, escaping from the more humdrum—and more difficult—task of trying to manipulate domain officials. Partly for this reason, the party rapidly broke up after 1863, when the national climate of opinion changed and Yōdō turned openly against it. Takechi was arrested, and most of his surviving followers fled to join their friends in other parts of Japan, becoming rōnin, or "lordless" samurai.

One can discern in these events an outline, if a distorted one, of something like the divisions we detected in Satsuma between "politicians" and "activists." Thus one Tosa group, of which twenty-two members, including Takechi, can be identified,[44] concerned themselves primarily with the politics of their own domain, much as

Ōkubo and his associates did, though less effectively. None of them were upper samurai, but seven were middle samurai and fifteen lower samurai, most of whom were gōshi (see Table 1). In age they were predominantly between twenty-five and thirty-five in 1862. Takechi himself was thirty-three, his chief allies among the officials rather older. So in this respect the parallel with the Satsuma "politicians" was close. Indeed, though the Tosa men in this category had a generally lower level of rank than their Satsuma equivalents, one must not assume that they were necessarily of lower economic standing: the landholding of the Tosa gōshi in general averaged a little over fifty koku, which was certainly as much as a good many hirazamurai in Satsuma had, especially the koshō-gumi to which Saigō and Ōkubo belonged. Takechi's family, for example, held land to the assessed value of fifty-one koku.

Another section of the Tosa loyalists, the "activists," chose to quit the domain and become rōnin so as to free themselves to take part in conspiracies and risings elsewhere in the country. It was a decision taken at various times, both before and after Takechi's fall, and for many reasons. The number of those who took it was large—significantly so, compared with Satsuma—for no fewer than fifty-five men are identifiable by name as having engaged in such activities. There were very few hirazamurai among them, probably no more than five (see Table 1).[45] By contrast, at least twenty-four were lower samurai, if one includes the nine gōshi; and several more, including the shōya, appear to have had in practice a not dissimilar position in society.

The list includes, to give some characteristic examples, Sakamoto Ryōma (born 1835), a castle-town gōshi with a merchant family background, who had been introduced to politics through the Edo fencing schools;[46] his brother-in-law, Chiya Takayoshi (born 1842), a village headman, who in 1863 became a student at Katsu Awa's naval training establishment, with which Ryōma himself was closely connected; Nasu Shigetō (born 1807), a relatively poor gōshi, who joined the extremists after his adopted son was killed in a loyalist rising; Nakaoka Shintarō (born 1838), the eldest son of a senior village headman (*ōshōya*), one of those who, like Sakamoto, came to be deeply involved in the politics of Kyōto and Chōshū; and a middle samurai, Mochizuki Yoshizumi (born 1838), a cousin of one of Takechi's friends among the domain officials and another of Katsu's students, who died in a clash with Bakufu security guards in 1864.[47] In age, two-thirds of these rōnin were under twenty-five in 1862 and only one was over thirty-five, which suggests that this kind of adventuring appealed mostly to the young. Only twelve of the fifty-five survived until after 1868.

From this summary of what happened in Satsuma and Tosa it is possible to draw some tentative conclusions. The majority of the upper and middle samurai in these domains—that is to say, those who do *not* appear in our lists—reacted cautiously and defensively to the pressures put on them by the Bakufu after Ii Naosuke came to power, despite widespread criticism of the signing of the treaties. Accordingly, the minority, who condemned this relapse into conservatism and wanted to reverse it in what they conceived to be the national interest, were forced to seek ways of restoring their domain's initiative in national affairs that did not depend in the first place on the daimyo and his close advisers: either by persuasion and intrigue, aimed at inducing a change of policy, or by acts of violence, calculated to produce a crisis in which domain officials would be forced, however reluctantly, to act. The choice of method typifies two different kinds of opposition group.

In both, the leaders, though not always the rank and file, were aged about thirty and came from the lower levels of the middle samurai or from families not very much below them. This similarity implies that the choice these men made between legal and illegal forms of politics cannot be explained exclusively in terms of age and social background. Temperament had a good deal to do with it, no doubt. So did local circumstance, in the sense that a man was much more likely to seek influence through the regular channels if he knew that others had been able to do so before him. Thus Saigō's experience of office in Satsuma before 1858 was an encouragement to Ōkubo, just as Chōshū's record of hirazamurai leadership since the Tempō period was to help men like Kido.[48] Against this, Takechi Zuizan of Tosa, knowing that he lacked the rank for significant promotion, was less firm in his own commitment to legality and had difficulty holding his followers to it, too.

Here, indeed, is the real relevance of rank, that below a certain point the lack of it disqualified a man for office. Ōkubo, as a koshō-gumi, had difficulty enough in establishing a personal relationship with Shimazu Hisamitsu, the father of his daimyo,[49] but at least he had the minimum status needed for appointment and could meet most upper samurai face to face. The gōshi, shōya, and ashigaru who were predominant among those rejecting orthodox political methods, lacked this qualification. They therefore lacked the freedom of choice that went with it.* If they were to act politically at all, they had either to accept a role subordinate to the hirazamurai politicians or to behave in ways that would bring them into conflict with authority. Hence ambition, coupled with ideals that were contrary to those of their society, almost of necessity meant defiance of their lord. Indeed, the decision often enough reflected not so much a dedication to radical politics as the qualities of youth: a sense of adventure, an impatience with delay, a willingness to abandon traditional virtues for the pursuit of a higher ideal. Sakamoto Ryōma, who had all these qualities, once said in a letter he wrote to the parents of a friend who had, like himself, fled from Tosa to become a rōnin: "The idea that in times like these it is a violation of your proper duty to put your relatives second, your *han* [domain] second, to leave your mother, wife and children—this is certainly a notion that comes from our stupid officials."†

There is a certain logic about the pattern that has so far emerged from this discussion: in Tosa and Satsuma, at least, involvement in the struggle for power within a domain by "political" means—they were not always "legal"—was associated with a higher spectrum of rank and age than is to be found among men who chose less reputable, if more exciting, alternatives.[50] Nevertheless, one is bound to ask how far this conclusion can be applied to the loyalist movement as a whole. It is not an easy question to answer, if only because

* Jansen, *Sakamoto*, p. 110, makes the further point that in Tosa the low rank of the loyalists prevented some upper samurai from joining them, despite sympathy for their cause.

† Jansen, *Sakamoto*, p. 118. Compare this with the letter one of Ōkubo's followers, Yoshii Tomozane, wrote to his father in 1859 justifying his plans to leave Satsuma and engage in loyalist activities in Kyōto: "I shall be acting entirely for Emperor and country, in accordance with the dying wishes of our former lord [Shimazu Nariakira], so I might be said to have died in battle. A samurai could ask for nothing more" (*Ōkubo Toshimichi monjo*, 1: 30–31).

not all domains have been, or can be, as thoroughly studied by historians as Satsuma and Tosa.

Yet there is a good deal of evidence that one can adduce. In Chōshū, for example, a major center of opposition to Bakufu policy and domain conservatism just after the signature of the treaties was the private school run by Yoshida Shōin. Fifteen of its students became known as "men of spirit" in later years.[51] All of them were young—three were only fifteen years old in 1858 and the oldest twenty-seven. Seven were middle samurai and eight were lower samurai, the latter including four ashigaru. Most of the fifteen took part in acts of terrorism or some form of illegal action on one occasion or another; but it is possible to distinguish those who fairly quickly abandoned this kind of life—as soon, it would appear, as they saw a prospect of office and power—from those who remained rebels until the end, the division corresponding in some respects to that between "politicians" and "activists" in the domains we have already discussed.

In the first category were two of the hirazamurai, Takasugi Shinsaku and Kido Kōin, who had stipends of 150 koku and 90 koku, respectively. Kido, it is to be noted, despite the extremism of the years of his youth, reached upper samurai rank before the Restoration. At the age of twenty-nine in 1862, he was six years older than Takasugi, three years younger than Ōkubo of Satsuma. Also in the "government" group, which effectively controlled Chōshū after early 1865, were Shinagawa Yajirō, one of the ashigaru, and two men of similar, if not lower, rank who were to become Japan's most famous statesmen of the later nineteenth century, Itō Hirobumi and Yamagata Aritomo. All three were roughly Takasugi's age, that is, under twenty-five in 1862. We might also mention here two others in the group who were *not* pupils of Yoshida Shōin: Inoue Kaoru, a middle samurai of 100 koku, born in 1835, and Hirosawa Saneomi, born, like Kido, in 1833 and apparently of similar rank.

From this it would seem that the men who fought their way to office in Chōshū in 1865 had more in common in terms of rank and age with those who *failed* in Tosa, Takechi Zuizan's party, than with those who *succeeded* in Satsuma, the followers of Ōkubo and Saigō, though in a sense all of them might be said to have come from the same broad segment of feudal society. So did the other students from Yoshida's school, those whose reputation is rather for rebellion than administration (possibly because they died young and had little opportunity to indulge any other tastes). The most famous of them was Kusaka Genzui, husband of Yoshida Shōin's sister. Born in 1840, one year after Takasugi, he came from a family of doctors who belonged to the lowest stratum of the hirazamurai and had a stipend of twenty-five koku. Among his associates, one a little younger, the other a little older than he, were Ariyoshi Kumajirō, a lower samurai of very respectable standing (twenty-one koku), and an ashigaru, Iriye Hirotake.

It is useful to note how these Chōshū loyalists compare with the men from other domains with whom they worked during 1862 and 1863.[52] Among the Tosa rōnin, they had especially close links with Sakamoto Ryōma and Nakaoka Shintarō, that is, a gōshi and a village headman, more or less of an age with Kido. At thirty-three, Takechi Zuizan of Tosa, another gōshi collaborator, was a year or two older. Their Satsuma connections were chiefly with Arima Shinshichi, a gōshi become hirazamurai by adoption, thirty-seven years old in 1862; they also had dealings with Saigō Takamori (hirazamurai, age thirty-four) and sometimes Ōkubo (hirazamurai, age thirty). Finally, they had links with two important loyalists from other domains: Maki Izumi of Kurume, a Shintō official of middle samurai status, who at forty-nine was much older than the rest, and Hirano Kuniomi, a middle samurai of Fukuoka (Chikuzen), aged thirty-four.

This is by no means a complete account of the loyalists—the evidence would not sustain completeness, even if space allowed us to attempt it—and it suffers from an undue emphasis on famous names. To supplement it, therefore, let us look in greater detail at the participants in one particular incident of these years, the so-called Yamato revolt of the autumn of 1863.[53] The rising (which will be discussed more fully in Chapter 9) was organized originally to support the Court, dominated at that time by the sonnō-jōi party, in its disputes with Edo over the issue of expulsion; and it took the form of an attack on a Bakufu steward's office in the province of Yamato, led nominally by a young Court noble, Nakayama Tadamitsu, but in reality the work of colleagues of Maki and Hirano, with local help.

TABLE 2
Age and Background of Known Participants in the Yamato Revolt

Background/age	Non-local participants (36)	Local participants (32)
FAMILY BACKGROUND		
Middle samurai	3	—
Middle or lower samurai	5	3
Lower samurai		
Ashigaru, etc.	7	—
Gōshi and shōya[a]	7	19
Other[b]	4	10
Not known	10	—
AGE IN 1862–63		
35 and over	3	9
26–34	9	6
25 and under	23	2
Not known	1	15

SOURCE: Hara, "Tenchūgumi kyohei shimatsu-kō," *Shigaku zasshi*, 48 (1937): 1115–51, 1223–51; *Kinnō resshi den* (Tokyo, 1906); *Junnan rokkō* (3 vols., Tokyo, 1933); Naramoto Tatsuya, *Meiji ishin jimbutsu jiten* (Tokyo, 1966).

NOTE: The same conventions have been adopted concerning age and background as in Table 1 (p. 158) except that a number of men who were clearly samurai but who cannot be attributed with confidence to either the middle or the lower samurai category (the evidence suggests that they were somewhere near the line dividing the two) have been so described. Of the 36 non-local participants, 14 came from Tosa; 5 from Kurume; 2 each from Shimabara, Fukuoka (Chikuzen), Tottori (Inaba), and Kariya; and 1 each from Awaji, Bitchū, Bizen, Edo, Higo, Hitachi, Kii, Kyōto, and Mito. Of the 32 local participants, 16 were Tōzugawa gōshi.

[a] In this case it is not always possible to distinguish between gōshi and shōya. Not all the shōya were necessarily lower samurai.

[b] There were, among the non-local participants, a Court noble, a farmer, a merchant/lower samurai, and a merchant; and among the local participants, there were 6 farmers, 2 doctors, and a Buddhist priest.

At least thirty-six of those who took part, including Nakayama, came from outside the area immediately affected by the revolt (see Table 2). Of these, twenty-three seem to have had pretensions to some kind of samurai or quasi-samurai status so far as inadequate records enable us to judge. Fourteen of the participants came from Tosa, including two gōshi, three shōya, and three ashigaru, their leader being Yoshimura Shigesato, a former village headman in his middle twenties. Twelve of this fourteen were under thirty years of age. Five of the other twenty-two outside participants came from Maki's domain of Kurume, two from Chikuzen (men who had connections with Hirano), and three from elsewhere in Kyūshū, making ten from Kyūshū in all. One of the ten was the son of a farmer of some apparent wealth, and nine were samurai of various kinds, at least six of them being clearly lower samurai. Their ages ranged from eighteen to thirty-four. The remaining eleven came from several different parts of the country and from backgrounds as varied as middle samurai and fortuneteller; but here again there was a preponderance of lower samurai. They were led by Fujimoto Tesseki, a lower samurai from Bizen (Okayama), who was over forty, and Matsumoto Kenzaburō, a thirty-three-year-old hirazamurai who had been a teacher in the fudai domain of Kariya in Mikawa. Altogether, twenty-three of the thirty-six non-local participants were no more than twenty-five years old at the time of the revolt, and only three were thirty-five or over.

Turning to those who lived in Yamato and its vicinity, the best known was Mizugōri Nagao, a steward (*daikan*) or village headman on estates belonging to a domain in Ise province.[54] He was thirty-eight years old and was of samurai rank. Mizugōri was the man who chose the place for the rising and did much of the detailed planning. Accompanying him were six men described as "farmers" from his own village or nearby, all presumably well-to-do, since they had family names. The remaining nine in this group comprised the younger brother of another local steward; three country doctors, two of them described as wealthy, one being of gōshi family; a doctor's son; a Shintō official, also of gōshi descent; a Buddhist priest; a "Dutch scholar," who had studied guncasting in Hizen; and a fencing expert from a neighboring domain. This made sixteen men (known to us chiefly because they were killed or executed when the rising failed) who might be described as constituting a fair cross-section of rural society at its upper levels. They were perceptibly older than those who came to the district from outside, only two being twenty-five or under, no fewer than nine being thirty-five or more. In addition, there were another sixteen local gōshi from Tōzugawa, of whom little is known beyond their names,* plus a large but indeterminate following of farmers who were called out to serve as auxiliaries after the rising had begun.

* The so-called Tōzugawa gōshi were a type of soldier-farmer, surviving from the 16th century, who worked their own lands in the Tōzugawa district. They were more akin socially and economically to the Satsuma gōshi than to the Tosa gōshi but were nevertheless in a privileged position as compared with mere unarmed farmers. For a brief account of them, see Ono, *Gōshi seido*, pp. 131–32.

The presence of such persons in the loyalist forces brings us back to the problem of the class character of the loyalist movement. On this evidence it was clearly much more than a simple response by a feudal class to a foreign military threat, notwithstanding the markedly "samurai" outlook of its leaders.* Indeed, there is no doubt that those loyalists who found themselves, whether from choice or necessity, seeking to coerce their superiors were able to secure support from men barely on the fringes of the samurai class, possibly even outside the ranks of aspirant samurai altogether. Often that support took the form, not of military help, but of financial contributions or simply an offer of shelter, which is to say, assistance of a kind consistent with a position of some affluence and dignity that the donor did not wish to sacrifice. Thus Hayashi Yūzō, a rich farmer of Chōshū, was Yamagata Aritomo's patron; Yoshitomi Kanichi, another Chōshū landlord, contributed to Takasugi's funds; and Furuhashi Kiji of Mikawa acquired a reputation for loyalism at little risk by befriending local loyalists, while quietly improving agriculture in his village.[55] One finds a number of such examples, if on a small scale, in reading the lives of the Tosa rōnin.

Nor is it only in a farming context that the point can be made. Some of the movement's sympathizers were wealthy merchants. A notable example was Mitake Sadatarō of Bitchū, who had interests in cotton, iron, and shipping enterprises. Mitake sheltered Hirano Kuniomi for over a year and was eventually forced to go into hiding himself because of his activities.[56] One of his business associates, Shiraishi Shōichirō of Shimonoseki, who acted as agent for Satsuma in the cotton and indigo trade, became more famous still, providing hospitality, it is said, for as many as 150 loyalists at various times in the years before 1868.[57] Mostly, as one would expect, these loyalists were men from Satsuma and Chōshū, but several came from Chikuzen, Kurume, Tosa, and other domains. Shiraishi's shipping business (and the fact that Shimonoseki had a famous brothel quarter) made a good cover for conspirators and messengers who wanted to move about in secret.

* The Yamato rebels gave themselves high-sounding feudal titles after their initial success, calling on the farmers of the area to follow them in terms that sound more like commands from lords to subjects than an appeal for popular support (*Ishin-shi*, 3: 592; Hara, "Tenchūgumi," 1: 1144–48).

Yamazaki Kyūzaburo, a cloth merchant avowedly of samurai descent, provided a different service, making his shop in Kyōto available as a meeting-place for visitors from the provinces. His guests included Kido and Takasugi from Chōshū, Sakamoto and others from Tosa, and several of those who took part in the preparations for the Yamato rising. He, too, had to take flight in the end, becoming a member of the Chōshū irregular forces.[58]

The implications of these social data concerning the loyalist movement are too far-reaching to be dismissed with this brief discussion. We must return to the subject again, first with respect to what happened to the loyalists after 1863–64, especially in connection with Chōshū, then in an examination of early Meiji policies. Yet it is desirable at this point to summarize some of the conclusions that can legitimately be drawn from what we have been saying.

First, those loyalist groups that concentrated their attention on the manipulation of domain politics had at their core men of middle samurai rank, usually from the lower levels of the hirazamurai. Around them were gathered a few upper samurai members who provided access to the really high-born, an essential if they were to influence policy as it was made, and a few lower samurai who were useful as a link with the extremists; but these elements did not alter the essential character of the group, the composition of which was related to its willingness to act within the rules of society as it was. From this point of view the loyalist "politicians" were not so very different from the moderates and conservatives.

Second, those loyalists who lacked the minimum degree of rank essential to castle-town politics in the usual sense, or who for other reasons considered legal methods to be inadequate or ineffective, were bound to work outside the regular centers of authority and hence to be drawn into kinds of political behavior that by their nature challenged the regime. A man might be prompted to act by a mixture of idealism, ambition, and adventurousness, as Sakamoto Ryōma was.* Yet having acted, he became through the act itself a

* On one occasion Sakamoto wrote in a letter from Nagasaki that "in a place like home [Kōchi], you can't have any ambition. You waste your time loafing around" (Jansen, *Sakamoto*, p. 173).

subversive. There is, therefore, a valid connection between low rank—rank below that of hirazamurai, which qualified a man for domain offices of some responsibility—and rebellion, terrorism, or the threat of violence. The rōnin who were the placard-posters, the demonstrators, the conspirators, the assassins were characteristically men of lower social standing than the "politicians."

Third, this argument applies also to those whose claim to samurai status was tenuous or even nonexistent: the village headmen, rich farmers, and merchants who had perhaps bought the right to use a family name and wear a sword. Given that these were men of influence in the community, well enough educated and informed to have opinions about the political issues of the day, the fact remains that Tokugawa society provided no channel through which their concern could legitimately be expressed. To be politically active was to act illegally, more so for them than for the samurai proper, and much more so than for feudal lords.* Hence it is not surprising that some of them—and the examples we have given are not necessarily evidence of a movement on a really large scale, when one considers how much modern Japanese research has gone into finding them—became politically linked with men who were in reality their equals, if in theory their superiors, that is, the lower-ranking samurai of the castle towns.

* Generally speaking, punishment under Tokugawa justice was the more severe the lower a man's rank; contrast the crucifixion of peasant rebels with the house arrest of supposedly subversive feudal lords. One might cite as an immediately relevant example the Noneyama incident of October 1864, when some local loyalists in the Aki district of Tosa organized a public demonstration against the imprisonment of Takechi Zuizan. There were twenty-three participants in all (gōshi, village headmen, and other men from families of some standing in rural society). Most were young, though their leader Kiyooka Masamichi, a gōshi, was forty years old. Their plan was to make their protest, then escape across the frontier to a neighboring province, presumably to become rōnin. However, the domain forces that were sent against them treated them as open rebels, killing some and capturing the rest, who were all subsequently executed. See Jansen, *Sakamoto*, pp. 111, 150; and Beasley, "Political Groups in Tosa," pp. 384–88.

CHAPTER VII

The Politics of Expulsion

To TURN FROM a consideration of the political character of the loyalist movement to a narrative of what its members actually did is to revert to the subject of jōi, the expulsion of the foreigner. This, above all, was the demand on which the shishi, the "men of spirit," insisted, the cause that the Emperor was to lead. Accordingly, most of the violence of the years after 1858 was related to it.

Violence offered by armed samurai to foreigners in the treaty ports was a characteristic of these years, as resentment of the unequal treaties imposed on Japan, coupled with frustration at an apparent inability to break the Bakufu's grasp of power, on which the privileges of the foreigners seemed to rest, led the "men of spirit" to seek victims for their wrath in a manner that endangered, and was meant to endanger, the treaty settlement. In the first two years the victims included a Russian naval officer, a Dutch merchant captain, a Chinese in French employ, and a Japanese attached to a British consulate. In January 1861 Townsend Harris's secretary, Heusken, was murdered in Edo, an incident that prompted the temporary withdrawal of the French and British ministers (but not Harris) to Yokohama. In the following July there was a night attack on the British legation at Tōzenji. Laurence Oliphant and another member of the staff were wounded, and several Japanese, both attackers and guards, were killed.*

* The bitterness this situation aroused is well illustrated by Rutherford Alcock's description of the kind of men he believed to be responsible for the attacks on foreigners: "Often drunk, and always insolent . . . the terror of all the unarmed population and street dogs" (*The Capital of the Tycoon*, 1: 126).

Nor was personal insecurity the only foreign grievance, for Japan's trade proved from the start disappointingly small in scale, not least, it was argued, because Japanese officials deliberately obstructed its growth.[1] Hence the risk that foreigners, too, might resort to force, out of simple anger or in the belief that samurai attacks had official patronage, was increased by their wish to maintain treaty rights and defend the commercial interests arising from them. In this situation, foreign affairs came to interact with Japanese politics in a much less hypothetical manner than before the opening of the ports. The clear danger now was that a major conflict would erupt, and that there would not be the time, even if there was the will, to avert it, should the representatives of the powers lose patience.

Awareness of this precarious situation itself became an element in politics. It encouraged the cautious, that is, the Bakufu and the lords, to moderate their differences, an end they pursued under the slogan kōbu-gattai, "unity of Court and Bakufu." But it also prompted the reckless to threaten catastrophe if they did not get their way: to insist on nothing less than expulsion of the foreigner and its concomitant, "respect" for the Emperor (sonnō). The struggle between them, complicated by a secondary trial of strength between Bakufu and lords, became the main thread of Japanese politics from 1860 to 1863.

UNITY OF COURT AND BAKUFU

Attacks on foreigners were accompanied by attacks on those Japanese who dealt with them, beginning with the assassination of Ii Naosuke outside one of the Edo castle gates, the Sakurada-mon, on March 24, 1860. His murder was the work of a band of samurai from Mito, helped by a few from Satsuma; and it was designed not only to exact revenge for the punishment Ii had inflicted on their lords, but also as the signal for a seizure of power. Their plan called for an attack by Mito on the foreign settlement at Yokohama and another by Satsuma on the Bakufu's troops in Kyōto; these attacks, it was hoped, would provoke an irresistible movement in favor of a change of policy toward the West.[2] None of this materialized, chiefly because domain officials proved unwilling to risk a move. Nevertheless, the notion itself—acts of terrorism by those without official responsibilities, calculated to force on authority a commitment to expel the foreigner—became a model for shishi everywhere in the next few years.

Though the plan to instigate a coup d'état proved ill-judged and unsuccessful, it at least opened the way for the surviving lords of the Hitotsubashi party to regain some of their influence. By removing the Regent it left the administration—almost inevitably, in view of the appointments Ii himself had made—in the hands of men with little strength of purpose or prestige, chiefly Andō Nobumasa and Kuze Hirochika, who now became the senior members of the Bakufu council. Facing pressures from the foreign representatives, critical of Edo's failure to protect their citizens on the one side, and from the samurai, hostile to the treaties and to the way they had been signed on the other, they sought urgently for a compromise.

Fortunately, the death of Tokugawa Nariaki in September 1860 made their task a little easier. Since Shimazu Nariakira and Ii Naosuke were also dead, it meant that three of the principals in the succession dispute, those about whom feelings were strongest, had been removed from the scene. In a gesture of conciliation, the rest, including Matsudaira Shungaku, Hitotsubashi Keiki, and Yamauchi Yōdō, were given a qualified pardon. As a more positive step, Andō and Kuze revived a proposal that Ii Naosuke had briefly considered at the end of 1858, namely, the idea of a marriage between the Shogun and one of the Emperor's relatives as a means of healing the breach with Kyōto. In May 1860 they formally proposed that Iemochi marry Kōmei's sister, Kazunomiya. In July they repeated the request, despite an initial rebuff.

In Kyōto, Iwakura Tomomi, one of the ablest of the Emperor's personal confidants, prepared a private memorial in late July or early August assessing the implications of the Bakufu approach, as well as the ways in which it might be exploited politically. The Tokugawa councillors, he said, were seeking "to make use of the prestige of the Court to bolster the authority of the Bakufu and quell the people's unrest." This made it now possible, as well as desirable, to force the Shogun to "return in private to the Court the substance of political power" and to base his decisions on "the views of the country at large," that is, on consultation with the feudal lords.[3]

At the same time, there was to Iwakura's mind little chance that the Tokugawa would surrender without a struggle or that the main body of the daimyo were ready to join an alliance against them. It might even be that the attacks on foreigners would bring double jeopardy, "domestic and foreign dangers" simultaneously. To avoid such a crisis was Kyōto's duty. It had only one method of doing so: "to concede in name what we retain in substance," in other words, to agree to the Kazunomiya marriage in return for Bakufu acceptance of the Emperor's wishes in foreign affairs. This would give the Court a real, if unacknowledged, voice in policy making.

Iwakura's conclusions, though not his reasons for them, were incorporated in a letter from Emperor Kōmei to the Kampaku on August 6, 1860, and forwarded by him to the Shoshidai, the Bakufu's representative in Kyōto, two days later. On September 14 the Shoshidai replied, communicating the Rōjū's comment, which was, in effect, an inversion of Iwakura's own. Setting out the case for the marriage as a means to unity, which was itself, the Bakufu argued, a prerequisite for handling the foreigner, it rejected outright the jōi position that a promise of expulsion was the condition on which unity must rest. "If our affairs are not in good order at home," the Bakufu claimed, "we shall be unable to strike successfully abroad. . . . The Shogun therefore wishes to demonstrate to the country without delay the accord that exists between Court and Bakufu."[4] To achieve that accord, he was willing to make a substantial concession to the jōi viewpoint, promising action against the West provided it was understood that there would be no hostilities before the country was properly prepared. "Within seven or eight to ten years from now," the document stated, "action will certainly be taken either to cancel the treaties by negotiation or to expel the foreigners by force."[5]

So qualified a commitment did not satisfy the extremer chauvinists, either at Court or in the domains, but it was enough for an Emperor who was at heart still anxious to avoid a breach with Edo. On October 2, officially but privately, he approved the marriage. This left the Bakufu free, or so it seemed, to pursue the other arm of its policy, an adjustment of its relations with the powers.

To this end, it was decided in March 1861 to send a mission to Europe. As announced, its object was to get the agreement of the powers to the postponement of the opening of Edo, Osaka, Hyōgo, and Niigata, due to take place within the next two years; the argument offered was that more time was needed to overcome popular anti-foreign feeling in Japan, bred by centuries of seclusion and exacerbated by the rising prices attributed to foreign trade.*

Rutherford Alcock, the British minister, was not initially much impressed by this argument. However, an attempt to assassinate Andō Nobumasa in February 1862, soon after the mission had sailed, finally convinced him that the political dangers of the situation were not mere figments of a Tokugawa imagination. Reluctantly, he concluded that "the Government of the Tycoon has real difficulties of no ordinary kind and actual dangers to contend with, threatening the dynasty and the existence of the Government," and that "vehemently pressed between two great dangers, the one from within, the other from without," the Bakufu was extremely unlikely to open the additional ports, unless the powers were "prepared to enforce their demand by material means of pressure adequate to the end in view."[6] Since Alcock thought the trade involved was hardly worth the effort this implied, he recommended acceptance of the Japanese proposals. In June 1862, while in London, he was himself given the responsibility for negotiating a protocol that postponed the opening of further ports until January 1, 1868, but reaffirmed the treaties in all other respects. The rest of the powers signed similar agreements in the next few months.

At this point it seemed as if the Bakufu might have found a satisfactory formula for dealing with its problems, even though it had given contradictory promises to Kyōto and London on the subject of foreign affairs. Certainly the policy of kōbu-gattai, "unity of

* Rōjū to Alcock, May 30, 1861, in Beasley, *Select Documents*, pp. 208–11. The question of whether or not there was a rise in prices due to foreign trade is a difficult one. Though not all records agree in detail, there is evidence of a fairly sharp rise in the price of rice and some other foodstuffs in 1861 (and of increasingly high prices in later years, especially 1865–67). See Tsuchiya, "Bakumatsu dōranki," p. 83; and Tanaka Akira, *Meiji*, pp. 93–94. It seems less certain that the increase was due to foreign trade. The volume of trade was still extremely small in 1861 (imports and exports totaled less than $6,000,000) and the recoinage undertaken in 1858 affords at least as likely an explanation. However, for the purpose of discussing Japanese politics it is less important to decide whether foreign trade was indeed to blame for the price rise than to recognize that many Japanese, including the "men of spirit," believed it was. The increase therefore acted as a stimulus to anti-foreign feeling, whatever its basis in fact.

Court and Bakufu," as manifested in the Kazunomiya marriage, had deprived samurai opposition of the Emperor's blessing, at least openly, while its corollary, the London Protocol, had slightly reduced the chances of an immediate conflict with the West. This seemed to provide time in which to rearm Japan and bring the turbulence, if not the chauvinism, of the extremists under control.

But the Bakufu was not to have that time, for by its very actions it had made possible a resurgence of the reforming lords. To Edo, as Iwakura had pointed out, "unity of Court and Bakufu" meant a bolstering of Bakufu authority by the use of the imperial prestige, no matter how "national" its stated objects. To some of the great lords, however, it implied a renewed possibility of intervening in politics in the Emperor's name so as to achieve, among other things, an increase in baronial privilege. They now attempted to exploit this possibility in what they took to be the more relaxed atmosphere resulting from Ii's death.

At the nucleus of the new movement were the men and the domains comprising the former Hitotsubashi party, though there had been changes in the intervening years. With Tokugawa Nariaki's death, Mito had fallen into disunity and a preoccupation with its own affairs. Tosa, under a reforming minister, Yoshida Tōyō, was concentrating on its own economic and military needs, as was Hizen. Accordingly, none of the three showed signs of taking an immediate initiative in Edo or Kyōto. On the other hand, Chōshū, the Mōri domain in western Honshū, was emerging for the first time on the national scene, rivaling Satsuma. In fact, it was Chōshū, at the instigation of a senior official, Nagai Uta, that first put forward an alternative version of kōbu-gattai in the spring and summer of 1861, one that accepted the impossibility of repudiating the treaties and even envisaged—as the Bakufu no longer did after the removal of its ablest officials in Ii Naosuke's purge—the development of national wealth and strength as a consequence of relations with the West, but sought "unity" through political proposals quite different in emphasis from the Bakufu's own. To quote Nagai:

Steps should now be taken by the Bakufu to carry on its administration by sending instructions to the domains in accordance with the orders of the Court. If this is done, the general lines of policy will be settled by the Court, while the Bakufu accepts responsibility for its execution, so that the proper relationship between ruler and minister will be observed. In this way, peace will quickly be ensured at home. . . . If, on the other hand, we continue in our present confused manner, having no agreement betwen Court and Bakufu and no clear policy, our difficulties at home will grow daily more severe, our people's livelihood will be destroyed, and we will eventually fall into the barbarians' toils.[7]

In July 1861 Nagai was sent to Kyōto, where his proposals were approved, and thence to Edo, where he secured orders for his domain to "mediate" between the country's two centers of authority;* but before he could do very much to implement these decisions, his plans were suddenly overshadowed by a move from Satsuma.

Under Shimazu Nariakira, as we have seen, Satsuma had been one of the most active of the reforming domains, but the purge and Nariakira's death had put power there into the hands of conservatives who had abandoned most of their former lord's policies.[8] So matters had remained until the end of 1859. Then Nariakira's half-brother, Hisamitsu, father of the new daimyo, Tadayoshi, began to gain influence and to reappoint some of the officials who had served before 1858. At the same time, he allowed the loyalist samurai of the domain, led by Ōkubo Toshimichi (who had also served Nariakira, to establish a connection with him.

The relationship between Ōkubo and Hisamitsu became closer in the spring of 1860, when news of Ii Naosuke's death emphasized to both men the dangers and potential uses of radical action, such as Ōkubo's followers demanded. In fact, that act provided the occasion for their first actual meeting, at which each was apparently impressed by the other's ability. There they struck a bargain: Ōkubo undertook to restrain the samurai hotheads by arguing for action by Satsuma, that is, by the domain as such, as a far more effective way of changing Bakufu attitudes toward the Court and the treaties than any ill-organized demarche by groups of impatient loyalists, while Hisamitsu promised to take an initiative in national affairs—by implication following his dead brother's example—when a safe opportunity arose. Soon after, Ōkubo was appointed to

* The term "mediation" or "good offices" (*assen*) was widely used in late-Tokugawa politics, reflecting the need for a political equivalent of the go-between in a society where status divisions were strict and politics operated through vertical relationships.

minor office and began the task of building a party of adherents in the administration and the daimyo's household.

The situation changed little in the following eighteen months, since Satsuma, like most of the other great domains, still respected Edo's powers of retaliation. Ōkubo, however, found it increasingly difficult to keep the extremists under control, especially in view of the prospect of reconciliation between Court and Bakufu with the Kazunomiya marriage. At the end of 1861 came news that the Princess had left Kyōto on her way to Edo. This—it was assumed to be against the Emperor's wishes—provoked a great outcry in Kagoshima, leading Ōkubo and his friends to demand that Satsuma follow Chōshū's example in offering its loyal services to the Court.

Fear of unrest, plus jealousy of Chōshū, made the idea acceptable to most of the officials, even those who were not of Ōkubo's opinion, so that by the end of December a plan had been worked out for Hisamitsu to take a strong force to Kyōto, ostensibly on his way to pay a visit to Edo, but in fact to secure the Court's approval for a new attempt at "mediation." It was to take the form (echoing Hashimoto Sanai in 1858) of a demand that Matsudaira Shungaku and Hitotsubashi Keiki be installed in Bakufu offices and given an effective role in the supervision of policy, in order to restore the country's confidence in the conduct of affairs. The Satsuma leaders were themselves to carry this demand to the Shogun's capital, thus ensuring that it would not be ignored.

As a first step, Ōkubo was sent to Kyōto to concert preliminary arrangements with Konoe Tadahiro, taking with him a long memorandum from Hisamitsu and his son, which he delivered on February 12, 1862.[9] Bakufu policies, it said, by alienating feudal opinion were endangering both the country's safety and "the fortunes of the Tokugawa house." They must therefore be changed. This was not to be achieved by overthrowing the Tokugawa, as extremists apparently wished—neither the Emperor nor the Shimazu would welcome such an outcome, the document claimed—but by substituting new men, sympathizers of the Court like Keiki and Shungaku, for those who had taken the Bakufu's decisions hitherto.

This time, Hisamitsu said, the great lords must take measures against the possibility that their attempt to make this change would provoke a defensive reaction from the fudai, as it had done in 1858. It was therefore his intention not only to come to Kyōto, but also to take precautions for its defense and to negotiate for the cooperation of other domains. It might even be neccessary in the last resort to call for a rising of loyal samurai against the Bakufu, though he would much prefer to achieve his object "without provoking hostilities or causing harm to the national polity [kokutai]."

The proposal, though much more moderate than some that were being canvassed among the samurai at this time, was greeted by Konoe and his colleagues with more alarm than enthusiasm. They had not forgotten that the great lords had done nothing to protect them from Ii Naosuke's wrath in similar circumstances a few years earlier. Their hesitation, however, was to no avail, for Satsuma was determined on a trial of strength. Saigō Takamori, Nariakira's former agent and a national hero to the loyalists, was recalled from exile. Hisamitsu with a substantial force set out for Osaka, then Kyōto.

On arrival in the capital on May 14, 1862, he at once communicated the details of his proposed measures to the Court officials.[10] They included a full pardon for both the kuge and the daimyo punished by Ii in 1858; the appointment of Keiki and Shungaku to posts of responsibility; the dismissal of Andō Nobumasa from the Bakufu council; a visit by the Shogun to Kyōto in order to settle questions of foreign policy; and the nomination by the Court of a small group of great lords to act as the Emperor's representatives in keeping the Bakufu to its promises.* By the beginning of June it was agreed that these items should form the basis of instructions to an imperial envoy, Ōhara Shigenori, and that Hisamitsu should escort him.

By this time word of what was going on had reached Edo, where attempts were made to avoid difficulties by anticipating some of the Court's demands. On May 9 Andō Nobumasa was relieved of office,

* The daimyo who were subsequently proposed to represent the Court as political commissioners were those of Satsuma, Chōshū, Tosa, Sendai, and Kaga. This interpretation of the Satsuma plan is said to have been Iwakura's contribution, aimed at reconciling the Chōshū and Satsuma initiatives while ensuring that the lords of these two powerful domains were associated with others who would be capable of keeping their ambitions in check. See *Ishin-shi*, 3: 101–5.

and two weeks later the remaining ban on meetings and correspondence between former members of the Hitotsubashi party was at last removed. On June 27, while Ōhara was on his way to Edo, it was announced that the Shogun would soon make a state visit to Kyōto in the interests of national unity. Next day Kuze Hirochika resigned as Rōjū.

Nevertheless, the Ōhara mission was not to find that all was plain sailing when it reached the city on July 3. The concessions, after all, had been designed to strengthen the Bakufu's hand, not pave the way for a Satsuma victory. First, Matsudaira Shungaku, struggling with the calls of family loyalty and not fully convinced of the purity of Shimazu's motives, had to be subjected to some persuasion before he would accept the post of Seiji-sōsai (equivalent to that of Regent). Then the hostility of the fudai to Mito, another heritage from 1858, made it difficult to get Hitotsubashi Keiki appointed as the Shogun's guardian (Kōken). In fact, it was not until Ōkubo and one or two other members of Hisamitsu's entourage threatened the use of force against obstructive officials that the Rōjū gave way. And it was well into August, almost a month after Keiki's appointment, before Matsudaira Katamori of Aizu (kamon; 230,000 koku), another Tokugawa relative, was made Kyōto Shugo, thereby superseding the Shoshidai as the principal Bakufu official in the Emperor's capital.

There can be no doubt that the main body of Edo officials, as their subsequent actions showed, had no intention of allowing the high-ranking triumvirate of Keiki, Shungaku, and Katamori to assume a genuine control of policy. Rather, they were to be a sop to Satsuma's Cerberus, a screen behind which things could go on much as before. This, however, was not the Shimazu view of things, as Hisamitsu made clear in the memorial he presented to Keiki on September 12, 1862.[11] It demanded, among other things, arrangements for the Shogun to make an early visit to Kyōto; an increase of 100,000 koku in the land designated for the Emperor's maintenance, together with smaller increases for the "loyal" kuge; and punishment for those Bakufu and Court officials who had cooperated in Ii Naosuke's purge. More important in the longer term, there were to be changes in the handling of both domestic and foreign affairs. These were to include a relaxation of sankin-kōtai and an end to Bakufu financial demands on the domains for the carrying out of public works, "since it is only in this way that we can achieve both defense against the foreigners and the pacification of unrest at home"; a drive to improve coast defenses, especially in the Kyōto area, and a reduction of "wasteful" government expenditure on matters other than defense; a change in guard duties at Kyōto, which were to be entrusted to four or five of the great domains, serving in turn, without which "there can be no basis for setting men's minds at rest"; and an arrangement by which day-to-day questions of foreign policy would be resolved, not by the Rōjū, but by a commission of daimyo, four tozama and four fudai, all with lands rated between 100,000 and 300,000 koku.

The document makes very clear the "great lord" bias of the Satsuma approach, which offered little more in the way of real authority to Kyōto than did the Bakufu's own concept of "unity" with the Court. To be sure, Shimazu's plan was much more positive than the Bakufu's; but this apart, the essential difference between the two was in the way they envisaged power as being exercised—whether by the Shogun and his officials, acting nominally with the approval of the Court, or through a process of consultation in which a number of powerful daimyo would have an effective voice as the Emperor's "representatives."

Not surprisingly, the second structure appealed more to tozama like Shimazu and kamon like Matsudaira Shungaku than it did to the fudai, few of whom had fiefs of as much as 100,000 koku. Indeed, the opposition of the fudai prevented much of the program from being carried out, despite some genuine attempts at administrative and military reform.* The one significant change was a modification of sankin-kōtai, announced early in October 1862, by which the period of residence in Edo was reduced for the great majority

* Tanaka Akira, *Meiji ishin*, pp. 72–86, outlines the reforms, noting that their effectiveness was limited by opposition or lack of enthusiasm among senior Bakufu officials, who were preoccupied with defending the Bakufu's authority from attacks by its rivals; and by the rigidity of the Bakufu structure, which made it difficult to secure any real promotion of "men of talent," even though some moves were made in this direction (especially in military affairs).

of feudal lords to a mere 100 days in every three years. As a consequence, according to *Genji Yume Monogatari*, "in the twinkling of an eye the flourishing city of Yedo became like a desert."[12]

That this was an exaggeration of Satsuma's achievements, as well as by implication a misrepresentation of its aims, is clear from Shimazu Hisamitsu's subsequent efforts to persuade the Court to give the new men in Edo a chance to prove themselves. Soon after he got back to Kyōto on September 30, he submitted a long memorial to the Emperor to argue that his own initial success could be exploited only if a temporary halt were called to demands for expulsion of the foreigner.[13] To order expulsion, even for the purpose of raising Japanese morale, would be to invite catastrophe, since the Bakufu might well refuse to carry such orders out, thus "putting at issue the whole question of the Court's authority"; and if samurai were thereby encouraged to try to put expulsion into effect, as was by no means impossible, they would bring on Japan the fate that had befallen China. Military action, in fact, must wait on reform at home. Only if the Bakufu failed to give a lead in this, Hisamitsu urged, only if it continued, as in the past, "merely to pursue ways of tyrannizing the domains," should the Court and the daimyo take the initiative from it.

Hisamitsu, then, remained consistent in his view that baronial independence was the only basis on which to create a united Japan, setting himself against the Tokugawa in a manner entirely feudal and traditional. He was nevertheless aware that the issue was no longer just the time-honored one of the respective rights of Shogun and daimyo. For one thing, there was an imminent danger of foreign attack, made more likely than ever by the action of some of his own retainers, who on the way back to Kyōto from Edo had killed an Englishman named Richardson at Namamugi, near Yokohama. For another, the daimyo themselves were divided: Chōshū, bidding for the Emperor's favor, was already pushing loyalty to a point at which it threatened to destroy the "unity" that Satsuma had achieved. Above all, the loyalist samurai could not be brought to accept the settlement as it stood. Their original high hopes in Hisamitsu had been shattered by the discovery that he intended neither to honor the Emperor nor to expel the barbarian, as they understood those terms. Hence they had turned once more to violence, terrorizing Kyōto in pursuit of their own ends.

EXPEL THE BARBARIAN

This part of the story begins in the winter of 1861–62, when the Satsuma leaders—including, although only at the margin, Ōkubo Toshimichi and one or two loyalist colleagues—were beginning to work out plans for Shimazu Hisamitsu's intervention in national affairs. As we have seen, this was intended primarily to serve the interests of "unity of Court and Bakufu" by imposing on Edo the appointment of former members of the Hitotsubashi party, notably Matsudaira Shungaku and Hitotsubashi Keiki, to senior posts. But it was widely understood by the "men of spirit" to be something much more.

For some time, Ōkubo had been seeking to persuade the Satsuma hotheads that "official" action would be much more effective than indiscriminate violence, independently pursued. This was to imply that the nature of what was done officially would be such as to meet at least some of the extremists' wishes. Hence when Hisamitsu eventually set out for Kyōto in the spring of 1862, many believed that he was taking the first step in an anti-Tokugawa loyalist coup—even in Satsuma, where hardly any of the loyalists, apart from Ōkubo, had a knowledge of the actual plans. Still more were such misapprehensions current in the rest of Kyūshū, since the principal sources of information were the extremists in Kagoshima and sympathizers at the Imperial Court, neither of whom were characterized by realism or caution.

Consequently, Satsuma's Arima Shinshichi, working closely with Maki Izumi of Kurume and Hirano Kuniomi of Chikuzen, devised a plot to promote a loyalist rising, timed to coincide with Hisamitsu's arrival in the neighborhood of Kyōto and intended to lend support to him if he meant to carry out an anti-Bakufu coup, or to force his hand, if not, by presenting him with the accomplished fact of one. As Hirano described it in a document of May 6, 1862 (when Hisamitsu was already approaching Osaka with a substantial force), the rising was to begin with an attack on Bakufu strongholds in Kyōto, Osaka, and Hikone, carried out by Satsuma at imperial orders and with shishi support. Victory would then be confirmed by an expedition against Edo. In this way, Hirano said, the Shogun could be stripped of office and reduced to "the same standing as the other great feudal lords."[14]

Maki and Arima, conferring in Osaka, saw the situation in even simpler terms. All that was needed, they maintained, was the assassination of the leading Bakufu spokesmen in Kyōto—Kujō Naotada, the Kampaku, and Sakai Tadayoshi, the Shoshidai—to set the country aflame. It was to this end that they directed their own activities.

There was little Ōkubo could do on this occasion to restrain them, since he was already suspect in the eyes of the extremists by virtue of his personal involvement in Hisamitsu's plans. Even Saigō Takamori, recently released from exile and more to be trusted, was unable to hold them back—indeed, there is some doubt about how hard he tried—and he was in any case disavowed by Hisamitsu on May 9.* This left the exercise of feudal discipline as authority's sole recourse, there being no longer any credible intermediaries through whom to use persuasion.

On May 13, Hirano Kuniomi, trying to argue matters with his lord, Kuroda Narihiro, who had just arrived in Kyōto, was arrested and sent back to Fukuoka. Encouraged by this, Hisamitsu, hearing on the evening of May 21 that Arima, Maki, and a number of others had gathered at the Teradaya Inn in nearby Fushimi to concert the final details of their plans, sent members of his entourage to instruct them to abandon the undertaking. The result was a confused encounter in the dark at the Teradaya, in which fighting broke out and Arima and several more were killed. The rest of the conspir-

* Saigō, who had only grudgingly accepted Hisamitsu's proposals in the first place, had been sent ahead to investigate what was happening in Osaka and Kyōto at the end of April. His reported association with the extremists in the next week or two, described by Saigō as an attempt to win their sympathy in order to moderate their plans, so angered Hisamitsu that he ordered Saigō back to Kagoshima on May 9 and thence once more into exile. There is a full but not very illuminating description of the incident in Shimonaka, *Dai Saigō seiden*, 1: 175–211. See also Iwata, pp. 52ff. Saigō's younger brother, Tsugumichi, was also punished for complicity with the plotters in this affair.

ators then submitted to Hisamitsu's orders. Maki Izumi was sent under arrest to his own domain, and twenty or so others were sent back to Kagoshima in disgrace.

Thus the attempt to exploit Shimazu Hisamitsu's presence in Kyōto to further the cause of sonnō-jōi ended in failure. The Court itself expressed its relief: the activities of the rōnin, it said, threatened national unity and were contrary to the Emperor's wishes.[15] More important, the incident marked the end of any serious breakaway plans among the Satsuma loyalists. This was partly, no doubt, because the affair had demonstrated that they were too weak to challenge directly the authority of the domain. But it was also because the failure of the plot enabled Saigō and Ōkubo quickly to reassert their leadership. Helped by Hisamitsu's willingness to play a national role and a dispute with Britain that led to fighting in 1863—both gave the Satsuma loyalists a new sense of patriotism and pride and made it easier for them to cooperate in policies of which they did not fully approve—the two men were again able to unite the movement behind the proposition that it was Satsuma, not its individual samurai, that had to act. Thus the rest of the story of Satsuma politics down to 1868 is principally the story of Saigō's and Ōkubo's efforts to take power from the conservatives, rather than an account of samurai turbulence and disaffection. It began almost at once, with Ōkubo's promotion to a higher office on June 17.

In Chōshū the situation worked out very differently.[16] On June 17, the same day that Ōkubo was promoted, Nagai Uta, Chōshū's principal advocate of unity between Court and Bakufu, finally succumbed to the pressure of those calling on him to resign. One reason for the opposition to him was his failure to maintain the domain's political initiative, which was passing, it seemed, to Satsuma. Another was that his concept of "unity" involved the sacrifice of "expulsion" and therefore a disregard of what the loyalists believed to be the Emperor's views, a circumstance that brought on him the wrath of all those samurai who acknowledged the leadership of Yoshida Shōin's successors, Kusaka Genzui and Kido Kōin. Indeed, the second argument was persuasive even to the Chōshū moderates, who abandoned not only Nagai, but also to some extent his policies.

Previously their declared aim had been to "show loyalty" toward the Court while "keeping faith" with the Bakufu. On August 1, 1862, however, after long discussions in which Kido played a leading part, it was formally resolved that the first must take priority over the second in any clash of interest between the two, in other words, that sonnō, "honor the Emperor," and jōi, "expel the barbarian," were for Chōshū the basis on which "unity" was to be achieved.

It is important to note that this decision was taken by the Chōshū men in Kyōto, which is to say, by those who were living in a heady atmosphere of imperial patronage and loyalist intrigues. On several occasions in the Restoration years this kind of circumstance was to contribute to the adoption of policies in the capital that those living farther from the scene, whether in Edo or the castle towns, found it difficult to accept. Certainly one should not assume from this resolution that the loyalists had already gained control of Chōshū, any more than Ōkubo's promotion is to be taken as evidence that they had been victorious in Satsuma.

Kido, it is true, like Ōkubo, now secured a valuable foothold in domain administration. But one gets the impression that both men held their place because of their ability to provide a link with and consequently a check of sorts on the extremists—or because of their capacity for making trouble, perhaps, which is almost the same thing—not because they were at the heart of things. In Satsuma the dominating force was Shimazu Hisamitsu, the daimyo's father, with whom Ōkubo had to work in a subordinate capacity. In Chōshū it was the more moderate middle samurai reformers, to whom by rank, if not by conviction, Kido himself belonged. In neither domain had there yet been an important change in the structure of power.

There had, however, been a change of emphasis, especially important for events in Kyōto. This was reinforced by what took place in Tosa during the summer months of 1862.[17] There, while the former lord, Yamauchi Yōdō, had been detained in Edo under Bakufu surveillance because of his participation in the Hitotsubashi party, the domain administration had been in the hands of Yoshida Tōyō, a reformer whose outlook had a good deal in common with that of Shimazu Nariakira in Satsuma and Nagai Uta in Chōshū. Tōyō had improved administrative efficiency, especially as it related to taxation and domain monopolies, had introduced new weapons and military methods, had encouraged "Dutch studies," and had even opened an agency for the conduct of Tosa's foreign trade at Nagasaki.

Toward the end of 1861 Tōyō set out in a memorial the advantages that he saw as deriving from all this—the creation of a Western-style navy, and the establishment of colonies overseas[18]—and early in 1862 he took steps to reorganize Tosa society as an essential preliminary to these wider aims. His reforms included a simplification of the samurai class system with a view to promoting "men of talent"; the abolition of the hereditary functions of traditional specialists, ranging from military experts to Confucian scholars, so as to create greater opportunities for men trained in Western skills; and the reorganization of the domain school to produce such men, who were to be recruited from lower as well as upper samurai. Several decrees initiating these measures were issued by the Tosa government in the two weeks beginning April 21, 1862.

One can see here an outline of much that the Meiji leaders were eventually to do, just as one can in the work of Shimazu Nariakira earlier. Certainly it was a program that gave no satisfaction to conservatives.* One must not conclude on this account, however, that it was one the "men of spirit" were automatically willing to support. In their eyes, reform at home was relevant only insofar as it might contribute to Tosa's effectiveness in the sonnō-jōi cause; hence Tōyō's failure to take up that cause condemned both man and program as pro-Bakufu. Accordingly, Takechi Zuizan's followers co-

* There is a story, recounted in Fukushima Nariyuki, pp. 58–59, that on one occasion Yamauchi Yōdō was discussing with two of his senior retainers, presumably in the context of Tōyō's reforms, the desirability of fixing the stipends of such specialists as Confucian scholars and doctors on the basis of life tenure instead of on the hereditary principle, that is, making their income in effect dependent on ability. One of the retainers pointed out that the same principle might be extended not only to Karō like himself, but even to daimyo and Shogun and perhaps the Emperor. The statement is treated as a joke; but it probably reflects a real fear among the privileged that meddling with the social order, even for lesser men like "specialists," might open the way to more far-reaching changes.

operated willingly in Tōyō's murder, an event that came, significantly enough, on May 6, 1862, immediately after the opening of the new domain school and just before Shimazu Hisamitsu's arrival in the capital.

Takechi, unlike Ōkubo and Kido, was, as we have seen, a gōshi, lacking the status for appointment to office in the domain. Nevertheless, he was now able to acquire a voice in the formulation of policy through colleagues of higher rank than himself and to press the demand that Tosa, like Satsuma and Chōshū, take a more active part in national politics. Even so, it was not until late July that he eventually got his way, and the young daimyo, Toyonori, left Kōchi for Kyōto. It was several more weeks (because Toyonori caught measles) before the mission entered the city. This at last put Takechi, who accompanied the young daimyo, into direct contact with the Chōshū loyalists and their allies at the Court.

The position in Kyōto toward the end of September 1862, then, was this. There was a large body of Chōshū samurai in the city, politically active and cooperating with members of the Imperial Court. Kido Kōin, because he held office, provided them with a channel of communication to their domain government; and the presence of their daimyo gave legality to what they did, regardless of occasional opposition from those officials who were still in Hagi, the Chōshū castle town. The young Tosa daimyo was also in the capital, increasingly in Takechi's power as his more conservative advisers withdrew to Kōchi. Like Mōri of Chōshū, he was accompanied by a considerable retinue, whose members added greatly to disorder in the streets and to the risk of serious trouble.

The Bakufu's representatives, it was clear, had neither the force nor the nerve to act against these loyalist groups, and the Court for its part was helpless in face of their unfailing readiness to interpret its wishes in the light of their own preconceived ideas. This was not least because the loyalists were developing methods of exerting an indirect control over the Court's decisions. Some shishi had been taken into the households of Court nobles who were sympathetic to their views, a situation that afforded them a measure of protection from their feudal superiors while enabling them to coordinate the activities of the samurai with moves by their kuge allies in the imperial council. Others, providing "bodyguards" for their daimyo, found it more and more possible to speak officially for them and hence to petition the Emperor in their names. Against a background of mounting terrorism,* it was difficult for senior Court officials, totally inexperienced in this kind of politics, to resist the double pressure.

Of the two men who might have had the will and the capacity to restore order in the capital, one, Yamauchi Yōdō, was still in Edo, where he had been working to prevent an open breach between the Bakufu and Satsuma over the Ōhara mission. The other, Shimazu Hisamitsu, was at this time on his way back from escorting Ōhara, but the interests of his own domain now largely superseded the loyalist struggle in his mind as the prospect loomed of a Satsuma clash with Britain over the murder of the English merchant Richardson. It is true that soon after he arrived in Kyōto on September 30 he firmly advised the Court to reject "reckless proposals" for punishing the Shogun and expelling the foreigners from the treaty ports;[19] but he quickly found that mere advice, however strongly worded, could not overcome the dominance Chōshū and Tosa had now achieved in the capital, backed as it was by threats. Nor was he prepared to commit himself to the sort of action that would have been needed to break their hold so long as Satsuma was in danger of foreign attack. On October 16 he left for Kagoshima, abandoning Kyōto to his rivals.

Just what it was that the loyalists were planning, once they had gained control of the Court, can be seen in the two important docu-

* A favorite technique was to murder relatively low-ranking retainers of the moderate or pro-Bakufu Court nobles as a warning to their superiors. There were, for example, three incidents of this kind in the middle of March 1863, when terrorism, which had been growing thoroughout the previous winter, reached its peak with the arrival of the kōbu-gattai lords in the capital. In the first, the ears of a murdered man were sent to two Court officials, Nakayama Tadahiro and Saga Sanenaru. Both resigned a few days later. In the second, the head of the victim was left outside Hitotsubashi Keiki's quarters, and one of his ears was sent to Iwakura Tomomi. In the third, a severed head was left at Yamauchi Yōdō's lodging, apparently after an attempt to get it to Matsudaira Shungaku had failed because he was too well guarded. In all cases there were warning notes to make sure that the recipients did not miss the significance of the deed.

ments we cited in the general discussion of the radical movement's aims.* One was the long memorial the twenty-two-year-old Kusaka Genzui of Chōshū had submitted to his lord at the end of August 1862 setting out his proposals for "the restoration of imperial prestige and the reform of Bakufu administration."[20] It called for determined action to make the Bakufu, in the persons of Hitotsubashi Keiki and Matsudaira Shungaku, adopt a policy of expulsion, punishing those officials who had disgraced the country by their pusillanimous attitude toward the foreigners. It also demanded that the Shogun express his respect for the throne by relaxing sankin-kōtai and surrendering to the Court the responsibility for framing national policy. As evidence of his acceptance of these terms, the Shogun was to come to Kyōto, attended by the great feudal lords.

The other document was the one Takechi Zuizan had written two months later, in October 1862.[21] In this, a draft of what he hoped would be a memorial submitted to the Court in his daimyo's name, Takechi too condemned the Bakufu for pursuing an unacceptable foreign policy and insisted on an increase of political authority for the Court; but his emphasis was different from Kusaka's, in that Takechi suggested an exercise of the new imperial authority by loyalist samurai, acting as officials, and by *several* of the great domains, not merely Tosa and Chōshū.

Kusaka's views carried the greater weight, since Chōshū had more influence at Court as well as with the samurai from other domains. Thus in November he was able to arrange a joint memorial, signed by Chōshū, Tosa, and Satsuma representatives in Kyōto,† urging that another imperial envoy be sent to Edo to demand an immediate end to "the unparalleled national dishonor" occasioned by the presence of the foreigners in Japan. The envoy was to require, in short, their "expulsion" forthwith, not a "withdrawal" after the lapse of seven or eight years, as the Bakufu had promised hitherto. Admittedly, there was no specific reference made to changes in po-

* See Chapter 6, pp. 152–54.

† The text is in *Ishin-shi*, 3: 276. The Satsuma signatures were those of the officials Hisamitsu had left in charge of the domain's Kyōto establishment. Consequently, Satsuma's participation did not reflect a change in policy but only an unwillingness to oppose the tide of opinion in the capital.

litical procedures or institutions, but it was obvious enough to all concerned that the mission would constitute a trial of strength between the Bakufu and its enemies. When Sanjō Sanetomi, a Court noble of secondary rank who was a sympathizer of the extremists and a relative of the Tosa daimyo, was appointed to carry it out, the Kampaku, Konoe Tadahiro, felt it necessary to caution him specifically to avoid an open breach with Edo.[22]

What eventually made the Sanjō mission a success was not Bakufu fear of the military support the Emperor might muster, but disagreement among those who should have been the Bakufu's defenders. Some weeks before Sanjō, escorted by Yamauchi Toyonori and 500 of his Tosa samurai, arrived in Edo in December 1862, news of his coming had already undermined the authority of the men Shimazu Hisamitsu had recently helped to power, substantially weakening resistance to the Court's proposals. On November 8 Matsudaira Katamori had threatened to resign as Kyōto Shugo unless a firmer stand was taken on foreign affairs. The Bakufu, he said, had given the impression of seeking not the punishment of foreign arrogance, but the suppression of criticism in Japan, thereby putting men's ideas in tumult. The first condition of political stability was that there be no more concessions to the treaty powers. More, because of the emotions that had been aroused, the Bakufu must show a public readiness to "act in conformity with the Imperial will." This would enable it, Katamori argued, "to calm men's minds, preserve the fabric of the State, and achieve harmony between ruler and ruled."[23]

Matsudaira Shungaku concurred in this conclusion, though he put the Bakufu's dilemma in even harsher terms. For his own part, he admitted, he regarded the opening of the country as both necessary and desirable, but the Bakufu had unquestionably gone about it in a way calculated to destroy the unity on which Japan's survival rested. By "submission to the strong and oppression of the weak" it had offended the Court and forfeited the respect of the feudal lords. By showing a preoccupation with its own narrow interests it had brought about a challenge to the Shogun's right to rule. To repair this damage, an attempt must first be made to persuade the Court to drop the demand for expulsion, on the grounds that it would inevitably bring defeat in a foreign war. If this proved successful, antiforeign turbulence could be quelled and an acceptable political arrangement negotiated with the lords. If not, then the Shogun ought to resign, loyally joining other daimyo, as one among equals, in carrying out jōi. After all, Shungaku argued, the Shogun could neither accept the responsibility for executing a policy with which he disagreed nor oppose the Emperor on whom national unity depended.[24]

Such a recommendation, coming from such a source, bitterly offended many of Edo's regular officials, leaving the Bakufu's policymakers in disarray for several weeks. The Rōjū, indeed, reversing Katamori's formula, insisted that upholding the treaties was more urgent than acknowledging the Emperor's prestige. However, a consciousness of the appalling consequences that might follow from disunity, together with Yamauchi Yōdō's constant efforts at mediation, eventually brought a compromise. Satisfying Sanjō's orders, if not the loyalists' hopes, the Bakufu accepted the principle of expulsion. It refused, however, to set a date for expulsion until the Shogun, preceded by Keiki and Shungaku, had had time to visit Kyōto. On January 26, 1863, following an exchange of letters to this effect, Sanjō left the city.

All this did, of course, was to transfer the scene of operations to the imperial capital, for nothing had really been settled. The reforming lords—Keiki and Shungaku invited Shimazu Hisamitsu, Date Muneki, and Yamauchi Yōdō to join them in Kyōto for the next phase of the discussions—looked to the Shogun's visit as an opportunity to restore order there. The "men of spirit" saw it as an occasion for extending to the Bakufu and its senior supporters the terrorist methods that had served them so well against the Court. The arrival of the great lords, therefore, beginning with Matsudaira Katamori's on February 12, 1863, and Keiki's ten days later, set the stage for a major confrontation between reformers and rebels. It involved in its wider aspects the issues of Bakufu authority and feudal discipline, as many contemporaries realized;* but it centered

* There is clearly an awareness of much that lay behind jōi in this comment on the rōnin in Kyōto in *Genji Yume Monogatari*: "During the long peace those in high places did not know the sufferings of those below them. Hence the lower samurai,

initially on the question of a date when the foreigners would be expelled.

During March 1863 the sonnō-jōi extremists, backed officially by Chōshū,* succeeded in forcing the resignation of several Court officials they distrusted, including Shimazu Hisamitsu's ally Konoe Tadahiro, the Kampaku. They also secured the appointment of a number of their own friends to office. Hence the Bakufu's representatives found it much more difficult than they had anticipated to obtain the Court's approval for the policies they proposed.

On March 29 they offered to effect the "withdrawal" of foreigners—the term expulsion (jōi) was substituted in a later draft at the Court's insistence—twenty days after the Shogun returned to Edo, that is, at the end of May or the beginning of June. This was fairly rapidly agreed to. On April 6, however, Hitotsubashi Keiki, Matsudaira Shungaku, and Matsudaira Katamori, in discussions with Yamauchi Yōdō and Date Muneki, decided that the issue of Court-Bakufu relations must also be squarely faced: either the Emperor must confirm the Shogun's right to govern Japan or the Shogun must surrender his authority entirely. This was a form of political blackmail that the Kampaku and other Court officials were by outlook and experience quite unable to resist. Accordingly, on April 24, shortly after Iemochi reached the capital, there was a public exchange of undertakings between Court and Bakufu, the one granting imperial confirmation of the Shogun's mandate, the other promising Bakufu consultation of the Court in carrying it out.

Yet the basis for this agreement was far from firm, as Shimazu Hisamitsu at once made clear when he arrived in the city on May 1, 1863. To compromise with extremists in this way, he said, would be fatal, an invitation to war both at home and abroad. The proposal for expulsion was rash, the views of the "men of spirit" violent and

who were better versed in conditions, aware of the dangerous situation in their provinces, constantly warned and advised those who had authority; but the senior officials, sunk in luxury and idleness, treated these men as turbulent agitators and would not take their advice." See Baba Bunei, 2: 33. Satow's translation in *Japan 1853–1864*, p. 65, differs in points of detail.

* With the arrival of Yamauchi Yōdō, Takechi Zuizan found his influence over the young Tosa daimyo, Toyonori, sharply reduced, with the result that the activists of Tosa played a much smaller part in these events than did those of Chōshū.

unacceptable, the Court's treatment of Keiki and his allies insulting. What was needed was a strong hand, not conciliation: a restoration of discipline over the lesser nobles; punishment of the shishi; orders that all daimyo and samurai without specific business in Kyōto return to their domains. Only on these terms was he willing to continue cooperating in kōbu-gattai, "unity of Court and Bakufu."[25]

The effect of this hard line was wholly negative. Though conviction and ambition made Hisamitsu reject a bargain that would reduce Edo's dependence on himself (and leave Chōshū's position in Kyōto almost unimpaired), he was unable, because of his quarrel with Britain, to devote troops and energy to imposing on the Court a solution of his own. Having made his declaration, therefore, he left for Kagoshima again on May 5, leaving behind him some embarrassed colleagues. Konoe Tadahiro withdrew from the affairs of the Court, and the daimyo (Matsudaira Shungaku, Yamauchi Yōdō, and Date Muneki) retired to their domains. Thus Hitotsubashi Keiki was left—at the age of twenty-six—to face Chōshū and the loyalists alone, able to look for support only to the members of Bakufu officialdom, whose power his own promotion had challenged.

Hisamitsu had shown that the particularism of the daimyo could overcome a consciousness of common interest. Keiki, for his part, was now to demonstrate an attempted subtlety that was characteristic of what the Bakufu's enemies called Edo "evasiveness." He recognized that with the departure of the great lords, the Court was more than ever at the mercy of the "men of spirit," who were demanding immediate fulfillment of the Shogun's promise of expulsion and even taking steps to put the Emperor in command of such a move. Unnerved by this and temperamentally disinclined to provoke a head-on clash, Keiki compromised. He fixed a date for expulsion, June 25, plainly meaning it to be the day on which the Bakufu would open negotiations to persuade the foreigners to leave Japan,[26] as indeed it eventually tried to do. The notice sent to the domains, however, was in some respects ambiguous on this point. Though it stated that June 25 was the date set for "withdrawal" of the foreigner (*kyozetsu*), it began by referring to their "expulsion" (jōi).* Consequently, it opened the way for a loyalist interpretation quite different from that which the Bakufu intended.

On June 25, the day appointed, Chōshū batteries fired on an American merchant ship at anchor in the Shimonoseki Straits. This was followed by attacks on French and Dutch vessels a few days later. Despite local punitive action by French and American squadrons, the Straits were closed to foreign shipping thereafter; and Chōshū defiantly informed the Bakufu that its belated orders to handle expulsion "peacefully" could do nothing to alter the fact of a conflict already begun.[27]

* The text of the announcement, dated June 9, 1863, is in *Ishin-shi,* 3: 406. The use of these apparently contradictory terms was probably due more to confusion than to conspiracy, since the Court's own announcement of June 7 (*ibid.*) omitted the preliminary reference to jōi.

CHAPTER VIII

The Failure of Expulsion

IN THE EARLY summer of 1863 the Bakufu's disunity and indecision, coupled with the self-interest of the feudal lords, especially Satsuma, provided the loyalists with the opportunity they wanted to attempt to expel the foreigner. Although they lacked an effective political structure or organized military force, they were nevertheless willing to put the country into what Aizawa Seishisai had called "the position of inevitable death" in order to rally "men of spirit" behind the Emperor's leadership and save Japan. The result was a major confrontation with the powers, leading to bombardments of the Japanese coast by foreign squadrons—twice in little more than a year.

Those Japanese who had all along described expulsion as madness were proved correct by these events. To demonstrate the superiority of Western military techniques was to demonstrate the impracticability of jōi. Accordingly, the men who had demanded expulsion had to seek a fresh outlet for the emotions on which their demand had been based: in some cases, action against those who had "betrayed" Japan; in others, a search for new forms of national strength, deriving from Western methods, which they summarized in the slogan fukoku-kyōhei, "enrich the country, strengthen the army." What is more, the failure of expulsion encouraged its opponents to rally and reassert themselves. Hence the years 1863 and 1864, with which we now have to deal, saw not only a transformation of the sonnō-jōi movement from within, but also an attack on it from without. Together they marked its end, at least in the form in which we have considered it so far.

CONFRONTATION WITH THE WEST

The announcement of June 1863 committing the Emperor and the Shogun to secure the withdrawal of foreigners from Japan, followed as it was by Chōshū's closing of the Shimonoseki Straits, brought a sharp deterioration in relations with the West and with Britain in particular. It was also a challenge to Bakufu power—and for both reasons was unacceptable in Edo.

As early as April 1863 Bakufu officials had described Keiki's acceptance of the expulsion policy as a dereliction of duty, a willingness to sacrifice "the interests of the empire as a whole" to political expediency.[1] In May, one of the Rōjū, Ogasawara Nagamichi, who was in attendance on the Shogun in Kyōto, put the point more strongly still: "Simply to obey the emperor's orders out of blind loyalty because they are the emperor's orders, making no attempt to assess their merits and demerits, would be the action of a woman. I could never believe it to be behaviour appropriate to the office of Shogun."[2] In other words, where "men of spirit" could find in loyalty to Emperor and country a duty that transcended obligations to Shogun or lord, some Bakufu officials, at least, could plead the defense of truly "national" interests as a responsibility that outweighed their respect for the Court and their own superiors.

Certainly, when Ogasawara was sent to take charge of the situation in Edo in June—and the choice of man, given the nature of the advice he had been tendering, suggests little real enthusiasm for expulsion within officialdom—he found a widespread sentiment there that any action likely to provoke "an unjust war" would be "an immense and irretrievable blunder."[3] This being so, he transformed the Court's inflammatory demands into a simple request for talks on the closing of the treaty ports, which was communicated to the foreign envoys on June 24. Even in this form it evoked language from the British chargé d'affaires that confirmed all the Bakufu's fears. Such an "indiscreet communication," the British representative stated, "is unparalleled in the history of all nations, civilized or uncivilized." It amounted, in fact, to "a declaration of war . . . against the whole of the Treaty Powers," which, if not withdrawn,

Japan would have "speedily to expiate by the severest and most merited chastisement."[4] Since Britain had at this time a substantial squadron anchored off Yokohama, the matter perforce rested there.

The fact was that Bakufu officialdom was facing two ways—not out of duplicity, as foreigners often thought, but from force of circumstance. In Kyōto Hitotsubashi Keiki, accompanied by members of the Shogun's entourage but abandoned by his former allies among the feudal lords, was aware principally of the danger of insurrection should the Court respond to the loyalist samurai pressure. Preoccupied with this, he sought to push the foreign problem to one side, to gain time, rather than pursue a settlement. By contrast, the men in Edo were more concerned at the spectacle of British warships gathering in the bay.

Earlier, when informed of the murder of Richardson at Namamugi in 1862, the Foreign Minister, Lord Russell, had stated categorically that Britain would require indemnities from both Satsuma and the Bakufu, the one for the killing itself, the other for failure to prevent it. If these were not forthcoming, he wrote, the naval commander was to take such measures "of reprisal or blockade, or both," as seemed appropriate.[5] It was the receipt of these orders in March 1863 that had led Neale, the British chargé, to exert pressure in Edo, a pressure no less great than that to which Keiki had been subjected at the Court. Indeed, once Neale made it plain that "Great Britain [would] not tolerate even a passive defiance of its power,"[6] there was little doubt of the outcome; and at the end of June Ogasawara had to promise to pay the Namamugi indemnity (almost certainly with Keiki's knowledge and complicity) before he could so much as get a hearing for his proposals concerning the future of the treaty ports.[7]

Throughout these months Satsuma had continued to ignore instructions to produce Richardson's murderers, treating the Bakufu with no more respect than did Chōshū in another context. Accordingly, having secured an indemnity from Ogasawara and rejected with indignation the proposal for the closing of the ports, Neale called on the British navy to take him to Kagoshima to present his demands to the Satsuma daimyo in person, as he had originally been ordered to do. There on August 15—the delay having been occasioned by Chōshū's activities in the Shimonoseki Straits—he began three days of fruitless talks, then ordered the seizure of some Satsuma steamers anchored offshore as a means of hastening a decision. This precipitated an exchange of shots that quickly developed into a general engagement.

In the next few hours, large parts of Kagoshima city were destroyed, including Shimazu Nariakira's famous industrial establishment, the Shūseikan. The British squadron, however, suffered damage that forced its withdrawal to effect repairs farther out in the bay. It retired to Yokohama two days later without attempting to renew either the bombardment or the negotiations that had brought it about, leaving a delighted Satsuma to acclaim the retreat as evidence of victory. Nor did the fact that at a meeting in Yokohama in December the domain's representatives agreed to pay an indemnity and to execute Richardson's murderers, if they were ever found, detract much from the success or the prestige that went with it.

The settlement of Satsuma's dispute with Britain, together with a coup d'état on September 30, 1863, that put Bakufu and Satsuma troops in command of Kyōto, made it possible for Edo and the lords to try again to reach agreement about outstanding problems. Incomparably the most important of these was Chōshū's defiance of the Bakufu in seeking a conflict with the powers. During the winter of 1863–64, therefore, at the request of Court and Shogun, the kōbu-gattai leaders gathered once more in the imperial capital. Shimazu Hisamitsu arrived on November 13 with an escort estimated at 15,000 men. He was followed by Matsudaira Shungaku (late November), Date Muneki (mid-December), Hitotsubashi Keiki (early January 1864), and Yamauchi Yōdō (early February). The Shogun himself arrived on February 22. By that date two preliminary steps had been taken to strengthen the lords at Court: Takatsukasa Sukehiro had been dismissed as Kampaku and replaced by Nijō Nariaki, and the great lords themselves—even the three tozama—had been admitted formally to participation in the imperial council. The stage was therefore set for policy discussions at the highest level.

Shimazu Hisamitsu had already made clear his own views about the decisions that needed to be taken. In December he had received through Konoe a private letter from the Emperor in which Kōmei reaffirmed his commitment to jōi but expressed his dislike for the ideas of ōsei-fukko, "restoration of imperial rule," which the loyalists had been urging. His own preference, the letter said, was for the kind of sonnō that would lead the Bakufu to show respect for the Court (so "the people at large would show respect for the Bakufu"), not for a change that would deprive the Shogun of his administrative functions.[8]

Hisamitsu, in a reply dated January 5, 1864, the day on which Hitotsubashi Keiki reached the capital, agreed that this was "entirely proper." The fact that the Bakufu had existed as an institution for so many centuries made it impossible now to restore imperial rule. Moreover, he said, "we must not cause upheaval in the government of the country while facing a foreign crisis." Therefore political extremists, whether samurai or kuge, had to be suppressed.[9] Yet Hisamitsu was no more willing on this occasion than he had been in the past—or than Bakufu officials were—to accept expulsion of the foreigners merely because it accorded with the Emperor's wishes. Rightly though the treaties were resented, he argued, they could not be overthrown, for the country lacked the necessary force. After 200 years of peace, her so-called military class was "military" in name alone, ignorant of the methods of modern warfare and deficient in morale, so that Japan had temporarily lost the ability to decide her own affairs. Only careful preparation would enable her to regain it: "The power to decide whether the country is to be open or closed has passed to the foreigners. . . . If we can resume that power, then I believe that the foreigners will come to fear *us* in their turn, but the only means of doing so is by first completing our defenses."[10] No Bakufu communication to the Court had yet put the point so brutally.

Certainly Edo was not prepared to make so open a bid to overthrow expulsion on this occasion. Chōshū's attacks on foreign ships in the Shimonoseki Straits, Satsuma's reports of victory over a British squadron at Kagoshima, news of anti-foreign unrest in Mito—all these seemed to make it more than ever necessary, for the sake of Bakufu prestige at home, to take a stand on the subject of the treaty ports. The demand that they be closed, rejected indignantly by the foreign envoys in June 1863, had already been modified into a proposal for the West's withdrawal from the one port of Yokohama.[11]

Predictably, the suggestion had been quickly dismissed by the representatives of the powers. Nevertheless, this time Edo had persisted, taking up the idea of a mission to Europe put forward by the French, which seemed to hold out the possibility of an appeal to governments over the heads of their envoys—the technique employed in 1862—or at least of a long delay in reaching a decision.

On February 6, 1864, shortly before the Shogun reached Kyōto, Ikeda Nagaaki, the Bakufu's chosen ambassador, left for France. His purpose was "to convince the foreigners of the inescapable fact that it is impossible for the Bakufu to maintain the treaties, since opposition to them is growing daily in Japan and there is bound eventually to be a complete breakdown of friendly relations if nothing is done."[12]

Senior Bakufu officials, less optimistically, saw the departure of the mission primarily as an opportunity to push the question to one side by reporting it to the Emperor as evidence that his orders were being obeyed. Almost at once they reaped their reward. On February 28 the Shogun had an imperial audience at which he received a letter, couched in the most extravagant terms, denying any wish that "the expulsion of foreigners be carried out recklessly" and calling on Iemochi to cooperate wholeheartedly with the Court and the great lords in "the great task of national revival."[13] A further letter on March 5 commended the Shogun for his efforts in military and administrative reform and for the respect he had shown the Court, and urged him to continue to promote policies that would give Japan military parity with the West, in readiness for an eventual confrontation: "Compared with the ships and guns of the arrogant foreigners, our own ships and guns will not yet suffice to quell their boldness." By contrast with this admirable behavior, the document said, Sanjō Sanetomi and other loyalist nobles had "given credence rather to the falsehoods of irresponsible *rōnin*." They had "misrepresented" the Emperor's instructions and "recklessly announced orders for the expulsion of foreigners"; and the Chōshū samurai, "without cause and in defiance of their lord," had acted on those orders. Beyond question, "the perpetrators of such violence must be punished."[14]

On the face of it this was a skillful reconciliation of the different viewpoints of Court, Bakufu, and lords. It was an assertion of the right of certain daimyo to be consulted—they were identified by name—together with an implicit recognition of the Shogun's responsibility for carrying decisions out. It was a reaffirmation of expulsion as an object of national policy, governed by the caution that it not be "recklessly" pursued. It was also a total repudiation of the imperial pronouncements of the previous summer (giving rise to suspicions that the Emperor's letters were being drafted by a Satsuma man, not by Kōmei or his ministers).[15]

The real difficulty, however, was that the imperial declaration did not effectively reconcile the ideas of Satsuma, representing the great lords, and those of Edo, reflecting the interests of Bakufu officialdom. Shimazu Hisamitsu's view of the matter can be seen in the following statement by his spokesman, the Karō, Komatsu Tatewaki: "Hitherto the Bakufu's authority has been exercised by Rōjū, who come from small domains. As things now stand, it is doubtful whether men will [continue to] bow to the Bakufu's will unless we reform the structure. Certainly we must devise a system that will elevate the lords of the larger domains."[16] Such observations gave color to the widespread belief among Edo officials that Satsuma's concern for the imperial dignity was just a cover for its own political ambitions. They therefore offered stubborn opposition to the proposal, made by Matsudaira Shungaku on March 20, that Shimazu, Yamauchi, and Date be formally admitted to the councils of the Bakufu, as they earlier had been to those of the Court.

Consequently, when Hisamitsu came forward, as he now did, with an argument against the closing of Yokohama, it was resisted by Edo on the grounds that for the Shogun meekly to carry out Chōshū's plans for expelling the foreigners one year and Satsuma's for opening the country the next would entirely destroy his prestige.[17] On March 21, 1864, when the Shogun submitted his formal acceptance of the imperial commands, he wrote: "I shall continue hereafter to carry out the emperor's stipulations: to reform the long-standing evils in administration and treat the feudal lords with the consideration due to brothers, so uniting all our strength and will in the path of duty as servants of the emperor; . . . to intensify military preparations; to establish order in the country and relieve the distress of the people; . . . and to press on with the construction of warships and cannon."[18] He also confirmed that "expulsion" would not be attempted "recklessly," adding that nothing more would be done until the outcome was known of the mission sent to Europe to negotiate the closing of Yokohama. He was, he claimed, "most anxious" that it should succeed.

To Hisamitsu, this response revealed a total misunderstanding of Japan's needs and problems. What is more, he said so at an imperial council called to discuss the matter next day, precipitating an open quarrel with Hitotsubashi Keiki—more and more becoming a spokesman for the Edo version of "Court-Bakufu unity"—in the Emperor's presence. A further meeting at Prince Asahiko's residence on March 25 completed the breach between them, for it culminated in Keiki subjecting his colleagues, including Hisamitsu, to what appears to have been a tirade of drunken abuse.[19]

The result was to break up the council of great lords once more. On April 14 they resigned their positions at Court, then withdrew to their domains, again leaving Hitotsubashi Keiki, as in 1863, to make what he could of the Bakufu's position. Events thereafter followed a familiar pattern: Edo announced its determination to close Yokohama and resisted proposals for closing the other ports; Kyōto confirmed the Shogun's rights and responsibilities while advising as usual a measure of consultation with the more powerful daimyo. The one new element, contained in imperial orders of May 25, was specific approval for the Bakufu to act against Chōshū, though it was coupled with an admonition to be "lenient," which took away some of its effect.

Equally a repetition of 1863 was the occurrence of a crisis in foreign affairs following immediately on deadlock in Kyōto. On May 30 identical letters from the French, American, Dutch, and British representatives reiterated earlier demands for the opening of the Shimonoseki Straits and the punishment of Chōshū, putting the responsibility for such action firmly on the Tokugawa government. A month later—the whole pace of events was slow, partly because Edo deliberately made it so—the Rōjū produced the standard response, citing unrest in Japan as a reason for delay and calling for the closing of Yokohama as the best means of overcoming it. Another month, or nearly, and the powers threatened to use force against Shimonoseki themselves unless the Bakufu gave convincing evidence of doing so within twenty days. Already by this time a considerable fleet was gathering in Edo Bay.

Two events intervened to extend the interval before action was taken on this ultimatum. The first was an opportunity to negotiate directly with Chōshū, afforded by the arrival at Yokohama of two Chōshū samurai, Inoue Kaoru and Itō Hirobumi, who had left Japan in 1863 to study in London. Reading of the crisis in the London papers, they had hurried back to offer their services as mediators. Rutherford Alcock, the British minister, accepted their proposal and sent them to Chōshū in a British warship, providing them with a memorandum setting out his position.[20] He was prepared, he said, to destroy the Shimonoseki batteries if necessary. Moreover, any general attempt at forcible expulsion of the foreigners by the Japanese would mean retaliation, possibly bringing a foreign army to Kyōto, "as similar conduct led the armies of Great Britain and France victoriously to Peking not five years ago." Against this, there was no desire on the part of the West to intervene in Japanese politics or "to call into question the rights and privileges of the ruling classes, so long as their existence is compatible with intercourse and trade." Hence there was no intention of harming Chōshū beyond what was necessary to maintain the treaties.

The document, if properly understood, can hardly have been reassuring to the Chōshū leaders, assuming that Inoue and Itō delivered it to them when they reached Yamaguchi on July 27. Nor was there much comfort in the opinion expressed by the two samurai that Britain had ample means of making good Alcock's threats. Inoue quoted Sun Tzu: "To know oneself and know one's enemy brings constant victory; to know one's enemy but not oneself brings victory and defeat in equal measure; to know neither one's enemy nor oneself brings defeat in every battle." The last of these was Chōshū's case, Inoue said.[21]

Yet so strongly was the tide of opinion running in the domain, now that it seemed to have been left to its fate as a result of Bakufu intervention at Court, that even this argument was to no avail. On July 30, therefore, a decision was taken that Chōshū must fight; and the British warship, which was waiting off the coast, had to return to Yokohama without a satisfactory answer. E. M. Satow, who accompanied Inoue and Itō as interpreter as far as the Chōshū coast, was privately warned by them before he left that matters had gone too far for their lord to be able to back down.[22]

The rebuff seemed to make inevitable the dispatch of a Western squadron to the Shimonoseki Straits. Before it could be made ready, however, there was yet another cause of delay, this one occasioned by the return to Japan of Ikeda's mission from Europe bringing news of an agreement signed in Paris in June. Its key provision was for the Bakufu to open the Straits within three months, using force and seeking the help of the French naval commander if necessary.[23] This clause produced consternation in Edo. Equally alarming, Ikeda insisted it was altogether justified because of the disparity of strength between Japan and Europe, and urged on the Bakufu a set of policies quite different from those it had been pursuing in recent months. What was needed, he said, was "that it [the Bakufu] will make every effort to suppress by force opposition at home and confirm the authority of the government; that it will give the foreigners no pretext for fresh demands nor any opportunity of which they could take advantage; that it will pursue a friendly policy towards them, strictly honouring the treaties and breaking none of their provisions; and that it will take steps at once to complete the equipment of our land and sea forces."[24]

This was more like Satsuma's policy than the Bakufu's and totally at variance with the bargain struck with the Court in May. If that was not enough, Ikeda had not even had the good sense to stay away longer from Japan, causing as much embarrassment by the timing of his return as by the document he brought. It is not surprising, therefore, that within a matter of days the Tokugawa council had repudiated the convention and dismissed its ambassador from his post. It also halved his stipend. The ministers of the powers promptly instructed their naval commanders to proceed against Chōshū.

Despite last-minute attempts by both the Bakufu and Chōshū to reopen negotiations, a squadron of seventeen foreign ships sailed from Edo Bay at the end of August 1864, bombarded coast defenses in the Shimonoseki Straits, and landed a force to destroy the batteries. Chōshū had undertaken urgent reforms in military organization and training in the previous year but was nevertheless unable to offer effective resistance. Accordingly, it agreed to an armistice on September 14 that provided for the opening of the Straits and a ransom for the city of Shimonoseki.

This done, the foreign representatives in Yokohama warned the Bakufu in the bluntest possible terms that they were no longer prepared to accept the argument about the dangers of public unrest in Japan as grounds for nonfulfillment of the treaties. Either the Shogun must assert his authority and carry out the agreements he had signed, they said, or they would stop making communications to him—"courteously listened to always, but wholly inoperative"—and seek satisfaction from the Emperor himself.[25] Moreover, since it appeared from documents obtained in Chōshū that the Bakufu had been a party to, if not actually responsible for, the issuance of orders calling for expulsion of the foreigners in 1863, under which Chōshū claimed to have acted, it was the Bakufu that must be held financially responsible for all that had followed from them. To this principle Edo reluctantly agreed.

Hence the final settlement of the affair, unlike that of the bombardment of Kagoshima the previous year, was made in a convention concluded in the Shogun's name. Dated October 22, 1864, it stipulated the payment of three million dollars as indemnity and ransom, subject only to the proviso that the Bakufu might offer instead the opening of Shimonoseki or another port to trade, since "the receipt of money has never been the object of the said Powers, but the establishment of better relations with Japan."[26]

ENRICH THE COUNTRY, STRENGTHEN THE ARMY

The Shimonoseki agreement, seen in retrospect, was decisive for the relations of the Bakufu with the treaty powers. From this time on, as was to be demonstrated at the end of 1865 and again in 1867, a clash between foreign demands and Kyōto chauvinism would immediately marshal the full weight of Edo's influence against the Court. No longer was it argued by the Bakufu that "troubles at home" (naiyū) were more to be feared than "dangers from abroad" (gaikan); and whatever the methods that might be employed to reduce Japan's dependence on the West, "the obstructive and disingenuous policy" of the past, as Alcock described it,[27] was not to be one of them. For the Bakufu, in fact, foreign policy almost ceased to be a matter of debate, except tactically.

The affair had an equal importance for the Bakufu's opponents. The bombardment of the Shimonoseki Straits and the destruction of the Chōshū batteries mark the end of a period in which the anti-Tokugawa movement was characterized essentially by the idea of expulsion (jōi) and the beginning of another in which the emphasis shifted to that of "enrich the country, strengthen the army" (fukoku-kyōhei). This is not to say that jōi prejudice vanished overnight simply because of a demonstration of naval superiority. Indeed, it remained a part of public sentiment for many years,* provoking, as we shall see, further attacks on foreigners and forming an important element in modern Japanese attitudes toward the outside world. Nevertheless, there *was* a change of atmosphere that one can plainly date from 1864. And since it contributed to the background against which political movements developed thereafter, it is desirable to give some preliminary consideration to it here.

Not all Japanese required the lessons of Kagoshima and Shimonoseki to convince them of Japan's need to learn from the West and abandon jōi as impracticable. In the 1850's Hotta Masayoshi, Matsudaira Shungaku, and Shimazu Nariakira had all adopted such a view and had transmitted it to a number of their subordinates and followers, including some who now counted as "men of spirit," like Ōkubo Toshimichi and Saigō Takamori. Similarly, the "Dutch" scholars of an earlier generation also had their successors, men who were sometimes able to persuade young hotheads to put their enthusiasms to more constructive use than in political violence. The relationship between Katsu Awa and Sakamoto Ryōma is an outstanding example: Katsu, the Tokugawa retainer of modest origins who became a naval expert, studying under the Dutch at Nagasaki in 1855 and founding the Bakufu's naval training establishment at Hyōgo in May 1863; Sakamoto, the Tosa gōshi of well-to-do mer-

* In Satsuma, for example, the young men sent to study in England in 1865 had to take false names and leave secretly because of the intensity of anti-foreign feeling in the domain. *Kagoshima-ken shi*, 3: 213–14.

chant stock who, pushed by his intense hatred of westernizers, had gone to Edo in December 1862 with the intention of murdering Katsu, only to be engaged by him in conversation and converted to his views.[28] Through Katsu, Sakamoto became a naval specialist, working toward what he saw as a long-term solution of the problem of foreign affairs and associating in this with men of like mind in the Bakufu, in Satsuma, and in Matsudaira Shungaku's fief of Echizen.[29] Through Sakamoto, Katsu was able to influence other Tosa rōnin to some degree and to build up a circle of friends among the "men of spirit," connections that made him an object of suspicion to Bakufu conservatives but ultimately enabled him to mediate between a defeated Bakufu and its enemies in 1868.

Other Japanese arrived at much the same conclusions by a different route, that is, through personal contact with the West and Westerners. This was not uncommon among Bakufu officials who were sent on missions abroad, for example. We have just cited the case of Ikeda Nagaaki, who returned from France in August 1864 with an agreement that he hoped would give Japan time to revolutionize her policies and position: to extend the range of her treaties, so as to find friends as well as enemies in Europe; to develop her foreign trade as the basis of national wealth; to send students abroad with a view to adopting the West's industrial and scientific skills.[30] Oguri Tadamasa, a Bakufu official not unlike Ikeda in rank and background, who had gone to America in 1860 with the embassy sent to ratify the treaty of 1858, also emerged during 1864 as an advocate of Western technology. However, he coupled this with pleas for political modernization on Western lines, designed primarily to strengthen the Bakufu's authority at home, which made his ideas more attractive to Edo than Ikeda's.[31] Oguri was put in charge of naval training at the end of the year, when Katsu Awa was dismissed because of suspected loyalist sympathies.

Among the loyalists themselves, one of the best documented examples of the persuasive effects of travel is that of Takasugi Shinsaku of Chōshū. He had never been in the true sense an advocate of national seclusion (*sakoku*), though he had opposed the opening of the ports;[32] but in 1862, when at the urging of Kido Kōin he joined a Bakufu vessel that was being sent to Shanghai to investigate the possibilities of trade, his ideas on the subject were greatly developed by the experience.

During the months of June and July Takasugi kept a diary of all he learned at what was by this time China's busiest treaty port: the great volume of foreign shipping, the size of the foreign trading establishments, the extent of the legal privileges that foreigners enjoyed. Shanghai, he noted, was like "an Anglo-French dependency," even though it belonged to China. Worse, Chinese "men of spirit" had withdrawn to Peking, leaving the city to the money-grubbers, merchants whose wealth came from their connections with British or French commercial houses. It was a depressing prospect, when he considered that it might foreshadow Japan's fate.

Yet Takasugi's response to the Chinese experience was not the negative one of rejecting all dealings with the foreigner, like so many of his contemporaries, but rather to urge that first Chōshū, then Japan, exploit the opportunities the situation offered. This meant trading at Shanghai and through Shanghai with the rest of the world, so as to acquire the wealth on which military strength depended. "However much we talk of serving the Emperor [kinnō]," he wrote, "we cannot do it without enriching the country and strengthening the army [fukoku-kyōhei]."[33] On his return he bought books for the study of mathematics, evidencing the interest in Western military science that was to bring him his first official post, commanding troops at Shimonoseki, in the following year. He also ordered a steamer for Chōshū from a Dutch trader at Nagasaki (an action taken on his own authority and subsequently repudiated by the government of the domain).

In view of Chōshū's consistent record of support for the jōi extremists in Kyōto in 1862 and 1863, it is instructive to find that Takasugi was encouraged in this visit to Shanghai, not only by the leader of the domain's moderates, Sufu Masanosuke, but also by Kido Kōin. Much the same is true of the circumstances surrounding the decision that Inoue Kaoru and Itō Hirobumi be permitted to study in England. In early 1863 Inoue had heard that Sakuma Shōzan, though refusing an invitation from Kusaka Genzui to enter Chōshū's service—an invitation that is in itself an interesting comment on the compatibility of jōi with a study of the West—had recommended that special attention be given to the creation of a navy, which in his view was the key to defense. At this Inoue and two other samurai proposed a plan for studying naval techniques abroad. Itō, who like the other three had already acquired some knowledge of English, joined in later. Sufu, Kido, and Takasugi supported the idea, and even Kusaka did not seriously oppose it. Accordingly on May 16 the plan was formally approved by the domain, which made a grant toward expenses. The young men's funds were supplemented later by a loan from the merchant representing Chōshū's interests in Edo, who also settled the details of the voyage with the British consul in Yokohama and the firm of Jardine, Matheson and Company. The party left in a Jardine's ship in June and reached London, via Shanghai, on November 4, 1863. There Matheson's arranged for the young samurai to be enrolled as students at University College London and scheduled them for a series of visits to museums, shipyards, and factories as well.[34]

We have already described how Itō and Inoue, impressed by what they saw in England, broke off their studies in 1864 in an attempt to prevent a further clash between their domain and the treaty powers. This underlines the fact that it was not so much the Shimonoseki bombardment itself as the increase in knowledge of the outside world in general, to which the bombardment contributed, that brought a number of important figures—in Chōshū, in the Bakufu, and in other parts of Japan—to recognize the impracticability of expulsion. Indeed, the result of Chōshū's military defeat was not to introduce attitudes toward the West that were new, even among the "men of spirit." It was to increase the pace at which those attitudes were extended from the few to the many. "Since the Chōshū fighting," Ōkubo Toshimichi wrote in September 1865, "the so-called irrational extremists have for the most part had their eyes opened, so that they have come to argue the impossibility of expulsion and even recommend the opening of the country; while the more enlightened domains—Hizen, Echizen, Tosa, Uwajima, and so on—are definitely inclining toward arrangements for trade."[35] Yet only a week or two later Kido Kōin, commenting on the opposition in Chōshū to his plans for obtaining ships and weapons through a British firm at Nagasaki, observed that irrationality was by no means dead, much though he disapproved of it. If the refusal to have dealings with foreigners continued, he said, jōi, which had brought Chōshū to disaster once in 1864, "will end by causing our destruction."[36]

From this it is clear that even after 1864 it was the leaders of the anti-Bakufu movement, rather than the rank-and-file, who showed the greater willingness to use Western methods for anti-Western ends. Gradually, however, they were able to overcome some of the suspicions that their policies aroused. Meanwhile, sending students abroad—the Bakufu, Satsuma, Kaga, Higo, and Hizen all did so in the next few years—together with appeals to a Confucian prejudice in favor of learning, helped to build up a nucleus of "experts" committed by self-interest to the new approach.

The cost of buying advanced types of ships and weapons proved an argument in favor of foreign trade that even the most conservative found it difficult to refute. Indeed, for many Japanese, particularly samurai, military reform was the indispensable starting point for a grudging acceptance of Western ways. Its relevance to national survival was immediately apparent to a self-styled military ruling class. More, the design and employment of modern weapons required a knowledge of science, their servicing and manufacture a training in technology, from which it was but a short step to a recognition of the organizational needs of industry and finance. In other words, through military problems it was possible to approach many of the fundamentals of contemporary Western society. This was the logic that eventually turned samurai into entrepreneurs and made fukoku-kyōhei a transmutation, rather than a flat denial, of jōi.

The impact of fukoku-kyōhei on the "men of spirit," when it was being put into practice by those whose political record they respected, like Saigō and Ōkubo in Satsuma and Kido and Takasugi in Chōshū, can be seen in a letter written by the Tosa loyalist Nakaoka Shintarō in early 1865.[37] After referring with admiration to the new leaders of Satsuma and Chōshū, he turned to the factors that had hitherto weakened Japan in her struggle with the West. They were, he said, a lack of fighting spirit, due to centuries of peace, and disunity, as reflected in the disputes between those who urged expulsion and those who sought a Western-style national strength. For his own part, Nakaoka admitted, he had moved from the first to the second of these groups, not least because of the events of 1863–64. The bombardments, after all, had been brought about by men who recognized the need for *action*, if morale were to be raised and something positive achieved; and they had attained their most important object, despite military defeat, since Satsuma and Chōshū, better led, were now moving through unity toward reform. Accordingly, if only the two domains could be brought together, it would at last be possible to secure the kind of changes—"returning all power to the throne and establishing a unity of government and worship"—that would make Japan "stronger than the enemy." For this result, the shock of defeat would have been well worthwhile: "We will look back on these days and recognise the foreign disease as a purgative that really did a great deal for our country."

There are two features of this letter that need particularly to be noted. First, it looked forward to a relationship with the West that would be much more one of equality—a prospect deeply satisfying to "men of spirit"—than anything that was likely to result from the Bakufu's apparently defeatist response to demonstrations of Western power. In other words, there was an expectation that the patriotic element in jōi could be retained even as its lack of realism was rejected. The second point is a similar one, but applies to political methods: an implicit recognition that domain governments, not "grass-roots heroes," were the proper instruments for putting such policies into effect. It was this recognition that was to characterize the next phase of the Restoration movement.

CHAPTER IX

The Failure of Terrorism

THE EVENTS OF two successive summers, those of 1863 and 1864, ended all hopes, not only of expelling the foreigners, but also of honoring the Emperor, in the sense in which the "men of spirit" had pursued these objectives hitherto. Satsuma, relieved of external pressure by the clash at Kagoshima—a paradox that did not go unnoticed by contemporaries—was left free to resume its lord's chosen task of rallying the men of moderate opinion, that is, the supporters of "the unity of Court and Bakufu," those who wished to reform Japan to the extent necessary for her defense against the West but not to disrupt society. Part of the process was a Satsuma move, in cooperation with the Bakufu, to restore order in the capital by force of arms. As a consequence, the closing months of 1863 saw an open confrontation between feudal authority and samurai extremists similar to the one Shimazu Hisamitsu had provoked among his own followers at the Teradaya in the previous year. This time, however, the conflict extended to much of Japan. In the end, the terrorists and their allies, who had controlled the Court for months, were almost everywhere defeated, suffering death, imprisonment, or house arrest, except where they escaped such punishment by flight. Only in Chōshū was this not the case, with the result that by the spring of 1864 Chōshū had become the sole refuge for the surviving adherents of sonnō-jōi.

The concentration of dissidents in Chōshū led to two further developments: one, a struggle for power within the domain between conservatives, reformers, and extremists; the other, a contest between the Bakufu and Chōshū over the extent of the Shogun's authority. Both were influenced by the foreign naval operations in the Shimonoseki Straits in the following summer; but, more important, they also played a part in shaping an anti-Tokugawa alliance, which was to achieve "the restoration of imperial rule" at the beginning of 1868.

One ingredient in the new situation was a weakening of the extremists, who now had to accept reformist leadership and control. Another, associated with it, was a transfer of emphasis from sonnō-jōi, "honor the Emperor and expel the barbarian," to fukoku-kyōhei, "enrich the country and strengthen the army," implying a change of political method as well as of policies toward the West. A third, which we will take up hereafter, was the estrangement of Satsuma from the Bakufu, growing out of Edo's attempts to exploit the failure of the loyalists to its own advantage. Together, these things made the years 1863–64 a significant turning point, a period in which the patterns of Meiji Japan—and of the forces that determined them—can first be clearly perceived.

THE REASSERTION OF AUTHORITY

As we have seen, some advocates of expelling the foreigner coupled that demand with a variety of proposals for increasing the power of the Emperor at the Shogun's expense. And because of their influence in Kyōto, they had even made some headway in giving such proposals effect. For example, in early 1863 they had persuaded the Court to create a new kind of deliberative body called the Gakushūin, which provided posts for extremist sympathizers among the Court nobles and gave the loyalist samurai themselves a channel through which they might directly—and legally—participate in the making of decisions. They had also won agreement in May for the formation of an imperial guard (*shimpei*), which was to consist of samurai, perhaps as many as 1,000, nominated by the larger domains to the number of one for every 10,000 koku of the assessed value of their lands.

Yet these measures, if ominous, nevertheless held dangers for the Bakufu that seemed more potential than real, so that little notice was taken of them during the debates about expulsion. Then, starting in June 1863, all was suddenly changed. The withdrawal of most of the great lords to their domains, followed by that of the Shogun to Edo, removed from the capital most of the troops who could have been used against the "men of spirit," as well as the commanders who might have ordered their deployment. Similarly, the departure of the Chōshū daimyo and his son, accompanied by their senior officials, ended what little restraint the Chōshū government had been able to exercise over its samurai in Kyōto. This left the field to activists like Maki Izumi of Kurume and Hirano Kuniomi of Chikuzen,* joined, once the first flurry of firing in the Shimonoseki Straits was over, by Kusaka Genzui and his colleagues from Chōshū.

Elated by the success of their efforts to bring about expulsion, the activists began to press on with plans for making good their advantage at home against a Bakufu apparently in full retreat. These plans, as Maki expounded them to the others on August 1, 1863, now foresaw: first, an announcement that the Emperor would take personal command of operations against the treaty powers (thereby arrogating to the Court the most important of the Shogun's functions); then, steps to make an imperial army a reality by furnishing Court nobles to "command" and shishi to "advise" the contingents of samurai and foot-soldiers that the domains were to provide; and finally, a major redistribution of fiefs in which the Bakufu would lose the whole of its rights in west Japan. These immediate measures were to be reinforced by a wide-ranging program of other reforms designed to secure popular support for the Court and increase the country's military strength.[1]

On August 24 the Chōshū representatives in the capital, acting in their daimyo's name, formally proposed the first step, an announcement that the Emperor would himself undertake jōi.[2] Despite hesitation on the part of Court officials and a growing coolness in the attitude of some of the great domains, fresh outbreaks of terrorism, including an attack on the residence of Matsudaira Shungaku, brought acceptance of this proposal on September 25. It was followed by the appointment of several loyalist samurai—Maki, Hirano, Kusaka, plus Kido Kōin and a number of others—

* Both men, previously arrested by their domain governments, had been released at the intervention of the Court, which in turn had been prompted by Chōshū.

to the Gakushūin to arrange the details of an imperial progress to the shrines at Uji-Yamada in Ise. This ceremonial, without precedent in many generations, was to signal the Emperor's resumption of command.

However, on the morning of September 30, anticipating this event, troops of Aizu (whose lord was Kyōto's military governor) and Satsuma seized the gates to the palace. They acted, it seems, with the knowledge of senior officials of the Court and even of the Emperor personally;[3] and they were immediately successful in bringing the loyalist "revolution" to an end. The Chōshū men on guard at the palace, their numbers already depleted by the withdrawal of some units to take part in the fighting in the Shimonoseki Straits, were driven from the capital. A group of allies among the kuge, led by Sanjō Sanetomi, retired with them. An imperial council, to which were summoned only those who were known to oppose the extremists, then abolished the posts connected with the Gakushūin. The progress to Ise was formally postponed, the shimpei ordered to disband. Nor were the rōnin forgotten. A wave of arrests directed against samurai who had quit their domains to engage in Kyōto politics, followed by decrees denying them access to noble households and instructing the domains to round them up and send them home, cleared several hundred from the city.[4] In fact, at the cost of some alarm among the general population—*Genji Yume Monogatari* noted that "just as on the occasion of a grand conflagration, there were many who abandoned the houses inhabited by their ancestors, and fled away"[5]—order was restored.

In May 1862 the Satsuma move toward Osaka and Kyōto had been enough to stimulate loyalist activity in a number of different areas: the Teradaya plot, the assassination of Yoshida Tōyō in Tosa, the overthrow of Nagai Uta in Chōshū. Similarly, in the autumn of 1863 the news of what had happened in the capital—by this time more than 70 domains possessed establishments there capable of passing the information on*—had repercussions throughout Japan. The "men of spirit," it was quickly recognized, had

* Oka, *Kindai Nihon*, p. 62. *Genji Yume Monogatari*, commenting on the change the increase in domain representation had made in the city's life, remarked that the "streets were crowded with samurai on foot and on horseback; pleasure and sightseeing became the order of the day, and the capital flourished as it had never done in any former reign" (Satow, *Japan 1853–1864*, p. 72).

overreached themselves, which made them vulnerable to attack. When they had urged expulsion, they had appealed to sentiments shared by many in high places, even the Emperor, notwithstanding an equally widespread recognition of its risks. Sonnō, too, was eminently respectable, provided it meant no more than adjusting the distribution of power in the Court's and the daimyo's favor. But ōsei-fukko, "the restoration of imperial rule," a phrase that had been occurring much more frequently in their writings during the summer months, had a revolutionary, and consequently unwelcome, ring, especially when it was a slogan in the mouths of lower samurai who plainly expected some part of the authority the Court acquired to be exercised at their own bidding, not that of their lords. Suspicion of the demand therefore prompted a wholesale closing of the daimyo ranks.[6] This ensured the extension of anti-rōnin measures on an almost national scale as soon as a lead was given.

In Tosa, for example, Yamauchi Yōdō, who had already been exerting his influence against the loyalists whenever opportunity offered, now broke openly with them.[7] Takechi Zuizan and his closest associates were arrested. Takechi was imprisoned for nearly two years before he was finally ordered to commit ritual suicide (*seppuku*). A half-hearted attempt by some of his rural followers to free him in October 1864 was savagely suppressed. By the end of that year the Tosa loyalist party had been virtually destroyed, its more determined members seeking safety in flight, the remainder lapsing into political quiescence.

Not all the shishi were prepared simply to await arrest, however, or to make their way to Chōshū in the hope of repairing their cause at some later time. Many chose, instead, to fight. This was the case, for example, in the Yamato revolt in the autumn of 1863, which we touched on in our discussion of the character and aims of the loyalists.[8] It had begun with a plan for a rising against the Bakufu during the imperial progress to Ise. Undeterred by the cancellation of the Emperor's journey and the displacement of the loyalists in Kyōto, the Yamato rebels decided to push ahead with their project. To this end a party of nearly forty rōnin, mostly from Tosa and domains in Kyūshū, had slipped away from Kyōto on the night of

September 26 and made their way into Yamato by a devious route. On the afternoon of September 29, together with about 100 local allies, they attacked the headquarters of the Bakufu steward at Gojō, beheaded the Daikan, and announced themselves, under the nominal leadership of a young Court noble, Nakayama Tadamitsu, to be taking over administration of the area in the Emperor's name. This done, they called on "the daimyo and other samurai of Yamato province" to rally to their aid, circulating for this purpose a document that is so characteristic of the extremist outlook as to be worth quoting nearly in full:

> In recent years, since the coming of the Western barbarians, the Emperor has been deeply concerned about the need to save our country from humiliation and disgrace. Yet the daimyo, by whom the land and people are held in trust, have acted as if blind and deaf to this situation. Forgetful of their duty, domains have even gone so far in evil as to oppose the imperial commands. Grievously, our country has fallen more and more into the barbarians' toils, has become a slave of the barbarian worms; and though it is the Emperor's wish to make a progress to Yamato . . . so as to put himself at the head of an army of chastisement, there are nevertheless those who seek to prevent him doing so. Overwhelmed with indignation at this, we are issuing orders for forces to assemble to meet the imperial chariot. The Court is ruler, the Bakufu [merely] lord. Those who know the relationship that should obtain between ruler and subject must join us and formulate plans.[9]

The tone and wording of this document owed much to the ideas of men like Maki and Kusaka. The proposed manner of putting those ideas into effect, however, caused the Kyōto radicals some concern. In their view, victory was to be achieved by manipulating the Court and the domains, not by isolated rebellions; and they went so far as to send Hirano Kuniomi to Yamato on September 29 in an attempt—which came too late—to forestall the rising. Indeed, even if he had not been too late, there is no certainty that Hirano would have been able to persuade the Yamato rebels to his own way of thinking, since they, especially the rōnin from the capital, were believers in a quite different doctrine: that it was the function of men of spirit to act, not to calculate, to sacrifice themselves for a cause, not to assess its chances of success.

Given this outlook, news of the coup d'état in Kyōto, which arrived soon after, did no more to get the rising abandoned than Hirano's arguments had done. But it did mean that the plan was doomed militarily. Nearby domains, acting much more promptly on Bakufu orders than they had been inclined to do in the past, sent troops against the rebels, and the embattled extremists, pressed from every side, found that there was little help to be had from the local rural population.* Moreover, their own unity did not long survive adversity. After defeat in an assault on the stronghold of Takatori on October 8, the principals began to think in terms of fighting their way to safety in other parts of Japan, rather than of extending the rebellion. Hence within a few weeks the force broke up. A few survivors, including Nakayama, made their escape to Chōshū. The rest were killed or captured by the 10,000 men who were eventually brought against them. Most of the prisoners were executed in Kyōto in the following year.

The autumn of 1863 also saw another loyalist revolt in the province of Tajima, west of Kyōto, which had similar characteristics and a similar fate.[10] There, too, the shishi had a long-standing connection with village headmen that provided a basis for the rising. The one important difference in this case was that the affair was specifically a response to the Kyōto coup d'état. It was organized by Hirano Kuniomi, who, having failed in his mission to stop the outbreak in Yamato at the end of September, found on his return to the capital that the conservatives were in control, and that the search for rōnin was being vigorously pressed. He therefore made his way secretly to Tajima, which he knew to be an area sympathetic to loyalist plans, and persuaded the leaders of a recently formed farmer militia there to agree to a rising in support of the Yamato rebels. It was to be timed for late November in order to give him time to find a suitable Court noble to act as leader and also, if possible, to win the backing of Chōshū.

Chōshū, Hirano discovered when he reached Mitajiri, was no more willing to countenance such proposals than the Court had been in Yamato. He did succeed, however, in getting Sawa Nobuyoshi, one of the nobles who had just fled from Kyōto with Sanjō,

* The fact that the Bakufu subsequently made no serious efforts to identify and punish those in the villages (apart from the gōshi) who had briefly supported the rebellion is itself evidence of how little "popular" support the rebels found.

to act as titular head of his revolt and was able to recruit some thirty or so young samurai hotheads, with whom, despite attempts by Maki and his colleagues to talk him out of the plan, he returned to Tajima.

By the time he arrived, news of the defeat of the Yamato force had reached the province, and Hirano tried to call his rising off. But the men he had brought with him from Chōshū would hear no talk of compromise. On November 22 they seized a local Bakufu office and summoned the militia to assemble, whereupon regular troops from the nearby fudai domain of Himeji began to move into the district against them. Sawa fled. The rest of the loyalists made ready to defend themselves but were promptly attacked by the farmers they had called to arms, who killed some of the shishi and captured others, then rioted through the area, venting their anger on village headmen, rich farmers, merchants, and brewers of saké. The rebellion, in fact, ended as a typical peasant revolt, which the Himeji samurai easily suppressed. Hirano was captured and was executed in Kyōto in the following year.

Events in Mito at this time, stimulated in some respects by news of the risings in Yamato and Tajima, also provide evidence of the loyalists' readiness to resort to arms.[11] After the death in 1860 of Tokugawa Nariaki, under whose patronage a sonnō-jōi party of largely middle samurai leadership had dominated Mito politics, three groups had engaged in a struggle for power there. One was a conservative, upper samurai faction, which resumed, in cooperation with the Bakufu, much of the authority of which Nariaki had earlier deprived it. Another comprised the "moderate" middle samurai reformers, led until 1863 by Aizawa Seishisai. Though reduced almost to helplessness by conflicting loyalties to Emperor and Shogun in a situation where the two seemed constantly at odds, they continued to urge, whenever they could, a "conformist" version of sonnō-jōi, not unlike that urged by Ōkubo in Satsuma. The third group consisted of the extremists, heirs to the assassins of Ii Naosuke, who found much of their support among gōshi and village headmen, as Takechi did in Tosa, for example. Unlike Takechi's followers, however, they had not been strong enough to make their domain take action on the Court's behalf during 1862 and 1863.

What changed this situation, it appears, was the widely held belief, which by the winter of 1863–64 had reached even the village level, that the events in Kyōto during the autumn had so strengthened the pro-foreign tendencies of Bakufu officialdom as to threaten the imperial decision for expulsion of the foreigner. As this suspicion deepened, funds were raised, mostly from local merchants and rich farmers, to finance an attack on the foreign settlements; a leader was found in the person of Fujita Tōko's son, Kōshirō; and on May 2, 1864, the standard of revolt was raised. Not that what followed was so very rebellious, at least initially. The force that was assembled made a kind of armed progress to the Nikkō shrines, where prayers were offered for the success of the anti-foreign crusade; a memorial was sent to the Bakufu calling for immediate action to put expulsion into effect; and letters were dispatched to Nariaki's sons, including Hitotsubashi Keiki, to remind them of their filial duty to a jōi father. Then the rebels settled down to live on the countryside and await the Emperor's commands.

These activities, though something less than radical in outward form, were an open enough challenge to authority to produce some remarkable results. The Mito daimyo, Tokugawa Yoshiatsu, wrote to Hitotsubashi Keiki to urge at least a token move of official resistance to the West—stopping trade at Yokohama, for example—lest the turbulence in Mito spread to the whole of Japan.[12] Meanwhile, the rising precipitated a renewal of political disputes within the domain that culminated a few weeks later in open civil war. The conservatives found allies in the Bakufu, which ordered other domains to intervene to help them. The moderates reluctantly came to terms with the extremists and their village supporters.

Since the farmer militia showed no taste for fighting regular samurai troops, the military outcome of such an alignment was never really in doubt. Still, it was not until late November that the main body of rebels, those led by the moderate middle samurai reformers, admitted defeat. And this was not the end of it. Several hundred irreconcilables, led by Fujita Kōshirō and another well-known loyalist, Takeda Kōunsai, were able to make their way westward through much of central Japan (in the hope of appealing to Hitotsubashi Keiki) before finally surrendering to the tozama domain of Kaga. Nearly 400 of them were then handed over to

Bakufu representatives and executed in early 1865. Another 100 were exiled, and many more were punished in less severe ways.*

There are a number of lessons to be learned from the story of what happened in Yamato, Tajima, and Mito. One, which was evident to some contemporaries even before the event, as Maki Izumi's reluctance to get involved in such affairs demonstrates, was that political action, to be successful, required the backing of one or more of the great domains. However weak the Bakufu might be in particular areas—and the ease with which the insurgents initially overcame local defenses puts such weakness beyond doubt—the strength of its counterattack was such as no mere militia could hope to contain. Hence the loyalists, if they were to move beyond terrorism to exert a genuine and lasting influence on events, had somehow to reconcile their activities with the prejudices of feudal authority, or work it to their will. After 1863–64 more of them were ready to face up to this reality.

A second point concerns the relationship between social structure and Restoration politics. The shishi, we have seen, comprised broadly two levels of society: middle samurai, men of no great wealth but respectable standing; and lower samurai, characteristically members of a rural elite that included a number of non-samurai village headmen and the richer farmers.† It was these lower samurai who provided a substantial proportion, if not the majority, of the rōnin who played a leading part in Yamato and Tajima. It is not surprising, therefore, that their local connections were with men very like themselves, the gōshi, the village officials, the well-to-do of the countryside. These rural leaders in turn were sometimes able to call the rest of the farmers to their aid because of the power

* By contrast only twenty-nine of the "moderates" were sentenced to death (*Ishinshi*, 4: 109–10). One is tempted to conclude that the disparity related more to the social status of the victim than his crime.

† I am conscious that the validity of this statement depends partly on the assumption that the pattern in Tosa (and to a lesser extent Mito) was characteristic of the movement as a whole. Some evidence to support it was given in the discussion of shishi social origins in Chapter 6. More can be adduced from what happened in Chōshū, as described later in this chapter. The situation in Satsuma can be held to be consistent with it, though less confidently. Nevertheless, I am left with a desire for more information about the social base of politics in other areas, especially those that were not so prominent in these years and have therefore been less studied.

they exercised over them; but they were also the common objects of village resentment and distrust, so that as soon as feudal authority was exerted against the rebels the poorer farmers were likely to attack them, too, or at least abandon them, as happened in Mito.[13] From this, one may conclude that there was no general peasant support for the loyalist movement as such. There is no clear indication that "samurai" leaders made themselves the representatives of "peasant" discontent, or that the rural rich sought to redress the grievances of the rural poor. Rather, the evidence of the risings strengthens the case for saying that a line of demarcation had already been drawn within the village between those the Meiji state was to favor—the landlords of modern Japan—and those whose disabilities it was to confirm.

Of more immediate relevance to pre-Restoration politics was the effect these events had on samurai thinking, that is, on the reactions of samurai as members of a dominant class to a form of unrest that seemed to threaten the social order. Essentially, they underlined the differences between middle and lower samurai. Because middle samurai had the status that made it possible for them to try to control, or at worst infiltrate, the governments of their domains, they tended to deprecate forms of radicalism that operated outside or in conflict with the regular feudal structure, since these were likely to alienate upper samurai opinion and so make more difficult the task of gaining power. Significantly, opposition to Hirano's proposals about Tajima came from his loyalist colleagues, not the domain conservatives. So did the attempt to hold back Nakayama from revolt in Yamato. In Mito, it was clearly with some reluctance that the moderates followed the extremists' lead in defying their lord. Consequently, the failure of all these enterprises, which served to discredit rebellion as a technique, also weakened the position of those, the lower samurai, who had insisted on it against the advice of their friends; and the new direction that the loyalist movement took after 1864, notably in Satsuma and Chōshū, was marked by an emphasis on hirazamurai status for its leaders (several who did not have that status by birth acquired it by promotion) as well as by a political method more in conformity with the needs of a feudal society.

Yet if the "men of spirit" had failed in their purpose and were to play little personal part in the final restoration of imperial rule, they still cannot be lightly dismissed. Much of what they did, it is true, was negative: they were men who were "against" things, not "for" them; men who destroyed, rather than built; men who would spend lives recklessly, including their own, but not make governments. They lacked organization, recognized too many "leaders," preferred slogans to policy. Nevertheless, they had wrought changes that were both important and, as it turned out, irreversible. This was not least because they helped to break down the "vertical" element in the structure of Japanese society, both politically and ideologically. On the one hand, they took the ideas of men like the Mito scholars and made them part of the common currency of debate, contributing to the development of a public opinion that was increasingly national, rather than regional, in its scope. On the other, they established political relationships that cut across feudal boundaries (even though they never entirely transcended feudal loyalties), thereby laying the basis for an alliance of domains that could operate at a level quite distinct from an alliance of lords.

What is more, because they condemned the men of authority in Edo and the castle towns, turning for support to those whom Yoshida Shōin had called *sōmō eiyū*, "humble heroes" (the lower samurai, perhaps, though it was a term that in its widest application could be used of many who were not really samurai at all), the loyalists, as we said at the beginning, had brought into active politics a segment of society that had not previously been entitled to a voice in the conduct of affairs: the members of a rural elite, men whose wealth and standing depended on the control of a changing countryside, including some who wielded power as landlords or entrepreneurs. For this reason it is tempting to see the "men of spirit" as critics of feudalism, as well as rebels against feudal government, signaling the emergence of a new ruling class within the lower levels of the old. Certainly they themselves had a certain consciousness of class and its relevance, as did those who suppressed them.

Against this, it is difficult to find anything like an avowal of social purpose in what the shishi said and did, a program, an organized idea of how to change the order of things to their own advantage. For all their talk of "men of talent," for all their denigration of inept daimyo and parasitic samurai, their proposals for reform never seem to have envisaged a fundamental transfer of authority *downward* through society, as distinct from a transfer laterally from Shogun to Emperor and lord. They were revolutionary in deeds, not in ideas, so that it is not easy to give them an ideological label. "Loyalists," "radicals," "extremists," "terrorists," we have called them, terms that are evocative and imprecise, not analytical. For the objective they ascribed to themselves was not revolution, but jōi, the expulsion of the barbarian, conceived as a first step to the salvation of Japan; and the fact that this reflected a patriotic emotion rather than coherent social aims made it easier to incorporate the surviving loyalists thereafter into a movement that diverted their emotions to the attainment of a new set of ends: national wealth and strength (fukoku-kyōhei) and the Bakufu's destruction (tōbaku). An important stage in this process was already beginning in Chōshū.

LOYALISM AND CHŌSHŪ

The manifestations of conservative reaction in late 1863 and 1864 —the attacks on rōnin in Kyōto, the campaign against Takechi's followers in Tosa, the suppression of the Yamato and Tajima revolts, the defeat of loyalists and reformers in the Mito civil war—had the effect of making Chōshū the sole remaining focus of loyalist hopes. Most of the rōnin who sought refuge there were permitted to establish themselves at or near Mitajiri, a port on the Inland Sea.[14] There they formed a number of irregular "companies" (*shotai*), which were to be available to assist the domain's troops in the event of foreign or Bakufu attack. These companies reinforced units of Chōshū irregulars, locally recruited since June 1863 among men with much the same attitudes and social background as the rōnin themselves, with the result that a new radicalism, stemming from a body of activists who were not only armed but organized, was introduced into Chōshū politics from this time.

The Chōshū companies proper, of which the most famous was called the Kiheitai, originated with a proposal by Takasugi Shinsaku, when he was appointed to a command at Shimonoseki in the summer of 1863. In a memorial submitted on July 22 of that year, he had argued for the creation of additional rifle units, trained on Western lines, to supplement the domain's military establishment. They should be composed mainly of ashigaru and other lower samurai, Takasugi suggested, among whom, after all, "there are many men of spirit." In these units, neither recruitment nor promotion was to depend primarily on status. Middle samurai would be permitted to serve in them, if they wished, but they would have to do so alongside rear-vassals (baishin) and lesser samurai of other kinds, with whom they would work "without distinction."[15] Yet the force so formed, if irregular in these respects, was to be a disciplined and semipermanent one, cooperating with the samurai of the castle town on something like equal terms. This made it quite unlike earlier militia units, which in Chōshū as elsewhere had been local, part-time levies commanded by the appropriate village or domain officials and called out only in emergency.

Once Takasugi's idea had been approved in principle—and this may well have been possible only in the context of plans for "expulsion"—several companies were formed,[16] some by samurai like Takasugi himself acting with the knowledge and support of the domain, some by enthusiastic loyalists financed by wealthy farmer or merchant sympathizers and only subsequently given recognition. In consequence, the units varied a good deal in size (anything from 100 to 500 men) and were often drawn from a single locality. In theory, their officers were chosen by ability, not rank; but in practice this usually meant, as it did also for promotion within domain officialdom, choosing from among those who had hereditary military standing, like hirazamurai and ashigaru, not from those who were outside the ranks of samurai entirely. Many of the rank-and-file, too, had samurai or quasi-samurai status, the proportion ranging from about 25 to 45 per cent, according to the units studied. Another 30 to 50 per cent can be identified as "commoners," drawn predominantly from families of well-to-do farmers and village officials.

So described, it is apparent that the recruits to these companies came from approximately the same segments of Japanese society as the Tosa rōnin and the rebels of Yamato and Tajima: men on the fringes of the samurai class, some within it, some outside, who accepted the canons of the ruling elite (though not always themselves accepted by it) and formed part of a network of families that exercised a good deal of authority in the countryside and the castle town.

Like the "men of spirit," most were first moved to act because of patriotism, albeit a patriotism attaching more to the domain than to Japan at large; that is, they recognized that the events of the summer made a foreign attack on Chōshū inevitable and offered themselves as ready to defend the domain, if need be to die for it. But once they had been mustered and brought into the major centers like Shimonoseki and Yamaguchi, this simple patriotism quickly acquired political overtones. The refugees from Tosa and Kyōto, the survivors from Yamato and Tajima, Chōshū's own loyalists, like Kido and Kusaka and Takasugi, who commanded them, all blamed the danger that Chōshū faced as much on Japanese who ought to have prevented it—the Bakufu and its allies in the domains—as on the foreigners. To them, expulsion was as inseparable from loyalism as it is was from gunnery and coast defense, was as much a matter of political duty as of military skills. To be sure, such ideas cannot have been altogether new to the recruits, even those from the villages, who had shown enough awareness of the world they lived in to have wanted to volunteer.* What *was* new, though, and exciting, was to mix with men to whom these ideas were not just words, but a framework within which to act. Their presence made the atmosphere in Chōshū as heady as that in Kyōto a few months earlier, contributing to an intensification of sonnō-jōi sentiment and a consequent increase in the influence of the loyalist leaders.

The effect of the change was seen as early as October 1863, when news of the September coup in Kyōto led to a successful demand by conservative samurai in Chōshū that the moderates, led by Sufu

* Except, perhaps, those whose financial position suggests a possible financial motive for volunteering; there were certainly some members of the rural poor in the shotai (see Craig, *Chōshū*, pp. 272–76). All the same, modern Japanese scholars (e.g., Seki, Tanaka Akira, Haga) tend to agree that such men were probably recruited by, and were firmly under the control of, leaders who were drawn from the village upper class.

Masanosuke, be dismissed. This was achieved by marshaling troops outside the daimyo's residence, a demonstration of the relevance of military force to bureaucratic power that was not lost on the shotai. Almost at once, by marching on Yamaguchi, the castle town,* they restored Sufu to office. More, they ensured that their own leaders, Takasugi and Kusaka, received official appointments, thereby indicating that Sufu's followers, though still controlling the domain government, could no longer do so without loyalist support. Two weeks later Kido Kōin, returning from Kyōto, was promoted to a key post on the daimyo's personal staff.

Yet if the support of the irregulars strengthened the hand of Takasugi and Kido in dealing with officialdom, it was also an embarrassment to them, since it could be mobilized in aid of policies that they condemned as reckless or naïve. This became clear in Chōshū's long dispute with the Bakufu and the Imperial Court arising from its attempt to carry out expulsion. In February 1864 the Court gave way to Bakufu demands to condemn Chōshū for its action in the Shimonoseki Straits, on the grounds that it had deliberately exceeded the intention of the orders issued. As a result, plans were formulated for the domain's punishment, if its leaders refused to submit, a step that aroused much anger in Yamaguchi. There it was held, not altogether honestly, that what was done was done at the Emperor's and the Shogun's own command. This made any attempt at punishment improper.

The shotai, in particular much incensed, demanded an armed foray against the capital to regain access to the Emperor's person, since it seemed obvious to them that his public utterances, so very different from those of the year before, could only be explained as being dictated by their daimyo's enemies. Kido and Takasugi—like Ōkubo, they were becoming more "responsible" in their attitudes with every promotion—urged that the wiser course would be to organize opinion among the lords, opposing one feudal coalition with another. They found, however, as others before them had

* The domain government of Chōshū moved on two or three occasions in these years between Hagi, the traditional (and conservative) center on the Japan Sea coast, and Yamaguchi, which was nearer the Inland Sea and the areas from which the shotai were mostly drawn. The change of location generally coincided with a shift in the balance of power in the domain. See Tanaka Akira, *Meiji*, pp. 131–32.

found in similar case, that wisdom appealed little to fanatics. Kijima Matabei, commander of the largest of the irregular companies, the Yūgekitai, arguing in favor of an expedition to Kyōto at a meeting with Takasugi at the beginning of March, was blunt about it. "The trouble with all of you is that you read too many books," he said. "Because you read books, the word 'afterwards' is always uppermost in your minds. How can one have an army with such lukewarm ideas?"[17] Indeed, Kijima was willing to take his men to the capital against the orders of his lord if necessary. Kido, by contrast, wanted the domain government to suppress the agitators and assert its authority. "Assuredly," he had written a few days earlier, "unless those above possess authority, all men will follow their own bent and we shall never attain our ends."[18]

There was an element of social prejudice as well as a difference of political attitudes in this disagreement, implicit in the remarks of Kijima and Kido, explicit on another occasion in Takasugi's reference to one of the Kiheitai leaders as "a baseborn fellow."[19] There was also a parallel with the earlier debates between the two groups we have distinguished as "politicians" and "activists," in that Kido and Takasugi, helped by Kusaka, tried for tactical reasons to restrain the extremists in the shotai, much as Ōkubo had done in Satsuma and as Kusaka himself had done in the case of the Yamato revolt. They failed, despite their own prestige as "men of spirit."

When the Kyōto talks between the Bakufu and the lords broke down in April 1864, it became obvious that Edo would exploit its dominance over the Court to pursue a vendetta against Chōshū. At this, Kusaka threw in his lot with the extremists. So did most of the rōnin and the seven Court nobles who had withdrawn to Chōshū from Kyōto the previous autumn. Takasugi was then arrested; Sufu and the other moderates were overborne; and on June 30, 1864, orders were given to send troops to the capital. In late July the first of them reached Osaka, spearheaded by irregulars, whence they moved to take up positions around Kyōto.

For nearly four weeks thereafter a dangerous state of watchfulness and suspense prevailed as men within the city urged the representatives of the Bakufu to compromise while moderates outside it sought to dissuade the Chōshū hotheads from attack. In the end, however, almost inevitably, the extremists lost patience. On August 20 three Chōshū columns moved on Kyōto, assaulting defenses manned principally by Satsuma and Aizu.[20] One, led by Kijima's Yūgekitai, fought its way almost to the palace gates. Another, which included Kusaka Genzui, Maki Izumi, and many of the rōnin, captured Takatsukasa's residence before being checked. A third, comprising the guard from Chōshū's office at Fushimi, turned back on meeting resistance in the suburbs. By afternoon the battle was over, the Chōshū forces scattered and in retreat, the Bakufu's authority, if not its dignity, preserved. Equally important, large numbers of the more radical loyalists were dead, for many who were not killed in the fighting preferred suicide to capture. Thus the death roll eventually included Kusaka and several of his closest colleagues from Chōshū, Maki and two of his companions from Kurume, and a dozen or so of the other rōnin leaders. This meant that the most famous of the remaining shishi had been removed from the political scene.

One result of these events was to confirm Edo's ability to dominate the Court, subject to Satsuma's cooperation. Another, related to it, was once again to disturb the political balance within Chōshū. Sufu's government, weakened by the "disgrace" of defeat in Kyōto and discredited still further by the foreign operations against Shimonoseki immediately afterward, was now threatened with disaster by Bakufu reprisals. Imperial orders of August 24 declared Chōshū rebel and called on the lords to furnish troops for a punitive expedition. This force assembled at Osaka in October under the command of Tokugawa Yoshikatsu of Owari and had the object, as many thought, of securing a reduction in Chōshū territory, in addition to the punishment of those who had attacked the palace. Certainly it had the effect of putting pressure on Chōshū, in face of which the alliance between the moderates and the loyalists crumbled. Kido, who might have done something to preserve it, had been in hiding since escaping from Kyōto in August and remained outside the domain. Takasugi, because he had signed the truce with the foreign naval commanders in September—he had been released from prison to take charge of the fighting against them—had incurred the hostility of the jōi extremists, which temporarily cost him much of his following. Sufu committed suicide, a gesture of atonement for policies that had failed. In these circumstances, by late October there was nothing to prevent the Chōshū conservatives under Mukunashi Tōta from returning to office; and before long they had given an indication of what this was to mean in terms of relations with the Bakufu by ordering the suicide of the three senior officials who had commanded the troops sent to Kyōto in July. The action, they hoped, might satisfy Edo and bring a more lenient settlement.

That they were successful in saving their lord from serious punishment and their domain from any substantial loss of lands they owed as much to Saigō Takamori as to their own efforts. Saigō, recalled from exile earlier in 1864, largely at Ōkubo's persuading, had commanded the Satsuma forces in Kyōto in August and had subsequently been appointed to Owari's staff for the campaign against Chōshū. It was a duty that he undertook at first with some enthusiasm, seeing it as an opportunity to break the power of a rival Satsuma had cause to fear.[21] However, a conversation with Katsu Awa early in October aroused in him the suspicion that in the end this might be less to Satsuma's advantage than it was to the Bakufu's,[22] so that news of the conservative resurgence in Chōshū found him ready to compromise. "Somehow to use Chōshū men to punish Chōshū men," he wrote to Ōkubo, would be better than fighting: first, such a policy would avoid strengthening Chōshū's will to resist, and hence be a more economical way of getting the domain to submit, and second, it would ensure that military resources, more urgently needed for use against the West, were not wasted in civil war.[23]

These arguments, especially the financial one, proved attractive to Owari, too, when Saigō put them to him on November 23. Accordingly, Saigō was authorized to mediate; and during the next few weeks, through messengers and by making a secret visit to Shimonoseki, he worked out an agreed set of terms: Chōshū was to make a formal apology, was to renounce the protection it had afforded the kuge refugees from Kyōto (who were to be transferred to a domain in Kyūshū), and was to promise to suppress the irregular companies, on whose members, together with the three Karō already dead, most of the blame for the affair was put. Owari accepted the terms for the Bakufu and announced from his headquarters at Hiroshima on January 24, 1865, that the expedition, having accomplished what it set out to do, would now disperse.

As one might expect, the whole trend of Mukunashi's policy, leading to this settlement, was anathema to the Chōshū irregulars, who from the first had been resolved to defend their domain against its enemies, whether Japanese or foreign. On December 2, 1864, the Kiheitai and other units therefore submitted a memorial condemning the growing signs of a submission to Bakufu demands, which they described as "contrary to the imperial wishes, a breach of loyalty toward the Court." They insisted that Chōshū's honor must be put before its safety. "The distinction between good and evil, the identification of right and wrong," they claimed, "do not depend on whether one lives or dies." More practically, they called for the promotion of "men of talent," the punishment of the conservatives, the return of the daimyo to Yamaguchi from Hagi, and the completion of preparations to fight. Threats to disband them (though ineffective because the shotai were largely self-sufficient in arms and could rely on the rural upper class for other kinds of support) exacerbated these discontents.[24]

Takasugi quickly proceeded to exploit this situation. On January 13, 1865, he persuaded the Yūgekitai, now under the command of Ishikawa Kogorō, together with a smaller company led by Itō Hirobumi, to make an attack on Shimonoseki. Despite some initial success, the two units were unable to maintain their position for lack of other help, so that Takasugi had to call the operation off. However, a similar raid, launched two weeks later, produced better results. This time the Kiheitai, led by Yamagata Aritomo, and Inoue Kaoru's company rallied to the insurgents. When domain forces were sent against them, other shotai joined the fray, precipitating general fighting. A major engagement followed on February 6 and 7. Though it produced no clear victory for either side, it enabled the irregulars to move on Hagi. At this point, middle samurai "neutrals" in the castle town, turning against the conservatives in the name of unity against external threat, forced a change of government and the opening of discussions with the rebels.*

* These two groups, the neutrals and the conservatives, are analyzed by Umetani in "Meiji ishin-shi," pp. 339–41. He notes that the conservatives were dominated by upper samurai, including six *yori-gumi* of 300 to 1,300 koku, whereas the leaders

Thus on March 12 the shotai forces entered the town. The daimyo was duly escorted back to Yamaguchi at the end of the month, and the loyalist leaders were gradually restored to office thereafter.

There are several things in the Chōshū story that deserve emphasis: the importance of Takasugi's initiative and of the backing he got from Itō, Inoue, and Yamagata at the moment of crisis; the reluctance of most of the irregulars to act against the daimyo's government, despite their objections to it, until Takasugi brought about a conflict in which they had virtually no choice; the extent to which "domain patriotism" provided a basis for the reassertion of unity, even in a situation like this. Nevertheless, these are matters of narrower significance than those that are raised by a consideration of the social and ideological character of the successful movement, especially since there is wide agreement that events in Chōshū provided "a scale model of what took place nationally three years later,"[25] that is, a kind of Meiji Restoration in miniature.

It is true that the experience of Chōshū was not in all respects typical. In no sense, for instance, can the daimyo, Mōri Yoshichika, be said to have played a positive role in politics, such as that played by Shimazu Hisamitsu in Satsuma, Yamauchi Yōdō in Tosa, and Matsudaira Shungaku in Echizen. This meant that a rather different set of conditions governed the struggle for office in Chōshū between conservative, moderate, and extremist samurai, compared with other politically active domains. Similarly, the loyalists seem at all times to have been stronger in Chōshū than elsewhere, with the result that they had to make fewer compromises with authority in 1862–64, just as they were able, as others were not, to seize power by force and hold it after January 1865. Yet despite these differences it can be convincingly argued that both the social basis of the loyalist movement in Chōshū and the policies to which its victory gave rise were closer to the patterns of "Meiji absolutism" than was the case in any other area. As Tōyama sees it, the Chōshū case involved

---

of the moderates, or neutrals, included thirteen middle samurai (of whom three had under 100 koku, five had between 100 and 200 koku, and five had over 200 koku, the highest being 363 koku). However, Craig, *Chōshū*, pp. 260–62, argues that the difference in status between the two groups was not really as significant as this might suggest; Mukunashi, after all, though the leader of the conservatives, was a middle samurai of only 46 koku.

an alliance in which a rural upper class, maintaining control of the countryside and suppressing peasant revolt, supported and was supported by a segment of the lower samurai, who were thereby enabled to acquire political authority—an authority that was then used to pursue a program of fukoku-kyōhei, "enrich the country, strengthen the army."[26] Craig, too, accepts much of this analysis, even though in general he emphasizes the continuing strength of traditional elements in Chōshū society and denies that the activities of the shotai were evidence of "a rising tide of revolution."[27]

Leaving aside at this point the question of whether the rural components in this alliance can properly be labeled either "bourgeois" or "revolutionary," as they sometimes are, it is clearly desirable to try to assess their influence and role. One way of approaching the problem is to examine the change in the structure and personnel of the Chōshū government after the civil war in early 1865, since this is what immediately resulted from the loyalists' actions. Another is to consider the nature of the policies that government pursued, in order to assess the extent, if any, to which these were relevant to, or directly reflected, the interests of the landlords and samurai in this putative coalition.

One fact becomes immediately apparent: that in Chōshū, as in Satsuma and Tosa, samurai birth was still the essential qualification for office of any consequence.[28] Many posts continued to be filled by the moderates, Sufu's successors, most of whom were hirazamurai; and the leading loyalists, more powerful now because of the support of the shotai, were in fact of similar status. In a key position, immediately below the two Karō, was Kido Kōin (born 1833), a middle samurai with a stipend of 90 koku and a good deal of bureaucratic experience, most recently in the daimyo's personal secretariat. Despite his reputation as a "man of spirit," Kido had argued against the attack on Kyōto in 1864 and had not returned to Chōshū until May 1865, when the struggle between the conservatives and Takasugi's companies was already over. So neither in background nor in outlook, except for his loyalism, did he differ greatly from a moderate like Sufu.

At the next level down came a group of posts concerned variously with local government, finance, and secretarial duties, which were all of approximately equal standing. Kido himself held one of them, concurrently with his other office. Among his colleagues were the moderates' leaders, Kaneshige Yōzō (60 koku) and Yamada Uemon (100 koku), together with the loyalists Takasugi Shinsaku, Maebara Issei, Hirosawa Saneomi, and Ōmura Masujirō. Takasugi (born 1839), son of a middle samurai of 200 koku, pupil of Yoshida Shōin, and founder of the shotai, has appeared often enough in this account to be familiar. Maebara (born 1834), also ranking as hirazamurai, had been closely connected with Kusaka Genzui and did not secure an appointment in the domain until 1863, though from then on he seems to have had a straightforward official career. Hirosawa (born 1834), a middle samurai of 104 koku, had surprisingly neither attended Yoshida Shōin's school nor joined the irregular companies, being simply an official of loyalist sympathies who had worked with Takasugi in military planning during 1863. The fourth member of the group, Ōmura (born 1824), was not only a good deal older than the rest, but also of a very different experience. Son of a fief doctor and student of Rangaku, he first served Date Muneki of Uwajima as a military reformer before being recalled to Chōshū and raised to hirazamurai rank in 1860. Indeed, if Hirosawa was principally a bureaucrat, Ōmura was preeminently an expert in Western skills.

Of these comparatively well-born loyalists, only Kido Kōin made a distinguished reputation in the Meiji government. Takasugi died prematurely in 1867; Ōmura was assassinated in 1869 and Hirosawa in early 1871; and Maebara, unable to adjust to a changing world after the Restoration, was executed for rebellion in 1871. Hence it was those who at this time filled some of the lesser Chōshū offices whose names are better known: Inoue Kaoru (born 1836), son of one hirazamurai, adopted by another (220 koku), who had studied in London and had commanded one of the shotai; Itō Hirobumi (born 1841), son of a farmer-turned-merchant with something like ashigaru rank but brought up as a samurai, who had attended Yoshida Shōin's school, then had been successively an activist, a student in London, and a shotai commander; and Yamagata Aritomo (born 1838), member of an ashigaru house of small stipend but long standing, who achieved political importance almost entirely because he rose to command the Kiheitai.

In social standing and experience, not least in an ability to bring together those who could manipulate feudal authority and those who could in some degree use Western skills, this group of men had much in common with the early Meiji bureaucracy as a whole.[29] They also had direct links with loyalists among the village headmen and local merchants.[30] For example, Inoue's family was friendly with that of the wealthy village headman (Ōshoya) Yoshitomi Tōbei, who helped to finance Takasugi and knew Sufu well enough for the latter to have committed suicide in his house; Yoshitomi's nephew Hayashi Yūzō, another village headman, was Yamagata Aritomo's patron; and Itō Hirobumi's father was descended from a branch of what may well have been the same Hayashi family. A network of relationships by marriage and adoption, such as existed between the Yoshitomi, Hayashi, and Akimoto houses—Akimoto Shinzō, village headman and merchant, organized and led one of the irregular companies—extended the scope of these contacts. Accordingly, the great social gulf that existed between "samurai" and "peasant" did not altogether preclude the possibility that in Chōshū, as in Tosa, men of each category, including some who were less than samurai on the one hand and more than peasant on the other, could work together for political ends.

Yet it does not follow that the ends in question were necessarily "revolutionary," however that term may be defined. The great issues in Chōshū during 1865, insofar as they are documented, centered on defense, conceived in terms of a likely resumption of attacks by the Bakufu or the foreigners, or both; and reform within the domain was subordinate to them, in that it was designed to further the defense effort, not to constitute an object of policy in itself.

In a memorial Kido submitted at the time of his appointment to office in June, he argued that what was needed was an effective distribution of military forces, including the irregulars (over whom proper discipline must be asserted), plus conscientious administration and an avoidance of waste.[31] In the long run, these measures would provide the unity and strength that Chōshū would need if it was to lead an alliance of domains against the Bakufu and remove the leadership that hampered the country in its efforts to resist the West. Edo had been provocative in its actions against Chōshū, he said in a later document, "driving our people more and more into a mood of desperation" when it ought to have been promoting national unity by "governing in peace."[32] Fortunately, Chōshū had survived the assault, as it had that of the foreigners in 1864. What is more, the experience had left it in a position to propose a "treatment" that might be effective in curing "the illness of Japan." "A skilled physician, who could now lay lasting foundations for peace at home and who could immediately initiate a national policy for enriching the country and strengthening the army, could bring relief to all Japan," he said. By contrast, to leave matters in the hands of the "unskilled physicians" in charge hitherto "may only make things worse."*

Like most policy statements in this period, Kido's letter and memorial were not at all precise about the ingredients of the "cure" he was proposing. It was clearly to include a reduction in the Shogun's authority, carried out in the Emperor's name. It might even go so far as "destruction" of the Bakufu (tōbaku), though that did not necessarily imply any specific institutional alternative, such as might lead to the destruction of the domains or of the feudal structure itself. Yet because the fact of victory in the civil war had imposed on Chōshū's loyalists the responsibility for day-to-day decisions, we can to some extent give content to Kido's phrases by examining what he and his colleagues actually did in their own domain.

One thing they did, as was to be expected from what we said of their views in the previous chapter, was to abandon jōi for fukoku-kyōhei, the pursuit of national wealth and strength. This, Takasugi argued, was *kinkoku*, "serving the country" (an apparent play on words, evoking the idea of kinnō, "serving the Emperor"), for wealth, which depended on opening Japan to foreign trade, produced military strength, without which "service" was not possible.[33] For this reason, he believed, as well as to avoid "falling into the

* *Kido Kōin monjo*, 2: 90. Kido's natural family—he was adopted as a small boy—was that of a fief doctor. Since a number of other Meiji leaders also had this medical element in their family background (e.g., Ōkubo and Ōmura), as did many of the shishi (e.g., Kusaka and several of the Tosa rōnin), one is led to speculate how far this made them part of an intelligentsia that was more likely than most of the population to recognize the superiority of certain newly available Western skills, other than simply medical ones.

foreigners' evil toils,"[34] Chōshū must open Shimonoseki. Itō put the emphasis a little differently—arguing that trade was at once essential to Japan's survival and dangerous without political unity at home[35]—but he, too, supported the Shimonoseki proposal, as did Inoue. However, fierce opposition from members of the irregular companies prevented realization of the plan. Indeed, Takasugi, Itō, and Inoue were all forced to go into hiding for a time at the end of April 1865 for fear of reprisals from advocates of expulsion. Nevertheless, Kido supported their proposal when he arrived back in the domain the following month, with the result that a decision was eventually taken to engage in foreign trade to the extent of importing ships and weapons through a British firm at Nagasaki.[36]

Steps were also taken, principally by Takasugi and Ōmura, to reorganize and re-equip the domain's military forces on Western lines, a process that involved among other things an attempt to bring the irregular companies under some degree of central control. That step has prompted a debate about how far the policy's motives were political, that is, aimed at detaching the shotai from the "bourgeois" who had helped to form them and putting them more fully under "bureaucratic-absolutist" leadership (a preview, it is asserted, of what happened generally throughout Japan after 1868).[37]

Clearly, an imposition of discipline of this kind had a logical place in strictly military reform. It was also a natural enough action for those recently come to power and conscious that some of their allies and followers did not agree with them on certain important issues, like expulsion. For this reason it is probably fruitless to try to settle the argument one way or the other on the evidence available. But at least the fact of what was done, regardless of its motive, casts doubt on any claim that Kido, Takasugi, and the other samurai leaders of the Chōshū government were the creatures of their shōya or merchant friends. It is more convincing to argue, as Craig does,[38] that the formation of the shotai was in the first place a military decision, taken by the samurai establishment in the face of external threat, and that through it some fairly affluent non-samurai were able to acquire a measure of samurai status they had always coveted, thus separating themselves to a greater degree than in the past from village society as a whole. This is to imply that the "alliance" between samurai and well-to-do commoners, insofar as it existed at all, was conceived as a form of "unity" called into being against the outsider and the dangers he posed, not an arrangement between equals pursuing similar political ends.

However this may be, it is certain that a group of men had now come to power in Chōshū who were determined to save their country and their domain by more sophisticated policies than had been proposed by the "men of spirit" earlier: by substituting fukoku-kyōhei for simple jōi as a technique of military survival; by securing office, instead of appealing to loyalist sentiment, as the means of arriving at unity. They had been able to win acceptance for these policies and for their own position from a substantial segment of what was in the widest sense the ruling elite in the countryside and in the castle town, so coming a stage nearer to an alliance against the Bakufu by overcoming the divisive effect of "expulsion" among its opponents. They had also sketched that alliance's prime aim: the creation of a strong Japan. The next few years were to see, first, the alliance made real and victorious; and second, a continuing debate about how its objectives could be attained. Both were important for the nature of the Meiji state.

CHAPTER X

The Restoration Movement

THE EVENTS OF 1863–64 heightened Japanese awareness of the foreign threat and spread it more widely through society. They also demonstrated that neither "expulsion" nor "loyalism" was a practicable solution to the problems that threat posed. This, as we have seen, led a critically important segment of samurai leaders to turn away from the negative attitudes associated with simple sonnō-jōi and replace them with the positive aims of fukoku-kyōhei, "enrich the country, strengthen the army," a program that was to be put into effect immediately in their own domains and then extended to the country as a whole. In consequence, the period between the end of 1864 and the beginning of 1868 was one in which Japan experimented with some of the ingredients of modernization.

Since this change weakened the jōi movement by depriving it of the support of those who could have been its most powerful advocates, it also contributed to a process of reshaping political alignments. Until this time there had been three issues in Japanese politics on which men had been divided: that of foreign policy, separating Chōshū and Court from Satsuma and Bakufu; that of Tokugawa authority, setting the great domains against Edo officialdom; and that of feudal discipline, pitting dissident samurai against their lords. The relegation of expulsion to a place of secondary importance reduced the divisive effect of the first of these issues, at least insofar as it had tended to isolate Chōshū. The fact that samurai activists had been successful in some domains, becoming respectable officials, and had been suppressed elsewhere, becoming prisoners or refugees, reduced the immediacy of the third. This left the question of Bakufu power as the focus of politics.

To put it differently, one might say that there now emerged a new polarization. Chōshū and Satsuma, committed more and more to similar policies under similar leadership, found that their separate causes of hostility toward the Bakufu, as it tried to punish one and dispense with the help of the other, were stronger than their mutual rivalry. They moved first toward cooperation, then toward alliance. This in turn prompted Bakufu attempts at "self-strengthening"—the parallel with what was taking place in China was in some ways very close—which, because they could be taken to be directed against domains in general, made it easier for Chōshū and Satsuma to win others to their side. In fact, the criteria of alignment became primarily feudal, that is, the relations of lord with overlord. So did the units of which the emerging anti-Tokugawa alliance was composed: domains, rather than the "right-thinking men" to whom the shishi had appealed. And once the leaders of opposition became convinced that only force would enable them to gain their ends, the Court itself reverted to an earlier, passive role as the source of legitimacy and the scene, rather than the arbiter, of struggle.

ALLIANCE BETWEEN SATSUMA AND CHŌSHŪ

In Satsuma there was no civil war, like that in Chōshū, to mark the rise of the loyalists to power. There, the daimyo had gradually promoted reformers into positions of influence in the hope of restraining samurai unrest. Thus Ōkubo Toshimichi's first really important office, which came at the end of 1862, though immediately a reward for his services during the Ōhara mission, was also a recognition of what he had done to preserve Satsuma's unity at a time when other domains were torn by loyalist violence. He certainly appears to have had a tacit understanding with Shimazu Hisamitsu to maintain discipline among his own turbulent followers provided Hisamitsu pursued a course that could be made acceptable to them. The success of this cooperation, which gave Satsuma internal peace, gave Ōkubo a share in the decision-making. On March 28, 1863, he was made Soba-yaku, becoming responsible for the daimyo's personal secretariat. He also gained allies in key positions within the domain administration proper. Accordingly, by April 1864, when Hisamitsu gave way to popular pressure and again pardoned Satsuma's most famous loyalist, Saigō Takamori, appointing him to a senior military post, it was already clear that Ōkubo's party, by working with feudal authority instead of challenging it, not only had avoided the fate that befell the "men of spirit" in Kyōto and Tosa, but had secured an opportunity to wield authority on its own behalf.

It will be useful at this point to sketch the background of some of those who were commonly accepted as members of the Saigō-Ōkubo party so they may be compared with the Chōshū leaders, whom we have already discussed.[1] Of Ōkubo himself, little more needs to be said here, save that he was born in 1830 to a middle samurai family of modest means and began his career in a minor office under Shimazu Nariakira in 1858.[2] His associate, Saigō (born 1828), had a similar background, if a poorer one; but his extra two years of age had meant a deeper involvement in Nariakira's activities, which brought him exile for the greater part of the time between January 1859 and the spring of 1864. The punishment made him a legend. However, it also put leadership of the Satsuma loyalists during that period in the hands of Ōkubo, subject only to the advice he received in Saigō's letters. Accordingly, once Saigō was pardoned in 1864, the two worked together on more or less equal terms, Saigō's prestige and military reputation being complemented by Ōkubo's greater political experience and skill.

Because Satsuma politics remained traditional in many ways, the two men found it necessary to seek out colleagues whose birth qualified them for offices to which they themselves, as middle samurai, could not aspire. The most active of these was Komatsu Tatewaki (born 1835), a younger son of the lord of Iriki, a Satsuma sub-fief, who had been adopted into the upper samurai house of Komatsu and who had held senior office as early as 1861. He was appointed Karō, or senior councillor, at the end of 1862 and acted thereafter as Ōkubo's chief ally in high places. Next to him in importance was Iwashita Masahira (born 1827), another upper samurai, who became Karō in January 1866 and represented Satsuma at the Paris Exposition in the following year. Unlike Komatsu, who died in

1870, Iwashita survived to achieve some distinction in the Meiji government, being eventually made a peer. Of the younger men, Machida Hisanari (born 1838), whose father held a sub-fief of 1,700 koku, became Ōmetsuke in 1864, a post of considerable importance in Satsuma. However, since he chose to go and study in England from 1865 to 1867, he played little part in the political movement we are discussing in this chapter.

Also cooperating with Saigō and Ōkubo in the domain administration were several men of their own rank and station, that is, hirazamurai. They included Yoshii Tomozane (born 1828), an official known for his loyalty to Saigō in particular; Ijichi Sadaka (born 1826) whose appointments closely followed those of Ōkubo; Kaeda Nobuyoshi (born 1832), who without any obvious or outstanding individual achievements to his credit seems always to have been near the center of things; and Ōyama Iwao (born 1842), Saigō's cousin, a military expert who was to be a field-marshal in the Meiji army.

All four, in fact, were to be of some consequence in the Meiji period. Yet they figure less largely in the history books than three other Satsuma officials of this time, men of less orthodox background and experience. The first of these, Matsuki Kōan, later known as Terajima Munenori (born 1832), was the younger son of a gōshi. Adopted into a family of hirazamurai, Terajima spent much of his boyhood in Nagasaki, studied Western medicine in Edo, then returned to become a Bakufu teacher of Rangaku, and, in 1857, one of Shimazu Nariakira's doctors. Thereafter he was successively adviser to Nariakira on Western scholarship and technology; naval expert, captured by the British at the bombardment of Kagoshima in 1863; joint supervisor of a party of Satsuma students sent to Europe at the beginning of 1865; and Foreign Minister in the early Meiji government.

Terajima's colleague in conducting the student mission to Europe was Godai Tomoatsu (born 1836), younger son of a hirazamurai. Godai had been one of those sent by Nariakira to study navigation and naval gunnery under the Dutch at Nagasaki in 1857, the start of a career that took him to Shanghai on a Bakufu ship in 1862, then made him Satsuma's shipping and trading representative at

Nagasaki and its commercial envoy in negotiations in Europe in 1865. After the Restoration he served briefly in the new government but resigned in 1869 to become one of the first of Japan's samurai entrepreneurs, concerned especially with railways and mines.

The last member of the group was Matsukata Masayoshi (born 1835). Matsukata's father was a gōshi who had turned to trade. Despite this commercial background, the son entered official service, rising from a minor clerical post, to which he was appointed in 1850, to become a useful ally to Ōkubo in domain politics after 1862. His outstanding achievements, however, came after 1868, when as one of the most capable of the new-style bureaucrats he rose to be Minister of Finance and subsequently Premier.

There are a number of differences between these men and those who were simultaneously coming to power in Chōshū. In the spectrum of rank they can fairly be described as "middle and upper," where Kido and his colleagues were "middle and lower." Their tenure of office depended on their ability to manipulate those who possessed authority rather than on the backing of an organized military force, such as Takasugi's irregular companies provided in Chōshū. Above all, they seem neither to have had, nor to have needed, a significant measure of support from gōshi, village headmen, or merchants. Notwithstanding the gōshi element in the family history of Terajima and Matsukata, there is no evidence that rural or commercial connections played an important part either in their individual careers or in the success of the group as a whole.

This poses a problem. If the Meiji Restoration movement was related to the aspirations of men who were outside or on the fringes of the samurai class, as is strongly suggested by our examination of the loyalists in other parts of Japan, how does it happen that Satsuma, remaining more traditional and "feudal," played such an essential role in it? Or, to put this more precisely in terms of a political narrative: when Satsuma and Chōshū came into alliance against the Bakufu early in 1866, what was the basis of their cooperation, if not an identity of class interest among those who controlled their policies?

One part of the answer is to be found in a growing community of outlook in the matter of Japan's relations with the West. Insofar as Chōshū abandoned jōi and turned to fukoku-kyōhei as an alternative way of ensuring national independence, it was reverting, at least in appearance, to a line of thinking that had been followed by Edo's Hotta Masayoshi, Tosa's Yoshida Tōyō, Chōshū's own Nagai Uta, and Satsuma's Shimazu Nariakira. Certainly there was nothing about it that was unacceptable to Satsuma men like Saigō and Ōkubo, who had served Nariakira, or like Terajima, who had advised him. Moreover, what differences there were between the ideas of national wealth and strength now being put forward and the earlier ones of kaikoku, or "opening the country," seem largely to be those of greater complexity and sophistication, founded on a fuller knowledge of the West.[3] This was reflected politically in the appointment to office of men with a new kind of expertise: Godai in Satsuma, Itō and Inoue in Chōshū.

What this meant in practice was exemplified in Satsuma by the mission to Europe in 1865–66. When Godai Tomoatsu had returned from his visit to Shanghai in 1862, he had been convinced of the need for Japan to develop a foreign trade, which could be carried in Western-style but Japanese-owned vessels. The strength of jōi feeling in Satsuma prevented him from making any headway with such proposals during the next two years, but in May or June 1864 he drew up a memorial that contained the seeds of most of the plans Satsuma later carried out. The domain must send an educational mission to Britain and France, Godai argued, made up of students from various elements of the feudal class: Karō houses, hirazamurai, young jōi enthusiasts, technical specialists. These should be ordered to apply themselves to a wide range of military, scientific, and administrative studies. In addition, trade must be opened with Shanghai, the proceeds of which—he calculated them in some detail—could be devoted to the purchase of arms and industrial investment, thereby providing for both immediate military needs and long-term economic advantage.[4]

These proposals, which Shimazu Hisamitsu and Ōkubo supported, were adopted by the domain government and put into effect, only slightly modified, in 1865. Fourteen students were selected and sent to London in charge of four officials, including Godai and

Terajima. On arrival there in June they were put to the learning of English, together with the study of some special field, like navigation, naval engineering, military science, or medicine (one, surprisingly, was allowed to choose literature). They were then sent on visits to America, Russia, and France. A further party of five joined them in 1866. Meanwhile, the officials who escorted them inspected factories and military establishments, organized the purchase of weapons and machinery, and even engaged in diplomatic discussions with the governments of Britain and France. Indeed, they behaved almost as if their domain was an independent state, arranging among other things for the inclusion of a separate Satsuma exhibit at the Paris Exposition of 1867.[5]

In Britain the Satsuma officials ordered machinery for a cotton-spinning factory, which was installed at Kagoshima in 1867 and continued in operation for thirty years, employing some 200 workers. English and Dutch equipment was also acquired for a steam-powered sugar-refining plant. It too began working in 1867 but proved unsuccessful, partly because of local resentment at the loss of employment it caused. It closed down in 1869 and the machinery was sold.

Both these undertakings were part of a much more ambitious scheme for Belgian help in the development of Satsuma, worked out by Godai and the Comte des Cantons de Montblanc and embodied in an agreement signed in Brussels on October 15, 1865. This created a joint company that was to supply equipment and technicians for Satsuma's industrial and mining operations in return for a monopoly of the Satsuma export and import trade conducted through the Ryukyu islands. Satsuma's share of the profits was to be devoted to the purchase of arms, including a steam warship of nearly 2,000 tons, mounting Armstrong guns in twin turrets. But personal difficulties with Montblanc, which began after Godai returned to Kagoshima in March 1866, together with financial problems and some indications of British opposition, greatly limited what was actually achieved, so that all Satsuma got in the end was 5,000 rifles. The entire arrangement was terminated in 1868, when abolition of the Bakufu destroyed the political basis for it.

The Godai mission was not an isolated incident but part of a consistent pattern linking trade with military reform. Godai, for example, in a memorial sent home from London, urged that the profits from trade (fukoku, as he saw it) be devoted to a kyōhei program encompassing not merely the reequipment, but also the reorganization, of Satsuma forces on Western lines.[6] It was a principle that his superiors in Kagoshima readily accepted. In 1865 they gave a new emphasis to Western subjects in samurai education, renaming the domain school the Yōgakusho (Institute for Western Studies) and awarding graded stipends to successful students. The following year they established a military school in Kyōto, where training was based on a translation of the British infantry manual, and separated out the naval arm of their forces, which was put under Komatsu's control. Ships, especially steamers, were purchased from abroad, including two of over 750 tons.

Inevitably, the cost of all this was greater than could be met from revenues founded on feudal dues. Part of it was raised by engaging in foreign trade: the production and sale of sugar was much increased, and additional profits were made by exporting tea, silk, and cotton (which were not Satsuma products) through Nagasaki and Yokohama. Even so, it proved necessary late in 1866 to introduce a 30 per cent cut in most samurai salaries and stipends. And soon after, in the spring of 1867, regulations were issued revising the scales of military equipment to be furnished by men of different ranks, so as to reduce the burden that would otherwise have fallen on official finances.[7]

Satsuma's adoption of a policy of "wealth and strength" not only had great political significance in establishing a set of objectives that were broadly similar to those envisaged by Chōshū; it also tended directly to exacerbate Satsuma's relations with the Bakufu. After all, it was a Bakufu trade monopoly and a Bakufu claim to authority that were being flouted in Satsuma's independent approach to the powers.* More, as men like Godai saw the situation,

* Godai and Terajima in London assured the British government (in an interview with Laurence Oliphant) that one element in the political disputes in Japan was the desire of some of the great domains to expand foreign trade, which the Bakufu was resisting in the interests of its own monopolies (see Fox, *Britain and Japan*, pp. 174–75). Tōyama, *Meiji ishin*, pp. 122–23, argues that statements of this kind, coupled with Satsuma's extensive trading operations in the treaty ports, indicate the opposi-

if the Bakufu could not be persuaded to accept these policies as its own—and this seemed almost certain in 1865—a domain like Satsuma had only two positive courses of action open to it: to fall back on *kakkyo*, "self-sufficiency," building up its own strength against a possible day of need, or to try to "unite all the great domains in a major reform of administration" so as to make Bakufu obstruction irrelevant.[8] By this estimate, fukoku-kyōhei, because Edo rejected it, could be a motive for tōbaku, "destroying the Bakufu."

Nevertheless, it took time before the men who mattered most in Satsuma politics were fully convinced of the necessity of a complete break with the Bakufu. Ōkubo, for one, had long been a supporter of Shimazu Hisamitsu's kōbu-gattai policies, aimed at producing "unity" by weakening the Shogun's hold over the great lords and so making possible a common front against the foreigner. Though there is some evidence that by late 1864, despairing of achieving anything useful in face of the Bakufu's "selfishness," he was tempted by the idea of self-sufficiency,[9] he was not yet committed to an outright attack on Edo's power. Saigō, too, was convinced of the importance of ensuring Satsuma strength; but he still put first, as he had ever since 1858, what he called *kyōwa-seiji*, "cooperative rule," in which a few powerful lords would assume the responsibility for advising the Emperor and the Shogun on major decisions.[10] In other words, though plainly hostile toward the Bakufu in 1864–65, neither man sought its destruction at that stage. Hence the fact that they were willing to enter into an anti-Bakufu alliance with Chōshū at the beginning of 1866 has to be explained by what happened during 1865: specifically, by Edo's policies toward Chōshū, and by Satsuma's failure, unaided, in an attempt to make the Court an anti-Bakufu instrument in a dispute at the end of the year. Let us look at these in turn.

---

tion to Bakufu monopoly in fact came from Japanese merchants, acting under the protection of the domains. However, on this question I am more inclined to accept the view attributed to Thomas Glover, the British merchant who acted as agent for both Satsuma and Chōshū at Nagasaki, namely, that neither of these domains really wanted to open their ports "to all foreigners indiscriminately," but rather sought "to secure to themselves just such an extent of communicating with foreigners as they may find convenient for promoting their own views or their own monopolies" (F.O. 46/67, Parkes to Hammond, private, Feb. 28, 1866, quoting Gower, the British consul at Nagasaki).

The compromise that Saigō had worked out between the Bakufu and Chōshū at the end of 1864, though accepted by Owari as commander-in-chief, was by no means welcome to those Bakufu officials who had planned exemplary punishment of Chōshū as a step toward reasserting the Shogun's authority.[11] Despite the settlement, they demanded that the Chōshū daimyo and his son be brought to Edo in token of submission. A few weeks later (February 20, 1865) they ordered the full resumption of sankin-kōtai in its pre-1862 form, requiring all the lords to spend half their time in the Shogun's capital, where they might be under stricter control. Chōshū, now firmly under the sway of the loyalists, responded to neither decision. Accordingly, on May 13 the Bakufu announced a further punitive expedition, to be commanded this time by the Shogun in person. He arrived at Osaka on June 15 to supervise the assembly of a suitable force.

Satsuma's initial reaction to these developments was one of suspicion. Ōkubo was sent to Kyōto in February 1865 to persuade the Court to oppose them and quickly secured an imperial decree, dated March 28, instructing the Bakufu to delay a final decision about Chōshū until the Shogun arrived. Meanwhile, it said, sankin-kōtai should revert to the pattern that had been adopted in 1862. The Bakufu did nothing to implement these instructions before Iemochi reached Osaka in June. Indeed, by then the Rōjū were urging that Mōri be executed and his domain confiscated because of his failure to submit, though a number of daimyo, among them those of Echizen, Bizen, Inaba, Kii, and Kumamoto, who regarded such a course as likely to lead to a catastrophic civil war, openly opposed the action Edo was urging.

In face of such Bakufu stubbornness, Ōkubo found it impossible to move the Court to do anything more. Nevertheless, he thought that Chōshū was in little military danger while so many great lords were unwilling to act. Saigō went further. Another expedition, he wrote in June, was more likely to damage the Bakufu than Chōshū: "It will not increase the Bakufu's prestige, but rather cause unrest throughout the country; the Tokugawa fortunes are in decline."[12] By October he was convinced that Edo would not be able to overcome the scruples of the lords. "The Bakufu is unable to conduct hostilities on its own," he claimed, "and lacks just grounds for levying troops from the domains."[13]

Ōkubo, writing to some of his colleagues who were then in Europe, set out more clearly still the implications for Bakufu power and Satsuma policy: "If the Shogun returns to Edo having achieved nothing after so bold a beginning, there is no doubt that his orders will more and more be disobeyed, and that the great domains will tend to hold themselves independent of him. Accordingly, we must set ourselves resolutely to the task of enriching the country and strengthening the army, so that we can devote all our strength, though it be but the strength of a single domain, to policies for defending the Court and making the imperial prestige resplendent beyond the seas."[14] Health and morale were poor in the force the Shogun had gathered at Osaka, he added, and it was costing half a million ryō a month to keep it in the field, so that there was little likelihood of holding it together long enough to overcome Chōshū.

From this it is evident that by the autumn of 1865 Ōkubo and Saigō believed the Bakufu's actions to be dangerously irrelevant to national needs as they conceived them. They therefore refused to cooperate in them. Nevertheless, they were not yet ready to seek an alliance with their traditional rival, Chōshū, preferring still to rely on "the strength of a single domain."

What moved them from this position, it seems, was the dispute over imperial ratification of the foreign treaties in November.[15] It had long been known to some of the Western representatives, through documents captured during the Shimonoseki operations in 1864, that the Court had encouraged hostility to foreigners on the part of the domains. Consequently, when Edo informed them in April 1865 that it wished to postpone payment of the second installment of the indemnity exacted on that occasion, they took the opportunity to formulate new demands. The early opening of the port of Hyōgo was one, a reduction in import duties was another. More important even than these, they called for a public acknowledgment by the Emperor that the treaties as a whole had his approval. The new British minister, Harry Parkes, who reached Japan in July, took the lead in pressing these claims; and since the Shogun had already gone to Osaka with most of his council, Parkes persuaded his colleagues to go there, too, ostentatiously backed by a squadron of warships.

The foreign terms, which were presented to Ogasawara Nagamichi at the anchorage off Hyōgo on November 7, 1865, caused consternation among Iemochi's advisers. Aware that the Court would give way only to the strongest pressure, they coupled a recommendation to accept the demands with an offer by the Shogun to resign, warning that a foreign war, coming when the Bakufu was in dispute with Chōshū, could mean calamity: a people "plunged in misery," the Tokugawa house "imperiled," the Emperor's safety "threatened."[16]

Thus panic, prompted by the fear that the foreigners might deal directly with Kyōto, had at last brought from Edo's representatives the kind of realistic and forthright public statement about foreign affairs that Shimazu Hisamitsu had been demanding for the past three years. The Bakufu's men in Kyōto—Hitotsubashi Keiki, Matsudaira Katamori, Ogasawara Nagamichi—declared their solidarity with Edo. Then, through their influence with the senior Court officials, they broke down the reluctance of the Emperor and the majority of the nobles, so that on November 22 imperial consent to the treaties was at last announced. On their own account, the Rōjū added a promise of tariff revision.*

For the Bakufu it was an expensive victory, not least because of its effect on the domestic situation. The Court and the domains, just as much as Edo, recognized that a foreign crisis, coming at a time when the Bakufu's dispute with Chōshū seemed likely to result in civil war, was exceedingly dangerous.† They saw this, however, as grounds for settling the Chōshū affair in order to unite the country against the West, not for evading foreign problems while

* A tariff convention reducing duties on foreign goods to a uniform 5 per cent was concluded without further difficulty on June 25, 1866. However, the question of Hyōgo was not resolved. The Court refused permission to open it; the Bakufu told the foreign envoys that it could not be opened *earlier than previously arranged*; and the whole matter had to be reopened in the spring of 1867.

† The foreign representatives were also aware of the precarious internal situation. In a memorandum to the Bakufu dated Oct. 30, 1865, they said that one motive for their actions was the hope that they might somehow help to prevent "le commencement des hostilités qui seraient peut-être le signal de la guerre civile, dont les conséquences, quelles qu'elles fussent, ne pourraient que nuire aux intérêts politiques et commerciaux des Puissances étrangères au Japon" (Beasley, *Select Documents*, p. 296).

the Bakufu restored its power. Ōkubo and Saigō, representing Satsuma at Kyōto and Osaka, respectively, made strenuous efforts to get this viewpoint accepted.

On November 9 Ōkubo had an interview with Prince Asahiko, one of the most influential members of the Court. He was told that Asahiko and others had done their best to persuade Hitotsubashi Keiki and Matsudaira Katamori that matters of such importance required a meeting of the great lords, but with little success, so that it now seemed likely the Court would accept the Bakufu's position. Ōkubo, as he later reported to Saigō, was highly critical of this statement. For the Court to lend its support to the Bakufu against Chōshū, he had told Asahiko, might well cause the domains to declare against it:

> If the Court were to approve this proposal, it would be issuing orders that were contrary to justice. Not one of the lords who give the Court their backing would obey them, . . . for an imperial order that is against justice is not an imperial order and need not be obeyed. At present the matter concerns only two provinces, Nagato and Suō [i.e., Chōshū]; but if the day comes when the domains refuse orders to act against them, . . . what then? Popular resentment at present focuses on the Bakufu. If that resentment should turn against the Court, it will be because the Court by its actions has brought the Bakufu's troubles on itself.[17]

Ōkubo went on to deny that he was defending Chōshū or proposing destruction of the Bakufu (tōbaku); but it is clear enough that he was threatening the Court with the loss of Satsuma's allegiance. Moreover, the manner of his doing so, even allowing for a measure of exaggeration in his reporting of the conversation, is a significant comment on his interpretation of loyalism (sonnō).

At this interview, and at a later one with the Kampaku, Nijō Nariaki, Ōkubo thought that he had succeeded in stiffening the Court's resistance to the Bakufu's ideas. He therefore proceeded to take steps to get the great lords to come to Kyōto. Saigō left for Satsuma to fetch Shimazu Hisamitsu, Yoshii for Uwajima and Date Muneki, and Ōkubo himself for Echizen and Matsudaira Shungaku. Events moved too fast for them, however. On the day Ōkubo got back to the capital came the Shogun's threat of resignation, precipitating a decision in the Bakufu's favor before any of the daimyo arrived. A last-minute attempt to send an imperial envoy to the foreign representatives—with a Satsuma escort—to get an extension of time, was overridden by the Bakufu's urgency. So the Court, lacking the resolution that only the presence of the great lords could have given it, had once more proved an ineffective instrument of anti-Bakufu politics.

Ōkubo recognized the failure for what it was. Instead of "a true opening of the ports," based on decisions taken by the daimyo and approved by the Emperor, Japan had again been condemned to the Bakufu's "irresolute" foreign policy. The moral: that Satsuma must redouble its efforts on the country's behalf; but also that it must pursue its own course—*sompan*, "honoring the domain"—regardless of the suspicions this might arouse among Court nobles, Bakufu officials, and other feudal lords.[18] Saigō agreed with him.[19]

In fact, the experience had brought both men to similar conclusions. First, they believed that the Bakufu, assisted, if not led, by Hitotsubashi Keiki and Matsudaira Katamori, was preoccupied with its own "selfish" interests to the exclusion of wider national ones. Second, they were convinced that in any attempt to make the Shogun's advisers act differently, the Imperial Court, though important because it could bestow legitimacy, was an unreliable ally. Third, they had become aware that in any future trial of strength their domain must be prepared, if need be, to stand alone. In other words, seeing themselves as the advocates of a plan for national survival, to be effected through fukoku-kyōhei, they came to see their relations with Edo as the key to the country's fate and kōbu-gattai, "unity of Court and Bakufu," as an inappropriate formula on which to rely. It was this assessment of the situation that inclined them more positively toward alliance with Chōshū.

The previous year had already seen some moves in that direction, which Saigō and Ōkubo must have had in mind during the November crisis.[20] Two Tosa rōnin, Sakamoto Ryōma and Nakaoka Shintarō, the first serving with Satsuma, the second with Chōshū, had been working toward this end ever since the spring of 1865, when Saigō's mediation between the Bakufu and Chōshū had seemed to create a favorable atmosphere for it. As Nakaoka wrote at the time, it was on these two domains that the surviving loyalists must pin their hopes "of establishing our national way of life [kokutai] some day and wiping out the barbarian insults."[21] Bringing them together, however, was not easy, given their traditional rivalry and the fact that the whole Tokugawa structure was designed precisely to prevent such "lateral" relationships. This was demonstrated when the Tosa men's first attempt, a proposal for a meeting between Kido and Saigō, came to nothing in June 1865. Undaunted, they then turned to an indirect approach, putting forward a plan for trade cooperation by which Chōshū's need for foreign military equipment for use against the Bakufu might be met through Satsuma's agent at Nagasaki, the British merchant Thomas Glover, in cooperation with a shipping organization, the Kaientai, which Sakamoto ran on Satsuma's behalf.

Sakamoto got Saigō's approval for the plan; and Inoue Kaoru took it up in Chōshū and persuaded Kido to give it his support. Kido then overcame the reluctance of other Chōshū officials, using the argument that since Satsuma, Hizen, and Higo, the most powerful of the Kyūshū domains, were all rearming apace, Chōshū "must not be allowed to fall behind them because of being preoccupied with loyalism [kinnō]."[22] As a result, Inoue and Itō Hirobumi were established at Nagasaki to handle the trade in arms with Satsuma assistance, in return for which Chōshū agreed to provide rice for Satsuma troops in central Japan.

Once these practical matters were decided, the road was paved for another direct approach. It came in October 1865, when the Chōshū daimyo and his son wrote jointly to the two Shimazu proposing formal talks.[23] From the tone of their letter, with its critical references to the Bakufu and its compliments to Satsuma's "loyalist" virtues, it was clear that what they had in mind was some kind of political agreement, but the crisis concerning imperial ratification of the treaties intervened before Satsuma had an opportunity to respond. By the time the crisis was over, attitudes had changed substantially. Satsuma's hostility toward the Bakufu had been confirmed, as had the Bakufu's decision to mount another expedition against Chōshū. In effect the two domains were being pushed into each other's arms.

Even so, the last formalities proved difficult enough. In January

1866 Saigō sent a messenger to invite Kido to join Ōkubo and himself in Fushimi for talks. Despite opposition from the Chōshū irregular companies, which still held Satsuma partly responsible for their defeat in Kyōto in 1864, Kido came, arriving late in February. However, there were still several days of quite inconclusive discussions before Sakamoto Ryōma intervened to bring them to a point, so that it was March 7 before an agreement was drawn up and signed. It comprised a promise by Satsuma to intercede with Court and Bakufu on Chōshū's behalf in the event of hostilities breaking out; a conditional military alliance to become effective if this intercession provoked Bakufu action against Satsuma, too; and a pledge to cooperate, once the struggle was over, in "restoring the imperial prestige." This was how Kido summarized it in a letter to Sakamoto Ryōma, in which he described the alliance as being "of the utmost importance in the regeneration of our imperial land."[24]

In the sense that this alliance was a decisive step toward the destruction of the Bakufu, Kido was right. To be sure, the arrangement was a secret one. But once events made it known, as they were bound to, it was inconceivable that the resulting struggle for power could end in the kind of compromise that had been worked out by the great lords on previous occasions. After all, this was a fundamental breach of Bakufu law, something far more specifically directed against the continuation of the Shogun's authority than anything the lords had envisaged under the name of "unity of Court and Bakufu." What is more, it had been arranged by hirazamurai, men who were not of high enough birth to avoid the worst consequences of failure, as their daimyo might. Having started, they had little choice but to go on.

THE BAKUFU UNDER ATTACK

Bakufu officials were quite sure by the end of 1865 that Edo's authority was at stake in the dispute with Chōshū.* They were also

* This attitude was not new. In August 1863 Hitotsubashi Keiki, referring to the clashes with the West that were then clearly impending, had written to the Rōjū as follows: "The action that the Bakufu takes about the two domains, Satsuma and Chōshū, is of great importance for the polity [kokutai]. . . . In the event of hostilities [between Satsuma and Britain] victory for the English would be a disgrace for the country, victory for Satsuma a blow to the Bakufu's prestige" (Shibusawa, *Tokugawa Keiki Kō den*, 5: 563–64).

beginning to doubt whether the threat of an expedition led personally by the Shogun would be enough to settle matters without fighting, which is what they had originally hoped. Then in early February 1866 the Chōshū leaders rejected any possibility of a settlement based on a surrender of Chōshū territory. Given the known reluctance of the great lords to take part in an expedition, the Bakufu decided in consequence to modify its terms, which on March 5, 1866 (two days before the conclusion of the Satsuma-Chōshū alliance), were agreed as follows: Mōri Yoshichika and his son were to retire in favor of a younger successor; Chōshū territory was to be reduced by 100,000 koku; and action was to be taken against the extremists and rōnin who had sought refuge in Chōshū. Ogasawara Nagamichi was sent to Hiroshima to convey these terms to the Chōshū representatives.

Once again, Chōshū played for time, determined not to give way, but returning no definite answer. This dragged matters out until early July; but by then Ogasawara's last ultimatum had expired and hostilities became inevitable. In a matter of days, the Bakufu's main force, including troops from Kii and Hikone, was advancing from Hiroshima along the Japan Sea coast. It was quickly checked. Another assault, launched from the island of Shikoku against southern Chōshū, was also halted (partly because of British objections to any operations that might interfere with maritime trade). A planned third invasion, to be mounted from Kyūshū, was anticipated by Takasugi, who forestalled it by seizing Kokura, a fudai stronghold across the straits from Shimonoseki. Within a few weeks, indeed, the Bakufu had been held or repulsed at every point of attack, and the campaign could be seen to have failed. The Edo council, therefore, thrown further into disorder by the death of the Shogun, Iemochi, on August 29, decided to abandon it; and on October 10 Katsu Awa, acting on the council's orders, concluded a truce that brought the rest of the fighting to an end.

Against the background of these events one can detect a rising tide of anti-Bakufu feeling throughout Japan. Even before the fighting began, rumors had been freely circulating—Echizen seems to have been a clearing-house for them[25]—that Katsu Awa, Ōkubo Ichiō, and the other Tokugawa officials who urged a conciliatory policy toward the great lords were steadily losing ground to a faction centered on Oguri Tadamasa that sought reform primarily as a means of strengthening the Bakufu against the daimyo. It was largely because of this that a number of domains, in addition to Satsuma, refused to contribute troops to the expedition against Chōshū or found excuses for delay in doing so.[26] Their uneasiness was increased by a deteriorating economic situation, due in great part to the financial strains the military costs were imposing. Rice prices doubled during 1865, then trebled again in the following year.* Not surprisingly, this brought rioting in the cities and the nearby countryside, especially in Osaka and its neighborhood, where the largest body of troops was assembled. As Matsudaira Shungaku noted in a letter to Katsu Awa in the middle of July, for the Bakufu to launch its expedition in the face of such evidence of popular unrest was to divide the country and risk total collapse: "It might well endanger the Bakufu's authority and eventually the state itself."[27]

It has been argued on the basis of this and similar statements that the effect of these riots (and contemporary peasant revolts of the more usual kind) was to bring a closing of the ranks within the ruling class, which saw in them a threat to its control of Japanese society.[28] For the lords, at least, there is probably some substance in the charge, since such a reaction would accord well enough with their view of "unity of Court and Bakufu" as we have described it. One must not forget, however, that even for them the whole question also existed in the context of the foreign threat. For example, Shimazu Hisamitsu and his son were stating a widely held belief when, in a memorial submitted to the Court on August 18, 1866, they charged Edo with recklessly exposing the country to external dangers in its determination to punish Chōshū.[29] Asserting that Bakufu foreign policy had "incurred general criticism and alienated opinion everywhere," they declared that to the domains, which wanted nothing more than "to support the Court, assist the Bakufu, and guard their territories," Edo now seemed incapable of

* Tsuchiya, "Bakumatsu dōranki," p. 83, gives the following series of prices for Higo rice, in silver momme per koku (for the first lunar month of each year): 1862, 144.5 momme; 1863, 177.5; 1864, 164.5; 1865, 207.5; 1866, 473.0; 1867, 1,475.0. On price increases in other commodities, see Tsuchiya, *Ishin*, pp. 39–42.

providing national leadership, above all because of its behavior toward Chōshū. Popular disturbances had also recently been reported from many areas, they noted. Even in Osaka and Hyōgo, where one would have expected the large concentration of Tokugawa troops at least to have been able to keep order among the local population, "merchants and the humblest classes have flouted the law, showing no respect for Bakufu authority." Rising prices and signs of drought in several places suggested that there might be worse to come. To have begun a civil war in these circumstances, the Shimazu argued (echoing Matsudaira Shungaku), was to have risked Japan being "torn to pieces by a mounting tide of disputes," an action that, in view of the constant danger of foreign attack, could only be called wholly irresponsible. Instead, Edo should have concentrated on "reforming administration and revitalizing the country." Since it had not, that task now fell by default to the Court and those who worked with it.

This is hardly evidence of class solidarity among feudal lords in the face of popular unrest. Just what else it signifies, apart from being a fulfillment of Satsuma's promises to Chōshū, depends on the meaning one gives to some other statements the document made about "revising the political structure," the nature of the revision not being specified. Judging from Saigō's declared admiration for Katsu Awa and Ōkubo Ichiō,[30] what he personally had in mind, and was presumably urging on the Shimazu at this time, was the inauguration of some kind of council of great lords, since this is what Katsu and his friends were known to favor. Support is given to this view by a private letter of the British minister, Harry Parkes, written just after a visit to Kagoshima. He reported the attitude of Shimazu's officials thus: "They owe the Tycoon no ill will and wish only for *a change of system and not of dynasty*; and that the peers of the land should be permitted a voice in the management of its affairs, or at least in its legislation."[31] This is not so very far from Satsuma's earlier ideas about "unity of Court and Bakufu." It implied, perhaps, a more formal framework of institutions, but it was still a long way short of "Meiji absolutism."

Nor can one argue that Chōshū, despite its longer record of anti-Bakufu activity, had taken its thinking on this subject any further.

Kido, for example, in a long letter to Shinagawa Yajirō in August 1866, discussed reactions to the civil war (waxing indignant about the Bakufu attack, and in particular about bombardments of the Chōshū coast, in which many women and children had died), but made little reference to what might follow *politically* from its failure. Policies that "reduced the whole people of the country to misery because of an ephemeral anger," he said, called in question the Shogun's right to rule.[32] However, he made no attempt to develop the implications of this judgment.

Indeed, in a letter written a few weeks later to an official of one of the Kyūshū domains, he dwelt more on foreign policy and the responsibilities of the feudal class than on the sins of Edo. As long as Japan remained unable to decide between seclusion, which had been ended by the Emperor's confirmation of the treaties, and opening the country in the full sense, which was not yet acceptable to national opinion, he argued, she would always be dragged along in the train of events. And where lay the fault for this indecision? With the daimyo, who "exploit the farmers of their territories and spend their days in idleness, enjoying women and wine," and "heedless of the dangers the country faces, lead lives of pleasure, behaving as if totally ignorant of the world about them." This situation was made even worse because "their retainers follow their example and menials follow that of the retainers." Under these circumstances, Kido said, "how can one tell when the skies will clear?"* There are echoes here of Yoshida Shōin, as well as indications of the line of thought that later led Kido to attack the feudal structure as a whole; but nothing practical is said about the Bakufu's fate.

If Kido was not at this stage seriously considering the larger question of the consequences of a struggle between the Bakufu and the domains, there was one man who was. This was the Court noble Iwakura Tomomi, who had begun to appreciate that such a struggle would not necessarily profit the Imperial Court, whatever its outcome. In a memorial written in the fall of 1866, shortly after that

* Kido Kōin to Watanabe Noboru, Oct. 6, 1866, in *Kido Kōin monjo*, 2: 224–26, at p. 225. It is interesting that in this document Kido makes use of the modern word Nihon for Japan rather than one of the more widely current expressions like *kōkoku*, "imperial land."

of the two Shimazu cited above, he took up the point they had made about the existence of widespread public condemnation of Edo's policy toward Chōshū and turned it into an argument for a Court initiative.[33] "Only by completing the subjugation of Chōshū," he said, "can the Bakufu maintain its authority over the great domains." In such a situation, one way in which Kyōto might protect itself was by declaring for the Bakufu and making Satsuma a rebel, too. Alternatively—and preferably, as he saw it—the Court could exploit the shift in feudal opinion in the interests of a restoration of imperial rule (ōsei-fukko). To quote him:

Today all questions of the country's government, such as whether there is to be peace at home or civil war, and whether we are to expel the foreigners or have friendly relations with them, depend on the Emperor's commands. If the Court will but act in the public interest, selflessly, reaching its decisions after listening to advice and carefully weighing conflicting views, then opinion everywhere will move irresistibly behind it, like water sweeping down a hill. . . . Since 1862 the imperial authority has been in the process of reviving, and Bakufu power has been in decline, . . . something that owes much to the energetic intervention and activities of the country's loyalists. . . . I submit, therefore, that the time has come when we might restore the fortunes of the imperial house. Recognizing this, the Emperor should issue orders to the Bakufu that from now on it must set aside its selfish ways, acting in accordance with public principle; that imperial rule must be restored; and that thereafter the Tokugawa house must work in concert with the great domains in the Emperor's service. In conveying these instructions, it should be pointed out that the purpose of requiring the Bakufu . . . to surrender its administrative powers is to make it possible to reassert our national prestige and overcome the foreigners. To achieve this requires that the country be united. For the country to be united, policy and administration must have a single source. And for policy and administration to have a single source, the Court must be made the center of national government. Thus may the will of the gods and the wishes of the people be observed.[34]

To this Iwakura added that the Shogun's principal advisers (Hitotsubashi Keiki, the daimyo of Aizu, and the Rōjū) were fully aware that opinion had moved against their retention of hereditary power. They were too deeply committed—"riding the tiger," he called it—to admit defeat voluntarily. But being realists, they might welcome the chance to escape from their dilemma by accepting an overture that would enable them to save the Tokugawa house, if not its prerogatives.

Given the caution that centuries of helplessness had ingrained in the attitudes of senior Court officials, there was little prospect of Iwakura's proposals being acted on, shrewd though they were. A shift of power within the Court was needed for that. Indeed, they were not even fully acceptable to the great domains: Shimazu Hisamitsu, reflecting more and more the ideas of Ōkubo and Saigō,[35] still put an emphasis on baronial independence that was potentially in conflict with true imperial rule; and Kido, insofar as he was representative of Chōshū, was already moving toward a brand of loyalism that went well beyond what Iwakura offered. For the rest, those lords who had strong Tokugawa links, like Tosa and Echizen, would certainly have been less ready to accept Iwakura's solution in 1866 than they were in 1867.

What altered this situation in the following twelve months was not fear of a revolution from below, caused by peasant unrest, but the prospect of a suppression of dissent under a revitalized Bakufu. Following the death of Iemochi in August 1866, Hitotsubashi Keiki was by common consent the obvious man to succeed him. However, Keiki was hesitant, chiefly because he had doubts about the Bakufu's own chances of success. He accordingly recommended instead that a new Shogun be elected by an assembly of daimyo; that this assembly be asked to make decisions on outstanding issues of policy, both domestic and foreign; and that there subsequently be initiated a program of administrative reform.[36] Encouraged in this course by "liberal" Bakufu officials like Ōkubo Ichiō and Katsu Awa—Katsu had commented earlier in the year that if Edo wanted to strengthen Japan, not merely perpetuate Tokugawa rule, then the Bakufu itself must step aside[37]—Keiki sent letters in October inviting the leading daimyo to join him in the capital for consultations. However, the majority, fearing involvement in matters too dangerous for them, preferred to stay away; and since Satsuma, at least, was openly hostile to it, the plan for a meeting was dropped.

The result was to leave Keiki more than ever isolated from his former kōbu-gattai colleagues and apparently convinced that reforms, if they were to be effected at all, must come from the Bakufu. His first thoughts on the subject, closely following suggestions made by Katsu Awa, were put to the Rōjū on October 10, 1866: promotion of men of talent among officials; military reform, including the separation of army and navy; financial economies; a more open attitude toward the treaty powers.[38] Later, when he became Shogun (January 10, 1867), he received a whole budget of advice along similar lines from the French minister, Léon Roches;[39] and he began to give his support to a group of reformers within the Bakufu whose proposals were designed as much to strengthen Edo against its domestic enemies as Japan against the West.

At the highest level these reformers included two Rōjū, Itakura Katsukiyo and Ogasawara Nagamichi, who had long been Keiki's associates in Kyōto politics. Of slightly lower rank were several "experts" holding key posts in the middle ranges of administration: Nagai Naomune, Hotta Masayoshi's adviser in the 1850's, who had been disgraced because of his Hitotsubashi connections in 1858 but had been restored to favor as Ōmetsuke and Gaikoku-bugyō at the end of 1864; Oguri Tadamasa, who had risen to prominence during the 1860's in the financial office of Kanjō-bugyō and in posts relating to military and foreign affairs; and Katsu Awa, friend to Saigō Takamori and the Bakufu's leading specialist on naval matters. By contemporary standards, these men had no lack of knowledge of the West. Katsu and Oguri had both gone to America with the diplomatic mission of 1860; and another member of the group, the Gaikoku-bugyō, Kurimoto Joun, was a friend of Roches' interpreter, Mermet de Cachon. In addition, they could command the services of several younger Japanese with European training, among them Nishi Amane and Tsuda Mamichi, who became Bakufu advisers in 1866 on their return from Leiden.[40]

Though they differed among themselves on the weight they were prepared to give to the political interests of the Tokugawa house, these men were in broad agreement with each other on matters of military and economic policy. Under their direction, steps were taken to increase the size of the Bakufu army and to reorganize it into infantry, cavalry, and artillery units on the Western model. In February 1867 a French military mission arrived to help train them. French help had already been sought in the building of an ironworks at Yokohama, which was associated with a school teaching French, mathematics, and other Western subjects to the sons of officials and local residents. In addition, work had been started in 1866 on an important dockyard at Yokosuka, again under the supervision of French engineers, though it was not finished until after the Restoration. To pay for all this, arrangements had been made for the formation of a Franco-Japanese trading company, backed by French and British capital, which was to have special privileges in the export of Japanese products, especially silk, and to organize in return the import of ships and weapons for the Bakufu's use.

This process of reform had started well before Iemochi's death. The agreement for constructing the Yokosuka dockyard was signed in February 1865, at about the same time as work began on the Yokohama ironworks. Kurimoto had been sent to Paris to arrange for machinery, engineers, and instructors the following summer, and the plan for a joint commercial venture had originated a few months later, in September. In other words, the Bakufu's plans for "enriching the country and strengthening the army" came into being at about the same time as those of Satsuma, which we discussed earlier. Moreover, there was much in common between Satsuma's arrangements with Belgian interests and the Bakufu's with France. Fukoku-kyōhei, for the Bakufu as for the domains, was essentially a response to the failure of "expulsion" in 1864.

Nevertheless, this fact was not *politically* a source of unity. In Satsuma, as we have seen—and it is true of Chōshū, Tosa, and Hizen as well—men held that their aim of saving Japan through "wealth and strength" could be attained only by first saving the domain. Bakufu officials argued similarly, but with the important difference that they could claim for their lord a national role, which made him a legitimate, not a rebellious, object of loyalty. This made it reasonable for them to accept, just as by Western law it was proper for diplomats to offer, foreign assistance. Hence when Roches, in meetings with Keiki and Itakura at Osaka in March 1867, put forward a radical plan for enabling the Bakufu to reassert itself against the domains, he was not immediately rebuffed.

Roches' proposals read like a preview of much that the Meiji government was to do: consultation with the great lords, coupled with their firm subordination to a reorganized central government; administrative changes, including the creation of specialized departments of finance, foreign affairs, justice, army, navy, and so on; the encouragement of trade, manufacture, and mining; a tax on merchant incomes and a reduction of samurai stipends; arrangements for samurai to enter farming and commerce; and cash levies from the fudai houses to support a full-time military establishment, which would be recruited from the more able and efficient Bakufu retainers.[41]

Some of this obviously accorded well with what had already been begun and could be acted on without much difficulty. Almost at once, some of the Rōjū were given responsibility for different governmental functions (finance, foreign and home affairs, the army, the navy) and began to build up departments appropriate to them. A number of promotions were made that broke through former barriers of status; Nagai Naomune, for example, was made a Junior Councillor (Wakadoshiyori). Something was also done to raise funds from the Bakufu's followers to pay for military reforms.

All the same, it was not easy to persuade a feudal regime to abolish feudalism, even as a means of preserving its power, which was effectively what Roches was trying to do. True, not every official wholly rejected the idea;* but it is evident that those who had the greatest influence, like Keiki, together with the large and powerful body of Bakufu conservatives, found it impossible to divorce their support of the Shogun's prerogatives from a more generalized preference for keeping things as they were. Roches' proposals about tax structure and about the role of the feudal class, as well as much of what he said about government, were more than they could stomach.

* As early as 1857 Iwase Tadanari, one of Nagai's colleagues in the treaty negotiations, had commented to Date Muneki that "even if trade is permitted, our methods of government will still be wrong without reform at home, since a feudal system [hōken-seido] like Japan's does not exist abroad" (Date to Matsudaira Shungaku, in *Sakumu kiji*, 2: 61). Moreover, in November 1865 it was reported that Oguri Tadamasa and others were proposing to overcome daimyo opposition by abolishing the domains and substituting a centralized prefectural system under a Shogun-President (Akizuki Taneki to Matsudaira Shungaku, in *Zoku saimu kiji*, 4: 357).

Nevertheless, it was the signs of serious efforts at reform that immediately mattered, since these were enough to cause alarm to the Bakufu's opponents. Iwakura Tomomi referred to Keiki in May 1867 as "an adversary not to be despised," and Kido said that if Keiki succeeded in his plans it would be "as if Ieyasu had been born again."[42] Harry Parkes, the British minister, wrote of Keiki that he "appears to me to be the most superior Japanese I have yet met and it is probable that he will make for himself a name in history."[43] And Satow, the British interpreter, went so far as to hint to Saigō "that the chance of a revolution was not to be lost," for if the Bakufu reached a settlement with the foreign powers, "then goodbye to the chances of the daimyôs."[44]

Nor, indeed, did Saigō and his friends need Satow to tell them this. Kido saw the situation as one requiring urgent action. Japan, he wrote, "will fall into the toils of the Bakufu and France unless authority is quickly restored to the Court."[45] Yamagata Aritomo, hearing at the end of February 1867 that Edo was planning still another attack on Chōshū, even proposed that Kyūshū be declared independent of the Tokugawa and put under the control of a federation of daimyo headed by Shimazu, into which the lords of Shikoku and western Honshū might subsequently be brought.[46] Saigō and Ōkubo, writing to Shimazu Hisamitsu, stated their own aims as follows: "The whole administration of the country to be entrusted again to the Emperor; the Shogun to be reduced to the status of one among the great lords and to work with them in supporting the Court; policy to be decided in the light of opinion in the country at large; and the handling of the foreign treaty question also to be left to the Court, to be dealt with in accordance with the usual international practice concerning treaties."[47]

The formulation of these ideas owed much to the influence of Iwakura Tomomi, who had now become Satsuma's principal ally at the Court, working closely with Ōkubo. Iwakura, however, put them in a wider context: "In the heavens there are not two suns. On earth there are not two monarchs. Surely no country can survive unless government edicts stem from a single source. If Court and Bakufu continue to coexist, as they do now, then we will be able to effect neither genuine expulsion of the foreigners nor genuine friendship with them. Hence it is my desire that we should act vigorously to abolish the Bakufu."[48] He, too, argued that the Tokugawa house ought properly to be "relegated to the ranks of the great domains."

It is clear from all this that the events of 1866 and early 1867 not only had given the anti-Bakufu domains a greater sense of urgency, raising as they did the specter of a Bakufu resurgence, but had also prompted them to think more precisely about alternatives to the existing structure. In place of vague thoughts about a consultative daimyo council, a scheme that would presumably have left the Bakufu to act as the executive arm, there was now a plan to abolish the Shogun's office and create a government centered on the Court in which the Tokugawa would play a part merely as feudal lords.

The gradualness of the change that had taken place is reflected in the correspondence of the British minister, Parkes, who was much the best informed of the foreign representatives in Japan.* In May 1866, shortly before the outbreak of hostilities between the Bakufu and Chōshū, Parkes had observed of Shimazu that he hoped "to depress the power of the Tycoon [Shogun], in whom he sees a rival, by raising that of the Mikado [Emperor], over whom he expects to exercise a predominant influence."[49] In October, when Parkes heard of the proposed meeting in Kyōto between Keiki and the lords, he identified their viewpoints as follows: Keiki "desired that his dignities, whatever these might be, should be substantial and not titular only," whereas the lords wished to settle "the relative powers of the Mikado and Tycoon . . . and the admission of their order to a deliberative voice in the national affairs on an intelligible footing."[50]

At this stage Parkes was fairly optimistic that the two sides could be reconciled. Keiki's succession as Shogun, he thought, would provide "a better opportunity than could otherwise have been looked for."[51] By the end of the year, however, when it was clear that the planned consultations had not in fact taken place, Parkes was be-

* Parkes visited Kagoshima and Uwajima in the summer of 1866. In addition, his interpreter, Satow, traveled extensively in central and west Japan and kept constantly in touch with anti-Bakufu samurai, as well as Edo officials.

ginning to have doubts. Keiki's Bakufu supporters "naturally lean to absolutism," he noted, though they had lost the power to coerce the lords since the revision of sankin-kōtai in 1862; and it remained to be seen whether Keiki could bring the daimyo round "by persuasion or by more vigorous measures."[52] Then came news of Keiki's installation as Shogun, apparently widening the breach. "Satsuma's people," said Parkes, "seem to regard his appointment as the defeat of their policy, which is to place the Tycoon's power under considerable restraint and to secure for some of the leading Daimios a share in the administration or in the deliberative portion of it."[53] This was followed by rumors of another Bakufu expedition against Chōshū, confirming Parkes in his view that the situation was getting steadily worse. "It is I fear by the force of the mailed hand and not of persuasion," he wrote, "that the Tycoon's Government seeks to keep down the Daimios."[54]

The tone of these reports makes it obvious that the British minister had a good deal of sympathy with what he believed to be the aims of Satsuma in particular. Since he had inherited from his predecessor specific instructions not to interfere in Japan's domestic politics, he was careful to declare to the Japanese "the absence of all disposition on our part to interfere with the form of government that they may elect"; but he also pointed out that the West's interest was in maintaining its treaty rights, which ensured that "the sympathies of the foreigners will naturally be given to that party which shows itself most ready to fulfil these obligations."[55]

In practice, this second principle gave grounds, if not for interference, at least for something that looked uncommonly like it. Parkes believed the exclusion of the daimyo from "a voice in the government of their country" might lead to an upheaval that would be detrimental to British trade. Accordingly, he attempted to forestall it by encouraging the Bakufu to accept a sharing of power. At the same time, he also established relations with the Bakufu's opponents in case it came to a fight and the lords won. This was a kind of political insurance. It also gave Parkes an opportunity to caution Satsuma and Chōshū "as to the care and deliberation that should mark the introduction of constitutional changes."[56] During the same period, Satow was writing articles in a treaty port newspaper to urge that the powers "give up the worn-out pretence of acknowledging the Tycoon to be sole ruler of Japan" and "supplement or replace our present treaties by treaties with the CONFEDERATE DAIMIOS." This, he argued, would not be a "political revolution, deposing the Tycoon," for that had "taken place already." It would merely recognize "the actual state of affairs."[57]

Given the effect of these activities on opinion in Japan (where both Japanese and foreigners were convinced that Britain was moving toward an anti-Bakufu position), as well as the growing involvement of the French minister, Léon Roches, in Bakufu politics, it is not surprising that the country's next major domestic crisis was again precipitated by a question of foreign affairs. Specifically, this was the matter of the opening of Hyōgo, which Roches raised in an audience with Keiki at Osaka castle on March 11, 1867. Under the terms of the London Protocol of 1862, Roches pointed out, the port was due to be opened on January 1, 1868. Not to open it would convince the powers that the Bakufu was either unwilling to carry out the treaties or unable to impose its decisions on Court and lords; and this might tempt them to use force against the Bakufu or enter into direct communication with its enemies.[58] Parkes tacitly underlined the warning in a letter written shortly afterward in which he took it for granted that the port would be opened but asked for discussion of the terms on which trade could be carried on there.[59]

Keiki's difficulty was that at the end of 1865, as we have seen, the Bakufu had accepted without protest an imperial ruling that Hyōgo should remain closed. This made it necessary, or at least wise, to apply to Kyōto before he acted. On April 9, 1867, therefore, he wrote to the Court confessing that nothing had been done to implement the Emperor's orders of November 1865 and asking that they be rescinded. There was a risk of foreign war if Hyōgo stayed closed, he argued, and also a need "to build up our national wealth and strength by adopting foreign methods."[60] The Court rejected both arguments; and the Shogun was promptly rebuked and commanded to reconsider, this time in consultation with the lords.

Keiki had nothing against this course in principle, but he thought it might take too long in view of British impatience, so on April 26 he repeated his request with greater urgency. On May 3 came another blunt refusal. It was received only twenty-four hours after a public audience in Osaka at which Keiki had promised the French, British, and Dutch envoys that the treaties as signed would be fully carried out.

Behind the Court's stubbornness lay something more than the continued strength of anti-foreign feeling, real though that was. Satsuma, it appears—the comments of Parkes bear directly on this—had been convinced by Keiki's acceptance of the office of Shogun that he had abandoned thoughts of compromise and could only be brought to terms by the formation of a domain alliance. Ōkubo accordingly used his influence at Court to prevent a decision about Hyōgo* while Saigō and Komatsu set out to fetch the lords. By June 3 Shimazu Hisamitsu, Yamauchi Yōdō, Date Muneki, and Matsudaira Shungaku had all arrived in the capital; and Saigō and Ōkubo set to work to concert a policy among them that could be jointly forced on Keiki in the Emperor's name.

Their substantive proposals were the pardoning of Chōshū (subject only to retirement of its daimyo), since the domain had acted "out of a sincere desire to maintain the interests of the whole country"; the opening of Hyōgo, accompanied by steps to make treaty relations "once and for all the responsibility of the Imperial Court"; and the punishment of the Shogun for the Bakufu's "great and unpardonable crime" of flouting the Emperor's orders over Hyōgo. The Shogun's sentence was to be a reduction of territory and a summons "to join the ranks of the feudal lords as one of themselves."[61] Shimazu Hisamitsu was with some reluctance brought to accept these proposals (and was given detailed instructions by his retainers on how he should present them to the "devious and wily" Keiki, including an injunction to talk in terms of respect for "public opinion," not "destruction of the Bakufu").[62] Iwakura then went about the business of persuading potential allies at the Court that the opening of Hyōgo ought now to be accepted as a means to the restoration of imperial rule. By negotiating an agreement on the matter

* See, for example, a letter from Ōkubo to Konoe Tadahiro arguing in effect that though it was clear Hyōgo would have to be opened sooner or later (this was in early May), the fact must not be admitted until the lords had been consulted about "a sound and enduring policy such as will pacify opinion throughout the Empire" (Beasley, *Select Documents*, pp. 311–12).

through its own envoy, he pointed out, the Court could demonstrate that the conduct of foreign affairs was the Emperor's prerogative, not the Shogun's.[63]

It remained only for the Satsuma men to overcome the doubts of the other lords. This proved to be no easy task, for what they this time proposed went far beyond the mere limitation of Bakufu authority to which the daimyo had earlier subscribed. In fact, their eventual success depended on emphasizing the importance of Chōshū, rather than Hyōgo or the Shogun's fate, for by putting the discussions with Keiki into the context of "national unity" they could avoid needlessly offending the anti-foreign party at the Court. In this sense, the Chōshū issue became the key to bringing about an anti-Bakufu alignment.

The common front, however, also depended heavily on Saigō's reputation and Ōkubo's political skills, as events soon showed. On June 16, 1867, when the first meeting with the Shogun was held, the four lords began by demanding that the Bakufu announce a policy of "leniency" toward Chōshū before agreeing publicly to open Hyōgo. To this Keiki replied that though he personally favored taking both decisions, he could not see how a Hyōgo settlement could be delayed without provoking the treaty powers. It was an argument that left the daimyo uncertain and divided during the next few days. When talking to Keiki they found his views persuasive; in the matter of foreign policy, after all, those views were their own. But outside the conference room, Ōkubo and Saigō were able to convince them, or at least to convince Shimazu and Date, whose connections with the Tokugawa were weaker, that the original demands about timing, even though Keiki made them seem unreasonable, were a political necessity. Out of this, at the end of a week's maneuvers, came compromise. Put forward by Matsudaira Shungaku, it provided for simultaneous announcements about Hyōgo and Chōshū.

But no sooner had the lords accepted the compromise than they repudiated it at Ōkubo's urging. In the circumstances, Keiki decided to wait no longer for unanimity and put the compromise as his own proposal to the Imperial Court. By so doing he changed the scene of the debate, but not its nature: senior Court officials, as they had often done before, dutifully stated the Bakufu's case; more junior ones, briefed by Ōkubo, repeated Satsuma's; and the lords, summoned to give testimony, revealed only that they disagreed. This left it open for the Bakufu to do what it had done in November 1865: to overbear a divided opposition and insist on its traditional rights. On the evening of June 26 the Sesshō, Nijō Nariaki, under pressure from Prince Asahiko and the former Kampaku Takatsukasa Sukehiro, accepted Keiki's recommendation and formulated it as an imperial decree: Hyōgo would be opened, since both Shogun and lords considered this inevitable; and as to Chōshū, "a lenient policy" would be pursued.[64]

In practice, the result was not so much a Bakufu victory as a fresh confrontation, since the lords at once united again against the Shogun. Two days later, on June 28, Shimazu, Date, Yamauchi, and Matsudaira Shungaku wrote formally to the Court to challenge the official version of events, putting on record their demand that the opening of Hyōgo should have followed the pardon of Chōshū and denying that they had agreed to Keiki's compromise. What Japan needed above all, they said, was evidence "that affairs were being handled in a just and straightforward manner," namely, a lenient policy toward Chōshū as a means of attaining "national stability," which was a prerequisite to dealing successfully with the West.[65] Within a very few months, the same argument was to be used as grounds for calling on Keiki to resign.

CHAPTER XI

Restoration

By the spring of 1867 it was clear to most politically active Japanese that what was chiefly at stake in disputes such as the one over the opening of Hyōgo was the extent, even the survival, of Tokugawa power. Three possibilities presented themselves for the immediate future. The first was that the Bakufu might so strengthen itself as to reassert its authority against the challenge from the lords, as the lords had mostly done against the dissident samurai. The second was that its principal opponents, Satsuma and Chōshū, might take the offensive, seeking to overthrow the regime by force. The third was that men of moderate views, represented chiefly by Tosa and Echizen, might find a formula of reconciliation to which all parties could subscribe in the cause of national unity.

The last was overwhelmingly the most likely. As Sir Harry Parkes commented in a letter to London in May, unless the Shogun gave the more powerful daimyo "a consultative voice in affairs," he would scarcely be able "to establish a general Government experiencing common control over all parts of the country."[1] Against that, he said, the "jealousies and divisions" among the lords made it difficult for them to maintain "an extensive combination,"[2] so that Keiki, by showing himself "willing to govern constitutionally" and "acknowledging the supremacy . . . of the Mikado," might again be able to make his authority effective.[3] Both by character and by experience—one has to remember that he had been a leading member of the party that advocated "unity of Court and Bakufu"—Keiki himself inclined in this direction. After all, such a policy would go some way toward satisfying the Tokugawa prejudices among Bakufu officials while rallying support from the great majority of the domains. In consequence, one strand in the events of the summer and autumn of 1867 is that which led to the Shogun's resignation, a step that both his friends and his enemies saw as a device for retaining the substance of power at the cost of relinquishing some of its forms.

To moderates, a persuasive argument in favor of such a plan was the Bakufu's continuing ability to control the Imperial Court, as manifested in the Hyōgo dispute during May and June. Most of them flinched from precipitating an open contest in which those who opposed the Tokugawa would incur the double stigma of rebelling against legitimacy and destroying unity in the face of foreign threat. This widespread reluctance to push matters to extremes underlines the importance of the ultimate decision of Satsuma and Chōshū to reject all compromise. They did so on the grounds that a perpetuation of Bakufu power, for which Keiki's constitutional proposals seemed no more than a disguise, was unacceptable as a response to the national need. In other words, to them the issue of leadership—whether there was to be a modified Tokugawa hegemony or a whole new system of daimyo-Emperor control—was critical. On this account they carried out a coup d'état that swept aside the possibility of agreement and precipitated civil war.

It is obviously necessary in any wider interpretation of the Meiji Restoration to decide whether this action was part of a straightforward struggle for power between rivals whose concepts of society were in other respects alike, or whether it implied the existence of more radical social ends. To some extent an answer must depend on an examination of the manner in which radical ends were brought about and on how radical they were. This is a topic to which we will turn in later chapters. But the answer rests as well on a detailed consideration of what took place in 1867–68, which we take up now.

THE SHOGUN'S RESIGNATION

The Tosa leadership, which took the first steps toward encouraging Keiki to resign, was not so very different in background and outlook from that of Satsuma, even though the two domains have commonly been described as pro-Bakufu and anti-Bakufu, respectively, in the disputes of 1867. Tosa's key figure was Gotō Shōjirō (1838–97), a middle samurai of 150 koku who was related by marriage to the reformer Yoshida Tōyō.[4] Gotō had first been raised to high office after the destruction of Takechi's loyalist party in 1864; he was then twenty-six years old. Three years later, as a reward for his services, he was promoted to the rank of Karō with 1,500 koku. Working closely with him was Fukuoka Kōtei (1835–1919), another middle samurai (56 koku) but one who came from a branch of one of the regular Karō houses and had held office as Yoshida Tōyō's colleague. Of about the same age and status was Itagaki Taisuke (1837–1919), a specialist in Western-style military reform and head of a well-to-do hirazamurai family (220 koku) with Yamauchi connections. Like Gotō and Fukuoka he had studied under Yoshida Tōyō and had held offices of some consequence as a result of Tōyō's patronage (despite his known loyalist sympathies). Other members of the group were Kōyama Kunikiyo (1828–1909), Saitō Toshiyuki (1822–81), and Sasaki Takayuki (1830–1910); all three were hirazamurai with stipends ranging from about 50 to 80 koku.

There is no trace here of the gōshi and shōya connections that had characterized the Tosa loyalists. Nor was there much enthusiasm for the Emperor-centered polity they had propounded. Nevertheless, these were reformers, not conservatives—at least in the sense that like Saigō and Ōkubo in Satsuma and Kido and Takasugi in Chōshū, they pursued the goal of "wealth and strength" by methods that were far from traditional. Itagaki was responsible for introducing Western-style weapons and organization into the Tosa armed forces, despite opposition from many samurai. To finance the changes, Gotō put Tosa into business, founding an institution, the Kaiseikan, to promote local production of camphor, paper, sugar, and tea, to develop mining, to operate fisheries, and to engage in foreign trade. His principal assistant in this task was Iwasaki Yatarō (1834–85), a gōshi protégé of Yoshida Tōyō, who helped to draw up the plans for the project in 1864–65 and then took charge of the domain's trading agency at Nagasaki (where he gained the commercial experience that enabled him to found the Mitsubishi shipping company after 1868).

These facts are relevant to Restoration politics not only because Tosa followed in all this a similar pattern to Satsuma—the relationship between Gotō and Iwasaki, for example, in which Gotō was concerned chiefly with political ends and Iwasaki with economic means, has much in common with the relationship between Ōkubo and Godai—but also because its policies created a direct link between the two domains. Gotō's reform program, which took him on visits to Nagasaki and Shanghai in 1866, also brought about a reconciliation with the Tosa rōnin Sakamoto Ryōma, who was then engaged in handling Satsuma's foreign trade. When the two men met, early in 1867, they quickly agreed to recruit Sakamoto's irregulars, the Kaientai, as the nucleus of a Tosa navy. This force was to finance itself as far as possible by engaging in transport and commerce (a reflection, perhaps, of Sakamoto's merchant and gōshi origins); but it had official support and established a valuable link with other exiled Tosa loyalists, especially Nakaoka Shintarō, who had been active in Chōshū. It certainly made possible a degree of cooperation with those who had come to recognize, as Sakamoto and Nakaoka did, that what was required by way of national policy was not expulsion of the barbarian in its cruder forms, but "learning of the strong points of other peoples" in military science and technology, so as to enable Japan to meet the West on equal terms.[5]

In other words, Tosa's reformers and surviving loyalists found common ground in a program of fukoku-kyōhei, much as their fellows in Chōshū and Satsuma had done. They also moved some way toward an anti-Bakufu position, despite the reluctance of their lord, Yamauchi Yōdō, to break his ties with the Tokugawa. Sakamoto would have liked to see his domain join the Satsuma-Chōshū alliance. So would Nakaoka and Itagaki. They recognized, however, as did Gotō, that Tosa's interests might be better served by following an independent line, mediating between Edo and its enemies. It was Sakamoto, in fact—drawing together ideas he had derived from "liberal" Bakufu officials like Katsu Awa and Ōkubo Ichiō, from Echizen reformers like Yokoi Shōnan and Yuri Kimimasa and from the experts in things Western he had met in Nagasaki—who produced a formula.[6] As he expounded it to Gotō in July 1867 it envisaged a formal recognition by the Shogun of the Emperor's authority;

the creation of a bicameral legislature to ensure that decisions had the widest possible support; the appointment to office of men of talent, chosen from Court nobles, feudal lords, and "the people"; and the founding of a modern navy and imperial guard. By such changes, he maintained, outdated laws and policies would be replaced by others more appropriate to the country's current needs.

On the basis of this plan, the Tosa leaders entered into discussions with those of Satsuma. On July 22, 1867, at a meeting in Kyōto attended by Gotō, Fukuoka, Sakamoto, and Nakaoka for the one side and by Komatsu, Saigō, and Ōkubo for the other, an agreement was drawn up stipulating that the two domains would work together to secure the resignation of the Shogun.[7] "There cannot," it stated, "be two rulers in a land or two heads in one family." Hence the fact that Japan's administration was entrusted to a Shogun instead of being conducted by the Emperor was "a violation of the natural order." This made it necessary to abolish the Shogun's office and relegate its holder to the ranks of the feudal lords. Thereafter, government should be carried on by a bicameral council in Kyōto, made up of an upper house of Court nobles and daimyo and a lower house of "retainers and even commoners . . . who are just and pure-hearted," which would devise means of revising the treaties, reforming institutions, and "setting men's hearts at rest."

We have here in essence the policies that were followed in the early part of 1868, except for the provisions about the fate of Keiki. However, it was precisely this point that was to divide the great domains during the next few months. As we shall see when we come to discuss them more fully later in this chapter, the Satsuma men, influenced by their failures in Kyōto in June, were already inclining to the view that Edo would surrender only to force. This implied a solution more drastic than the Tosa plan—which had earlier been Satsuma's—of allowing Keiki to step down to become a daimyo of much the same standing as Shimazu. Nevertheless, Satsuma was not unwilling to let Tosa try its hand provided there was no commitment to accept an unsatisfactory outcome. So it agreed to wait until Gotō had made his effort to get Keiki to resign. For its own part, Tosa promised to contribute troops to an anti-Bakufu military operation if its mediation failed.

It was not easy to convince Yamauchi Yōdō, who was still in Kōchi, that this was Tosa's best course. On August 12, however, he gave in to Gotō's arguments and agreed to play his part, which was to write to Keiki. But there was then a further delay because of a dispute with Britain over an alleged attack on British seamen in Nagasaki by men from Tosa's Kaientai. As a result, it was not until September 17 that Yōdō announced his decision to his senior retainers.* A memorial to the Bakufu was then drawn up, consisting of a general covering statement signed by Yōdō and a detailed set of proposals from Gotō and his colleagues.[8]

Yōdō's personal statement concerned itself chiefly with the question of national unity. The divisions between Court and Bakufu, it said, as well as those between nobles and feudal lords, weakened Japan at a time when strength was her greatest need. Only "the restoration of imperial rule" (ōsei-fukko) would rally "the whole people of the country" (*tenka banmin*) so as to reform the polity (kokutai) and make possible a solution to the problems of foreign affairs.† The memorandum of the Tosa officials pursued a similar theme, though at greater length, echoing the agreement Gotō had made with Satsuma. There should be a transfer of administrative responsibility to the Emperor, exercised through a bicameral council; "a fundamental revision" of feudal authority and of the institutions of the Court; an imperial guard based near Kyōto; new treaties negotiated in the Emperor's name and in consultation with the lords; a system of schools "appropriate for those of various ages"; and the appointment of officials who would "avoid the controversies of the past and concentrate on the problems that lie ahead." In sum, Japan must do what was necessary for national revival so

* The announcement reflected his reservations about what was being done. In it he specifically denied any intention of "destroying the Bakufu" (tōbaku) and coupled the proposal to seek Keiki's resignation with plans for developing navigation and trade, implying fukoku-kyōhei (see *Ishin shiryō kōyō*, 7: 222).

† There are two interesting points of terminology here. Notwithstanding the use of the expression "the whole people of the country," the only specific references are to segments of the ruling class, which makes it difficult to argue that Yōdō was thinking of popular support in the modern sense. Moreover, the term kokutai, which in later (and some contemporary) usage implied an Emperor-centered polity, is here clearly being used of the *existing* structure, i.e., that comprising Bakufu and domains. The document is therefore more feudal in tone than the translation might suggest.

that she might "stand unashamed before all nations and all ages to come."

Gotō left Tosa with these documents on September 22, 1867, and after delays due to bad weather reached Kyōto on October 1, which is to say more than two months after his meeting with the Satsuma leaders. He found Saigō and Ōkubo on the point of moving troops to the capital, having apparently given him up; and when he explained to them that Yamauchi Yōdō, despite the earlier agreement, could not be persuaded to cooperate in any attempt to overthrow the Bakufu by force, they refused to wait any longer for a Tosa initiative. Nevertheless, at Komatsu's urging they agreed that Gotō should go ahead on his own while they completed their preparations.[9] On October 29 the Tosa memorial was duly handed to the Rōjū Itakura Katsukiyo for transmission to the Shogun. It was followed a few days later by a private warning from Sakamoto to Nagai Naomune about Satsuma's military arrangements.

Keiki was in fact well aware that the Bakufu's relations with Satsuma and Chōshū were again moving toward crisis. Moreover, he was already under some pressure from Bakufu officialdom to adopt the kind of policies that Tosa now proposed. Two of his ablest officials, Ōkubo Ichiō and Katsu Awa, had long been urging some such step.* The Rōjū Inaba Masakuni, in a memorial written in early November 1867, recommended that the office of Shogun be abolished, but that the head of the Tokugawa house take office as Kampaku, establishing himself in Kyōto and governing through a council that would include both Court nobles and feudal lords.[10]

Another senior official, Ōgyū Noritaka, put forward a much more elaborate proposal: that the Shogun remain the chief executive of government but act on the advice of a bicameral national assembly or council, which in turn would be supported by local assemblies of a similar kind. This, he argued, would be ōsei-fukko, "the restoration of imperial rule," not merely in the sense of eliminating the

* Ōkubo Ichiō had proposed to Matsudaira Shungaku in 1862–63 that the Shogun resign his office and revert to daimyo status, retaining the lands the Tokugawa had held before Ieyasu's rise to power; that a bicameral assembly, meeting in Kyōto or Osaka, be established to discuss general policy; and that five daimyo, selected from the upper house, serve as an executive committee. See Osatake, *Ishin,* 1: 76–81.

Bakufu as an administrative structure, but also in the sense of creating a centralized state. It could then be strengthened by depriving the daimyo, including the Tokugawa, of their private armies and requiring them to put two-thirds of their revenues at the disposal of the central power. In addition, they would be required to allot part of the remaining third to education and industrial development. If this program was followed, the Bakufu's enemies would no longer be able to maintain that the national interests were being subordinated to those of the Tokugawa house: "Government would be efficient, the people would be united, the country's interests would be served. . . . The whole country's strength would be used to defend the country as a whole, the whole country's wealth would be applied to the country's expenditure as a whole. . . . None would be able to say that government was personal and the country put to private use."[11]

Another plan, drawn up at Keiki's request by Nishi Amane, recently returned from his studies at Leiden, put something of the same ideas into Western dress. Under his plan, the Emperor would possess the right to sanction laws, supervise ceremonials and religion, conscript an army, and require service from the daimyo. The Shogun, who would still control his own lands and conduct the administration of the country, would appoint officials and act as president of the upper house of a bicameral assembly, to which daimyo and samurai (but not commoners) would belong. This assembly—that is, the representatives of the domains—would legislate on general policy, but its decisions would be subject to the Emperor's approval. Securing that approval would be one of the Shogun's functions.[12]

Some of these proposals envisaged the perpetuation of the Bakufu in fresh guise, whether as the executive arm of a feudal assembly or as the nucleus of a more centralized bureaucracy. Others hinted that Bakufu officialdom might in the last resort have to be sacrificed to appease the Shogun's enemies. All, however, sought ways of using the Tosa overture in such a manner as to retain in the new order a key position for the Tokugawa house.

This seems to have been Keiki's attitude, too.[13] Although he later maintained that he saw resignation in favor of an assembly as the only means of carrying on the administration in view of the country's growing disunity,[14] there is little doubt he saw himself as the effective head of any government that might eventually emerge. So did many others. Satsuma and Chōshū, as we shall see, regarded the idea of his resignation as a mere device, another variant on kōbu-gattai, "unity of Court and Bakufu." Fukuchi Genichirō, the Bakufu's historian, reports that the same impression was current—albeit in terms of approval, not rejection—among senior Court and Bakufu officials.[15] Sir Harry Parkes, reflecting the sentiment in Edo, said of Keiki: "I doubt very much whether he would abandon the large party and large interests which he doubtless represents, and throw the game of Government into the hands of his opponents. It would be a misfortune for Japan and for foreign interests if he were to do so, as the country eminently needs a strong man at the helm to prevent a flood of anarchy."[16] Later, when Parkes received more accurate news of what was going on, he gave Keiki credit for courage in acting "against the manifest wishes and interests of his own supporters";[17] but he noted that nothing was likely to destroy the Shogun's influence so long as he held "the power of the purse," as he inevitably would while he retained control of almost a third of the country's revenues.[18]

In view of all this, it is not surprising that on November 8, after private consultations with Matsudaira Shungaku and those senior Bakufu officials who were available—significantly, there was no general canvassing of Bakufu opinion—Keiki announced to the representatives of Satsuma, Tosa, Aki, Bizen, and Uwajima his decision to surrender his administrative functions as Shogun (but not his title) to the throne. Next day he submitted a memorial to the Emperor in these terms. By taking this step, he said, he wished to ensure that "government is directed from one central point," in order that Japan might "hold her own with all nations of the world."[19]

The Bakufu, explaining the change to the ministers of the powers, stated the motive for it even more explicitly: the current unrest in Japan was due to a mistaken notion of Edo's "submission to foreign demands for fear of hostilities," and it was partly for the sake of maintaining the treaties that Keiki now intended "to surrender to the Court the administrative authority he inherited from his ancestors." He would then "petition the Mikado to convene an assembly of the heads of the great houses, that they may discuss fully the present state of affairs and join forces in laying down laws concerning government."[20]

Parkes reported that Edo was caught by surprise by the news, but for his own part he approved it. Foreign interests needed above all stability within Japan, he claimed. Had Keiki not taken this step there might well have been civil war; but now there seemed "a fair chance of the unworkable Government of Japan being replaced by an intelligible system" centered on Kyōto instead of Edo. "It is rather saddening," he wrote to Edmund Hammond of the Foreign Office, "to see the glory of government depart so suddenly from this fine city, but it derives its ornament and consequence from a system which we must desire to see ended—a system of feudality ill organized and acknowledging no control."[21]

That Parkes could write in this vein is evidence of the extent to which opinion in Japan, even in Edo, by this time accepted the inevitability of substantial institutional change. It did not follow, however, that the idea of a transfer of power from the Bakufu to its opponents was equally acceptable. Many fudai were willing to use force against Satsuma and Chōshū, treating Keiki's resignation as no more than a tactical move that might lead in the end to an imperial renewal of the Shogun's mandate and a restoration of his prestige. Senior officials of the Court, who were faced with the task of framing a reply to Keiki, held much the same views; but they also came under pressure from Satsuma men, acting with "opposition" kuge who were seeking to exploit the occasion in the interest of a true "restoration of imperial rule."

As ever, their response to such a situation was equivocal. On November 10 an imperial decree announced the acceptance of the submission (but not specifically the proposal) that Keiki had made. Simultaneously, the great lords, together with those, like Shimazu Hisamitsu and the daimyo "retired" during Ii Naosuke's purge, who remained the real, if not the titular, heads of their domains, were summoned once again to confer on policy. Pending their discussions, the Court decided, things were to go on much as before: "The territories and cities heretofore under Bakufu control will continue to be administered as in the past, though subject to orders which shall be issued in due time."[22] Ominously, it seemed to some, there was an implication here that the Shogun might eventually lose his lands; but when Keiki asked for clarification of the document two days later, he was promptly—and improbably—assured by the Kampaku that only the lands providing the Emperor's revenues were in question, that is, those the Bakufu supposedly administered on the Court's behalf, not those the Tokugawa held in fief.

A week later, on November 19, Keiki went even further and submitted his resignation as Shogun. Again the Court put off a decision pending consultation with the lords. In the meantime he was to continue in his duties as before. Indeed, it seemed at this point that the portentous event of the Shogun's resignation was to come and go without wreaking any of the great changes that had been expected of it. The lords showed little sign of coming to Kyōto to take decisions.[23] Keiki remained inactive, making no move against his enemies. The Court was uncertain and divided. At the end of the month, a despairing Gotō set out for Tosa again to see if he could persuade Yamauchi Yōdō to come and break the deadlock, while the representatives of Satsuma and Chōshū continued to prepare for the very different solution that they had come to regard as both necessary and their own.

COUP D'ÉTAT

During 1865 and 1866 the new leaders of Satsuma and Chōshū—chiefly Saigō and Ōkubo in the one, Kido and Takasugi in the other—had been confirmed in their hostility to the Bakufu. Its "selfish" policies, they insisted, threatened national disaster. Yet the Bakufu retained enough of its traditional authority to withstand all the pressures they could marshal in favor of change, whether exercised through the Court, as at the end of 1865, or through the lords, as in the spring of 1867. Therefore, the Bakufu must be "destroyed." The argument enabled personal ambition, local patriotism, and a growing national consciousness—sentiments proper to domain bureaucrats who styled themselves "men of talent" and "men of spirit"—to be brought together in shaping an anti-Bakufu alliance.

One must, however, distinguish here between ends and means. Down to the middle of 1867, certainly, most of those who thought about the subject at all had only the haziest notion of an institutional alternative to the Edo structure. Some kind of Emperor-centered feudalism, operating through a baronial council, was as far as their ideas went; and wisely so, perhaps, for this very vagueness made it possible to incorporate into the movement a great variety of social groups, ranging from Court nobles and feudal lords to lesser samurai and even well-to-do commoners. It also left room for a variety of attitudes (from traditionalism to Western-style reform), as well as of specific policies (both the plans of Tosa and those of Satsuma-Chōshū).

The Tosa proposals, as envisaged in Gotō's agreement with Satsuma in July 1867, were in substance an attempt to persuade the Shogun to adjust the balance of power between himself and the lords to the advantage of the latter. Inasmuch as the lords acting together had failed to achieve this during the Hyōgo crisis only a month before, Ōkubo, for one, had doubted from the start whether such a démarche could succeed. Still, he did not want gratuitously to offend his potential allies, and so, as we have seen, he agreed that the Tosa attempt be made. At the same time he continued to consider what other action might be needed in the event the Tosa initiative failed. As he wrote to a colleague in Kagoshima at this time: "It is absolutely clear that the Bakufu intends at all costs to pursue its own selfish interests, bringing pressure to bear on the loyal domains to cow and overawe them. This leaves us no choice. . . . It is quite possible that the Bakufu could eventually bring the Imperial Court wholly within its power. . . . Hence we must make ready our troops, rally support in the country, and show ourselves resolute in the Emperor's service. Without this we can effect nothing."[24] The rest of the letter was about moving troops, which suggests that this was not mere idle talk. All the same, there was still much to do before so experienced a politician as Ōkubo would be willing to proceed to the use of force. After all, in the Imperial Court, in the other great domains, even within Satsuma and Chōshū, there remained many hostile and uncommitted groups whose influence could not safely be ignored.

On July 17 the Chōshū representatives in Kyōto, Shinagawa Yajirō and Yamagata Aritomo, were told in the course of discussions with the Satsuma leaders that Satsuma contemplated using force, if it came to that, to secure the Court's backing for its policy.[25] What was in mind, presumably—the wording of the statement was, as ever, imprecise—was a seizure of the palace, such as Satsuma and Aizu had carried out in 1863 and Chōshū had attempted in 1864. Kido and Takasugi were quickly informed of this. Soon afterward, however, they also received news of the Tosa-Satsuma agreement, which raised doubts in their minds about what Ōkubo really intended. Shinagawa, sent to query the point in August, was assured that the agreement made no difference because Tosa would certainly fail; but it was not until Ōkubo visited Yamaguchi himself two months later that trust between the allies was finally restored. In meetings with the Chōshū leaders on October 15,[26] he emphasized that Shimazu Hisamitsu was aware of having too often in the past submitted memorials to no avail and would not rest content with such action again; he would use troops and hoped Chōshū would do the same. In private talks, Ōkubo warned that the palace must be seized without delay for fear the Bakufu might forestall the move, perhaps with foreign help. Kido agreed. "If we are robbed of the jewel," he commented—meaning the Emperor's person—"we shall be helpless indeed."[27]

Two things emerge from the accounts of these discussions: first, that the initiative was now Satsuma's, and second, that there were still many in Chōshū who, though united in their determination to resist a Bakufu attack, hesitated to risk another offensive like that of 1864. Largely because of Kido's influence, the reluctance of the Chōshū leaders was overcome. But the margin of victory was a narrow one at best, making it necessary to continue to move with caution lest the decision be suddenly reversed.

What is more, an almost identical problem existed with respect to Satsuma, which had also to be solved before any military action could begin. The plans we have been discussing had been formulated not in Kagoshima, but in Kyōto, where Shimazu Hisamitsu was surrounded by activists like Ōkubo, Saigō, and Komatsu. In his castle town the balance of political forces was very different: adherents of "unity of Court and Bakufu" (his own former policy) resisted what seemed to be a move toward the very loyalism they had thought to have defeated in suppressing the "men of spirit"; and conservatives, preoccupied like their counterparts in Chōshū with the narrow parochial interests of daimyo and domain, argued against any step that might endanger them.[28]

Hence, while Ōkubo went to Chōshū Hisamitsu went to Kagoshima to make sure that the orders for the movement of troops were carried out. Persuasion, as well as authority, had to be called on before they were. An announcement of October 24, signed jointly by Hisamitsu and his son, suggested—quite dishonestly—that the troops were needed to defend the Court in the event of disturbances. Another, dated three weeks later, said that in the existing state of unrest within Japan it was necessary to be ready for emergencies, including violence in Kyōto, and that Satsuma might have to act quickly to preserve national unity, since the new Emperor, fifteen-year-old Mutsuhito—his father, Kōmei, had died in February 1867—was too young to be able to pacify the country on his own. In any case, it promised, Satsuma would not be the first to appeal to force.[29] This was a flat contradiction of what Ōkubo was simultaneously saying in Chōshū, but it served its turn. The activists, with support from most of the younger samurai, got the decision they wanted.

To do so, they had had to appeal to the sentiment of loyalty to Emperor, as well as duty to lord, a circumstance that showed how vital it was to them, in holding their followers together, to be able to manipulate the public statements of the Court. Iwakura Tomomi, who had gradually been emerging from enforced inactivity during 1866 and early 1867, proved a useful ally in this. He had in fact already begun to build a party of sympathizers among the kuge, men who would be available to provide a change of Court leadership when the moment came: Sanjō Sanetomi (who had changed his place of exile from Chōshū to Kyūshū); Saga Sanenaru, acknowledged leader of the extremist group among lesser officials in Kyōto; Nakamikado Tsuneyuki, one of his colleagues; and perhaps most important of all, Nakayama Tadayasu, maternal grandfather to the new boy-Emperor.

Iwakura's general strategy was set out in a long memorandum

that he prepared for Saga and Nakayama at the end of May 1867, on the eve of the discussions about the opening of Hyōgo.[30] It was essential, he argued, that the Court overcome its own disunity and be ready to act whenever the chance arose. For it to call openly for overthrow of the Tokugawa would be to invite disaster, since it could not count on the support of friendly lords with the same degree of confidence that Edo could expect the backing of the fudai. Neither the justice of its cause nor the prestige attaching to an imperial decree was enough to balance this. To succeed, there had to be an actual or potential use of force, which only Satsuma, Chōshū, Tosa, and a few other domains could possibly provide. Thus, pending the time when the lords could be brought to realize this themselves, Kyōto could do no more than maintain relations with them—"its hands and feet," Iwakura called them—keeping in mind its long-term "grand design" of bringing about a situation in which "the Court would be respected, the Bakufu and the great domains controlled."[31]

By this estimate, Iwakura was setting out to exploit the military strength of Satsuma and Chōshū on the Court's behalf while maintaining such political balance as would prevent the substitution of a Shimazu or Mōri hegemony for a Tokugawa one. His aims might well be compared with those of Tosa, though directed to imperial, not baronial, ends. There was little opportunity to accomplish them, however, while the Bakufu seemed strong and confident, as the Hyōgo dispute showed.

By the autumn, the difficulties the Satsuma and Chōshū leaders were experiencing in maintaining the resolution of their followers, together with the risk that the Tosa initiative might rally "neutral" domains like Aki and Bizen behind what could prove in the end to be no more than another abortive compromise, caused Saigō and Ōkubo, along with Hirosawa Saneomi of Chōshū, to seek secret imperial sanction for their plans. On November 3, less than a week after Gotō submitted the Tosa memorial to Itakura, Ōkubo drafted another document, this time in Satsuma's name, requesting orders from the Emperor for the Shogun's overthrow.[32] It began by reciting briefly the history of Edo's failures: its weakness in foreign policy, the rise in prices, the widespread unrest among both samurai and commoners. It then turned to the Bakufu's policy toward Chōshū, charging that this had culminated in a punitive expedition so unjust as to have alienated daimyo opinion and provoked an open breach between Keiki and Shimazu. The danger now was that the Shogun might attempt to "seize the Court and govern by arbitrary will," thereby precipitating a civil war. Since that war would be carried on in the face of foreign threat, there could be only one outcome: the destruction of Japan. To avert this the Shogun must be removed from office, a task that Satsuma and its allies were ready to undertake. Given the imperial command, they would "punish his offenses by force, eliminating traitors and laying lasting foundations for the state, so that the Emperor's mind might be put at rest and the distress of the people eased."[33]

Iwakura at once supported this application, though not in quite the same terms that Ōkubo had used. In a memorial of his own, which he got Nakayama to put before the Emperor, he emphasized that during centuries of feudal rule "the people as a whole have become unaware that there is a Son of Heaven above them."[34] Accordingly, he said, the case for abolishing the Shogun's office was not merely that it would be a punishment for recent government errors, but also that it would make possible "a major reform of political institutions" and the adoption of measures for promoting "national wealth and strength."

Such a formulation, envisaging far more than a redistribution of feudal power, would certainly have frightened senior Court officials, even Satsuma sympathizers like Konoe Tadahiro, had they known of it. But it had great appeal for the small group of kuge loyalists who had, through Nakayama, access to Mutsuhito (Meiji).* On November 8 they secured a secret pardon for the Chōshū daimyo and his son. Next day, also in secret, they obtained—or manufactured, since there has always been a doubt about its authenticity—the edict for which Ōkubo had asked. Keiki was to be dismissed and two of his associates, the lords of Aizu and Kuwana, punished. (The two lords seem to have been singled out because they were the Bakufu officials responsible for controlling Kyōto and the Court;

* It was not until 1868 that the era-name Meiji was adopted for Mutsuhito's reign.

Matsudaira Katamori of Aizu was Kyōto Shugo, Matsudaira Sadaaki of Kuwana was Kyōto Shoshidai.)

Whether genuine or not, the decree served one of the purposes for which it had been designed: Satsuma and Chōshū closed their ranks and began to move troops toward the capital.* Moreover, rumors of it may well have influenced Keiki's resignation, which coincided almost exactly with it in time. Then, on November 16, while Saigō and Ōkubo were away from the capital (using the imperial orders as a means of keeping their more conservative colleagues in Kagoshima and Yamaguchi up to the mark), their allies at Court lost their nerve and withdrew the document, on the grounds that the Shogun's resignation made it superfluous. Soon after, Matsudaira Shungaku reached Kyōto and began to organize support for the Tosa plan among the lords who were known to favor "unity of Court and Bakufu," pointedly omitting Satsuma but including the Tokugawa branch house of Owari as well as Uwajima.

Thus Ōkubo, returning on December 10, found the situation moving rapidly against him. Feeling he had to give ground, he told Shungaku that if it could be shown that Keiki was serious about relinquishing his power, Satsuma and Chōshū would be willing to let Owari and Echizen act as intermediaries in arranging a settlement.[35] However, Shungaku was unable to get an equivalent concession from the Bakufu, largely owing to the stubbornness of Aizu, which still demanded action against Chōshū. Meanwhile, Ōkubo was having little better success in restoring his influence over the Court nobles. Apart from Iwakura, they seemed only half-persuaded by his insistence that this chance might be the loyalists' last. To add to the confusion, Gotō Shōjirō, trying desperately to get Yamauchi Yōdō to the capital in time to play an effective role, told Shungaku

* It was well over a month, however, before any actually arrived there. The first unit of Satsuma troops reached Mitajiri, in Chōshū, on December 10. It was followed two days later by the main body, some 3,000 men, commanded by Saigō and accompanied by the daimyo, Shimazu Tadayoshi. This force reached Kyōto on December 18. Meanwhile, Chōshū troops had also begun to move east, reaching the vicinity of Nishinomiya, outside Osaka, on December 31. Some Tosa troops reached the capital two days later. See *Ishin shiryō kōyō*, 7: *passim*. One pretext offered for all this activity was that there might be conflict with the foreigners when Hyōgo was opened in accordance with treaty obligations on Jan. 1, 1868. *Ibid.*, p. 387.

what he knew of Ōkubo's plans, information that Shungaku promptly passed on to Keiki.

In all this, two facts stand out: that Satsuma and Chōshū had gone too far to withdraw safely, whatever might be said of the rest; and that their prospects depended largely on an ability to demonstrate that they were acting in accordance with the Emperor's wishes. This meant controlling the palace, at almost any cost. As Kido wrote from Chōshū to his representative in Kyōto, Shinagawa Yajirō: "It is of the utmost importance that we should first get the Emperor into our custody. Should the Bakufu seize him, then no matter what resolution we may show, the morale of loyalists and activists would crumble on every side, and our plot would end in failure. That this would mean destruction for the domains concerned goes without saying. Yet it is also clear that it would bring such harm to our imperial country as could never be repaired."[36] These were the sentiments of Ōkubo and Iwakura, too. They therefore decided that on the morning of January 3, 1868, with or without the endorsement of other domains, they would make public and official the kind of anti-Bakufu pronouncement that had already been secretly issued and withdrawn.

On January 2 Iwakura summoned to his house samurai from Satsuma, Tosa, Aki, Owari, and Echizen and invited them to help in the task of "restoring imperial rule" (ōsei-fukko). (The three other Court nobles involved in the conspiracy, Nakayama, Saga, and Nakamikado, were to have joined him, but at the last moment each found a reason for being elsewhere.)[37] The stated grounds for the step, now described as being the Emperor's own, were essentially those that Ōkubo and Iwakura had given in the memorials in November, namely, the national crisis and the Bakufu's failings at home and abroad. Because of them, Keiki was to be stripped of office. And in order that there might be no disturbance when a new council, to which the lords of the five domains would be invited, issued the decree, the palace gates were to be seized next morning.

That night the imperial council met to consider once again the long-standing issue of the punishment of Chōshū. Keiki, Aizu, and Kuwana, presumably forewarned—after all, the troops to be employed in the coup included units from the fiefs of some of their relatives—pleaded illness and stayed away, but members of the Court engaged in a long discussion. It was so long, in fact, that it upset the arrangements for taking over the gates at dawn, bringing a premature incursion into the palace of men from Owari (who withdrew, apologizing), then a hurried revision of plans. Despite all the confusion this produced, the palace was firmly in loyalist hands by ten o'clock in the morning. Nakayama, Saga, Matsudaira Shungaku, and the lords of Aki and Owari had remained there after the council ended. Iwakura now joined them, bringing the draft of an imperial decree, and secured the Emperor's permission to announce it at a hastily summoned meeting. Bakufu adherents, including most of the high officials of the Court, were refused admission.

The announcement authorized at this meeting[38] accepted Keiki's proffered resignation and stated that the Emperor proposed to resume his ancient responsibilities for government because of the need to "restore the country's prestige." To this end, it said, there would have to be new men as well as new policies. Therefore, all existing senior offices of the Court and the Bakufu would be abolished in favor of a new three-level structure of offices consisting of a Chief Executive (Sōsai), Senior Councillors (Gijō), and Junior Councillors (Sanyo). Most of the initial officeholders were specified in the decree: as Chief Executive it named Prince Arisugawa, a politically "neutral" choice; as Senior Councillors, two imperial princes plus the men who were nominally responsible for the coup, i.e., the three Court nobles Nakayama, Saga, and Nakamikado and the daimyo (or distinguished members of their houses) of Satsuma, Tosa, Aki, Owari, and Echizen; and as Junior Councillors, five Court nobles, including Ōhara Shigenori and Iwakura Tomomi. In addition, three Junior Councillors (by implication, samurai) were to be appointed from each of the domains that furnished Senior Councillors. Chōshū was not at this stage represented at either level, since its lord had not yet been formally pardoned. Sanjō Sanetomi was excluded for the same reason.*

* The kuge appointments are an interesting reflection of how the strict barriers of rank were already being ignored, albeit in a modest way. The eight kuge named in the decree to offices in which their colleagues would be either daimyo (Senior

This administrative structure hinted that there would be changes in the way decisions were made. The document itself promised that "past evils would be swept away," that "men of talent" would be promoted, and that steps would be taken to relieve the hardships resulting from the rise of prices in recent years, whereby "the rich have steadily amassed more wealth, the poor plunged further into misery." In other words, for all that the event had the appearance of a palace revolution—news of it was not communicated even to the feudal lords until five days later—and that most of what was said in the decree was expressed in familiar clichés, there was also in it an indication of a willingness to initiate reform. It remained to be seen, however, whether those who wrote the document could remain in power long enough to give effect to the promises they had made.

CIVIL WAR

Palace revolution though it may have seemed, it would be wrong to suggest that the Restoration and the long weeks of intrigue that preceded it went completely unnoticed by a wider public. In Kyōto, posters and placards had provided a running commentary on current politics for some years. Mostly the work of young "men of spirit" and hence in the tradition of sonnō-jōi, these public displays criticized the Bakufu for its dealings with foreigners, the Court for its subservience to Edo, the officials for accepting bribes and approving "disgraceful" policies.[39] In other words, they were consistently "loyalist" in tone. So were a number of street demonstrations that took place in late 1867, known to historians by the slogan the crowds chanted as a comment on the Emperor's expected resumption of power: "e ja nai ka," or "isn't it good?" It has been argued that these demonstrations were organized by the anti-Bakufu party to provide evidence of popular support for their

Councillors) or samurai (Junior Councillors) all belonged to the middle levels of the Court nobility, not its upper ones, though some were well-to-do by Court standards: Saga, Nakamikado, Nakayama, and Iwakura had stipends ranging from 150 to 350 koku. The one truly high-ranking kuge among the loyalists was Sanjō (469 koku), who belonged to one of the *kuge dōjō* houses from which senior Court offices were traditionally filled. He was later made Gijō, as was Iwakura (presumably because of their close connections with Chōshū and Satsuma, respectively). On the ranks and stipends of these men, see Fukaya, *Kashizoku*, pp. 96–97.

cause.[40] But the British diplomat Algernon Mitford (later Lord Redesdale), who witnessed one in Osaka on December 13, 1867, failed even to recognize it as a political act at all. He reported seeing thousands of "happy fanatics," who were "dancing along the streets dressed in holiday garb" and "shouting till they must have been hoarse." When he inquired what it was all about, he was told that it was because of a "miraculous shower" of slips of paper bearing the names of Shintō gods. As a result, he was led to dilate in his memoirs on "the sacred traditions of a glorious past," not on Japanese politics.[41]

In one respect, Mitford's impressions may have been correct: to contemporaries who were reasonably well informed the events of December 1867 and early January 1868 probably seemed less decisive than they do to us. Parkes commented in a dispatch to London that the crisis did not appear to be "of an alarming nature as regards ourselves," though he added that there was "always danger of many evil passions being let loose, when once the sword is drawn —especially in a semi-civilised country."[42] The historian Oka Yoshitake quotes a samurai from Sakura as having noted that in the capital "people showed no surprise . . . and seemed generally to doubt whether the new administration would last."[43]

Some such belief probably lies behind the Bakufu's failure to act at once to counter the palace coup d'état. To revert to Parkes again, his view of events, based on a subsequent meeting with Keiki, was that the proposals for the Shogun's resignation had been widely believed to be "a plan to bring him in again to a chief if not sovereign position by the vote of a small packed assembly"; that in consequence "the party of action . . . had thought it necessary to strike a blow"; and that Keiki appeared "not to have cared to struggle" against this, possibly because "he looks upon his opponents as a coalition which may soon dissolve of themselves."[44] Certainly this account of Keiki's attitudes—they led Parkes to describe him as "more subtle than bold"[45]—is borne out by what the Bakufu did, or failed to do. Essentially, it relied on the family loyalty of Owari and Echizen, plus the good offices of Tosa, to isolate Satsuma and Chōshū and to ensure that Tokugawa interests were properly represented in the imperial government.

At the first meeting of the reformed council, which took place on January 3, only a few hours after the Emperor had been "restored," the principal topic for discussion was what, if anything, should be done about Keiki, apart from dismissing him. Ōkubo's argument was that there could be no reality in the new arrangements unless the Shogun surrendered not only his office, but also his lands, or at least the greater part of them. If he continued to own a quarter of the country, he would inevitably dominate, whatever the regime's form. Iwakura agreed with this. Yamauchi Yōdō and Matsudaira Shungaku, however, urged that Keiki be invited to join the council without more ado. Since Aki backed Satsuma, and Owari backed Tosa and Echizen, the council was soon hopelessly split. There followed an adjournment for private consultations (and some strongly worded Satsuma threats), which brought compromise, though not until far into the night: Keiki's dismissal alone was to be officially decided at this time; and before anything else was done, Owari and Echizen would be given an opportunity to persuade him to surrender his lands. Unless he did so, he would not be allowed a place in the government.[46]

Next day, Matsudaira Shungaku and Tokugawa Yoshikatsu of Owari conveyed this decision to Keiki at Nijō castle. Keiki expressed a willingness to negotiate, if not precisely in these terms. Thus encouraged, Tosa and Echizen continued their efforts, producing during the next week or so a series of proposals for widening the membership of the council to include not only Keiki, but also a number of other lords, and for financing the imperial administration by a levy on the revenues of daimyo generally, instead of by confiscating Keiki's lands. Meanwhile, on January 6 Keiki withdrew to Osaka, ostensibly to remove his followers from a situation in which they might be tempted to precipitate a clash.

Initially, Satsuma's position was a good deal weakened by these moves. Iwakura was ill. Shimazu Hisamitsu was in Kagoshima and his son, Tadayoshi, proved no match in the council for the more experienced lords from Tosa and Echizen. Saigō and Ōkubo, as mere Sanyo, had no direct access to the highest levels of debate. However, the apparent drift toward a compromise solution, to which these factors seemed to be contributing, was halted by the formal pardoning of Chōshū. On January 21 Sanjō Sanetomi arrived in Kyōto with a Chōshū escort and was at once made Gijō. Six days later the two Chōshū hirazamurai Hirosawa Saneomi and Inoue Kaoru were appointed Sanyo. Moreover, though Matsudaira Shungaku and Yamauchi Yōdō gained the support of the daimyo of Sendai, Fukuoka, Higo, and Hizen (four of the largest domains in the country), Ōkubo was able to win over the Ikeda houses of Inaba and Bizen and to secure the cooperation of powerful loyalist parties in a number of other areas as well. In fact, since the great majority of the lords (including the fudai, despite their attachment to the Tokugawa) had shown themselves reluctant to take sides,* sending an impressive list of excuses to explain their failure to come to the capital, the balance was a great deal more evenly poised than it might have seemed. This, at least, was Ōkubo's belief.[47] And it led him to the conclusion that a trial of strength was a worthwhile gamble.

The fact was that, notwithstanding the mediation of Tosa and Echizen and the paralysis of will shown by many Bakufu officials,† there were irreconcilables on both sides who saw fighting as the sole solution to their rivalries. For the Bakufu, Matsudaira Katamori of Aizu and Matsudaira Sadaaki of Kuwana had only with the greatest difficulty been prevailed on to leave Kyōto for Osaka; and once there they continued to press for a military showdown with Satsuma and Chōshū against those who favored withdrawal to Edo (where the Shogun could presumably stand on the defensive in the midst of his lands).[48] Nor was it certain that Aizu and Kuwana could indefinitely be kept under Keiki's control. Satow records a revealing conversation he had with Kubota Sentarō, one of the Bakufu's military officers, in Osaka on January 7. To the suggestion that imperial orders forbidding hostilities, if issued, would have to be obeyed, Kubota replied: "Yes, by the Tycoon, but not by his retainers."[49]

There were Satsuma men who were equally hotheaded. In Edo,

* Bakufu officials, too. One of them, Ikeda Nagaaki, later commented: "Although it caused me anguish, I looked on in idleness because I had no fixed idea; no policy such as the occasion demanded" (Burks, "A Sub-leader," p. 290).

† Fukuchi, *Bakufu suibō ron*, Chap. 30, comments that many in the Bakufu who were still loyal to the Tokugawa house itself had been sufficiently offended by Keiki's reform program to be hesitant about supporting him fully.

some of them, supposedly acting on Saigō's orders, precipitated rioting in the hope of prompting a rising against the Bakufu in nearby provinces, only to be suppressed with heavy loss of life.[50] When news of this affair reached Osaka, it was a spark to tinder, for it finally convinced Keiki and his more moderate advisers that they must seize the initiative to prevent it falling further into Satsuma hands. On January 26 they began to move troops toward the capital along the roads through Toba and Fushimi, ostensibly to make a show of force to strengthen Tosa and Echizen in their mediation.

Ōkubo once again played a key role in the resulting crisis. In a memorial written for Iwakura on January 27 urging the Court to forbid Keiki's entry to the city, he argued that two serious mistakes had been made since the coup d'état at the beginning of the month. The first had been to allow Tosa, Echizen, and Owari to involve the government in a long series of discussions about the Shogun's fate, instead of stripping him at once of his office and his lands. The second had been to let Keiki remove himself to Osaka and go on behaving as if he ruled the country, especially in his dealings with the foreign representatives. A third mistake of that magnitude now—allowing him to return to Kyōto and take part in politics—would be decisive, for it would encourage his wavering supporters and enable him to regain his influence and power. Indeed, only by bringing matters to the point of war could this be prevented, Ōkubo maintained. And since neither the Gijō nor the Sanyo could be relied on in a situation of this kind, Satsuma and Chōshū must be willing to take the decision themselves, even if the result might make it seem that this was "a Satsuma-Chōshū Court."[51]

Significantly, troops from the two domains went into action before the imperial response to this memorial reached the Satsuma and Chōshū leaders. At Toba and Fushimi some 6,000 of their men (the total includes small contingents from Tosa and elsewhere) met and defeated a Bakufu force about 10,000 strong, driving it back toward Osaka. Both militarily and politically, it proved a crucial victory. Keiki at once decided to withdraw to Edo by sea, refusing permission for a counterattack. As he later told the story, this was because he had made up his mind for the country's sake to submit (though he did not reveal this fact, even to the Rōjū, until he was well on his way, leaving it to be assumed that he was falling back to a position of strength).[52] Whatever the truth of the matter—and there is certainly evidence of a strong desire in many quarters, including the Bakufu, to avoid full-scale civil war lest it bring foreign intervention[53]—the effect was to give Keiki's opponents a clear run.

On January 31, the day of Keiki's departure, the Court issued a decree blaming the Shogun for the hostilities and relieving his followers of their duty toward him. Three days later Osaka castle surrendered. Aizu and Kuwana forces fell back along the Tōkaidō, the road to Edo, but in the provinces around the capital the Bakufu's supporters lost no time in making their peace. Some, like Hikone, had already done so before Toba-Fushimi. Others even went so far as to punish their men for pro-Bakufu activities. In Edo representatives of forty-three domains of the east and northeast drew up a petition calling on the Court to show clemency to Keiki personally, but there were a number who refused to sign even this, preferring to retire to their territories and await developments. It is not so surprising, then, that when an expedition under Prince Arisugawa began to move against Edo at the end of February, its eastward march seemed more a triumphal progress than a military campaign.[54]

Keiki now put matters in train for a negotiated settlement, working through Katsu Awa, who was given military command and was made a Bakufu Junior Councillor (Wakadoshiyori) so as to have rank appropriate to his task. On March 28 he sent a letter to his old friend Saigō Takamori, now Arisugawa's chief of staff, proposing talks. As one who "although a retainer of the Tokugawa house" was also "a subject of the imperial land," he wrote, he believed an early return to peace to be in the best interest of both.[55] At this, Saigō and Arisugawa, whose headquarters had been moved to Shizuoka, a little over 100 miles from Edo, proposed a truce, asking that the Shogun surrender himself into the custody of the daimyo of Bizen (his brother) and hand over his castle, his warships, and his arms. On April 6 Katsu sought a meeting with Saigō and accepted these terms, subject to Mito replacing Bizen. Saigō agreed. Calling a halt to military operations, he left at once for Kyōto, where Iwakura put the agreement in due form: Keiki was to resign the headship of the

Tokugawa house, which was to pass to the Tayasu branch, holding not more than 700,000 koku; and only officials who had openly offended against the Court were to be punished. On May 3, once Keiki had confirmed his acceptance of the formula, Edo castle capitulated. Ten days later Arisugawa made a state entry into the city.

Neither side found it easy to impose this agreement on its followers. In Kyōto, Iwakura, Ōkubo, and Kido had to work hard to overcome the opposition of loyalists who called for something more severe, with the result that a public announcement of the terms was delayed for several weeks. In Edo, Saigō had to use force against 3,000 Tokugawa retainers protesting the treatment of their lord. Part of the Bakufu fleet, commanded by Enomoto Takeaki, fled to the north, rather than surrender. More serious, an alliance of domains in the northeast, led by Sendai and Aizu, showed a willingness to resist the new regime in an organized way. Arguing that Satsuma and Chōshū were "evil advisers" and that the Emperor was being misled, they prepared to defend their feudal rights. But in September Saigō took command of large-scale operations against them, and their main stronghold, Aizu's castle of Wakamatsu, eventually capitulated at the beginning of November. By the end of the year the northeast was pacified, albeit at considerable cost.

This left only Enomoto, who escaped with eight ships and about 2,000 men—among them the senior Bakufu officials Itakura Katsukiyo, Ogasawara Nagamichi, and Nagai Naomune—to Ezo (Hokkaidō), which they requested be made a Tokugawa fief. This was more than Kyōto could grant, for all that Enomoto was respected there, so in 1869 a strong force was sent to suppress the "rebels" as soon as spring made fighting possible. Hakodate fell on June 29, thus restoring peace to the whole of Japan. Appropriately, Enomoto signaled the event by sending the notes on navigation he had made as a student in Holland to the commander of the force that had defeated him. They would, he said, "be of use to the country," whatever happened to him.[56]

Nor were his opponents any less ready to assert that patriotism was a higher ideal than feudal loyalty. On November 1, 1869, Keiki was pardoned (though not restored) in the name of national unity. For the same reason, if more slowly, pardons were also granted to those who had served him, even men like Enomoto, who had fought for his cause. Some of them—Ōkubo Ichiō, Nagai Naomune, Enomoto himself—eventually gained high office in the Meiji bureaucracy; and it was thereby demonstrated that the pursuit of national strength, necessitating the reconciliation of the vanquished as well as the use of "men of talent," wherever found, had left the politics of "destroying the Bakufu" behind.

CHAPTER XII

Problems of Government

THE EVENTS OF late 1867 and early 1868 had two characteristics that need to be emphasized. First, they were feudal in manner and personnel: rivalries of great lords, who in the last resort could call on private military force. Second, they represented a struggle for power, not a war of ideologies. What was immediately at stake was not whether there should be a change of fundamental institutions in Japan, but whether those who exercised authority in the Shogun's name, the Tokugawa vassals, were to be displaced by others, chiefly from Satsuma and Chōshū, who would exercise it in the name of the Emperor. For this reason, the Bakufu's opponents were more interested in slogans than in programs, quick to speak in general terms of ōsei-fukko, "the restoration of imperial rule," or fukoku-kyōhei, "enriching the country and strengthening the army" (amplified, perhaps, by a reference to the Bakufu's "selfishness" and "arbitrary" power), but slow to spell out the precise steps they would like to take when in office. It is a not unfamiliar feature of political controversy.

Victory, or the expectation of victory, changed all this, as it commonly does. Once the new leaders had to issue orders, rather than exhortations, they were confronted with the task of deciding the uses to which to put their power. And this led them to initiate a policy debate in much more concrete terms. They began it with some agreed objectives and some shared assumptions: that national unity, on which defense in the face of foreign threat depended, required political change; that this must in some sense give a new role to the Imperial Court; and that there must be a willingness to "use the barbarian to control the barbarian," that is, to adopt Western techniques in the service of military and economic strength. In other words, their attitudes reflected, at least in part, the interests of the elements in society that supported them: the technological modernizing of the reforming lords and the political ideals of the "men of spirit" of 1863.

Thus to argue that at the beginning of 1868 the policies of the imperial government had still to be determined is not to say that we have no prior indications of the direction they might take. For one thing, the nature of the traditional polity and the strength of the sentiment surrounding it set limits to the practicable alternatives to Bakufu rule. For another, the character of the new leadership implied certain kinds of political and social change rather than others; and even though this had not been made explicit, members of the group had engaged in the discussion of a number of proposals from which decisions eventually emerged. An account of early Meiji politics might usefully begin, therefore, with an examination of this background of ideas, both specific and general.

It also requires, however, a consideration of circumstance, in that decisions were taken by men who did not perfectly control events. What they tried to do and when they tried to do it were often determined by what they felt able to do. Accordingly, before we turn to the wider theme of the shaping of Meiji society, which will be the subject of the remaining chapters of this book, we should first look at the everyday problems of government in the immediate aftermath of Restoration, that is, at the pragmatic, as well as the conceptual, components in the process by which "absolutism" was evolved. For it was the interaction of the two, rather than the supremacy of either, that gave Japan, somewhat improbably, a centralized, Western-style, bureaucratic state presided over by an avowedly "traditional" Emperor whose authority was ratified by the tenets of a Shintō faith.

INFLUENCES AND IDEAS

The central issue of Japanese politics in the first few weeks of 1868 was whether, or to what extent, the Tokugawa should retain a measure of influence after imperial rule had been "restored." Of almost equal importance, however, was the question of how far the relationship of domains to central government would have to be transformed. In other words, the debate that contemporaries conducted was political in a fairly narrow sense, raising questions about the organization of government and the nature of its institutions—including the merits of feudalism (hōken-seido) as against a provincial system (gunken-seido) staffed by imperial nominees—but not, initially, raising questions of social or economic structure, except insofar as they related directly to the locus of power. Logically, it was a debate that began by examining the position of the Emperor, since control of his person had been the focus of the preceding struggles.

For centuries the Japanese Emperor had been a symbol, not a ruler, the embodiment of "national independence, national historic continuity, national unity, harmony within the government, and harmony between rulers and ruled."[1] As such he was immensely important to the Restoration leaders because he could give them legitimacy, as his predecessors had to Shogun for nearly 700 years. Like the Tokugawa, therefore, they accorded him great ceremonial respect. By so doing, they were able to assert a cultural continuity in the name of a sovereign "uncontaminated by responsibility for Tokugawa policies"[2] while they in fact pursued a course for which there were no true precedents. In the long run this was vital to their ability to effect profound changes in Japanese life with a minimum of psychological shock. In the shorter term, it was the key to holding together an unwieldy alliance of domains. As a contemporary observer put it, for some time the new government existed "simply by the halo surrounding his [the Emperor's] sacred name."[3]

It did not follow, however, that these governmental functions could be performed only within a centralized administrative framework, any more than loyalism as expounded by the shishi in earlier years had precluded the continuation of a feudal state. Men like Maki Izumi and Takechi Zuizan, though often contemptuous of their superiors, had not planned to abolish the whole structure that sustained them; they had proposed rather to replace the Bakufu with an Emperor-centered feudalism and create an imperial domain in which they and the Court nobles might find suitable rewards. Thus their hostility to Edo, stemming from a wish to see foreigners expelled, did not of necessity imply a call for revolutionary innovation. For this, indeed, one must turn to a different tradition, one more scholarly than political, which saw feudalism as a departure from a Chinese norm that had been established in Japan in very ancient times.

Tokugawa scholars could not fail to be aware that they lived under a system of government quite distinct from that of China, not only in the duality of Emperor and Shogun, but also in matters of vassalage, feudal tenure, and hereditary status.[4] They clearly distinguished the personal and separatist tendencies of the one system (hōken) from the centralizing emphasis of the other (gunken). They quite naturally compared their respective virtues and defects as well. Vassals themselves, the Confucian scholars of Bakufu and domains saw a better basis for military strength in feudalism than in the Chinese system; and they also believed the feudal class structure provided a kind of continuing social stability that China lacked. Yet as Confucianists they had a professional stake in the respectability of what they taught, coupled with an envy, natural to those of only modest rank, of the fact that in China, as one of them put it, "a man born among the peasantry" could "advance to the position of one of the chief ministers of the State."[5] They therefore had no total commitment to either tradition.

This fact had some significance for Japan's entry to the modern world. In the first place, because both systems were known and in part acceptable, it was possible to transfer allegiance from the "feudal" to the "bureaucratic" without great emotional strain. Second, because knowledge of the bureaucratic system was only intellectual —the reality was either historically or geographically remote—it was not difficult to recast it in new terms. At the time of the Opium War, Japanese writers blamed China's defeat on the military defects of a provincial type of organization, from which they believed feudalism to be free. Then, when their own country's dealings with the West proved no more successful, they began to argue that feudalism had its weaknesses, too, notably that the cherished independence of domains made for a fragmentation and disunity imperiling the safety of the whole. This was in effect an argument for centralized bureaucracy couched in "Western" terms. Nevertheless, the possibility of equating it with a familiar gunken-seido, not some European model, made it that much easier to accept.

Most of those who wrote about these matters in Japan were samurai scholars serving feudal lords, but it was in the Imperial Court that there existed the rudiments of a structure to which a Chinese pattern of centralization might most easily be attached. Significantly, this was a survival of eighth-century models, subsequently superseded, not the contemporary range of senior Court posts, like that of Kampaku, through which the Bakufu exercised its power. Hence in this context an appeal to the past—the word fukko means restore antiquity—implied a shift of authority away from the Fujiwara within the Court, as well as away from the Tokugawa within the country. No doubt for this reason the call for ōsei-fukko held great attractions for lower-ranking nobles like Iwakura Tomomi, who could not aspire to the highest offices as things stood.

Certainly it was Iwakura who worked out constitutional plans based on this particular feature of the Japanese tradition. In a memorial written in the spring of 1867, anticipating the arrival of the great lords in Kyōto to discuss with Keiki the questions of Hyōgo and Chōshū, he had addressed himself to the problem of how Japan was to be made politically strong in a situation in which her rulers were all too often preoccupied with "competing for petty power."[6] There could be only one solution, he said: "to make the sixty-odd provinces of the country into a single imperial stronghold and so ensure the people's unity."

All the same, Iwakura felt the strength of feudalism was too great to be ignored: "Since the beginning of the Kamakura Bakufu [in 1192] the military houses have held their own territories, each lord conducting his administration within them. It will be no easy matter to try to regulate them suddenly now. Yet if we do not regulate them, then we shall be unable to lay foundations for manifesting to the world the imperial prestige."[7] Accordingly, he envisaged merely the subordination of the domains to the Court, not their destruction. He proposed the creation of regional governments, which would administer areas larger than domains—a revival of the eighth-century "circuits," of which there had been seven outside the home provinces (Kinai)—and would be staffed by "men of talent appointed from among the imperial princes, Court nobles, and feudal lords." These men, who would serve in rotation for a fixed term of years, would "assume direction and control of all feudal lords within the circuit, . . . coordinating their administration," and would implement the policies, old and new, that were necessary to national wealth: the promotion of agriculture and the cultivation of marginal land to finance welfare programs and expand the tax base; the development of foreign trade; and the establishment of a local university, in addition to primary schools, where instruction would be so informed by Confucian values as to ensure that the country's youth would not be "seduced by the path of profit" even as they were encouraged to follow it.

In this document Iwakura put forward proposals that foreshadowed many of the early problems and policies of the Meiji government. The only thing missing, in fact, was the specifically Western ingredient that was eventually to color the modern bureaucracy, industry, and military establishment. In matters of government, too, where he sketched an imperial alternative to the Bakufu such as would neither transfer power outside the existing ruling class nor mount a fully Western-style attack on feudalism and its political forms, it might fairly be argued that he went as far as the Japanese tradition, taken by itself, was able to go.

On the other hand, of course, Japan was no longer limited to her own or China's experience, culturally and politically. A long record of "Dutch studies," greatly extended in scope during the middle years of the nineteenth century under the shadow of danger from abroad, had by now been reinforced by the willingness of foreign consuls and missionaries to lecture the Japanese on Western ways of running a society, as well as by the observations of Japanese envoys and students who had gone overseas. In all the Bakufu's diplomatic missions, beginning with that of 1860, there were men charged specifically with acquiring such information about the West as might be useful to themselves and their superiors.[8] Several domains had obtained permission to add their own men to these missions. Others had sent abroad students or even missions of their own, as Satsuma had done in 1865. On rarer occasions, enthusiastic individuals—there were several from Chōshū, for example—had been able to take the initiative themselves, subject only to official blessing. As a result, by the time of the Restoration Japan possessed a core of "experts," their knowledge based in some cases on no more than a single visit to Europe or America, but in others reflecting years of study, including perhaps a stay at a Western university, who could supplement her own tradition not merely in science and technology, but also in law, government, economics, and philosophy.

Thanks to the didactic outlook commonly possessed by Western officials and residents in Japan on the one hand and the memorializing habit that Chinese practice had instilled in samurai officials on the other, Japan's rulers were ensured of receiving quantities of advice from both groups, whether solicited or not. Often it came from Japanese whose status was low and who consequently could influence decisions only insofar as what they recommended was attractive. Nishi Amane, despite his training at Leiden, had the frustrating experience in the Bakufu's last years of being largely ignored.[9] Sometimes, however, the man with ideas was also a man of standing, able to argue his views in person in the councils of the great. It was partly because the Restoration marked a transition, or at least a shift of emphasis, from the former situation to the latter, that it opened the way for dramatic change.

As we have seen, one strand of modernizing ideas inherited by the Meiji government had developed within the Bakufu, where it centered on the proposals made by the French minister, Léon Roches. Aimed at strengthening the Shogun's authority over the daimyo by changes in military organization, taxation, and administration generally, it was expounded chiefly by a group of officials of middle rank who had had some experience of foreign countries; but they were also able to win over several of their seniors to the view that feudalism—by which they meant the existing relationship between Bakufu and domains—would have to give way to the need for a stronger central power. Thus Matsudaira Shungaku commented to Itakura Katsukiyo in November 1867 that a restoration of imperial rule must inevitably cause the creation of a provincial system (gunken-seido).[10] He opposed it on that account. Keiki himself was reported as saying a few weeks later that if Japan wanted to be strong, she would sooner or later have to follow England's example in abandoning feudal institutions.[11] Parkes, after a dinner with Keiki earlier in the year ("served entirely in foreign style" and followed by coffee), reported how impressed he had been by the Shogun's openness to suggestion in such matters, as well as by his interest in steamers, coal mines, railways, and telegraphs.[12]

The recognition implicit in these comments, that there was a question to be asked about how *efficient* political institutions were, as well as how they distributed power, is reflected in the constitutional plans that were discussed by the Bakufu's leaders at the end of 1867. In particular, the memorial submitted by Ōgyū Noritaka on November 13 seems in this respect more Meiji than Tokugawa.[13] In a world that was moving toward "enlightenment" (*kaika*), it said, when many in Japan would like to "sweep away at a blow our former habits" and introduce those of the West, it was necessary to think clearly about how the traditional order could be preserved. Politically—his chief concern—Noritaka believed it could be done only by adopting a system that convincingly put the country's interests first. The Shogun's authority could be maintained, to be sure. But it would have to be modified (by creating advisory assemblies, both national and regional, in which daimyo and samurai played a part) and also strengthened against local particularism (by abolishing the private armies under daimyo control and instituting a tax system in which the lords would contribute two-thirds of their revenues to a central treasury). As corollaries, there would have to be a modern army and navy, recruited from physically fit and intellectually capable members of the samurai class; a government acting in the Emperor's name; and a policy of "enlightenment" by which the lords would be required to devote part of their remaining revenue to founding schools, setting up factories, building railways, and the like.

Comparing this with the ideas put forward by Iwakura a few months earlier, it is striking that it is the Bakufu official who is the more "modern" and "Western" of the two, despite his loyalty to the Tokugawa house and a commitment to the class interests of the feudal lords. Clearly, he was aware of issues wider than those raised by the struggle for power in which the Shogun and his enemies were engaged. So were other Bakufu men, like Katsu and Enomoto, who were to serve the Meiji government in later years, when the passions provoked by the civil war had had time to subside. In other words, modernization, even political modernization, was not simply a function of political alignment or a monopoly of Satsuma and Chōshū. This point made, however—and it is an important one—we must also recognize that the Bakufu's adherents were deprived by history of the ability to determine their country's future course. Their proposals were discredited by the attempt to preserve a substantial element of Tokugawa power, and their influence on policy was ended by defeat at Toba and Fushimi, with the result that in the end they did more to engender an atmosphere than to build a new state. That task fell to their opponents, who were also their heirs.

Still, it can be argued that despite the discontinuity of authority, the Bakufu's ideas on constitutional reform were transmitted to the Meiji government through Tosa and Echizen. Sakamoto Ryōma, who played an important part in drawing up the Tosa document calling for the Shogun's resignation in October 1867, had long been a friend of Edo's Katsu Awa, from whom he acquired the vision of a Japan made rich and strong in the Western manner. The relationship also provided a connection with Yuri Kimimasa of Echizen. All three men envisaged a society in which office would depend on ability, not birth, and in which government would include some kind of representative assembly.[14] This implied an attack on feudalism.

Indeed, the point was made explicit in a memorial shown to Sakamoto by an Echizen samurai at Nagasaki in 1867, expressing views that Sakamoto accepted as "almost identical" with his own. "In the 66 provinces there are 263 lords," it said, "each conducting administration independently within his own domain. While this kind of disunity exists, how can we attain national strength, how promote national prestige? Feudalism [hōken] must quickly be abolished, and districts and prefectures [gunken] established under a single imperial government to control the country."[15] The essence of this statement was incorporated in Tosa's memorial to Keiki, together with arguments for founding schools, for securing treaties "which are reasonable and explicit," and for eliminating "self-interest" and "outmoded customs."[16] Thus the proposals became a matter of public debate, influencing policy both before and after January 1868.

Another form of continuity was provided by the advice that was so freely given to Japanese governments by the British minister, Sir Harry Parkes. Parkes was outstandingly a man of his age, to whom Victorian Britain was the pinnacle of civilized achievement. Moreover, though he had no doubt that the West's privileged position in Japan was as merited as it was advantageous to both sides, he knew also that it needed law and order for its preservation. "In the general interests of the country," he wrote to London on November 27—the day he heard that Keiki had resigned—"no less than with a view to the maintenance of a friendly understanding with foreign powers, the necessity of a consolidated Government, whose authority shall be recognised throughout the Empire, is daily becoming more evident."[17] To this end, the great lords must be made to recognize "a supreme authority in all matters relating to general legislation, judicature and national defence." Parkes was doubtful, however, whether this could be accomplished unless "the tenure of land under military service" gave way to "a system which is better suited to the establishment of civil government." In another letter, written the next day, he observed that the Bakufu's proposals for constitutional change must in the end "strike at the power of the Daimios." The beneficiaries, he thought, would be their samurai followers, on whom the anti-Bakufu movement depended. They had "but little faith in their chiefs" and were unlikely to be satisfied "until they find that their class can give free expression to its views."[18]

These anti-feudal prejudices and expectations Parkes expressed no less forcefully to the Meiji leaders, some of whom he had known and dealt with before they came to office. For example, to quote his own account of what he said to Iwakura in January 1869: "The government of the country having now been reconstituted under the Mikado, it is obvious that the latter must be supported by a central organisation and by material power; and although much may still be left to local administration, still certain cardinal functions of government, such as legislation, national defences, foreign affairs, etc., should be conducted from the centre." Only in this way, he said, would it be possible "to correct the disintegration which has so long been the leading feature of the Japanese polity."[19]

Nor did these political recommendations stand in isolation. To Parkes, as to other foreigners, good government was but one mark of a civilized country, which ought also to enjoy the social and material advantages to be derived from economic growth. "It has been an object with me," he wrote of Bakufu officials in 1867, "to divert their attention from military glitter to industrial enterprize."* Foreign trade, too, would "enrich the country greatly, by introducing a spirit of enterprize and industry, and creating capitalists—both of which are much wanted in Japan."[20] Pursuing this line of argument, he found opportunities after the Restoration to advise or help the Meiji government, sometimes by request but often not, on subjects as far removed from his diplomatic duties, strictly defined, as lighthouses, railways, currency, agricultural rents, samurai stipends, factories, and education.

It is not surprising that those Parkes tutored in this way eventually found it more than they could bear, so that his influence waned. Before that happened, however, his role had been taken over—more persuasively because more patriotically—by Japanese. Many who visited Europe, or studied there, became so convinced of the superiority of its culture that they returned to their own country determined to spread "enlightenment" and raise Japan from its semi-barbarous condition to a civilized one.[21] What they meant by this was the civilization of Herbert Spencer and Samuel Smiles,† of Free Trade, Progress, and Social Darwinism, that is, the civilization of contemporary Western Europe, especially Britain. In its name they attacked their own civilization: feudalism, in both its

* F.O. 391/14, Parkes to Hammond, Yedo, June 14, 1867. This is an oblique reference to the activities of Léon Roches, who preferred, Parkes said in another dispatch, "to minister to the military aspirations or vanities of the Japanese rather than to their commercial prosperity" (*ibid.*, March 16, 1867).

† Samuel Smiles (1812–1904) was most famous as the author of a number of tracts expounding the virtues appropriate to an industrial society, with titles like "Character," "Thrift," "Duty," and so on. The best known, "Self-help" (1859), was translated into Japanese in 1871.

political and its social manifestations; and the Confucianism that was its ethic and rationale. Unremittingly they urged the adoption of everything Western, from railways to parliaments, from hair styles to philosophy. Yet they denied that to do so was unpatriotic or un-Japanese. Fukuzawa Yukichi said, "My great wish has always been to lead the whole country into the ways of civilisation, and to make Japan a great nation, strong in military might, prosperous in trade."[22] Similarly, Taguchi Ukichi refuted the charge that he was merely copying the West by asserting the *universality* of the patterns he wanted to impose: "We study physics, psychology, economics and the other sciences not because the West discovered them, but because they are the universal truth. We seek to establish constitutional government in our country not because it is a Western form of government, but because it conforms with man's own nature."[23]

Books on the West and its institutions like Nishi Amane's *Bankoku kōhō* (International Law) and Fukuzawa Yukichi's enormously popular *Seiyō jijō* (Conditions in the West), published just before the Restoration, were available to those engaged in politics —Nakaoka Shintarō is known to have given a copy of Fukuzawa's book to Iwakura Tomomi in May 1867[24]—and helped to form a climate of opinion within which Japan's problems were discussed. All the same, they did not lead to a specific form of pressure, exerted where it could count. Neither Nishi nor Fukuzawa were themselves politically active at this time, holding aloof from Satsuma and Chōshū because of the extreme anti-foreign views with which those domains were associated, yet reluctant to give support to a Bakufu they believed to be obscurantist.[25] Accordingly, for at least the first year or two of the Meiji era they had no access to the centers of power. Nishi, in fact, remained in the service of the Tokugawa until 1870. Like several other modernizers who had received Bakufu salaries,* his importance, both as bureaucrat and publicist, be-

* Most of the men who founded the Meirokusha in 1873—a club devoted to publicizing the ideas of the Enlightenment—were ex-samurai, members of the Meiji bureaucracy, and formerly connected with the Bakufu's institutes of Western learning, the Bansho-shirabesho and Kaiseijo. They had more influence as intellectuals than they had as officials (presumably because of their Tokugawa connections, at least initially). See Havens, *Nishi Amane*, pp. 164–69.

longed to the later years, when the main lines of policy had been laid down and the task was to work out detailed programs of reform.

This means that for the initial steps we have to look within the Meiji leadership itself, especially to men like Godai Tomoatsu and Terajima Munenori of Satsuma and Inoue Kaoru and Itō Hirobumi of Chōshū, who had visited the West and drawn conclusions from what they saw, though lacking the fuller knowledge that comes from years of study. Godai, impressed by Britain's stability in contrast to Japan's disunity, had begun urging political reform as the prerequisite for national wealth and strength as early as 1865.[26] Terajima was more specific, at least as regards institutions. Writing to the Satsuma authorities on the eve of the Restoration, he said that everything he had learned in Europe convinced him the feudal system must be destroyed. "That authority came to be transferred to the Bakufu was due to the existence of fiefs," he maintained, "and it is my belief that all fief-holding lords must be removed if there is to be true imperial rule."[27] Ultimately the lords should surrender their lands to the Emperor, becoming commoners; but a start could be made by handing over part of their revenues to the Court, by providing contingents for a national army under imperial control, and by ensuring that officials in the new government received salaries, not fiefs.

In Chōshū, Itō put forward very similar views. In January 1868 he wrote to Kido urging the necessity of getting away from local and feudal loyalties to national ones, to a proper "consideration of the public interest."[28] A year later, as an official of the new administration, he was arguing that national unity, which would enable Japan "to meet countries overseas on equal terms and have a civilized and enlightened government," depended on abolishing the domains, by force if necessary.[29] Soon after, he prepared a list of the policies he would wish the government to follow, which was signed by several other officials in Hyōgo, where he was governor. It emphasized the importance of maintaining friendly relations with foreign countries, in conformity with universal "natural law"; of studying the West, in order that Japan might "open her eyes and ears to the world, reforming the outdated customs bequeathed to us by the centuries"; of establishing an effective government by abolishing the domains, so "the people can be freed from one-sided laws and without exception made subject to a rule that is uniform and just"; and of ensuring to all men, "without distinction of high and low," freedom from all feudal regulations that restricted rights of occupation and residence.[30]

From this it is clear that within a year of the Restoration Itō had made himself a spokesman for the more "progressive" of his contemporaries. Nevertheless, he had not yet become a figure of the foremost consequence, any more than Godai and Terajima were. Their service and abilities had won them the right to be heard; but it was not until they began to come together after late 1869 under the leadership of Ōkuma Shigenobu of Hizen, who also brought into the group some of the more talented former Bakufu men, like Shibusawa Eiichi and Kanda Kōhei, that they became a considerable political force.[31] Once this stage was reached, they were able to press on the government a program of Western-style reforms. Before that, they could do no more than try to influence their seniors, those who had gained power by the part they had played in overthrowing the Tokugawa: Ōkubo, Saigō, Kido, Iwakura.

Ōkubo and his associates were not by any means opposed to political change, of course. However, none of them had been outside Japan or knew the West well, so that they approached innovation cautiously, having to be persuaded that nothing else would serve before they would use their skills and experience to promote modernization (or Westernization) of the extremer kind. It was through them, in fact, that the modernizers' plans were subjected to pragmatic test, that what seemed to be desirable came to be examined in the light of what was possible politically. The process took several years.

ESTABLISHING A GOVERNMENT

Governing is an untidy business, not least because circumstance has a way of making its own priorities. Japan in 1868 was no exception. Sincerely though they believed that their task was national salvation, which could be achieved only through "wealth and strength," the men who came to power in January of that year had also to solve a number of problems that were not immediately relevant to it. They had to win, or successfully end, a civil war; to find means of financing the war; and to devise machinery for administering those parts of the country that came under their control. All these things were necessary to their own survival, on which, in turn, they believed the country's survival to depend. Such preoccupations did, however, divert attention initially from institutional reform.

By overthrowing the Bakufu, the new leaders found they had fallen heir to its responsibilities, some of which had to be acted on at once. Not least was this true in foreign affairs, where the issues were as urgent as they were embarrassing. After all, given the events of previous years and the tone of the various documents the Court had issued, it was logical that most samurai, especially those who now saw their cause as won at home, should have expected the change of regime to be followed by some kind of "expulsion" of the foreigners. As Kido had said of his supporters in Chōshū in the spring of 1867: "Our young men of spirit see only the enemy in front of their eyes; about the world at large they are absurdly misinformed."[32] In consequence, the early weeks of 1868 saw a number of attacks on foreigners. There was one by Bizen troops in Hyōgo on February 4, another by Tosa samurai at Sakai on March 8, then an attempt to kill Parkes in Kyōto on March 23 by two typical rōnin (one a former priest, the other the eighteen-year-old son of a village doctor).

What made these incidents particularly unwelcome to the imperial government was the risk that they might provoke the West to intervene in the civil war or delay its recognition of the transfer of power. Parkes, who professed himself willing to recognize any "regular government," whatever its form,[33] had succeeded in getting the foreign representatives to issue a declaration of neutrality, but he had done so over the opposition of Roches, some of whose military advisers had continued to serve with the Tokugawa forces. This made the situation delicate, especially since it was the French who were attacked at Sakai.

At the same time, the attacks on foreigners also provided an opportunity to demonstrate that imperial rule was a reality, as Iwakura pointed out. In May 1867, when the opening of Hyōgo had been under discussion, he had urged the Court to take over responsibility for negotiations as a means of depriving Keiki of one of his prerogatives: "Seeking the return to the Emperor of administrative authority over the country, under the guise of handling foreign affairs," was how he had described it.[34] Together with Ōkubo, he now applied the argument to the position in 1868, thereby persuading a reluctant Court to promise to punish the offenders and apologize to the foreigners, as well as to declare publicly (on February 8) that the treaties made by the Bakufu would be maintained subject to the revision of unsatisfactory clauses.[35] Expulsion, in fact, was to be transmuted into treaty revision. Nor was the matter left there. On February 29 a joint memorial from the lords of Echizen, Tosa, Satsuma, Aki, and Kumamoto, accompanied by a separate one from Chōshū, urged the government to manifest its rejection of jōi by arranging an imperial audience for the envoys of the treaty powers. This, they said, would mark Japan's abandonment of the outlook of "the frog looking at the world from the bottom of the well" and indicate her willingness to learn from the Western powers, "adopting their best points and making good our own deficiencies."[36] The Court, as was hardly surprising, since these lords furnished the whole of its military strength, acceded to the request without much delay.

Notwithstanding the fact that the attack on Parkes came when he was on his way to the audience arranged as a result of these exchanges—and that the Japanese Foreign Ministry found it necessary to continue its attempts to educate samurai opinion on the subject for many months to come[37]—this decision won the new leaders a respite from the problem of foreign affairs. Instead, they were able to turn their attention to the equally pressing problem of confirming their own power. Their position in the country as a whole was tenuous at best, for the rapid submission of domains to the imperial government after Toba-Fushimi had been the result of apathy and indecision, not an upsurge of loyalism. Meanwhile, in the capital itself, the restiveness of the Court nobility over the new direction of Japanese foreign policy, added to the continuing resentment of Tosa and Echizen at the refusal of Satsuma and Chōshū to let Keiki keep the greater part of his lands,[38] threatened the victors' unity almost from the start. As Kido put it: "Too much talk of Satsuma and Chōshū makes those who distrust us all the more suspicious. We may believe that it is for the sake of the Court that we act as we do, but to convince the country at large of this is extremely difficult."[39] The argument led him, as it also led Ōkubo and Iwakura, to seek ways of reinforcing the ruling coalition.

At one level, it was possible for them to do so by exploiting traditional alliances and family ties with lords who might be willing to take office in the central government, like the daimyo of the powerful Kyūshū domain of Kumamoto (tozama; 540,000 koku). Lower in the social scale they could count on the support of loyalists and reformers in many different areas with whom the shishi had forged bonds in the previous decade; men like themselves, who were now in a position to increase the pressures on their lords to declare for the imperial cause, or who as individuals could be drawn into the new bureaucracy. Thus in Hizen (tozama; 357,000 koku), where the daimyo, Nabeshima Naomasa, had preserved a careful neutrality in national politics while pursuing "wealth and strength" through the application of Western technology, the loyalist party greatly increased its influence in the early weeks of 1868; and its leaders—Ōkuma Shigenobu, Etō Shimpei, Soejima Taneomi—men of the same stamp as those who had gained control in Satsuma, Tosa, and Chōshū, soon became important figures in the Meiji government.[40]

In the announcement of January 3, 1868, abolishing the Court and Bakufu offices and establishing new positions,[41] virtually all those appointed to office had been directly concerned in the coup d'état. That is to say, apart from a few imperial princes, all the Senior Councillors (Gijō) and Junior Councillors (Sanyo) were either anti-Bakufu nobles or representatives of the breakaway domains. In the next week or so, however, the number of councillors was vastly expanded in an attempt to widen the base of the government's support. Inevitably, Chōshū men were added as soon as their domain was pardoned. In addition, fresh allies were recruited wherever they were to be found, so that by June 11, when there was a major reorganization (following the surrender of Edo), well over 100 men were serving in one or other of these posts.

Altogether, thirty men were appointed Gijō during the period: five imperial princes; twelve other Court nobles (mostly known loyalists, though there were also two former Kampaku, Konoe Tadahiro and Takatsukasa Sukehiro); and thirteen daimyo or their relatives (the five named originally, from Satsuma, Owari, Aki, Echizen, and Tosa, the daimyo and ex-daimyo of Hizen, and representatives from Chōshū, Kumamoto, Bizen, Uwajima, Awa, and Tsuwano). The Sanyo were even more numerous, totaling 102 in all. They included forty-three Court nobles and six Court officials not of noble rank. The remaining fifty-three were all from the domains, chiefly those that provided Gijō: twenty-three upper samurai (significantly, only three from Satsuma and none at all from Chōshū, Tosa, and Hizen); twenty-one middle samurai; two men (Itō Hirobumi of Chōshū and Terajima Munenori of Satsuma) who might count as lower samurai because of their origins, though they were hirazamurai at this time; and seven others who cannot be classified, except in general as members of the samurai class.

In the next phase, which lasted from June 1868 until a further reorganization of the administrative structure in August 1869 (after the fighting in Hokkaidō ended), the number of councillors was substantially reduced. Where there had been thirty Gijō, there were now only twenty-one, mostly daimyo and loyalist kuge (but no imperial princes). The number of Sanyo was cut even more severely, from 102 to twenty-two. Three of the twenty-two were Court nobles (against the earlier forty-three); the other nineteen were domain representatives (against the earlier fifty-three): two daimyo and a daimyo's heir; two other upper samurai; thirteen middle samurai; and one lower samurai. In other words, most of the upper samurai from the earlier list were now omitted. Equally interesting, only seven domains were now represented among the Sanyo; and the failure to include any domain representatives from Owari, Uwajima, and Bizen, in particular, even though their lords remained Gijō, hints at a narrowing of the geographical, as well as the social, base. It was not only the upper levels of traditional society, but also some of the recently powerful domains that were becoming less important to the ruling group.

A similar concentration of power was being reflected in the administrative structure, that is, in the very nature of the posts themselves. In mid-February 1868 the Court had established seven departments of state, those that had existed in the supposedly golden days of imperial rule: Shintō religion; home, foreign, and military affairs; finance; justice; and "organization." An eighth department (Sōsaikyoku), to exercise general supervision, was added at the end of the month. All of the department heads and their chief subordinates were Gijō or Sanyo, thus giving members of the council an executive function.

In June this system was replaced by a more elaborate one, the Seitaisho. In the name of a Western-style separation of powers, a legislative body and an executive (Gyōseikan) were established. The legislature consisted of an upper chamber of Gijō and Sanyo and a lower chamber of nominees from the domains and imperial territories. The departments of state, reduced to five (religion, military affairs, foreign affairs, justice, and finance), were supervised by the executive, which was also responsible for the lands that had been seized from the Tokugawa. It was laid down that the senior ministers of these departments had to be imperial princes, Court nobles, or daimyo, but in practice most key decisions were taken by Gijō and Sanyo (by this time, as we have seen, a fairly small number). The Gyōseikan itself was put under Sanjō Sanetomi and Iwakura Tomomi, two Court nobles who were closely connected with Chōshū and Satsuma, respectively. Both were Gijō. Within the departments, it was the vice-ministers, mostly Sanyo, who exercised real power, continuing their dual role as councillors and bureaucrats.

With these changes, we see taking shape by the middle of 1869 a group of about thirty men who can justly be called the first generation of Meiji leaders. It included men of three kinds: senior members of the pre-Restoration ruling class who survived in the new order in part because they were sympathetic representatives of the Court and baronial interest and in part because they had greater talent than their fellows; the samurai who had led the Restoration movement in its later stages, or, more specifically, those who had dominated Satsuma, Chōshū, and Tosa politics in 1867; and, finally, those recruited into the government from other domains, notably from the politically "neutral" domain of Hizen, but also including one or two men from elsewhere who had gained a reputation as reformers.

As Court nobles in the first group I would name principally Sanjō and Iwakura, though Nakayama Tadayasu (1809–88) and Tokudaiji Sanenori (1840–1919) continued to have an important role within the Court itself. Among the daimyo, Nabeshima Naomasa (Hizen), Date Muneki (Uwajima), and Matsudaira Shungaku (Echizen) held major offices down to 1871, when the domains were abolished. Most of the rest, including Yamauchi Yōdō (Tosa) and Shimazu Tadayoshi (Satsuma), ended their effective participation in the central government in 1869.

Nearly all the names in the second group are familiar ones by now: from Satsuma, Ōkubo and Saigō, together with their chief supporters, Yoshii Tomozane, Terajima Munenori, Matsukata Masayoshi, and Ōyama Iwao; from Chōshū, Kido and Hirosawa, then Maebara Issei, Ōmura Masujirō, and Inoue Kaoru, plus two younger men just emerging into prominence, Itō Hirobumi and Yamagata Aritomo; and from Tosa, Gotō and Fukuoka, who were soon to be joined in the inner councils by Itagaki Taisuke, Saitō Toshiyuki, and Sasaki Takayuki.

In the third group were two famous middle samurai reformers, Yokoi Shōnan of Kumamoto, who was murdered by a reactionary in 1869, and Yuri Kimimasa (1829–1909), a specialist in finance and economic policy from Echizen. Both had been advisers to Matsudaira Shungaku. The rest, as we have said, were mostly from Hizen. Their leader, Ōkuma Shigenobu (1838–1922), who was a little younger than Kido and Ōkubo, was the eldest son of a well-to-do (400 koku) gunnery specialist.[42] His background was respectably loyalist, but the chief reason for his rise to position was his usefulness as an "expert" in matters relating to "wealth and strength": as a young man he had studied Rangaku, then English; and from 1864 on, he had been in charge of Hizen's trading activities at Nagasaki, through which he had acquired commercial contacts and experience. In later life, as diplomatist, modernizer, bureaucrat, party politician, Prime Minister, and publicist, he was to be an outstanding personality of Meiji history. Several of the men he had worked with in Hizen before 1868 also became officials of considerable standing in later years. Among them were Soejima Taneomi (1828–1905), who had studied English with Ōkuma; Ōki Takatō (1832–99), Ōkuma's cousin; and Etō Shimpei (1834–74), a man of lower samurai origins,[43] who had been punished for loyalist activities before the Restoration and was to be executed for rebelling against the imperial government in the cause of feudalism in 1874.

As the presence of Etō in the list conveniently emphasizes, the first-generation Meiji leaders were not men with a single view of how Japan's future should be shaped. They included both "conservatives" and "progressives" who were subsequently to engage in bitter quarrels. Nevertheless, the group had coherence in a number of ways. Its samurai members, at least, were much of an age and sufficiently alike in family background to be able to meet on roughly equal terms. In dealing with each other they were more conscious of regional differences than class ones.* Equally, they had much in common temperamentally: ruthlessness, a readiness to use violence, but also a political realism that made them calculate the consequences of what they did. Few, if any, were shishi, "men of spirit," in the sense that one uses the term for the years 1862 and 1863. Rather, they were men of affairs, usually with experience in domain bureaucracy, whose political skills had brought them through turbulent times to a place in national government. Since the shishi, if they had survived at all, were more likely to be found in the army, fighting the Tokugawa, one can conclude that the process by which the Meiji government was gradually formed included not only a pushing to one side of high-born nonentities, but also the exclusion of loyalist hotheads from positions of power. The loyalist extremists were released and pardoned, if they lived; they were often rewarded; they were invariably honored, even if dead; but they were rarely given responsibility.[44]

The nature and outlook of the new leadership were reflected in the way in which it went about the task of persuading the rest of the country to accept the authority it had acquired. Partly this was a matter of manipulating the domain alliance: choosing domains

* Ōkubo, recognizing that because of the differences of domain origin the samurai members of the new government did not know each other very well, went out of his way to meet them socially in the early days (Katsuda, *Ōkubo,* 2: 508).

to be represented; and choosing men within the domains, that is, backing loyalists who might be expected to keep local policy in line with government wishes. The technique came naturally to samurai politicians who had had constantly to overcome feudal rivalries in order to defeat the Bakufu. Similarly, they knew at first hand about samurai unrest, which gave them some idea of how to handle it. As early as February 1868 provision was made for domains to send delegates to a samurai assembly, thereby giving some kind of voice, though not a controlling one, to those not represented on the council. The inclusion of a bicameral legislature (Giseikan) in the Seitaisho structure the following June was a development from this. Only five months later the Giseikan was absorbed into the executive, to be replaced early in 1869 by the Kōgisho, a body of over 200 samurai, which met on several occasions in the next few months to discuss such matters as the abolition of domains, the wearing of swords, forced loans, and the proscription of Christianity.[45] The discussions were far from constructive, but they served their purpose, which was to serve as a sounding board for feudal opinion at a critical time. They came to an end in July.

To a government that depended on contingents from the domains for its military force, such processes of consultation were logical and necessary. They continued until the regime felt strong enough to do without them. Equally important was the ability to exploit the Emperor's prestige—and equally natural, since samurai who had often used their daimyo as instruments of policy within the domain had little difficulty in seeing the Emperor in an equivalent role on a wider stage. They therefore gladly cooperated with those who were led by tradition, or self-interest, to emphasize the imperial labels, rather than the feudal realities, of Japanese political life. Major acts of state, like the punishment of the Tokugawa, were made public in ways designed to make it seem that they were the *Emperor's* decisions, not those of faceless officials. For the first time in many generations the sovereign showed himself to the people outside his capital. And much was made of Shintō and its ceremonial. The department of religion had high formal status and an imperial prince at its head; and throughout the country Shintō doctrines and teachers were given encouragement.[46]

Characteristic of the new policy was a pamphlet issued in March 1869 for circulation to various localities, where "all well-disposed men" were ordered to study it and instruct the population in its principles.[47] The first of these was that Japanese, as Japanese, owed a debt of gratitude to the Emperor because he protected and sustained them. That debt must be paid with loyalty: "Reverently receiving the Imperial will, we will humbly obey his commands; we will set our hearts upon serving him for his sake." The second principle was that the Japanese must behave in the manner the Emperor's government enjoined. In particular, they must observe the treaties with foreign powers, which the Emperor had now approved. To avoid the "shame and disgrace" of "violent and lawless acts," such as might incur "the scorn of foreign nations," Japan had to be "penetrated by the Imperial precepts" and "united in one whole."

The outstanding example of the use of the Emperor's dignity to bolster the regime in the early months of its existence was the so-called Charter Oath of April 1868. In large part this was an attempt to reassure the domains about the attitudes and objectives of those who had carried out "restoration." Its general theme had already been sounded in a notification issued on January 16, which stated: "All matters will [hereafter] be decided by the Imperial Court. Opinion will be widely consulted and action will be based on the general view, not the private interests of a particular faction [i.e., the Bakufu]. The good features of the traditional Tokugawa system and its laws will be left unchanged."[48] The Oath itself, however, coming at a time when the defeat of the Tokugawa was fairly certain, went a good deal further than this, sketching a framework of policy within which the government proposed to act.

Several hands went into the making of it.[49] The first draft was prepared by Yuri Kimimasa of Echizen after a meeting on February 2, 1868, at which Court officials, including Sanjō and Iwakura, had discussed the government's need for support, political and financial. In addition to repeating the promise made earlier, that policies would be decided by "public discussion," Yuri asserted that in order to prevent discontent the people must be allowed to "fulfil their aspirations"; that samurai and commoners alike must unite in promoting the national welfare; and that the foundations of "the imperial polity" must be strengthened by seeking "knowledge throughout the world."

At this stage the document was a very summary one, though reflecting clearly enough its author's interest in the economy (and perhaps also his earlier links with rich farmers and merchants). A revised version, drawn up a day or two later by Fukuoka Kōtei of Tosa, contained substantial changes. It made specific reference to an assembly of feudal lords and stated that the aspirations of "civil and military officials" were to be fulfilled in addition to those of commoners. Here was plainly a new emphasis: unity within the ruling Court and feudal groups, rather than "popular" participation. Fukuoka himself later said of the change: "It was not that I held the masses lightly, but I just did not consider them an important political factor."[50]

The matter was allowed to rest there for the next several weeks, possibly because the new leaders were preoccupied with questions of foreign policy and the civil war. At all events, nothing further was done until after the Court's announcement on March 10 of an imperial audience for the foreign envoys. Kido then refurbished Fukuoka's draft in points of detail and added a new clause relating to foreign affairs. "Base customs of former times" must be abandoned, it said, meaning by this the policy of seclusion; and "universal reason and justice" (i.e., international law) must be observed. So modified, and after a few changes of wording by Iwakura and Sanjō—at some stage, for example, though it is not clear when, Fukuoka's assembly of lords became an assembly "widely convoked"—the document was finally issued on April 6, 1868. It read as follows:

1. An assembly widely convoked shall be established and all matters of state shall be decided by public discussion.
2. All classes high and low shall unite in vigorously promoting the economy and welfare of the nation.
3. All civil and military officials and the common people as well shall be allowed to fulfil their aspirations, so that there may be no discontent among them.
4. Base customs of former times shall be abandoned and all actions shall conform to the principles of international justice.
5. Knowledge shall be sought throughout the world and thus shall be strengthened the foundation of the Imperial polity.[51]

It would be unrealistic to take this handful of worthy generalizations as evidence that the Meiji leaders now had firmly in mind the reforms they intended to carry out. But it would also be unduly cynical to dismiss the declaration as a mere exercise in public relations, a set of platitudes designed to win popular approval for a claimed authority. The seniority of the men who drafted it and the care they gave to it suggest something more than that. Moreover, its wording reflects, if not with ideal clarity, the policies to which they had committed themselves in detailed memorials (Iwakura) or in domain administration (Kido and Ōkubo): political unity, implying something more widely based than in the immediate past; and national wealth and strength, involving Western technology and the abandonment of expulsion. To this extent the Charter Oath manifests attitudes from which a realistic program could evolve.

CHAPTER XIII

The New Political Structure

INTERESTINGLY, the Charter Oath announced in April 1868 scarcely hinted at one set of changes much canvassed among the Meiji leadership earlier in the year, namely those that led first to the surrender of domain registers (*hanseki-hōkan*) in 1869, making the daimyo imperial governors of the lands they had held in fief, and then, in 1871, to the outright abolition of the domains (*haihan*) in favor of prefectures governed by the Emperor's nominees. The process, which was a key step in the creation of "Meiji absolutism," is important enough to be called "a second Restoration."

It is also a focus of controversy among historians. George Sansom sees it as "mainly an afterthought," made necessary by the inability of the new ruling group to wield effective power through "an administration already obsolete."[1] In the view of Herbert Norman it was an inevitable consequence of the *nature* of the movement that had overthrown the Tokugawa, put into effect as soon as the victors in the struggle realized that their choice was between "shifting the hegemony from the Tokugawa to some other clan or coalition of clans" and establishing "a centralized state."[2] Many of the post–World War II Japanese historians would probably emphasize instead that the essential factor was the willingness of the members of the feudal class to surrender their rights to an acceptable kind of central government implicitly because this would still guarantee them a substantial measure of privilege which might otherwise be lost to "popular" unrest.[3]

In the previous chapter we looked at some of the influences and ideas that formed a background to the working out of political institutions after 1868. We now turn to the politics of the process, examining in particular the stages by which men in authority were brought to believe that radical change was needed, and that it was within their power to carry it out. Since most of them were samurai who had risen to positions of influence by manipulating the techniques of feudal rule, they were not easily persuaded that the entire system on which they had hitherto depended should be jettisoned, still less that it should be replaced by something alien in origin and clearly bound to provoke conservative discontent. Their decisions were therefore a test of their nationalist resolution.

THE SURRENDER OF DOMAIN REGISTERS

There was evidence from the beginning that some members of the Meiji government did not want simply to substitute for the Bakufu an Emperor-centered feudalism. Iwakura, for example, had always wished for more, though he was realist enough to be cautious about saying so. Similarly, in 1868 Ōkubo was urging the removal of the Emperor and his capital from the stultifying atmosphere of Kyōto and the Court, explicitly because he thought this was the only way of making the imperial institution an effective instrument for governing Japan. The Court nobles, he said, were with few exceptions "like women of the harem," incapable of bearing responsibility.[4] And the Emperor, because he was treated with excessive respect, had come "to think of himself as honorable and illustrious in a quite exceptional degree, until in the end he is alienated from both high and low."[5] The domains were "insubordinate," opinion unsettled, "all things in confusion." In this situation, the overriding need was to unite the country and "reform the dilatory habits which have been indulged for several hundred years," a task that made it imperative for the Emperor to emerge from behind the screen. He must "take simple and direct steps to clear away the many abuses," "discharge the duty of a prince," and become more like monarchs in other countries, who "walk about accompanied by only one or two attendants and pay attention to the welfare of their people."[6]

By arguments of this kind, Ōkubo, backed by Kido, eventually got his way, and Edo, now Tokyo, or "eastern capital," was made the seat of imperial government.* This was one example of how practical considerations (in this case, the fear that an Emperor detached from politics and subject to pressure from a reactionary entourage might become a center of opposition to essential reforms) precluded the continuation of traditional patterns. Another, tending to similar conclusions, was the difficulty of reaching and enforcing decisions through a domain alliance, such as existed in the first half of 1868. Every time a question of substance had to be decided, the central group first had to reach its own agreement about what needed to be done. This in itself was by no means easy, given the group's diversity. As Parkes put it, "Perhaps the great difficulty in the way of the restoration of order in Japan and the establishment of general Government lies in the inaptitude for combination which must characterize men who have hitherto been debarred from all association and who are moreover actuated by feelings of jealousy and distrust."[7] Once agreed among themselves, the policy-makers still had to win the support of their lords and manipulate interests at Court to secure the Emperor's blessing. Finally, they had to ensure that the decisions were carried out locally. For this they relied on the Court's prestige, the example given by their own domains, and the persuasions of their friends throughout the country. All in all, it was a method that was as uncertain as it was slow. To men of authoritarian habit, brought up in the disciplined atmosphere of the great domains, it was barely tolerable.

As we have seen in the previous chapter, during the course of 1868 they made steady progress in shaping the structure of the central government itself, reducing the number of figureheads and "empty" offices until the identity and authority of those who had to be consulted in reaching a decision became relatively clear. This left the second part of the problem, that of how policies, once decided, were to be imposed on the rest of Japan. Assuming that this problem was not to be solved by creating another Bakufu—the

* Edo was renamed on Sept. 3, 1868. The Emperor lived in Tokyo after mid-1869, but his residence there, the former Shogun's castle, was not formally declared "the imperial palace" until 1873. There is a long account of the debates concerning these decisions in *Ishin-shi*, 5: 447–71. See also Iwata, pp. 117–19.

rivalry between Satsuma and Chōshū, if nothing else, made such a step unlikely—then the solution had to involve a new relationship between central and local power, that is, between government and domains.

The first practical step in this direction was the reassertion in a modified form of some Tokugawa principles. As part of the governmental changes carried out in June 1868, the daimyo were forbidden, as they had been by the Bakufu, to form alliances with each other or to issue coinage. At the same time, the lands taken over from the Shogun (to which were added nine million koku confiscated from his supporters after the defeat of Aizu later in the year) were brought directly under the Court's control as *fu* (cities) and *ken* (prefectures) administered by imperial officials. The wording of the announcement of this move implied a break with feudal practice. In reality, however, what was done was little more than to make the Emperor his own Shogun, the most powerful of the country's feudal lords.

The Emperor's administrative arrangements, like those of the Tokugawa, now became a model for all Japan. On December 11, 1868, just five days after the army announced the complete pacification of the northeast, an imperial decree was issued instructing the daimyo to bring a degree of uniformity into the "three types of local organization," cities, prefectures, and domains.[8] It spelled out in detail how this was to be accomplished: a clear separation was to be maintained between the affairs of each domain and those of its daimyo house; a standard (and new) terminology was to be adopted for senior posts, which were to be filled by men chosen for their ability, not their birth; and one official was to be appointed to represent the domain in the capital, where he would belong to a consultative assembly.

All this, once it had been carried out, greatly increased the government's means of influencing the domains, since it strengthened the hands of those who were expected to sympathize with its objectives, the "men of talent." Put in the simplest terms, a link between Court and local reformist groups had been substituted for the link between Bakufu and conservative upper samurai. To some, like Terajima Munenori of Satsuma and Itō Hirobumi of Chōshū, whose knowledge of Western ways led them to regard the very existence of domains as inhibiting progress and weakening unity, this was far from enough. To others it was as much as was acceptable, or more. As an Echizen samurai put it—doubtless expressing the views of Matsudaira Shungaku—any proposal that all the lords, not just the Shogun, surrender their lands would "bring the country into confusion and disorder." The suggestion was improper in itself, he said: "A country's land is undoubtedly the ruler's land; but even though it is the ruler's land, it would not be right for the ruler to take it into his own hands at will."[9]

Shimazu Hisamitsu felt much the same way, as did the other "enlightened" lords, who had never associated the need for reform with an attack on their own political and social privileges. Their samurai, recognizing this, felt it unwise to provoke them, at least so long as they remained an important ingredient in the anti-Bakufu alliance. Thus the samurai officials who drew up a memorial offering to surrender 100,000 koku of Satsuma land to the Court as a contribution to the costs of the imperial army showed themselves to be at least as realistic as they were loyal. Though "it would have been proper to surrender [the whole], as was the case before the Kamakura period," they observed, ". . . conditions are not such as to make this possible."[10] With equal realism, the Court, aware of the embarrassment that acceptance might cause in its relations with the daimyo generally, thought it best to thank the Satsuma officials for the sentiment but refuse the offer.

It was Kido Kōin who took the initiative in trying to overcome daimyo conservatism in this matter. Perhaps because of Itō's influence, perhaps because he had less taste for intrigue than Ōkubo, Kido quickly became impatient with the complexities of Kyōto politics and sought an alternative to them. The new government, he wrote in early 1868, had two tasks: to "promote men of talent on every side, devoting itself fully to the welfare of the people," and to put Japan on "an equal footing with other countries of the world." Neither could be achieved without effective authority at home. And since authority rested on creating an imperial army instead of continuing to rely on separate domain contingents, no real progress could be made until the lords surrendered land and people to the Emperor.[11]

Itō agreed with him. More, he saw a way in which the policy

might be carried out. Force might have to be used against those daimyo who could not see for themselves the importance of subordinating their personal interests in the cause of national unity, he said; but those who *did* offer to surrender their domains could be rewarded with membership in a newly formed aristocracy, carrying stipends as well as rank, and given access to office if their abilities warranted. As for their followers, those who were qualified could have posts in the army or the bureaucracy. The rest could return to the land in their former provinces, helped financially, in case of need, by special relief programs.[12]

From this it is evident that by about the end of 1868 the Chōshū leaders in the Meiji government—though not necessarily those who remained in Chōshū—had already worked out the broad lines of the plan that was later adopted for abolishing the domains. They had also received their daimyo's permission, grudgingly given, to discuss the matter with their colleagues, especially those from Satsuma without whose cooperation little could be done. Some of the Satsuma leaders were already known to be in sympathy, notably Terajima. So was Gotō of Tosa, who had remarked to the British interpreter Mitford during the summer that however difficult it might be "to do away with a whole feudal system," he would for his own part declare in the end for Emperor rather than lord.[13] Against those who dissented a number of arguments could be employed. As Kido put it, to allow each domain to go on being preoccupied solely with its own affairs would so weaken the government that Japan would become nothing more than a conglomeration of "little Bakufus,"[14] a situation as bad as the one that the Restoration had been designed to end. Or in Itō's words, "if we cannot rule at home, we will be unable to set matters to rights abroad";[15] it was thus Japan that was at stake, not merely victory in a domestic struggle.

Kido first broached the matter to Ōkubo on November 2, 1868, though he noted in his diary that he was not yet ready at this time to reveal the full extent of what he had in mind.[16] Ōkubo, equally cautious, agreed to sound out other Satsuma men while Gotō did the same in Tosa. They met a mixed reception, however; and by the beginning of 1869 Ōkubo, at least, was coming around to the view that the only way to make any progress was to do what they had done in the conspiratorial closing months of 1867—preempt a decision by presenting the lords and the domains with a *fait accompli*. The country needed firm direction, he noted in a letter to Iwakura. Instead, "what is done today is changed tomorrow, what is done this year is changed next year,"[17] so that the turmoil continually increased. On February 24 Ōkubo had a meeting with Hirosawa of Chōshū and Itagaki of Tosa to discuss once again what should be done about the domains. Within a few days, joined now by representatives of Hizen, they had decided to submit a memorial in the name of their lords, putting their lands at the Emperor's disposal.

Presented to the Court on March 5, 1869, the document began by referring briefly to the Emperor's supersession in the distant past by the Shogun, who had held power "by stealth under pretense of the imperial authority." Under all of the Shogun, it stated, including the Tokugawa, this "boundless despotism" had led to the sequestration of lands that were properly the Emperor's own. These ought therefore to be restored.

The lands in which we live are the Emperor's lands. The people we govern are the Emperor's people. How, then, can we lightly treat them as our own? We now surrender our registers to the throne, asking that the Court dispose of them at will, bestowing that which should be bestowed, taking away that which should be taken away; and we ask that the Court issue such orders as it may deem necessary, disposing of the lands of the great domains and deciding changes in them, as well as regulating all things, from institutions, statutes, and military organization down to regulations concerning uniforms and equipment, so that state affairs, both great and small, may be in the hands of a single authority. Thus will name and reality be made one and our country put on a footing of equality with countries overseas.[18]

The interpretation of this document presents certain difficulties. Its tone was feudal, implying the kind of submission appropriate at a change of overlord, who might be expected to confirm or vary the landholding of vassals by way of reward or punishment. There was nothing in it to suggest that the lands, once surrendered, would not be returned to those who already held them in fief, where this was merited. Yet Parkes, who was in close touch with the men who drafted the memorial, was quite sure that it was an omen of radical change. "I am glad to say," he reported to London, "that light breaks out through the cloud. . . . Several of the leading Daimios have come forward and offered to surrender the Government of their own territories—their revenues, forces, jurisdiction, etc.—into the hands of the Mikado's Government in order that a strong Central Power may be created."[19] The references in the memorial to "a single authority" and making "name and reality" one seem to bear this judgment out.

It seems highly probable that the ambiguity of the document was deliberate, for it enabled Ōkubo and Iwakura to feel their way toward a solution without abandoning the chance of compromise, should conservatism prove too strong. Certainly the Court's reply on March 6, for which they were chiefly responsible, suggests as much. The loyalty shown by the four lords was commendable, it said. However, a final decision on a matter of such importance must wait on the consultation of opinion, such as could conveniently take place when the Emperor went to Tokyo in May or June.[20] In other words, the leadership proposed to take time to test the ground.

The response of the domains to this initiative was very mixed.[21] Several that had been cooperating closely with the new government, including Echizen, Tottori, and Kumamoto, hastened to follow the example of Satsuma, Chōshū, Tosa, and Hizen by submitting memorials. Thus prompted, most of the rest also came into line, so that by the time a decision was taken at the end of July only fourteen still stood out. There was, in fact, little open opposition anywhere.

But this is not to suggest that there was widespread support for the idea of abolishing the domains. When the question was put to the Kōgisho in June and July, representatives of about forty domains, led by Echizen, expressed themselves in favor of the arrangement Itō had proposed, that is, prefectures governed by imperial officials, chosen—"for the time being"—from daimyo and upper samurai. Another 60 favored the kind of compromise that was eventually adopted: the appointment of daimyo as imperial governors of their own former lands, coupled with the continuation of samurai fiefs and stipends. Yet over 100 advocated the retention of "feudalism" in one form or another. Some, arguing that things were well enough as they were, believed the lands should be formally surrendered and then restored to the domains, subject to a minimum of imperial inspection. Others sought merely to substitute the Emperor for the Shogun, keeping everything else unchanged. Indeed, Mitford was told by a samurai that it was doubtful whether the domains could be abolished "without a revolution," since to do so would "interfere with too many vested interests." Even the daimyo only gave lip service to the idea, the samurai said; "their heart was not in the work."[22]

A memorial prepared by the Kōgisho on August 2, 1869, largely at the urging of Kumamoto (which now repudiated those who had earlier spoken for the domain in the capital), gave color to this. It argued that the coexistence of two different systems of local administration, one based on domains, the other on prefectures, would lead to confusion and unrest; and that the provincial system had not served China well in offering resistance to the West, suggesting there were no military grounds for adopting it in Japan. Furthermore, since the existence of domains had never yet prevented the Court's orders from being carried out, present relationships should not be disturbed merely for the sake of administrative uniformity, however desirable in theory this might be.[23]

The Meiji leaders were well aware of this undercurrent of opposition. Ōkubo, writing to Iwakura in April 1869, noted that "an uneasy peace prevails; the daimyo are stricken with doubt and the people are filled with confusion."[24] Sanjō reported from Tokyo that samurai turbulence there made him fear further attacks on foreigners, causing "a situation of the utmost danger." Men, he said, were "beginning on every side to express a longing for the former government and show contempt for the failures of the new one."[25]

Against this background, Ōkubo, Kido, and Iwakura had little difficulty in agreeing that they must take steps to ensure order in the capital before the future of the domains was publicly discussed. One step, as Ōkubo pointed out in June, was to streamline the government and change its personnel in the interests of efficiency and popularity. As it was, he said, the government was despised by Parkes, "who ridicules us as if we were children," and insulted by samurai, "who treat us like slaves."[26] At his suggestion, an "election" was held within officialdom. When it was over, the number of senior posts had been reduced to ten, which were filled by four Court nobles (including Sanjō and Iwakura), one daimyo (Nabeshima of Hizen), and five samurai (including Ōkubo, Kido, and Gotō). A week or two later over 700,000 koku of imperial stipends were distributed in reward for military service in the civil war, most of it to men from Satsuma and Chōshū.* Finally, several units of "reliable" troops were moved into Tokyo.

Nevertheless, it was still not clear what policy these preparations were intended to support, since officialdom was as divided as the Kōgisho. Itō, Inoue, and those who later became known as the "student party," because they had studied abroad, continued to insist that a mere change of name was not enough, and that the domains must be abolished. Many of the daimyo and upper samurai, however, were as insistently against anything but superficial change. In consequence, Ōkubo, as he revealed in a letter on July 12, was convinced the proposal to extend the prefectural system to the whole of the country was "unrealistic." It was, he said, "a matter for gradual action, for keeping within bounds, not acting rashly."[27] The other "politicians," Kido and Iwakura, tended to agree with him.

Once again it fell to Iwakura, now clearly emerging as the most able of the Court nobles, to formulate a compromise. In a document drafted at about the beginning of July, he proposed that the lords be made governors or vice-governors of provinces, each remaining responsible for his former territories, and that they then appoint "men of ability and education" among their retainers as their lieutenants. The lords were to forward one-tenth of their revenues to the Court, where it would be used initially for the redemption of domain debts, and to allocate the rest to specified local costs, such as household expenses, samurai stipends, and administration. In mat-

* The largest rewards, announced on July 10, went to various daimyo, including the lords of Chōshū, Satsuma (100,000 koku each), Tosa, Hizen, Tottori, and Bizen. Samurai recipients included Saigō Takamori (2,000 koku), Ōmura Masujirō (1,500 koku), and Itagaki Taisuke (1,000 koku). The decision to allocate funds for this purpose, despite opposition from officials responsible for finance, had been made much earlier in the year (Katsuda, *Ōkubo*, 2: 683–88), so the timing of the actual announcement is probably significant. Certainly it was not until October 30 that rewards for political services (presumably less important as a means of winning support) were announced. They included 5,000 koku each to Sanjō and Iwakura; 1,800 koku each to Kido, Ōkubo, and Hirosawa; and 1,000 koku to Gotō. There is a full list of both sets of rewards in the appendix to *Ishin-shi*, vol. 5.

ters of general policy they were to be subject to imperial direction. In this way, "the idea of a prefectural system could be fulfilled in the guise of feudalism." In addition, the social order was to be unified, first, by asserting that the duties of vassalage were owed (through provincial governors) to the Emperor, and second, by instituting a new nobility made up of former kuge and daimyo, who would belong to it by right of birth, plus such samurai (and possibly others) as could earn their place in it as "men of repute in the locality, men who have performed outstanding services, or men of virtue and learning."[28]

It was basically this plan that Iwakura put to the inner group of senior officials on July 9, 1869. Hirosawa Saneomi of Chōshū and Soejima Taneomi of Hizen supported it, as did Ōkubo. Kido at first argued for more sweeping changes but gave way when it was agreed that the appointment of provincial governors would not be made specifically hereditary. So modified, Iwakura's plan became government policy.

It was soon made public. On July 25 the Court announced that it was accepting the daimyo's offers to surrender their lands and ordered all who had not made the offer to follow suit. The daimyo were to become governors (Chiji), the announcement informed them, and were to retain one-tenth of former domain revenues for their household expenses. Other decrees, issued at the same time, brought Court nobles and feudal lords together in a single order of nobility, to be called *kazoku*; divided the samurai into two broad segments, *shizoku* (gentry) and *sotsu* (foot-soldiers), replacing the existing multiplicity of ranks; instituted a review of hereditary stipends; and revised the regulations concerning local office and finance. It was, the British minister observed, "a great step": "The Mikado may gain but little in purse by the change, and the Daimios may still retain much of their authority, but henceforward they govern as *national officers*, and not for *themselves*."[29]

THE ABOLITION OF THE DOMAINS

The decision to accept the surrender of land registers and make the daimyo into governors of their former domains was followed on August 15, 1869, by a further reorganization of the central government.[30] One characteristic of it was a greater emphasis on the imperial derivation of authority, marked by the high place accorded to the Board of Religion (Jingikan) and by the introduction of a new system of Court ranks, with which the holding of office at different levels was equated. Another was a strengthening of the executive (known hereafter as the Dajōkan), together with a reduction in the number of those who had effective power within it.

The top post, Minister of the Right (Udaijin), went to Sanjō Sanetomi. Below him were three Great Councillors (Dainagon); these positions went initially to two Court nobles (Iwakura Tomomi and Tokudaiji Sanenori) and one former daimyo (Nabeshima Naomasa of Hizen). Nabeshima withdrew after a year (and died in early 1871), but two more Court nobles were appointed to this office in December 1869 and November 1870, respectively. Next came the Councillors (Sangi), all of whom were samurai: initially two (Soejima Taneomi of Hizen and Maebara Issei of Chōshū), then four (by the addition of Ōkubo Toshimichi of Satsuma and Hirosawa Saneomi of Chōshū a week or two later). During the next two years the number of Sangi varied (from a minimum of two to a maximum of seven), and six other samurai held office at one time or another (Kido Kōin of Chōshū, Ōkuma Shigenobu of Hizen, Saigō Takamori of Satsuma, and Sasaki Takayuki, Saitō Toshiyuki, and Itagaki Taisuke, all of Tosa).

Responsible to the Dajōkan were six departments: Civil Affairs (Mimbushō), Finance (Ōkurashō), War (Hyōbushō), Justice (Kyōbushō), Imperial Household (Kunaishō), and Foreign Affairs (Gaimushō). They were usually headed by imperial princes, Court nobles, or daimyo (e.g., Matsudaira Shungaku and Date Muneki), but generally it was the samurai deputies who had effective control. Ōkuma Shigenobu served in this capacity in the Mimbushō and the Ōkurasho, with Itō Hirobumi of Chōshū and Yoshii Tomozane of Satsuma acting as his immediate assistants in both (for overlapping periods). Ōki Takatō (Hizen) was a deputy in the Mimbushō; Ōmura Masujirō, Maebara Issei, and Yamagata Aritomo of Chōshū succeeded each other during the next two years at the Hyōbushō; and Terajima Munenori of Satsuma was at the Gaimushō. In other words, a handful of men, samurai from the four domains that had taken the initiative in proposing the surrender of registers, monopolized the key positions of government, continuing the process by which control of the council and the administration was concentrated into fewer hands. On September 15, 1869, the six men currently holding senior posts (the Udaijin, two Dainagon, and three Sangi) pledged themselves in writing to work closely together and uphold collective decisions.[31]

Assuming that this settled the question of the government's unity, at least for the time being, there remained the question of its authority outside the capital. The Kōgisho was now replaced by another consultative assembly, the Shūgiin, which for about a year—it was adjourned in October 1870 and never met again—allowed the airing of samurai opinion. More important, however, were the steps that were taken to impose conformity on the domains.

In the summer of 1869, as we have seen, the decision about land registers was accompanied by instructions concerning the allocation of domain revenues, the simplification of samurai class structure, and the revision (by implication, a reduction) of stipends. On October 4, 1870, these were amplified by further regulations, which brought together and supplemented those that had been issued in the past two years.[32] They provided, as before, for a standard pattern of local administrative offices and terminology. They required the governor (the former feudal lord) to attend meetings in the capital every three years, remaining for three months (a variant on sankin-kōtai); established procedures for the control of accounts and local currency; reiterated the rule that household finance was to be kept separate from public expenditure; and set limits to the power of provincial officials in such matters as legal punishment and the granting of stipends. December brought yet another regulation, this one restricting the size of local armed forces to 60 men for every 10,000 koku, much as the Bakufu had done.

The extent to which this program was given effect varied widely from place to place. For example, in the fudai domain of Sakura the senior posts in the new administration seem to have remained firmly in the hands of upper samurai, but there was a sharp reduction of stipends at all levels, so that a man's economic standing came to depend more on office—and hence to some extent on ability, especially in the middle and lower range—than on hereditary rank. This increased the bureaucratization of the samurai, widening the gap between officeholders and the rest, and drove many families to seek additional income from agriculture or commerce. It therefore went some way toward dismantling the privileges of the samurai as a class, though the power structure was almost unchanged.[33]

By contrast, in Kumamoto the actions of the central government greatly strengthened the position of lower samurai reformers, who, together with their allies among the gōshi and richer farmers, were able for a time to dominate policy in a manner reminiscent of the "men of spirit" (shishi) in 1862 and 1863. They forced tax reductions, the dismissal of many samurai officials, the breakup of local monopolies, and even the resignation of the daimyo in favor of his son.[34]

Predictably, there was a greater consistency of aims, if not always of results, in the domains that were represented on the Meiji council. Hizen, prompted by Etō and Soejima, committed itself openly to diminishing the importance of status by promoting "men of talent" while continuing its pre-Restoration policies in pursuit of "wealth and strength."[35] In Tosa, too, reformers (in this sense), backed by Yamauchi Yōdō, had long been in power; but the growing influence of Itagaki Taisuke led to proposals in 1870 for a much more radical attack on traditional society than anything that had gone before. By a decree issued on December 26, 1869, the Tosa gōshi, ashigaru, and many senior village headmen had been included in the ranks of shizoku, or gentry. What was now envisaged was the abolition of status distinctions based on hereditary occupation; the opening of office to men of all social groups; the creation of a professional army, replacing samurai; and the termination of such privileges and restrictions as tended to prevent or inhibit economic choice and competition.[36] Thus Tosa became the scene of an experiment designed to make the samurai into productive members of society in the interest of both social unity and national wealth.

The situation in Satsuma was complicated by the fact that Ōkubo Toshimichi and his closest associates felt it necessary to spend most of their time in the national capital. This weakened the leadership in Kagoshima, which proved unable to cope with the disputes arising between activists of fairly low rank, who on their return from the northeast campaign demanded access to power, and conservative upper samurai, who were unwilling to grant it. Ōkubo had to go back to try to resolve these difficulties in the spring of 1869. As a result of his persuasions, Saigō Takamori agreed to accept local office, together with some of the loyalists, to carry out a program of reforms. One of their first steps was to replace the rule linking official position to status with one providing for promotion by ability and for stipends pegged to the duties of office. In addition, the administrative system was overhauled to increase specialization of function; offices were more clearly defined, and the number of officials was reduced. Later in the year the surviving samurai fiefs were abolished and stipends were cut. The Shimazu branch houses were limited thereafter to a maximum of 1,500 koku, other upper samurai to 700 koku, and middle samurai to 200 koku. Stipends of under 200 koku were not affected.[37]

A similar pattern was followed in Chōshū, where as early as December 1868 the domain had announced its objectives as "wealth and strength," a career open to talent, and a revised official structure. In the following October came a reduction of stipends, much more severe than that in Satsuma, which brought the highest (those over 1,000 koku) down to 10 per cent of their former value and established a ceiling of 100 koku for the rest. Soon after came a reorganization of military units, then the abolition of status subdivisions within the samurai class. Finally, in July 1870 samurai families were given permission to engage in agriculture or commerce.[38]

One thing is apparent: a common thread running through all the early Meiji reorganization in domains was the use of the central government's influence to make certain that local power was in the hands of men who would implement its plans. If domains were not to be abolished, they must be made to conform in order that national unity could be achieved. Unhappily, to achieve that conformity it was necessary to effect two different kinds of change, each likely to provoke hostility. The first, based on the not unreasonable expectation that the government's sympathizers were to be found in the middle and lower ranges of the samurai class, was the emphasis on ability rather than birth in officeholding. This opened the way for "men of talent" to gain positions of authority where they had not done so before, or to consolidate such positions where they had already been won. Such an attack on the hereditary principle of position quite naturally incurred the opposition of those who were being robbed of a traditional predominance. The second change, a corollary of the first, was the extension of the new policy to the samurai as a whole, again with the goal of ensuring that in the future wealth and privilege would be earned, not just inherited. Implicit in both changes was a functional (not an egalitarian) approach to rank and office, designed to produce military and administrative efficiency; but the second also had the effect of depriving many quite ordinary samurai families, not belonging at all to the upper levels, of the modest competence or comfortable sinecure that had long protected them from the worst consequences of disadvantageous economic trends. Stipends, for example, were severely cut back almost everywhere, more sharply in the domains that had been defeated in the civil war, but also very substantially, except for the lowest income groups, among the victors.[39] As a result, resistance to government policies did not come only from the few who were being displaced from power. It came also from the many who suffered small, but important, losses of income and position. In addition, traditionalists and conservatives—not necessarily much affected in this way themselves—were offended by what they saw as the concomitants of these policies, that is, an emphasis on commerce and an aping of foreign ways.[40]

In Satsuma, Shimazu Hisamitsu and Saigō Takamori both became increasingly critical of the central government during 1870, refusing to cooperate in its modernizing program. This encouraged others to express their dissatisfaction. For example, one of Kagoshima's restless samurai publicly committed suicide in August in order to underline his grievances, leaving a memorial in which he listed his complaints. At the head of the list was the question of appointments; office, he said, went to men who were "intent only upon increasing their own reputation" and was "regulated by partiality, not by merit." He went on to complain of high prices, high taxes, railways, and the treaties, and to deplore the prevalence everywhere of expediency, leading men to "pronounce good today that which yesterday they denounced as evil."[41] In all this he fairly represented much samurai feeling, especially the feeling of those in Satsuma who had supported the anti-Bakufu movement out of a simple belief in loyalism and expulsion, only to find that these had little place in contemporary politics. Saigō alone, or so it seemed, was able to prevent them from venting their anger on the ministers in the capital who were to blame for this state of affairs.

Elsewhere there was no such restraint. Three men who had reputations as reformers were attacked and killed: Yokoi Shōnan on February 15, 1869; Ōmura Masujirō toward the end of the same year; Hirosawa Saneomi early in 1871. During the winter of 1869–70 there was serious trouble in Chōshū, arising directly from attempts to disband the irregular units (shotai) and incorporate them into regular battalions, but also reflecting a more general resentment about foreign policy and samurai stipends. Some 2,000 men rebelled and attacked Yamaguchi, forcing those who had formerly led them, Kido, Inoue, and Shinagawa (Takasugi had died in 1867), to come down from Tokyo and suppress them with loyal samurai troops.[42] Some of the rebels escaped into northern Kyūshū, where they joined other disaffected groups in Kumamoto and Maki Izumi's former home domain of Kurume, keeping the whole area in a state of unrest until the spring of 1871. Eventually, forces from Satsuma, Chōshū, and Kumamoto hunted them down.

Much of this turbulence, Parkes was told in Tokyo, was due to the resentment of lower samurai over the government's financial demands on the domains, coupled with a naïve understanding among the farmers that "after the revolution they were to pay no taxes at all."[43] In other words, the "disbanded soldiery" was "making common cause with the agricultural or industrial classes."[44] Parkes's senior subordinate, F. O. Adams, later wrote of the situation: "Whenever the ignorant peasants rose, under the infliction of some injustice at the hands of officials, there were, since the restoration, never wanting [to lead them] men of the samurai class, who were deeply irritated at their fallen state [and] could not comprehend the friendly attitude towards foreigners which was the ruling policy of the Mikado's advisers."[45]

As this suggests, the Meiji leaders had inherited some of the Bakufu's more intractable problems. The social and economic upheavals of late-Tokugawa Japan, manifested in samurai debt and peasant rebellion, had not magically vanished with the change of regime, any more than a transfer of power had made the "unequal treaties" suddenly acceptable; and insofar as these were grievances to be blamed on "the government," they were as much a source of weakness to the new one as the old. More, it is clear that up to this point the post-Restoration attempts to revise the structure of domains had done little to improve political stability. Indeed, though undertaken in a search for unity, they had proved contentious enough to undermine it, not least in those areas that the council rightly regarded as the chief prop to its power. Hence despite the surrender of registers and the reforms founded on it, the same three political issues remained to be resolved as in 1869: the government's own unity of purpose; the extent to which it could rely on Satsuma and Chōshū for support; and the degree of authority it could exert over the country at large.

Put another way, what was at stake was not just the government's policies, but the very survival of the government itself. In Kido's words, taken from a letter to Ōkuma in September 1869: "Unless the government settles its major policies firmly and on a permanent basis, it will without question prove quite impossible to save our country. Constant shilly-shallying, which serves to confuse men's minds, can only lead in the end to disaster."[46] A year later he could still have said the same.

Part of the difficulty lay with a group of determined modernizers, led by Ōkuma Shigenobu and Itō Hirobumi, that had established itself within the Finance Ministry. Gaining a measure of responsibility for local government when the Ministry of Finance was amalgamated with the Ministry of Civil Affairs in the autumn of 1869, these men took the opportunity to press for a number of domain reforms, especially in connection with finance and stipends, that incurred the displeasure of conservatives everywhere, including some of their colleagues. As Sanjō commented, for all their ability they were not tactful men: "They have no spirit of moderation or capacity for tolerance, so they are inevitably censured."[47] And Kido, who in large measure supported what they tried to do, once noted in his diary that Itō "understands what is far away, but is not yet versed in the state of affairs in our own country. As a result, what he says is sound in theory, but in practice he cannot assess its merit in relation to present possibilities."[48]

These were not qualities that appealed to Ōkubo, who was much more concerned with maintaining his political fences; and in the summer of 1870 he joined Maebara and Matsukata in an attempt to restrict the apparently divisive influence of Ōkuma and his friends by separating the two ministries. They got their way, though only after a major confrontation, which did little to restore the council's unity.[49] Then in late October and early November Ōkubo held a series of discussions with Kido, Sanjō, and Iwakura to see what could be done about restoring the old anti-Bakufu alliance, which had fallen sadly into disrepair. They reached two decisions: first, that the authority of the Councillors (Sangi) must be strengthened within the administration, especially their control over the ministries of Finance and Civil Affairs, and second, that a fresh effort must be made to secure the cooperation of their former colleagues in Satsuma and Chōshū.

Broadly, this was to say that the balance between progressives and conservatives must be tilted to the conservatives for the sake of the government's authority overall. In practice, it became a plan for an imperial mission to Kagoshima and Yamaguchi, headed by Iwakura, under cover of which Ōkubo and Kido could conduct the necessary talks. Their arguments proved convincing. In Satsuma in early February 1871 both Shimazu Hisamitsu and Saigō Takamori were persuaded to take office in Tokyo. Then in Chōshū Mōri Yoshichika agreed to come to the capital to give the administration countenance. Finally, while Iwakura returned to Kyōto, the others went on to Tosa to enlist Itagaki into the cause. By the end of March the whole party was back in Tokyo.

Despite a wealth of documentation, it is extraordinarily difficult to discover what these comings and goings were really about (apart from the obvious issue, that of political power). Only two things were directly mentioned by the men concerned: a public reassertion of unity within the central group of domains, and a program of administrative reform designed to increase the efficiency of the

Tokyo government. Nevertheless, it is reasonably certain that during these fews months one crucial and specific decision was taken, that is, to abolish the domains. Indeed, it is often assumed—rather too readily, I believe—that this was the primary object of the exercise.[50]

There were several factors that made such a decision easier to take in 1871 than in 1869. One was that a number of the domains, embarrassed on the one hand by the fiscal demands of the Ministry of Finance and on the other by the objections of samurai to a reduction of stipends, had requested that they be made into prefectures (ken), as the Tokugawa lands had been. Most of these were small domains, on which economic pressures were greatest, though a few larger ones—Morioka, Nagoya, and Tokushima—also favored the idea.[51] Then there was evidence, provided chiefly by debates in the Shūgiin, that many individual samurai found the earlier compromise about the surrender of registers unsatisfactory because it involved anomalies of status and personal loyalty in their relations with the daimyo-governors. A different kind of outside prompting came from Harry Parkes, who never ceased to remind the men in power of the need to make Japan "into one firm and compact State, governed by uniform and just laws,"[52] not merely because this was the way to be civilized, but also because it would give the council a means of intervening in local affairs in order to punish samurai who attacked foreigners. Some members of the council saw the force of this, though their reasons were not quite the same as those of Parkes.

Within the government coalition, the Tosa men saw the abolition of the domains as a way to achieve the goal they had sought in their earlier proposals for a feudal assembly: diluting the domain-based dominance of their colleagues from Satsuma and Chōshū.[53] Iwakura was also attracted by this argument. In a long memorandum he wrote in the late summer of 1870, surveying many aspects of national policy, he argued for a change to prefectures on two grounds: first, because it was the only way of ending the weakness caused by internal divisions, of producing a government that was "above" domains instead of one based on territorial factions; and second, because national defense required a national army, not one made up of contingents from different domains with many types of organization and training.[54]

In principle, these arguments appealed also to those close to Ōkubo and Kido, men who had chosen a career in the central bureaucracy over working in their own domains, and could hardly turn back now. Ever since 1869, in fact, they had been concerned, not about whether abolition was desirable, but about whether the circumstances were right for carrying it out. And this consideration still made them cautious in the spring of 1871.

Kido, some months earlier, had advocated a gradual approach, based on example. "A beginning should be made in the areas under direct Court rule," he wrote to Sanjō, "easing the restrictions hitherto placed on the generality of the people and letting them acquire the right to freedom [*jiyū no ken*]. In this way the Court's administration will inevitably establish itself, until the domains find themselves unable to maintain their old habits and therefore place themselves peacefully under the Court's control."[55] Ōkubo, too, opposed unnecessary haste, fully aware that the government depended as much on the conservative Saigō's influence in Satsuma as on the progressive Kido's ability to manipulate Chōshū.[56] One danger that he saw was personal: the risk of imperiling the inner group's authority, which rested partly on their position as spokesmen for the components of a domain alliance. Another was national: the risk of provoking samurai disorder on an extensive scale and so destroying the regime. Significantly, Iwakura, discussing the domestic situation with Parkes on May 20, 1871, linked three things: the abolition of the domains, the formation of an imperial army from units that would no longer be under domain control, and a substantial reduction of samurai stipends.[57]

What all this amounts to is that the debate within the government was about means, not ends, about implementation, not the political goal of national strength itself. On the one side were those like Ōkuma and Itō who saw no possibility of national unity without abolishing the domains, and on the other those like Ōkubo and Iwakura who saw no way of abolishing the domains without destroying the government's own unity in the process. Kido hovered uneasily in the middle, sympathizing with the arguments of the first, accepting the realism of the second. None of the five men in question, as far as the documentation shows, was at this point concerned with anything but tactics and timing (which may explain why no decision in principle seems ever to have been recorded).

Lacking such a record, we can only conclude that the decision to complete the process of unification was probably taken during the winter of 1870–71. Certainly it was made before May 20, 1871, when Iwakura told Parkes that the government was determined to bring about a state of affairs in which "Higo may no longer be Higo, nor Satsuma Satsuma."[58] Nevertheless, there was still a good deal to be done before this resolve was translated into law. Although it had been agreed at the end of March that troops would be moved to Tokyo from Satsuma, Chōshū, and Tosa in case the reforms were resisted, several things happened thereafter to cause delays: it became clear that Shimazu Hisamitsu was not willing to come to the capital after all; there was disagreement between Chōshū and Satsuma over the suppression of unrest in northern Kyūshū; and the death of Mōri Yoshichika forced Kido to return to Yamaguchi to make fresh arrangements there. It was not until the middle of July that these matters were settled and the key members of the government were back in Tokyo, supported by several battalions of loyal troops.

Their first concern was a reallocation of posts that would put a decisive concentration of power in their own hands. That goal was fulfilled in a major reorganization on August 11, 1871, by which Kido and Saigō became the only Councillors (Sangi) and Ōkubo stood down to make way for them, becoming Minister of Finance. A month later the Ministry of Civil Affairs was abolished and its functions again transferred to the Ministry of Finance, that is, to Ōkubo. This began a process by which, within the next year or two, samurai emerged as titular heads of the principal ministries, replacing the Court nobles and daimyo who had held those offices hitherto. More immediately, it gave Saigō and the other conservatives a guarantee that the hotheads of the Ōkuma faction would be under control.

Almost simultaneously, the final steps were taken for abolishing the domains. Kido had raised the question formally with Sanjō, the senior minister, on July 21, arguing that the opportunity now existed to carry matters a stage beyond what had been done in 1869. Ōkubo and Saigō supported him. After the government reorganization, they began to get down to details.[59] At a meeting on August 24, attended only by the Satsuma and Chōshū leaders—neither the Tosa leaders nor the Court nobles were invited—it was decided that action would be taken by decree, not by consultation, and that Saigō would be ready to suppress all opposition. This agreed, Sanjō and Iwakura were informed of what was to be done, and Ōkuma and Itagaki were made Councillors to ensure the cooperation of Hizen and Tosa. Finally, on August 29 such daimyo as were in the city were summoned to imperial audiences and peremptorily informed that the prefectural system was to be extended forthwith to the whole of Japan. The full edict was read to them. "In order to preserve the peace of Japanese subjects at home and to stand on an equal footing with countries abroad," it explained, ". . . We deem it necessary that the government of the country be centred in a single authority."[60]

The way in which this matter was handled makes plain the predominance of the central samurai group. They were willing not only to dispense with most of their kuge and daimyo allies, even to the point of not consulting them, but also to risk a head-on clash with those of their samurai colleagues who still remained committed to domains. That this was a gamble, they knew; witness their military precautions. And the stakes were high. The dangers were minimized in one direction by offering "substantial monetary advantages" to the daimyo,[61] who were allowed to retain one-tenth of their former revenues as income. As an added inducement, all were to become members of a peerage, which ensured their continuing social prestige. The two things together prompted the daimyo to accept the change without demur, except for a few, like Shimazu Hisamitsu, who still wanted power. However, many of the samurai, as we shall see, did not fare as well. In fact, their grievances were one of the government's enduring problems.

Leaving aside for later consideration the wider issue of changes in Japanese society, of which the decision to abolish the domains was a part, let us look in conclusion at the political consequences of the decision, more narrowly defined. In the central government, it marks a vital stage in the development of a modern bureaucracy and a political style dependent on it. This is chiefly because it changed the process of policy-making from one that required the manipulation of both central and local interests (Court, feudal lords, domain governments) to one in which feudal and regional loyalties, where they survived, became elements in a struggle between factions operating at the center. In other words, those loyalties became influences on, not objects of, government policy. In this context, men of ability and appropriate experience who lacked "feudal" power, in the sense of being unable to command the resources of a domain, were able to become key figures by virtue of office or a bureaucratic following,* while the reforming lords and others whose hereditary status had gone far to explain their initial importance faded from the scene.

The change was in this respect anti-feudal. It was not, however, anti-feudal in the sense that it constituted an attack on feudal society emanating from outside, that is, from merchants or peasants. Rather, the attack was made by men who emerged from within the feudal class (by ostensibly traditionalist means), and was directed against those feudal institutions that hampered them in the task of creating a strong Japan. The result was that they jettisoned those elements that determined the nature of government but retained a good deal of the concomitant social framework. Overwhelmingly, senior officials were still of samurai origin for the rest of the century. The twenty-two men who held office as Councillor (Sangi) between 1871 and 1885 were without exception former samurai. So (on the basis of a random sample) were 86 per cent of those appointed to the post of prefectural governor before 1900.[62] At the same time, expertise, especially Western-style expertise, became more important

* Mutsu Munemitsu is a good example. A moderately prosperous samurai of Kii (Wakayama), a senior Tokugawa domain, he had joined forces with the Tosa rōnin after 1864 and moved on to become a Meiji bureaucrat (eventually serving as Foreign Minister). Even he, however, felt it necessary to restore his links with Wakayama in 1869 in order to provide himself with some kind of domain "base." See Jansen, "Mutsu," especially pp. 311–20.

than family rank or even regional affiliation.* Thus a privileged background, represented by samurai birth, remained important, but inherited status as such no longer determined the shape of a man's career. This was a logical outcome of the promotion of "men of talent." It was also a natural extension of the trend toward samurai control that had been manifested in the government reorganizations of 1868 and 1869.

Similarly, the abolition of the domains was the last stage in a move away from feudal separatism as an ingredient in reform, that is, away from the lingering traces of "unity of Court and Bakufu" and ideas of a feudal assembly. Before the end of 1871 the lords had been ordered to reside in Tokyo, most being replaced as governors by samurai, usually from other areas. In the following January the domains lost their identities, as well as their names, when the 302 prefectures formed on their abolition were reduced to a mere 72. Subsequently these were subdivided into districts, wards, towns, and villages. At the end of 1873 they were all brought under the control of a newly created Home Ministry (Naimushō), headed by Ōkubo, which had extensive powers to intervene in local matters; and before long, politicians were beginning to complain of the "evil of centralization" as one of the less desirable products of the new regime.[63] This led to the formation of prefectural assemblies in 1878, but these did little to modify the character of the system. For Japan as a whole, local autonomy had vanished with feudal rule.

* Silberman, *Ministers*, Table 12, p. 70, shows that of 69 men studied who achieved important office between 1875 and 1900, no fewer than 47 had some kind of Western education or experience. Table 11 (*ibid.*, p. 68) shows a correlation between Western influence and lower samurai origin. Sidney Brown, "Ōkubo Toshimichi," pp. 221–23, notes that despite the enormous preponderance of men from Satsuma, Chōshū, Tosa, and Hizen among the councillors and ministers, their immediate subordinates did not necessarily conform to the same pattern; in the War Ministry over a third of those in the highest grades came from these four domains, but in the Home Ministry under Ōkubo only 5 out of 51 senior bureaucrats came from Satsuma or Chōshū.

CHAPTER XIV

Wealth and Strength

THE ABOLITION OF the domains was not an end in itself. To most members of the Meiji council it was a decision designed to complete the work of "restoration" by providing a political structure within which the business of government could be carried on. It was therefore a further step toward political unity, seen as a precondition of national strength. Yet it worked no magic; it could not at a blow resolve all the problems of formulating policy. It is true that in the most general terms the nature of Meiji objectives had been set out in what the new leaders had done in their own domains, both before and after 1868: fukoku-kyōhei, "enriching the country, strengthening the army," manifested in the adoption of Western military technology and new kinds of economic activity to finance it; and the promotion of "men of talent," by which was emphasized the functional, rather than the hereditary, basis of samurai power. All the same, experience had differed from domain to domain, so that trying to apply it on a national scale was not always a route to unanimity. Similarly, the men who undertook the task, though broadly alike in background and career, differed greatly in outlook and temperament—some cautious, others eager, some conservative, others radical—with the result that they often had difficulty in agreeing among themselves.

In these circumstances, the work of turning slogans into policies was sometimes slow, continuing through much of the Meiji era. It also raised major issues. One was that of cultural heritage: How far could Japan maintain a national identity, based on traditional culture, while introducing the Western-style institutions that seemed to be an essential element in national strength? This was to pose the old question of jōi and kaikoku in a more sophisticated form, in which it was to be debated for several more generations. Another problem was the social one: Was the pursuit of new goals, like unity and efficiency, to destroy Japanese society as it had existed for the past 200 years? More specifically, would the search for social, as distinct from administrative, cohesion entail the destruction of the samurai so that non-samurai "men of substance" could be mobilized behind the regime? All these were matters about which Japanese felt deeply. As a consequence, the process of spelling out the *content* of policy, making it necessary to identify the *extent* of the change that was proposed, involved great controversy. Only when this process had been completed—at least provisionally—can one say that the Restoration had ended and the history of the Meiji period had begun.

FORMULATING POLICY

In considering the formulation of early Meiji policy, it is instructive to examine the way in which Iwakura Tomomi's ideas developed, since he was frequently a spokesman for the government's inner group. In the spring of 1867, during the complex maneuvering in Kyōto over the opening of Hyōgo and the punishment of Chōshū, he had drafted a memorial that foreshadowed many features of the Meiji state: a form of imperial rule that would impose controls on the daimyo through regional governors; the stimulation of economic growth in agriculture and foreign trade; an education system designed to teach useful skills and traditional ethics; the renegotiation of the treaties on an equal footing.[1] To this was added, once Iwakura and his colleagues came to power, a more specifically Western element, arising from greater knowledge of the West. In January 1869 Iwakura sought the British minister's advice about how "we may profitably adopt in Japan the institutions which obtain in Europe," for, he said, "although Japan has a civilization of her own, still we recognize . . . that in many respects our civilization is inferior to theirs."[2] Parkes was not the man to miss such a didactic opportunity. Nor did others, when it came their way, whether they were foreigners in Japan or Japanese who had been to Europe and the United States.

As a result, by the late summer of 1870, when Iwakura prepared another long statement on questions of general policy, his ideas were taking a more definite shape. First, he now proposed the outright abolition of domains, arguing that a Japan fragmented by feudal separatism would be too weak to defend her people and their livelihood against the foreign threat: "The country's safety is the individual's safety, the country's danger is the individual's danger."[3] As corollaries, he held that tax collection must be unified under a central authority in order to ensure financial stability and an equalization of burdens between one region and another; that samurai privilege must be brought to an end, since those who no longer gave military or administrative service to the state should not be paid stipends from public funds; and that Japan must be given a modern, national army to withstand the "national" enemy she had to contend with. By the same token, education must be made an instrument of government policy, contributing to wealth and strength. This implied that it must not be in the old form of Confucian academies instructing samurai, but a whole new system: primary schools, to raise the level of literacy among the people; commercial schools, because of the importance of trade; and schools for girls, who as mothers would eventually play the greatest part in shaping moral attitudes within the family.

In putting forward this kind of blueprint for a new Japan, with its emphasis on the need to attain equality with the West, Iwakura had wide support within the Meiji leadership. The typically conservative daimyo of Kumamoto, Hosokawa Yoshiyuki, had expressed many of these ideas (albeit in much more Confucian dress) in a memorial of June 1869.[4] Among those who were closer to the heart of things, Ōkuma Shigenobu of Hizen, already a recognized "progressive," was urging in the autumn of 1870 the need for unity in a threefold sense: an administration united under the Ministry of Civil Affairs; an army united under the Ministry of Military Affairs; a tax system united under the Ministry of Finance.[5]

Ōkubo Toshimichi, too, accepted that Japan must move toward "civilization and enlightenment," though as a more cautious politician than Ōkuma he was aware that any change likely to offend deep-rooted prejudice must be approached with care. "We must not look on things with favor just because they are new," he had commented in the previous year. "Rather, we must proceed in due order and at a deliberate pace, not putting our aims in jeopardy through an anxiety for progress."[6] In the spring of 1870 he warned Ōkuma specifically that the reformers were trying to move too fast in view of the unrest the program of centralization was bound to engender.[7] Iwakura had similar reservations. As Parkes reported to London, members of the council were "sadly in fear of the reactionary party, who attack them fiercely on any innovation they sanction."[8]

This is a reminder that by 1870, when Iwakura was drafting his proposals, there had emerged within the government a party of reform, or renovation (ishin), which was pressing for a more thoroughgoing and Western type of "wealth and strength" than most of those who had belonged to the anti-Bakufu alliance of 1867 were ready to accept.[9] It had as its nucleus those members of the Meiji oligarchy who combined a reputation for loyalist politics with some first-hand knowledge of the West, including Ōkuma himself, whose tenure of office as vice-minister at the Ministry of Finance (August 1869 to September 1870) made that department the center of "enlightenment" in the administration; Itō Hirobumi and Inoue Kaoru of Chōshū, who served under him there and in the Ministry of Civil Affairs; and Godai Tomoatsu, Satsuma's naval and industrial expert, who had been Ōkuma's colleague at the Foreign Ministry during 1868. This core group was reinforced by a number of "experts" in things Western, whose politics were in some cases tainted by prior service to the Bakufu, but whose Western-style training had been much more thorough: men like Nishi Amane, Shibusawa Eiichi, and Kanda Kōhei. According to Parkes, they were commonly known as the "students' party" because they had been abroad.[10] The British chargé Adams, who succeeded Parkes temporarily in 1871, reported Iwakura's comment on them: They wanted "to adopt foreign inventions at once and advance the country as it were at telegraphic speed," in contrast to the conservatives, who were "opposed to making a number of changes suddenly and without much reflection."

His own view, Iwakura had added, was that "the true policy probably lay between these two extremes."[11]

In fact, Iwakura and Ōkubo had a key role in the debates that followed, since they were at once alert to the political risks of offending the conservatives and open-minded enough to effect radical change where they were persuaded that nothing less could serve the government's purpose. This made their opinions a touchstone of practicality, to be applied to any given proposal for reform; and it made their willingness to back the reformers in 1873, when an open confrontation came, decisive.

But before we turn to a discussion of that controversy and of the manner in which it was resolved, it will be useful to take a closer look at some of the issues raised in 1871–73. Since those concerning railways, education, and conscription serve well enough to illustrate the various differences of approach, they will be considered here, leaving the questions of stipends and land-tax reform, which are also relevant, to the next chapter, where they can be put in the context of finance and social change.

The improvement of communications was something that was urged on the Meiji government by all kinds of groups and for a variety of reasons. As a contribution to the growth of industry and commerce, it had the support of those who wanted Japan to enter an age of "civilization and enlightenment." Politically, it could be justified on grounds of unity and administrative efficiency; militarily, as a means of maintaining order and defense. In one way or another, therefore, it was attractive to men of many different views. By the same token, it drew opposition from those who objected to new-fangled gadgets or who feared that Western-style innovation of almost any kind must inevitably benefit the foreigner more than the Japanese. Hence it provides a convenient test of attitudes toward imported technology.

All these arguments were brought to bear, for example, in connection with the telegraph, which was first introduced through the influence of Itō Hirobumi, acting on the advice of an English engineer. A line from Tokyo to Yokohoma was completed in January 1870 and another from Osaka to Hyōgo in the following December; the network was extended to most major provincial centers during the next five years and was provided with an international connection, linking Nagasaki to Shanghai and Vladivostok, in 1871.

All the same, the construction of a telegraph network did not prove as controversial as the building of railways, partly, no doubt, because railways seemed more symbolic of cultural change. The mid-nineteenth century was, after all, the Railway Age in Europe and America. By the West's own estimation, railways meant progress. This fact had been hinted at in the very beginning of its dealings with Japan, when a "Lilliputian locomotive" (as well as a telegraph) was among the gifts brought by Perry in 1854. According to his report on the formal presentation, the train was an instant hit. Indeed, some of the Bakufu officials, "not to be cheated out of a ride, . . . betook themselves to the roof" of the miniature carriage, so that the ceremonial was enlivened by the sight of "a dignified mandarin whirling around the circular road at the rate of twenty miles an hour, with his loose robes flying in the wind."[12]

The "new toy" was soon taken seriously enough, however, and a number of proposals were made for building railways in Japan during the remaining years of Tokugawa rule.[13] Godai Tomoatsu's dealings with Belgian businessmen in 1865–66 produced an abortive Satsuma plan for a line connecting Osaka and Kyōto, designed to improve the facilities for possible military intervention in the capital by the domains of the southwest (using the sea route to Osaka). On similar grounds though from an opposite viewpoint, Bakufu modernizers, backed by the French minister, Léon Roches, canvassed the idea of an Edo-Kyōto railway in 1866–67, seeing it as a means of strengthening their own position at the Court. This, too, came to nothing, as did discussions with American interests for a line between Edo and Yokohama to promote foreign trade.

After the fall of the Bakufu, some of these proposals were renewed. In 1868 the Hizen members of the new government—representing a domain that had pioneered the casting of iron cannon in Japan—suggested that the problem of administering the country from two centers, Tokyo and Kyōto, might be solved by building a railway between the two. At the same time, American diplomats began to press for confirmation of the arrangements they had been discussing with the Shogun's officials earlier. This prompted action by Sir Harry Parkes, who offered British engineering and financial help if the Japanese would undertake the railway project themselves instead of leaving it to the Americans. Carried out in this way, he said, the building of a railway could do nothing but good: it would be "a *Japanese* measure," not "a concession to a foreign company"; and it would thereby avoid becoming a badge of foreign domination, as all such operations must if they were to gain Japanese support.[14]

Parkes's plan was backed up by detailed recommendations in April 1869 from a British engineer, R. H. Brunton (who had been employed by the Japanese government to supervise the construction of lighthouses). They envisaged a main trunk line from Tokyo to Osaka, managed by the state and financed by government funds, of which the section from Tokyo to Yokohama would be the first to be completed. In this form the proposal was supported by most of the reformers in the Meiji government, especially Ōkuma and Itō. Significantly, however, in view of Parkes's activities, it was the Foreign Ministry—under Shimazu Nariakira's former adviser on Dutch studies, Terajima Munenori—that took the initiative in securing its formal adoption. In a memorandum for the council (Dajōkan) dated November 14, 1869, the ministry made a general case for railways as a contribution to national wealth and strength, declaring: "They would make it possible to even out inequalities of distribution, so easing the difficulties that now arise for our country through shortages and price increases in commodities like rice and grain [a reference to the poor harvest of 1869]. Moreover, they would have the advantage of enabling us to bring under cultivation tracts of land that are now empty and barren; and in times of grave emergency they would make possible the rapid dispatch of troops."[15] To clinch the argument, it was claimed that the cost of building the first section, Tokyo to Yokohama, could almost certainly be borne by Yokohama merchants, who would profit by the great increase in the city's prosperity that the railway would bring.

The Foreign Ministry memorandum, supplemented by further lobbying from Parkes,[16] led to an agreement in principle that the railway be built, followed by the opening of negotiations to obtain British capital. There were still a number of obstacles to be overcome, however, since difficulties about the British loan, arising in part from personality clashes, caused a delay, which gave opponents of the scheme time to marshal arguments against it. Thus in early 1870 a group of conservative officials, including two influential Satsuma men, Yoshii Tomozane and Kaeda Nobuyoshi, and the former daimyo of Bizen, Ikeda Mochimasa, tried to get the original decision set aside on the grounds that the large sums of money involved would be better spent on defense and the relief of distress at home. There were also objections from the Ministry of Military Affairs, especially from its vice-minister, Maebara Issei, to starting with a Tokyo-Yokohama link. He and his colleagues argued that the line would create a potential source of unrest by impoverishing Japanese now engaged in transport in the area, and at the same time make it more difficult than ever to defend the capital from foreign attack, since French and British troops were already stationed at Yokohama as legation guards. Under the circumstances they thought it would be preferable to start with a line to northeast Japan. This would open up the underdeveloped region of Hokkaidō and provide access to the frontier under Russian threat. Indeed, so strongly did the ministry feel about the matter that for some weeks it refused to hand over the site chosen for the Tokyo terminal of the Yokohama line, which was one of its own establishments.

To counter these and similar moves, advocates of the railway project in the Ministry of Finance, notably Shibusawa Eiichi, drew up a fresh memorial on the subject in April 1870, which they submitted to the government jointly with the Foreign Ministry.[17] It first rehearsed the arguments put forward by the Gaimushō, namely, that local variations in prices due to poor communications weakened the country's economy and kept Japan from competing effectively with the Western world. It then took up the objection that expenditure on railways would be wasteful at a time when things like welfare and defense were much more needed. This, it said, was contradicted by the examples of Britain and France. Far from being wasteful, what they had spent on railways had become a primary source of their wealth and power. In fact, it was the cost of traditional transport along the Tōkaidō that was wasteful, impoverishing those who lived along the route by imposing on them costs of as much as two million ryō a year. Five years of such costs would pay for a railway. Another five would finance relief measures for the local population on a considerable scale. And with it all, by linking the country's major political centers, the line would ensure stability and coordination, as nothing else could.

Despite Maebara's objections, these arguments persuaded the council that work on the Tokyo-Yokohama line should go ahead. It was constructed under British supervision and was opened two and a half years later, in September 1872. Meanwhile, in July 1870 work had also begun on an Osaka-Kōbe section, which was completed in 1874. In December 1870 responsibility for these operations was assumed by a newly created Ministry of Public Works (Kōbushō). Once that portfolio passed to Itō Hirobumi (November 1871), the plans for railways were never again challenged in principle, though they were sometimes held up for lack of funds. As a result, by the end of the century Japan possessed a network of trunk lines extending from the northern port of Aomori to Nagasaki in Kyūshū, via Tokyo and Osaka, with spurs extending to the Japan Sea coast. Almost all of it, except the first section, had been paid for by capital raised within Japan.

Since railways were the alien product of an alien technology, it is not surprising that many Japanese viewed them with disfavor. But education was quite a different matter. By Confucian axioms, education was an activity that ranked with benevolence and filial piety, to which, indeed, it contributed. Generations of lords had therefore recommended it to their retainers and established schools for them; by so doing they had bequeathed to the Meiji leadership an almost unquestioned belief, not only that education was a good in itself, but also that it was properly a function of the state. Iwakura, as we have seen, consistently included new schools in his list of desiderata.

Hence what was at issue after the Restoration was not *whether* there should be an education system, but what kind it should be. Under the Tokugawa, Court nobles and samurai, together with a good many men whose wealth, if not status, put them on the fringes of the ruling class, had received a training in Chinese literature and thought, often quite an elaborate one. A few, especially later in the period, had added to this a knowledge of some quite different cultural and philosophical values, those of "Dutch" learning; and a very much larger number, drawn from the ranks of commoners, had acquired a basic literacy and some practical skills, plus an acquaintance with the chief maxims of approved Confucian behavior. All this gave Japan a substantially literate (and numerate) society, which was a valuable groundwork for creating a modern state. There had even been pre-Restoration proposals for establishing a more general educational system in order to bolster authority by moral training and marshal talent in the country's service.[18] These were characteristically Meiji principles.

From the viewpoint of a modernizing, centralizing government, an education that would combine useful skills with appropriate civic virtues was clearly desirable. The first Meiji efforts to achieve it, however, were far from successful.[19] The three schools the Bakufu had established, concerned with Confucian, Western, and medical studies, respectively, were continued and were opened to a wider range of students than before. In July 1869 they were brought together in a single organization, the Daigakkō, later renamed Daigaku (the modern word for university), which in the following March was divided into five sections, namely, religion, law, science, medicine, and literature. In addition to training an elite, the new institution in theory was to supervise education in the provinces, but in practice neither task was ever properly fulfilled. Lack of authority to intervene outside the imperial territories limited the geographical scope of the Daigaku's work, leaving the existing domain and private schools to continue much as before. In Tokyo itself, bitter quarrels about the type of education to be provided brought the whole arrangement into disrepute. There were constant internal divisions, with adherents of the Chinese tradition (*kangaku*) and the Japanese tradition (*kokugaku*) clashing, then turning together on the "Western" scholars. Finally, in August 1870 Matsudaira Shungaku, the institution's nominal head, resigned, and the Daigaku as such was abolished, leaving its component parts to go their separate ways.

Abolition of the domains reopened the matter, as it did so many others, by transferring to the central government the duties formerly performed by feudal lords. This prompted the establishment of a Ministry of Education (Mombushō) in September 1871 under Ōki Takatō of Hizen, who took over the task of framing a national educational plan. Significantly, the process seems to have been an entirely bureaucratic one. It occasioned no apparent controversy within the government and was based on the study of foreign models, which had begun when a group of scholars from the Daigaku had been sent to Europe earlier. As a result, the Education Law, issued on September 5, 1872, owed its character in the main to the westernizing predilections of officials.

The nature of its preamble shows how firmly the new bureaucrats had taken control. Education, it said, was to be useful both to the citizen and to the state:

> The only way in which an individual can raise himself, manage his property and prosper in his business and so accomplish his career, is by cultivating his morals, improving his intellect, and becoming proficient in arts. . . . This is the reason why schools are established; from language, writing and reckoning for daily use, to knowledge necessary for officials, farmers, merchants and artisans and craftsmen of every description, to laws, politics, astronomy, medicine, etc., in fact for all vocations of men, there is none that is not to be acquired by learning. . . . Hence, knowledge may be regarded as the capital for raising one's self.[20]

To these largely utilitarian concepts was added an attack on the idea of education as a monopoly of the samurai class, an attack that has much in common, as we shall see, with bureaucratic writings on the subject of conscription. Because Japan had had the wrong kind of schools, the document stated, "people have made a mistake of thinking that learning is a matter for those above samurai rank." Farmers, artisans, and merchants, as well as women, "have no idea of what learning is and think of it as something beyond their sphere." This situation must now end. "It is intended that henceforth universally (without any distinction of class or sex) in a village there shall be no house without learning and in a house no individual without learning."[21]

Apart from enunciating these "modern" principles, the Education Law established a pattern for a network of universities, middle schools, and primary schools, within which existing institutions were to be absorbed and new ones created. By 1880, it is estimated, 40 per cent of the children were attending primary school, by 1900 almost all. Nevertheless, some of the essential characteristics of what is now regarded as the Meiji education system—the combination of Western skills with Japanese ethics, the assertion of tight central control over what was taught—only took shape over the years. That is, they were a product of Meiji society as it developed, not directly of the Education Law itself. One might even say of them, indeed, that they were a response to the Law's existence, not an ingredient in it; for the absence of a public debate in 1872, which gave the ministry's modernizers a clear field at the time, simply delayed the kind of traditionalist opposition that the railways and conscription elicited from the start.

Certainly a nationalist reaction in the 1880's was to give the officially stated purposes of education a very different tone; and though the Imperial Rescript on Education of 1890 falls well outside the period we are studying, we might usefully conclude this section by quoting a passage from it, partly to point the contrast with the document of 1872, but also to illustrate the kind of conservative attitudes that had been pushed aside at the time, rather than overcome. In 1890 the Emperor enjoined his subjects: "Be filial to your parents, affectionate to your brothers and sisters; as husbands and wives be harmonious; as friends true; bear yourselves in modesty and moderation; extend your benevolence to all, pursue learning and cultivate arts, and thereby develop intellectual faculties and perfect moral powers; furthermore, advance public good and promote common interests; always respect the Constitution and observe the laws."[22] Clearly, the emphasis in educational policy had by then shifted from utilitarianism to the making of useful and *law-abiding* citizens.

Military reform had this much in common with the reform of education: both were principles to which samurai unmistakably subscribed, however controversial they found the attempts of their fellows to define them. The issue of how an army should be equipped was perhaps the least of the difficulties; for though it aroused, as one would expect, the same kind of prejudices about technology that we have already discussed in the context of railways, it was not a subject likely to divide the members of the Meiji government from each other or from their rank-and-file. Most men had long since decided that Japan must fight fire with fire. So in the choice of weapons, at least, the nature of Meiji plans was never seriously in doubt.

This was far from being the case with matters of military organization, since these raised important political and social questions. In some domains, as we have seen in earlier chapters, the experiences of the decade after 1858 had brought a recognition that the samurai class structure in its existing form was not necessarily the most efficient basis for a military force. Yoshida Shōin's call for the recruitment of humble heroes; Takasugi Shinsaku's initiative in forming irregular companies in Chōshū; Yoshida Tōyō's attack on traditional military expertise in Tosa; Satsuma's attempts to organize army and navy units in the Western manner; the Bakufu's reforms, based on French methods and advice—all these are examples of the search for some new formula that would reconcile the samurai inheritance with current needs. Nor did the restoration of imperial rule solve the problem, since the samurai continued to see themselves as their country's first defense.

For a government born in civil war and faced with the problem of asserting its authority over its own people, the control of the armed forces was bound to be a major preoccupation, especially since most of its military units were provided by daimyo. It was largely in this context that Iwakura, envisaging in his memorial of August-September 1870 the creation of an army formed from domain contingents, insisted that ways must be found sufficiently to detach units from their regional affiliations to ensure that they were truly under government orders.[23] Similarly, Ōkubo argued for military reviews conducted by the Emperor "so that men may forget the fact of belonging to domains and seek to become soldiers of the Court."[24] There are hints that this may have been one of the reasons for abolishing the domains. Certainly their abolition ended the problem, at least in this particular form.

It did not, however, decide what kind of army the national army was to be, specifically how it should be officered and recruited; and since this put in question the whole future of the samurai class, it was an issue for debate at the highest levels.[25] Some men wanted to protect the position of samurai by entrenching it formally in the military structure. For example, Tani Kanjō, an army officer from Tosa, urged that all sons of samurai be required to undergo a period of military training, forming an elite corps to which commoners would be added only if the need arose. Maebara Issei of Chōshū held similar views, in the sense that he, too, wanted to make samurai the nucleus of a modern army. So did Shimazu Hisamitsu of Satsuma and some of Saigō Takamori's followers.

Many other Meiji leaders were just as firmly bent on creating a conscript army on the European model. Two Chōshū men led this campaign. The first was Ōmura Masujirō, who as vice-minister of Military Affairs in 1868–69 put forward a detailed plan to this effect. It proposed that men be selected from the domains—not necessarily samurai—to serve the Emperor for a five-year term; that they be clothed and equipped at the expense of the central government during this tour of duty; and that when their service was over they be paid a terminal bonus, which would serve in part as a substitute for stipends. The plan was blocked by Ōkubo, who thought it premature,[26] but knowledge of it helped to bring about Ōmura's murder by disgruntled samurai toward the end of 1869. Thereafter it fell to Yamagata Aritomo to continue and complete his work.

In August 1869 Yamagata had left Japan with Saigō's younger brother, Tsugumichi, for a visit to Europe, arranged at their own request. What they saw there, especially in France and Germany, convinced them that conscription was as necessary to military strength as modern weapons were, with the result that when they returned in September 1870, to be appointed almost at once to senior posts in the Ministry of Military Affairs, they became the center of a reforming group.

Until the abolition of the domains their activities were focused on the technical details of organization and training, not least because Saigō Takamori, resuming his place in Tokyo, refused to countenance sweeping changes at a moment when the government's authority was about to be put to the test. Once the domains were abolished, however, this constraint was removed. Accordingly on February 2, 1872, Yamagata, now vice-minister, together with his two Satsuma assistants, Saigō Tsugumichi and Kawamura Sumiyoshi, submitted a memorial urging the formation of a conscript army.[27] The "immediate concern" of the ministry, it said, was with security at home, but it must also prepare in the long term to meet foreign attack. Both contingencies required a regular conscript army and a trained reserve. Citing the example of Prussia, recently so successful against France, the document recommended calling up men at age twenty, "regardless of whether they be samurai or commoners," to be trained for a period of two years in the Western manner, then put in the reserve.

Opposition from men like Tani Kanjō and Maebara Issei prevented immediate acceptance of this plan, but by appealing to the authority of Europe's example and pointing to the achievements of the non-samurai troops Takasugi had led in Chōshū, Yamagata eventually got his way. On December 28, 1872, the government promulgated an imperial edict establishing conscription, together with a separate explanatory announcement of its own.[28] A Conscription Law followed on January 10, 1873, providing for three years' service with the colors and four with the reserves, though with liberal exemptions.[29]

The imperial edict, observing that the distinction between soldier and peasant in Japan had arisen only under feudalism, sought to make the reform more readily acceptable by describing it as a return to the past, modified, but no more than that, by a knowledge of what was being done abroad. By contrast, the Dajōkan document made this the occasion for a remarkably intemperate attack on the samurai as a class. In the Tokugawa period, it said, the samurai had been obdurate and turbulent, living at the expense of others. Now, as a result of the abolition of domains and the introduction of conscription, they were at last to be put on a level with commoners, "both alike as subjects of the Empire": "After living a life of idleness for generations, the samurai have had their stipends reduced and have been authorized to take off their swords, so that all strata of the people may finally gain their rights to liberty. By this innovation the rulers and the ruled will be put on the same basis, the rights of the people will be equal, and the way will be cleared for the unity of soldier and peasant."[30]

One can detect behind this attack a number of influences: the Court's long-standing resentment of samurai dominance; the impatience of low-born "men of talent" with their social superiors (Yamagata was born an ashigaru); the rationale of Western anti-feudal prejudice (much of the drafting was done by the Leiden-trained, ex-Bakufu bureaucrat Nishi Amane).[31] What cannot be shown is that the object of the measure was democratic or egalitarian, despite some of the wording the documents used. With conscription, as the later history of Japan makes clear, the government provided itself with an instrument not only for effecting its policies overseas, but also for keeping order at home, that is, for suppressing samurai rebellion and peasant revolt.[32] Conscription was therefore a measure that strengthened the government's authority, making it less, rather than more dependent on popular support. And there is no doubt at all from the records that this object had been in the minds of the reformers all along. To them, conscription was a part of the mechanism that was to sustain the Meiji state at home as well as abroad. It was not *primarily* a social policy; but because it involved the destruction of the samurai's military function, it forced an adjustment to the class basis of political power. Hence the samurai was attacked—but he was attacked for the bureaucrat's benefit, not the peasant's, however much the bureaucrat spoke of the people's "rights."

DEBATING PRIORITIES

This brief survey of how decisions about railways, education, and conscription were taken serves to emphasize that the proposals contained in Iwakura's memorandum of the late summer of 1870, to which we referred at the beginning of this chapter, did not represent a statement of collective purposes previously agreed on. Neither the content nor the extent of reforms had at that time been fully debated; and the advocates of the solutions that were eventually to characterize "modern" Japan had to work hard thereafter to get them adopted. Much the same was true with respect to samurai stipends and land-tax reform, which we shall consider later. In all these matters, prejudice was aroused by particular proposals for reform, reflecting sometimes traditionalism, sometimes the entrenched interests of a class or group; a prejudice that often divided members of the government from each other as much as it divided them from their common enemies.

The consequence was a debate about priorities that determined both the dominant themes and the dominant men of the next several years. It was a continuing debate, centering first on one problem, then on another; but it came to a head—inevitably, one might suggest, in view of all that had happened in the previous decade—in a dispute over the relationship between domestic politics and foreign affairs. The question raised was a familiar one: How far and how long must Japan continue to compromise with the foreigner while she made the changes at home that would give her equality? And there were both "responsible" and "irresponsible" answers to it, just as there had been before 1868. But the question was set now in a different diplomatic context, the controversy being focused in part on treaty revision and the pursuit of "enlightenment," involving a mission to Europe and America under Iwakura, which left at the end of 1871, and in part on a deterioration of relations with Korea, which reached a crisis point shortly before the Iwakura mission returned in 1873.

The earliest reference to sending an imperial mission overseas came in fact before the Restoration, in two documents written by Iwakura himself in the spring of 1867.[33] He urged it, first, as a public assertion of the Emperor's authority, designed to deny the Shogun's treaty-making powers; second, as a means of giving the imperial cause the protection of international recognition, thereby according Japan a breathing spell, free of diplomatic pressures, in which to effect reforms; and third, as an opportunity to study the civilization of the West, especially those aspects of it that might be turned to Japan's advantage. The first of these aims ceased to be relevant with the Bakufu's overthrow. The others persisted, however, and if anything seemed even more desirable after the events of 1868–69.

The decision to confirm the treaties and to grant the foreign representatives an imperial audience early in 1868, which were necessary steps if the risk of foreign intervention in the civil war was to be forestalled, so offended anti-foreign jōi sentiment as to make it politically expedient to bid for "equality" as soon as possible. In consequence, Iwakura's original idea of a mission came gradually to be related to a project that had been independently under consideration in the Foreign Ministry during 1869 and 1870. Article XIII of the American treaty of 1858, stating that the agreement should be "subject to revision" after July 4, 1872, gave the proposals a diplomatic starting point.

At the same time, the notion of studying the West for the purpose of reforming Japan—in the tradition of embassies to China in the sixth and seventh centuries—was being pressed by the modernizers and their Western, or Western-trained, advisers. An American missionary, Guido Verbeck, hearing rumors about some such proposal in the summer of 1869, sent a paper to Ōkuma Shigenobu, one of his former pupils, suggesting that the mission, if sent, should incorporate separate sections for the study of Western law, finance, education, and military matters.[34] This earned him a number of interviews with Iwakura late in 1871. Within the council, Kido supported the plan, though not entirely for Ōkuma's reasons. Anxious to see Europe, as so many of his younger colleagues were doing, but told by Iwakura in 1870 that the political situation made it unwise for him to go, he now saw in the idea of an embassy a way of fulfilling his ambition.[35] Finally, Ōkubo Toshimichi and Inoue Kaoru at the Finance Ministry expressed themselves in favor of the mission, observing that tariff reform, which greatly concerned them because of its importance for taxation generally, depended in the long run on the willingness of foreigners to accept that Japan was "civilized."[36]

It is clear, then, that a good many influences came together in shaping Iwakura's mission, which was formally approved in October 1871, as soon as the abolition of the domains gave a respite from domestic crises. Most of those influences are reflected in the envoys' instructions.[37] Signed by Sanjō as senior minister, these began by contrasting Japan's international position with that of the countries of the West. She had "lost her equal rights and been made subject to the insults and wrongs of others," so that "the principle of equality between Japanese and foreigner, of reciprocity between East and West, is not maintained." The government's first task must therefore be to end this inferiority. "We must restore our country's rights and remedy the faults in our laws and institutions; we must abandon the arbitrary habits of the past, returning to a rule of clemency and straightforwardness; and we must set ourselves to restore the rights of the people . . . seeking thereby to achieve equality with the Powers." Consequently, the embassy would have a double purpose: to conduct exploratory talks about treaty revision with a view to later negotiations, which would be undertaken after the proper foundations had been laid; and to pave the way for those reforms within Japan that Western governments saw as a necessary preliminary to treaty revision, namely, those that would make her society "acceptable" by international standards.

To this end, the instructions continued, the mission was to have a special staff, organized in three sections. One would study "the constitutions, laws, and regulations of the most enlightened countries of Europe and America." Another would collect economic information: about systems of banking, taxation, and currency; about trade and industry; about railways, telegraphs, and postal services. The third would concern itself with education, including the curriculum and administration of "schools for officials and people," as well as commercial and technical schools. All these things were to be studied "with the object of adopting them in Japan and establishing them here." In addition, all members of the mission were expected to keep on the alert for any knowledge "that will be of benefit to our country," especially with respect to the organization, equipment, and training of military and naval forces and such related operations as the administration of bases, arsenals, and dockyards.

There was some delay in deciding the composition of the mission, partly because of factional in-fighting, partly because the weaker members of the council, like Sanjō, felt that it was too soon after the abolition of the domains to risk having several senior statesmen absent from the country at once. This hesitation was overcome, however, by the argument that the envoys must be distinguished enough to speak authoritatively for Japan and to impress by their rank the peoples they would visit. As a result, Ōkubo, Kido, and Itō were all appointed to accompany Iwakura. Adams entertained them at the British legation before they left and commented on them in dispatches to London. Itō, he said, was "a clever, useful fellow, but easily got hold of by foreigners not always of the best class."[38] Ōkubo, little known to foreigners, was "not very communicative." Kido was quiet in manner but "one of the most zealous members of the party of progress." And the head of the mission, Iwakura, the very model of "a Japanese gentleman," was not only unusually able and plain-spoken, but also conservative enough to act as "a wholesome check upon the almost republican tendencies of some of the ultra-progressive members of the Government."[39]

The ministers of the treaty powers having been duly given formal notice, the mission left Yokohama by steamer on December 23, 1871; there were 107 in the group, 48 officials and 59 students (including 5 girls). They reached San Francisco on January 15, 1872, then went by rail to Washington, arriving on February 29. Here there was an interruption of the original plans, for they found in the capital some prospect of actual negotiations about the treaties. Since Iwakura had no plenipotentiary powers, Ōkubo and Itō returned to Japan to get the necessary authorizations while the rest remained in Washington. But there was reluctance in Tokyo (on the grounds that action at this stage would be premature because ill-prepared) and then a lack of enthusiasm in America (implying still greater difficulties in Europe), so that in the end the talks were never seriously pressed. Instead, when Ōkubo got back to Washington in July the party decided to move on to Europe and sailed from Boston on August 6, bound for Liverpool. This was the beginning of a tour that took the mission to London for the autumn, to Paris in December, to Brussels and the Hague in February 1873, and to Berlin in March, the whole punctuated by audiences with monarchs and heads of state, dinner with statesmen, sightseeing, and a lot of hard work.

For our purposes, the most important consequence of all this was its effect on Kido and Ōkubo, who as the senior representatives of Chōshū and Satsuma, respectively, had a decisive voice in making Japanese policy. Both were a good deal changed by what they saw and heard. Kido, writing from America in January 1872, confessed that he had not previously realized how far ahead of Japan the Western world was in matters of civilization and enlightenment (*bummei-kaika*): "Our present civilization is not true civilization, our present enlightenment is not true enlightenment."[40] Only education, in "true schools," could close the gap, he said. It was also at this time that he began to think in terms of parliamentary institutions for Japan, believing these, too, to be hallmarks of a higher civilization.[41]

Ōkubo, by contrast, thought more of strength than of enlightenment. Bismarck impressed him enormously. "I think there is nothing this man cannot achieve," he wrote to Saigō in Japan.[42] So did British industry. In a letter from London to Ōyama Iwao, dated December 20, 1872, he wrote:

> Our recent travels have taken us to many very interesting and famous places, law courts, prisons, schools, trading companies, factories—from shipyards and ironworks to those manufacturing sugar-refining machines, paper-making machines, wool and cotton textiles, silver cutlery, glass, etc.—as well as coal mines, salt mines, even temples and castles. There is nowhere we have not been. And everywhere we go, there is nothing growing in the ground, just coal and iron.... Factories have increased to an unheard-of extent, so that black smoke rises to the sky from every possible kind.... This is a sufficient explanation of England's wealth and strength.... And it is said that this great growth of trade and industry in the cities has all happened in the last fifty years.[43]

For both Kido and Ōkubo, experiences such as this changed the relative importance of commerce and industry in their scheme of values, just as earlier contacts with the West had affected a number of the men who now counted as "reformers," notably Itō Hirobumi, Inoue Kaoru, Godai Tomoatsu, and Fukuzawa Yukichi. For Godai and Shibusawa Eiichi, indeed, this kind of exposure brought a commitment to economic, rather than governmental, activity, reflected in their decision to leave the bureaucracy for the business world. Many others followed suit. A student, Inoue Shōzō, explaining in a letter from Germany in 1873 why he was turning from military science to industry, provided a rationale that many of them would have accepted. Though there was talk of bummei-kaika and fukoku-kyōhei on everyone's lips in Japan, even those of children, he wrote, few realized that "if the country is to be enriched, the army strengthened, and education established, then first production must be encouraged among the people, products of every kind manufactured and exported overseas, goods imported that our country lacks"; for this was "the tree on which was borne the fruit of civilization and enlightenment in Europe."[44]

Kido and Ōkubo, if they did not go quite so far—certainly not to the point of abandoning politics—at least now came fully to accept that the growth of industry and commerce was an object in its own right, not merely a means of financing military reform. From this was eventually to stem a policy of government intervention in economic matters that was to be a marked feature of Meiji industrialization in the following decade. More immediately, it led them to espouse the cause of the reformers in the crisis that was already developing in Japan.

This crisis had a complex set of origins. In part it grew out of a disagreement that had arisen between the reformers and the rest of the government officials in Tokyo while the Iwakura mission was away. Before the mission's departure at the end of 1871, several decisions had been taken concerning the steps that had to follow the abolition of the domains, including agreement in principle about such questions as conscription and land-tax reform. It was clearly necessary to go ahead with these programs, even in the absence of the envoys. At the same time, since the new machinery of government was still relatively untried, it also seemed necessary not to put it under too much strain. Hence those who were going and those who were staying signed an elaborate twelve-point note in December 1871 defining with some care the powers to be enjoyed by the "caretaker" administration. It included a pledge of unity, a promise to exchange information with the absent members of the council on all important matters, and a restriction on Tokyo's freedom to appoint new men to senior posts or recruit more foreigners. In addition, it contained this promise: "Since it is our intention to carry out major reforms in home affairs when the mission returns, the introduction of further reforms will in the meantime be avoided as far as possible."[45]

A glance at the list of reforming measures that were introduced in 1872 and early 1873—they included the abolition of the Tokugawa ban on the sale and purchase of land, the separation of the army and navy departments, the promulgation of the Education and

Conscription laws, the adoption of the Gregorian calendar, and the institution of several reforms bearing on land tax—makes one question whether this self-denying promise was kept. And even if one concludes that, strictly speaking, there was nothing in this list that went outside the principles already agreed on, there was certainly ample scope for disagreement about the manner in which those principles should be put into practice. In particular, it was the modernizers of the Finance Ministry, with their demands that samurai stipends be abolished, that land tax be standardized and made payable in cash, that a whole range of "westernizing" devices be adopted in support of such reforms (see Chapter 15), who put the point at issue. For their ideas aroused hostility among samurai, alarm among peasants, and animosity from all the spokesmen for these groups within officialdom.

Sanjō, less able and less flexible than Iwakura, lacked the qualities to hold his team together. So did Saigō, the senior samurai representative in the government, who in any case had reservations of his own about the way things were going. As a result, the confrontations between conservatives and progressives mounted, coming to a head in May 1873, when Inoue Kaoru and Shibusawa Eiichi resigned from the Finance Ministry on the grounds that "civilization by decree" was costing more than the country could afford in the present state of the economy. Interestingly, they also complained that reform was proceeding too fast for the people to assimilate, producing opposition, not progress. "While our legal system gets better our people get more exhausted," they said, warning that "before success has been achieved our country will be in a state of poverty."*

The quarreling in government circles over the pace and extent of reform increased, until at last Kido and Ōkubo were asked to return from Europe to bring their colleagues under control. But these disputes were not the immediate cause of the crisis that faced the members of the Iwakura mission when they eventually got home.

* Inoue's and Shibusawa's letter of resignation, dated May 7, 1873, in *Segai Inoue Kō*, 1: 549–61, at p. 553. The specific issue involved was the claimed overspending of the departments headed by Etō (Justice) and Ōki (Education). In view of what followed, it is important to note that Ōkubo was still Finance Minister, though *in absentia*.

Rather it arose in a foreign policy issue, specifically, Korea's rebuff of the Meiji government's attempts to secure recognition of Japan's new regime (a very traditional piece of diplomacy, customary between China's satellites). In 1869 Korea had rejected Japanese overtures, showing little courtesy.[46] Thereafter, there was much indignant debate in Tokyo, but occasional diplomatic moves as well, culminating in a mission to Pusan in the summer of 1872. It too proved unsuccessful.

Many in Tokyo simply saw Korea's actions as a blow to Japanese pride for which she should be punished; there was no need, after all, to accept insults from an Asiatic neighbor, even though one had to stomach them from the West. Others, Saigō among them, saw the dispute in a different light—as an opportunity to find employment for a samurai class that was rapidly being stripped of its privileges at home, including its military ones. An expedition to Korea would be an outlet for samurai energies and ambition, "a far-reaching scheme," as Saigō described it to Itagaki in 1873, "which will divert abroad the attention of those who desire civil strife."[47] He was paraphrasing something Kido had said in 1869, when he had observed that the forcible opening of Pusan to trade, designed to make Korea follow Japan's example, "would probably bring us no profit in terms of goods or currency. Indeed, I believe we would suffer loss. But it would set our country on its course, turning the people's eyes from domestic to foreign affairs and giving our army and navy practical experience. Only thus can we ensure that our country will one day rise again and be preserved forever."[48]

In fact, as seen from Tokyo in the spring of 1873, there was no real question whether an attack on Korea was desirable, only whether it was wise. Saigō thought it was, provided the Koreans were shown to be the first to give offense. Accordingly (perhaps because he sought a task for which he felt temperamentally better suited than running a government) he proposed himself as envoy to make a fresh approach, believing that he would be killed and so provide the excuse for a punitive expedition. Itagaki supported him, chiefly from a concern about the fate of the samurai. So did the Foreign Minister, Soejima. Gotō, Etō, and Ōki followed suit, though this would appear to have been partly out of rivalry with the Finance Ministry officials, who opposed hostilities on the grounds of cost. At all events, whatever the different motives of its members—and accounts of them vary a good deal—the council finally decided, on August 17, 1873, to accept Saigō's plan. This was tantamount to deciding on war with Korea. Only the Emperor's insistence that confirmation of the decision must await Iwakura's return, which was expected shortly, prevented arrangements from being put in hand at once.

Kido and Ōkubo were by this time back in Japan. Ōkubo had left France in April and had been in Japan since May 26. Kido, who had insisted on accompanying Iwakura to Russia first, regardless of Tokyo's quarrels, had returned late in July. Both, therefore, were in the country for the closing stages of the Korean debate, though they had become estranged in Europe and could not now work closely together. Ōkubo, though Minister of Finance, was not a member of the council. Indeed, he described himself as helpless to influence events—"like a mosquito trying to carry a mountain" was how he put it to Ōyama[49]—and took care to remove himself from Tokyo. Kido, by contrast, did what he could to restrain the hotheads, though without actually attending any of the council's meetings. In August he submitted a memorial to the Court in which he argued strongly that Japan was not yet in a position to undertake a military adventure of the kind being proposed. She "lacked civilization"; her "wealth and strength were not developed"; she had "independence in name, but not independence in fact." Nothing could be more important at such a stage in her development, he said, than "conducting our finances with economy," certainly not pursuing dangerous and discreditable activities overseas attended by great diplomatic risks. Better "to give heed to our own affairs and build our national strength," leaving it until the reform program had had time to take effect before attempting more.[50]

It seems highly probable that Kido's arguments were reinforced by Ōkubo's intrigues, for the Emperor, when he took the vital decision to await Iwakura before confirming the council's plans, was at Hakone, as was Ōkubo (ostensibly on his way to climb Mount Fuji).

In any case, the Emperor's reluctance—or that of his entourage—held matters up until the arrival of Iwakura and Itō on September 13, which was quickly followed by efforts to get the government's previous decision about Korea overturned.

The first step, accomplished on October 12, was to get Ōkubo made a councillor again. Two days later, Sanjō and Iwakura reopened the council's discussions of the question, having already pledged their support to Ōkubo. The meeting was opened by Iwakura, who called for abandonment of the plan for an attack on Korea on the grounds that dealing with the Russian threat in the north and developing Japan's resources at home were both more urgent. Itagaki disagreed, as did Saigō. Kido was ill and did not attend the meeting, but Ōkubo now put the case that had been stated in Kido's August memorial, namely, that no large-scale military activities should be envisaged until the foundations of "wealth and strength" had been firmly laid at home. The result was deadlock, and the meeting was adjourned until next day.

Before it could be resumed, Saigō wrote to Sanjō and Iwakura in the strongest possible terms, forcing them to move some way toward his position. However, when their defection became apparent in the council's subsequent proceedings, Ōkubo and Kido both offered to resign (October 17), apparently to put pressure on Sanjō. It undoubtedly did so, if not quite in the way that was intended, for on October 18 Sanjō collapsed under the strain, leaving Iwakura as acting head of the government and so tilting the balance between the contending groups once more. This time, Iwakura acted with decision. Despite threats of resignation from Saigō, Itagaki, Etō, and Gotō, he summoned the council on October 23 and announced his intention of advising the Emperor to reverse the decision about sending an envoy to Korea. The members of the "war party" thereupon resigned.

There is no doubt that there were many crosscurrents in all this: personal animosities, feudal and local rivalries, genuine differences over policy. The whole affair affords a fascinating example of the forces at work in Japanese politics and the way in which political institutions functioned after the abolition of domains. However, what chiefly concerns us here are the results, for the crisis determined the nature of the Meiji government and its policies for the next two decades.

In the first place, it marked the final stage in the disintegration of the loose and widely based Restoration alliance of Court nobles, feudal lords, and samurai of every rank and region, leaving in its stead a small nucleus with a relatively coherent view of the country's future. Saigō's resignation split the Satsuma contingent, more than half of which withdrew to Kagoshima. Since this included many army men, the army became more of a Chōshū preserve than ever. Chōshū was less seriously divided, because it was involved in no such clash of personalities as that between Saigō and Ōkubo; but Etō's withdrawal from the government was followed by the resignation of several of his domain colleagues, mostly samurai, who had little sympathy with reforms that cost their class its standing. Itagaki and Gotō of Tosa turned to party politics, seeking a new kind of following to pit against the power of the bureaucrats.

In other words, all those who were out of sympathy with the policies of the central group, whether because of a sentimental view of the past or a radically different concept of the future, took other roads, leaving Ōkubo, now entrenched in the newly created Ministry of Home Affairs (Naimushō), as the government's strong man. Iwakura still worked closely with him, as did Ōkuma, Matsukata, Itō, and Yamagata. Kido was less to be counted on, though he never made an open break. And together they trained a generation of officialdom in the habits and ideas that were to characterize the next phase in the modern history of Japan.

In a final chapter we shall consider further some aspects of the society they were creating, together with the kind of opposition that their policies provoked. First, though, as a means to a better understanding of those policies, it is worth giving a little more attention to the views expressed by Ōkubo at this time, since he was in a position to impose them on his colleagues. The best place to begin is with a memorandum he wrote about the Korean crisis, apparently in October 1873.[51] It made seven points, specifically argued with respect to the immediate issue; but as a guide to his attitudes in more general terms, it can better be treated as falling into two main parts, one dealing with international factors, the other with domestic ones (though one has to bear in mind that the essence of his argument is the relationship between the two).

To start with the former: Japan, Ōkubo said, had signed treaties with the countries of Europe and America on terms of patent inequality, to the point, indeed, where France and Britain had even established garrisons on Japanese soil (i.e., at Yokohama) on the pretext that the Japanese government was unable to protect their citizens properly. They treat us, he complained, "almost as if our country were one of their dependencies." Revising treaties that could impose this kind of disgrace was therefore an urgent national task. Success in that task, however, depended on the caution with which it was approached. In the north, Russia was awaiting just such an opportunity for spoils as a war between Japan and Korea might provide. More dangerous still, Britain would seize any excuse to intervene in Japanese affairs to secure her financial interests. In India, as everyone knew, she had first created a company to trade, then used its profits to establish a colonial army and navy, and finally exploited the quarrels between various Indian rulers in order to establish a territorial empire. "We in Japan must give careful thought to this, taking steps quickly to stimulate domestic production and increase our exports, so as to repair our weakness by attaining national wealth and strength."

Turning to the domestic situation, Ōkubo recognized that the many radical changes of the last five years, including the abolition of the domains, had caused much disquiet, imperiling unity. Moreover, they had occasioned heavy expenditure on the government's part, which any hostilities with Korea would certainly increase. Raising extra revenue for this purpose, whether by way of heavier taxes, a foreign loan, or issues of paper money, would carry a danger of spreading the unrest, "producing confusion and disorder in the circulation of the goods needed for everyday use and so inflicting hardship on the people." This "might in the end even prompt them to rebel." It would be better by far to wait until the country had reaped the fruits of "the undertakings already put in hand to contribute to our national wealth and strength," which "unnecessary hostilities" would undoubtedly force the government to abandon. War, in fact, by diverting resources from production and increasing the import of costly weapons from overseas, would so hamper the economy as to cause a return to the situation existing in 1868: "a disparity between imports and exports, involving the greatest difficulties for Japan."

In one respect, this statement was an exercise in realpolitik, as the opening appeal for realism in foreign affairs makes clear: "Shameful though it be, a thing may have to be endured; just though it be, it may not always be pursued." But more than that, it was a statement that put the whole Meiji program into a nationalist context. Accepting that Japan could only be saved by abandoning tradition, it implied that the past must be sacrificed to the future for the country's sake. Domains had to be abolished, samurai replaced by conscripts, the economy developed in quite new ways. A whole range of reforms had to be adopted that were alien in concept and radical in effect. Indeed, they had not only to be adopted, but even to be imposed—by force if necessary—on those who felt themselves to suffer by them. Unquestionably, everything possible ought to be done to avoid rebellion. But this was only because rebellion was a source of weakness in the international sphere, not because it was a symptom of injustice and distress.

CHAPTER XV

Finance and Society

IN ONE RESPECT, the position adopted by Ōkubo at the end of 1873 marks a convenient point at which to end a study of the evolution of Restoration policy. The slogan fukoku-kyōhei, "enrich the country, strengthen the army," which had earlier been transposed from its traditionally agrarian and feudal context into the context of Western-style modernization, had also by this time become the official program of the Meiji government, geared to achieving the strength with which Japan could resist the West.

This was not the whole of the story, however. There was another element in Meiji reform, the fiscal element, that linked government policies to pre-Restoration socioeconomic change, i.e., to some of the problems with which this book began. It involved both the samurai and the farmer, the twin pillars of Tokugawa society; and by modifying their position in the social structure it brought about a redistribution of power that was an important characteristic of the new "absolutist" state. A discussion of this topic does not lend itself quite so readily to the chronological limits we have so far observed. Nevertheless, its importance to an understanding of the Meiji Restoration, plus the fact that many of its essential features took shape in 1871–73, makes it a theme we must now pursue.

SAMURAI STIPENDS

Abolition of the domains had given the Meiji government financial responsibilities as well as political gains. These included the responsibility for collecting land tax throughout the whole of the country and deciding the rate at which it should be paid, a subject we have yet to discuss. More immediately, they laid on the government, rather than on daimyo, the duty of funding feudal debt and of paying stipends to samurai. This, it has been said, was the price the feudal class had to be offered in exchange for political power.[1] It was certainly an acute financial embarrassment to the Meiji leadership.

During the first year or two of the regime's existence, Meiji finances were bedeviled by civil war and political uncertainties, exacerbated by the fact that only about eight million of the country's thirty million koku of land were under the Court's control, that is, what had once been the Tokugawa territories.[2] The revenue from this holding was relatively small, both because tax was difficult to collect in the circumstances and because dues on Bakufu lands had in any case been lower than the national average. As a result, the high level of military costs produced huge deficits. These could be met only by large-scale borrowing, mostly from Mitsui and the other financial houses of Osaka and Edo (at 18 per cent interest), and by issuing unbacked paper money,[3] devices that put the government heavily in debt from the outset. The charges on the debt were still considerable in 1870 and 1871, by which time the situation had in other respects settled down. In those years revenue and expenditure came approximately into balance (see Table 3), though only by virtue of continued borrowing and paper issue, which plainly could not go on indefinitely.

In some ways, abolition of the domains improved the position. Measured in the new unit of currency, the yen (which replaced the ryō), the land tax yield increased from ¥11.3 million, or 51 per cent of total revenue, in 1871 to ¥60.6 million, or 71 per cent, in 1873 (ignoring 1872, when the problems of transition from one system to another distorted the figures). Against this, the costs of administration rose by about ¥20 million and those of stipends and similar expenses by about ¥16 million, so that in taking over the domains the government gained more in revenue than it lost. To put it differently, in 1871 the *whole* of its land tax receipts was required to meet the cost of stipends and administration—a situation no better than that of the Bakufu before it—whereas in 1873 the propor-

TABLE 3
Government Revenue and Expenditure, 1870–1874
(in million yen)

Financial year	Revenue: Total	Revenue: Major sources: Land tax	Revenue: Major sources: Paper money and loans	Expenditure: Total	Expenditure: Major outlays: Administration (central and local)	Expenditure: Major outlays: Military	Expenditure: Major outlays: Stipends
1870	20.9	8.2	10.3	20.1	6.7	2.9	4.2
1871	22.1	11.3	6.5	20.2	5.8	3.3	5.5
1872	50.4	20.0	24.0	57.7	20.9	9.5	20.6
1873	85.5	60.6	12.5	62.7	25.8	9.7	21.7
1874	73.4	59.4	1.2	82.3	26.7	13.6	36.1[a]

SOURCE: Seki Junya, *Meiji ishin to chiso kaisei* (Kyoto, 1967), tables, pp. 21, 51.

NOTE: The accounting period varied from time to time, partly because of changes in the calendar. I have used here the year that most closely corresponds to the government financial year. The figure labeled "stipends" includes various other "feudal" commitments of the Bakufu that were taken over by the Meiji government.

[a] About one-fifth of this amount consisted of lump sum payments to those who chose to accept a commutation of stipend.

tion had dropped to a little under four-fifths. Even if one attributes the concurrent increase in military expenditure entirely to items formerly paid by the domains, adding this to the two other main categories, one still gets a total for 1873 rather smaller than the yield of land tax in that year.

This does not necessarily lead to the conclusion that the new position was a satisfactory one. After all, the domain debts, which the government now took over, amounted to a considerable sum: as originally reported, about ¥74 million was owed to domestic creditors, about ¥4 million to foreign ones.* After study of the question by a special department of the Finance Ministry, begun

* The geographical distribution of the debts varied a good deal but seems not to have reflected differences of political alignment to any great extent. For example, Tosa was at about the national average, measuring its debts against its kokudaka. So was Chōshū, though this was apparently a result of the costs of fighting the Bakufu after 1864. Satsuma was very much below the average, but so also were some of the pro-Bakufu domains. The clearest distinction is to be found between the large domains and the small domains, no doubt reflecting the importance of problems of scale. Niwa, *Meiji ishin*, pp. 10–13, estimates that of 182 domains of less than 100,000 koku, only 62, or about a third, had debts below the national average, whereas over half of those over 100,000 koku (20 of 38 domains) were below it. There is a useful table showing domain debts in *Nihon kindaishi jiten*, pp. 647–54.

in early 1872, it was decided in March 1873 to cancel without compensation all domestic debts incurred before 1844. The remaining ¥34 million was then reduced to ¥23 million, chiefly by the adjustment of interest rates. Similarly, foreign debts were reduced by negotiation to ¥2.8 million, so that the final total the government had to pay was a little under ¥26 million. To this, however, had to be added the ¥22 million required to redeem the domain paper money still in circulation, making the cost to the Treasury, payable over a period of years, not far short of the ¥48 million it spent on stipends and administration in that year.

Faced with the need to raise this sum, plus a growing expenditure on Western-style reforms, especially military ones, the Meiji leaders viewed with the same alarm as the domain administrators to whose responsibilities they had succeeded the fact that regular annual stipends siphoned off about a third of the revenue derived from land tax, which was the regime's principal resource. As we have seen, the total would have been even greater had not the domains, urged on by the imperial government, already done everything they could to trim it. Almost everywhere, the highest stipends had been reduced in recent years to 10 per cent of their former value, or even less; and in many of the medium and small domains, in particular, the stipends of middle and lower samurai had also been cut back, sometimes to what was barely a subsistence level.[4] By these means the amount required for stipends in the country as a whole (including the expenditure of domains as well as that of the central government) had been brought down from an estimated ¥34.6 million in the period just before the Restoration to about ¥22.6 million at the time the domains were abolished in 1871.* This meant that in and after 1872 the government had to pay out only about three-fifths of what had been chargeable against the revenues of the Bakufu and the lords a year or two earlier, or a good deal less if one allows for inflation. Most of it was paid in small amounts to very large numbers of samurai families.†

* These figures are taken from Fukaya, *Kashizoku*, p. 250. The same work cites a different estimate (p. 27) without trying to reconcile the two sets of figures: stipends totaling 13 million koku before 1868; 9 million koku in 1869; 4.9 million koku in 1871. Variations in the price of rice would account for at least some of the discrepancy.

† Niwa, *Meiji ishin*, pp. 24–25, analyzes the stipend structure in Fukuoka in 1870 and Chōshū in 1874. In the first case stipends of less than 100 koku accounted for 81

The significance of this is that it left very little scope for further reduction, not at least without causing real and widespread hardship to a politically powerful segment of the population representing some 5 or 6 per cent of Japan's thirty million people. In fact, only three courses were open to the Meiji government. It could acquiesce in the continuation of stipends and the consequent limitations on its own freedom of choice in economic policy. It could seek alternative sources of revenue, from which new kinds of expenditure could be met, while effectively leaving land tax in large part mortgaged to stipend payments. Or it could abolish stipends, accepting the risk of unrest or even rebellion. Choosing between them proved a long and difficult process.

A number of factors went into the making of the final decision. Some of them arose from the policy of promoting "men of talent," which began as a process of selection by ability *within* a status system and ended by destroying that system in the name of efficiency. The policy had been given effect in a number of domains before 1871, often in the form of increasing the salaries paid to civil and military officials *pari passu* with a reduction of stipends, so shifting the emphasis to function, not birth, as a determinant of samurai income. In conservative Satsuma, for example, stipends had been greatly reduced in 1869 for all men who had 200 koku or more. Thereafter, however, salaries ranging from the equivalent of 50 koku to 1,200 koku had been introduced for the five highest ranks of local officials (commanders of companies and assistant magistrates of districts at the bottom, senior domain councillors at the top).[5] Much the same was done elsewhere, sometimes more radically. Thus in the Hotta domain of Sakura, only thirty-three samurai families out of nearly 500 still had stipends of thirty koku or more by 1871, the highest being 200 koku for branches of the daimyo house. Yet the top salaries paid were between 60 and 150 koku, that is, as much as (or even more than) those who received them might otherwise have had as stipends.[6]

One result of this was to give economic substance to the differences between the able minority and the less able majority among samurai at every level, a situation that was confirmed by the man-

---

per cent of the total paid out; and in the second, stipends of under 25 koku accounted for 63 per cent.

ner in which the central government bureaucracy was built up after 1871 and by the adoption of conscription as the basis of army recruitment. For the fact was that throughout much of the country the samurai class no longer commanded, either by interest or by sentiment, the loyalty of many of its most active members, who were finding outlets for their energies—and appropriate rewards—in serving the Emperor's government. They had abandoned local ties, much as the shishi had done, committing themselves to a world of opportunity and vigor. In the process some of them had acquired, directly through their own studies and experience or indirectly through those of others, a belief that they must not just abandon, but completely destroy, the privileges of the class from which they came. With that belief went a Western-style rationale to justify what they wanted to do. We have already seen an example of it in the announcement about conscription, which was the work of a former Chōshū lesser samurai, Yamagata, and the better-born (but Western-trained) former Bakufu adviser Nishi Amane.

One of the most forthright statements of their point of view came from Itagaki Taisuke, whose class loyalties (as head of a well-to-do middle samurai family) seem clearly here to have taken second place to his modernizing preferences. In a memorial submitted to the Tosa authorities at the beginning of 1871, he argued that human skills were the result of natural endowment: "None of them depend on a division into classes, as samurai, farmers, artisans, and merchants."[7] Hence the samurai, by monopolizing the offices of government in the past, had preempted a role that belonged to all human beings, "debasing the lower classes." The time had come for this to be changed, he wrote: "We should seek above all to spread widely among the people the responsibility for the civil and military functions hitherto performed by the samurai ... so that each may develop his own knowledge and abilities ... and have the chance to fulfill his natural aspirations."[8]

The success of French popular resistance against Prussia had shown, Itagaki continued, how important it was to national strength to devise institutions that accorded the people their rights in this way. "In order to make it possible for our country to confront the world and succeed in the task of achieving national prosperity, the whole of the people must be made to cherish sentiments of patriotism, and institutions must be established under which people are all treated as equals. There is no other course. . . . After all, the people's wealth and strength are the government's wealth and strength, and the people's poverty and weakness the government's poverty and weakness."[9] Inherent in all this was Itagaki's later argument for creating a parliament, namely, that it would be a means of marshaling the popular will behind the actions of the state. Immediately, however, his proposals were directed to achieving social unity—as one ingredient in fukoku-kyōhei—by eliminating some of the inherited symbols that divided man from man.

Insofar as this implied a willingness to accord to others some of the privileges hitherto reserved to samurai, it was readily accepted by the Meiji government. Its members were conscious that they had been brought to power with the help of non-samurai groups—Itagaki himself later commented that "the richer farmers and merchants" had "produced the leaders of the revolution of 1868"[10]—and that these groups had to be given recognition. In consequence, a number of decrees about class designations and privileges were issued between 1868 and 1873.[11]

On August 2, 1869, immediately after the surrender of domain registers, the various labels used for different samurai ranks were formally replaced by two new ones, *shizoku* (for middle samurai and above) and *sotsu* (for lower samurai), which domain officials were to assign to individual samurai in accordance with local conditions. This opened the way for a good deal of readjustment of status classification and allowed some of the gōshi and rural upper class to gain a designation more in keeping with their influence. In Tosa, for example, there were thereafter five numbered ranks of shizoku, the gōshi being put in the fourth and senior village headmen (Ōshōya) in the fifth.* In addition, commoners (heimin), who still included many of Itagaki's rich farmers and merchants,

* In fact, the dilution of the shizoku category was eventually even greater than this implies. Partly because so many anomalies arose by leaving the implementation of this change in local hands, the government decided to carry out a further revision after the abolition of domains, issuing instructions on March 8, 1872, that did away with the sotsu category. All those of permanent sotsu status became shizoku, and the rest, those who held only life status, became heimin. See Fukaya, pp. 154–57.

were given the right to have family names (October 1870) and to marry into samurai or noble families (September 1871). Shizoku were permitted to leave off their swords (September 1871) and to engage in agriculture, commerce, or industry without loss of status (January 1872). The attribution of certain kinds of dress or hair style to particular social groups was also brought to an end.

Inevitably, these changes aroused a certain amount of resentment among former samurai; but as long as the changes were confined to raising the status of others, not directly lowering their own, that resentment remained within bounds. Stipends were quite a different matter. On these most shizoku depended, and knew themselves to depend, for the income to maintain their social pretensions. Consequently, their anticipated sense of grievance had to be taken into account in any attempt to go beyond what had already been done by the domains to reduce the burden that stipends laid on government finance.[12] Kido, for example, though he believed it was the government's duty to eliminate "unnecessary" expenditure, of which the expenditure on stipends was a case in point, also maintained that it would be wrong to discard and impoverish those who for so many centuries had been the state's protection and support. To do this would be a breach of faith, he wrote in a long and emotional memorial at the end of 1873.[13] It would damage the government's reputation both at home and abroad, and possibly even provoke a revolt. He proposed instead a kind of compulsory savings plan, by which stipend-holders would be required to surrender one-third of their annual receipts to the Treasury for a period of years in return for government bonds. By this means they could accumulate enough capital in time to make the stipends themselves unnecessary.

Iwakura, too, was aware that stipends were an anomaly in a situation where the recipients were no longer regular servants of the state, and was equally cautious about ending them because of fears of unrest. His solution, put forward in the survey of policy he wrote in the summer of 1870, was to pay stipends in the form of vouchers, which would be subject to taxation but which could be sold by those wishing to raise capital to buy land or enter commerce. In other words, he wanted to give the government an opportunity to reduce its commitments over time, gradually redeeming the vouchers on the market while also encouraging the samurai to take up "useful occupations." Like so much else in the document, this was close to the policy that was adopted at the end of 1873.[14]

The first direct move toward that policy came in early 1872, when the reform-minded officials in the Finance Ministry began to insist that something must be done about government finance. Inoue Kaoru (Chōshū) and Yoshida Kiyonari (Satsuma), backed by Ōkuma, urged that Japan raise a foreign loan, part of which (¥10 million) would be used to reduce stipends. Specifically, they recommended that one-third of each stipend be discontinued and the remaining two-thirds paid by marketable bonds, which the government would then redeem in six annual installments: that is, capitalizing the stipends at a figure equal to six years' payments but using for this purpose an annual value only two-thirds of what it had been before. This was much more drastic than the plan Iwakura had proposed; and since it was a major issue, not covered by the agreements made before the Iwakura mission left, it had to be referred to the absent members of the council, then in America.

Both Iwakura and Kido objected to it, Kido noting indignantly in his diary, "the shizoku are not criminals, they are people of our imperial land."[15] Apparently Ōkubo and Itō also expressed some doubts about it when they returned briefly to Tokyo that summer over the matter of plenipotentiary powers. In any case it was certainly to them that Ōkuma and Inoue suggested an amendment in September, providing for more gradual redemption (lasting fifteen years, not six) and giving holders the option of an immediate lump sum payable in bonds and equal in value to eight years' stipends.

Even this proved too controversial, and the question was dropped until November 1873, that is, after the mission had returned and the Korean crisis had been settled. There was then brought forward a Finance Ministry proposal that stipends be taxed. It was supported by Ōkubo but opposed by both Kido and Itō. Ōkuma, together with the former Bakufu official Katsu Awa, argued that such a step would be extremely unpopular and proposed instead that a samurai be permitted to surrender his stipend for cash if he so wished, permanent stipends being capitalized at the equivalent of six years' normal payments and lifetime stipends at four years'. However, Ōkubo still insisted, despite Kido's objections, that stipends must also be taxed, and in the end both decisions were announced simultaneously (December 27, 1873).

The central government established taxes on a sliding scale, ranging from 35 per cent on a stipend of 50,000 koku to only 2 per cent on a stipend of 5 koku, thereby penalizing upper samurai more than lower samurai, much as the domains had done when cutting stipends before 1871. The tax was estimated to yield an annual revenue of about 500,000 koku on the 4.7 million koku in stipends still being paid. The justification offered for it was the traditional one for stipend cuts in the Tokugawa period: the cost of military reform. By contrast, the optional commutation of stipends, which was limited to those of less than 100 koku, was presented as an economic opportunity, not a contribution to government funds. It was being introduced, the government announcement said, because many samurai had found it impossible to avail themselves of the permission, granted a year before, to engage in farming or trade, "owing probably to the want of the necessary capital."[16]

After this there was little hope left for the main body of the samurai. Among the Meiji leaders, the reformers, preoccupied with finance, gave fiscal problems priority over feelings of gratitude; the politicians, like Itagaki, continued to be concerned with unity, hence with the interests of respectable non-samurai; and the centralizers, like Iwakura and Ōkubo, recognized that having a professional bureaucracy and a conscript army meant the end, or at least the transformation, of the samurai inheritance. Only Kido continued to object—and his influence was on the wane. In November 1874 optional commutation was extended to stipends of over 100 koku; in November 1875 all payments were converted to cash; and finally, in March 1876, Ōkuma proposed the compulsory commutation of the remaining stipends. This course was agreed on in May, against further opposition from Kido, and was announced in August.

For permanent stipends valued at ¥1,000 or more a year, bonds bearing interest at 5 per cent were to be issued at a capitalization value of from five to seven and a half years' income. For lesser sums the valuation was higher, rising at maximum to fourteen years' income at 7 per cent interest. Thus, at the highest level a former feudal lord having an annual stipend of ¥100,000 would now be issued bonds with a face value of ¥500,000 (i.e., five years' income), bearing interest at 5 per cent and giving him an income of ¥25,000, but toward the other end of the scale a samurai with a stipend of ¥100 would receive bonds of ¥1,100 (i.e., eleven years' income), bearing interest at 6 per cent and therefore yielding ¥66 a year. Life stipends were to be commuted at half the rates applicable to permanent ones.[17] In all, a total of ¥173 million in bonds and ¥730,000 in cash was paid out to 313,000 individuals under these regulations. The result was to reduce the government's expenditure in stipends for the period 1877–80 to about ¥15 million a year, that is, to roughly 70 per cent of what it had been in 1873.[18] Taking into account the continuous inflation of these years, the disparity, which is a measure of the samurai's loss, was even greater.

The importance of this decision to Japan's economy was considerable. James Nakamura has estimated that interest payments on bonds represented less than 2 per cent of agricultural income by 1878–82, no more than a tenth of the proportion that had been allotted to stipends under the Tokugawa.[19] Thus the dispossession of the samurai left more to be divided between landlord and government, if not more for the farmer. It also provided many shizoku with modest amounts of capital to invest, whether in land or in new financial institutions like the national banks,[20] and forced still others—those who quickly lost their capital—into productive employment. For these reasons, it played a considerable role in modernization.

Equally important, however, is the fact that it marked a change in the nature of Japanese society. Although it was the entrenched and privileged position of samurai as a group that was destroyed, not the more pervasive influence of samurai in society, the step was an essential one if the formal composition of the country's ruling class was to reflect more accurately the real distribution of power. In this sense, dismantling samurai privilege was the resolution of one of the Tokugawa "contradictions," the failure of wealth, status, and office to cohere. Yet the movement that resolved it was not in any obvious respect class based. The change was the work above all of a group of samurai, men who were willing not only to attack their superiors in the name of the promotion of men of talent, but also to attack their fellow samurai in the name of national need; and though a few of them had connections among, or even a personal background as, non-samurai, there is no convincing evidence that those few represented the interests of non-samurai groups. In other words, the victory was not one of lesser samurai over upper samurai or of non-samurai over samurai so much as a victory of a particular *kind* of samurai over all the rest.

LAND-TAX REFORM

In discussing the abolition of feudalism in Japan, Herbert Norman observes that "the commutation of *daimyo* pensions, while symbolizing the political compromise between a former governing class and the new government resting largely upon merchant and landed interests for its support, represents at the same time a far-reaching social process in which the interests of usurer, landlord, merchant, financier and *ci-devant daimyo* were melted down, transfused and solidified into a homogeneous mass in which the original elements became indistinguishable."[21] He also notes that land-tax reform played a major part in this process, especially because it contributed to the "further consolidation of a landlord class which could become the political foundation for the government in the countryside." The Japanese scholar Seki Junya, pursuing a similar theme, has described land tax as the price that landlords paid for feudalism's land, just as stipends were the price the government paid for feudal authority.[22] Other Japanese historians, though differing in emphasis, are equally clear about the importance of land-tax reform in the growth of landlordism and therefore in the shaping of Japan's society.[23]

There is obviously substance in the claim that the Meiji leaders, having taken control from a feudal class of which they were themselves only a fragment, found it desirable, even necessary, to seek the cooperation of other social groups, including landlords and merchants. It is equally obvious that by so doing they determined how Japan's ruling class would evolve in the following decades.

Nevertheless, these statements do not fully answer some of the questions with which we have been concerned; in particular, whether such social changes were part of the leadership's aims, or whether they were so inherent in the situation with which it had to deal as to be inescapable. Properly speaking, these are questions that involve a study of Meiji society, not merely Restoration politics. Nevertheless, some attempt must be made to consider them, even within the narrower compass of this book.

One might begin by observing that any government of Japan in 1870, whatever its character, would have found it necessary to tackle the problems of the village, which was its greatest source of tax and the home of the vast majority of the population it undertook to govern. These problems were of two kinds, or rather, centered on two different sources of discontent, both stemming from economic changes in the Tokugawa period.

In the first place, as we have often had occasion to note, the financial embarrassments of samurai and feudal lords had increased the fiscal pressures on the cultivator everywhere, causing great distress. Secondly, in the more advanced areas—the regions close to Edo and the Tōkaidō, the provinces around Kyōto, the coastal belt along the shores of the Inland Sea, some parts of northern Kyūshū—there had been a redistribution of wealth within the village, associated with the appearance of landlordism and commercial growth, which had distorted the incidence of tax and threatened to divide the community.

Moreover, events in the middle decades of the nineteenth century had made this situation worse: the costs of indemnities, defense preparations, and finally civil war, which increased the needs of government for revenue; and the effects of foreign trade, which created new demands for goods and hence new opportunities for those who were able to take advantage of them. As a result, the incidence of peasant revolt, reflecting resentment of hardship however caused, was only briefly reduced by the expectations that came with Restoration. Within a matter of months it had been resumed at a mounting level: 177 outbreaks in the years 1868–73, of which 66 were concerned with tax.[24] And to the familiar protests against the tax collector and the usurer was now added a traditionalist reaction against some of the reforms that Tokyo sought to carry out: railways, offending the village's gods; conscription, taking away its men; education, demanding its money.

It was against this background that the Meiji government had to set its considerations of the need for revenue. Even before the abolition of the domains there had been some consideration of land-tax reform for the territories acquired from the Tokugawa, enough to establish that there were varying attitudes toward the matter within officialdom. Dues, always inadequate to government requirements, were being made more so by inflation, since many had been commuted for cash. They also varied widely from place to place. From this situation there developed a conflict of interest between different departments of the Meiji government as the Finance Ministry, concerned to maximize revenue, insisted that the yield from dues be maintained or even increased, while district and prefectural administrators, faced with the prospect of peasant revolt, sought to reduce unrest by making local concessions on tax wherever a case could be made for a claim of exceptional hardship.

From their differing premises, both kinds of officials began to raise the question of reforms.[25] Characteristically, Matsukata Masayoshi of Satsuma, acting as governor of Hida (Ōita) in 1869–70, called for tax relief and the elimination of the injustices arising from regional variations so as to remove a major source of unrest. His arguments were reflected in a memorial from the Ministry of Civil Affairs to the Dajōkan in August 1870 and found an echo in Iwakura's memorandum on general policy in the following month.

Earlier, one of Matsukata's colleagues, Mutsu Munemitsu, governor of the Settsu (Osaka) region, had proposed a quite different approach: the standardization of tax throughout the country as a move toward administrative unity, applying to domains as well as the imperial territories; the payment of all dues in cash; and the imposition of a greater share of the tax burden on commerce. Much the same program was envisioned by Kanda Kōhei, formerly a "Western" expert in the Bakufu's service, now a Finance Ministry bureaucrat. In the early summer of 1869 and again in July 1870, he put forward plans for a land tax in cash, to be based on a valuation of holdings derived, initially, from the records of tax yields over the previous twenty or thirty years. He argued that such a tax would be easier to administer than the existing multiplicity of local customs; would provide a stable and predictable revenue for the central government; and because it depended on current land values, adjusted constantly by the free working of the market, would in the long run give greater justice to the farmer than feudal methods of survey (*kenchi*) and periodic crop assessment.

Like Matsukata's, Kanda's ideas were taken up by his superiors, in particular Ōkuma Shigenobu, who urged the cause of fiscal unity during the closing months of 1870. They became more directly influential in the following year, however, when the abolition of the domains faced the government with the task of devising a tax machinery for the country as a whole, not just the 25 per cent or so that had been administered by Tokyo previously.

The Finance Ministry was very conscious that it would now have heavy new commitments to meet, especially for domain debts and samurai stipends. Against that, the former domains were being reorganized into prefectures (*ken*) and urban areas (*fu*); and since there were only 75 of these from January 1872, compared with nearly 300 domains, many new units included several of the old ones (in fact, twenty-nine of them incorporated five or more domains). Given the existing variations in local practice with respect to feudal dues, this amalgamation involved prefectural officials in a risk of greater rural unrest, for as villagers became aware that they were being differently treated from residents of nearby areas they tended to demand "justice" from officialdom. The government's representatives found these demands difficult to ignore, lacking as yet the support of a modern army or police. At the same time, they knew that the Finance Ministry would not countenance a general tax cut to the lowest levels obtaining, since this would reduce the revenue to the point of endangering stability. Tax reform therefore acquired a greater appeal as a possible means of escaping this dilemma.

It was the Finance Ministry that took the initiative in pushing the issue. Toward the end of 1871 Matsukata, then deputy head of the tax section, prepared an important memorial on the subject.[26]

In it he spelled out unambiguously the dangers that might arise from failing to equalize the tax burden in different areas. He also noted the natural suspicion of farmers, wise in the habits of Tokugawa land surveyors, that any attempt to change or regulate customary ways was likely to be for the purpose of raising the effective level of tax, and warned that every step must be cautiously approached and clearly explained if any kind of local cooperation was to be won.

From this traditionalist beginning, he proceeded in the main body of his statement to expound an entirely nontraditional view of the relationship between taxation and economic policy that made few concessions to rural prejudice in general. Under feudal rulers, he said, the object of policy had been to achieve local self-sufficiency and provide against bad harvests, that is, to exercise control over the land and the crops grown on it in the interests of security and stability. Tax laws had been intentionally restrictive, not designed to stimulate growth. In Japan's new situation, this had to be changed so that production could be increased for the sake of the country's and the people's wealth. In particular, restrictive rules must be abolished: those that prohibited the sale and purchase of land; those that limited the cultivator's choice of crops; even those that banned the import and export of grain. In other words, land-tax reform was to be an inherent part of a new agrarian policy.

The point was expanded in another ministry memorandum in the following month, signed by Inoue Kaoru and Yoshida Kiyonari. Outdated practices of cultivation must be brought to an end, they argued, whether caused by restrictive rules or the farmer's obscurantist habits, because they were to the detriment of tax revenue and the national wealth. In addition, there must be a tax system designed to "lighten the taxes levied on the land in general, thereby encouraging an increase in production."[27] The British chargé Adams, reporting a conversation with Iwakura, recorded one interpretation of the Finance Ministry's moves, namely, that the government was preparing to lighten the burden of tax on the peasantry by taxing the merchant class.[28]

An outline of the land-tax proposals was put to the council by Ōkubo Toshimichi and Inoue Kaoru, Minister and Vice-Minister of Finance, respectively, just before the departure of the Iwakura mission.[29] Emphasizing the need to avoid inconsistencies between different localities to prevent unrest, they recommended a land tax payable in cash and representing a percentage of an agreed valuation of the land. As a preliminary, they noted, this would necessitate the issue of certificates of ownership and the formal lifting of the ban on the sale of land—which was already widely disregarded—in order that a market in it might be created, on which valuations could be based.

The general principle was quickly accepted, as were the document's specific proposals. Accordingly, the Finance Ministry was left to make more detailed studies and preparations while the Iwakura mission was away. Freedom of cropping was announced immediately. The ban on the sale of land was abolished on March 23, 1872, followed two weeks later by regulations for the issue of land certificates when a holding changed hands. During August this regulation was extended to all land, whether put up for sale or not, and the right to pay tax in cash, which had been granted to the inhabitants of the imperial territories in 1871, was extended to areas that had been part of domains. By the time the land-tax regulations themselves were published in July 1873, only a minority of farmers still paid their dues in kind.

This is not to say, however, that the progression from a decision in principle to a system fully worked out was a simple matter of bureaucratic action devoid of debate. It is true that most of the work was done in the tax section of the Finance Ministry, headed successively by Mutsu Munemitsu and Matsukata Masayoshi, both of whom were modernizers with experience as prefectural governors and capable, therefore, of balancing fiscal advantage against the risks of rural discontent. Nevertheless, their drafts of regulations met with considerable opposition. Much of it was technical; but as a survey of the discussions will show, some of the opposition had a wider significance, involving attempts to maintain the separate interests of samurai and landlords.

The earliest important drafts of actual land-tax regulations, though mostly undated, appear to belong to the autumn of 1872.[30] The first concerned land valuation, a subject that was already causing problems, not only because there was popular suspicion about the government's motives, leading men to distort or suppress their figures about yield, but also because the sale price of land inevitably included an element based on assumptions about tax liabilities. As a result, the Finance Ministry proposed the following procedure: an initial valuation by the owner; a confirmation of this figure by a village assembly, if the original amount was questioned; and then, if this still revealed disagreement, a valuation by officials, arrived at by multiplying the net annual value of the crop by ten in the case of an owner-cultivator, or an equivalent calculation based on rent in the case of a tenant. The owner would be required to accept either the final, official estimate or any offer to purchase his land at his own (presumably lower) valuation. A draft to this effect was circulated to local officials for comment. So was another, proposing a tax level of 3 per cent, that is, an equivalent of 30 per cent of the net value of the crop, which judging from the ministry records was seen as a reasonable average of what had formerly been paid in dues across the country as a whole.

Among the criticisms that were voiced in response to the circulation of these documents,[31] two are of special interest. One grew out of the apprehensions of those of the rich farmers whose wealth depended on landholdings that were undertaxed relative to yield. Their spokesmen sought to ease the transition to the new system by establishing an interim period during which no increase or decrease of tax in a given case would be greater than 40 per cent. Other critics, speaking on behalf of the former samurai, held that the existence of stipends was evidence of the feudal class's legal claim to the land, and that therefore the samurai's interests must be defended when land certificates were issued. One way of doing this would be to insist that the "public rights" in land—apparently meaning those rights of lordship formerly held by the Bakufu and domains—be sold to private persons instead of simply passing to the occupant or his landlord, the purchaser being required to pay for them in twenty equal annual installments. The funds so raised, it was claimed, could be used to finance samurai stipends (which could themselves be pledged against the purchase of land) as well as to provide for the costs of modernization (railways, schools, and so on). Moreover, once land had passed into private ownership in this way, it could be taxed at 4 per cent of its value, as established by the price that had been paid.

In the hope of resolving the underlying conflicts revealed in such arguments, the whole question, together with that of stipends, was put to a conference of local officials, summoned to meet in Tokyo in April 1873. Inoue Kaoru presided over the early meetings, Ōkuma Shigenobu over the later ones, which were attended by about ten members of the Finance Ministry, including Mutsu, and 65 men from the prefectures and urban areas. The stipends issue proved insoluble, since the local officials continued to urge the dangers of samurai unrest and the ministry representatives to insist on the government's financial needs. A similar division emerged on the subject of land-tax proposals, which were put to the conference on April 13 and severely criticized. But in this case agreement in principle was eventually reached. This done, a committee was formed to settle final details in consultation with the Finance Ministry. It set to work on April 15 and put its recommendations to the full conference within a month, on May 10. After minor amendment, they were accepted two days later.

During these weeks, several drafts were prepared. The first, prepared in the ministry though produced in consultation with the committee and others, proposed a tax rate of 3 per cent, but at the same time expressed the hope that the taxation of commerce would soon make possible a lower rate. Discussion of this draft brought a number of modifications. One was the watering down of the reference to a possible land-tax reduction, apparently at the instigation of Matsukata, who believed it to be dangerous for a government to make such promises when it was already heavily in debt. A second was the introduction (at the request of prefectural officials) of a supplementary tax for local use, established at one-third of the national rate, bringing the total rate to 4 per cent. A third was in the matter of official calculations of land values in cases of local disagreement, a point on which much of the subsequent argument turned.[32]

The ministry, seeking to maximize revenue, was able to get the committee's acceptance of a method of calculation that in effect increased the tax on owner-cultivator land (through three successive drafts) from 31.4 per cent to 34 per cent of the assessed value of the crop. This was achieved by adjusting such items as allowable expenses while keeping the tax rate constant at the 3 per cent figure that had already been agreed on. For tenants the calculation was more complex, since it involved assumptions about levels of rent; but by arguing the importance of strict comparability in the treatment of different kinds of farmer, the ministry was again able to increase its share, this time from 26.3 per cent in the first draft to 34 per cent in the third. Since the landlord's share remained almost constant (moving only from 33.7 per cent to 34 per cent), the effect was to reduce the share of the crop remaining in the tenants' hands from 40 per cent to 32 per cent in the final version.

Local officials, in fact, were more successful in defending the landlord than the tenant from the central government's demands. No doubt they fought harder on the landlords' behalf, perhaps from a feeling of social affinity, perhaps from a belief that unrest among the village upper class, like unrest among samurai, was more to be feared than the ordinary forms of peasant revolt. Certainly landlords, in addition to having gained an advantage in the methods of calculation used, proved better able in the event to dispute land valuations with officials. Thus the effect of these supplementary regulations was to create a situation that encouraged landlordism, which began to spread into areas where it had not previously been strong.

Issued on July 28, 1873, the tax-reform edict emphasized the Emperor's desire "that the tax be levied impartially in order that the burden may be shared equally among the people."[33] Its actual provisions, however, revealed a far greater devotion to the government's own fiscal interests than to any principle of tax equity. A standard tax, paid regularly in cash and bringing in a known amount of revenue broadly equivalent to what had been received before—this is what the Finance Ministry had always sought. It was approximately what it got.[34] It was, moreover, as much as agriculture and the agriculturalist could be expected to bear, especially since the new laws drove more farmers than ever into selling crops for cash. This was an undertaking for which many of them showed little skill, making one by-product of the reform an increase in tenancy and loss of land, due to financial failures. Another was that the vexing question of ownership was settled—because of the way in which land certificates were issued—not only in favor of commoners rather than samurai, but also in favor of landlords rather than cultivators as such. In these respects, the law was truly a landlord's bill of rights.

Much of this was the product, not of the law as written, but of the manner in which it was implemented during the next few years: estimating values and making surveys took until 1876 for arable land and until 1881 for forest and wasteland. Throughout this period the government, bent on maintaining revenues, exerted considerable pressure on the villages to get them to accept its estimates—for example, by setting target totals for different prefectures—and in the process aroused a good deal of resentment. So much, in fact, that it was forced to reduce the tax rate to 2.5 per cent in January 1877.[35]

In the long term, the decisions that were taken fixed the trend toward tenancy in Japanese rural society by making high-rent landlordism profitable while inhibiting improvement or rationalization of holdings.[36] They also confirmed the new social relationships that late-Tokugawa economic change had brought to the villages, since they gave the wealthier members of the community an opportunity to manipulate land valuations, much as they had previously been able to manipulate feudal tax assessments by Bakufu and domain. William Chambliss, for instance, has shown that in Chiaraijima the nominal tax burden was increased more sharply for small landholders than for large; that the larger landowners also benefited substantially by the ending of feudal demands for forced loans (*goyōkin*); and that they retained a considerable measure of control in village affairs, notwithstanding the creation of a centralized bureaucratic machine.[37] It should be said, however, that the further separating out of rural rich and poor was not the only consequence of the government's tax policies. By favoring the landlord in this way they also contributed to the accumulation of capital in the hands of those who might use it to modernizing ends and in that sense aided the development of a modern economy.*

These comments on what was to happen to rural society in the Meiji period, though relevant, have taken us away from our original subject, which is the nature of the government's policy decisions in the years 1871–73. Here I am inclined to accept Seki's argument—that the compelling *motive* of policy, no matter what its results, was the need for revenue, above all, money to pay for modernization and stipends.[38] Certainly it is difficult to see the class interests of either samurai or landlord as a direct and decisive influence at this stage. The interests of the samurai were clearly made subordinate to the requirements of national strength, just as they were in the context of conscription and stipends; the samurai's claim to the land, though mooted, was never seriously entertained. As for the interests of the landlord—or better, the rich farmer (*gōnō*)—the evidence of the 1873 discussions suggests that by and large their actions were defensive, which is to say that the village well-to-do were more concerned with defending themselves against the government's demands for revenue than with seeking to impose a tax pattern of their own; and that insofar as they subsequently gained by land-tax reform, it was because they were able to exploit an opportunity which they had not consciously made.

OPPOSITION

One test of the social character of the Restoration (though not necessarily of the purpose of its leaders) is to examine the opposition it provoked, which might be said to hold a mirror to its policies. For some of the decisions we have discussed in these last two chapters were inevitably divisive, despite the constant reiteration of the theme that unity is strength. It was, after all, a particular kind of unity that most men had in mind. Kido, reflecting at the

* James Nakamura, *Agricultural Production*, pp. 159–69. Nakamura associates this argument with another: that the overall effect of land-tax reform (and inflation) by the end of the Meiji period had been greatly to reduce the demands of the state on the agricultural community, leaving a larger proportion of what was produced in private hands, counting both landlords and cultivators.

end of 1873 on the lessons he had learned in Europe, put it in the context of destroying feudalism:

A single rod, even though a stout one, may be broken by a young child, but if ten rods, though weak ones, are made into a bundle, they cannot be broken by a full grown man. . . . In the same manner, if a country is divided among a multitude of petty rulers, each one having full authority in his own district, . . . each prince will seek his own advantage and devise schemes for his own gain. Under such a system the national strength is dissipated. . . . How could they ever withstand a powerful enemy whose forces were harmoniously united?[39]

Itagaki, writing in the following year to urge the creation of representative institutions in Japan, saw it rather differently: "How is the government to be made strong? It is by the people of the empire becoming of one mind. . . . The establishment of a council-chamber chosen by the people will create community of feeling between the government and people, and they will mutually unite into one body. Then and only then will the country become strong."[40]

Even Ōkubo, who opposed Itagaki on the particular point of the early granting of a constitution, nevertheless recognized that political forms were crucial to national unity and strength. The example of England, he said, which with a population and area no greater than Japan's had "spread its power overseas and brought many lands under its control," demonstrated "that a nation can rise or decline according to the ability of the people who support it and the system of government which will nourish such ability." In Japan, "when the people and the government are united," modernization would not be without result.[41]

These are the words of a man to whom nationalist objectives were more important than social change, except insofar as social change was a means to greater efficiency or to the elimination of popular grievances. Much the same was true of his colleagues. Even Kido, in the document quoted above, said of their decisions: "The truth was there was no change made which had not become unavoidable, chiefly owing to the internal condition of the country, but also, though in a less degree, to our relations with foreign countries."[42] This raises, of course, the question of what was to be regarded as "unavoidable," an issue on which many of the debates within the leadership turned; but it does not suggest that reform, in the sense of "improving" society, was the primary object of government policy. In what sense, then, was policy opposed?

It is easiest to identify the nature of opposition when it emanated from samurai, most of whom lost their privileges, including stipends, and found themselves governed by men who often flouted their most cherished beliefs. Not surprisingly, in view of their military tradition, many protested under arms. What is more, in doing so they were led on a number of occasions by disgruntled oligarchs, men who had fallen out with their fellows in the government about many of the same matters. Thus early in 1874 Etō Shimpei raised the flag of revolt in Hizen, partly because of the decision that had been taken about Korea, partly in belated protest at the abolition of domains. Over 3,000 men took part in the affair, including local officials, and Ōkubo himself took charge of the operations by which the rising was crushed.[43]

In 1876 the announcement that the commutation of stipends was to be made compulsory brought new and more widespread trouble. In October, samurai attacked government offices in Kumamoto, and killed the prefectural governor. A few days later there were disturbances in nearby Akizuki. In November Maebara Issei led a rebellion in Chōshū. Finally, in January 1877 the Satsuma samurai, resentful of Tokyo policy and of Ōkubo, the Satsuma "renegade" who made it, rebelled, placing themselves under the leadership of Saigō Takamori.[44] They were not finally suppressed until September, when the remnants of Saigō's army, which had at one time been 40,000 strong, were defeated by a government force that was half as big again. Saigō committed suicide on the field of battle. Eight months later, on May 14, 1878, some of his sympathizers (from the former domain of Kaga) avenged him by killing Ōkubo in Tokyo.

The fact that most samurai unrest occurred in "loyalist" domains—Satsuma, Chōshū, and Hizen—tells us something about the character of the Meiji Restoration movement. Of the rank-and-file samurai who had contributed to the downfall of the Tokugawa, the great majority had not done so with the idea of introducing anything like the kind of program their leaders had adopted by the end of 1873. Equally, however, they lacked the organization to make their wishes felt, just as the "men of spirit" had in the 1860's, with the result that violence (if not acquiescence) was their only recourse. Because it failed, they ceased from this time to be a decisive factor in Japanese politics. In almost all fields, it is true, their education, family links, and inherited prestige continued to give them an influence out of proportion to their numbers. Moreover, their attitudes and ideas had a pervasive effect on social behavior, setting norms to which others aspired. In some instances they bequeathed codes of conduct to specific successors, many of whom were ex-samurai themselves, notably army officers and the police. In other instances they contributed to the growth of special pressures within society, outstandingly in the demand for a "strong" foreign policy, which was descended from "expulsion." Nevertheless, one cannot say that in the old sense the samurai hereafter "ruled" Japan. In protesting against modernization, they had correctly identified a threat to themselves and their position.

Unhappily, if one can identify samurai protest with some of the men who left the Meiji government, one cannot equally tidily associate the "new" forces in Japanese society with those who stayed. A consequence of the Korean dispute, as we have seen, was that some members of the oligarchy left it to organize a constitutional movement through which they might weaken the hold of Ōkubo and his allies on the reins of power. Led at first by Itagaki, Gotō, and other Tosa samurai, and later by Ōkuma as well, it eventually came to represent the interests of those "men of substance," chiefly landlords and businessmen, who though no longer as completely excluded from affairs as they had been under the Tokugawa, did not feel that they were properly represented in the emerging bureaucratic state. To this extent, the political parties of the middle Meiji years were more directly a manifestation of long-term social change than was the turbulence of Restoration.

All the same, we need to be clear about the nature of their opposition to the Meiji government. Because the principle of promoting "men of talent" had given them a limited access to power—the second generation of leadership had a less exclusively samurai background than the first—and because the pursuit of "wealth and strength" gave greater opportunities to those who had economic expertise, whether in agriculture or in industry and commerce, the landlords and businessmen were for the most part able and willing to pursue their ambitions *within* the system, not by trying to demolish it. One might even say that the symbiotic relationship they had enjoyed with feudal authority had in essence been transferred to Meiji's imperial government, with the difference that their interests were better served by the new regime's policies, so that they were no longer even potentially subversive. The contrast with the samurai is striking.

Finally, what of the peasants? Whereas the Restoration gave landlords unprecedented opportunities by making them members of the ruling class—if widely defined—the lowest stratum of village society profited little, if at all, and certainly not politically. Peasants, like samurai, protested violently at many of the reforms (as well as at the continuation of older grievances). Like the samurai's, their protests were ruthlessly suppressed. Indeed, the greater efficiency of a modern army and police force, aided by telegraphs and railways, plus the fact that men in the upper levels of the village structure had readier access than in the past to the support of those in power, eventually deprived the peasantry even of rebellion as a form of restraint on what a government could do. After the revolts of the 1880's were put down, the peasant became an object of policy, not a participant in its making, lacking even the vote; and it was not until the twentieth century, with the emergence of an industrial society in Japan, that this situation changed.

CHAPTER XVI

Conclusions

THE HISTORY OF the Meiji Restoration, as we said at the beginning of this book, is relevant to a number of themes that are important not only for Japan. In part it was a response to the nineteenth-century expansion of the West in Asia. Hence studying it raises questions about the nature of imperialism and nationalism and of their relationship to change in the modern world. Equally, the Restoration was at least in some respects a revolution. One must therefore ask, what kind of revolution was it? How does it compare with other great political upheavals in other parts of the world at other times? And are the features that mark it off from them idiosyncratically Japanese, or do they arise from the fact and nature of the West's involvement? Finally, since the Restoration is the historical starting point for the modernization of Japan, a process that is highly significant for theories of economic growth, it poses yet another question, to wit: How far is a radical restructuring of society a necessary condition—and not merely a consequence—of the transformation of a pre-modern into a modern economy.

Clearly, though the example of Japan is an element in the discussion of all these matters, it is not necessarily a decisive one. Therefore a book like this, which approaches the Restoration from inside, as it were, that is, as a part of Japanese history, ought not to offer itself as providing answers that are universally valid. What it *can* do, what these closing remarks are intended to do, is to present its conclusions in such a way that others might be able to use them to these ends. As a preliminary to this, it might be helpful to recapitulate the story in a rather more generalized form than was possible when setting out the detailed narrative.

* * *

Under the Tokugawa, Japanese society was gradually modified by economic change in such a way as to bring about by the nineteenth century a disjunction between contemporary reality and the inherited ideal. This was manifested in a number of phenomena for which the traditional order had no place: samurai whose debts turned them into ambitious office-holders or impoverished umbrella-makers; farmers abandoning subsistence agriculture to become commercial producers and rural entrepreneurs or laborers and quasi-tenants; and city merchants enjoying feudal patronage in a kind of symbiosis with authority or escaping into an urban subculture of their own.

Because these things happened at different speeds in different areas, they disturbed the balance of power between the Bakufu and the domains, which had depended originally on a carefully calculated distribution of land. Because they happened at all, they produced social upheaval: a blurring of status distinctions, stimulating samurai unrest; and economic disruption, provoking peasant revolt. These were reflected in turn in a "what-is-wrong-with-the-world" literature and attempts at "reform," the latter seeking either to reconstitute an ideal past (a restoration of feudal authority and its agrarian base) or to exploit commercial growth for the benefit of the ruling class (if at some cost to its ethos). One result was to give more samurai a degree of participation in active politics than hitherto. Another was to make the concept of "reform" familiar and to prompt a feeling that society was in danger of destruction from within.

Yet the country's social and political institutions proved to be remarkably durable: eroded but far from demolished, they did not seem in 1850 to be on the point of being swept away. Not least, this was because the system of institutional checks and balances coupled with deliberate regional fragmentation that had been devised to restrain the anticipated disaffection of samurai and feudal lords proved capable also of imposing controls on the new "men of substance" who might have challenged the established order from outside the samurai class. Accordingly, most of these men sought their opportunities of advancement through conformity, not revolution, acquiring status by purchase or marriage, but remaining politically passive.

It was into this situation that there was injected the West's demand for trade relations in the years 1853–58, leading to "unequal" treaties. The manner in which the treaties were obtained, that is, by gunboat diplomacy, was as important as their content, for it helped to produce in Japan an upsurge of emotion greater than any that had been aroused by domestic issues. Its importance was not merely that the blow to Japanese pride led to a call for "action" (not necessarily of any specific kind); it was also that this was a "national" dishonor in the sense that it could be felt in all areas and at all levels in Japanese society. It thereby helped to break down the regional and social fragmentation that had been one of the foundations of Tokugawa power.

Moreover, the humiliation at the hands of the West precipitated struggle and controversy. The struggle arose when men questioned the efficiency of the country's leaders, especially their ability to defend Japan; and it brought to the surface many of the latent divisions in the national polity by asking, if only implicitly, who their replacements should be in case they failed. The controversy concerned both short-term diplomatic issues and long-term cultural ones, but it had a single, central thread: the extent to which Japan must abandon custom in order to save herself, first in the context of technology, or particular institutional devices to serve particular ends, and then, more generally, in the context of radical changes in society, such as industrialization had induced in the countries of the West.

It was the Tokugawa Bakufu that had first to grapple with these problems, since it was the self-styled treaty-making and executive authority with which the foreigners had to deal. Partly from conviction, resting on self-interest, partly from a recognition of superior force, it moved toward compromise. By so doing, however, it made itself a target for both anti-foreign and reformist feeling. The first to attack it was a group of feudal lords, led by those of Mito,

Satsuma, and Echizen, who subscribed to a reform program based on two propositions: that the country must rally its resources for defense against the West, and that in order to make this possible the great lords must be relieved of some of their obligations to the Shogun. In other words, they related national survival to political rivalries in the service of baronial power. The disputes in which they engaged about the treaties and the Tokugawa succession brought the Imperial Court and a number of their own samurai followers into the arena of politics. What is more important in the longer term, their activities paved the way for a new opposition movement made up of lower-ranking samurai and some whose claim to samurai status was no more than marginal. Insisting that the lords were no more capable than the Shogun of saving Japan, these men turned instead to the Emperor as a focus of loyalty and to "men of spirit" as the instruments to carry his wishes out.

The actions of Ii Naosuke in 1858, when he tried to enforce both the treaties and the Bakufu's authority against both opposition groups, precipitated a triangular struggle that lasted for a decade. In the course of it, both the Bakufu and the lords were handicapped by their appreciation of the risks of foreign war. The "men of spirit," by an unvarying commitment to the slogan "honor the Emperor, expel the barbarian"—which was important for its emotional appeal rather than as a policy—and by a fanaticism that led them to disregard all dangers to life, were able for a time to seize the initiative. In particular, they were able to precipitate just such a dispute with the powers as both the Bakufu and the lords had sought to prevent, bringing about the bombardments of Kagoshima and Shimonoseki in 1863 and 1864. Yet they had neither the organization that would have enabled them to exploit the turmoil they created nor a program that would have given them effective "revolutionary" support among the masses. In fact, they were rebels to the end, hoping to bring about by violence the conditions in which others would shape things to their liking, not planners of something radically new. For this reason, when their extremism united the Bakufu and the lords against them, they were quickly suppressed.

Conceivably, at this point there could have been a minimal redistribution of power within the upper levels of the feudal class—

a sort of Japanese Magna Carta—reinforced by a compromise with the foreigner and a limited introduction of Western technology in its military application, such as was then taking place in China. China, after all, faced the same Western threat as Japan did, in a domestic situation that was certainly no less explosive than Japan's. Her officials produced a range of proposed solutions to the crisis that were not unlike those put forward by Japanese samurai, in both variety and tone.[1] From these various proposals they evolved a policy of "self-strengthening," which though designed eventually to provide defense against the West, just as the Japanese proposals were, gave initial emphasis to the task of restoring order at home, that is, reasserting the authority of the Confucian state. Tseng Kuo-fan expounded the priorities as follows in a diary entry dated June 1862: "If we wish to find a method of self-strengthening, we should begin by considering the reform of government service and the securing of men of ability as urgent tasks."[2] Most of Japan's reforming lords would have accepted some such statement (if expressed in feudal terms). Similarly, it is possible to ascribe to the reforming lords much the same objectives as Mary Wright ascribes to China's T'ung-chih leaders: that they sought to modify the state so as to make it function efficiently in a new kind of world "without revolutionary changes in traditional . . . values or in the institutions that embodied them."[3]

The purpose of this digression has not been to suggest that there was an exact equivalence in these matters between China and Japan —there are important differences that I have not touched on here— but rather to emphasize the significance of Japan's departure from this apparently "Chinese" pattern after 1864. The Bakufu, it is true, persisted with its own version of self-strengthening during its remaining years: a conciliatory policy toward the treaty powers coupled with Western-style reforms that were intended to restore its authority over domestic rivals. For the rest, however, the "men of spirit"—China had no obvious counterpart—had succeeded in changing the character of Japanese politics in significant ways.

Despite defeat, the "men of spirit" revealed the existence of powerful sentiments that could not subsequently be ignored in making policy. Nor could their own turbulence be forgotten, especially against a known background of peasant revolt. In consequence, they contributed to two changes of focus in the opposition movement: from "honor the Emperor" to "destroy the Bakufu" (tōbaku), an object to which both feudal lords and dissident samurai could subscribe; and from "expel the barbarian" to "enrich the country, strengthen the army" (fukoku-kyōhei), a formulation in which anti-foreign prejudice and modernizing came together. More, the events of 1863–64—an unmistakable demonstration of Western military strength, plus a reassertion of feudal discipline by the most powerful lords—in some degree united the Tokugawa's enemies, since the daimyo were now able, because of the restatement of their aims, to recruit to their cause the surviving "men of spirit."

This, at least, was how it seemed on the surface. In practice, however, the daimyo were only able to do so by sharing, or even losing, the leadership of their domains. In both Chōshū and Satsuma, which had the key role in these years, there came to power during 1864 and 1865 groups of middle samurai bureaucrats capable of mediating between an upper samurai "establishment" and lower samurai activists while themselves substantially controlling (and modifying) policy. Chōshū, which was a refuge for "men of spirit" and a natural center for tōbaku because of its disputes with Edo, moved as a result toward acceptance of the doctrine of "wealth and strength." In Satsuma, where that doctrine seemed a natural extension of the modernizing activities of Shimazu Nariakira, the former lord, it was the relationship with the Bakufu that changed; a gradual recognition that Edo could not be influenced or browbeaten into accepting "satisfactory" policies, even with the help of the Imperial Court, increasingly brought cooperation with Chōshū. The alliance of the two domains early in 1866 completed this realignment, symbolizing a marriage of tōbaku with fukoku-kyōhei, an association of anti-Bakufu politics with the pursuit of national strength.

Since the Tokugawa (in the person of Hitotsubashi Keiki) also espoused the last of these aims, the contest centered thereafter on a debate about who could best carry it out. The Bakufu accused its opponents of dividing the country in the face of foreign threat. The Satsuma and Chōshū leaders argued that Bakufu self-interest was distorting fukoku-kyōhei, making it more a weapon against the lords than against the foreigner. This proved the more convincing argument of the two; and by making it possible for the Satsuma and Chōshū men to exploit sentiments of feudal separatism in other domains, as well as their own, it brought into existence a wider anti-Bakufu alliance, through which they succeeded in forcing the Shogun to resign. Six weeks later (January 3, 1868), despite efforts at mediation by Tosa, they achieved the destruction of the Bakufu itself. This was ōsei-fukko, "the restoration of imperial rule," confirmed by victory in a short-lived civil war.

One can easily exaggerate the importance of these events. It is true that they closed the door on one aspect of Japan's past, that is, they abolished the central institutions through which the Tokugawa had exercised and perpetuated their authority. It is also true that they were carried through by men who acknowledged the urgency of increasing the country's wealth and strength in nontraditional ways. For the most part, however, they still left the shape of the future obscure, dependent above all on the extent to which different groups within the victorious alliance would be able to agree upon, then impose on others, definitions of the slogans to which they had subscribed. This was to involve thinking out an alternative to the Bakufu as a machinery for governing the Japanese state; giving content to ideas about "reform," primarily in the military and economic context; and adjusting the social structure in ways that would contribute to stability. In the event, all this imposed a further imperative: that Japan's leaders decide how far to follow Western models, not merely in matters of technique, but also in those fundamentals that were thought to determine the nature of "civilization" and explain the West's preponderance of power.

It was in this constructive stage, rather than in the destructive one preceding it, that the importance of the socioeconomic changes of the previous hundred years or so became fully apparent. A conviction that good government needed "men of talent," who were rarely to be found among the high-born, together with an awareness that over much of the country a class of rich farmers, landlords, and village officials had successfully interposed itself between the samurai and the land, turned the new rulers away from feudalism as well as from the Bakufu. One consequence was the abolition of the domains, signifying the application of a Western rationale to a Japanese reality for the purpose of creating a centralized, bureaucratic state. Another was conscription, in which Tokugawa condemnations of samurai "decadence" came together with a European-style concept of military strength to produce a recognition that an army's effectiveness rested on organization as much as on weapons. Both changes were an incentive to the dismantling of samurai privilege, to the substitution of achievement for inherited rank. As a corollary, the government's needs also forced an acceptance of village society as it was, not as Confucian officials might have liked it to be, thereby putting an end to protection of the middle farmer–cultivator and confirming the position already won by a rural elite.

It was precisely because the changes implicit in the "wealth and strength" policy proved so much more radical in practice than men had expected them to be that they provoked controversy and crisis. Among both lords and samurai, those who supported the regime as a means of defending Japan against the foreigner were offended by what seemed an international subservience worthy of Edo and an aping of foreign ways. Others, ready enough to welcome Western technology, denied the need for major social change or resented an attack on their own vested interests. In consequence, the later months of 1873 saw a challenge to the government's policies, by then well in train, followed by a variety of protests from those who had failed to overturn them. The leadership's success in resisting this challenge set the pattern of Japan's history for the next few generations.

* * *

History offers many different examples of the kind of motivating force that is capable of overcoming inertia and the bonds of tradition: imperial ambition, religious faith, the pursuit of social justice, the aspirations of a newly emergent class. For Japan in the nineteenth century, nationalism had this function. Again and again in the documents of the years we have been considering there are phrases that put policy of every kind—economic and political, as well as diplomatic—into the context of the "national" interest, justifying proposals on the grounds that they would "restore our national strength" or "make the imperial dignity resound beyond the seas." What is more, most of the major political crises centered on the question of Japan's relations with the outside world: that of 1858, when the signing of the treaties became linked with the question of the Tokugawa succession; that of 1863–64, when the fate of the "men of spirit" was decided against a background of foreign bombardment; that of 1873, when the debate about Korea brought into the open a struggle about priorities at home. Throughout, Japanese opinion was moving from a consciousness of foreign threat to an awareness of national identity, expressed in demands for unity and independence.

The contrast with China underlines the extraordinary speed and thoroughness of Japan's response. Despite widespread anti-foreign feeling among gentry and officials, Chinese continued to behave, at least until the end of the nineteenth century, as a people defending a civilization that was threatened, not a nation defending a country that was under attack.[4] Long before then, the Japanese, subscribing to a more articulate and sophisticated version of the Restoration's search for "wealth and strength," had found in nationalism a means of reconciling the conflict between cultural tradition and imperative circumstance.

The "liberal" constitutional movement was heavily influenced by that new-found nationalism. "The one object of my life is to extend Japan's national power," Fukuzawa Yukichi wrote in 1882. "Compared with considerations of the country's strength, the matter of internal government and into whose hands it falls is of no importance at all. Even if the government be autocratic in name and form, I shall be satisfied with it if it is strong enough to strengthen the country."[5] This is Fukuzawa the nationalist overcoming Fukuzawa the liberal, if only temporarily.

Taking a wider framework, the newspaper *Nihon* celebrated the announcement of the Meiji Constitution in 1889 by urging that a limit be set to the adoption of foreign ways. It had no desire "to revive a narrow xenophobia," *Nihon* declared, for "we recognise the excellence of Western civilisation. We value the Western theories of rights, liberty and equality. . . . Above all, we esteem Western science, economics and industry." Nevertheless, it continued, these things "ought not to be adopted simply because they are Western; they ought to be adopted only if they can contribute to Japan's welfare."[6] In Tokyo in 1889 this was a conservative warning not to go too fast or too far. In contemporary Peking it would have been reformist.

One is bound to ask, why did Japan evolve in a generation a nationalism that in China came much more slowly and with much less effect, given that both countries had long traditions of political and cultural unity? Difference of size was a factor, of course. In Japan, which was smaller and had a very long coastline, the presence of the foreigners and their ships was evident to a higher percentage of the population, making the danger from them easier to believe and act on. China was not only larger, but more varied—in spoken language, social patterns, types of crop—so that there were great practical obstacles to imposing administrative and economic unity in the nationalist sense, just as there were in India and the Ottoman Empire, for example. China did not lend herself very readily to being made into a "country." Japan did.

In addition to all this, however, there are historical differences between the two that have a particular relevance to the study of the Meiji Restoration. One is Japan's relative freedom of cultural choice: she was less bound than China to a single view of her society and her place in the world. Japan had already imported elements of Chinese civilization, which coexisted with others that were her own; thus to adopt a part of Europe's civilization was not to damage an entity that was whole and unique, but to add a third possibility to an existing two, one of which was in any case "foreign." For instance, medicine was a Chinese science in pre-modern Japan, using many Chinese drugs, hence accepting a Western alternative was not so very shocking. Warfare, the samurai's trade, was studied in a Chinese classic text (albeit embodied in a thoroughly Japanese mystique) and was conducted with the help of a seventeenth-century "Dutch" technology. There was nothing in this to inhibit following alien models. As Rutherford Alcock noted of the Japanese when he first became acquainted with them, "they have little of the stupid conceit of the Chinese, which leads them to ignore or deny the superiority of foreign things."[7]

It was the same with political institutions. No educated Japanese of the Tokugawa period could fail to be aware that the political structure of his country differed from that of China, which the philosophers he read upheld as an ideal. His country had a Shogun as well as an Emperor; it was administered through a feudal system, not a bureaucratic one. This helped to heighten his sense of Japaneseness, which was an element in nationalism, but it also made him aware that substantial variations could exist within the limits of what was known and acceptable.

In other words, in abolishing the Bakufu, reasserting the Emperor's authority, and instituting a centralized bureaucratic state, the Japanese could see themselves as making a fresh set of choices among the variables that their history already contained, however much they reinterpreted them. Hence renovation (ishin) could be coupled with restoration (fukko) in a manner that caused the least offense. This was especially so because of the nature and ethos of the ruling class. In China, civil officials held office by virtue of being Confucian, that is, as exemplars of a structure of belief on which their whole society was founded. To tamper with part of that structure was to undermine the whole, weakening their power. This was not so in Japan. The samurai, it is true, had accepted the Confucian ethic and some of the bureaucratic habits that went with it. He did not depend on these, however, to validate his rule. As a feudal lord or retainer, his position rested on birth, on inheritable status received as a reward for past military prowess. His code, Bushidō, though it coexisted with Confucianism, emphasized different virtues, the specifically military ones. Accordingly, he did not feel a need to accept or reject Confucianism as a whole. He could employ it—as Meiji society did—in the context of personal and family behavior while turning to other concepts for his political and economic life: nationalist ones, which could be given a Shintō coloring; or Western ones, explaining the new phenomena of industry and commerce. And the fact that the new amalgam was not a conspicuously logical one worried him less because of the equal irrationality of the old.

Finally, one must note the significance of Japan's having entered this phase of her history, unlike China, under a *military* ruling class. This relates to nationalism to the extent that soldiers were more inclined to think of defending a territory than defending a system of ideas, more of defending country than culture. It also relates to modernization, since it contributed to the identification of agreed priorities, where individuals had a multiplicity of views. Indeed, it may well be that a military habit of mind, variously applied, was the samurai's most important contribution to Meiji society—and hence to the making of the modern Japanese state.

What has been said above amounts to an assertion that nationalism had a double function in Japan in the twenty years after 1853: first, that it provided a motive compelling men to act; second, that it shaped their aims and priorities. Unhappily, this pleasingly simple explanation of what took place is incomplete. Side by side with the story of nationalism and the foreign threat, there is another, that of social change; and in turning to it, we move from a discussion of men's purposes to a discussion of the circumstance in which they found themselves. It was from the interaction of the two that history was made.

One aspect of this "circumstance" was the stress that economic growth had imposed on the Tokugawa class structure. At the lowest levels, peasant revolt had become a regular part of the Japanese scene by 1850, a response both to the tax demands of feudal rulers and to the gradual reshaping of village life. Nevertheless, its political role was indirect, its influence on the country's leaders much less marked than the rebellions in China had on the leaders there. The existence of peasant revolt, the possibility that it might increase, these had a ghostly presence in Japan in many situations. Peasant uprisings threatened the finances of the feudal lords and implied in Confucian terms a criticism of their administration. They also aroused fears that at a crucial moment the country might be critically weakened, so that they were an element in the formula "troubles at home, dangers from abroad." All the same, they do not seem to have become a *primary* determinant of the actions of the ruling class. And rightly so, for the peasants found neither the doctrines nor the leaders to make themselves into an effective political movement, with the result that they remained a problem to be solved, not a force to be reckoned with.

Those who might have led them—the emerging rural elite of landlords, local moneylenders and entrepreneurs, village officials, and lesser samurai—in the event pursued quite contrary ambitions. Under the Tokugawa, they had a love-hate relationship with the samurai proper, which led them on the one hand to emulate samurai education and style of life, seeking rank and status by a variety of devices, and on the other to provide a high proportion of the terrorists and conspirators of the 1860's. A similar ambiguity persisted after the Restoration, when they helped to transmit a samurai code to the Meiji ruling class even as they were actively engaged in dismantling samurai privilege. What is more, whereas they had sometimes been prepared, if unsuccessfully, to call for peasant support against a regime that denied their aspirations (as in the cases of the Yamato and Tajima revolts and the Mito civil war), the fact that they were always the residual targets of peasant attack as the nearest testimony to exploitation, plus the new opportunities that were opened to them through the Meiji doctrine of promoting "men of talent," inclined them in the last analysis to seek control of the village in the name of authority rather than put themselves at the head of a demand for peasant "rights."

Indeed, if one can define a ruling class in its widest sense as including all those who contribute substantially to governing the polity, then one result of the events of the years 1853 to 1873 was to widen the boundaries of Japan's ruling class so as to place these men within it rather than just outside it. There was, it would seem, a logical progression. Initially, upper samurai incompetence opened a route to power for middle samurai (like Ōkubo and Kido). This in turn paved the way for the emergence of able lower samurai, usually a little later in time (Itō, Yamagata, Matsukata). Finally, though slowly, mere commoners acquired a measure of influence, collectively, at first, through the bureaucracy or party politics, but in the end as individuals. However true it may be that these commoners were "men of substance"—landlords' sons—this plainly marks a significant shift in the locus of power.

There remain for consideration the samurai themselves. By the middle of the nineteenth century their position was already in some respects an anomaly, since they were neither a *landed* gentry—though the daimyo might be described perhaps as a landed aristocracy—nor a *salaried* bureaucracy. Moreover, one cannot simply treat them as a privileged group, concerned only to retain its own advantages. They did not respond in a uniform manner to either of the great issues of the age, those of financial and foreign crisis; and there is little sign in the disputes we have examined that they felt a community of class interest strong enough to override their disagreements with each other. Discontent certainly provoked a minority of them into taking more part in politics, both nationally and locally, than before; and it made them far and away the most conspicuous feature of contemporary turbulence, an influence on policy incontestably more important than peasants or rural elite. Yet what they did can hardly be called "a samurai movement," if only because it took such a diversity of forms. Men who had the minimum status to participate legally in the domain bureaucracy engaged in a quite different kind of politics from those who had not, the first becoming factions within officialdom, the others acting outside it at the risk of their lives.

Similarly, because of the strict vertical divisions in political society, fostered by the Bakufu to minimize any prospect of a daimyo challenge to its power, there was no necessary equivalence of pattern from domain to domain. In Satsuma, the presence of an able and reforming lord gave middle samurai an indirect, but effective, voice in the decision-making process without breaking down the status system as applied to senior posts. As a result, they were able to push through policies that prevented any large-scale defection of the "men of spirit." In Tosa, another reforming lord helped the middle samurai to gain high office as well as influence; but the course they then pursued divided them from a loyalist movement led by rural samurai and village headmen, many of whom fled to take part in terrorism. In Chōshū, the middle samurai loyalists, in this case supported by men who were barely samurai, or not even that, made their bid for power against the resistance of upper samurai and conservatives, first through the bureaucracy, then by seizing control of their lord. Nor does this exhaust the list of variants. In many domains, reformers and loyalists, despite encouragement from their fellows elsewhere, were able to make little or no progress until after 1868.

The picture, in fact, is not one of samurai asserting themselves against the rest of society, but of various samurai groups acting in different relationships to feudal authority and nonfeudal pressures. This is confirmed by the result: the promotion of "men of talent" became in the end an instrument for creating a genuine salaried bureaucracy, not for the bureaucratization of the samurai class. Granted that samurai, because of educational opportunity or family connection, frequently retained a greater access to positions of advantage than their ability strictly warranted, making ex-samurai or those of samurai descent an important element in Japanese elites; and granted also that certain samurai, the ablest of them, were to dominate politics and policy-making for another generation; yet the decisions of the years 1868–73 deprived samurai as a group of their inherited monopoly of office, both civil and military, and soon after of the stipends that went with it.

At this point in the discussion, having suggested that the phenomena we have been considering cannot easily, or exclusively, be explained in terms of social class, let us look at two characteristics of the politics of nationalism that we considered earlier. First, it is clear that political affairs engaged the attention of only a few. Peasants had no real part in them: their political activities, such as they were, were concerned with the problems of rural society, not the country's fate. What is more, among the several hundred thousand families that made up the samurai and village elites, the great majority did not *actively* behave as loyalists, patriots, or even traditionalists.* Nationalism was not at this stage a mass movement. Second

* Tōyama, *Meiji ishin*, pp. 37–39, notes that of a total of 1,070 "men of spirit" and others who were later rewarded for their loyalist activities, about two-thirds were samurai of one kind or another. Even allowing for the fact that most of these samurai came from a few active domains, the proportion is not large; and a study of the actual

—and this is inherent in the use of the label "nationalist"—the politics of the Restoration did not *directly* put at issue conflicting concepts of society, for all that policies like conscription and land-tax reform had important social effects. Hence the struggle for power was not openly about the distribution of "rights" between competing interests. It was not about "democracy."*

Leaving these largely negative conclusions and turning to more positive ones, how, then, are we to set political struggle and social change in relation to each other? I would suggest, as follows:

1. The class composition of the politically active minority in late-Tokugawa Japan already reflected the results of economic change in that it did not accord with the *formal* allocation of authority in society: a few daimyo, a few upper samurai, a good many middle samurai, a much larger number of lower samurai and "men of substance" from outside the samurai class. Proportionately, this corresponds fairly well with the number of men within each of these groups. Yet no Japanese of the time would have been prepared to argue that participation in decision-making should be proportional to numbers in this way; traditionally, it should have been almost entirely the prerogative of lords and senior retainers. Departure from traditional norms in this respect therefore suggests that at the *beginning* of the period with which we have dealt, the outlines of a new ruling class were emerging from within the old. It was *within* this class that most of the crucial debates took place.

2. In the various proposals for curing the country's ills after the

domains in which activity was greatest (Mito, Satsuma, Tosa, and Chōshū) suggests that there were never more than a few hundred men taking part in "politics" at any one time, including those who did no more than sign memorials and petitions. In the case of Tosa, for example, there is a list of Takechi Zuizan's loyalist followers that contains only 192 names. Neither conservatives nor reformers were as numerous. In contrast, the domain reported over 10,000 households of shizoku and sotsu in 1869 (*Hansei ichiran*, 1: 152).

* Itagaki's party in the 1880's claimed (retrospectively) that the Restoration had been "not merely a restoration of imperial rights of government, but also a restoration of the people's liberties" (*Jiyūtō-shi*, 1: 4). By this estimate, the Restoration was an incomplete struggle of Emperor and people against samurai privilege. Given Itagaki's use of the term "the people" as virtually a synonym for "the richer farmers and merchants," there is some substance in this claim if it refers to what was eventually brought about (and what was therefore *latent* in political events). It would be difficult, however, to substantiate a claim that this was the kind of thing men believed themselves to be fighting for in the years just before and after 1868.

conclusion of the treaties, there was usually an element of class or group interest, though not necessarily a dominant one. Bakufu and feudal lords, despite their rivalries, both sought to defend Japan without much disturbing its society; by promoting "men of talent," the middle samurai meant principally themselves; and the "men of spirit," despite an inability for the most part to get away from feudal terminology, clearly envisaged that the success of their plans would bring them a status they did not already have. Thus the defeat of kōbu-gattai, "unity of Court and Bakufu," and of kinnō, "serving the Emperor," were defeats for socially conservative and politically radical formulations of reform, respectively, as well as for particular ideas about how Japan could best be defended from the foreigner.

3. The men who emerged as leaders in succession to the reforming lords and dissident samurai, mostly after 1864, were realists, pragmatists, bureaucrat-politicians whose social origins matched their role: that is, they were nearly all middle or lower samurai, not high enough in the feudal hierarchy to be bent on preserving it, nor excluded from it to the point of wanting above all to break it down. Moreover, they were convinced that national defense required national unity. Accordingly, they believed as much in conciliation as reform, and so began to bring together the components of what was a social, as well as a political, alliance. Edo intransigents and rebellious peasants they would not tolerate, because both were obstacles to order and unity in their different ways. But the rest could all find a place: Court nobles, feudal lords, samurai, landlords, influential merchants, even servants of the Shogun in the end. To belong, one needed only to subscribe to the national objectives, as the inner group defined them.

4. Victory over the Tokugawa made these men responsible for government, that is, for implementing on a national scale the policies that would bring Japan "wealth and strength." In much of what they then did they acted still as samurai-bureaucrats trained in Confucian ideas: manipulating the Emperor as they had their lords; caring for the people's welfare, subject to the tax needs of the state; framing an education system that contributed to good order and to the citizen's skills. Concepts of government and its functions did

not change as much from Tokugawa to Meiji as the emphasis on modernization sometimes makes us think. Yet some of the differences were vital. Since feudalism contributed nothing to efficiency and was an obstacle to military strength, it had to go. Equally, since land tax was an essential resource and defining it involved the recognition of what had happened in the village, landlords got confirmation of their landed rights. Indirectly, they also obtained an extension of their economic opportunities. In fact, though the purpose of it all was not to change society, but rather to identify the least degree of social adjustment that would make possible fukoku-kyōhei—a militarily strong Japan rich enough to sustain a position of independence in the world—the application of these policies produced something very different from the Japan of twenty years before. For the minimal change, once identified, proved to be substantial. Consciously, there was an attack on samurai privilege; but consequentially this made possible the emergence into a position of influence of a new class, the well-to-do commoners whose power had until then been only latent.

5. Several factors came together to ensure that the society which emerged at the end of these years would be a capitalist one. Some of the long-term trends in the Tokugawa period were already moving in that direction, providing a basis on which to build. They were given a stimulus by contact with the capitalist West, initially through the effects of foreign trade, then because of the nature of the advice Japan received and the models she studied; the Western solutions that were applied to Japanese problems were inevitably those of the contemporary industrial state. Development was also given a particular direction by the nature of the policies that were devised for the promotion of national strength—the encouragement of industrial and commercial growth, coupled with an unusual degree of government intervention in the country's economy—so that Japan's transition from the "centralized feudalism" of Tokugawa days was to a similarly centralized form of capitalism. This resolved one Tokugawa anomaly, that of merchant wealth, by bringing the entrepreneur, like the landlord, into the dominant class and giving him a means to fulfill his aspirations legally. It left another, that of peasant unrest, aside. In the short term the second issue was settled

by force; but as the pressures on the cultivator increased with the growth of industry it re-emerged to become a problem of the twentieth century in a different form.

Does all this amount to a revolution? Perhaps to ask the question is to invite an argument about the meaning of words, since the reader is likely to have and to apply criteria of his own in finding an answer. Nevertheless, there are a number of points that can be made by way of a final gloss on what has been said above. For example, the Bakufu had some of the classic characteristics of an ancien régime: it had grave financial problems; it tried unsuccessfully to effect reform; it was indecisive and ineffective at the end in suppressing opposition; and for a variety of reasons it lost the confidence of a considerable segment of the ruling class. Also, those who overthrew it included men of many social origins (but not the lowest); they were generally of some respectability and experience; and they produced what might well be called "a dictatorship in commission." One could even argue that Restoration politics moved through appropriate stages of moderation and extremism before eventually bringing about, not "a brand-new ruling class," but "a kind of amalgamation, in which the enterprising, adaptable or lucky individuals of the old privileged classes [were] for most practical purposes tied up with those individuals of the old submerged classes, who, probably through the same gifts, were able to rise."[8]

There are other tests, too. There was a considerable shift in the locus of political power, which was downwards by pre-Restoration standards. Broadly speaking, there was—if one takes a long enough time base—a change from feudalism to capitalism as the organizing principle of Japanese society. There was even an application of force to politics to bring about these things, or at least to bring about some of the specific decisions that went to make them up.

Yet despite it all, I am reluctant to call the Restoration a revolution in the full meaning of the term. In part, this is because what happened in Japan lacked the avowed social purpose that gives the "great" revolutions of history a certain common character. But it is also because of the nature of the society to which the Restoration gave rise, in which "feudal" and "capitalist" elements worked together in a symbiosis dedicated to acquiring national strength. The political movement that brought this society into being cannot properly be called "bourgeois" in view of the dominant role samurai played in it and the power they retained when it was done. It was certainly not "peasant," given the fate of peasant revolt. Nor was it "absolutist" or "rightist," if that is to imply that the primary stimulus was a fear of popular unrest. What then is left, when none of these standard categories satisfactorily apply? Only to call it a nationalist revolution, perhaps, thereby giving recognition to the nature of the emotions that above all brought it about.

Appendixes

APPENDIX A

Glossary of Japanese Terms

ashigaru. Foot soldier. Regular member of the feudal class; below the rank of samurai.

baishin. Rear-vassal, i.e., the retainer of a subvassal.

Bakufu. See under *Shogun.*

bummei-kaika. "Civilization and enlightenment." Usually taken to mean the state of development that Western society had reached by the second half of the nineteenth century.

Daikan. Samurai official who administered a district or estate on behalf of the Shogun or a daimyo.

daimyo. Feudal lord who held 10,000 *koku* or more of land and was not a subvassal. Cf. *fudai daimyo; tozama daimyo.*

Dajōkan. The executive council of the early Meiji government.

fu. City. Urban local government unit established by the Meiji government.

fudai daimyo. Daimyo (feudal lord) who was a hereditary vassal of the Tokugawa. Cf. *tozama daimyo.*

fukoku-kyōhei. "Enrich the country, strengthen the army." Classical description of feudal-agrarian policy, which became transformed into a slogan signifying the adoption of Western methods to strengthen Japan against the West.

Gaikoku-bugyō. Bakufu officials responsible for the conduct of foreign relations; first appointed in 1858. Of about the same standing as *Kanjō-bugyō.*

Gijō. Senior councillors in the early Meiji government.

gokenin. Tokugawa retainers; samurai below the status of *hatamoto.*

gōshi. "Rural samurai." Samurai of low formal status (below *hirazamurai*), who were permitted to live in the countryside instead of the castle town.

goyōkin. "Forced loans." Levies made from time to time by the Bakufu and the domains, usually on merchants but sometimes also on farmers.

gunken-seido. Prefectural system, i.e., an administration based on local units under officials of the central government (and especially such a system as it was known to exist in China). Contrasts with feudal system (*hōken-seido*).

haihan-chiken. The abolition of domains (*han*) and establishment of prefectures (*ken*). Policy carried out by Meiji government in 1871.
han. The territory held by a daimyo. Translated in this book as "domain," but is also translated as "fief" and sometimes as "clan."
hanseki-hōkan. Surrender of daimyo registers of land and population to the Emperor. Policy enforced by the Meiji government in 1869.
hatamoto. Tokugawa retainers; upper and middle samurai, immediately below the *fudai daimyo* in status, often holding fiefs rather than stipends.
heimin. Commoner. Usually means a person below the status of samurai.
hirazamurai. "Middle samurai." Retainer of full samurai status; clearly superior to *ashigaru* but not belonging to the small group of upper samurai who were close to the daimyo.
hōken-seido. "Feudal system," i.e., a polity based on fief-holding. Contrasts with prefectural system (*gunken-seido*).
hondaka. See under *kokudaka.*
ishin. "Renovation." Term that came to signify the innovating policies adopted after the Restoration.
jitsudaka. See under *kokudaka.*
jōi. See *sonnō-jōi.*
kaikoku. "Open the country." Term commonly used to designate a willingness to establish treaty relations with the West before 1858.
kamme. Measure of weight; equal to 1,000 *momme.* Standardized as equivalent to 8.27 lbs. or 3.75 kg. Commonly used to measure large quantities of copper coin (*mon*).
kamon. Daimyo houses whose lords were collaterals of the Tokugawa and bore the family name of Matsudaira.
Kampaku. Senior official of the Imperial Court who exercised the powers of a regent even though the Emperor was adult. Cf. *Sesshō.*
Kanjō-bugyō. Bakufu official responsible for finance. The highest level of office open to *hatamoto,* coming just below the posts reserved for *fudai daimyo.*
Karō. Senior official of a domain (*han*), usually the local equivalent to a *Rōjū.*
kazoku. In the early Meiji period, term for a nobility composed of both *kuge* and daimyo. Later the peerage (established in 1884 on Western lines).
ken. Prefecture. Local government unit established by the Meiji government.
kōbu-gattai. "Unity of Court and Bakufu." Slogan of those who sought a basis of accommodation between the Bakufu and the great lords after 1858; its advocates envisaged also reaching a settlement with the West. Contrasts with *sonnō-jōi.*
koku. Measure of capacity, used especially of rice. Standardized as the equivalent of 4.96 bushels or 180 liters. For its use in land assessment, see *kokudaka.*
kokudaka. Land valuation; an assessment of the annual crop expressed in

koku of rice. Applicable to domains (*han*), villages, and individual holdings of samurai or farmer. When used of domains, there were two types of *kokudaka*: (1) the official valuation for purposes of record by the Bakufu, usually a 16th- or 17th-century figure (known as *hondaka*, "original" assessment, or *omotedaka*, "public" assessment); and (2) the tax collector's valuation, which took some account of subsequent changes (known as *jitsudaka*, "true" assessment, *uchidaka*, "private" assessment, or *kusadaka*, "total" assessment).

kokugaku. "National learning." Scholarship emphasizing Japan's national traditions, especially Shintō.

kokutai. "National polity." An emotive term for Japan's system of government, which by implication distinguished native from imported institutions. In the Restoration period, increasingly associated with the idea of rule by the Emperor.

kuge. Nobles of the Imperial Court.

kusadaka. See under *kokudaka*.

Kyōto Shoshidai. The Shogun's representative, or governor, in Kyōto. Post usually held by a senior *fudai daimyo*.

Kyōto Shugo. Military governor of Kyōto. Post created in 1862; senior to the position of *Kyōto Shoshidai* and held by one of the Tokugawa collaterals.

Metsuke. Bakufu official chiefly responsible for investigation of maladministration and related matters, hence often called Censor. Ranked just below *Kanjō-bugyō*.

momme. Measure of weight, normally applied to silver when used as money. Standardized as equivalent to 3.75 grams. Cf. *kamme*.

naiyū-gaikan. "Troubles at home, dangers from abroad." Term signifying simultaneous domestic unrest and foreign attack: a Chinese formula for dynastic disaster.

omotedaka. See under *kokudaka*.

ōsei-fukko. "The restoration of imperial rule." Term for the overthrow of the Bakufu and the resumption by the Emperor of direct responsibility for the government of the country.

Rangaku. "Dutch studies." The study of the West through Dutch books.

Rōjū. Senior councillors of the Bakufu, appointed from among the *fudai daimyo*.

rōnin. Lordless samurai. In the late-Tokugawa period, used especially of those samurai who quit their domains to engage in loyalist activities.

ryō. Gold coin. Approximately equal in value to 60 *momme* of silver. Replaced by the yen after the Restoration.

samurai. Retainer of a daimyo. More loosely, any member of the feudal class.

Sangi. Councillors in the Meiji government. Replaced the earlier offices of *Gijō* and *Sanyo*.

sanke. The three senior branches of the Tokugawa family—Kii, Owari, and Mito.

sankin-kōtai. "Alternate attendance." System by which daimyo were required to spend much of their time in Edo (usually alternate years); used to strengthen Bakufu control over the feudal lords.

Sanyo. Junior councillors in the early Meiji government.

Sesshō. Regent; the senior official of the Imperial Court when the Emperor was a minor. Cf. *Kampaku.*

shishi. "Men of spirit." Term used to describe the activists of the *sonnō-jōi* movement in the 1860's.

shizoku. Gentry. Term that officially replaced the word "samurai" in the early Meiji period.

Shogun. Abbreviated form of *Sei-i-tai-shōgun,* "barbarian-subduing generalissimo," the Emperor's military deputy. The title under which the Tokugawa acted as de facto rulers of Japan. The Shogun's government was known as the Bakufu.

Shoshidai. See *Kyōto Shoshidai.*

shotai. Military units. Commonly used to describe the irregular forces raised by Chōshū in and after 1863, of which the *Kiheitai* was the most famous.

Shōya. Village headman (especially in western Japan).

sonnō-jōi. "Honor the Emperor, expel the barbarian." Slogan associated with the loyalist movement, especially in the decade after 1858.

sotsu. Soldier. In the early Meiji period, term used for former lower samurai, i.e., those below the *shizoku.*

tōbaku. "Destroy the Bakufu." Slogan describing the political aims of the anti-Tokugawa movement in the late 1860's; used by those who wanted to indicate a more precise immediate objective than was implied by *sonnō.*

tozama daimyo. Daimyo who was not a vassal of the Tokugawa house. Often known as "outside" lords. Cf. *fudai daimyo.*

uchidaka. See under *kokudaka.*

yen. Modern unit of Japanese currency, introduced in 1871 as an equivalent to the U.S. dollar (though it soon declined in value from that level). Replaced the *ryō* as the principal unit for tax records.

APPENDIX B

Biographical Notes

A brief guide to some of the men who were active in Japanese politics between 1853 and 1873. Family names are in capitals; given names (or their equivalents) are in lower case.

ABE Masahiro (1819–57).
Fudai daimyo (Fukuyama; 100,000 *koku*; 1837–57). Rōjū, 1843–57. Senior member of Bakufu council at time of Perry negotiations.

AIZAWA Seishisai (1781–1863). Also: Hakumin.
Mito samurai and famous loyalist. Author of *Shinron*. Adviser to Tokugawa Nariaki. Leader of middle samurai reform party in Mito.

ARIMA Shinshichi (1825–62).
Son of Satsuma *gōshi*, adopted by *hirazamurai*. Active loyalist; plotted rising in Kyōto, 1862. Killed at Teradaya.

Asahiko, Prince (1824–91). Also: In-no-miya.
Imperial prince; influential supporter of *kōbu-gattai* policies at Court.

DATE Muneki (1819–92). Also: Munenari.
Tozama daimyo (Uwajima; 100,000 *koku*; 1844–58). Reformer; member of Hitotsubashi party, then *kōbu-gattai* party. Senior offices in early Meiji government; councillor (Gijō).

ENOMOTO Takeaki (1836–1908).
Son of a *gōshi* who bought status as *gokenin*. Student of naval science under Dutch at Nagasaki, then in Holland (from 1862). Senior Bakufu naval post, 1867. Fled to Hokkaidō and resisted Restoration, 1868–69. Pardoned in 1872 and appointed to office under Meiji government; rose to cabinet rank.

ETŌ Shimpei (1834–74).
Low-ranking samurai of Hizen; punished for loyalist activities in Kyōto, 1862. Member of early Meiji government. Led revolt in Saga after Korea dispute of 1873. Executed.

FUJITA Tōko (1806–55).
Mito *hirazamurai*; adviser to Tokugawa Nariaki; advocate of *sonnō-jōi*.

FUKUOKA Kōtei (1835–1919). Also: Takachika.
Tosa *hirazamurai* (56 *koku*). Associate of Yoshida Tōyō and Gotō Shōjirō in domain government. Senior posts in early Meiji government.

GODAI Tomoatsu (1836–85).
Satsuma samurai (apparently *hirazamurai*). Studied naval science under Dutch at Nagasaki, becoming Satsuma naval and shipping expert. Advocate of *fukoku-kyōhei*. Mission to Europe with Terajima Munenori, 1865–66. Councillor (Sanyo) in early Meiji government. Later entrepreneur, with interests in transport, mining, and textiles.

GOTŌ Shōjirō (1838–97).
Tosa *hirazamurai* (150 *koku*), related by marriage to Yoshida Tōyō. Leader of Tosa after 1864; raised to Karō rank (1,500 *koku*). Active in intrigues leading to Restoration. Senior member of early Meiji government. Later engaged in party politics and business enterprises.

HASHIMOTO Sanai (1834–59).
Son of Echizen official doctor (25 *koku*). Specialist in Western studies; given samurai rank as adviser to Matsudaira Shungaku. Shungaku's agent in Kyōto intrigues, 1858. Executed.

HIRANO Kuniomi (1828–64). Also: Jirō.
Chikuzen samurai (apparently *hirazamurai*). Loyalist; fled domain to engage in Kyōto politics, 1862–63; associate of Maki Izumi. Raised revolt in Tajima, late 1863. Captured and executed.

HIROSAWA Saneomi (1834–71). Earlier: HATA.
Chōshū *hirazamurai*. Loyalist sympathizer; official colleague of Kido Kōin after 1864; military reformer. Senior posts in early Meiji government. Assassinated.

HITOTSUBASHI Keiki, see Tokugawa Keiki.

HOTTA Masayoshi (1810–64). Also: Masahiro.
Fudai daimyo (Sakura; 110,000 *koku*; 1825–59). Rōjū, 1855–58. Senior member of Bakufu council at time of treaty negotiations, 1857–58.

Iemochi, Shogun, see Tokugawa Iemochi.

Iesada, Shogun, see Tokugawa Iesada.

II Naosuke (1815–60).
Fudai daimyo (Hikone; 350,000 *koku*; 1850–60). Tairō (Regent), 1858–60. Signed 1858 treaties and instituted "Ansei purge." Assassinated at Sakuradamon.

IKEDA Nagaaki (1837–79). Also: Chōhatsu.
Hatamoto (1,200 *koku*). Bakufu official; Gaikoku-bugyō, 1863–64. Bakufu special envoy to France, 1864.

INOUE Kaoru (1836–1915). Also: Bunta. Earlier: SHIJI.
Chōshū *hirazamurai* (100 *koku* by birth; 220 *koku* by adoption). Loyalist.

Studied in London, 1863–64. Active in *shotai* with Takasugi Shinsaku, 1865. Senior posts in Meiji government, becoming finance expert, Genrō. Close links with Itō Hirobumi.

ITAGAKI Taisuke (1837–1919). Earlier: INUI.
Tosa *hirazamurai* (220 *koku*). Loyalist and military reformer; associate of Yoshida Tōyō and Gotō Shōjirō. Councillor in early Meiji government (Sanyo, then Sangi). Resigned over Korea dispute, 1873. Thereafter political party leader (Jiyūtō).

ITAKURA Katsukiyo (1823–89).
Fudai daimyo (Matsuyama; 50,000 *koku*; 1849–68). Rōjū, 1862–64, 1865–68. Worked closely with Tokugawa Keiki.

ITŌ Hirobumi (1841–1909). Also: Shunsuke.
Chōshū loyalist; son of a farmer turned castle-town merchant. Student of Yoshida Shōin. Made samurai, 1863. With Inoue Kaoru, studied in London, 1863–64. Led a *shotai*, working with Takasugi Shinsaku, 1865. As "Western" expert and colleague of Kido Kōin, rose steadily in Meiji government, becoming Prime Minister and Genrō.

IWAKURA Tomomi (1825–83). Also: Tomoyoshi.
Court noble of middle rank; minor Court posts before 1868. Supporter of *kōbu-gattai* party. Later closely linked with Satsuma, especially Ōkubo Toshimichi. After Restoration, key member of Meiji government; councillor (Gijō); senior minister. Led mission to America and Europe, 1871–73.

IWASE Tadanari (1818–61).
Hatamoto (700 *koku*). Bakufu official; Metsuke, 1854–58; Gaikoku-bugyō, 1858. Advocated opening ports to foreign trade.

KATSU Awa (1823–99). Also: Kaishū; Rintarō.
Hatamoto (41 *koku*). Studied naval science under Dutch at Nagasaki. Bakufu's leading naval expert in 1860's. Advocate of *fukoku-kyōhei*; links with Saigō Takamori and other loyalists. Negotiated surrender of Edo, 1868. Appointed to naval and other posts in Meiji government from 1869, reaching cabinet rank.

KATSURA Kogorō, see Kido Kōin.

Keiki, Shōgun, see Tokugawa Keiki.

KIDO Kōin (1833–77). Also: Takayuki. Earlier: KATSURA Kogorō.
Chōshū loyalist; son of official doctor (20 *koku*); adopted by *hirazamurai* (150 *koku*; then 90 *koku*). Student of Yoshida Shōin. Official posts in Chōshū from 1862. With Takasugi Shinsaku, effective leader of Chōshū from 1865. Key member of early Meiji government.

KOMATSU Tatewaki (1835–70).
Upper samurai of Satsuma. Senior ally of Ōkubo Toshimichi in domain politics; Karō, 1862. Senior posts in early Meiji government.

Kōmei, Emperor (1831–67).
Succeeded to throne, 1846. *Kōbu-gattai* sympathizer.

KONOE Tadahiro (1808–98).
Senior Court noble, related to Shimazus of Satsuma. Kampaku, 1862–63.

KUJŌ Naotada (1798–1871).
Senior Court noble. Kampaku, 1856–62.

KURIMOTO Joun (1822–97). Also: Sebei.
Son of Bakufu official doctor. Bakufu official; Gaikoku-bugyō, 1865–68. Member of Bakufu reform party. Links with French minister to Japan, Léon Roches.

KUSAKA Genzui (1840–64). Also: Michitake.
Chōshū loyalist; son of fief doctor (25 *koku*). Student of Yoshida Shōin. Active in Kyōto politics, 1862–63. Died in Chōshū attempt to seize Kyōto, 1864.

MAEBARA Issei (1834–76). Earlier: SASE.
Chōshū loyalist; apparently son of lower samurai. Student of Yoshida Shōin. Promoted to office and samurai rank. Associate of Takasugi Shinsaku. High office in Meiji government, but retired to Chōshū, 1871. Led unsuccessful samurai revolt, 1876.

MAKI Izumi (1813–64).
Loyalist from Kurume; son of Shintō official of middle samurai status. Advocate of *sonnō-jōi*; leader of loyalist *shishi* in Kyōto, 1862–63. Committed suicide after failure of Chōshū attack on Kyōto, 1864.

MATSUDAIRA Katamori (1836–93).
Kamon lord (Aizu; 230,000 *koku*; 1852–69). Member of Bakufu *kōbu-gattai* party. Kyōto-shugoshoku, 1862–64, 1864–68. Resisted Restoration in 1868 but defeated in civil war.

MATSUDAIRA Sadaaki (1846–1908). Also: Sadataka.
Fudai daimyo (Kuwana; 110,000 *koku*; 1859–68). Kyōto-shoshidai, 1864–68. Resisted Restoration in January 1868. Defeated at Toba-Fushimi.

MATSUDAIRA Shungaku (1828–90). Also: Keiei or Yoshinaga.
Kamon lord (Echizen, or Fukui; 320,000 *koku*; 1838–58). Leader of Hitotsubashi party, then *kōbu-gattai* party. Senior offices in early Meiji government; councillor (Gijō); departmental minister.

MATSUKATA Masayoshi (1835–1924).
Son of Satsuma *gōshi* turned merchant (Ryukyu trade). Modest official career in Satsuma before 1868; promoted *hirazamurai*, 1863. After 1868, posts in local and central government; finance expert; eventually Prime Minister and Genrō.

MATSUKI Kōan, see Terajima Munenori.

Meiji Emperor (1852–1912). Given name: Mutsuhito.
Son of Kōmei. Succeeded to throne, February 13, 1867.

MIZUNO Tadanori (1810–68).
Hatamoto. Bakufu official; Kanjō-bugyō, 1855–58, 1859; Gaikoku-bugyō, 1858–59, 1861–62. One of the treaty negotiators, 1857–58.

MŌRI Yoshichika (1819–71). Also: Katachika.
Tozama daimyo (Chōshū; 369,000 *koku*; 1837–69).

Mutsuhito, Emperor, see Meiji Emperor.

NABESHIMA Naomasa (1814–71). Also: Kansō.
Tozama daimyo (Hizen, or Saga; 357,000 *koku*; 1830–61). Patron of technological innovation. Supporter of *kōbu-gattai*, but held aloof from political disputes before 1868. Senior posts in early Meiji government; councillor (Gijō).

NAGAI Naomune (1816–91).
Younger son of *fudai* daimyo, adopted by *hatamoto* (3,000 *koku*). Bakufu official; Metsuke, 1853–58; Gaikoku-bugyō, 1858–59, 1865–67. Member of Edo reform group in Bakufu's closing years; raised to junior council (*wakadoshiyori*), 1867–68. Fought under Enomoto Takeaki in Hokkaidō; pardoned, 1871; given post in Meiji government.

NAGAI Uta (1819–63).
Chōshū *hirazamurai* (150 *koku*). Rose to senior office in domain; shaped Chōshū *kōbu-gattai* policy, 1862; dismissed because of loyalist attacks. Committed suicide.

NAKAOKA Shintarō (1838–67).
Tosa loyalist; son of *gōshi*. Fled to Chōshū, late 1863; worked with Sakamoto Ryōma to bring about Satsuma-Chōshū alliance. With him, killed by Bakufu agents, December 1867.

NAKAYAMA Tadayasu (1809–88).
Court noble. Maternal grandfather to Meiji Emperor. Cooperated in Restoration coup d'état. Gijō in early Meiji government.

NARIAKI of Mito, see Tokugawa Nariaki.

NARIAKIRA of Satsuma, see Shimazu Nariakira.

NIJŌ Nariaki (1816–78).
Senior Court noble. Kampaku, 1864–67; Sesshō, 1867–68.

NISHI Amane (1829–97).
Son of fief doctor in Tsuwano domain; student of Rangaku. Employed by Bakufu in Bansho-shirabesho; sent to study in Leiden, 1862–65; then Edo adviser. Later Meiji bureaucrat; specialist in Western law, military administration, philosophy.

OGASAWARA Nagamichi (1822–91).
Eldest son of *fudai* daimyo (Karatsu; 60,000 *koku*; never succeeded). Bakufu official; Rōjū, 1865–66, 1866–68. Worked closely with Tokugawa Keiki. Joined Enomoto Takeaki in Hokkaidō, 1868–69.

OGURI Tadamasa (1827–68).
Hatamoto (2,500 *koku*). Bakufu official; Gaikoku-bugyō, 1860–61; Kanjō-bugyō, 1863, 1864–65. Member of Edo reform group in Bakufu's closing years, especially as military and naval expert. Executed 1868, after Restoration.

ŌHARA Shigenori (c. 1810–79).
Court noble. Imperial envoy to Edo in association with Satsuma, 1862. Councillor in early Meiji government (Sanyo; Gijō).

ŌKI Takatō (1832–99).
Hizen samurai (apparently *hirazamurai*); related to Ōkuma Shigenobu. Loyalist sympathizer. Came to prominence in Meiji government.

ŌKUBO Ichiō (1817–88). Also: Tadahiro.
Hatamoto and Bakufu official; Metsuke, Kanjō-bugyō, Gaikoku-bugyō. Associate of reformers, including Iwase Tadanari and Katsu Awa. With latter, took part in arranging surrender of Edo, 1868. Later served in Meiji bureaucracy, notably as prefectural governor.

ŌKUBO Toshimichi (1830–78). Also: Ichizō.
Satsuma *hirazamurai*. Loyalist and domain bureaucrat; with Saigō Takamori, largely controlled domain policies after 1864. After Restoration, key figure in Meiji government; councillor (Sanyo; Sangi); minister. Dominant figure after Korea dispute of 1873 until assassinated, 1878.

ŌKUMA Shigenobu (1838–1922).
Hizen *hirazamurai* (400 *koku*). Student of Rangaku, then of English; held domain offices connected with finance and foreign trade before 1868. Senior Hizen member of early Meiji government; leader of modernizing group. Later, political party leader, cabinet minister.

ŌMURA Masujirō (1824–69). Earlier: MURATA.
Son of Chōshū fief doctor. Student of Western military science; adviser to Date Muneki of Uwajima. Returned to Chōshū, 1856; carried out military reforms; made *hirazamurai*. Post in war ministry after Restoration. Assassinated late 1869.

SAGA Sanenaru (1816–1909). Also: ŌGIMACHI SANJŌ; Jitsuai.
Court noble; loyalist sympathizer. Court offices of some importance, 1860–68. Councillor (Sanyo) in early Meiji government.

SAIGŌ Takamori (1828–77).
Satsuma *hirazamurai*. Agent of Shimazu Nariakira in Edo, 1858; exiled; recalled, 1862; again exiled; pardoned, 1864. With Ōkubo Toshimichi, leader of Satsuma thereafter. After Restoration, senior member of Meiji government. Broke with other leaders over Korea dispute, 1873; leader of samurai revolt, 1877. Committed suicide on battlefield.

SAITŌ Toshiyuki (1822–81). Also: WATANABE Yakuma.
Tosa *hirazamurai* (50 *koku*). Senior domain official; associate of Yoshida Tōyō and Gotō Shōjirō. Councillor (Sangi) in early Meiji government.

SAKAMOTO Ryōma (1835–67).
Tosa *gōshi* (merchant origins). Loyalist; associate of Takechi Zuizan. Fled to Satsuma, 1862; organized Kaientai shipping group. Active in bringing about Satsuma-Chōshū alliance. With Nakaoka Shintarō, killed by Bakufu agents, December 1867.

SAKUMA Shōzan (1811–64). Also: Kunitada.
Samurai of Matsushiro. Student of Rangaku; specialist in Western military science; Bakufu adviser. Advocate of *kaikoku* and *kōbu-gattai*. Killed by *jōi* fanatic.

SANJŌ Sanetomi (1837–91). Also: Saneyoshi.
Court noble; related by marriage to Yamauchi Yōdō. Court offices of moderate importance, 1862–63. Loyalist sympathizer; imperial envoy to Edo, 1862. Fled to Chōshū, 1863; later to Kyūshū. Returned after Restoration to become senior minister in Meiji government.

SASAKI Takayuki (1830–1910). Also: Sanshirō.
Tosa *hirazamurai* (48 *koku*). Loyalist sympathizer; official colleague of Gotō Shōjirō. Senior posts in Meiji government; councillor (Sangi).

SHIMAZU Hisamitsu (1817–87). Also: Saburō.
Half-brother to Shimazu Nariakira; father of Tadayoshi, Nariakira's successor as daimyo of Satsuma; as such, effective head of domain in 1860's. Leader of *kōbu-gattai* party; patron of Ōkubo Toshimichi and Saigō Takamori. After 1868, a conservative opponent of Meiji reform program.

SHIMAZU Nariakira (1809–58). Also: Saburō.
Tozama daimyo (Satsuma, or Kagoshima; 770,000 *koku*; 1851–58). Reformer, especially in importing Western technology. Leader of Hitotsubashi party.

SOEJIMA Taneomi (1828–1905).
Hizen samurai; family with *kokugaku* connections. Student of Rangaku, later English (with Ōkuma Shigenobu). Loyalist sympathizer; came into prominence as Hizen representative in early Meiji government; diplomatic specialist; later cabinet minister.

TAKASUGI Shinsaku (1839–67).
Chōshū *hirazamurai* (150 *koku*). Student of Yoshida Shōin. Loyalist activities, 1862–63. Organized Kiheitai, 1863. Led loyalist seizure of power in Chōshū, early 1865. Died of illness, 1867.

TAKATSUKASA Masamichi (1789–1868).
Senior Court noble; brother-in-law to Tokugawa Nariaki. Kampaku, 1823–56.

TAKATSUKASA Sukehiro (1807–67).
Senior Court noble; son of Masamichi. Kampaku, 1863–64.

TAKECHI Zuizan (1829–65). Also: Hampeita.
Tosa *gōshi*; leader of Tosa loyalists in 1861–63. Arrested and imprisoned on orders of the former daimyo, Yamauchi Yōdō, late 1863; later ordered to commit suicide.

TERAJIMA Munenori (1832–93). Earlier: MATSUKI Kōan.
Son of Satsuma *gōshi*; adopted into *hirazamurai* family. Studied medicine and Rangaku; doctor and adviser to Shimazu Nariakira. Mission to Europe with Godai Tomoatsu, 1865–66. Senior posts in Meiji government, especially diplomatic ones.

TOKUGAWA Iemochi (1846–66). Earlier: Yoshitomi.
Head of *sanke* house (Kii; 550,000 *koku*; 1849–58). Nominated Shogun after succession dispute, 1858; 14th of Tokugawa line, succeeding Iesada.

TOKUGAWA Iesada (1824–58).
Shogun, 1853–58; 13th of Tokugawa line.

TOKUGAWA Keiki (1837–1913). Earlier: HITOTSUBASHI. Also: Yoshinobu.
Younger son of Tokugawa Nariaki, adopted into Hitotsubashi house (*sankyō*; 100,000 *koku*; 1847–59, 1862–67). Unsuccessful candidate in succession dispute, 1858. Leader of Bakufu *kōbu-gattai* party after 1862. Succeeded as Shogun, January 1867; 15th and last of Tokugawa line.

TOKUGAWA Nariaki (1800–60).
Sanke lord (Mito; 350,000 *koku*; 1829–44). Advocate of military reform and *jōi*. Leader of "reforming lords" before 1858.

YAMAGATA Aritomo (1838–1922).
Chōshū *ashigaru*. Succeeded to command of Kiheitai; supported Takasugi Shinsaku in seizure of power, 1865. Offices in Chōshū, then Meiji government; became outstanding figure of late Meiji period; Prime Minister; Genrō.

YAMAUCHI (or YAMANOUCHI) Yōdō (1827–72). Also: Toyoshige.
Tozama daimyo (Tosa; 242,000 *koku*; 1849–59). Member of Hitotsubashi party, 1858; then of *kōbu-gattai* party. Senior posts in early Meiji government.

YOKOI Shōnan (1809–69). Also: Heishirō.
Younger son of Kumamoto *hirazamurai* (150 *koku*). Through influence of Hashimoto Sanai, invited to act as adviser to Matsudaira Shungaku of Echizen. Advocated *kōbu-gattai* and reform of Bakufu system. Strong influence on ideas of anti-Bakufu groups. Councillor (Sanyo) in early Meiji government.

YOSHIDA Shōin (1830–59). Also: Torajirō.
Low-ranking samurai of Chōshū. Student of Sakuma Shōzan; influenced by Mito writers. Loyalist and teacher. Executed 1859 for plot to assassinate a Rōjū.

YOSHIDA Tōyō (1816–62). Also: Genkichi.
Tosa *hirazamurai* (200 *koku*). Reformer, who rose to high office through favor of Yamauchi Yōdō; followed *kōbu-gattai* and modernizing policies. Assassinated by loyalists, 1862.

YURI Kimimasa (1829–1909).
Echizen *hirazamurai* (100 *koku*). With Hashimoto Sanai and Yokoi Shōnan, adviser to Matsudaira Shungaku; finance specialist. Links with anti-Bakufu leaders, especially those of Satsuma. Senior posts in early Meiji government, but little political activity after 1871.

Notes

Notes

Complete authors' names, titles, and publication data can be found in the Bibliography, pages 483–95. I have used two abbreviations in the Notes: F.O. for British Foreign Office documents and *BGKM* for *Dai Nihon Komonjo: Bakumatsu Gaikoku Kankei Monjo.*

INTRODUCTION

1. I have used the Iwanami Bunko edition of Taguchi's book (Tokyo, 1934), in which the sections on the Restoration appear on pp. 243–61.

2. Taguchi made two points that originated with the Bakufu's own apologists: first, that by opening the ports, even though it did so as a result of weakness, not of foresight, the Bakufu had done the country great service; second, that the last Shogun, Keiki, had sought by his resignation to avoid a civil war that might have afforded opportunities for foreign meddling. Both points were made much of in histories like Fukuchi Genichirō's *Bakufu suibō ron,* first published in 1892, and Shibusawa Eiichi's *Tokugawa Keiki Kō den* (1918), though in other respects neither departs very much from Taguchi's argument.

3. The most succinct statement of Inobe's views is to be found in his 1929 article "Seijishi-jō yori mitaru Meiji ishin." The interpretation has remained influential ever since. For example, it is reflected in the work of Oka Yoshitake, especially his *Kindai Nihon no keisei* (1947), which is still one of the clearest and most balanced accounts of late Tokugawa and early Meiji history.

4. *Jiyūtō-shi* 1: 4. The Jiyūtō version of Restoration history in general is to be found in *ibid.,* pp. 3–14.

5. In particular, his study of feudal finance: Tsuchiya, *Hōken shakai hōkai katei no kenkyū.*

6. Takahashi, "Keizaishi-jō ni okeru Meiji ishin."

7. It is usually said to have begun with Hani Gorō's plea for an "objective" study of modern Japanese history, by which he meant one that saw the stages of development not merely as moving from feudal to bourgeois-capitalist, but

as part of a progression from feudal to capitalist to proletarian. This was argued in his article "Meiji ishin kaishaku no hensen," which appeared in the same volume as those by Inobe and Takahashi cited above: *Meiji ishin-shi kenkyū*. Another important work was a collection of articles on the history of Japanese capitalism (*Nihon shihonshugi hattatsu-shi kōza*), published in Tokyo in 1932–33, which initiated a long-drawn-out dispute on the nature of pre-Meiji economic development and its effect on capitalism in Japan.

8. Tōyama, *Meiji ishin*. I am conscious that the brief summary of Tōyama's argument given here does a great deal less than justice to the complexities and originality of his work.

9. See, for example, Horie Hideichi; and Seki, *Hansei kaikaku*.

10. For example, *Meiji ishin to jinushi-sei*; Fukushima Masao; and Seki, *Meiji ishin*.

11. See Shibahara.

12. Sakata's principal work on the subject is *Meiji ishin shi*, but his views are usefully summarized in the introductory essay to a volume he edited later: *Meiji ishin-shi no mondai-ten*. They are also given in part in an article in English he authored with J. W. Hall: "The Motivation of Political Leadership in the Meiji Restoration."

13. A notable example is Ishii Takashi, [*Zōtei*] *Meiji ishin no kokusaiteki kankyō*. Some of this work's argument was first stated by Ishii in his study of late-Tokugawa foreign trade: *Bakumatsu bōeki shi no kenkyū*.

14. The present state of writing about the Restoration, including this aspect of it, has recently been the subject of an interesting discussion in which leading Japanese scholars, among them Tōyama and Ishii, took part under the chairmanship of Konishi Shirō. It is recorded in *Meiji ishin-shi kenkyū kōza*, supp. vol., 1969, pp. 3–19.

15. Outstanding (though it does not deal exclusively with the Restoration) is G. B. Sansom, *The Western World and Japan*.

16. One might include in this category E. H. Norman's pioneer work *Japan's Emergence as a Modern State*, as well as Barrington Moore's *Social Origins of Dictatorship and Democracy*. Of the many studies of modernization, the important Princeton series should be mentioned, especially M. B. Jansen, ed., *Changing Japanese Attitudes Toward Modernization*; and W. W. Lockwood, ed., *The State and Economic Enterprise in Modern Japan*.

17. Since I wrote this passage, the question of the interaction of ideas and late-Tokugawa politics has been taken up in an important new book: H. D. Harootunian, *Toward Restoration*.

CHAPTER I

1. The most recent and authoritative accounts in English of the Bakuhan system, as it is usually called, are Totman, *Politics*; and the multiauthor volume edited by Hall and Jansen. Of the many Japanese studies of the subject, I

have made most use, in this introductory discussion, of Kanai, *Hansei*; and the first volume of *Ishin-shi*.

2. For a full-scale study of this system, see Tsukahira.

3. On the difficulties and complexities of Bakufu administration, see especially Totman, *Politics*, pp. 181–86, where he describes the emergence of the "vertical clique," that is, a number of officials acting at different levels within the bureaucratic machine who could collectively control the main aspects of policy-making and its execution. The mere fact that such a device was necessary says much for the clumsiness of governmental procedures.

4. On village government, see Befu, "Duty."

5. On some of the fudai domains, however, those that were means of support for senior bureaucrats rather than old, established personal fiefs, the Bakufu's powers of intervention were considerably greater. Hotta Masayoshi's domain of Sakura is an example. See Totman, *Politics*, pp. 154–62.

6. Details of some han governments (choosing as examples the domains that were of greatest importance in Restoration politics) can be found in the following works: on Satsuma, *Kagoshima-ken shi*, 2: 95–119; on Chōshū, Suematsu, *Bōchō*, 1: 49–68, and Craig, *Chōshū*, pp. 107–10; and on Tosa, *Kōchi-ken shiyō*, pp. 264–65, and Jansen, *Sakamoto*, pp. 23–24.

7. See the list in Kanai, pp. 60–74. On the subject of samurai fiefs and stipends generally, see also Shimmi, pp. 15–21.

8. Craig, *Chōshū*, pp. 102–6. See also Seki, *Hansei kaikaku*, pp. 15–19.

9. On the kuge, see Fukaya, pp. 92–101; and Webb, *Japanese*, pp. 89–99.

10. For a brief discussion, see Kanai, pp. 30–35. See also Totman, *Politics*, pp. 34–37, 110–30, 153–78.

11. On Tokugawa population figures, see Honjō, *Social and Economic History*, pp. 145–58. Strayer, pp. 6, 9, notes the contrast with medieval England, where there were at most 6,000 knights' fees and even fewer knights. This goes far to explain the more structured and bureaucratic features of feudal society in Japan as compared with that of Europe. It also meant that Meiji Japan did not in numerical terms need to go outside the samurai class in recruiting for a modern bureaucracy.

12. Hall, *Government*, p. 371.

13. Craig, *Chōshū*, pp. 13–17. The figures include lesser samurai, which, as we shall see, raises certain problems of classification. Consequently, they can be taken only as a broad indication of variations in the percentage of samurai in the population. I have given some consideration to regional variations in this percentage in my article "Feudal Revenue in Japan," pp. 265–66.

14. Complete figures for 1826 are given in *Sappan seiyō roku*, a kind of Satsuma official handbook. See also *Kagoshima-ken shi*, 2: 10–17. Adding together figures for families of castle-town samurai and all types of lower samurai, one gets a total of 241,157 persons out of an overall population (excluding Ryukyu) of 724,592.

15. For a useful discussion of this topic, see Craig, "Restoration," pp. 363–67.

16. The material on Satsuma and Chōshū samurai cited in this discussion is taken chiefly from the following works: on Satsuma, *Kagoshima-ken shi,* 2: 18–25, and Hayashi, Part 2, pp. 19–26, 113–40; on Chōshū, Craig, *Chōshū,* pp. 98–102, 261, and Suematsu, *Bōchō,* 1: 35–47. Also useful in this connection is *Hansei ichiran,* which gives population and revenue figures reported by the domains in 1868–69.

17. On the Tokugawa samurai, see Fukaya, pp. 50–55; and Totman, *Politics,* pp. 131–45.

18. On Tosa samurai, see Jansen, *Sakamoto,* pp. 24–26; *Kōchi-ken shiyō,* pp. 265–66; and Irimajiri, pp. 111–29.

19. Kimura, pp. 1–5.

20. The fullest study of gōshi is Ono Takeo, *Gōshi seido no kenkyū.* On the Satsuma gōshi, see especially pp. 73–90 of that work. On Tosa, see also Jansen, *Sakamoto,* pp. 27–30; and Irimajiri, pp. 76–141.

21. Based on lists in *Tosa-han gōshi chōsha-sho.*

22. Shimmi, pp. 3–10, cites a number of examples contrasting the attitude of Tosa, which was relatively generous in according shizoku status, with that of Owari, which was just the reverse.

23. The Chōshū figures come from Suematsu, *Bōchō,* 1: 41–47; and the Satsuma ones from *Kagoshima-ken shi,* 2: 78–79. Tables in *Sappan seiyō roku,* pp. 97–102, show that in 1826 only 125 Satsuma families had more than 200 koku. A table in Totman, *Politics,* pp. 134–35, shows that of the total of 22,547 Tokugawa hatamoto and gokenin, only 6,234 had fiefs or stipends of 100 koku and over. Craig, *Chōshū,* p. 75, quotes Murata Seifū on the household budget of a samurai of 100 koku to the effect that even this might well be insufficient.

24. See Sasaki, pp. 130–38. Sasaki is one of the few contemporary writers who specifically identifies the hirazamurai as the middle stratum in a three-part samurai class structure.

25. Blacker, *Japanese Enlightenment,* p. 2.

26. It is not easy to document the statements made here about social mobility. They derive principally from the study of a large number of individual biographies I consulted in the course of preparing the following articles: "Councillors of Samurai Origin in the Early Meiji Government, 1868–9"; "Political Groups in Tosa, 1858–68"; and "Politics and the Samurai Class in Satsuma, 1858–1868."

27. Hayashi, Part 2, p. 138.

28. Fukaya, p. 53.

29. On this whole question, see Smith, *Agrarian Origins,* especially pp. 166–79.

30. Jansen, *Sakamoto,* pp. 30–32; Seki, *Hansei kaikaku,* pp. 19–22. See also Jansen, "Tosa." On the subject of village government in general, see Befu, "Village."

31. Some examples are given in *Ishin-shi,* 1: 337–41. See also Honjō, *Social and Economic History,* pp. 202–10.

32. On this subject in general, see Sheldon, especially pp. 25–63, 144–49. See also Chap. 2 below.

33. Ono, pp. 155–57, cites the example of the Homma family of Sakata in northern Japan. The profits it derived from the rice trade were invested in land, until its holding at the time of the Restoration was estimated at no less than 100,000 koku. The head of the family had gōshi rank, granted for financial services, which meant that he was not supposed to engage in trade. The rule, however, was circumvented by allowing him to do so in the name of his dead father.

34. Webb, "Development," p. 177. The implications of this attitude for the relationship of Emperor and Shogun will be considered further in Chap. 6.

35. For a discussion of Bushidō, see Bellah, pp. 90–97.

36. Dore, p. 42.

37. *Ibid.,* p. 293. See also *ibid.,* pp. 84–89, 115–21; and McEwan, pp. 84–94, 132–44.

38. Dore, pp. 276–77, 303–4.

39. *Ibid.,* pp. 219–26.

40. *Ibid.,* p. 217.

41. The difficult question of the extent of literacy in Tokugawa Japan is discussed in *ibid.,* pp. 317–22.

42. Craig, "Science," pp. 147–48.

43. Bellah, pp. 157–60.

44. E. H. Norman, for example, has commented on the difficulty he had in finding an outspokenly antifeudal treatise; see his *Andō Shōeki,* 1: 3–10. In the end he had to be content with the work of an obscure 18th-century writer whose chief book no longer exists in complete form.

45. Most of the writers mentioned in this paragraph will be discussed later in appropriate chapters. A good idea of the range of their ideas, however, and of those of Tokugawa thinkers in general, can be gained from Tsunoda et al., Chaps. 16–18, 21–23.

46. There is an interesting discussion of the Neo-Confucian view of Tokugawa political structure in Harootunian, *Toward Restoration,* pp. 8–14.

47. Some Tokugawa discussions of the point are summarized in Asai, pp. 16–28.

CHAPTER II

1. On the development and nature of castle towns, see Hall, "Castle Town."

2. See Sheldon, pp. 25–63.

3. There is a detailed table of prices for the period down to 1825 in *Tokushi biyō,* pp. 743–73, and a less detailed one that includes the years down to 1866 in Borton, pp. 208–9. The most recent and convenient price series is in

Chihōshi kenkyū hikkei, pp. 157–59. There are a good many differences of detail between these various series, but the general pattern is the same.

4. McEwan, p. 40. For an early-18th-century view of samurai impoverishment generally, see *ibid.*, pp. 35–56. *Ishin-shi*, 1: 321–33, also gives a useful account of the subject.

5. *Segai Inoue Kō*, 1: 9–10. It must be said, however, that with hirazamurai rank and a kokudaka of 100 koku the family can hardly be called poor. On samurai poverty in Chōshū generally, see Naramoto, *Kinsei*, pp. 111–13.

6. Katsuda, *Ōkubo*, 1: 6–8. See also Hayashi, Part 2, pp. 127–29.

7. Tokutomi, *Kōshaku Matsukata*, 1: 59–64. This was presumably as much a search for wealth as an escape from poverty.

8. The subject is examined in some detail in Tsukahira, pp. 88–102. The best general discussion of domain finances in this context is Tsuchiya, *Hōken shakai*, pp. 4–51.

9. Craig, *Chōshū*, p. 39. The assessed value in this case is the *uchidaka*, or *jitsudaka*, that is, Chōshū's own figure for administrative use, not the figure reported to the Bakufu.

10. *Kagoshima-ken shi*, 2: 68–77. Again the total given is the jitsudaka.

11. Tsuchiya, *Hōken shakai*, pp. 53–63.

12. Matsuyoshi, pp. 41–47. The kamme was a unit of weight equal to 1,000 momme.

13. Tsukahira, pp. 96–102.

14. Craig, *Chōshū*, p. 42; Seki, *Hansei kaikaku*, pp. 2–10; Naramoto, *Kinsei hōken*, pp. 202–5.

15. The figures for Tosa and Satsuma are in *Hansei ichiran*, 1: 151–52. Others can be found in my article "Feudal Revenue in Japan," pp. 256–61, where I consider also the question of regional variations.

16. Beasley, "Feudal Revenue," pp. 261–65.

17. See, for example, the information on this point in the 1690–91 list printed in Kanai, pp. 60–74.

18. Ōe, pp. 15–20, gives a tax rate of under 40 per cent for Kumamoto in the 18th century. Naitō, pp. 292–96, gives 50–55 per cent as the rate for a village in Bitchū in the same period. Chambliss, pp. 47–56, estimates an average of 27–29 per cent for a village in Musashi for the period 1825–73. See also the examples given in Smith, "Land Tax." Smith examined tax returns for 11 villages in different parts of the country for most of the Tokugawa period and found that in all but three—which were higher—tax rates ranged between about 30 and 45 per cent.

19. Ōyama, pp. 300–328, gives an example of failure to do so on a Bakufu holding in Kyūshū at the end of the period.

20. *Kagoshima-ken shi*, 2: 87–90, 250–54.

21. Tsuchiya, *Hōken shakai*, pp. 113–23.

22. Matsuyoshi, pp. 114–47.

23. Tsukahira, pp. 84–85.
24. Tsuchiya, *Hōken shakai*, pp. 18–25, 123–62.
25. *Kagoshima-ken shi*, 2: 243–47, 250–54.
26. Naramoto, *Kinsei hōken*, pp. 110–11. See also Craig, *Chōshū*, pp. 38–42.
27. Tsuchiya, *Hōken shakai*, p. 41.
28. The most useful discussion of Bakufu finances is to be found in Horie Yasuzō, "San dai-kaikaku." See also Totman, *Politics*, p. 79.
29. I discuss this in my article "Feudal Revenue," especially pp. 257–65. See also Hall, *Government*, pp. 357–59.
30. Sheldon, p. 128.
31. Ōyama, pp. 350–74, which includes a detailed analysis of the types of contributor and the sums they provided.
32. Chambliss, pp. 56–57, 61.
33. For a general account of domain monopolies, see Horie Yasuzō, *Waga kuni*, pp. 16–104.
34. Matsuyoshi, pp. 224–78, gives a detailed description of the Tosa paper monopoly.
35. Tsuchiya, *Hōken shakai*, pp. 354–60. Of Satsuma's rice revenue, only about 10,000 koku was available for use in Edo, whereas by 1830 something like seven times this amount was coming from sales of sugar, wax, rape-seed, etc. *Ibid.*, pp. 26–33.
36. On this subject in general, see especially Smith, *Agrarian Origins*, pp. 157–79; also his "Japanese Village." Smith has more recently published a valuable case study of one of the period's agricultural innovators: "Ōkura Nagatsune and the Technologists."
37. For example, Shibusawa Eiichi's father, who was in the indigo trade, was able to subscribe heavily to goyōkin (this being an index of wealth), though his actual landholdings were less than 2 *chō*. Two chō would have yielded 20 to 30 koku, so that in terms of land he counts as a middle farmer, or not much above it. See Chambliss, p. 36.
38. Tsuchiya, *Ishin keizai-shi*, pp. 11–14. There is no good reason for accepting the actual figure, but it is important as representing an estimate by a shrewd and much-traveled observer.
39. Naitō, pp. 296–314, shows that in a cotton-growing village in Bitchū it is possible to identify both "rich" farmers (30 koku) and "poor" farmers (under 3 koku) by the end of the 18th century.
40. Examples are given in Smith, *Agrarian Origins*, pp. 180–87; and Naitō, pp. 314–30. See also Furushima, pp. 3–10, 21–27.
41. On Kumamoto and Tosa, see Ōe, pp. 27–32, and Jansen, *Sakamoto*, pp. 30–32; on Aizu, see Nagakura, pp. 107–17; and on Chōshū, see Seki, *Hansei kaikaku*, pp. 80–89, 110–19.
42. Tōyama, pp. 37–39. It will be necessary to revert to this question later in the discussion. See especially Chap. 6.

43. A summary of the frequency and geographical spread of the revolts, as well as the grievances they expressed, based on the work of Japanese historians, is most conveniently available in Borton, pp. 17–28, 39, 88n, 121n, 205–7. Much of the material cited on the subject here is taken from Borton's work. See also Tōyama, pp. 25–32.

44. For additional information on Ōshio, see Najita.

45. Borton, pp. 84–86; Craig, *Chōshū,* pp. 55–57; Naramoto, *Kinsei hōken,* pp. 114–16; Seki, *Hansei kaikaku,* pp. 89–101; and Tanaka Akira, pp. 31–38.

46. See Ono, pp. 39–61; Tsukahira, pp. 106–13, 119–23; and McEwan, pp. 57–74.

47. Ono, pp. 112–18, cites examples of limited experiments in Saga (Hizen), Kumamoto (Higo), and Yonezawa. It is also clear that in both Satsuma and Chōshū impoverished samurai were permitted to return for a time to the land. All these examples, however, were measures of samurai relief designed to meet the problems of insolvency for particular groups. None envisaged a wholesale dispersal of the population of the castle town.

48. Honjō, *Economic Theory,* pp. 101–2.

49. *Ibid.*, pp. 105–6. On other aspects of Yamagata's hostility to commerce, see *ibid.*, pp. 98–99, 205–6.

50. See, for example, the arguments of Kaiho Seiryō (1755–1817) cited in *ibid.*, pp. 108–10. The nationalist scholar Motoori Norinaga (1730–1801), though he condemned the abuses of unrestrained profit-making, recognized the importance of trade and saw the solution to peasant revolt not merely in suppression, but also in the removal of grievances. *Ibid.*, pp. 96–98, 103–5.

51. Tsukahira, p. 105.

52. McEwan, p. 31.

53. Keene, p. 189; rev. ed. (1969), p. 199.

54. *Ibid.*, p. 182; rev. ed. (1969), p. 193.

55. *Ibid.*, pp. 197–98; omitted from rev. ed. (1969).

56. See Harootunian, "Jinsei," pp. 87–94, where the point is made that the obvious contrast between orthodox doctrine and actual practice had much to do with making this a political issue. See also on this subject Dore, pp. 190–93, 198–213.

57. Tsunoda et al., p. 433.

58. Quoted in McEwan, p. 78.

59. Dore, p. 210.

60. The process by which the middle samurai, at least, found their way into the higher posts of the domain bureaucracy seems to have begun in some areas —Tosa and Kumamoto are examples—in the second half of the 18th century. See Fukushima Nariyuki, pp. 254–55; and Ōe, pp. 20–23. We shall have occasion to discuss the 19th-century situation, especially as it applies to Tosa, Satsuma, and Chōshū, in subsequent chapters.

61. Dore, p. 197.

62. Harootunian, "Jinsei," p. 113.
63. My account of Mizuno's reforms is based principally on Horie Yasuzō, "San dai-kaikaku," pp. 67–78; Honjō, "Tempō"; and Miyamoto, "Tempō."
64. Jansen, *Sakamoto*, pp. 43–46.
65. On the Hizen reforms, see Shibahara, pp. 28–75.
66. The Mito reforms are summarized—from a rather traditional historiographical viewpoint—in *Ishin-shi*, 1: 384–87. They are discussed in greater detail and with greater attention to their social background in Shibahara, pp. 133–64.
67. On the economic development of Chōshū, see Seki, *Hansei kaikaku*, pp. 24–54, 66–79; Craig, *Chōshū*, pp. 38–43, 62–67; and Tanaka Akira, pp. 31–38.
68. Murata's reforms are discussed in Craig, *Chōshū*, pp. 54–67; Seki, *Hansei kaikaku*, pp. 98–107; and Naramoto, *Kinsei hōken*, pp. 117–23.
69. The most detailed study of Zusho's reforms is to be found in Tsuchiya, *Hōken shakai*, pp. 389–445. See also Tōyama, pp. 35–36; and Sakata, *Meiji ishin shi* (1960), pp. 58–61.
70. On the Satsuma sugar trade, see Tsuchiya, *Hōken shakai*, pp. 446–80; and Craig, *Chōshū*, pp. 69–72.
71. See, for example, Tōyama, pp. 25–44; and Craig, *Chōshū*, pp. 72–73, 353–54, 360.
72. See Tōyama, p. 35; Sakata, *Meiji ishin shi* (1960), pp. 61–63; and Umetani, pp. 310–17.
73. Tanaka Sōgorō, *Kindai Nihon*, pp. 80–82; *Kagoshima-ken shi*, 2: 278.
74. Craig, *Chōshū*, pp. 110–11.
75. Shibahara, pp. 133–34.
76. *Ibid.*, pp. 42–46.
77. Tōyama, pp. 42–43; *Ishin-shi*, 1: 145–46.
78. *Kagoshima-ken shi*, 2: 272–79; Katsuda, *Ōkubo*, 1: 29–33, 43–47; Sakai, pp. 224–32.
79. Chōshū politics after 1840 are discussed in some detail in Craig, *Chōshū*, pp. 78–83, 94–98; Naramoto, *Kinsei hōken*, pp. 123–30; Seki, *Hansei kaikaku*, pp. 119–27; and Umetani, pp. 318–22.
80. See variously Horie Hideichi; Seki, *Hansei kaikaku*; Shibahara; and Tōyama.
81. Summarizing Tanaka Akira, pp. 27–53.

CHAPTER III

1. Tsunoda et al., p. 602. On the seclusion policy in general, see the useful brief discussion in Oka, pp. 14–17.
2. Tsunoda et al., p. 544.
3. Earl, p. 46.
4. Tsunoda et al., p. 595.
5. For detailed accounts of Russian, British, and American activities insofar

as they affected Japan in the period before 1853, see Lensen; Beasley, *Great Britain*; and Sakamaki.

6. On Rangaku, see in particular two recent works: a special issue of *Monumenta Nipponica* (vol. 19, no. 3-4 [1964]), comprising articles on different aspects of the subject by Japanese scholars; and G. K. Goodman, *The Dutch Impact on Japan*. Goodman, p. 122, quotes one of the most famous Rangakusha, Sugita Gempaku, as follows: "Until now [1783] China was considered the most civilised country. Holland, however, is superior because next to [in addition to] literature it possesses science."

7. The best study of these two men is Keene, *Japanese Discovery*. On Honda, see also Tsunoda et al., pp. 553–61.

8. Keene, p. 196; omitted in rev. ed. (1969).

9. On Satō, see Tsunoda et al., pp. 561–78; Tsuchiya, "Bakumatsu shishi," pp. 161–62; and Inobe, "Mito," pp. 134–36.

10. Tsunoda et al., p. 577.

11. On Sakuma, see *ibid.*, pp. 603–16; Earl, pp. 149–53; and Inobe, "Sakuma Shōzan." Two valuable recent studies are Harootunian, *Toward Restoration*, pp. 136–83; and Chang, pp. 99–186.

12. Sansom, p. 258.

13. Tsunoda et al., p. 610.

14. *Ibid.*, p. 611.

15. Chang, pp. 141–44.

16. *Ibid.*, pp. 172–73, quoting a letter of early 1858.

17. *Ibid.*, p. 178.

18. The Mito scholars have been extensively studied. In English, see especially Tsunoda et al., pp. 592–603; Earl, pp. 86–106; and Harootunian, *Toward Restoration*, pp. 47–128.

19. Tsunoda et al., p. 601.

20. *Ibid.*, pp. 593–94.

21. Quoted in Earl, pp. 95–96. The Mito concept of loyalism is also discussed in Webb, *Japanese*, pp. 182–95. The subject of loyalism is one to which we will return later; see Chap. 6.

22. On Tōko's view of Christianity, see Chang, pp. 54–59.

23. Van Gulick provides a valuable introductory discussion of the outlook of Japanese Confucian scholars generally. See also Blacker, *Japanese Enlightenment*, pp. 17–19.

24. Van Gulick, p. 488.

25. *Ibid.*, p. 534.

26. On his work, see Blacker, "Ōhashi"; Harootunian, *Toward Restoration*, pp. 258–78; and Tsuchiya, "Bakumatsu shishi," pp. 162–63.

27. Blacker, "Ōhashi," p. 165. There are close parallels with the arguments that conservative scholars in China advanced against the Treaty of Tientsin in 1858. See Hsü, pp. 57–66, 111–12.

28. Hawks, 1: 256. The text of the letter is also in Beasley, *Select Documents*, pp. 99–101.

29. Hawks, 1: 238.

30. *Ibid.*, pp. 258–59.

31. Satow, *Japan 1853–1864*, p. 4.

32. Sakai, pp. 214–19.

33. Inobe, pp. 348–65. See also Kanno, pp. 382–89.

34. Only an undated summary of Hotta's views at this time is extant. It is printed in *BGKM*, 3: 591–92. This work contains the Japanese texts of all the memorials concerning the negotiations of 1853–58 translated in Beasley, *Select Documents* (which are referred to below in translation only).

35. Beasley, *Select Documents*, p. 117.

36. *Ibid.*, p. 118.

37. *BGKM*, 1: 575. The whole text of Kuroda's memorial, which was dated Aug. 21, 1853, is there given (pp. 566–78).

38. His memorial is translated in Beasley, *Select Documents*, pp. 112–14. For a discussion of Shimazu's attitudes, see Chap. 5, pp. 124–27.

39. Hirao, *Yamauchi*, pp. 20–21.

40. The text is in *BGKM*, 1: 509–22. I have translated much of it (omitting the long section dealing with detailed military proposals) in *Select Documents*, pp. 102–7.

41. Beasley, *Select Documents*, p. 103. Cf. the views of Aizawa Seishisai, pp. 83–84, above.

42. Date Yoshikuni of Sendai (625,000 koku) condemned trade in terms very reminiscent of Nariaki's own, describing it as an exchange of Japan's real wealth for "mere foreign curiosities," which made "the foreigner's profit our country's loss" (*BGKM*, 1: 639–42). His views were echoed by other influential lords, notably Mōri Yoshichika of Chōshū (369,000 koku) and Nabeshima Naomasa of Hizen (357,000 koku), whose memorials appear in *ibid.*, 2: 260–62 and 104–6, respectively.

43. Beasley, *Select Documents*, pp. 114–17, at p. 115. Shungaku is also known as Keiei (Yoshinaga).

44. *BGKM*, 1: 686–724, at p. 722.

45. See text in Beasley, *Select Documents*, pp. 107–12.

46. The text is in *Sakumu kiji*, 1: 83–84. See also Chang, pp. 82–86.

47. Tabohashi, *Kindai Nihon*, pp. 506–7. On the relations between Abe and Tokugawa Nariaki in the years prior to this, see Totman, "Political Reconciliation."

48. The decree was issued on Oct. 17, 1853. See Akao, 2: 780.

49. The text is in *BGKM*, 3: 221.

50. Letter of Feb. 12, 1854, in *Sakumu kiji*, 1: 105–6.

51. Hawks, 1: 345.

52. English texts of the treaty can be found in *ibid.*, pp. 377–79; and Beasley,

Select Documents, pp. 119–22. Japanese and Chinese texts are to be found in *BGKM*, 5: 449–60.

53. Hawks, 1: 388.

54. *Ibid.*, p. 359. This appears as a comment on the interest aroused by the official presents Perry took to Japan, which included a small steam locomotive, a telegraph, clocks, and agricultural implements.

55. Official report of the Japanese negotiators, in Beasley, *Select Documents*, pp. 122–27, at p. 123.

56. *Ishin-shi*, 1: 609–10. On May 6 Abe actually offered to resign, partly on this account, but his resignation was not accepted. *Ibid.*, 2: 107–8.

57. Inobe, "Sakuma Shōzan," 1: 474–79, 484–86.

58. In the context of a study of Japanese politics, which is our principal concern, the story of the negotiation of these two treaties adds little that is of value. It is given in some detail in Lensen, pp. 311ff; and Beasley, *Great Britain*, pp. 113ff.

CHAPTER IV

1. For an account of Hotta's policies in Sakura, see Kimura and Sugimoto, pp. 196–205, 262–79.

2. They are usefully discussed in Sakata, *Meiji ishin shi* (1960), pp. 88–95.

3. For his two letters, dated Aug. 10 and Aug. 23, 1856, see *Ishin-shi*, 2: 192, 232–33. On the Dutch negotiations in general, see *ibid.*, pp. 192–98, 232–49.

4. Rōjū circular of March 19, 1857, in Beasley, *Select Documents*, pp. 130–31.

5. Hotta memorandum of March–April 1857, in *ibid.*, pp. 131–34, at p. 133.

6. *Ibid.*, pp. 134–36, at p. 136.

7. *Ibid.*, pp. 137–39, at p. 138.

8. *Ibid.*, pp. 139–44.

9. The various memoranda and drafts of instructions of Sept.–Oct. 1857 are to be found in *BGKM*, 17: 466–502.

10. Letter of Oct. 14, 1857, in Beasley, *Select Documents*, pp. 146–49, at p. 148.

11. Harris's negotiations are fairly fully described in his journal. The diary of his secretary, Hendrik Heusken, has also been published, though it adds little to the story. A detailed account in Japanese, making use of Bakufu documents, is to be found in *Ishin-shi*, 2: 251–72.

12. Documents on the Bakufu discussions of this question in Aug. 1857 are given in *BGKM*, 16: 437–40, 497–501, 506–11, 653–61.

13. Beasley, *Select Documents*, pp. 163–64. There are two accounts of what Harris said on this occasion, one in Harris, pp. 485–86, the other, from which this quotation is taken, a translation of a Japanese account, printed in *Select Documents*, pp. 159–65. The two do not disagree in substance, though the latter is more threatening in its tone, as well as more detailed.

14. Harris, pp. 485–86.

15. Beasley, *Select Documents*, pp. 165–68, at p. 167.
16. Harris, p. 490.
17. *Ibid.*, p. 505. Harris refers to the entries for Jan. 25 to Feb. 23 (*ibid.*, pp. 505–53), in which his account of the talks is given, though the comment itself probably derives from his previous experiences at Shimoda. His sentiments would certainly have been echoed by many British consuls on the China coast as a comment on the practices of Chinese officials. Indeed, they are almost clichés of Far Eastern diplomacy at this time.
18. The text of the treaty, as signed on July 29, 1858, is given in Beasley, *Select Documents*, pp. 183–89. The Japanese text is in *BGKM*, pp. 474–84.
19. See, for example, two memorials, dated c. Dec. 19 and Dec. 25, 1857, in *BGKM*, 18: 249–51, 345–46, recording the views of a large body of officials who felt the treaty would have to be signed—but only because there was no alternative.
20. Quoted in Beasley, *Select Documents*, pp. 170–74, at p. 171.
21. *BGKM*, 18: 399–401. For his attitude in 1853, see note 42 to Chap. 3, p. 451, above.
22. Beasley, *Select Documents*, pp. 176–79.
23. *BGKM*, 18: 886–92. The parallel with the arguments used by the Bakufu to try to secure British consent to postponing the opening of further ports in 1861–62 is very close. See the papers in Beasley, *Select Documents*, pp. 208ff; and also Chap. 7, above, pp. 175–77.
24. *BGKM*, 18: 360–68. Nariaki's proposal is translated in part in Beasley, *Select Documents*, pp. 168–69.
25. Beasley, *Select Documents*, pp. 174–76, at p. 176.
26. *Ibid.*, pp. 179–80, at p. 180.
27. *BGKM*, 18: 884–86.
28. *Ibid.*, pp. 750–52 and 415–19, respectively. Here again, both were more forthright now than in 1853, when Tachibana had advocated continued seclusion (*ibid.*, 2: 264–66) and Shimazu had urged postponement of treaty relations until defense preparations were complete.
29. *Ibid.*, 18: App., pp. 4–7. Kuroda (who was Shimazu Nariakira's brother) had expressed similar views in 1853–54.
30. Harris, p. 543.
31. *Ibid.*, p. 539. The Bakufu interpreter, Moriyama, commented that if all else failed the Court could always be bribed (Heusken, p. 191).
32. A detailed account of the subsequent discussions with the Court is given in *Ishin-shi*, 2: 320–46. See also Inobe, "Ansei jōyaku"; and Chap. 5, below.
33. Emperor Kōmei to Kampaku, March 11, 1858, in *BGKM*, 19: App., pp. 4–7.
34. Beasley, *Select Documents*, pp. 180–81, at p. 181.
35. *Ibid.*, pp. 181–83, at p. 183, quoting from the journal of Ii's secretary, which gives an account of the council meeting and related discussions.

CHAPTER V

1. On this subject, see especially Jansen, *Sakamoto*, pp. 82–89. See also Dore, *passim*.

2. Inobe, "Sakuma Shōzan," 1: 480–84; 2: 609–17.

3. Earl, p. 207.

4. *Iwakura Kō jikki*, 1: 349.

5. Satow, *Japan 1853–1864*, p. 14.

6. Letter of Hirano Kuniomi, May 6, 1862, in *Junnan rokkō*, 1: 346–49.

7. Memorial by Takechi Zuizan, Sept.–Oct. 1862, in *Takechi Zuizan*, 1: 119–24.

8. Oliphant, 2: 245–46.

9. Dore, p. 171.

10. The spread of these studies in the domains is described in Goodman, pp. 158–81. See also Dore, pp. 161ff.

11. Kanai, pp. 120–21.

12. Oliphant, 2: 208.

13. On Takashima, see Sansom, pp. 248–53. There is a recent biography in Japanese: Arima Seiho, *Takashima*.

14. See *Kagoshima-ken shi*, 2: 265–72; and 3: 84–92. See also Tanaka Sōgorō, *Kindai Nihon*, pp. 62–69.

15. Numata, pp. 83–86.

16. Tsunoda et al., p. 625. However, foreign experts were nevertheless on board in case of need.

17. A brief account is given in Smith, *Political Change*, pp. 1–11. More detailed studies in Japanese include the following: on the Bakufu, *Ishin-shi*, 2: 125–52; on the domains generally, *ibid.*, pp. 152–74. As to individual domains: on Satsuma, *Kagoshima-ken shi*, 2: 48–67; on Hizen, Egashira; on Chōshū, Horie Yasuzō, "Yamaguchi-han"; and on Mito, Miyamoto, "Mito-han."

18. For information on Nariakira's ideas—outside the matters on which he wrote specific memorials—we are chiefly indebted to a collection of his "conversations" compiled by one of his retainers, Ichiki Shirō, and first published in 1884. This is most readily available as *Shimazu Nariakira genkōroku*. The passages relevant to his views on foreign relations, as discussed here, are at pp. 100–104, 115–28 in the 1944 edition.

19. *Ibid.*, pp. 159–63, 166–67, 170–71, 180. See also *Kagoshima-ken shi*, 3: 97–99, for his memorial on education, dated Nov. 23, 1857.

20. *Kagoshima-ken shi*, 3: 30–32.

21. *Shimazu Nariakira*, pp. 191–93, 201–2.

22. Draft memorial of the summer of 1857, *Kagoshima-ken shi*, 3: 247.

23. Tokugawa Nariaki's views are usefully discussed in Tōyama, pp. 68, 76–79; Sakata, *Meiji ishin shi* (1960), pp. 37–47; and Shibahara, pp. 133–48. Since Nariaki relied heavily on Fujita Tōko, who drafted many of his memorials, it

is also useful to consult the discussion of Tōko's ideas in Harootunian, *Toward Restoration*, pp. 119–28.

24. In *Shinron*; see Tsunoda et al., p. 601.

25. Tōyama, p. 76. Italics mine.

26. *Ibid.*, p. 78.

27. Tanaka Akira, pp. 56–57.

28. This is the argument of Fujita Yūkoku. See Harootunian, *Toward Restoration*, pp. 58–85.

29. Sakata, *Meiji ishin shi* (1960), p. 71, notes that they considered (and rejected) other possible candidates for membership. He cites a correspondence between Tokugawa Nariaki and Date Muneki about the possibility of including Mōri Yoshichika of Chōshū.

30. Beasley, *Select Documents*, p. 180.

31. George M. Wilson, pp. 244–46.

32. Matsudaira Shungaku to Hotta Masayoshi, Dec. 2, 1857, in *Sakumu kiji*, 2: 201–6.

33. Shimonaka, 1: 73–77. The most recent account of Matsudaira Shungaku's part in the affair is to be found in Kawabata, pp. 94–114. See also George M. Wilson, pp. 250–58. For a general account of the succession question and its politics, see *Ishin-shi*, 2: 380–431.

34. See *Kagoshima-ken shi*, 3: 161–65, for letters by Nariakira on this subject. On Shungaku, see *Ishin-shi*, 2: 367–73.

35. On the activities of Ii and Nagano, see Yoshida Tsunekichi, pp. 220–24.

36. Sakata, *Meiji ishin shi* (1960), pp. 97–98. See also Inobe, "Ansei jōyaku," pp. 482–85.

37. Political events between Hotta's departure from Kyōto on May 17, 1858, and the appointment of Ii Naosuke as Tairō on June 4 are discussed in Yoshida Tsunekichi, pp. 233–43. It must be noted, however, that the intrigues were by their nature secret and the details concerning them are still not entirely clear.

38. On the "Ansei purge," see *Ishin-shi*, 2: 498–500, 608–62.

39. Yoshida Tsunekichi, p. 280.

40. Emperor Kōmei to Kujō Naotada, Dec. 13, 1858, in *BGKM*, 21: 702–4.

41. Beasley, *Select Documents*, pp. 189–93.

42. *Ibid.*, pp. 193–94.

CHAPTER VI

1. See Jansen, *Sakamoto*, pp. 98–102, where this point is made with special reference to Tosa.

2. These problems of interpretation are set out more fully in the Introduction, and to some extent in Chap. 2, where bibliographical references are given.

3. The topic is discussed at some length in Earl, pp. 16–65; and Webb, *Japanese*, pp. 168–73, 248–52.

4. Hall, *Government*, p. 403.

5. *Ibid.*, p. 351.
6. See Earl, pp. 67–81; Tsunoda et al., pp. 506–51; and Satow, "Revival."
7. Satow, "Revival," p. 13.
8. In *Naobi no mitama,* written in 1771. See Earl, p. 75.
9. On the Mito school and loyalism, see Webb, *Japanese,* pp. 182–95, 213–16; Earl, pp. 94–106; and Harootunian, *Toward Restoration,* pp. 47–128.
10. Webb, "Development," p. 177. Cf. Tokugawa Nariaki's views, above, pp. 127–28.
11. Tsunoda et al., p. 600.
12. From *Shinron.* See Earl, p. 95. See also Asai, pp. 57–60; and Shibahara, pp. 127–28.
13. See the account of Rai Sanyō's *Nihon gaishi* by Carmen Blacker, in Beasley and Pulleyblank, pp. 259–63. The book was much more widely read than the monumental history *Dai Nihonshi* (*ibid.*, pp. 245–53 *passim*) produced by Mito scholars in the 17th and 18th centuries, which had a similar loyalist theme.
14. There have been a good many studies of Yoshida Shōin (also known as Yoshida Torajirō), including an essay by R. L. Stevenson. For the account given here I have relied largely on Earl, pp. 109–210; and Craig, *Chōshū,* pp. 156–64. Harootunian, *Toward Restoration,* pp. 184–245, is a more recent and in many ways more penetrating study of his thought than the cited works.
15. Hawks, 1: 421.
16. Earl, p. 147. The influence of Sakuma is very apparent in Shōin's attitudes at this time. At the end of 1853 he had described Sakuma in a letter as "the hero of the present day; he is the one man of all in the capital" (*ibid.*, pp. 147–49).
17. *Ibid.*, p. 173.
18. *Ibid.*, p. 203, quoting a letter of Sept. 16, 1856.
19. *Ibid.*, p. 209.
20. Tsunoda et al., p. 622.
21. Craig, *Chōshū,* pp. 161–62.
22. Harootunian, *Toward Restoration,* p. 193, describes Shōin as "a nihilist, who saw in action and destruction an antidote to compromise and accommodation." In other words, Shōin was shocked by the treaties into rejecting the values of a world that had failed him, substituting for them not alternative values, but action itself.
23. *Iwakura Kō jikki,* 1: 349. The text of the memorial and the letter accompanying it are given at pp. 342–50.
24. On this point the most useful discussion, though brief, is in Asai, pp. 60–64. On shishi political ideas in general, see Inobe, "Bakumatsu shishi"; and Harootunian, *Toward Restoration,* pp. 246–320.
25. Asai, pp. 61–62. The pre-Taika titles to which Maki referred (e.g. *kuni no miyatsuko*) are not usually regarded as feudal by modern scholars, though they might be so described in Chinese terms.
26. Tanaka Sōgorō, *Meiji ishin,* pp. 9–19.

27. Memorial of May 6, 1862, in *Junnan rokkō,* 1: 346–49.
28. Tanaka Akira, pp. 90–91.
29. Asai, pp. 63–64. There is a summary of the memorial in Suematsu, *Bōchō,* 3: 329–30. It is interesting to compare these proposals (and also those of Takechi Zuizan, outlined in the following pages) with Shimazu Nariakira's views on the subject. See Chap. 5, pp. 126–27, above.
30. The text is in *Takechi Zuizan,* 1: 119–24. A number of apparently earlier drafts are also included at pp. 109–19.
31. Harootunian, *Toward Restoration,* p. 318.
32. Jansen, *Sakamoto,* p. 98.
33. *Ibid.,* p. 189.
34. Iwata, p. 39.
35. *Kagoshima-ken shi,* 3: 267–71.
36. *Ibid.,* pp. 275–77.
37. Saigō to Ōkubo, Feb. 4, 1859, in *Dai Saigō zenshū,* 1: 137–46, observing that reckless courage, though admirable in itself, reflected "an inability to distinguish the great from the small." From this Saigō argued that Satsuma must act only in cooperation with other great domains, notably Mito, Echizen, Chōshū, Tosa, and Owari, with whose representatives there must be prior consultation.
38. The affair is described in great detail in Katsuda, *Ōkubo,* 1: 117–51.
39. For further details of the analysis, as well as information on materials on which it is based, see Beasley, "Politics," pp. 50–55. The terminology of samurai class divisions generally is discussed in Chapt. 1.
40. On Tosa politics and the social background thereof, see the following writings of Jansen: "Tosa During the Last Century of Tokugawa Rule"; *Sakamoto Ryōma,* pp. 30–40, 104–23; and "Takechi Zuizan and the Tosa Loyalist Party."
41. This subject is briefly discussed in Jansen, "Takechi Zuizan," pp. 200–202. See also his *Sakamoto,* pp. 27–36, where references are given to the extensive Japanese writings on the subject.
42. Jansen, "Tosa," p. 341.
43. A translation of the pledge the members signed is given in Jansen, *Sakamoto,* pp. 108–9.
44. Fortunately, the background of the Tosa loyalists is very well documented, making it possible to arrive at conclusions more precise than those stated with respect to Satsuma, above. See my article "Political Groups in Tosa."
45. In view of the relative completeness of Tosa records, it is not likely that any of the 11 given as "not known" were in fact hirazamurai.
46. Sakamoto's background is discussed in Jansen, *Sakamoto,* pp. 77–86. Since about 10 per cent of the Tosa gōshi lived in or near the castle town of Kōchi, one has to be wary of putting too much emphasis on their "rural" label.
47. Biographical information about these men is to be found principally in the following collections of biographical notes about Restoration heroes and

martyrs (the first three concern men from all parts of the country, the fourth has particular reference to Tosa): *Kinnō resshi den*; *Zōi shoken den*; *Junnan rokkō*; and *Zoku Tosa ijin den*. More easily accessible, but less complete, is Naramoto, *Meiji ishin jimbutsu*.

48. Craig, *Chōshū*, pp. 110–11, points out that the leaders of *all* parties in Chōshū since the Tempō reforms had been hirazamurai of quite modest means; Murata Seifū, 91 koku; Sufu Masanosuke, 68 koku; Tsuboi Kuemon, 100 koku; Mukunashi Tōta, 46 koku.

49. He had to work through intermediaries who were in Hisamitsu's confidence for some time before he could even secure an audience with Hisamitsu himself. See *Kagoshima-ken shi*, 3: 306–8; and Katsuda, *Ōkubo*, 1: 177–81.

50. One might note in passing that differences in the legality of political action do not seem to have been related to different degrees of responsibility within the family, though one might have expected, given the nature of the Japanese family system, heads of households to have been more reluctant to put *family* interests at risk by engaging in what were clearly illegal acts. Of the 121 men from Tosa and Satsuma about whom information is given in Table 1 (p. 158), 40 are recorded as having been heads of families or eldest sons (including heirs by adoption) and 37 as having been younger sons; the family status of the remaining 44 is unknown. There is no significant difference in this respect between "politicians" and "activists." In fact, ignoring those in the "not known" category, more than half of the men in the Saigō-Ōkubo party were younger sons, whereas there were more heads of families and eldest sons in each of the other three groups.

51. This is to follow the list given by Umetani, especially the table on p. 325. See also Craig, "Kido Kōin," pp. 268–90.

52. There is a useful survey in Haga, pp. 57–65.

53. The rising is described in detail in Hara. The biographical information given here is derived chiefly from *Kinnō resshi den*; *Junnan rokkō*; and Naramoto, *Meiji ishin jimbutsu*.

54. This is to follow *Junnan rokkō*, 1: 333–37. Haga, pp. 58–61, discussing the leaders of the revolt, describes Mizugōri as a "rich farmer" holding land assessed at 300 koku.

55. Haga, pp. 49–52, 55–57, 138–39. Furuhashi's reputation has something of an ex post facto look about it.

56. Naitō, pp. 338–40.

57. Haga, pp. 132–38; Tanaka Akira, pp. 91–92.

58. *Zoku Tosa ijin*, pp. 61–65.

CHAPTER VII

1. A contemporary commented that the Japan trade, in comparison with that of China, "wore something of the air of a comic opera, or as if children were playing at being merchants" (Michie, 2:27). Foreign grievances are set

out in some detail in Fox, pp. 45–87. The best account of Japan's foreign trade in this period is to be found in Ishii Takashi, *Bakumatsu bōeki*; see especially pp. 325–29 on the subject of Bakufu restrictions on trade.

2. The plan is set out in *Ishin-shi*, 2: 710–14.

3. Beasley, *Select Documents*, pp. 198–200, at p. 198.

4. Rōjū to Court, undated, submitted in Kyōto on Sept. 14, 1860; *ibid.*, pp. 200–204, at p. 202.

5. *Ibid.*, p. 203. A later memorandum made it clear that force would be used only if persuasion failed. See Shoshidai to Kampaku, c. Jan. 8, 1861, *ibid.*, pp. 206–8.

6. F.O. 46/21, Alcock to Russell, confidential, no. 23, Yedo, March 17, 1862. The negotiations, which are treated very summarily here, can be studied in greater detail in Ishii Takashi, *Zotei Meiji ishin*, pp. 55–138; Fox, pp. 87–96; and Beasley, *Select Documents*, pp. 208–21.

7. Memorial by Nagai Uta, dated 1861, 5th month [June 8–July 7], in *Iwakura Kō jikki*, 1: 526–34, at pp. 533–34. On Nagai's policies in general, see Craig, *Chōshū*, pp. 168–72.

8. My account of Satsuma politics is based largely on the very detailed information in *Kagoshima-ken shi*, vol. 3; Katsuda, *Ōkubo*, vol. 1; Shimonaka, vol. 1; and *Shimazu Hisamitsu*, vols. 1 and 2. Kaeda, *Ishin zengo jitsu rekishi den*, vol. 4, is also useful.

9. The text, dated Jan. 1862, is printed in *Shimazu Hisamitsu*, 1: 18B–22B.

10. The proposals are listed in *ibid.*, pp. 38A–39B.

11. The text is in *ibid.*, 2: 35A–38A; also in Shibusawa, *Tokugawa Keiki*, 5: 268–73.

12. Satow, *Japan 1853–1864*, pp. 61–62. On the changes in sankin-kōtai, see Tsukahira, pp. 132–37.

13. Memorial of Oct. 14, 1862, in *Shimazu Hisamitsu*, 2: 50A–56B.

14. Hirano's memorial of May 6, 1862, submitted to the Imperial Court through Ōhara Shigenori, in *Junnan rokkō*, 1: 346–49.

15. Imperial message to Hisamitsu, May 23, 1862, in Katsuda, *Ōkubo*, 1: 267–68.

16. On Chōshū politics at this time, see principally Craig, *Chōshū*, pp. 172–92. See also Umetani, pp. 322–26.

17. On Tosa, see principally Jansen, *Sakamoto*, pp. 72–77, 104–23, 130–34. There are useful accounts of Yoshida Tōyō's reforms in Fukushima Nariyuki, pp. 255–71; and Hirao, *Yoshida*, pp. 110–52.

18. Memorial of Oct. 11, 1861, in *Yoshida Tōyō ikō*, pp. 268–70.

19. Memorial of Oct. 14, 1862, in *Shimazu Hisamitsu*, 2: 50A–56B.

20. It is summarized in Suematsu, *Bōchō*, 3: 329–30.

21. *Takechi Zuizan*, 1: 119–24.

22. Letter of Dec. 2, 1862, quoted in *Ishin-shi*, 3: 284. For Sanjō's official instructions, dated the previous day, see *ibid.*, p. 282. They imply that any action

decided on as a result of the mission would be a matter for Bakufu consultation with the feudal lords, which suggests that there was still resistance at the Court to the more radical ideas of the shishi.

23. Memorial of Nov. 8, 1862, in Beasley, *Select Documents*, pp. 225–27.

24. Memorial of Dec. 4, 1862, *ibid.*, pp. 227–34.

25. Statement of May 1, 1863, summarized in *Shimazu Hisamitsu*, 3: 7A–7B.

26. This was clear from the orders Keiki sent to Edo: Keiki to Rōjū, June 12, 1863, in Beasley, *Select Documents*, pp. 246–48.

27. Chōshū note to Bakufu, July 20, 1863, in *Kawakatsu-ke monjo*, pp. 278–81. A Bakufu minute on the document stated that the explanation was unacceptable: Chōshū had acted knowingly in contravention of Bakufu orders and should be punished.

CHAPTER VIII

1. Bakufu memorandum of early April 1863, in Beasley, *Select Documents*, pp. 234–36.

2. Memorial of early May 1863, *ibid.*, pp. 243–46.

3. Bakufu memorial of June 21, 1863, *ibid.*, pp. 248–49. Hitotsubashi Keiki, in a letter to the Kampaku on July 9, recounted his own experience in trying to get a commitment to expulsion from the Edo officials at this time: "They answered that the Bakufu could not accept the imperial orders, for they did not think it in the best interests of the country to expel the foreigners" (*ibid.*, p. 252).

4. Neale to Bakufu, June 24, 1863, encl. in Neale to Russell, same date, "Correspondence Respecting Affairs in Japan (No. 1)," in Great Britain, House of Commons, *Parliamentary Papers 1864*, 66: 73–75.

5. Russell to Neale, Dec. 24, 1862, *ibid.*, pp. 179–80. There is a detailed account of the Namamugi indemnity affair in Fox, pp. 97–116.

6. Neale to Bakufu, April 6, 1863, in Beasley, *Select Documents*, p. 237.

7. Ogasawara's explanation of what took place is given in his memorandum of July 27, 1863, *ibid.*, pp. 254–56.

8. *Shimazu Hisamitsu*, 3: 65B–71B.

9. *Ibid.*, pp. 71B–77A.

10. *Ibid.*, at p. 74A.

11. *Ishin-shi*, 3: 648, cites a Court pronouncement of Oct. 26, 1863, approving the decision but stating that this was the minimum Kyōto would accept.

12. Ikeda's memorial of Jan. 19, 1864, which was in effect a draft of instructions for the mission, in Beasley, *Select Documents*, pp. 260–63.

13. Emperor to Shogun, Feb. 28, 1864, *ibid.*, pp. 263–64.

14. Emperor to Shogun, March 5, 1864, *ibid.*, pp. 264–66.

15. *Ishin-shi*, 3: 683. In my view, the whole trend of Court pronouncements at this time suggests an attempt by the Emperor's senior ministers to find some way of healing the rift between the Bakufu and Satsuma, rather than a Satsuma dominance.

16. Tōyama, p. 134. See also Sakata, *Meiji ishin shi* (1960), pp. 160–62, citing a discussion between Hisamitsu and Matsudaira Shungaku on Nov. 29, 1863.

17. According to Hitotsubashi Keiki's own later account of the dispute, this was the argument being urged on him by the Rōjū (Shibusawa, *Tokugawa Keiki*, 6: 46–50).

18. Shogun to Emperor, March 21, 1864, in Beasley, *Select Documents*, pp. 266–67.

19. There is a colorful, if one-sided, account of these events in a letter by one of Keiki's retainers, Hara Tadanari, which I have translated in part in *Select Documents*, pp. 268–72. It needs to be compared with the version in Date Muneki's diary, *Date Muneki zaikyō nikki*, pp. 337–42.

20. It is printed *in extenso* in Fox, pp. 133–34.

21. There are accounts of the discussions Itō and Inoue had with domain officials between July 27 and July 30 in their respective biographies: *Itō Hirobumi den*, 1: 125–29; and *Segai Inoue Kō*, 1: 116–19. There is no direct reference to delivery of the memorandum in these accounts. Satow, Alcock's interpreter, reports only that the memorandum was translated into Japanese and taken by the two men when they landed in Chōshū (*Diplomat*, p. 97).

22. Satow, *Diplomat*, p. 99.

23. The text of the agreement is printed in Beasley, *Select Documents*, pp. 273–74. On the mission in general, see Burks.

24. Ikeda et al. to Bakufu, c. Aug. 18, 1864, in Beasley, *Select Documents*, pp. 274–82, at pp. 277–78.

25. Minutes of meeting between foreign envoys and Bakufu officials, Sept. 18, 1864, *ibid.*, pp. 282–88.

26. The text of the convention is printed in *ibid.*, pp. 288–89.

27. Alcock to Russell, Nov. 19, 1864, in *Parliamentary Papers 1865*, 57: 696–702.

28. For information on the connections between the two men, as well as the incident itself, see Jansen, *Sakamoto*, pp. 154–84.

29. Many of the ideas incorporated in the later versions of fukoku-kyōhei were worked out by Yokoi Shōnan, a Kumamoto samurai who for some time served Shungaku as an adviser in Echizen. His views are fully discussed in Harootunian, *Toward Restoration*, pp. 325–79.

30. In addition to the report on his mission (Beasley, *Select Documents*, pp. 274–82), Ikeda wrote a series of memorials setting out these proposals in detail. For the texts, see *Zoku saimu kiji*, 3: 199–217.

31. On Oguri, see Jansen, *Sakamoto*, pp. 181–82; also Chap. 10, pp. 263–65, above.

32. Naramoto, *Kinsei hōken*, p. 214, quotes a letter from Takasugi to Yoshida Shōin in 1858, emphasizing that his opposition to the treaties arose from his fear of their practical consequences for Japan, not from a preference for seclusion.

33. Quoted in Haga, p. 102, in the course of an account of Takasugi's experiences (*ibid.*, pp. 97–108).

34. *Itō Hirobumi den,* 1: 84–97; *Segai Inoue Kō,* 1: 82–93.

35. Letter of Sept. 23, 1865, in *Ōkubo Toshimichi monjo,* 1: 298.

36. Letter to Yamada Uemon, Oct. 16, 1865, in *Kido Kōin monjo,* 2: 108.

37. The letter is summarized and in part translated in Jansen, *Sakamoto,* pp. 208–11.

CHAPTER IX

1. Maki's proposals are stated at length in Tanaka Sōgorō, *Meiji ishin,* pp. 9–19.

2. The events of this period are usefully summarized in Craig, *Chōshū,* pp. 204–7.

3. *Shimazu Hisamitsu Kō,* vol. 3, includes the texts of several apparently panic-stricken appeals for Satsuma help against the extremists from Prince Asahiko and Konoe Tadahiro. These were accompanied by personal letters from the Emperor to very much the same effect. See also Sakata, *Meiji ishin shi* (1960), pp. 152–55; Tōyama, pp. 116–19; and Katsuda, *Ōkubo,* 1: 469–76.

4. On the anti-rōnin measures, see Hirao, "Bakumatsu," especially pp. 542–46.

5. Satow, *Japan 1853–1864,* p. 119.

6. Nabeshima Naomasa of Hizen, who supported a kōbu-gattai policy like Satsuma's, was much disturbed by the disruptive moves of the extremists and welcomed steps to bring them to order. Shibahara, pp. 99–101. Moreover, *Ishin-shi,* 3: 549, notes several other lords, among them those of Inaba and Bizen, also opposed the shishi plans. This suggests, as one would expect, a degree of solidarity among daimyo, even those who were relatively inactive in politics, on the subject of challenges to feudal authority as such.

7. See Jansen, *Sakamoto,* pp. 143–50.

8. The fullest account is Hara, "Tenchūgumi."

9. Text in *ibid.,* 2: 1229–30.

10. See the account in *Ishin-shi,* 3: 602–21.

11. My account of the Mito situation is based on *Ishin-shi,* 4: 92–110; and Shibahara, pp. 149–83.

12. The text of the letter, dated May 22, 1864, is in Shibusawa, *Tokugawa Keiki,* 6: 93–94.

13. The point is emphasized in Haga, pp. 58–61.

14. Some details are given in Umetani, pp. 326–30; and Hirao, "Bakumatsu," pp. 565–67.

15. The text of Takasugi's memorial is in Tokutomi, *Kōshaku Yamagata,* 1: 312–14.

16. This account of them is based on Seki, *Hansei kaikaku,* pp. 128–37; Tanaka Akira, pp. 118–21, 128–30; Haga, pp. 63–65; and Craig, *Chōshū,* pp. 199–204. In addition, Craig, *Chōshū,* pp. 271–72, gives details of the social composition of three of the shotai.

17. Craig, *Chōshū,* p. 215.

18. Memorial of Feb. 27, 1864, in *Kido Kōin monjo,* 2: 1–7, at pp. 3–4.

19. Craig, *Chōshū,* p. 280.

20. There is a detailed and vivid account of the fighting in *Genji Yume Monogatari,* where it is represented simply as a Chōshū attempt to dislodge Aizu. The palace was attacked, by this account, only because Matsudaira Katamori's troops had taken up positions there (Satow, *Japan 1853–1864,* pp. 173–219). Giving a Satsuma viewpoint, Shimonaka, 1: 271–86, suggests that Satsuma defended the Bakufu on this occasion only because of imperial orders to do so, secured by Hitotsubashi Keiki when the Chōshū plans to attack were leaked by kuge sympathizers on the previous day.

21. Saigō to Ōkubo, Oct. 7, 1864, expressing the hope that victory over Chōshū would make it possible to reduce the daimyo's territory and transfer him to eastern Japan, in *Dai Saigō zenshū,* 1: 471–76.

22. Saigō to Ōkubo, Oct. 16, 1864, *ibid.,* pp. 490–504.

23. Saigō to Ōkubo, Nov. 11, 1864, *ibid.,* pp. 548–53, at p. 549. See also Saigō's letter of Nov. 7, *ibid.,* pp. 522–33.

24. The text of the shotai memorial is in Tokutomi, *Kōshaku Yamagata,* 1: 455–59. On the support available to the shotai from village headmen in certain areas, see Tanaka Akira, pp. 166–69; and Craig, *Chōshū,* pp. 281–85.

25. Craig, *Chōshū,* p. 269.

26. The argument is stated in Tōyama, pp. 139–50. See also Seki, *Hansei kaikaku,* pp. 132–37.

27. Craig, *Chōshū,* p. 276, in the course of a detailed examination of these issues (pp. 268–301).

28. On the status and background of the Chōshū leadership at this time, see Craig, *Chōshū,* pp. 264–67; Tanaka Akira, pp. 186–89; and the standard biographies of the principal figures. Tanaka gives a long list of offices and their holders, dating from a major reallocation of posts made on May 31, 1865.

29. Compare the analysis of the Meiji bureaucrats given in Silberman, "Elite transformation."

30. On the cases cited here, see Craig, *Chōshū,* pp. 286–88; Umetani, pp. 331–39; and *Itō Hirobumi den,* 1: 3–5.

31. The text of the memorial, undated, is in *Kido Kōin monjo,* 8: 22–24. For information on the circumstances in which it was submitted, see *Shōkiku Kido Kō,* 1: 465–71.

32. Kido to Ōshima Tomonojō, Sept. 7, 1865, in *Kido Kōin monjo,* 2: 89–93. Note that this letter was written to an official in another domain (Tsushima) in an attempt to excuse Chōshū's actions and is to that extent a piece of special pleading.

33. Tanaka Akira, p. 194n.

34. Takasugi to shotai commanders, April 18, 1865, in Tokutomi, *Kōshaku Yamagata,* 1: 566–67. Presumably because he anticipated a hostile response, Takasugi was careful to suggest that opening Shimonoseki (which had actually

been proposed by the foreign representatives) was necessary to prevent further foreign attacks.

35. *Itō Hirobumi den,* 1: 202.

36. Kido argued the case for doing so in a letter to Yamada Uemon on Oct. 16, 1865, in which he roundly condemned jōi (*Kido Kōin monjo,* 2: 105–9). The whole affair is recounted at length in *Itō Hirobumi den,* 1: 194–203. See also Haga, pp. 143–46, where it is stated that the plan for opening the port was strongly backed by the loyalist Shimonoseki merchant Shiraishi Shōichirō, presumably for commercial reasons.

37. For a discussion of the point, see Craig, *Chōshū,* pp. 324–26; and Tanaka Akira, pp. 235–36.

38. Craig, *Chōshū,* pp. 274–81, 292–95.

CHAPTER X

1. Much of the material on which this summary is based is cited in my articles "Politics and the Samurai Class in Satsuma," and "Councillors of Samurai Origin in the Early Meiji Government."

2. There is a succinct account of Ōkubo's career before 1868 in Craig, "Kido Kōin," pp. 282–90.

3. However, as we shall see, the political implications of fukoku-kyōhei were different from those of kaikoku. The point is well made in Harootunian, *Toward Restoration,* pp. 354–79.

4. Quoted and summarized by Tanaka Akira, pp. 197–209, in the course of an admirable discussion of Godai's modernizing attitudes.

5. Generally on Godai's background, early career, and mission to Europe, see *Godai Tomoatsu den,* pp. 7–16, 36–100. There is a useful account of the mission in *Kagoshima-ken shi,* 3: 212–34.

6. *Godai Tomoatsu den,* pp. 56–57.

7. On military reform and finance in Satsuma at this time, see Tanaka Sōgorō, *Kindai Nihon,* pp. 69–71; and *Kagoshima-ken shi,* 3: 26–27, 68–72, 111–20.

8. Ishii Takashi, *Gakusetsu,* pp. 194–96, quoting Godai's memorials.

9. Katsuda, *Ōkubo,* 1: 588–91, cites Ōkubo's recommendation to Saigō in late 1864 to give up his part in the expedition against Chōshū and return to Satsuma, where there were matters of military reform to be dealt with that were more urgent and would better repay his efforts.

10. Saigō to Ōkubo, Oct. 16, 1864, in *Dai Saigō zenshū,* 1: 490–504, at pp. 496–99.

11. My account of Bakufu policies toward Chōshū in 1865–66 and Satsuma reactions to them is based chiefly on Craig, *Chōshū,* pp. 302–11; Iwata, pp. 85–88; and Katsuda, *Ōkubo,* 1: 598–99, 607–49.

12. Saigō to Komatsu, June 27, 1865, in *Dai Saigō zenshū,* 1: 645–46.

13. Saigō to Ōkubo and Minoda Dembei, Oct. 12, 1865, *ibid.,* p. 647.

14. Ōkubo to Niiro Hisanaga and Machida Hisanari, Sept. 23, 1865, in *Ōkubo Toshimichi monjo,* 1: 297–99. Niiro and Machida were senior officials with the Satsuma mission then in Europe. Iwata, p. 88, gives a slightly different translation of this passage and describes the addressees as Ishigaki and Ueno (the false names that Niiro and Machida had taken for their visit to Europe in order to avoid jōi criticism).

15. For accounts of this affair, see Fox, pp. 164–70; and Beasley, *Select Documents,* pp. 290–305.

16. Shogun to Emperor, Nov. 18, 1865, in Beasley, *Select Documents,* pp. 297–99.

17. From a detailed description of the meeting in a long letter from Ōkubo to Saigō, Nov. 11, 1865, in *Ōkubo Toshimichi monjo,* 1: 307–21, at p. 311.

18. Ōkubo to Ijichi Sadaka, Nov. 30, 1865, *ibid.,* pp. 337–42.

19. Saigō to Minoda Dembei, Jan. 22, 1866, in *Dai Saigō zenshū,* 1: 678–86, where Saigō repeats his belief that the authority of the Bakufu was "in decline" and expresses confidence in Satsuma's ability to act independently of it.

20. Accounts of the Chōshū-Satsuma alliance negotiations are to be found in Jansen, *Sakamoto,* pp. 211–22; and Craig, *Chōshū,* pp. 311–19.

21. Jansen, *Sakamoto,* p. 210.

22. Kido to Hirosawa Saneomi, Oct. 16, 1865, in *Kido Kōin monjo,* 2: 103–5.

23. The text, dated Oct. 27, 1865, is in *Ishin-shi,* 4: 458–59.

24. Kido to Sakamoto, March 9, 1866, in *Kido Kōin monjo,* 2: 136–42. The agreement was signed by Kido for Chōshū; by Saigō, Ōkubo, and Komatsu for Satsuma; and by Sakamoto as witness.

25. See the various letters and conversations recorded in Matsudaira Shungaku's records under dates ranging from Nov. 30, 1865, to April 2, 1866, in *Zoku saimu kiji,* 4: 356–58; and 5: 54–57, 71–74, 80–82.

26. *Zoku saimu kiji,* 5: 210–13, reporting a conversation between Matsudaira Shungaku and Hitotsubashi Keiki on Aug. 17, 1866.

27. Matsudaira Shungaku to Katsu Awa, July 15, 1866, *ibid.,* pp. 172–75, at p. 174.

28. See especially Tōyama, pp. 179–83, 193.

29. The text is in *Shimazu Hisamitsu Kō,* 5: 49A–59B.

30. In a letter to Minoda Dembei on April 3, 1866, Saigō commented that the Bakufu, by giving no heed to the advice of Katsu Awa and Ōkubo Ichiō, was risking its own destruction. See *Dai Saigō zenshū,* 1: 727.

31. F.O. 46/69, Parkes to Hammond, private, Nagasaki, Aug. 2, 1866.

32. Kido to Shinagawa Yajirō, Aug. 23, 1866, in *Kido Kōin monjo,* 2: 208–18, at p. 210.

33. Memorial of 1866, 8th month [Sept. 9–Oct. 8], in *Iwakura . . . monjo,* 1: 249–55.

34. *Ibid.,* pp. 251–54.

35. Ōkubo's statement of Satsuma objectives at about this time was "to bring about peace [with Chōshū], to destroy the Bakufu's authority, and to lay the basis for a resurgence of Court prestige" (Ōkubo to Saigō, Oct. 16, 1866, in *Ōkubo Toshimichi monjo,* 1: 410).

36. Keiki expressed these ideas at a meeting with Matsudaira Shungaku and others in Kyōto on Sept. 5, 1866. See *Zoku saimu kiji,* 5: 255–63.

37. Tanaka Akira, pp. 242–43.

38. The text of Keiki's proposals is given in Shibusawa, *Tokugawa Keiki,* 6: 460–61. Katsu Awa's memorial on the subject, dated Sept. 1, 1866, is in *Zoku saimu kiji,* 5: 275–77. It was framed in more forthright terms than Keiki's document and included some additional items: cooperation with the great lords in order that policy might be based on common consent, the manufacture of Western-style ships and guns, the promotion of trade, science, and industry.

39. The activities and advice of Roches are discussed in Ōtsuka; and in Sims, pp. 67–114.

40. On Nishi and Tsuda in Leiden and later as Bakufu advisers, see Havens, pp. 48–65.

41. See Honjō, "Léon Roches," pp. 188–93; and Honjō, *Economic theory,* pp. 179–82.

42. Both quotations are given in Oka, p. 95. Kido's reference is to Tokugawa Ieyasu, founder of the family line.

43. F.O. 391/14, Parkes to Hammond, May 6, 1867.

44. Satow, *Diplomat,* p. 200.

45. Kido to Shinagawa Yajirō, June 18, 1867, in *Kido Kōin monjo,* 2: 300. On the general subject of Kido's ideas concerning ōsei-fukko, see especially Umetani, pp. 341–50.

46. Tokutomi, *Kōshaku Yamagata,* 1: 710–11.

47. Memorial by Saigō and Ōkubo, 1867, 5th month [c. June 12–16], in *Dai Saigō zenshū,* 1: 840.

48. Iwakura Tomomi to Nakayama Tadayasu and Saga [Ōgimachi-Sanjō] Sanenaru, May 29, 1867, in *Iwakura Kō jikki,* 2: 35. There is also a long memorial by Iwakura, dated 1867, 3d month [April 5–May 3], that shows how far ahead of his contemporaries he was in working out the detailed administrative implications of all this. See *Iwakura ... monjo,* 1: 288–300. Its content will be discussed later, in the context of the development of ideas about a new regime.

49. F.O. 46/68, memorandum enclosed in Parkes to Hammond, private, May 29, 1866.

50. F.O. 46/71, Parkes to Stanley, no. 180, Oct. 31, 1866.

51. F.O. 391/14, Parkes to Hammond, Oct. 31, 1866. The opportunity in question was one to achieve "union" between "the Tycoon and the liberal Daimios" against "the old conservative Daimios and the functionaries of the Mikado's Court."

52. *Ibid.*, Dec. 31, 1866.

53. *Ibid.*, Jan. 16, 1867.

54. *Ibid.*, Feb. 1, 1867.

55. F.O. 46/68, memorandum enclosed in Parkes to Hammond, private, May 29, 1866.

56. F.O. 391/14, Parkes to Hammond, Aug. 14, 1866.

57. Quoted in Fox, p. 568. Two of Satow's three articles, dated March 16 and May 19, 1866, are there printed *in extenso* (pp. 566–75). Satow translated the articles into Japanese (with the help of his Japanese assistant), and they circulated in Japan as a pamphlet entitled *Eikoku sakuron* (English Policy). See variously Fox, pp. 179–82; Satow, *Diplomat,* pp. 159–60; and Ishii Takashi, *Zōtei Meiji ishin,* pp. 505–13. Satow always claimed to have acted without Parkes's knowledge in this matter, though I doubt whether he would have dared to go clean contrary to his senior's wishes.

58. *Ishin-shi,* 4: 627–28.

59. *Ibid.*, p. 629.

60. Keiki to Imperial Court, April 9, 1867, in Beasley, *Select Documents,* pp. 308–10. The other documents exchanged between the Court and the Bakufu on this subject are given at pp. 310–11.

61. The points are listed in Ōkubo to Shimazu Hisamitsu, c. May 15, 1867, in Beasley, *Select Documents,* pp. 312–13.

62. The various memorials Saigō and Ōkubo prepared for Hisamitsu at this time are printed in *Dai Saigō zenshū,* 1: 822–49. The one quoted here, dated mid-June 1867, is at pp. 835–42.

63. The argument is stated in Iwakura's letter to Nakayama and Saga, May 29, 1867, in *Iwakura Kō jikki,* 2: 36–37.

64. Court to Bakufu, June 26, 1867, in Beasley, *Select Documents,* p. 319. Accounts of the preceding discussions at the Court are also given in *ibid.*, pp. 314–19. A detailed account of the whole affair will be found in *Ishin-shi,* 4: 634–43.

65. Memorial by the four lords to the Imperial Court, June 28, 1867, in Beasley, *Select Documents,* pp. 319–20.

CHAPTER XI

1. F.O. 391/14, Parkes to Hammond, Osaka, May 6, 1867.

2. F.O. 46/67, Parkes to Hammond, private, Feb. 28, 1866.

3. F.O. 391/14, Parkes to Hammond, Yedo, July 27, 1867.

4. Much of the account of Tosa politics that follows is based on Jansen, *Sakamoto,* especially pp. 241ff. See also my article "Political Groups in Tosa," *passim,* on the nature of Gotō's political following.

5. Jansen, *Sakamoto,* p. 252, quoting a memorial by Nakaoka, written in the autumn of 1866.

6. *Ibid.*, pp. 294–302.

7. The text, based on a draft by Gotō, is translated in *ibid.*, pp. 299–301. For the Japanese text, see Katsuda, *Ōkubo,* 2: 131–35.

8. There is a complete translation in Ishii Ryosuke, pp. 708–11. Jansen, *Sakamoto,* pp. 316–17, summarizes Yōdō's statement and translates the enclosure. The Japanese texts of both documents are to be found in *Iwakura Kō jikki,* 2: 75–78, where they are dated 1867, 9th month [Sept. 28–Oct. 26]. I follow Jansen's translation wherever possible.

9. *Kagoshima-ken shi,* 3: 453–54. Significantly, the Satsuma leaders were at this time encountering opposition in Kagoshima, which was delaying the movement of troops. See Jansen, *Sakamoto,* pp. 324–25.

10. The text is in *Yodo Inaba-ke,* pp. 328–31.

11. Ōgyū Noritaka memorial of Nov. 13, 1867, *ibid.*, pp. 334–42, at p. 337.

12. Havens, pp. 61–64. See also Asai, pp. 45–56. The Japanese text of Nishi's draft is in Osatake, 1: 87–99.

13. The fullest discussion of Keiki's views is in Osatake, 1: 147–64.

14. Shibusawa, *Tokugawa Keiki,* 4: 79–80.

15. Fukuchi, Chap. 30.

16. F.O. 46/82, Parkes to Hammond, private, Yedo, Oct. 15, 1867.

17. F.O. 391/14, Parkes to Hammond, Yedo, Nov. 28, 1867.

18. *Ibid.*, Dec. 16, 1867.

19. There are translations (with minor differences) in Gubbins, p. 305; and Ishii Ryosuke, p. 712. The Japanese text is in *Iwakura Kō jikki,* 2: 74–75.

20. Bakufu memorandum in Shibusawa, *Tokugawa Keiki,* 7: 212–20, at p. 218. There is a not very exact translation of the document in Gubbins, pp. 306–11.

21. F.O. 391/14, Parkes to Hammond, Yedo, Nov. 28, 1867. In passing, one might note that Parkes's dispatches made it clear his sympathies at this time were for something like the Tosa solution, not for the Satsuma-Chōshū one as has sometimes been asserted.

22. Ishii Ryosuke, p. 713.

23. Tanaka Sōgorō, *Meiji ishin,* pp. 47–53, gives a long list of the replies they sent to the Court, excusing themselves for failing to attend.

24. Ōkubo to Minoda Dembei, 1867, 6th month [July 2–30], in *Ōkubo Toshimichi monjo,* 1: 475–76.

25. *Kagoshima-ken shi,* 3: 442–43; Katsuda, *Ōkubo,* 2: 124–26, 202–5; Craig, *Chōshū,* p. 339.

26. They are described in some detail in Ōkubo's diary, *Ōkubo Toshimichi nikki,* 1: 392–96. See also the Kido biography *Shōkiku Kido,* 1: 810–16.

27. *Ōkubo Toshimichi nikki,* 1: 395.

28. On the situation in Satsuma at this time see Katsuda, *Ōkubo,* 2: 205–8, 214–20; and *Kagoshima-ken shi,* 3: 449–50, 457–58.

29. The texts of the two announcements are in Katsuda, *Ōkubo,* 2: 214–17.

30. Memorandum of May 29, 1867, in *Iwakura Kō jikki*, 2: 33–39.

31. *Ibid.*, p. 37.

32. There were in fact two documents: a short statement, addressed to Nakayama, Saga, and Nakamikado Tsuneyuki and signed by Komatsu, Saigō, and Ōkubo; and a longer explanatory memorandum. The text is in Katsuda, *Ōkubo*, 2: 171–75.

33. *Ibid.*, p. 175.

34. The text, dated only 1867, 10th month [Oct. 27–Nov. 25], but apparently written on Nov. 3, is in *ibid.*, pp. 179–81.

35. Katsuda, *Ōkubo*, 2: 237–42. This was at an interview between the two men on Dec. 22.

36. Kido to Shinagawa, Dec. 17, 1867, in *Kido Kōin monjo*, 2: 338.

37. The most detailed account of these events is in Katsuda, *Ōkubo*, 2: 263–89.

38. The text, dated Jan. 3, 1868, is in *Iwakura Kō jikki*, 2: 148–50. There is a translation in Ishii Ryosuke, pp. 714–16. This version was addressed only to the Court. A notification issued to daimyo on Jan. 8 was in similar terms, though it omitted the list of appointments.

39. Examples are given in Haga, pp. 46–47, where the originators of the placards are mostly identified as village headmen visiting Kyōto to engage in politics, i.e., the political heirs to the shishi of 1863; and in Shimonaka, 2: 99.

40. Oka, pp. 105–7.

41. Redesdale, 2: 414. He identifies the chanted slogan as "i ja nai ka."

42. F.O. 391/14, Parkes to Hammond, Osaka, Jan. 5, 1868.

43. Oka, p. 115.

44. F.O. 391/14, Parkes to Hammond, Osaka, Jan. 10, 1868.

45. *Ibid.*

46. The most detailed account of the meeting is in Katsuda, *Ōkubo*, 2: 294–98. On the political maneuvers of January 1868 generally, see Osatake, 1: 164–77; and Asai, pp. 105–11.

47. For his assessment of the situation, see Ōkubo to Minoda Dembei, Jan. 22, 1868, enclosing a detailed account of Kyōto politics, in *Ōkubo Toshimichi monjo*, 2: 128–45.

48. *Yodo Inaba-ke*, p. 329, makes it clear that this debate had begun even before the Satsuma-Chōshū coup.

49. Satow, *Diplomat*, p. 299.

50. There is a detailed account in *Junnan rokkō*, 3: 1–4.

51. *Ōkubo Toshimichi monjo*, 2: 154–58.

52. Shibusawa, *Tokugawa Keiki*, 7: 341–49.

53. Katsuda, *Ōkubo*, 2: 485, gives the text of a letter that Katsu Awa, then in Edo, sent to Kyōto by an Echizen samurai appealing to the Court to avoid hostilities, which would only serve, he said, to give the powers a pretext to intervene. See also Oka, pp. 129–32; and Sakata, *Meiji ishin shi* (1960), p. 208.

54. On fudai reactions generally, see Kimura and Sugimoto, pp. 306–10.
55. *Ishin-shi*, 5: 201.
56. Quoted in Fukuzawa, pp. 276–77.

CHAPTER XII

1. Webb, "Development," p. 187. On the same topic, see also Hall, "Monarch."
2. Hall, "Monarch," p. 41.
3. Adams, 2: 132.
4. Some of their writings on the subject are discussed in Asai, pp. 16–38.
5. McEwan, p. 22.
6. Memorial dated 1867, 3d month [April 5–May 3], in *Iwakura . . . monjo*, 1: 288–300.
7. *Ibid.*, p. 297.
8. On the collection of "political" information by diplomatic missions, see Osatake, 1: 42–56.
9. Havens, pp. 57–59.
10. Asai, pp. 74–75.
11. *Ibid.*, p. 37.
12. F.O. 46/80, Parkes to Stanley, no. 78, Osaka, May 4, 1867.
13. The text is in *Yodo Inaba-ke*, pp. 334–42.
14. Jansen, *Sakamoto*, pp. 338–41.
15. Asai, p. 37.
16. Jansen, *Sakamoto*, pp. 316–17.
17. F.O. 46/82, Parkes to Stanley, no. 194, Yedo, Nov. 27, 1867.
18. F.O. 391/14, Parkes to Hammond, Yedo, Nov. 28, 1867.
19. F.O. 46/106, Parkes to Stanley, confidential, Yokohama, Jan. 13, 1869.
20. F.O. 46/82, Parkes to Hammond, private, Yedo, Oct. 15, 1867.
21. This is to touch on a very large subject, which cannot be considered properly here. It is discussed more fully in Sansom; Blacker, *The Japanese Enlightenment*; Haven; and Pyle.
22. Blacker, *Japanese Enlightenment*, p. 121, quoting Fukuzawa's autobiography.
23. Pyle, p. 90.
24. Jansen, *Sakamoto*, p. 250. A more detailed survey of the availability of political information about the West is given in Asai, pp. 92–103.
25. Havens, pp. 66–70; Blacker, *Japanese Enlightenment*, pp. 25–27.
26. Tanaka Akira, pp. 202–5.
27. Memorial by Terajima dated Nov. 27, 1867, in Katsuda, *Ōkubo*, 2: 606–8, at p. 606.
28. Itō to Kido, Jan. 29, 1868, in *Itō Hirobumi den*, 1: 332–33.
29. Itō memorial, c. Dec. 1868 or Jan. 1869, in *Itō Kō zenshū*, 1: Part 1, pp. 165–68.

30. The text, dated 1869, 1st month [Feb. 11–March 12], is in *Itō Hirobumi den*, 1: 420–25. One of the signatories of the document was Mutsu Munemitsu, through whom there was a link with Tosa: Mutsu, though a fairly well-born samurai of the Tokugawa domain of Kii, had served with Sakamoto Ryōma in the Kaientai. See Jansen, "Mutsu," pp. 311–13.

31. See Sakata, *Meiji ishin shi* (1960), pp. 229–32, 235–39.

32. Kido to Kuroda Kiyotsuna of Satsuma, April 23, 1867, in *Kido Kōin monjo*, 2: 286–87. In February 1868 (in a letter to Itō Hirobumi) Kido extended the criticism to include those samurai of other domains who were making attacks on foreigners. See Sakata, *Meiji ishin shi* (1960), p. 217.

33. F.O. 391/14, Parkes to Hammond, Osaka, Jan. 5, 1868.

34. Iwakura memorial of May 29, 1867, in *Iwakura Kō jikki*, 2: 36.

35. The text of the decree is given in Katsuda, *Ōkubo*, 2: 431–32. See also Oka, pp. 139–42.

36. Memorial of Feb. 29, 1868, in *Iwakura Kō jikki*, 2: 315–17. There is a rather uneven English translation in Black, 2: 178–81.

37. For example, Redesdale, 2: 487–91, gives the text of a paper the Foreign Ministry prepared for discussion by a samurai assembly in 1869 that was clearly aimed at bringing the assembly to reject any lingering sentiments of jōi.

38. A memorial by Yamauchi Yōdō, dated Jan. 6, 1868, in *Iwakura Kō jikki*, 2: 168–69, complains of the high-handedness of Satsuma and Chōshū and of the failure of the inner group to consult properly with the lords.

39. Kido to Sanjō Sanetomi, secret, Jan. 22, 1868, in *Kido Kōin monjo*, 2: 353–56, at p. 356.

40. On Restoration politics in Hizen, see especially Shibahara, pp. 91–96, 102–3, 107–12. There are also two useful recent biographies: Nakamura Naomi, *Ōkuma Shigenobu*; and Sugitani Akira, *Etō Shimpei*. Hizen technology was discussed in Chap. 5, pp. 123–24.

41. The most useful account of the offices created in 1868–69 and the appointments made to them is to be found in Robert A. Wilson, pp. 9–46; lists of senior officials are given, *ibid.*, pp. 105–19. See also my article "Councillors of Samurai Origin" for a discussion of the regional and social origins of the new leadership.

42. On Ōkuma's background and early career, see Nakamura Naomi, pp. 1–43.

43. Sugitani, pp. 1–3. His father was a minor district official (reputedly a negligent one, more interested in saké and the puppet theater than in his duties).

44. For some examples, see my articles "Political Groups in Tosa" and "Politics and the Samurai Class in Satsuma."

45. Robert A. Wilson, pp. 49–54.

46. See Oka, pp. 144–48; and Delmer Brown, pp. 101–3. Tanaka Sōgorō, *Meiji ishin*, pp. 27–37, quotes a long memorial from the Ōsu samurai Yano

Gentō, later an official of the department of religion, setting out a view of imperial rule in terms of the Shintō tradition.

47. The pamphlet is translated in Redesdale, 2: 503–10.

48. Addressed by the Court to daimyo; text in *Iwakura Kō jikki*, 2: 199.

49. The most detailed discussion of the various drafts is to be found in Inada, 1: 1–22. In English, see Ishii Ryosuke, pp. 141–45; and Pittau, pp. 12–13.

50. Akita, p. 8.

51. I follow the wording given in Ishii Ryosuke, p. 145. There are several variants in English. See, for example, Sansom, pp. 318–20.

CHAPTER XIII

1. Sansom, pp. 338–39.

2. Norman, *Japan's Emergence*, p. 91.

3. See, for example, *Meiji ishin-shi kenkyū kōza*, 4: 83–87.

4. Ōkubo letter of May 23, 1868, quoted in Tanaka Sōgorō, *Meiji ishin*, p. 125.

5. Ōkubo memorial of Feb. 16, 1868, arguing the case for moving the capital to Osaka, in *Ōkubo Toshimichi monjo*, 2: 191–95, at p. 193. There is a translation, which I have slightly modified, in Black, 2: 184–87.

6. Black, 2: 184–87. Interestingly, Sir Harry Parkes shared Ōkubo's distaste for Kyōto, partly perhaps because it was there that he had been attacked. It was, he said, "a second Mecca," from which the "very prejudiced and narrow-minded" Court nobles would have to be removed before they could be brought to "more intelligent views" (F.O. 391/14, Parkes to Hammond, Aug. 8, 1868).

7. F.O. 391/14, Parkes to Hammond, Oct. 7, 1868.

8. The text is translated in McLaren, *Japanese Government Documents*, pp. 26–27. See also Asai, pp. 84–86; and Tanaka Sōgorō, *Meiji ishin*, pp. 132–34.

9. Asai, pp. 109–10.

10. *Ibid.*, p. 117, where the text of the memorial (March 4, 1868) is quoted.

11. Memorial of 1868, 2d month [Feb. 23–March 23], in *Kido Kōin monjo*, 8: 25–26.

12. Memorial of Dec. 1868/Jan. 1869, in *Itō Kō zenshū*, 1: Part 1, pp. 165–68.

13. Memorandum by Mitford, Aug. 6, 1868, in F.O. 410/12, pp. 337–38.

14. Kido to Sanjō and Iwakura, March 13, 1869, in *Kido Kōin monjo*, 3: 237–43. Iwakura seems to have taken over the phrase and modified it in talking to Parkes a few weeks later, when he referred to the difficulties arising from the fact that each daimyo was "a little Mikado in his own right" (as Parkes reported it). See F.O. 391/15, Parkes to Hammond, Yedo, June 7, 1869.

15. Itō to Kido, May 5, 1869, in *Itō Hirobumi den*, 1: 438–40.

16. *Kido Kōin nikki*, 1: 99–100.

17. Ōkubo to Iwakura, Feb. 6, 1869, in Tōyama, pp. 265–66.

18. Translated from the text in *Iwakura Kō jikki*, 2: 671. There are con-

temporary translations of the memorial, differing from this in points of detail, in McLaren, *Japanese Government Documents*, pp. 29–32; and Gubbins, pp. 313–15.

19. F.O. 391/15, Parkes to Hammond, Yedo, April 6, 1869.

20. *Iwakura Kō jikki*, 2: 672.

21. This subject is discussed in some detail in Asai, pp. 159–71, 190–99; and in Kimura and Sugimoto, pp. 329–32.

22. F.O. 46/109, memorandum by Mitford, May 20, 1869, enclosure in Parkes to Clarendon, no. 114, confidential, May 28, 1869.

23. Kōgisho memorial of Aug. 2, 1869, in *Higo-han*, 10: 31–33.

24. Ōkubo to Iwakura, April 26, 1869, in Akita, p. 6.

25. Sanjō to Iwakura, May 17, 1869, in *Iwakura Kō jikki*, 2: 706.

26. Memorial of June 6, 1869, in *Ōkubo Toshimichi monjo*, 3: 161–65.

27. Ōkubo to Katsura Hisatake, July 12, 1869, in Katsuda, *Ōkubo*, 2: 692–94. The discussions within officialdom are treated in Asai, pp. 173–90.

28. Iwakura memorial of 1869, 5th month [June 10–July 8], in *Iwakura Kō jikki*, 2: 728–30. Cf. his earlier proposals, discussed in Chap. 12, pp. 304–5.

29. F.O. 391/15, Parkes to Hammond, Yedo, Aug. 28, 1869.

30. See Robert A. Wilson, pp. 66–86, and the list of appointments at pp. 120–25.

31. Iwata, pp. 132–33; Katsuda, *Ōkubo*, 2: 702–8 (which gives the text). Its preamble, a statement about the need for national unity, was couched in very "loyalist" terms.

32. The October laws are summarized in Ishii Ryosuke, pp. 94–95.

33. See Kimura and Sugimoto, pp. 323–47.

34. See Ōe, pp. 51–60.

35. See Shibahara, pp. 111–12.

36. Tosa reforms are discussed in Jansen, *Sakamoto*, pp. 361–68. Itagaki's criticisms of inherited privilege were expressed in a memorial of 1870, 11th month [Dec. 22, 1870–Jan. 20, 1871], the text of which is given in *Jiyūtō-shi*, 1: 7–9.

37. See *Kagoshima-ken shi*, 3: 522–50.

38. See *Ishin-shi*, 5: 727–31.

39. There is a detailed examination of stipend cuts in Niwa, *Meiji*, pp. 16–21.

40. On the general subject of this opposition, see especially Asai, pp. 221–43.

41. Memorial of Yokoyama Shōtarō, Aug. 21, 1870; translation enclosed in F.O. 46/138, Parkes to Granville, no. 31, March 17, 1871.

42. *Shōkiku Kido Kō*, 2: 1217–43. See also Tōyama, pp. 272–74, where the point is made that the shotai were in this case behaving not only as sonnō-jōi adherents, but also typically as samurai, despite the rich farmer and merchant elements to be found in their ranks.

43. F.O. 46/138, enclosure in Parkes to Granville, no. 38, confidential, March

25, 1871, reporting talks with the Gaimushō's Date Muneki and Terajima Munenori on March 8 and 23 concerning unrest as a possible threat to foreign interests.

44. *Ibid.*, no. 31, March 17, 1871.

45. Adams, 2: 246.

46. Kido to Ōkuma, Sept. 5, 1869, in *Ōkuma*, 1: 120.

47. Sanjō to Sasaki, July 11, 1870, in *Itō Hirobumi den*, 1: 504.

48. Entry in Kido's diary, July 28, 1871, in *Kido Kōin nikki*, 2: 52.

49. The dispute is treated at some length in Sakata, *Meiji ishin shi* (1960), pp. 245–57.

50. See, for example, Robert A. Wilson, pp. 96–98, and the authorities there cited; also Asai, pp. 272–78.

51. Asai, pp. 245–58. On the financial difficulties of the domains (a topic that will be treated in more detail in a later chapter), see especially Niwa, *Meiji*, pp. 9–47.

52. F.O. 46/139, Parkes to Granville, no. 72, May 22, 1871, reporting what he had said to the Emperor at a private audience on May 18.

53. Asai, pp. 265–72.

54. Memorial of 1870, c. 8th month [Aug. 27–Sept. 24], in *Iwakura . . . monjo*, 1: 338–62. The document is said to have been drafted by Etō Shimpei of Hizen, but Iwakura signed it as his own.

55. Kido to Sanjō, Sept. 15, 1870, in *Kido Kōin monjo*, 4: 102–6, at p. 104.

56. The difficulty this presented was underlined at a meeting of the three men at Osaka on March 15, 1871, when they were on their way to Tokyo from Tosa. There was a sharp disagreement between Kido and Saigō, and it was only with the greatest difficulty that Ōkubo prevented another open breach. See *Shōkiku Kido Kō*, 2: 1375–76.

57. F.O. 46/139, enclosure in Adams to Granville, no. 7, most confidential, June 12, 1871.

58. *Ibid.*

59. Katsuda, *Ōkubo*, 2: 856–59; *Shōkiku Kido Kō*, 2: 1457–60. The tone of the documents suggests that the question of abolishing the domains was an issue that had been held in abeyance and was now being reactivated, rather than an end to which all the group's recent actions had been directed.

60. Edict of Aug. 29, 1871, translated in Ishii Ryosuke, p. 717.

61. The phrase is that of McLaren, who gives a useful account of the whole affair. See his *Political History*, p. 82.

62. Silberman, "Bureaucratic development," pp. 352–55.

63. Steiner, pp. 33–34.

CHAPTER XIV

1. Memorial of 1867, 3d month [April 5–May 3], in *Iwakura . . . monjo*, 1: 288–300.

2. F.O. 46/106, Parkes to Stanley, confidential, no. 5, Jan. 13, 1869.

3. Memorial of 1870, c. 8th month [Aug. 27–Sept. 24], in *Iwakura . . . monjo,* 1: 338–62, at p. 348.

4. Memorial of June 13, 1869, in *Higo-han,* 9: 794–97.

5. Niwa, *Meiji,* pp. 131–32, quoting a memorial by Ōkuma dated 1870, 9th month [Sept. 25–Oct. 24].

6. Memorial of 1869, 1st month [Feb. 11–March 12], in *Ōkubo Toshimichi monjo,* 3: 8–13, at p. 11.

7. Sidney Brown, p. 203.

8. F.O. 391/15, Parkes to Hammond, March 26, 1870.

9. See Sakata, *Meiji ishin shi* (1960), pp. 229–43; Tōyama, pp. 301–4; Sidney Brown, pp. 199–202.

10. F.O. 391/15, Parkes to Hammond, March 26, 1870.

11. F.O. 46/139, Adams to Granville, no. 7, most confidential, June 12, 1871.

12. Hawks, 1: 357–58.

13. My account of railway politics is based largely on the careful and detailed study by Tanaka Tokihiko, *Meiji ishin,* much of which is summarized in English in his two-part article "Meiji Government."

14. F.O. 391/14, Parkes to Hammond, Dec. 18, 1868.

15. Text of memorandum in *Dai Nihon Gaikō Bunsho,* 2: 3 (vol. 5), pp. 73–76.

16. F.O. 391/15, Parkes to Hammond, April 22, 1870, reports that Parkes had had a dinner with some 20 Japanese entrepreneurs believed to be hostile to the railway plan—the arrangements for it were made by Japanese officials—in an attempt to persuade them to put up money for the Tokyo-Yokohama railway. He had earlier conferred with both Ōkuma and Itō on the question.

17. Memorial of April 14, 1870, in *Meiji zenki zaisei,* 2: 83–84.

18. Dore, pp. 249–51.

19. For an account of them, see *Ishin-shi,* 5: 600–610.

20. From the complete translation of the preamble in Kikuchi, pp. 68–69.

21. *Ibid.*

22. Translation in *ibid.*, pp. 2–3.

23. *Iwakura . . . monjo,* 1: 357–58.

24. Ōkubo to Iwakura, Oct. 1, 1870, in Katsuda, *Ōkubo,* 2: 777.

25. The best accounts of the introduction of conscription are to be found in Chapter 2 of Hackett's *Yamagata* and in the same author's article "Meiji Leaders."

26. Katsuda, *Ōkubo,* 2: 726–27.

27. The text is in Tokutomi, *Kōshaku Yamagata,* 2: 183–87.

28. Both documents are translated in Ishii Ryosuke, pp. 723–24; and also in Tsunoda et al., pp. 704–5 (where the date is wrongly given). The Japanese texts are in Tokutomi, *Kōshaku Yamagata,* 2: 195–96.

29. Details are in Hackett, *Yamagata,* pp. 66–67; and Ishii Ryosuke, pp. 194–96.

30. Ishii Ryosuke, pp. 723–24.
31. Havens, pp. 194, 196–97, 207–8.
32. The argument is stated at length in Norman, *Soldier*, pp. 41–47.
33. Memorial of 1867, 3d month [April 5–May 3], in *Iwakura . . . monjo*, 1: 288–300, at pp. 290–92; and letter to Nakayama and Saga, May 29, 1867, in *Iwakura Kō jikki*, 2: 33–39, at pp. 36–37. The best account in English of the mission and its origins is Mayo, "Rationality in the Meiji Restoration."
34. Altman. It is clear from the text of Verbeck's note that one advantage he hoped for as a result of such studies was a Japanese decision in favor of tolerating Christianity.
35. *Shōkiku Kido Kō*, 2: 1321–24.
36. Ōkubo and Inoue joint memorial, 1871, 8th month [Sept. 15–Oct. 13], in *Ōkubo Toshimichi monjo*, 4: 361–63.
37. The text, dated Oct. 16, 1871, is in *Iwakura Kō jikki*, 2: 927–34.
38. F.O. 46/143, Adams to Hammond, private, Dec. 8, 1871.
39. F.O. 46/151, Adams to Granville, no. 13, confidential, Jan. 12, 1872.
40. Kido letter of Jan. 26, 1872, in *Kido Kōin monjo*, 4: 319–21.
41. Pittau, pp. 41–48.
42. Letter from Berlin, March 21, 1873, in Katsuda, *Ōkubo*, 3: 54–55.
43. Ōkubo to Ōyama Iwao, Dec. 20, 1872, in *Ōkubo Toshimichi monjo*, 4: 467–70, at p. 468.
44. Ienaga, p. 260.
45. Text, dated Dec. 18, 1871, in Katsuda, *Ōkubo*, 3: 21–25. See also Iwata, pp. 150–54. Among the signatories were Sanjō, Iwakura, Saigō, Kido, Ōkubo, Ōkuma, Gotō, Itagaki, Soejima, and Itō.
46. The best account of the Korean affair is Conroy, *The Japanese Seizure of Korea*, pp. 17–77. See also Iwata, pp. 164–72.
47. Saigō letter of Aug. 1873, in Tsunoda et al., p. 657.
48. Kido to Sanjō and Iwakura, March 13, 1869, in *Kido Kōin monjo*, 3: 237–43, at p. 241.
49. Letter to Murata Shimpachi and Ōyama Iwao (in Europe), Aug. 15, 1873, in *Ōkubo Toshimichi monjo*, 4: 521–23.
50. Memorial, dated Aug. 1873, in *Shōkiku Kido Kō*, 2: 1580–84.
51. *Ōkubo Toshimichi monjo*, 5: 54–64. There are translations of substantial parts of the text in Tsunoda et al., pp. 658–62; and Conroy, pp. 47–49. The former follows the Japanese original more closely.

CHAPTER XV

1. Seki, *Meiji ishin*, pp. 105–6.
2. My account of early Meiji finance is based largely on *ibid.*, pp. 21–25, 105–17; and Niwa, *Meiji ishin*, pp. 9–30, 119–25, 155–60.
3. Tanaka Sōgorō, *Meiji ishin*, pp. 110–15; Honjō, *Social and Economic History*, pp. 323–32, 342–44.

4. Niwa, *Meiji ishin*, pp. 16–26, puts the domains into five classes, ranging from those (mostly the defeated) whose cuts reduced *all* samurai to somewhere near subsistence level, regardless of former stipend, to those in which the highest stipends were cut to 10 per cent but others little or not at all. The last category included Satsuma, Tosa, and Hizen. Fukaya gives details of stipend cuts for former Bakufu retainers (pp. 168–81) and in a number of domains (pp. 201–27). One should also note that stipends of Court nobles were reduced in January 1871 (by 37.5 per cent across the board), the cut being applied to Restoration rewards for political services as well as to hereditary incomes (Fukaya, pp. 230–39).

5. *Kagoshima-ken shi*, 3: 539–40, 544–48.

6. Kimura and Sugimoto, pp. 335–47.

7. Memorial by Itagaki Taisuke, 1870, 11th month [Dec. 22, 1870–Jan. 20, 1871], in *Jiyūtō-shi*, 1: 7–9.

8. *Ibid.*

9. *Ibid.*

10. Memorial of Feb. 20, 1874, in McLaren, *Japanese Government Documents*, p. 445. Interestingly, the French minister Maxime Outrey, no doubt basing his statements on the local knowledge of those who had served his predecessor, Roches, commented in a report to Paris on July 9, 1868, that "le pays traverse une crise sociale des plus sérieuses, et insensiblement une classe intermédiaire de la population semble tendre à se substituer à la classe supérieure qui seule jusqu'à ce jour a occupé la scène politique" (Sims, p. 171).

11. See chiefly Ishii Ryosuke, pp. 102–6; and Fukaya, pp. 145–51.

12. The most detailed account of the government discussions of stipends is in Fukaya, pp. 259–397. I have depended heavily on it in preparing the summary given here.

13. Memorial of Dec. 7, 1873, in *Shōkiku Kido Kō*, 2: 1640–48. Kido had spoken to Adams, the British chargé, in similar terms at an interview two years earlier. See F.O. 46/141, Adams to Granville, no. 80, confidential, Sept. 18, 1871.

14. *Iwakura . . . monjo*, 1: 338–62, at pp. 349–54.

15. Entry for May 14, 1872, in *Kido Kōin nikki*, 2: 175.

16. Text in McLaren, *Japanese Government Documents*, p. 557.

17. Details of the arrangements are given in *ibid.*, pp. 562–66.

18. See table showing items of government finance, 1872–80, in Niwa, *Meiji ishin*, pp. 156–57. The actual interest paid on the bonds was only ¥11.6 million annually.

19. James Nakamura, p. 159.

20. Norman, *Japan's Emergence*, pp. 99–100.

21. *Ibid.*, p. 97.

22. Seki, *Meiji ishin*, pp. 120–21.

23. There is a useful summary of their views in *Meiji ishin-shi kenkyū kōza*, 4: 229–35.

24. *Nihon kindaishi jiten*, p. 774. See also Seki, *Meiji ishin*, pp. 45–48, 52–54; and Norman, *Japan's Emergence*, pp. 72–77.

25. The following material on the discussions that took place before 1871 is based largely on Fukushima Masao, pp. 16–62; and Seki, *Meiji ishin*, pp. 17–20, 25–34.

26. The text dated 1871, 9th month [Oct. 14– Nov. 12], is in *Ōkubo Toshimichi monjo*, 4: 394–99.

27. Seki, *Meiji ishin*, pp. 135–36.

28. F.O. 46/141, Adams to Granville, no. 63, confidential, Sept. 8, 1871.

29. Memorial to Dajōkan, 1871, 9th month [Oct. 14–Nov. 12], in *Ōkubo Toshimichi monjo*, 4: 392–94.

30. The most detailed account of government discussions leading to the final decisions of 1873 is in Fukushima Masao, pp. 84–105 and 123–98. See also Seki, *Meiji ishin*, pp. 133–36, 150–83; and Niwa, "Jinushi-sei," especially pp. 250–54, 258–70.

31. See Fukushima Masao, pp. 137–54.

32. Details are given in *ibid.*, pp. 189–93; and Niwa, "Jinushi-sei," pp. 266–68.

33. Text in Ishii Ryosuke, p. 722.

34. Fukushima Masao, pp. 183–84, notes that the Finance Ministry expected the yield of land tax to be reduced by ¥5.4 million as a result of the reform. In the event, however, the implementation of the law resulted in the identification of enough hitherto untaxed arable land to offset this anticipated loss and even show a small gain. The problem of underreporting and undermeasurement (which still persisted) is discussed at length in James Nakamura, pp. 52–104. Niwa, *Meiji ishin*, table, pp. 156–57, gives figures for the later yield of land tax that show a decline from a peak of ¥60.6 million in 1873 to ¥43 million in 1875–76, by which time the work of implementing the reform was largely complete. One must bear in mind that the last of these figures presumably excludes the local land tax, amounting to a further third.

35. Seki, *Meiji ishin*, pp. 186–93; Ishii Ryosuke, pp. 184–86; James Nakamura, pp. 185–92. Perhaps significantly, the decision came when samurai unrest about stipends was at its greatest.

36. Seki, *Meiji ishin*, pp. 122–33. Hirano, p. 28, points out that the tax reduction further increased the profitability of landlordism, since the savings of the landlord, who paid the tax, were not necessarily passed on to the tenant.

37. Chambliss, pp. 72–77, 94–96. This village was in the Bakufu territories, where pre-Restoration dues were below the national average.

38. Seki, *Meiji ishin*, pp. 392–93.

39. McLaren, *Japanese Government Documents*, p. 570.

40. *Ibid.*, p. 430.

41. Memorial of late 1873, in Beckmann, p. 113.

42. McLaren, *Japanese Government Documents*, p. 571.

43. See Tōyama, pp. 337–38; Iwata, pp. 180–83; and Conroy, pp. 51–53.

44. There are detailed contemporary accounts of the rebellion in Black, 2: 476–99; and Mounsey.

CHAPTER XVI

1. See, for example, the documents translated in Teng and Fairbank, especially those by Wei Yüan, Feng Kuei-fen, Tseng Kuo-fan, and Li Hung-chang, which might well be compared with the statements of Japanese officials like Ii Naosuke, Hotta Masayoshi, Mizuno Tadanori, and Iwase Tadanari (see examples in Beasley, *Select Documents*, sections I, II, and III).

2. Teng and Fairbank, p. 62.

3. Wright, p. 8. This work gives much the best analysis of Chinese self-strengthening in the 1860's, especially at pp. 2–10, 43–67.

4. See, for example, the analysis of culturalism and nationalism in China in Levenson, especially pp. 109–25.

5. Blacker, *Japanese Enlightenment*, p. 134.

6. Pyle, p. 94.

7. Alcock, 2: 259–60. This was part of an estimate of Japan's economic potential, in the course of which Alcock commented that the Japanese would learn quickly from the West and could soon be expected to export "swords and cutlery to rival Sheffield" or silk textiles to match the best Britain and France could offer.

8. Crane Brinton, *The Anatomy of Revolution* (New York, 1957), p. 257.

Annotated Bibliography

Annotated Bibliography

This book is based almost entirely on published materials, most of them Japanese. Apart from a very considerable body of modern histories, monographs, and articles, these include much that is contemporary to the events described. Some of the Bakufu's records have been published, especially those concerning foreign affairs (see *Dai Nihon Komonjo: Bakumatsu Gaikoku Kankei Monjo*). So have extracts from early Meiji archives (e.g., *Dai Nihon Gaikō Bunsho*). There are a few published domain records (e.g., those of Matsudaira Shungaku's domain of Echizen, starting with *Sakumu kiji*). The letters and papers of many of the participants in Restoration politics have also been made available in print, as have the diaries of men like Ōkubo Toshimichi and Kido Kōin (chiefly in the Nihon Shiseki Kyōkai series). In addition, there are one or two older compilations, called *jikki*, or "true records," which consist of documents strung together with a minimum of narrative (e.g., those for Iwakura Tomomi and Shimazu Hisamitsu); and a number of "authorized" biographies, though frequently exercises in filial piety, follow Chinese practice in giving many relevant documents in full. Detailed local histories are numerous, too: older ones, like Suematsu's *Bōchō kaiten shi*, dealing with Chōshū; and more recent ones, like *Kagoshima-ken shi*, covering Satsuma.

All this amounts to several hundred volumes, of which I have been able to use only a part. A few of these works I have read in full. For the rest, however, I have followed a process of sampling: sometimes by identifying what seemed to be key topics or events, then seeking out as much as possible of the material concerning them; at others, by following up the references and quotations given by Japanese historians over as wide a range as was practicable. This could be done only because of the completeness and variety of the scholarly literature available in Japanese, both that which provides detailed narrative (especially the monumental six-volume *Ishin-shi*, an "official" history published in 1939–41) and that which gives the often conflicting viewpoints of individual scholars (like Oka Yoshitake. Tōyama Shigeki, Sakata Yoshio, and Tanaka Akira).

I am aware that there is much that I have not used, or have used inadequately. Specialists will no doubt notice omissions in the list that follows. It is, however, intended only to provide details of works that have been cited in the notes, along with a minimum of descriptive comment, not to give a reference bibliography of Restoration history.

The following abbreviations are used in the Bibliography:

BGKM *Dai Nihon Komonjo: Bakumatsu Gaikoku Kankei Monjo*

BSOAS *Bulletin of the School of Oriental and African Studies,* University of London

JAS *Journal of Asian Studies* (formerly *Far Eastern Quarterly*)

TASJ *Transactions of the Asiatic Society of Japan*

F.O. Foreign Office archives in the Public Record Office, London. (In each F.O. citation, the relevant series number—F.O. 46, F.O. 391, or F.O. 410—is given first, then an oblique stroke followed by the volume number, e.g. F.O. 46/82.)

Adams, F. O. *The History of Japan.* 2 vols., 2d ed. London, 1875. Includes an account of events during the period of his own diplomatic service in Japan; especially useful for the early years of Meiji.

Akao Tōji. "Perry torai zengo ni okeru taigai kokumin shisō no kōsatsu," *Shirin* (2 parts), 22 (1937): 529–54, 753–82.

Akita, George. *Foundations of Constitutional Government in Modern Japan, 1868–1900.* Cambridge, Mass., 1967.

Alcock, Rutherford. *The Capital of the Tycoon. A Narrative of a Three Years' Residence in Japan.* 2 vols. London, 1863.

Altman, A. "Guido Verbeck and the Iwakura Embassy," *Japan Quarterly,* 13, 1 (1966): 54–62.

Arima Seiho. *Takashima Shūhan* [biography]. Tokyo, 1958.

———. "The Western Influence on Japanese Military Science, Shipbuilding, and Navigation," *Monumenta Nipponica,* 19 (1964): 352–79.

Asai Kiyoshi. *Meiji ishin to gunken shisō.* Tokyo, 1939.

Baba Bunei. *Genji Yume Monogatari.* 5 books. N.p., [1864]. An account of events in Japan from 1853 to 1864, written from a loyalist and Kyōto viewpoint. Translated in 1905 by E. M. Satow under the title *Japan 1853–1864* (q.v.).

Beasley, W. G. "Councillors of Samurai Origin in the Early Meiji Government, 1868–9," *BSOAS,* 20 (1957): 89–103.

———. "Feudal Revenue in Japan at the Time of the Meiji Restoration," *JAS,* 19 (1960): 255–72.

———. *Great Britain and the Opening of Japan, 1834–1858.* London, 1951.

———. "Political Groups in Tosa, 1858–68," *BSOAS*, 30 (1967): 382–90.

———. "Politics and the Samurai Class in Satsuma, 1858–1868," *Modern Asian Studies*, 1 (1967): 47–57.

———. *Select Documents on Japanese Foreign Policy, 1853–1868.* London, 1955.

Beasley, W. G., and E. G. Pulleyblank, eds. *Historians of China and Japan.* London, 1961.

Beckmann, G. M. *The Making of the Meiji Constitution. The Oligarchs and the Constitutional Development of Japan, 1868–1891.* Lawrence, Kans., 1957.

Befu, Harumi. "Duty, Reward, Sanction, and Power: Four-Cornered Office of the Tokugawa Village Headman," in Silberman and Harootunian, eds., listed below, pp. 25–50.

———. "Village Autonomy and Articulation with the State: The Case of Tokugawa Japan," *JAS*, 25 (1965): 19–32. Reprinted in Hall and Jansen, eds., listed below, pp. 301–14.

Bellah, Robert N. *Tokugawa Religion. The Values of Pre-industrial Japan.* Glencoe, Ill., 1957.

Black, J. R. *Young Japan. Yokohama and Yedo. A Narrative of the Settlement and the City from the Signing of the Treaties in 1858 to the Close of the Year 1879.* 2 vols. London, 1880–81.

Blacker, Carmen. *The Japanese Enlightenment. A Study of the Writings of Fukuzawa Yukichi.* Cambridge, Eng., 1964.

———. "Ōhashi Totsuan. A Study in Anti-Western Thought," *TASJ*, 3d Ser., vol. 7 (1959): 147–68.

Borton, Hugh. "Peasant Uprisings in Japan of the Tokugawa Period," *TASJ*, 2d Ser., vol. 16 (1938): 1–219.

Brown, Delmer M. *Nationalism in Japan: An Introductory Historical Analysis.* Berkeley, Calif., 1955.

Brown, Sidney D. "Ōkubo Toshimichi and the First Home Ministry Bureaucracy: 1873–1878," in Silberman and Harootunian, eds., listed below, pp. 195–232.

Burks, Ardath W. "A 'Sub-leader' in the Emergence of the Diplomatic Function: Ikeda Chōhatsu (Chikugo no Kami), 1837–1879," in Silberman and Harootunian, eds., listed below, pp. 289–322.

Chambliss, W. J. *Chiaraijima Village: Land Tenure, Taxation, and Local Trade, 1818–1884.* Tucson, Ariz., 1965.

Chang, Richard T. *From Prejudice to Tolerance. A Study of the Japanese Image of the West, 1826–1864.* Tokyo, 1970.

Chihōshi kenkyū hikkei. Iwanami Zensho no. 171. Tokyo, 1968 [1952].

Conroy, Hilary. *The Japanese Seizure of Korea: 1868–1910. A Study of Realism and Idealism in International Relations.* Philadelphia, 1960.

Craig, Albert. *Chōshū in the Meiji Restoration.* Cambridge, Mass., 1961.

———. "Kido Kōin and Ōkubo Toshimichi: A Psychohistorical Analysis," in Craig and Shively, eds., listed below, pp. 264–308.

———. "The Restoration Movement in Chōshū," in Hall and Jansen, eds., listed below, pp. 363–73.

———. "Science and Confucianism in Tokugawa Japan," in Jansen, ed., *Changing Japanese Attitudes,* listed below, pp. 133–60.

Craig, A., and D. Shively, eds. *Personality in Japanese History.* Berkeley, Calif., 1970.

Dai Nihon Gaikō Bunsho. Edited by Japanese Ministry of Foreign Affairs (Gaimushō); multivolume work, in progress. Tokyo, 1936 to date. A valuable, though selective, edition of documents on Japanese foreign policy, starting in 1868, drawn from the archives of the Gaimushō. Later parts appear under the title *Nihon Gaikō Bunsho.*

Dai Nihon Komonjo: Bakumatsu Gaikoku Kankei Monjo. Edited by Shiryō Hensanjo; multivolume work, in progress. Tokyo, 1911 to date. A very full collection of documents on Japanese foreign policy, drawn from various sources and starting from the Perry negotiations of 1853.

Dai Saigō zenshū. 3 vols. Tokyo, 1926–27. The standard edition of the collected works of Saigō Takamori; includes both letters and memorials, but is by no means complete.

Date Muneki zaikyō nikki. Tokyo, 1916.

"Diary of an Official of the Bakufu," *TASJ,* 2d Ser., vol. 7 (1930): 98–119. Translation of a Japanese account of negotiations with Perry in 1854.

Dore, R. P. *Education in Tokugawa Japan.* London, 1965.

Earl, D. M. *Emperor and Nation in Japan. Political Thinkers of the Tokugawa Period.* Seattle, 1964.

Egashira Tsuneharu, "Saga-han ni okeru yōshiki kōgyō," in Honjō, ed., *Bakumatsu keizaishi kenkyū,* listed below, pp. 59–100.

Foreign Office, Great Britain. *Confidential Prints, Japan* (F.O. 410). Public Record Office, London. Foreign Office correspondence printed for the information of the Cabinet (chiefly from F.O. 46, below).

———. *General Correspondence, Japan* (F.O. 46). Public Record Office, London. Archive of the British Foreign Office, including correspondence with its representatives in Japan, starting from 1859.

———. *Hammond Papers* (F.O. 391). Public Record Office, London. Manuscript correspondence of Edmund Hammond, Permanent Under-Secretary at the British Foreign Office. Includes most of his semiprivate correspondence with British representatives in Japan (the rest being in F.O. 46, above).

Fox, Grace. *Britain and Japan, 1858–1883.* Oxford, Eng., 1969.

Fukaya Hakaji (Hiroharu). *Kashizoku chitsuroku shobun no kenkyū.* Tokyo, 1941.

Fukuchi Genichirō. *Bakufu suibō ron.* Tokyo, 1926 [1892].

Fukushima Masao. *Chiso kaisei no kenkyū.* Tokyo, 1962.

Fukushima Nariyuki. *Yoshida Tōyō* [biography]. Tokyo, 1926.

Fukuzawa Yukichi. *The Autobiography of Fukuzawa Yukichi.* Translated by E. Kiyooka. Tokyo, 1934.

Furushima Toshio. "Seiritsu-ki kisei jinushi-sei no seikaku," in *Meiji ishin to jinushi-sei,* listed below, pp. 3–27.

Godai Tomoatsu den [biography]. Edited by Godai Ryūsaku. Tokyo, 1936 [1933].

Goodman, G. K. *The Dutch Impact on Japan (1640–1853).* Leiden, 1967.

Gubbins, J. H. *The Progress of Japan, 1853–1871.* Oxford, Eng., 1911.

van Gulik, R. H. "*Kakkaron,* a Japanese Echo of the Opium War," *Monumenta Serica,* 4 (1939–40): 478–545.

Hackett, Roger F. "The Meiji Leaders and Modernization: The Case of Yamagata Aritomo," in Jansen, ed., *Changing Japanese Attitudes,* listed below, pp. 243–73.

———. *Yamagata Aritomo in the Rise of Modern Japan, 1838–1922.* Cambridge, Mass., 1971.

Haga Noboru. *Bakumatsu shishi no seikatsu.* Tokyo, 1965.

Hall, John W. "The Castle Town and Japan's Modern Urbanization," *Far Eastern Quarterly,* 15 (1955): 37–56. Reprinted in Hall and Jansen, eds., listed below, pp. 169–88.

———. "Feudalism in Japan—a Reassessment," *Comparative Studies in Society and History,* 5, 1 (1962): 15–51. Reprinted in Hall and Jansen, eds., listed below, pp. 15–51.

———. *Government and Local Power in Japan, 500 to 1700. A Study Based on Bizen Province.* Princeton, N.J., 1966.

———. "A Monarch for Modern Japan," in Robert Ward, ed., listed below, pp. 11–64.

Hall, J. W., and M. B. Jansen, eds. *Studies in the Institutional History of Early Modern Japan.* Princeton, N.J., 1968.

Hani Gorō. "Meiji ishin kaishaku no hensen," in *Meiji ishin-shi kenkyū,* listed below, pp. 772–92.

Hansei ichiran. 2 vols. Tokyo, 1928–29. Returns of revenue, population, etc., made to the Meiji government, c. 1869.

Hara Heizō. "Tenchūgumi kyohei shimatsu-kō," *Shigaku zasshi* (2 parts), 48 (1937), 9: 1115–51; and 10: 1223–51.

Harootunian, Harry D. "*Jinsei, Jinzai,* and *Jitsugaku*: Social Values and Leadership in Late Tokugawa Thought," in Silberman and Harootunian, eds., listed below, pp. 83–119.

———. *Toward Restoration. The Growth of Political Consciousness in Tokugawa Japan.* Berkeley, Calif., 1970.

Harris, Townsend. *The Complete Journal of Townsend Harris, First American Consul General and Minister to Japan.* Edited by M. E. Cosenza. New York, 1930.

Havens, T. R. H. *Nishi Amane and Modern Japanese Thought.* Princeton, N.J., 1970.

Hawks, F. L. *Narrative of an Expedition of an American Squadron to the China Seas and Japan, Performed in the Years 1852, 1853, and 1854, Under the Command of Commodore M. C. Perry.* 3 vols., Washington, D.C., 1856.

Hayashi Yoshihiko. *Sappan no kyōiku to zaisei narabi gumbi.* Kagoshima, 1939.

Heusken, Henry. *Japan Journal: 1855–1861.* Edited by J. C. van der Corput and R. A. Wilson. New Brunswick, N.J., 1964.

Higo-han kokuji shiryō. 10 vols., Kumamoto, 1932. Records of the Kumamoto domain.

Hirano Yoshitarō. *Nihon shihonshugi shakai no kikō.* Rev. ed. Tokyo, 1950.

Hirao Michio. "Bakumatsu rōnin to sono hogo oyobi tōsei," in *Meiji ishin-shi kenkyū,* listed below, pp. 527–78.

———. *Yamauchi Yōdō* [biography]. Tokyo, 1961.

———. *Yoshida Tōyō* [biography]. Tokyo, 1959.

Honjō Eijirō. *Economic Theory and History of Japan in the Tokugawa Period.* Reprint. New York, 1965 [1943].

———. "Léon Roches to Bakumatsu no shosei kaikaku," in Honjō, ed., *Bakumatsu no shin-seisaku,* listed below, pp. 178–214.

———. *The Social and Economic History of Japan.* Kyoto, 1935.

———. "Tempō no kaikaku," in Honjō, ed., *Kinsei Nihon,* listed below, pp. 161–86.

———, ed. *Bakumatsu keizaishi kenkyū.* Tokyo, 1935.

———. *Bakumatsu no shin-seisaku.* Tokyo, 1935.

———. *Kinsei Nihon no san dai-kaikaku.* Tokyo, 1944.

Horie Hideichi, ed. *Hansei kaikaku no kenkyū.* Tokyo, 1955.

Horie Yasuzō. "San dai-kaikaku to zaisei," in Honjō, ed., *Kinsei Nihon,* listed above, pp. 51–82.

———. *Waga kuni kinsei no sembai seido.* Tokyo, 1933.

———. "Yamaguchi-han ni okeru yōshiki kōgyō," in Honjō, ed., *Bakumatsu keizaishi kenkyū,* listed above, pp. 133–52.

Hsü, Immanuel C. Y. *China's Entrance into the Family of Nations. The Diplomatic Phase, 1858–1880.* Cambridge, Mass., 1960.

Ienaga Saburō. *Gairai bunka sesshu shiron.* Tokyo, 1948.

Inada Masatsugu. *Meiji kempō seiritsu-shi.* 2 vols. Tokyo, 1960–62.

Inobe Shigeo. "Ansei jōyaku chokkyo sōsei ni kansuru ichi-kōsatsu," *Shigaku zasshi,* 42 (1931): 469–90.

———. "Bakumatsu shishi no shisō-teki haikei," in *Bakumatsu kinnō shisō no kenkyū* (Tokyo, 1937), pp. 83–100.

———. "Mito gaku-ha no jōi-ron," *Shirin*, 5 (1920): 125–53.

———. "Perry torai no sai ni okeru kokuron no kisū," *Shirin*, 13 (1928): 343–70.

———. "Sakuma Shōzan no taigai iken," *Kokugakuin zasshi* (2 parts), 30 (1924): 455–86, 608–37.

———. "Seijishi-jō yori mitaru Meiji ishin," in *Meiji ishin-shi kenkyū*, listed below, pp. 48–75.

Irimajiri Yoshinaga. *Hōkensei hōkai katei no kenkyū*. Tokyo, 1948.

Ishii Ryosuke. *Japanese Legislation in the Meiji Era*. Translated by W. J. Chambliss. Tokyo, 1958.

Ishii Takashi. *Bakumatsu bōeki shi no kenkyū*. Tokyo, 1942.

———. *Gakusetsu hihan Meiji ishin ron*. Tokyo, 1961.

———. [*Zōtei*] *Meiji ishin no kokusaiteki kankyō*. Tokyo, 1966.

Ishin-shi. Edited by Ishin Shiryō Hensan Jimukyoku. 6 vols. Tokyo, 1939–41. The standard political history; traditional in methodology.

Ishin shiryō kōyō. 10 vols. Tokyo, 1937–39. A guide to historical materials, which are listed under events, arranged chronologically.

Itō Hirobumi den [biography]. Edited by Shumpo Kō Tsuishōkai. 3 vols. Tokyo, 1940.

Itō Kō zenshū. 3 vols. Tokyo, 1927. An early and very incomplete collection of the papers of Itō Hirobumi.

Iwakura Kō jikki. 3 vols. Tokyo, 1927. A valuable collection of Iwakura Tomomi's papers and materials concerned especially with the Court. First published in 2 vols. in 1906.

Iwakura Tomomi kankei monjo. Edited by Nihon Shiseki Kyōkai. 8 vols. Tokyo, 1927–35. Iwakura's letters, memorials, and related papers.

Iwata Masakazu. *Ōkubo Toshimichi: The Bismarck of Japan*. Berkeley, Calif., 1964.

Jansen, Marius B. "Mutsu Munemitsu," in Craig and Shively, eds., listed above, pp. 309–34.

———. "New Materials for the Intellectual History of Nineteenth-Century Japan," *Harvard Journal of Asiatic Studies*, 20 (1957): 567–97.

———. *Sakamoto Ryōma and the Meiji Restoration*. Princeton, N.J., 1961.

———. "Takechi Zuizan and the Tosa Loyalist Party," *JAS*, 18 (1959): 199–212.

———. "Tosa During the Last Century of Tokugawa Rule," in Hall and Jansen, eds., listed above, pp. 331–47.

———, ed. *Changing Japanese Attitudes Toward Modernization*. Princeton, N.J., 1965.

Jiyūtō-shi. Edited by Uda Yūi and Wada Saburō. 2 vols. Tokyo, 1910. The party's "official" history, prepared under the direction of Itagaki Taisuke.

Junnan rokkō. Edited by Kunaishō. 3 vols. Tokyo, 1933. Collection of short biographies of loyalists "martyred" in the Restoration movement.

Kaeda Nobuyoshi. *Ishin zengo jitsu rekishi den* [autobiography]. 10 vols. Tokyo, 1891–92.

Kagoshima-ken shi. 5 vols. Kagoshima, 1939–43. Includes a detailed history of Satsuma for this period.

Kanai Madoka. *Hansei.* Tokyo, 1962.

Kanno Kazutarō. "Shokō to gaikoku bōeki," in Honjō, ed., *Bakumatsu keizaishi kenkyū,* listed above, pp. 375–419.

Katsuda Magoya. *Ōkubo Toshimichi den.* 3 vols. Tokyo, 1910–11. The standard biography, if old-fashioned. Gives the complete text of many relevant documents.

Kawabata Tahei. *Matsudaira Shungaku* [biography]. Tokyo, 1967.

Kawakatsu-ke monjo. Edited by Nihon Shiseki Kyōkai. Tokyo, 1930. The papers of a Bakufu official family.

Keene, Donald. *The Japanese Discovery of Europe: Honda Toshiaki and Other Discoverers, 1720–1798.* London, 1952; also rev. ed., Stanford, Calif., 1969. The 1969 edition adds some new material but also omits some. Hence the pagination of the two editions differs.

Kido Kōin monjo. Edited by Nihon Shiseki Kyōkai. 8 vols. Tokyo, 1929–31. The only modern edition of Kido's papers.

Kido Kōin nikki [diary]. Edited by Nihon Shiseki Kyōkai. 3 vols. Tokyo, 1932–33.

Kikuchi Dairoku. *Japanese Education.* London, 1909.

Kimura Motoi. "Hagi-han no baishin ni tsuite," *Rekishigaku kenkyū,* 220 (June 1958): 1–10.

Kimura Motoi and Sugimoto Toshio, eds. *Fudai hansei no tenkai to Meiji ishin: Shimōsa Sakura-han.* Tokyo, 1963.

Kinnō resshi den. Tokyo, 1906. A collection of short biographies of Restoration loyalists, arranged by provinces.

Kōchi-ken shiyō. Kōchi, 1924.

Lensen, George A. *The Russian Push Toward Japan. Russo-Japanese Relations, 1697–1875.* Princeton, N.J., 1959.

Levenson, Joseph R. *Liang Ch'i-ch'ao and the Mind of Modern China.* Rev. ed. Berkeley, Calif., 1967.

Lockwood, William W., ed. *The State and Economic Enterprise in Modern Japan.* Princeton, N.J., 1965.

McEwan, J. R. *The Political Writings of Ogyū Sorai.* Cambridge, Eng., 1962.

McLaren, W. W. *A Political History of Japan During the Meiji Era: 1867–1912.* London, 1916.

———, ed. *Japanese Government Documents* (*TASJ,* vol. 42, Part 1), Tokyo, 1914.

Matsuyoshi Sadao. *Tosa-han keizaishi kenkyū.* Tokyo, 1930.

Mayo, Marlene. "Rationality in the Meiji Restoration: The Iwakura Embassy," in Silberman and Harootunian, eds., listed below, pp. 323–69.

Meiji ishin-shi kenkyū. Edited by Shigakkai. Tokyo, 1929. An important collection of articles.

Meiji ishin-shi kenkyū kōza. Edited by Rekishigaku Kenkyūkai. 6 vols. Tokyo, 1958–59. Plus an additional volume, 1969.

Meiji ishin to jinushi-sei. Edited by Rekishigaku Kenkyūkai. Tokyo, 1956.

Meiji zenki zaisei keizai shiryō shūsei. Edited by Ōuchi Hyōe and Tsuchiya Takao. 21 vols. Tokyo, 1931–36. A major collection of materials on Meiji economic history.

Michie, A. *The Englishman in China During the Victorian Era as Illustrated in the Career of Sir Rutherford Alcock*. 2 vols. Edinburgh and London, 1900.

Miyamoto Matatsugu. "Mito-han ni okeru Bakumatsu no shin-jigyō," in Honjō, ed., *Bakumatsu keizaishi kenkyū*, listed above, pp. 153–92.

———. "Tempō kaikaku to kabu-nakama," in Honjō, ed., *Kinsei Nihon*, listed above, pp. 187–233.

Moore, Barrington. *Social Origins of Dictatorship and Democracy. Lord and Peasant in the Making of the Modern World*. London, 1967.

Mounsey, A. H. *The Satsuma Rebellion, an Episode of Modern Japanese History*. London, 1879.

Nagakura Tamotsu. "Aizu-han ni okeru hansei kaikaku," in Horie Hideichi, ed., listed above, pp. 61–117.

Naitō Seichū. "Bakusei kaikaku no shakaiteki kiban: II, Bitchū tenryō Kurashiki-mura," in Horie Hideichi, ed., listed above, pp. 281–340.

Najita Tetsuo. "Ōshio Heihachirō (1793–1837)," in Craig and Shively, eds. listed above, pp. 155–79.

Nakamura, James. *Agricultural Production and the Economic Development of Japan, 1873–1922*. Princeton, N.J., 1966.

Nakamura Naomi. *Ōkuma Shigenobu* [biography]. Tokyo, 1961.

Naramoto Tatsuya. *Kinsei hōken shakai shiron*. Tokyo, 1952.

———, ed. *Meiji ishin jimbutsu jiten: Bakumatsu-hen*. Tokyo, 1966.

Nihon Gaikō Bunsho. See *Dai Nihon Gaikō Bunsho*.

Nihon kindaishi jiten. Edited by Kyōto Daigaku Kokushi Kenkyūshitsu. Tokyo, 1958. Particularly useful for its statistical and other tables.

Niwa Kunio. "Jinushi-sei sōshutsu no seiji katei ni tsuite," in *Meiji ishin to jinushi-sei*, listed above, pp. 247–91.

———. *Meiji ishin no tochi henkaku: ryōshuteki tochi shoyū no kaitai wo megutte*. Tokyo, 1968 [1962].

Norman, E. H. *Andō Shōeki and the Anatomy of Japanese Feudalism* (*TASJ*, 3d Ser., vol. 2). 2 vols. Tokyo, 1949.

———. *Japan's Emergence as a Modern State*. New York, 1940.

———. *Soldier and Peasant in Japan: The Origins of Conscription*. New York, 1943.

Numata Jirō. *Bakumatsu yōgaku shi*. Tokyo, 1950.

Ōe Shinobu. "Kumamoto-han ni okeru hansei kaikaku," in Horie Hideichi, ed., listed above, pp. 15–60.

Oka Yoshitake. *Kindai Nihon no keisei.* Tokyo, 1947.

Ōkubo Toshimichi monjo. Edited by Nihon Shiseki Kyōkai. 10 vols. Tokyo, 1927–29. The standard edition of Ōkubo's papers, supplementing the material in Katsuda's biography.

Ōkubo Toshimichi nikki [diary]. Edited by Nihon Shiseki Kyōkai. 2 vols. Tokyo, 1927.

Ōkuma Shigenobu kankei monjo. Edited by Nihon Shiseki Kyōkai. 6 vols. Tokyo, 1932–35. This edition of Ōkuma's papers is now being superseded by a much fuller one (which I have not used).

Oliphant, Laurence. *Narrative of the Earl of Elgin's Mission to China and Japan in the Years 1857, '58, '59.* 2 vols. Edinburgh and London, 1859.

Ono Takeo. *Gōshi seido no kenkyū.* Tokyo, 1925.

Osatake Takeshi. *Ishin zengo ni okeru rikken shisō.* Rev. ed. 2 vols. Tokyo, 1929 [1925].

Ōtsuka Takematsu. "Fukkoku kōshi Léon Roches no seisaku kōdō ni tsuite," *Shigaku zasshi* (2 parts), 46 (1935): 809–50, 982–1001.

Ōyama Shikitarō. "Bakumatsu ni okeru denso oyobi jōnōkin," in Honjō, ed., *Bakumatsu keizaishi kenkyū,* listed above, pp. 298–374.

Pittau, Joseph. *Political Thought in Early Meiji Japan, 1868–1889.* Cambridge, Mass., 1967.

Pyle, Kenneth B. *The New Generation in Meiji Japan. Problems of Cultural Identity, 1885–1895,* Stanford, Calif., 1969.

Redesdale, Lord [A. Mitford]. *Memories.* 2 vols. London, 1915.

Saimu kiji. Edited by Nihon Shiseki Kyōkai. Tokyo, 1922. The records of Matsudaira Shungaku of Echizen for the period May to Sept. 1862, with a brief narrative of events from Aug. 1858 to May 1862. Cf. *Sakumu kiji* and *Zoku saimu kiji.*

Sakai, Robert K. "Shimazu Nariakira and the Emergence of National Leadership in Satsuma," in Craig and Shively, eds., listed above, pp. 209–33.

Sakamaki, S. *Japan and the United States, 1790–1853* (*TASJ,* 2d Ser., vol. 18). Tokyo, 1939.

Sakata Yoshio. *Meiji ishin shi.* Tokyo, 1960.

———, ed. *Meiji ishin-shi no mondai-ten.* Tokyo, 1962.

——— and John W. Hall. "The Motivation of Political Leadership in the Meiji Restoration," *JAS,* 16 (1956): 31–50.

Sakumu kiji. Edited by Nihon Shiseki Kyōkai. 4 vols. Tokyo, 1920–21. The records of Matsudaira Shungaku of Echizen for the period July 1853 to Aug. 1858. Cf. *Saimu kiji* and *Zoku saimu kiji.*

Sansom, G. B. *The Western World and Japan. A Study in the Interaction of European and Asiatic Cultures.* New York, 1950.

Sappan seiyō roku (*Kagoshima-ken shiryō-shū,* vol. 1). Kagoshima, 1960. Reprint of the 1826 text.

Sasaki Takayuki. *Kinnō hishi: Sasaki rōkō sekijitsu dan.* Tokyo, 1915. Memoirs of one of the Tosa men; a useful commentary independent of the Satsuma-Chōshū viewpoint.

Satow, E. M. *A Diplomat in Japan. The Inner History of the Critical Years in the Evolution of Japan When the Ports Were Opened and the Monarchy Restored.* London, 1921.

———. "The Revival of Pure Shintau," *TASJ*, vol. 3 (1875), App. pp. 1–87.

———, trans. *Japan 1853–1864, or Genji Yume Monogatari.* Tokyo, 1905. A translation of Baba Bunei's work.

Segai Inoue Kō den. 5 vols. Tokyo, 1933–34. The standard biography of Inoue Kaoru.

Seki Junya. *Hansei kaikaku to Meiji ishin: han taisei no kiki to nōmin bunka.* Tokyo, 1956.

———. *Meiji ishin to chiso kaisei.* Kyoto, 1967.

Sheldon, Charles D. *The Rise of the Merchant Class in Tokugawa Japan, 1600–1868. An Introductory Survey.* Locust Valley, N.Y., 1958.

Shibahara Takuji. *Meiji ishin no kenryoku kiban.* Tokyo, 1965.

Shibusawa Eiichi. *Tokugawa Keiki Kō den.* 8 vols. Tokyo, 1918. The standard biography, to which are appended some volumes of documents, including extracts from Keiki's memoirs.

Shimazu Hisamitsu Kō jikki. 8 vols. Tokyo, 1910. An important collection of Shimazu's papers, chiefly memorials and political correspondence.

Shimazu Nariakira genkōroku. Compiled by Ichiki Shirō. Tokyo, 1944 [1884]. A collection of Nariakira's "conversations," compiled after his death by one of his retainers.

Shimmi Kichiji. *Kakyū shizoku no kenkyū.* Tokyo, 1953.

Shimonaka Yasaburō. *Dai Saigō seiden.* 3 vols. Tokyo, 1939–40. The fullest biography of Saigō Takamori, but a traditionalist and not very satisfactory one.

Shōkiku Kido Kō den. Edited by Kido Kō Denki Hensanjo. 2 vols. Tokyo, 1927. The standard biography of Kido Kōin, including texts of many useful documents.

Silberman, Bernard S. "Bureaucratic Development and the Structure of Decision-making in Japan, 1868–1925," *JAS*, 29 (1970): 347–62.

———. "Elite Transformation in the Meiji Restoration: The Upper Civil Service, 1868–1873," in Silberman and Harootunian, eds., listed below, pp. 233–59.

———. *Ministers of Modernization. Elite Mobility in the Meiji Restoration, 1868–1873.* Tucson, Ariz., 1964.

———, and Harry D. Harootunian, eds. *Modern Japanese Leadership: Transition and Change.* Tucson, Ariz., 1966.

Sims, R. L. *French Policy Towards Japan, 1854–1894.* Unpublished Ph.D. thesis. London, 1968.

Smith, Thomas C. *The Agrarian Origins of Modern Japan.* Stanford, Calif., 1959.

———. "The Japanese Village in the Seventeenth Century," reprinted (from *Journal of Economic History,* 1952) in Hall and Jansen, eds., listed above, pp. 263–82.
———. "Land Tax in the Tokugawa Village," *JAS,* 18 (1958): 3–19. Reprinted in Hall and Jansen, eds., listed above, pp. 283–99.
———. "Ōkura Nagatsune and the Technologists," in Craig and Shively, eds., listed above, pp. 127–54.
———. *Political Change and Industrial Development in Japan: Government Enterprise, 1868–1880.* Stanford, Calif., 1955.
Steiner, Kurt. *Local Government in Japan.* Stanford, Calif., 1965.
Strayer, Joseph R. "The Tokugawa Period and Japanese Feudalism," in Hall and Jansen, eds., listed above, pp. 3–14.
Suematsu Kenchō. *Bōchō kaiten shi.* 12 vols. Tokyo, 1911–20. An account of the part played by Chōshū in Japanese politics from the 1830's to 1871.
Sugitani Akira. *Etō Shimpei* [biography]. Tokyo, 1962.
Tabohashi Kiyoshi. *Kindai Nihon gaikoku kankei shi.* Rev. ed. Tokyo, 1943.
Taguchi Ukichi. *Nihon kaika shōshi.* Tokyo, 1934 [1877–82].
Takahashi Kamekichi. "Keizaishi-jō ni okeru Meiji ishin," in *Meiji ishin-shi kenkyū,* listed above, pp. 112–48.
Takechi Zuizan kankei monjo. Edited by Nihon Shiseki Kyōkai. 2 vols. Tokyo, 1916. Takechi's letters, memorials, and related papers.
Tanaka Akira. *Meiji ishin seiji-shi kenkyū.* Tokyo, 1965 [1963].
Tanaka Sōgorō. *Kindai Nihon kanryō shi.* Tokyo, 1941.
———. *Meiji ishin taiseishi.* Tokyo, 1941.
Tanaka Tokihiko. "Meiji Government and the Introduction of Railways," *Contemporary Japan* (2 parts) 28 (1966–67): 567–88, 750–88. A fairly full summary in English of the author's 1963 book on this subject (below).
———. *Meiji ishin no seikyoku to tetsudō kensetsu.* Tokyo, 1963.
Teng Ssu-yu and J. K. Fairbank, eds. *China's Response to the West: A Documentary Survey, 1839–1923.* Cambridge, Mass., 1954.
Tokushi biyō. Edited by Shiryō Hensanjo. Tokyo, 1933. A useful compilation of factual data about Japanese history.
Tokutomi Iichirō, ed. *Kōshaku Matsukata Masayoshi den.* 2 vols. Tokyo, 1935. The standard biography of Matsukata.
———, ed. *Kōshaku Yamagata Aritomo den.* 3 vols. Tokyo, 1933. The standard biography of Yamagata.
Tosa-han gōshi chōsha-sho (Tosa Shiryō Sōsho, no. 3). Kōchi, 1958. Lists of *gōshi* landholdings in Tosa in the late-Tokugawa period.
Totman, Conrad. "Political Reconciliation in the Tokugawa Bakufu: Abe Masahiro and Tokugawa Nariaki, 1844–1852," in Craig and Shively, eds., listed above, pp. 180–208.
———. *Politics in the Tokugawa Bakufu, 1600–1843.* Cambridge, Mass., 1967.
Tōyama Shigeki. *Meiji ishin.* Tokyo, 1951.

Tsuchiya Takao. "Bakumatsu dōranki no keizaiteki bunseki," *Chūō Kōron*, 47, 11 (Oct. 1932): 75–91.

———. "Bakumatsu shishi no mita Shina mondai," *Kaizō*, 20, 7 (July 1938): 154–67.

———. *Hōken shakai hōkai katei no kenkyū*. Kyōto, 1927.

———. *Ishin keizai-shi*. Tokyo, 1942.

Tsukahira, T. G. *Feudal Control in Tokugawa Japan: The Sankin-Kōtai System*. Cambridge, Mass., 1966.

Tsunoda Ryusaku et al. *Sources of Japanese Tradition*. New York, 1958.

Umetani Noboru. "Meiji ishin-shi ni okeru Chōshū-han no seiji-teki dōkō," in Sakata, ed., *Meiji ishin-shi no mondai-ten*, listed above, pp. 307–54.

Ward, Robert, ed. *Political Development in Modern Japan*. Princeton, N.J., 1968.

Webb, Herschel. "The Development of an Orthodox Attitude Toward the Imperial Institution in the Nineteenth Century," in Jansen, ed., *Changing Japanese Attitudes*, listed above, pp. 167–91.

———. *The Japanese Imperial Institution in the Tokugawa Period*. New York, 1968.

Wilson, George M. "The Bakumatsu Intellectual in Action: Hashimoto Sanai in the Political Crisis of 1858," in Craig and Shively, eds., listed above, pp. 234–63.

Wilson, Robert A. *Genesis of the Meiji Government in Japan, 1868–1871*. Berkeley, Calif., 1957.

Wright, Mary C. *The Last Stand of Chinese Conservatism. The T'ung-chih Restoration, 1862–1874*. Stanford, Calif., 1957.

Yamaguchi Muneyuki. *Hashimoto Sanai* [biography]. Tokyo, 1962.

Yodo Inaba-ke monjo. Edited by Nihon Shiseki Kyōkai. Tokyo, 1926. The papers of a senior Bakufu official at the time of the Restoration.

Yoshida Tōyō ikō. Edited by Nihon Shiseki Kyōkai. Tokyo, 1929. Some memorials and other papers of Yoshida Tōyō.

Yoshida Tsunekichi. *Ii Naosuke* [biography]. Tokyo, 1963.

Zōi shoken den. 2 vols. Tokyo, 1927. A collection of short biographies of participants in the Restoration movement.

Zoku saimu kiji. Edited by Nihon Shiseki Kyōkai. 6 vols. Tokyo, 1921–22. Records of Matsudaira Shungaku of Echizen for the period Sept. 1862 to Oct. 1867. Cf. *Sakumu kiji* and *Saimu kiji*.

Zoku Tosa ijin den. Kōchi, 1923. A collection of short biographies of Tosa men, mostly related to the Restoration.

Index

Index